A Spectrum of Innovation

A Spectrum of Innovation

Color in American Printmaking

1890–1960

David Acton

with contributions by

Clinton Adams

Karen F. Beall

Worcester Art Museum

W. W. Norton & Company

New York • London

Copyright © 1990 by Worcester Art Museum
All rights reserved.

Printed in Hong Kong by South China Printing Co.

The text of this book is composed in Gill Sans.
Composition by Trufont, Inc.
Book design by Katy Homans.

First Edition.

ISBN 0-393-02901-8

W. W. Norton & Company, Inc., 500 Fifth Avenue, New York, N.Y. 10110
W. W. Norton & Company, Ltd., 37 Great Russell Street, London WC1B 3NU
Worcester Art Museum, 55 Salisbury Street, Worcester, Ma. 01609

1 2 3 4 5 6 7 8 9 0

Exhibition Itinerary

Amon Carter Museum
July 28–September 23, 1990

The Nelson-Atkins Museum of Art
October 14–December 2, 1990

Worcester Art Museum
September 22–November 17, 1991

COVER:
Stuart Davis
Detail Study for Cliché, c. 1957
Lithograph on cream wove paper
32.0 × 37.9 cm. (image)
35.8 × 41.9 cm. (sheet)
Private collection

Contents

Foreword

The greatest strength of the collection of graphic arts at the Worcester Art Museum is in its holdings of color prints. This important collection had its inception in 1901 with the bequest of John Chandler Bancroft. At that time, the collection was comprised of Japanese prints, including rare, hand-colored "primitives" and outstanding examples of *ukiyo-e* by such masters as Haronobu, Utamaro, and Hiroshige, as well as florid *nishiki-e* or "brocade prints" by Kunisada and Kuniyoshi.

In 1926, the museum received another extraordinary gift from the bequest of Mrs. Kingsmill Marrs, the former Laura Norcross. A prominent Bostonian of discrimination and means, Mrs. Marrs had collected prints for many years under the guidance of Sylvester Rosa Koehler, the curator of graphic arts at the Museum of Fine Arts in Boston. This remarkable scholar passed on to Mrs. Marrs the benefits of his connoisseurship skills and an enthusiasm for his favorite subject, printmaking in color. An astounding collection was assembled, ranging from the first color woodcuts of the Renaissance through Baroque chiaroscuro woodcuts and color engravings, and included outstanding examples of eighteenth-century French intaglio prints by LeBlon, Bonnet, Deboucourt, Decourtis, and Janinet. Among the treasures gathered by Mrs. Marrs were also prints of her own day, such as the elegant color intaglios of Mary Cassatt.

Through the 1930s and 1940s, insightful directors and curators at Worcester lovingly added to the growing collection, often with American color prints purchased soon after they were created, such as works by Werner Drewes and Robert Gwathmey. With the recent revived interest in American prints, which brought long-forgotten material into the market, the museum has been able to further supplement its holdings with color prints of our own century.

The allure of color is strong, and color prints have always been popular in this country. In the nineteenth century, as a school of printmaking in the United States distinguished itself from the graphic arts traditions around the world from which it had evolved, the characteristic American spirit of individuality and self-reliance quickly became perceptible in the artwork. Unlike the doctrinaire traditions of Europe and Japan, where prints had long been the product of regimented divisions of labor, American artists, by necessity or preference, were compelled to carry out every step of the creative and technical process themselves. The resulting works of art were wholly the creations of the artist, free from the homogenizing mechanical perfection imposed by professional printers.

This exhibition presents a selection of American color prints organized as a chronological survey. The review begins with works from the last decade of the nineteenth century, when American artists traveled to Europe to learn traditional printmaking methods in academies and professional printing shops. The *terminus ante quem* for our selection is 1960, the year in which the first color prints were produced at the Tamarind Lithography Workshop in Los Angeles, heralding the era of collaborative American printmaking workshops and a vital new tradition that continues today.

The range of subjects and styles in the prints is as broad as our country is vast and its history varied. In American printmaking, aesthetic creativity has always been accompanied by technical innovation. Particularly with the advent of modernism, as stylistic individuality became *de rigueur*, American printmakers sought to accompany their distinctive personal styles with their own unique techniques for making prints. This exhibition explores the varied solutions that American artists have brought to the challenge of printing in color, a whole "spectrum of innovation."

James A. Welu
Director, Worcester Art Museum

Acknowledgments

Throughout the researching and writing of this book and the organization of its accompanying exhibition, a great many individuals generously shared with me their time, their works of art, their insights and knowledge. It has been a privilege to work with outstanding scholars in the preparation of this catalogue. I am most grateful to Clinton Adams and Karen Beall for their important contributions of the catalogue's introductory essays. Their able research and thoughtful organization of a vast amount of materials helped to make complicated subjects more comprehensible and accessible.

I am indebted to many people who generously made prints available in my visits to museums, private collections, and galleries and with art dealers. Much information was passed by telephone and by letter, and many individuals went to great lengths to search out obscure facts. I am grateful to many museum colleagues across the country: Missy Anderson, Georgia Barnhill, Kathie Bennewitz, Cynthia Burlingham, Barbara Butts, Bruce Davis, Ellen D'Oench, Kevin Donovan, Richard S. Field, Ruth Fine, Betsy Fryberger, Sinclair Hitchings, Audrey Isselbacher, John Ittmann, Una E. Johnson, David Kiehl, Judy Larson, John T. McGill, George McKenna, Lisa Messinger, Joanne Moser, Jane Myers, Martina Norelli, Martha Oaks, Thomas O'Sullivan, Mary-Ellen Earl Perry, Carol Pulin, Robert Rainwater, Ann Severs, Barbara Shapiro, Graham Smith, Michael O. Smith, Andrew Stevens, Christine Swenson, Marilyn Symmes, Carol Troyen, Roberta Waddell, Barry Walker, and Judith Zilczer.

The base for my research has been the library of the Worcester Art Museum, where the staff has been diligent, patient, and perseverant, and to Kathy Berg, Cynthia Bolshaw, and Patricia Kelly I give many thanks. Among the many other librarians and museum registrars who went to special trouble to provide information to me are Eleanor Barefoot, Mary Jane Benedict, Joanne Guest, Pamela R. McKay, Karen Papineau, Margaret Welch, Jeanine K. Wing, and Sarah B. Ziegenbein.

I am obliged to many other individuals who provided me with observations, facts, ideas, and boundless encouragement. They include Doris Adams, Richard Axsom, Will Barnet, Fred Becker, James Bergquist, William P. Carl, Gala Chamberlain, Lee Chesney, Sylvan Cole, Robert P. Conway, Margo Dolan, Gil Einstein, N. Michael Fishman, Janet Altic Flint, Donald Fox, William Greenbaum, Arthur Halliburton, Jane Haslem, Ann Havens, Norman and June Kraft, Tina Letcher, Stephen Long, Vincent Longo, Edith McCullough, John C. Menihan, Tobey C. Moss. Nancy Myrick, Roy Pederson, Krishna Reddy, Mary Ryan, Michelle Russel, Susan Sheehan, Alice Simsar, Tobin Sparling, Nesta and Anne Spink, Edward T. and Roslyn K. Stempel, Linda Sweeney, Susan Teller, Steven Thomas, Tom Veilleux, Anthony Velonis, Carey Mack Weber, Mrs. Gerald Wexler, Connie Wirtz, and Murray Zimiles.

My colleagues at the Worcester Art Museum have been steadfast and hardworking through this long and demanding campaign. Director James A. Welu has been an enthusiastic supporter of the project from its inception. Susan E. Strickler, director of curatorial affairs, and Tony King, deputy director, made incalculable contributions in guiding me through the mystifying complexities of organization and administration, and in their tolerance of my frequent dereliction of daily responsibilities. Elizabeth De Sabato Swinton, curator of Asian art, and Stephen B. Jareckie, curator of photography, provided supportive research, bore long discussions over the prints, read early drafts of the catalogue, and offered many helpful facts and comments. Several fascinating and useful discussions were shared over months of research and writing with Judith C. Walsh, paper conservator at the Worcester Art Museum, who offered many ideas and observations concerning matters not only technical.

This catalogue has also benefited greatly from the efforts of Jennifer K Layton, intern in the Department of Prints, Drawings, and Photographs at the Worcester Art Museum, whose position was jointly funded by Charles and Kitty Sawyer and the John Sloan Memorial Foundation. She contributed to the book as an able research assistant and exacting proofreader, and above all in her careful preparation of the extensive bibliography. Photography for the catalogue, funded by the Mellon Foundation, was done mostly by Ron White, with contributions by Dirk Bakker and Patrick Young. The monumental task of producing and refining typescript was ably undertaken by Margaret Avery, Jill Burns, and Virginia Harding.

Support for this project was provided in part by the Members' Council of the Worcester Art Museum and by the Heald Foundation. Special thanks are due to the lenders of the exhibition, who included Clinton Adams, Garo Antreasian, the Amon Carter Museum, James and Margaret Heald, Reginald Neal, Nathan Oliveira, and Charles and Kitty Sawyer. The logistics of the traveling exhibition were expertly managed by Sally Freitag; John R. Reynolds prepared the prints for the exhibition and oversaw its installation; John Rossetti prepared the traveling crates; and Joanne Carroll and Cynthia Gilliland prepared the exhibition labels. Other important contributions to the project were made by Jaqui Bazin, Susan Courtemanche, Anne Gibson, Sandra Petrie Hachey, Clare O'Connell, and Jennifer Weininger.

The book was skillfully edited by Robin Jacobson, who worked with diligence and remarkable patience against a hectic schedule. Its production was accomplished with enthusiasm and expertise by Eve Picower and James L. Mairs of W. W. Norton. I am very grateful to Katy Homans for the catalogue's elegant design.

I am also indebted to James N. Heald II, whose fascination with this subject diverted my attention from the Old Masters. His exacting connoisseurship and contagious enthusiasm have been formative for my own interest in American prints. Finally, I am grateful to Roberta Gordon, without whose tolerance and support over the past few years this project would have been a far more formidable task.

David Acton

Relief

Figure 1
Ugo da Carpi (Italian, about 1460–1523), after Parmigianino (Italian, 1503–40), *Diogenes* (detail), about 1530. Woodcut. Worcester Art Museum, Mrs. Kingsmill Marrs Collection, 1926.334.

Figure 2
Ando Hiroshige (Japanese, 1797–1858), *The Whirlpool of Awa*, from *Famous Places in the Sixty-Odd Provinces*, 1853–56. Woodcut. Worcester Art Museum, The John Chandler Bancroft Collection, G1449.

In the twentieth century, the techniques most popular with American artists making color prints have been those of the relief media. Perhaps because of their simplicity and accessibility, these methods have been the focus of the broadest range of experimentation and innovation. Relief printmaking in America has, in general, progressed from a commercial process to an illustrative and reproductive one closely allied with the production of books and periodicals, to a highly specialized, creative artistic medium.

The printing matrix is created by carving away from a flat surface—usually that of a block of wood—areas that are meant not to print. Ink is then deposited on the uncarved areas and transferred to paper under pressure, either by hand rubbing or in a printing press. Woodcut, the most prevalent among the different techniques, utilizes materials that are universally and cheaply available, and offers infinite possibilities for technical variation. Artists can make woodcuts by themselves, and the technique encourages personal adaptation.

Historically, woodcuts were printed in oil-base printing inks, and their pigments were derived from the same colorants as used in contemporary oil paints. These sticky inks were applied to the blocks with leather-covered tamping pads; later, rollers covered with leather or a similar material such as gelatin or rubber were used. Relief blocks were printed in a variety of mechanical presses, which generally applied pressure vertically against the block, rather than laterally from a moving roller. Traditionally, with prints of multiple colors, each color was printed from a separate block. Registration was achieved by locking the printing blocks and paper into fixed positions in the press. Woodblocks of identical size and shape were clenched in the vicelike chase of the press, and the paper was held in a hinged tympan frame, having been pressed onto pins that perforated the margins.[1]

In formulating their practices of color relief printmaking, American artists drew from the perfected wisdom of two traditions—those of Western Europe and Japan. In Europe during the Renaissance, woodcuts evolved in conjunction with book printing, and the first color relief prints in the West were produced in Germany during the early sixteenth century.[2] These chiaroscuro woodcuts were meant to imitate the current manner of drawing on toned paper with pen, wash, and white heightening. Along with a conventional linear woodcut, a supplementary block printed a neutral color. Grooves in this tone block created highlights by allowing portions of the white paper to remain unprinted. The chiaroscuro woodcut, an Italian variation of this technique, was developed in Venice by Ugo da Carpi in about 1515. This process eliminated the linear matrix and represented light and shadow with two or three tones of a single hue, each printed from a different block (Fig. 1). Occasionally, an etched plate was used for the outlines in order to imitate more precisely a washed pen drawing.[3]

In Japan, color printing developed into a commercial method for producing popular, inexpensive ephemera. *Ukiyo-e*, or "pictures of the floating world," originally depicted the realm of worldly delights, the pleasure quarter of the eighteenth-century urban center of Edo, the domain of stylish actors and fashionable courtesans. Later, printmakers represented images from legend and literature as well as landscapes of dreamlike beauty. In contrast to Western artisans, Japanese printmakers applied ink to carved woodblocks with brushes, deftly painting washes onto the block for each impression.[4] Mixing natural pigments with water and a medium of rice paste on the surface of the woodblocks, they achieved modulation,

color blending, and subtleties of hue and tone that were very different from Western woodcuts (Fig. 2). Dampened paper was placed face down on the woodblock and then printed by rubbing the back of the sheet with a *baren*, a flat pad made from a palm leaf. Multicolor woodcuts, printed from several blocks, were registered by careful alignment of the paper in guide marks carved at exactly the same position in the lower corners of each block.

In both the Western and Eastern printmaking traditions, a division of labor governed the production of relief prints. The designers were distinct from the craftsmen, who cut the blocks; the printers, who actually produced the works; and the publishers, who financed production of the prints and managed their distribution and sales.

European papers, traditionally made from cotton and linen fibers of recycled rags, differ in substance and quality from Japanese papers.[5] *Washi*—commonly called "Japan" papers in the West—were usually composed of the long fibers of the inner bark of several varieties of the Asian mulberry bush.[6] With the rise in interest in Japanese prints during the nineteenth century, these soft, absorbent papers became popular in Europe. In the mid-twentieth century, American woodcut artists also came to prefer these papers for their resistance to printing stresses and for their translucent appearance.

Many different woods were used for relief printing blocks. They ranged, according to the needs of the process, from soft varieties such as pine and basswood to harder box, pear, and sycamore. The creative artist, working alone, usually favored soft, workable materials; commercial printers preferred harder and more durable woods for making large editions. In Japan, printing blocks were customarily carved in planks of cherry wood.

Figure 3
Gustav Sigismund Peters (1793–1847), *General Invitation*, from *The Courtship, Marriage, and Pic-Nic Dinner of Cock Robin and Jenny Wren*, 1837. Wood engraving. American Antiquarian Society.

Chiaroscuro woodcuts were produced steadily in Europe, albeit not in profusion, through the seventeenth century by such artists as Ludolph Büsinck and Bartolommeo Coroliano. The practice was carried through the eighteenth century by Nicholas Le Sueur in Paris, Antonio Maria Zanetti in Rome, and John Baptist Jackson in London, all of whom made multiblock color woodcut reproductions of the works of famous bygone artists.[7] In 1764, the English poet, painter, and engraver William Blake developed a unique method for printing in color from metal plates etched in relief, which he seems to have inked using an offset method. His unique experiments produced forerunners of the type-metal line block or chromotypographic print, a technology that was utilized in the nineteenth and twentieth centuries more for commercial printing than by artists. Blake's methods were essentially forgotten until the middle of the twentieth century, when artists in New York explored these innovations as the basis for their own experiments.[8]

Early in the nineteenth century, color relief printmaking in the United States evolved from traditional European methods. Employed chiefly for commercial and illustrative purposes, American methods trailed some years behind transatlantic achievements. The first color woodcut made in the United States seems to have been the *Plan of Boston*, printed in 1814 by the flamboyant inventor Benjamin Dearborn.[9] He modified a large letterpress to accommodate four woodblocks of the same size, one at a time— essentially as printers of the Renaissance had done—to produce a print in three colors with black. The "typographically coloured" map carried an advertisement for the new printing process. Despite this confident promotion of his capabilities, Dearborn must have attracted little attention, for he made just three color woodcuts.

It had long been known that by carving a block of very hard wood across rather than along its grain, much thinner lines could be cut and finer details achieved. A burin, the copperplate engraving tool, could even be used to gouge thin furrows in the wood. But printing a clear image from such a block required great pressure, and soft papers could not withstand this stress. However, late in the eighteenth century, the Englishman Thomas Bewick successfully printed minutely carved blocks of end-grain boxwood on mechanical presses that could exert strong, even pressure on newly available hard-surfaced papers; thus wood engraving was developed. The longevity of engraved wood blocks made the process most appropriate for reproductive and commercial purposes, in which its use was soon concentrated.

At the beginning of the nineteenth century, William Savage, one of the most accomplished printers in London, focused his talents on color printing from engraved woodblocks, combining the achievements of his English predecessors. He developed an alternative to linseed oil–base inks, which had discolored the papers of John Baptist Jackson's prints. Savage's treatise *Practical Hints on Decorative Printing*, first published in 1818, presented the state of the technology of relief printing and revealed his own refinements.[10·]Six charts displayed Savage's own colored inks, which were also utilized in thirty-three full-page color plates. Printed in as many as thirty colors, these technical tours de force exemplified the high level of refinement that chromoxylography had attained in Britain.

In Germany at this time, the craft of color wood engraving was developed with equal zeal by Friedrich Wilhelm Gubitz, who created sophisticated, expensive prints conceived for an audience of bibliophiles and collectors. His best-known works were exacting facsimiles, complete with gold ink, of the imperial productions of Renaissance artist Lucas Cranach. Besides working his boxwood blocks with traditional

knives and gouges, Gubitz tried working with punches and roulettes, tools more commonly used on intaglio plates.[11]

By contrast, the few American wood engravings printed in color were behind in style and technique, and far rarer. The earliest were produced between 1826 and 1847 by Gustav Sigismund Peters. Born in Langebruck, Germany, in 1793, Peters was active by 1823 in Carlisle, Pennsylvania.[12] There, in partnership with John B. Moser, a townsman from Germany, he created an array of German-language ephemera, including broadsides, a German-English dictionary, and—as did most rural printers of the day—a newspaper, *Der Pennsylvanische Anzeiger*. In 1826, the shop produced *Der Lutherisches ABC, und Namen Buchlein für Kinder* (*The Lutheran Alphabet, and Little Book of Names for Children*), which was illustrated with color wood engravings. Although the partnership dissolved soon after moving to nearby Harrisburg, Peters went on to produce several children's books in both German and English, including *The Courtship, Marriage, and Pic-Nic Dinner of Cock Robin and Jenny Wren* (Fig. 3). Printed on a letterpress, the books were liberally illustrated with four-color wood engravings. The style of these illustrations places them in the popular book printing tradition of Europe; technically, Peters's prints are quite masterful.

Although wood engraving soon became the standard method for illustrating newspapers, magazines, and books in nineteenth-century America, it was used by craftsmen rather than academically trained artists. The decorative fillers and illustrations that they produced very rarely appeared in color.

Figure 4
Joseph W. Morse (active about 1830–60), *Great Golden Menagerie*, 1853. Woodcut. American Antiquarian Society.

Early in the nineteenth century, color printing techniques were used in the production of wallpaper. However, this specialized field seems to have developed in isolation, and its methods were not used for printing books or broadsides. The first woodcuts used to print repeated patterns on rolls of paper were colored by hand with stencils of paper or tin, a method that grew out of the colonial practice of painting stenciled decorations directly onto walls. Although inexpensive domestic wallpapers were printed in one color from relief blocks, it was customary for complex colored wallpapers to be imported. The manufacture of wallpaper with printed colors remained rare in the United States until the advent of machine-made relief printed wallpapers around 1840.[13]

Perhaps the most visible color woodcuts of the day were large, colorful posters that advertised circus and theatrical performances. A pioneer of this genre was Jonas Booth, a printer who emigrated from England to New York in 1822.[14] This craftsman revolutionized commercial printing in America when he built mechanical presses from his memories of the machines with which he had worked in England. Shortly before 1840, after years as a printer of books and ephemera, he made the first big color posters for the circus from multiple woodblocks. Booth was the patriarch of a large family, which carried on this business after his death in 1850.

Designed to be bold, arresting, and legible from a distance, circus posters combined striking typography with dynamic action and bright colors. Images and type were printed on separate sheets, in modules of various forms and sizes that could be adapted to the odd shapes and dimensions of walls and fences. Sometimes the images were engraved in blocks composed of many small pieces of boxwood bolted together. More often, however, large planks of mahogany, basswood, or clear white pine were used, planed to the thickness of type. Like sign painters, poster designers worked directly on these woodblocks, which were placed end to end on a large easel, plotting out the compositions of the key block with crayon or charcoal and filling the outlines with India ink. Impressions from the linear matrix were used to transfer the design to the other blocks, one of which was carved for each color.[15]

This technique of working directly on planks of pine was perfected by Joseph W. Morse shortly before 1845.[16] He was probably the apprentice of Shubael D. Childs in New York during the 1830s. Later, Morse worked in the shop of Thomas W. Strong, whose specialty was greeting cards, and he may have contributed illustrations to the illuminated Bible published by Harper's in New York in 1846. Morse designed and probably cut the blocks for the *Great Golden Menagerie* for Van Amburgh's Circus in 1853 (Fig. 4). Along with several lines of type, this dramatic fantasy was printed on a steam-driven press at the jobbing plant of Clerry and Reilly in New York. In this image, the artist used parallel hatching systems to modulate tone and model forms, revealing experience as a wood engraver. Such pictorial posters as this were usually printed in black, three primary colors, and a neutral tint. By overlapping, tinting, and isolating these colors, artisans could produce a remarkable range of hues. For large posters, however, simplicity and impact were preferable to sublety and complexity.

Color woodcut posters required big presses, and because it was time-consuming to clean and reink the machines in changing from black to colors, this kind of printing was a labor-intensive business. Thus, production of posters quickly became a specialty of large companies, usually concentrated in the biggest cities. By about 1848, these printers also made posters for theaters and music halls. Soon the railroads and the state and county fairs also used color posters extensively. The expression "billed like a circus," which was first used at this time to describe a gaudily advertised performance, came by extension to mean any ostentatious display. Traditional woodcut posters continue to be made for fairs and circuses to this day.[17]

In England, the field of chromoxylography reached its technical and commercial summit by the mid-nineteenth century. Many large, flourishing firms produced full-color prints to illustrate books and for reproductions of fine art. Edmund Evans and Walter Crane designed color wood engravings to illustrate children's books. George Baxter received a patent for a process that combined many colors printed by individual relief blocks with an intaglio plate printed in a neutral color to add details and modulation. These expensive prints were meant to be framed.[18]

Color wood engravings of this quality remained rare in the United States because of the expense and technical demands and costliness of the process. The few American chromoxylographs were released in the most sophisticated publications and sold in the most exclusive shops, though they varied widely in technical and aesthetic quality. These expensive prints were often made by craftsmen who had been schooled abroad, such as Alfred Bobbett.[19] Born in England in about 1824, Bobbett trained in London as a wood engraver and worked in partnership with Charles Edmonds in New York from 1848 to 1854, in a company that produced high-quality bills, broadsides, and illustrations. He contributed wood engravings to John Gadsby Chapman's *American Drawing Book*.[20]

Figure 5
Alfred Bobbett (active 1824–about 1880) and Edward Hooper (active 1829–70), after Albert F. Bellows (1829–83), *Spring,* from the *Atlantic Almanac,* 1868. Wood engraving. American Antiquarian Society.

In 1855, Bobbett entered into partnership with Edward Hooper, another immigrant, who had trained in London and was an adept watercolorist and wood engraver. By 1865, Bobbett and Hooper had moved to Brooklyn, where from 1868 to 1870 they concentrated on chromoxylography, producing some of the most sophisticated American color wood engravings of the day. They illustrated the *Atlantic Almanac,* a gracious literary annual that utilized color wood engravings for its covers and its reproductions of paintings by famous artists (Fig. 5).[21]

Like their European counterparts, these prints were characterized by myriad layers of overlapping translucent colors. Minute details and subtle tonal variations were achieved by fine crosshatching in the blocks with a burin. The difficulties of the reproductive process and the hard, inhibitive materials generally gave these images a stiff, mechanical quality; their vitality came mostly from their delicately modulated colors. An exhibition of prints by Bobbett and Hooper was mounted in 1869 at the National Academy. But it seems that demand for their products was limited, for the partnership was dissolved in 1870, and both craftsmen abandoned commercial chromoxylography. Afterward, the *Atlantic Almanac* stopped publishing color reproductions.

Also significant among American firms that produced color wood engravings were those of Thomas R. Holland (later Holland and Stinson) in Boston, and Adrian and Sharp and the H. H. Lloyd Company in New York. The requirements of expertise, time-consuming precision, and labor intensity precluded creative printmakers from using the technique in the nineteenth century. Furthermore, around 1845, the cheaper chromolithograph began to replace the color wood engraving as the most common form of color print, especially in the lucrative fields of

book illustration and commercial printing. The relief techniques of color line block and half-tone chromotypograph came to dominate commercial printing through most of the twentieth century.

Just before the turn of the century, American artists, directed by the French fashion for oriental design and culture, became interested in Japanese printmaking. This interest was further stimulated by color prints exhibited in the Japanese pavilion at the Centennial Exposition in Philadelphia in 1876, and at the World Columbian Exposition at Chicago in 1893. In 1889, the Smithsonian Institution in Washington, D.C., proudly displayed a collection of prints, woodcutting, and printing equipment given to the national museum by the Japanese government.[22] Cosmopolitan Americans such as Captain Frank Brinkley, Ernest Fenollosa, Charles L. Freer, and Frank Lloyd Wright began collecting Japanese prints, forming the foundation for what became the world's finest collections of this material. At this time, a handful of American artists studied the traditional techniques of *ukiyo-*e in order to create their own color woodblock prints in that style.

These artists transferred to color woodcuts Western ideals of the print as an art object, giving them a value they had never had in Japan. The esteem of American collectors for Japanese prints coincided with the Etching Revival in the West, and its respect for these graphic works of art. Notions of art for art's sake, of the renaissance of the methods of the Old Masters, and of precious limited editions were applied to these hybrid productions. Color woodcuts by American artists were given some of the cachet of prints by Rembrandt, Whistler, Harunobu, or Hiroshige.

Arthur Wesley Dow (cat. 6) was probably first exposed to Japanese art while studying in France. After his return to Massachusetts in 1889, he became closely associated with Fenollosa, the curator of oriental art at the Museum of Fine Arts in Boston. Exchanging ideas freely and working with the collection that the curator had compiled, these two aesthetes combined principles of Japanese composition with elements from the Arts and Crafts movement to create a new style. His prints, mostly representing New England landscapes, were experiments with color relief printmaking as an expressive tool. Through Dow, color woodcut came to the forefront of the development of abstraction in American art. Dow was an influential teacher, and his theories, practices, and writings molded a generation of art teachers, who in turn spread his ideas and educational systems across the country. Among his students were Max Weber (cat. 15), Pedro J. Lemos (cat. 24), May Gearhart (cat. 22), photographer Alvin Langdon Coburn, and painter Georgia O'Keeffe. These artists extensively used Japanese compositional models and the technique of color woodcut.

Helen Hyde (cat. 8) seems to have been the first important American artist to produce color woodcuts in Japan. This painter and etcher moved to Tokyo to study art in 1899. She learned the fundamentals of traditional *sumi* painting with the venerable Kano Tomonobu, and her adept brushwork is apparent in woodcuts of her design, which were carved and printed in the customary manner by specialist craftsmen. Over a period of several years, Hyde depicted Japanese children and their mothers in sentimental woodcuts that reflected both her training as an illustrator and ideas derived directly from *ukiyo-*e prints. Widely exhibited and sold in the United States, these prints established her considerable reputation.

In 1897, while living in Paris, the American painter Charles Hovey Pepper had his first solo exhibition at L'Art Nouveau, a gallery run by

Figure 6
Bertha Lum (1879–1954), *Temple Portal*, about 1925. Raised-line woodcut with watercolor. Private collection.

Figure 7
Ethel Mars (1876–about 1956), *Untitled*, about 1916. Woodcut. National Museum of American Art, Smithsonian Institution, gift of Mrs. B.J.O. Nordfeldt, 1976.93.

Siegfried Bing, the famous dealer of *ukiyo-e* prints. In this way Pepper was introduced to Japanese woodcuts, which he then studied and collected. Traveling to Japan in 1903, he met Hyde and the craftsmen who worked with her.[23] Japanese artisans produced several color woodcuts from Pepper's watercolors. Several other Americans traveled to Japan to learn the techniques of color woodcut, among them Edna Boies Hopkins, Elizabeth Keith, Lillian Miller, and Bertha Boynton Lum.

After studies at the Art Institute of Chicago and the Frank Holme Studio of Illustration, also in Chicago, Bertha Lum worked for two years in the stained-glass studio of Anna Weston.[24] When Lum first visited Japan on her honeymoon in 1903, she doggedly sought out craftsmen practicing the traditional woodcut techniques. She observed these shy and protective artisans at work, and purchased woodblocks, cutting tools, and brushes. Arriving home, she learned the process through diligent and patient practice. Lum returned to Japan in 1908 to study woodcut techniques firsthand. On her next visit, in 1911, the artist rented a house and engaged artisans to print her own woodblocks, much as Hyde had done before her. She returned to Japan regularly every three or four years to make prints during visits of five to six months.

In November 1920, the first of two solo exhibitions of Lum's prints was mounted at the Los Angeles County Museum.[25] In 1922 the artist traveled to China; she returned there many times, and soon established a second residence in Peking. Her later prints represent Indian, Balinese, and Chinese subjects. Inspired by the works of Lafcadio Hearn, Lum also wrote about oriental life and folklore, and provided the illustrations for her writings.[26]

From her studies of Japanese and Chinese art, Lum developed her original "raised line" printmaking method. She adapted the Japanese method of *ishizuri-e*—a printmaking technique developed to simulate Chinese stone rubbings—in order to imitate the effect of Chinese screens of carved and lacquered coromandel wood, with their raised outlines separating flat areas of color (Fig. 6). Lum never disclosed the technique of these remarkable works, but they were probably unique rather than multiple productions. It seems that the embossments were made from carved woodblocks, in which the linear designs were deeply cut in the manner of an intaglio plate. When the artist pressed thin, thoroughly wetted bamboo fiber paper into these grooves, the linear composition was cast in high relief. These pieces were then strengthened by laminating other layers of paper to the verso. The linear design isolated shapes that were afterward painted by hand in gouache.

The influence of Asian art came indirectly to many other American artists who were working and studying in Europe, particularly in Paris.[27] Soon after the beginning of World War I, hundreds of them returned to the United States, many gathering at the artists' colony in Provincetown, Massachusetts.[28] Here several artists were reunited who had known each other in Paris and who shared an enthusiasm for printmaking. Although their styles were diverse, each was influenced by both Japanese printmaking and contemporary European art.[29]

Maud Hunt Squire and Ethel Mars met when they were students at the Art Academy of Cincinnati. Together, in about 1906, they moved to Paris, where they painted, made prints, and enthusiastically adopted a bohemian life-style, attending Gertrude Stein's famous salon.[30] The influence of French art is apparent in the evolution of their work. Squire created color intaglios in the manner of Eugène Delâtre, representing images of Parisian café life. Mars made

color woodcuts, apparently having learned the process before going to France. Her prints depicted genre scenes, often placid and contemplative, which reflected the influence of the Nabis (Fig. 7). Mars preferred flat, decorative shapes printed in bright hues, in the manner of contemporary German multiple-block color prints.[31] These prints were favorably received by the French and prompted Mars's election to the Société de la Salon d'Automne, in which she showed her work from 1907 to 1913 and served on selection juries. She also taught the process of color woodcut to Ada Gilmore (cat. 12) and Mildred McMillen, two young artists from Chicago.

After studying with Dow in New York, Edna Boies Hopkins (cat. 9) learned the technique of *ukiyo-e* in Japan in 1904. Afterward, settling in Paris, she dedicated herself to mastering this process and to forging her own style by combining this technique with the current French manner. In the summers between 1914 and 1920, Hopkins often went on extended visits to Provincetown, where she made prints and taught color woodcut to other artists.

In 1900, B.J.O. Nordfeldt (cat. 11) had learned the Japanese printmaking techniques from Frank Morley Fletcher in Reading, England. Nordfeldt's well-received woodcuts of the ensuing decade were closely inspired by *ukiyo-e* prints in composition and palette as well as technique. In the winter of 1915, he originated a simplified technical innovation that transformed the look of his prints and became the hallmark of color woodcut printmaking in Provincetown. Frustrated with the tedium of carving several blocks and with the laborious process of inking, registering, and printing from them, Nordfeldt used a single block prepared in a manner akin to the inking of an intaglio plate *à la poupée*.

Dedicated to making relief prints, the Provincetown artists formed the nucleus of a group who shared ideas and worked and exhibited together. Many of them contributed to a show in May of 1916 at the Berlin Photographic Company, a gallery in New York that showcased avant-garde art. When they exhibited again in Provincetown that summer, numerous other artists were drawn to relief printmaking and to this growing coterie. Painter Oliver Chaffee—who later married Ada Gilmore—taught the single-block color process to Blanche Lazzell (cat. 18), who instructed Agnes Weinrich (cat. 20). Gustave Baumann (cat. 23), Eliza Draper Gardiner (cat. 19), Tod Lindenmuth (cat. 25), and Margaret Jordan Patterson (cat. 14) were among the many artists who, using a range of color relief techniques, contributed to the exhibitions of the Provincetown group. In 1918, at the height of this period of enthusiasm and before these artists began to disperse, the Provincetown Printers, the first woodblock printmaking society in America, was formed.

Although color relief printmaking in New York City during this period was oriented to book illustration, its diversity can be seen by comparing prints of Alfred J. Frueh with those of Max Weber. Born in Lima, Ohio, in 1880, Frueh worked as a painter, illustrator, and craftsman in New York.[32] He is best known for his satirical cartoons, which he regularly contributed to *The New Yorker*, *Variety*, and *Life* magazines. His caricatures of actors in and out of character present a lively vision of the world of music halls and theaters. Many of these were carved in linoleum, a fairly new material, and printed in color, and were published in compilations of 1917 and 1922.[33]

A committed and inspired painter, Max Weber (cat. 15) had directly experienced the development of modernist styles in Paris. Despite a lack of critical or financial support, he continued to paint in an avant-garde style in New York in the 1910s. In 1919 and 1920, he created a series of woodcuts, many of which were in color, that synthesized his European modernist style with the influences of primitive and ethnographic arts. The artist employed the most basic process and modest materials to make innovative woodcuts of great sophistication and vitality. Like Gauguin and the group of German printmakers known as *Die Brücke*, Weber attempted to exploit the distinctive graphic character of the material itself. He exhibited with the Provincetown Printers, probably having been introduced to the group through his long friendship with artist William Zorach, who also made relief prints, a few of them in color.

Simultaneously, a community of color woodcut artists was thriving in California. This group had also been ultimately stimulated by Arthur Wesley Dow's *japonisme*.[34] Their work was featured in 1915 at the Panama-Pacific International Exposition in San Francisco, a world's fair organized in celebration of the opening of the Panama Canal and the entry of California into world markets. Art was assembled from all over the world for exhibitions, which were an important part of the fair. There were several print shows, including installations of contemporary works by American and European printmakers as well as an exhibition of Japanese prints, traditional and contemporary. Several of the Provincetown Printers, including Baumann, Hopkins, Nordfeldt, and Patterson, were among the prizewinners at the exposition.[35]

The exhibition of prints by California artists at the fair was organized by Pedro Lemos (cat. 24), who had by this time become a prominent figure in printmaking in the state. A student of Dow and an active creator of woodcuts, linocuts, and intaglios in color, Lemos was also a teacher, the author of many instructive books and pamphlets, founder of the Rionido Summer Art School, and a

museum director. In 1911, he helped found the California Society of Etchers. One of his most prolific students of printmaking was William Seltzer Rice (cat. 28), whose widely exhibited color prints reveal the aesthetic of the Arts and Crafts movement. Rice was also a schoolteacher, and passed on his method to many students.

After studies in Britain and Paris, Frank Morley Fletcher traveled to Japan to learn traditional printmaking methods.[36] Returning to England, he taught the process to many students. Fletcher was director of the Edinburgh College of Art from 1907 to 1923, when he moved to California. There, he established the Santa Barbara School of Art, which offered a curriculum that was influenced by Asian philosophy and included the Japanese traditional method of color woodcut.

In Los Angeles, brothers Howell C. and Benjamin C. Brown founded the Print Makers Society of California, later known as the California Print Makers, with the aid of May Gearhart and her sister Frances Hammell Gearhart (cats. 22, 16). This organization sponsored annual traveling print shows and commissioned the yearly publication of a print for distribution to all of its associate members. In 1932, the California Print Makers sponsored the first of their exhibitions entitled "Fifty Colour Prints of the Year," a show circulated by the American Federation of Arts. Frances Gearhart, the champion of the color woodcut in southern California, favored landscape views that represented the magnificent scenery of the American West. She made use of Eastern techniques and adapted her style from Japanese models; her work of the 1910s anticipated that of later Japanese artists who became popular in the United States, such as Chiura Obata and Hiroshi Yoshida.

Yoshida had already had a successful career in Japan as a Western-style painter by 1920, when he was induced by Watanabe Shozaburo, the publisher of prints in Tokyo, to begin making woodcuts.[37] Yoshida's reputation as a printmaker became greater in the United States than in his homeland, and a number of his woodcuts parallel in subject those of Frances Gearhart. He derived many of his images from his travels in the American and Canadian West. The artist became prominent in the *shin hanga*, or new prints movement, in which Western-influenced Japanese artists utilized traditional *ukiyo-e* techniques. Yoshida was also instrumental in the organization of the landmark exhibition of contemporary Japanese prints at the Toledo Museum of Art in Ohio in 1930.[38]

Many other printmakers of the American West, including Anders Aldrin, Cora Boone (cat. 29), Cornelis Botke (cat. 30), Jessie Arms Botke, Meta Cohen Hendel, Frank Holme, Florence Lundborg, and Elizabeth Norton, made color relief prints that were conservative in style. While in the South, Alice Ravel Huger Smith and Henrietta Bailey worked in this genre, and in the northwestern United States and Canada, Waldo Corwin Chase and Walter J. Philips made excellent color woodcut landscapes. A number of artists who exhibited with the Prairie Printmakers, including Glenn Wheete, Ernest Watson, and Eva Auld Watson, also produced color relief prints.

A valiant attempt to chronicle the quickly growing interest in color relief, the remarkable exhibition "Woodcut Prints in Color by American Artists," was organized by the Detroit Institute of Arts in 1919.[39] Works by the American *japonistes*, the Provincetown Printers, and artists working in California and New York City were included in this show, which comprised 160 works by twenty-two artists. The exhibition contained a didactic component in the inclusions of Japanese cutting and printing tools, and all of the technical materials related to a print by Gustave Baumann (cat. 23), including the original sketch and the complete set of woodblocks along with progressive proofs. The introductory essay accompanying the checklist underscored the range of technical demands required of the woodcut artist, clearly showing that he undertook the process alone. These distributable, affordable, multiple original works of art were shown to have had a democratizing effect upon the visual arts.

Baumann exemplified an array of American commercial artists and book illustrators who derived their style and technique from European illustrators. These craftsmen used color relief methods as the means for creating their own printing matrices. Trained in the European tradition of color printing for books and for commercial purposes, for a time Baumann used color woodcuts in commercial contexts. Although the artist knew American printmakers working across the country and well understood their technical innovations, he always printed his woodcuts from multiple blocks on a press, in his own version of the method of book illustrator.

Rudolph Ruzicka (cat. 26), another artist who was oriented to the bookish aspects of printmaking, forged his technique out of a dedication to craftsmanship, a love of typography, and personal respect for the virtuoso American wood engravers of the nineteenth century. Ruzicka studied the history of color printmaking in European and American museums and libraries and became quite an expert on the subject.

The new material of linoleum came into use for relief printmaking in the United States shortly after 1910, introduced it seems, by the Czechoslovakian artist Vojtěch Preissig.[40] Born in the village of Světec, near Teplitz, on July 31, 1873, Preissig was a student of Friedrich Ohmann at the Art Academy in Prague. In 1898, he went to Paris to continue his studies with Franz Kupka and Alphonse Mucha.[41] There, Preissig became adept in a range of printmaking techniques, especially color intaglio. Returning to Prague in 1903, he worked as a designer in a type foundry, while maintaining his independent printmaking activity. The artist may have taken up linocut under the influence of the Wiener Werkstätte, where printmaking experiments with the synthetic material were undertaken in the first decade of the century. In 1910, he came to New York to work as a commercial artist and illustrator; two years later, he was teaching classes in the graphic arts at the Art Students League, including the method of linocut.

Although Preissig's poster designs were bold and decorative, his prints, often in color, generally represented picturesque views and genre scenes in a Barbizon-related style. He often depicted Czechoslovakian subjects in his intaglios and linocuts. In 1914, Preissig met Arthur Wesley Dow, who persuaded him to teach a course in "The Arts of the Book" at Columbia Teachers College. The two artists showed prints and paintings in a joint exhibition at the Montclair Art Museum in New Jersey in 1914–15. During World War I, Preissig created propaganda posters for distribution in Czechoslovakia. He joined the faculty of the Wentworth Institute of Technology in Boston in 1916, where he taught graphic design, typography, and printmaking until 1924. After a period as a freelance designer, Preissig returned to Prague before 1930.[42]

Linoleum was composed of powdered cork and linseed oil bound together with resin and molded onto burlap or canvas. Produced primarily as a floor covering, it was inexpensive and readily available. Preissig preferred this material for its workability and for its uniformity, which facilitated the printing of large, even areas of color in posters. The softness of linoleum, its consistency, and its absence of grain made it easier to cut than wood, simplifying relief printmaking and the teaching of the technique. Dow recognized the significance of linocut for education,

and its suitability to the schoolroom was the focus of enthusiasm in the 1920s, reflected in instructional books about the medium by William Seltzer Rice (cat. 28) and Ernest Watson. Many printmakers oriented to book illustration, including Edward Penfield (cat. 4), Wuanita Smith, and Allen Lewis, favored the material for its resilience and durability.

Born in Mobile, Alabama, in 1873, Allen Lewis studied at the Buffalo (New York) Art Students League under George Bridgman, and afterward in Paris at the Ecole des Beaux-Arts with Gèrome.[43] In 1903, Lewis's color relief prints won awards from the Chicago Society of Etchers and the Buffalo Society of Etchers, and in 1915 at the Panama-Pacific International Exposition in San Francisco. His early prints were wood engravings, influenced by the new school of American wood engravers. Most of his color prints were in the chiaroscuro manner, although they often used two or three tone blocks. Lewis taught wood engraving and color printing from blocks at the Art Students League in New York in the 1920s. He also designed and cut his own typefaces in wood.

Paul Honoré was an artist whose career was divided between mural painting and the production of wood-engraved book illustrations. After studying at the Pennsylvania Academy of Fine Arts and with Frank Brangwyn in London, he settled in Detroit, Michigan.[44] Working in a style that combined a decorative, illustrative quality with sketchy spontaneity, Honoré specialized in color prints, utilizing four blocks, and he often printed in a range of bright, saturated colors (Fig. 8).

Howard McCormick, Percy Grassby, Thomas Nason, Rockwell Kent, Norman Kent, and James D. Havens (cat. 40) numbered among the virtuosi of wood engraving, whose activities grew out of the American tradition of book illustration, and who occasionally experimented with color. Like Ruzicka and Lewis, these artists often straddled the boundaries between illustration and fine printmaking, and they exhibited their works in the group shows of printmaking societies. The audience for illustrated books began to dwindle in the 1930s, and it was almost extinguished by the onset of World War II, an era during which the print media adopted cheaper photographic reproductions for illustration. The rise of modernism also contributed to changing the face of printmaking in this country.

The Arts and Crafts movement—which conceived of printmaking as an applied art that should be available to amateurs—had its final flourish in the late 1920s, when a spate of instructional books by artists about color relief printmaking were published. Primers by Pedro Lemos and William Rice were aimed at instruction in schools, while those by Frank Morley Fletcher and Ernest Watson presented the process as an amusement which could be easily pursued at home for the hobbyist's own pleasure.

In the spring of 1933, at the Brooklyn Museum, a definitive exhibition presented American color prints in many media, including woodcuts by artists from all over the country.[45] This event marked the end of an era In American printmaking, for the reign of realistic, illustrative styles—which had their origin in the Etching Revival of the late nineteenth century and which put great value on technical competence—was also coming to an end. Although modernist prints by Arthur B. Davies, Max Weber, and Agnes Weinrich (cats. 13, 15, 20) were included, most of the nearly three hundred works in the Brooklyn exhibition were conservative and naturalistic in style. In the next decade, American art underwent profound changes in conception, purpose, and practice, all of which were reflected in printmaking.

During the depression, the graphic arts divisions of the Works Progress Administration's Federal Arts Project (WPA/FAP) provided jobs for printmakers who would otherwise have been out of work. This organization also exerted profound influences on printmaking, particularly in color.[46] In the New York City workshop, the most influential of the graphic arts divisions, color relief prints were produced by many artists between 1935 and 1943, under the supervision and technical direction of Albert Heckmann, Isaac Sanger, and Louis Schanker (cat. 41). The workshop offered instruction, equipment, and printing assistance as well as its guaranteed system of remuneration and distribution.

Schanker became the leader in the development of the creative color woodcut in the New York City workshop. Employed by the FAP mural division in 1934, he began experimenting with color relief printmaking after his studies of Japanese and German Expressionist woodcuts. By the middle of 1938, he was working in the FAP graphic arts division, in which he soon became the supervisor of block printing, and in which he remained until 1943. A founding member of the American Abstract Artists group, Schanker was committed to an expressive mode of abstraction, and his approach to technique was exploratory. He led the trend that replaced Social Realist and semiabstract styles with expressive abstraction, and his attitudes toward the creative process and technique influenced many other artists.

Hyman Warsager also distinguished himself by making color woodcuts in the FAP.[47] After studies at the Hartford Art School in Connecticut, the Metropolitan Art School in New York, and the Pratt Institute in Brooklyn, this young painter and illustrator began working in the New York City FAP graphic arts division in 1935. Although he made prints in other media, Warsager specialized in woodcut. His generally figurative style progressed from Social Realism toward a more expressive mode during his experience in the workshop, and he participated in some of the technical experiments undertaken there.[48]

Working in proximity to engravers and lithographers, the woodcut artists sought to emphasize the distinctive quality of their medium by accentuating their materials. Wood grain was deepened by scraping with wire brushes and sandpaper, and printing surfaces were raised with cement in order to enhance texture and manipulate color intensity. By printing some layers of color from engraved end-grain blocks and others from open-grained planks, the artist achieved interesting effects of color, transparency, and luminosity. After his dismissal from the FAP, Warsager joined with Anthony Velonis (cat. 42) in a commercial printing business that made use of his practical experienced gained in the workshop.

Gustave von Groschwitz was the first director of the New York City FAP graphic arts division; he was succeeded by Lynd Ward, Werner Drewes (cat. 55), and Oscar Weissbuch, artists who all worked in relief printmaking. Although they did not make color prints in the FAP workshop, their presence and support was certainly encouraging. In particular, Drewes contributed to the development and spread of the color woodcut in America by sharing his firsthand experiences of German Expressionism and the Bauhaus. Aside from his long and distinguished teaching career, the artist consistently produced block prints, many in color, from his arrival in New York in 1930 until his death in 1985. In 1939, Will Barent (cat. 69) began experimenting with the addition of tone and color blocks to his woodcuts, which he produced sporadically in the midst of a steady output of lithographs and intaglios.

Many changes in American printmaking were introduced by the achievements of the FAP. Gradually, a new audience grew up for this relatively affordable and accessible art. Artists working in other media now found it worthwhile to make prints. Prints became progressively bigger, and color prints became far more common. No longer consigned to library albums and boxes, they were now conceived for the wall, like paintings. New attention was given to surface texture, whether illusionistic or realistic. This new aesthetic went hand in hand with modernist, Surrealist, and Expressionist styles, which tapped the artist's introspective, intuitive vision. As printmakers insisted upon the legitimacy of their works as art, a higher degree of creative inspiration and technical innovation was demanded of them. In all of the graphic media, this attitude gained impetus through the influence of Stanley William Hayter's Atelier 17 (cat. 60), which moved from Paris to New York and opened under the aegis of the New School for Social Research in 1940. There, Hayter encouraged a spirit of experimentation, inviting painters and sculptors to learn printmaking and contribute fresh points of view. Students commingled with established artists who came from far and wide to work at the studio.

In the 1940s, a remarkable group of woodcut artists was assembled in New York, which was fast becoming the center of the postwar art world. This group, which included Will Barnet (cat. 69), Leonard Baskin, Fred Becker (cat. 62), Worden Day (cat. 72), Werner Drewes (cat. 55), Misch Kohn, Seong Moy (cat. 74), Anne Ryan (cat. 65), and Louis Schanker (cat. 41), was supplemented by the arrival of immigrant artists. Bernard Reder joined them in 1943, Antonio Frasconi (cat. 89) in 1945, and Adja Yunkers (cat. 81) in 1947.

Bernard Reder was born near Czernowitz, Austria (now Romania), in 1897.[49] He was introduced to printmaking when he was a student of sculpture in Prague between 1919

and 1922. In Paris in the late 1930s, he worked in a style similar to that of his friend Aristide Maillol. In 1945, two years after his immigration to the United States, Reder suffered an illness that prevented him from working strenuously on sculpture, so he returned to woodcuts. Reder inked his vigorously carved relief blocks in the manner of a monotype. The blocks themselves were like low-relief sculptures, deeply gouged with a variety of tools. The artist printed his woodcuts with oil paints in very thin veils of color, applied at once to a single block, from which only one impression was pulled. Drawing on ancient mythology, stories from his Hasidic Jewish background, and his own romantic imagination, Reder created his own fabulous universe. The people, animals, and musical and mystical celebrations of this realm found further expression in the 1950s and 1960s in color woodcuts, lithographs, and expressionistic sculpture, which were similar in style to the works of Jacques Lipchitz.

Experimental approaches to style and technique spread throughout the print world in the 1950s. Artists often gathered in groups—such as VANGUARD, the Graphic Circle, Studio 74, and 14 Painter-Printmakers—where they hoped to share ideas and encourage inspiration.[50] They also attempted to stimulate broader popular interest in modern graphic art by organizing group exhibitions. In some sense, all of these groups were dedicated to sharing ideas and developing free creative attitudes toward style and technique. The groups exhibited together, in dealers' galleries and in museums, and all of them included artists working in color relief printmaking.

In 1947, the Society of American Graphic Artists expanded its activities, holding yearly exhibitions to

Figure 9
Alfred Sessler (1909–63), *Look Heavenward Tree III*, 1958. Woodcut. Elvehjem Art Center, gift of Mrs. Alfred Sessler, 67.9.68.

showcase the works of a selection of its members. In the same year, the Brooklyn Museum instituted its National Print Annual exhibitions, and relief prints in color were presented in each exhibition over the following thirteen years.[51] Una E. Johnson, the remarkable curator of prints and drawings at the Brooklyn Museum, worked closely with artists on a series of solo exhibitions, many of which focused on relief printmaking in color.

Beginning in the late 1940s, several new graphic workshops were established at art schools and universities across the country. They were led by the printmaking program established by Mauricio Lasansky (cat. 67) at the University of Iowa, where intaglio was most avidly pursued. In a sense the progeny of Atelier 17, they also ushered in their own era of experimentation and productivity. In 1944, Alfred Sessler joined the faculty at the University of Wisconsin in Madison.[52] Having studied in the Milwaukee FAP and with Robert von Neumann, the artist began offering classes in lithography, etching, and woodcut in 1946, thus establishing one of the most vital university printmaking programs in the nation. In the early 1950s, he concentrated on expressive, brightly colored, multiple-block woodcuts (Fig. 9). Sessler's best-known color relief prints, produced late in the decade, were powerful compositions in which organic forms twisted themselves into expressive, surrealistic abstractions. In 1957, Sessler seems to have been the first to develop a reduction block method for color woodcuts.[53] This process, in which a single relief block was progressively cut away for subsequent printings of different colors, was utilized soon afterward by Picasso.

In the 1950s, the revival of interest in color woodcut spread worldwide. American artists were prominent in an important exhibition of relief prints in color organized by the Victoria and Albert Museum in London in 1956, which subsequently traveled

around Britain.[54] Artists and collectors in the United States also became aware of a thriving modern school of color woodblock printmaking in Japan. *Nippon Sosaku-hanga kyokai*, or the Japanese "creative print" movement, had been growing gradually since its organization in 1918. Artists of this school strove to synthesize Western, modernist aesthetics with those of traditional Japan. They broke decisively from the past in that they did their own carving and printing. They often leaned toward spontaneous methods of cutting and used the full range of inking techniques. In the postwar occupation of Japan, Americans began to collect, study, and organize exhibitions of these prints. Their Western popularization reached its zenith in 1960, when the Art Institute of Chicago mounted a landmark exhibition of *Sosaku-hanga*.[55]

Ansei Uchima (cat. 99) represents an instance of direct intercourse between Japanese and American printmakers. Born and raised in California, this artist worked for nearly fifteen years in Japan before returning to the United States. In the succeeding years, he passed on his broad experience in this flourishing artistic mode through a career in printmaking, exhibiting, and teaching.

Individualism characterized American printmaking in the 1950s. Experiments with printmaking processes were natural outgrowths of the searching, intuitive nature of abstraction, and the spectrum of technical exploration was astounding. Yunkers, Ryan, and Reder willfully varied their prints from impression to impression, varying inking and even adding or altering blocks, so that their woodcuts were often monotypes rather than multiple, editioned objects. Robert Conover added colors to his woodcuts by printing from plates of cardboard. This technique also was used by James Forsberg and Dorothy Bowman, while Edmond Casarella (cat. 98) pushed the process furthest by using cut-paper collages for his printing matrices. Vincent Longo produced a handful of large, vivid, energized color prints from plywood blocks.[56]

Aside from her innovative activities in painting and intaglio printmaking, Worden Day (cat. 72) also made relief prints directly from the cross sections of trees with rugged sawed textures, which she supplemented with thin layers of color printed from other blocks. Erik Hoberg worked in a method that combined rubbings from carved woodblocks with colored crayons, melted to fuse their wax with passages of painted inks.[57] Carol Summers (cat. 92) developed his unique manner of applying ink to the face of his carved blocks and then chemically drawing the ink into the paper fibers. Louis Schanker (cat. 41) poured plaster into his inked woodcut blocks to produce multiple bas-relief castings. Arthur Deshaies and Harold Paris were among the printmakers who experimented with carving relief and intaglio plates in Plexiglas; these were printed in color only occasionally, however. Boris Margo (cat. 66) continued to print his own innovative Surrealist cellocuts, from plates he made from synthetic materials. New acrylic materials were also used for relief collagraph prints in color by Clare Romano, Glen Alps, and other artists.

After 1960, fine arts printmaking flourished as never before in the United States, and an extensive print establishment grew up comprising craftsmen, publishers, dealers, curators, critics, and a growing legion of collectors. However, compared with the vigorous production and experimentation of the preceding decade, activity in relief printmaking all but ceased. The dominance of Abstract Expressionism led to the dismissal of the woodcut. Although relief techniques were used for gestural prints in the 1950s, the marriage was never a comfortable one. Most artists preferred media that could capture the spontaneity of creation, like drypoint and lithography. Intaglio was favored in the university print shops, and lithography was revived through such enterprising collaborative workshops as Tamarind and Universal Limited Art Editions (ULAE). Subsequently, Pop Art, eschewing the personal and handmade, adopted process-oriented media with links to advertising, especially screen print. With their intellectual objectives and orientation to scientific precision, Op Art and Minimalism also preferred meticulously controllable mechanized print media. The craft of relief printmaking seemed lax and unsophisticated by comparison, and fell progressively into obscurity.

In the early 1980s, a healthy print establishment reawakened wide interest in relief prints.[58] Many fledgling print workshops and publishers established themselves as independent businesses in the 1970s. Seeking inexpensive ways to make prints and fresh imagery to distinguish their products in the market, several among them—including Brooke Alexander, Crown Point Press, Landfall Press, Solo Press, and Diane Villani—embraced relief printmaking. Printers such as Chip Elwell and Kathy Caraccio introduced relief printmaking techniques to young artists, and a reactionary revival began.

Despite stylistic diversity, several qualities that had characterized American woodcuts of the past reappeared. Once again, the movement began with the re-examination and adaptation from time-honored printmaking traditions. In the 1980s, as at the turn of the century, American artists had their designs carved and printed by virtuoso Japanese craftsmen. There was great interest in the formal qualities of the materials, and in the "primitive" appearance of woodcut with all its expressive implications. The presence of the artist was appreciated and emphasized in the prints. Although these printmakers exploited thriving publishing and marketing systems, many were impressed by the liberty that relief printmaking allowed. The compulsion to experiment ensued, and a range of captivating color prints appeared. This satisfying freedom of creativity distinguished the finest American woodcuts of the 1980s.

Notes

1. Moran 1973, pp. 17–26.

2. Haverkamp-Begeman 1962, pp. 7–14; van Hasselt 1965, pp. 7–13.

3. Reed/Wallace 1989, pp. 16–17.

4. See Uchima 1976, pp. 153–155, and Saff/Sacilotto 1978, pp. 53–68, for explanations of the traditional processes of *ukiyo-e* printmaking and their contemporary adaptation.

5. Hunter 1943.

6. Hughes 1978.

7. Haverkamp-Begeman 1962, pp. 25–28; van Hasselt 1965, pp. 47–52, 67–69.

8. Todd 1948.

9. Waite 1951; Lippencott 1941.

10. Savage 1818; see also Friedman 1978, p. 17.

11. Thieme/Becker 15 (1922), p. 184.

12. Stapleton 1906; Bryan 1957.

13. McClelland 1924, pp. 272–274; Lynn 1980, pp. 305–315.

14. Pasko 1894, p. 102.

15. *Boston Sunday Herald* 1886.

16. Groce/Wallace 1957, p. 456; Linton 1882, pp. 20, 24.

17. Pasko 1894, p. 102.

18. Friedman 1978, pp. 19–23, 36–37.

19. On Alfred—or Albert—Bobbett, see Groce/Wallace 1957, p. 58.

20. Chapman 1857.

21. Hamilton 1958, p. 154.

22. Tokuno 1893.

23. Smith 1945, pp. 15–17; Pepper 1905.

24. Falk, p. 383; Hughes, p. 285; Wright 1916; Lum 1981; see also Gravalos.

25. Los Angeles 1920; see also Los Angeles 1921.

26. Lum 1922.

27. Barbin 1976.

28. Flint 1983.

29. Chaffee 1952.

30. Flint (1983, p. 11) observed that Squire and Mars were the models for Gertrude Stein's short story "Miss Furr and Miss Skeene."

31. Ibid., p. 12.

32. Silverman 1972; Bruhn 1983.

33. Frueh 1917; Frueh 1922.

34. Dailey 1989; Harlow/Keats 1984 also discusses several California woodcut artists.

35. Prizewinners for prints at the Panama-Pacific International Exposition are listed in the *American Art Annual* (1915), p. 59.

36. Hughes, p. 157; LeJeune 1970; Knowles 1970.

37. Jenkins 1983, pp. 48–50; Smith 1983, p. 102; Yoshida 1939.

38. Toledo 1930.

39. DIA 1919.

40. See *Teachers College Record* 17 (January 1916), p. 183; Moffatt 1977, pp. 122–123.

41. Bowles 1927, pp. 161–190.

42. Preissig died in the Nazi concentration camp at Dachau on June 1, 1944; Vollmer 3 (1956), p. 624.

43. Falk, p. 370; Bowles 1927.

44. Falk, pp. 290–291; de Salle 1929.

45. Brooklyn 1933.

46. Kainen 1972.

47. Michigan 1985, pp. 208–209.

48. Velonis 1930.

49. Cummings 1988, pp. 535–536; Rewald 1953; Baur 1961.

50. Brooklyn 1946; Kup 1947; *Art Digest* 1949; Gordon/Johnson 1955.

51. Johnson 1956.

52. Sessler 1988.

53. Watrous.

54. V & A 1956; Floud 1955.

55. AIC 1960.

56. Baro 1970.

57. Johnson 1956, p. 21.

58. Field 1972; Capasso 1988.

Intaglio

Artists and craftsmen first turned their attention to color printmaking during the Renaissance. Because woodcuts were often used as book illustrations, they developed alongside the technology of book printing. Chiaroscuro, or multiblock color woodcut, was intended to reproduce the effect of heightened drawings on tinted paper. Later, Italian Baroque etchers occasionally printed their plates in a single colored ink on tinted paper, or touched them with pigment; however, it was the Netherlandish who, in the seventeenth century, first attempted multicolor intaglios. Hercules Seghers printed his etched plates in colors on a variety of supports, often supplementing them with watercolor and oil, and amateur etcher Johannes Teyler of Nijmegen experimented with multiple inkings of single etched and engraved plates (Fig. 1).[1]

Figure 1
Johannes Teyler (Dutch, 1648—after 1697), *Round Landscape*. Engraving. Worcester Art Museum, bequest of Mrs. Kingsmill Marrs, 1926.1196.

The intaglio technique offers marvelous opportunities for artists to create images both brilliant and incisive. There is something in the resistance of the metal plate that, when overcome by the engraver or etcher, permits very direct and personal expression; the process of cutting into a hard metal plate can become a catalyst for the artist's creative ideas. The Italian word *intaglio* (incising, engraving) has come to describe several processes and combinations thereof, all of which involve cutting into a surface, usually of metal. A print comes into being when the incised areas of the plate are filled with ink and, under the pressure of the press, the image is transferred to the paper—a principle exactly opposite to that of relief printing. Intaglio techniques involve the use of cutting tools, acid solutions, and grounds, materials that vary depending on the results desired.

Figure 2
Louis-Marin Bonnet (French, 1736–93), *Tête de Flore (Head of Flora)*, 1769. Crayon-manner etching and engraving. Worcester Art Museum, bequest of Mrs. Kingsmill Marrs, 1925.149.

Although the principles of intaglio were known earlier than the fifteenth century, only then did paper become widely available, allowing the printing of images to become a widely practiced art. The various intaglio techniques include engraving, stipple engraving, drypoint, etching, soft-ground etching, aquatint, and mezzotint (and variations and elaborations on each).

An engraving is produced by cutting the plate directly with a sharp tool called a burin; the resulting lines are then inked and printed under pressure. In stipple engraving, tonal effects are created by making closely spaced, incised dots. For drypoint, a sharp needle scratches the plate, depositing fragments of displaced metal, or burr, alongside each line; the burr creates a particularly rich, soft line when printed.

In etching, the plate is first covered with an acid-resistant ground such as wax; the plate is then drawn upon with a metal needle, which scratches away the ground to expose bare metal. Placing the plate in an acid bath causes the exposed metal to be eaten away, creating depressed lines that are inked and printed. To create a soft-ground etching, the metal plate is covered with an acid-resistant compound of asphaltum, beeswax, resin, and tallow. Various textured materials, such as fabric, are pressed into the soft ground; when removed, they pull away the sticky ground, exposing the metal. The plate is then placed in an acid bath, which etches this pattern into the metal.

Aquatint is a process in which resin is used to create a textured or tonal surface. Heat fuses the design to the plate, which is then etched with acid. Because in this process spaces, rather than lines, are etched and printed, the results resemble wash drawings and watercolors. Aquatint has often been combined with etching. With the "sugar-lift" technique of lift-ground aquatint, the image is drawn on the plate with a water-soluble solution (generally containing sugar). When the plate is covered with a ground and placed in water, the solution dissolves, lifting the ground to reveal the image areas, which can then be etched.

The use of miniature toothed wheels, or roulettes, to simulate the stippled effect of crayon line became popular in the late sixteenth century. In mezzotint, sometimes called *manière noire* (black manner), the plate is first roughened all over with a rocker; if a print were to be made after the initial preparation, the result would be a continuous, rich black. Instead, gradations of tone are created by scraping or burnishing away the microscopic barbs of metal loosened by the rocker, thus producing an image with an infinite variety of values.

An explosion in color intaglio techniques occurred in France during the eighteenth century.[2] There, a huge market had sprung up for affordable facsimiles of paintings and drawings by the most famous artists of the day; these were manufactured in quantity to satisfy collectors and decorators. A search for printed tonal color, meant almost exclusively for use in making these reproductive prints, resulted in the development of several techniques—including mezzotint, aquatint, and stipple and crayon-manner engraving—for biting or engraving tone, rather than line, in the copperplate. Jakob Christof LeBlon developed and patented a process for making three-color mezzotints in which he aimed at achieving a full range of hues. Crayon-manner engraving, developed by Jean-Charles François for the reproduction of drawings, was perfected in multicolor prints by François, Louis-Marin Bonnet, and Gilles Demarteau. Bonnet combined the multiplate mezzotint process with the crayon-manner technique, utilizing as many as eight plates in his remarkable facsimiles of François Boucher's color pastels (Fig. 2).

Because the intaglio processes require specialized equipment and more expensive materials than does

Figure 3
Edward Savage (1761–1817), *Eruption of Mount Etna*, 1779. Mezzotint. Worcester Art Museum, The Charles E. Goodspeed Collection, 1910.48.3871.

relief printmaking, the former were established more slowly in colonial America. Many of the earliest professional printmakers in the New World were immigrants trained in the European system of workshops and apprenticeships. These colonial craftsmen established print shops in larger cities, where artists and book publishers, as well as the market and distribution systems, were located. These printers began training apprentices and reproducing the works of American artists. The English-born mezzotint engraver Peter Pelham, for example, made intaglio prints after his arrival in Boston in 1727 that were technically identical to those he had created in London. American painter Edward Savage made an early attempt at color printing in his mezzotint *Eruption of Mount Etna* (Fig. 3). The colors and inking of this large plate are similar in manner to LeBlon's work, albeit less sophisticated. By the 1830s, William James Bennett had printed city views in color aquatint after works in other media.[3]

In the nineteenth century, color printing came to be dominated by the newly invented technique of lithography. Although it required even more specialized equipment and more sophisticated technical skills, this process produced large quantities of prints more cheaply and more easily than color intaglio could. A vast market developed for inexpensive genre, portrait, and topographical images; big lithographic firms such as Currier and Ives and Louis Prang & Company satisfied most of the demand.

Intaglio was still confined primarily to commercial reproductive engravings after paintings, but in Europe a few prominent artists, such as Camille Pissarro, made original etchings in color. This concept of artists' prints—from a long and distinguished European tradition that included such masters as Rembrandt and Goya—came to America late in the century.

Beginning in the 1870s, in response to the Etching Revival in Europe, intaglio printmaking emerged as an important creative technique for American artists. Amateur and professional etching societies sprang up around the country, encouraging original printmaking through camaraderie, teaching, and exhibitions. Although much of their work had a mediocre monotony, these pioneers of the craft launched a new era of interest in the graphic arts that has persisted to the present day. American painters Winslow Homer and Thomas Moran made wonderful monochrome intaglio prints, and several in the group of painters known as "The Ten," including Childe Hassam and J. Alden Weir, made superb etchings, but none of these conservative printmakers ever attempted color intaglios. Artists such as James A. M. Whistler and Mary Cassatt, who had directly experienced the sphere of European printmaking and were able to progress beyond it, ultimately provided the impetus for a new American tradition of intaglio printmaking.

The only American to exhibit with the French Impressionists, Mary Cassatt made remarkable aquatints that stand as hallmarks of nineteenth-century color printmaking quite apart from nationality. The artist's first solo exhibition, at the Durand-Ruel Galleries in Paris in 1891, included color prints, among then *In the Omnibus* (cat. 1). Cassatt's fine draftsmanship, her notions of composition and asymmetry derived from *ukiyo-e* prints, and her color sense, garnered both from those Japanese prints and from French Impressionism, assured the distinction of her outstandingly innovative prints. In close collaboration with printer M. Leroy, she achieved an elegant and seamless integration of drypoint and aquatint. In Chicago in 1893, the artist painted murals for the Columbian Exposition, the most comprehensive exhibition of American art assembled to date and a turning point for the visual arts in this country. Nonetheless, during her lifetime, the influence of Cassatt's paintings and prints in her homeland was limited, although she was able to persuade Americans to buy works by the Impressionists.

In the United States, the period between the turn of the century and World War I was turbulent and optimistic, characterized by tremendous economic growth and social change. Although there was no longer a Western frontier, massive immigration continued, and a vast cultural coalescence began. Multitudes clustered in the cities, and ethnic neighborhoods came into being, both preserving a broad range of traditions and gradually infusing them into American culture. People lived in closer proximity, but they also enjoyed greater mobility. The railroads expanded, automobiles became available, and dramatic changes of lifestyle began. William Randolph Hearst introduced the mass circulation of sensationalist newspapers that featured photographs and colored comics. Between 1900 and 1910, the United States held five world's fairs and regional expositions, and their visitors experienced a new access to burgeoning knowledge, technology, and culture.

Three dominant styles—academic, Social Realist, and avant-garde—coexisted in the visual arts of this period. Etching, tied to traditions of realistic genre and landscape, remained conservative in the midst of this diversity. Still rare in the United States, particularly in comparison with multicolor relief printmaking, color intaglio was the object of some very interesting isolated experiments. Curiously, these were conducted by traditionally trained printmakers, most of whom had visited Europe. These exercises may have been inspired by European printmaking, but contrary to the conventional practice of collaboration—exemplified in the prints of Cassatt and Whistler—American artists, partially out of necessity, worked on their own.

Many American women were drawn to intaglio by the popularity of the Etching Revival. Gabrielle De Vaux Clements, a pupil of Thomas Eakins and Stephen Parrish, and her friend artist Ellen Day Hale traveled to Europe together in 1884, and there

Figure 4
Charles F. W. Mielatz (born in Germany, 1864–1919), *A Balcony in Pell Street*, 1908. Etching, soft-ground etching, and roulette. Print Collection, Miriam and Ira D. Wallach Division of Art, Prints, and Photographs, New York Public Library, Astor, Lenox and Tilden Foundations.

first encountered color etchings. However, not until after the turn of the century did these artists begin producing color intaglio prints on their own press (cat. 7). Like Mathilde de Cordoba, they remained conservative in their imagery, though their private technical experiments with color were quite innovative. Helen Hyde studied privately in New York, Paris, and Berlin. An illustrator of children's books, she became enthralled by East Asian art and imagery when she visited Chinatown in San Francisco; she took extended trips to Japan and there studied woodblock printmaking. In addition to her popular woodcuts in the Japanese manner, Hyde also made etchings with color aquatint. Using only a few colors, she passed her plates through the press several times to achieve subtle tints (cat. 8).

James D. Smillie, a student of his father, who was a professional steel engraver, taught at the National Academy of Design in 1868 and helped found the New York Etching Club in 1877. He printed some of his original etchings and mezzotints in color. The German immigrant artist Charles F. W. Mielatz experimented with etchings and aquatints printed in color *à la poupée*, that is, by the application of several colors to a single copperplate using small felt pads (Fig. 4).

George Senseney used several colors of ink in successive printings of his intaglio plates, creating pleasant harmonies and increasing the opportunity for chance effects. He was concerned with the selection of inks, preferring to grind his own colors; with the combination of etching, aquatint, drypoint, and soft-ground etching; and with the problems of registration. Thus his work anticipated future experiments.

After studies at the Art Institute of Chicago, landscapist George Elbert Burr spent five years in Europe, where he became interested in—and ultimately inspired by—experimental color prints from earlier times. Returning to the United

States in 1904, Burr settled in Toms River, New Jersey, where he made his first color etching, representing an Italian view. He worked out his own personal method for printing color monotypes from his intaglio plates. These prints attracted so much interest that he was prompted to issue an explanation of his technique.[4] His mastery of color, plate tone, and chiaroscuro effects captured subtleties of light, weather, and atmosphere (cat. 10).

Although many prominent Social Realist and avant-garde artists were active as printmakers, none made color intaglios of significance in the 1910s. Nevertheless, their work revolutionized American printmaking, and their students and followers became active in color printmaking in several media. The most prolific printmaker among the Ash Can painters, who were prominent among the socially conscious artists of the period, John Sloan made unmistakably American etchings, alternately humorous and biting, representing the realities of city life. The style and imagery of Sloan and other politically aware artists were widely disseminated in popular magazines as various as the *Saturday Evening Post* and *The Masses*.

The American avant-garde began as a result of European influences in the 1910s. In this time of profound change—of World War I, the women's suffrage movement, the Model T Ford, and landmark films—these artistic attitudes slowly came to be understood and assimilated. In New York, the Armory Show of 1913 presented the American public with its first comprehensive view of European modernism, and of the work of American artists in related styles. Notable among the Americans represented in this exhibition were Max Weber (cat. 15) and project organizer Arthur Bowen Davies (cat. 13).

An eminent painter and tastemaker, Davies exerted a great influence on American art. Sometimes described as "American Symbolism," his figurative style was lyrical and classical, far more traditional than that of the avant-garde works he promoted. A member of "The Eight" for political rather than stylistic reasons, Davies was interested in printmaking throughout his career. He made color lithographs beginning in about 1919, and in about 1924 he began to work with master printer Frank A. Nankivell, who aided him and encouraged him to print his intaglio plates in colors. Ultimately the painter and printer together created fifteen soft-ground etchings with aquatint, one drypoint, and one mezzotint in color.[5] These figurative prints are characterized by the same lyricism and careful manipulation of line and tone that are typical of Davies's paintings.

In 1915, at the Panama-Pacific International Exposition in San Francisco, an entire gallery was devoted to American color paints in several media. Among the intaglios shown there were color etchings by Benjamin Brown and Earl Horter and color aquatints by Maud Squire, George Senseney, and Pedro Lemos (cat. 24). However, it was not San Francisco but the Los Angeles area that became the center of color printmaking on the West Coast. There, brothers Benjamin C. and Howell C. Brown both worked in color intaglio, founding the Print Makers Society of California in 1914. This organization commissioned the annual publication of a print and produced annual traveling exhibitions. In 1932, it sponsored the first of its exhibitions entitled "Fifty Colour Prints of the Year," which was circulated by the American Federation of Arts. Benjamin Brown's color work achieved harmony and balance between linear and tonal areas. In Pasadena, Frances and May Gearhart also worked with color printmaking. Frances made woodcuts (cat. 16), but May, a student of Benjamin

Figure 5
George Overbury "Pop" Hart (1868–1933), *Orizaba, Mexico*. Soft-ground etching. Brooklyn Museum, Museum Collection Fund, 25.76.

Brown, concentrated on color intaglio (cat. 22). Supervisor of art programs for the Los Angeles City Schools from 1903 through 1939, May made brilliantly colored soft-ground etchings influenced by Park French's tinted motion pictures and by the artist's own trips to Mexico.[6]

The establishment of the Brooklyn Society of Etchers (later known as the Society of American Graphic Artists, or SAGA) in 1915 provided evidence of the enduring preeminence of etching. Initially interested in the diversity and national character of American printmaking, which they sought to represent in their prominent annual exhibitions, this group showed their work at the Brooklyn Museum until 1930. Their first exhibition, which opened in November 1916, included works by sixty-five etchers, among them Mary Cassatt, Childe Hassam, John Marin, and John Taylor Arms (cat. 21). The exhibition of 1918 featured a group of color etchings, and that of 1922 had an international representation, demonstrating that Americans were again willing to show their work beside the best from abroad. Nevertheless, as late as 1942, the *New York Times* review of that year's SAGA exhibition stated: "Several of the prints demonstrate the uses to which color may be put. However fine, color plates cannot affect the status of work in plain black and white."[7] Thus, even at this late date, etching was still seen by some as a conservative medium.

In the 1920s, a decade that opened with an economic boom and closed with the great stock market crash, American printmaking showed little change. A thriving automobile industry characterized the initial prosperity and increasing disposable wealth of average Americans during this period. Cars became available in colors; suburbs sprouted up. Many challenges to the status quo surfaced during this prosperous time: the

ideas of Albert Einstein and Sigmund Freud, the phenomena of jazz and Art Deco. A growing number of consumers purchased a greater volume of prints in a slightly wider range of styles. However, in the years of crisis that followed, the arts receded from public attention and became dominated once again by more accessible, less sophisticated styles and by technical conservatism. Intaglio printmaking remained relatively conventional, predominantly oriented to draftsmanship and to the now academic, Barbizon-influenced style and technique of the Etching Revival. A scattering of pioneer artists were active in color intaglio, but change came slowly.

Master printer Frank Nankivell made his own color aquatints in the 1920s. He continued to produce editions of color intaglios from plates by Arthur Bowen Davies (cat. 13); in turn, Davies's stylistic power exerted itself on the printer; after 1920, Nankivell created many plates of his own, representing svelte, Symbolist nudes. An exhibition of his color prints was mounted in 1929 at Ferargil Galleries in New York. In the 1930s, Nankivell printed for the Federal Arts Project.

John Taylor Arms (cat. 21) gained great popularity and a loyal following of collectors during this period. Like his approach to printmaking in general, Arms's use of color was thoughtful and methodical. Early in his career he attempted color printing, but, failing to achieve the effects he desired, he quit in discouragement—and even tried to recall etchings already on the market. Still, inspired by eighteenth-century color aquatints, the artist thought that this medium might suit him. Arms understood the potential of aquatint for rendering and modulating tone; when done in color, such prints could achieve subtle effects, at times similar to those of Japanese woodcuts. Although the artist conceived his aquatints in color, he also printed them quite successfully in black ink. Together with his collaborator, New York master printer Frederick Reynolds, he created true masterpieces of tone, texture, and detail.

Russian-born William Meyerowitz, also active in New York, became one of the most prolific printmakers of his time; nearly three hundred color intaglios have been attributed to him.[8] This artist preferred to use a single plate, which he carefully inked, wiped, and passed through the press, for each of several colors. As a student, he was first drawn to color etching by the prints of Charles Mielatz. Meyerowitz's color prints range from abstract Cubist images to contemplative, naturalistic views of Rockport, Massachusetts, and New York City (cat. 27).

David Milne came to New York from his native Canada in 1903. He studied briefly at the Art Students League, and made a living for himself as an illustrator and through sales of his oils and watercolors. After serving in Europe in the Canadian Army during World War I, Milne settled in upstate New York and in Ontario, Canada; the landscape of this region provided the subjects for his first multiplate color drypoints. Their designs scratched into zinc plates with a darning needle and printed between the rollers of a laundry wringer in bright, often arbitrary colors, these spare prints were products of true inspiration and imagination.[9]

Dorsey Potter Tyson and George Overbury "Pop" Hart also made color intaglios in the 1920s. Little interested in New York art circles, Hart traveled through much of his life, and he remains an enigmatic figure. His prints reflect his journeys to such exotic places as Oaxaca, Mexico, and Tahiti, and they often portray people and situations in a gently satirical way (Fig. 5). Although Hart had assistance in printing his lithographs, he probably printed his intaglios himself. Notable for their technical complexity, these prints combined soft-ground etching, aquatint, and drypoint with a sandpaper ground on zinc plates to create spontaneous, painterly results.

Figure 6
Louis O. Griffith (1875–1956), *Landscape*, about 1930. Etching. Indiana University Art Museum, 70.15.

Hart's acquaintance Jules Pascin was an exceptional draftsman, both of drawings and of prints (some of them with color). Pascin's linear comments, often satirical though sometimes reportorial, reveal his great compassion for people. Mortimer Borne worked in color drypoint, using three metal plates and combining only a few hues to create a wide range of color. Rather than superimpose tonal areas in aquatint or mezzotint, he used color exclusively in the line itself.

Marked by the unprecedented participation of the federal government, the depression years were a turning point for American art. When Franklin Roosevelt moved to stabilize the economy after the collapse of banking in 1933, his New Deal programs included schemes to support artists. The process began when the College Art Association asked the Emergency Works and Relief Bureau to employ out-of-work artists with money donated from private sources, for the purpose of producing works that could decorate nonprofit institutions.[10]

The most significant development came late in 1935, when the Works Progress Administration established the Federal Arts Project, which organized an active printmaking workshop program. Particularly in the New York area, this organization gave attention to print production, including innovations in color printmaking techniques. Some artists, including Augustus Peck and Blanche Grambs, experimented with color intaglio in the FAP graphic arts division, but for the most part project artists attained more concrete results in color relief, lithography, and serigraphy. Largely owing to the impetus provided by achievements in the latter techniques, the American Color Print Society was founded in 1939. Many artists and craftsmen trained in the FAP went on to careers in teaching, perpetuating the benefits of federal investment for generations. The absence of color intaglio prints in this decade is an enigmatic and fascinating phenomenon.

Most of the prints created by artists in the FAP represented accessible, humanistic themes. The American Scene artists, heirs and students of the Ash Can group who orbited around the Art Students League, dominated this era. Many of these artists—including Edward Hopper, Martin Lewis, and Reginald Marsh—made social comments in eloquent black ink etchings. Parallel to this focus on the city, the style of Regionalism developed, with artists representing rural themes in related expressive means. The originators of the idiom, Midwesterners John Steuart Curry, Thomas Hart Benton, and Grant Wood, worked in monumental painting styles influenced by the Mexican muralists. They found lithography better suited to their plastic manner than the essentially linear intaglio techniques.

In Nashville, Indiana, however, a school of color intaglio printmakers thrived, producing prints that were Regionalist in the truest sense of the term. These members of the Brown County Art Gallery Association found their subjects in the rural landscape of Indiana and in the streets of its small towns; they also strove to capture on paper the colors of the changing seasons. Louis O. Griffith, president of the association, was its most prolific etcher (Fig. 6). Trained at the Art Institute of Chicago, he had also visited Paris. The artist exhibited his prints as early as 1915 at the Panama-Pacific International Exposition, and his plates often combined drypoint and aquatint with soft-ground etching.

Though relatively few in number, printmakers across America, among them Mathilde de Cordoba, Philip Cheny, Maurice Bebb, Augusta Rathbone (cat. 31), and Beatrice Levy, continued to work in color intaglio in the 1930s and 1940s. These artists took mild encouragement from a steadily expanding market. Prints had become accessible to a broad public

through national companies that sold them by mail order at minimal prices. The Contemporary Print Group and the Associated American Artists, established in 1933 and 1934, respectively, often distributed editions of some 250 impressions; therefore, they did not always find intaglio techniques appropriate to their publication activities.

The gradual growth of public print consumption was interrupted by World War II. The United States received a wave of immigrant artists from Europe with the approach of the war, and with the attack on Pearl Harbor, the country shed its last vestiges of isolationism. Although the early 1940s were fraught with the problems of war, American printmaking began to move into a more central, more recognized position in the arts.

Paradoxically, in America in the 1940s, when the other print media stagnated by comparison, color intaglio saw unprecedented growth, owing to the establishment of Atelier 17 in New York and to the predominance of its proprietor, Stanley William Hayter. Trained in the sciences, this Englishman had founded a workshop by the same name in Paris, where from 1928 to 1938 the intaglio print media were explored as vehicles for creative expression. Printmakers, painters, and sculptors—Picasso, Miró, Chagall, Lipchitz, Tanguy, and others—had come from all over Europe and across the Atlantic to work there. Fleeing the war, Hayter reopened his workshop at the New School for Social Research in New York in 1940. There, Atelier 17 became a meeting place for refugee European masters and American students. Hayter's own energetic personality, combined with the famous experimental and collaborative atmosphere of the workshop, became a monumental force in American printmaking.

Hayter's personal preference for an Abstract Surrealist style, along with his distinctive formal vocabulary, exerted a strong influence over the workshop, by virtue of which he was faulted for encouraging imitation. He approached intaglio printmaking as both a tactile, creative act and a visual experience, bringing with him from Paris interests in free-form imagery and the exploitation of materials. Hayter found the burin more responsive to his intention than were most drawing instruments, and the infinite possibilities of engraving fascinated him. Both subtle refinements and radical experimentation occurred as artists sought new methods for self-expression at Atelier 17, germinating a movement that would soon dominate all others: Abstract Expressionism.

Of the many developments at that studio, methods of simultaneous color printing were among the most important. Hayter focused his color experiments on a means of printing several transparent colors from a single plate in one pass through the press, thereby avoiding problems of registration, which are so bothersome in working with large metal plates.[11] From his study of William Blake's eighteenth-century experiments with color relief etching, Hayter developed a method for applying color to an intermediary surface before transferring it to the plate, allowing for the use of more than one color on a single surface. Following this experiment, he hit on the notion of using silkscreens to stencil several colors onto a single copperplate that had already been inked in the normal way for intaglio printing. The artist perfected this process in 1946 with the printing of his complex *Cinq Personnages* (cat. 60).

Many students from Atelier 17 went on not only to develop very distinctive personal styles but also to make further technical innovations in the intaglio techniques. In the mid 1940s, they began teaching and developing print workshops at universities nationwide. American artists were no longer compelled to go abroad, and European art ceased to be the standard by which American printmaking was judged.

When Hayter turned his attention to color printmaking, the focus of his entire workshop shifted from soft-ground etching and engraving in black ink to a range of experimental color intaglio techniques. When, in 1944, the Museum of Modern Art in New York sponsored a traveling exhibition of work from Atelier 17 entitled "New Directions in Gravure," the studio's reputation rose meteorically; the workshop was deluged with requests from artists wanting to work there. The creation of color prints from plates had entered an energetic new period in America.

Sue Fuller experimented with the sugar-lift method and with stenciled color at Atelier 17 (cat. 58), and Fred Becker devised new methods for three-color prints and for the accurate registration of several plates (cat. 62). One of the most versatile technicians in the shop, Becker went onto an influential teaching career at Washington University in St. Louis and at the University of Massachusetts, Amherst. He later continued his experiments with shaped plates and with embossing from uninked intaglio plates. The artist also experimented with photoengraved plates and often combined intaglio and relief printing processes. Elaborating on a statement by Picasso, Becker underscored the point that "the artist must work with what he gets, as well as for what he wants. Each step of the way is a commitment, and may suggest several different directions. Even one that did not occur to him at the start."[12]

Karl Schrag, who took over as director of Atelier 17 after Hayter's departure in 1950, derived very personal approaches to printmaking that paralleled his painting. He combined the vocabulary of the painted lift-ground with that of the burin (cat. 80). Along with Raoul Ubac, Schrag tried purposely overprinting a single plate out of register, using various colored inks to create effects

of vibration and depth. Although his prints were thematically related to his paintings, the artist understood that the textural and tonal capabilities of the intaglio media differ fundamentally from those available in painting. Throughout his career, Schrag has sought to discover and exploit the unique and exclusive characters of these very different media.

Minna Citron, a lithographer who had also created murals for the Tennessee Valley Authority, felt a need to break away from the traditional, representational style in which she had long made prints. She found it comfortable to explore her own emotions and her ideas of abstraction in the new style of Atelier 17. In her multiple-plate soft-ground etchings with aquatint, the artist carefully balanced line, texture, and color. In the bold and lively *Squid under Pier* (cat. 68), Citron achieved watery, three-dimensional effects by superimposing lacy veils of soft-ground textures on layers of translucent color. The title of the print derives from the sense of drama and tension present in the forms.

Although Atelier 17 prevailed in intaglio printmaking, elsewhere artists persevered with other stylistic trends in printmaking in the 1940s. For example, the print exhibition "America and the War," sponsored by the Artists for Victory, was presented concurrently at twenty-six museums throughout the country in 1942 and 1943, taking full advantage of its morale-boosting prints.[13] Included in this widely attended exhibition was the powerful *River of Blood* by Beatrice Levy, who had been actively producing color intaglios since the 1920s. A review of the catalogues from print competitions held annually by the Library of Congress during the 1940s reveals that many other artists—including Eda Spoth Benson, Kathleen Macy Finn, Joseph Margulies, Leon Pescheret, Nicholas Hornyansky, William Meyerowitz, Elizabeth McHenry, and Seymour Tubis—experimented independently with color intaglio.

Gabor Peterdi (cat. 79) had worked at Atelier 17 in Paris from 1933 to 1939 and was well acquainted with European modernism before he emigrated to the United States. Initially drawn to engraving, he was introduced by his experiences in Paris to the great range of possibilities in other intaglio techniques, and he became one of the most creative experimenters in the New York workshop. Peterdi rejoined Atelier 17 in 1946, just as its members began combining intaglio and stencil techniques in color; his first color print was *Sign of the Lobster* (1947). One of the first artists to make intaglio prints in color, Peterdi focused his experiments more on expressionist effects than on technical problem solving. Though he was interested primarily in personal expression, he strove to develop complete technical mastery in order that process might become almost incidental to creation. Ever captivated by nature, whether in microscopic detail or cosmic expanse, Peterdi was also sensitive to color, light, movement, and texture. His teaching activities at the Brooklyn Museum, Hunter College, and Yale University extended not only his own influence in American printmaking but that of Atelier 17

This sort of perpetuation is also apparent in the career of Mauricio Lasansky. A native of Argentina, Lasansky was always a vocal proponent of printmaking as a major creative art form. He used the metal plate as a matrix for personal expression charge with social content; his work is often compared with Goya's. Lasansky came to Atelier 17 in 1943, and two years later he established the now-legendary graphics workshop at the University of Iowa. Within a couple of years, works by his students were being accepted into such major shows as the National Exhibition of Prints at the Library of Congress (instituted in 1943) and the Brooklyn Museum Print National (begun in 1947). By the early 1950s, Lasansky's students,

in keeping with the "Iowa mission," were teaching in art departments across the country, spreading their knowledge of and appreciation for intaglio techniques.

Lasansky began to incorporate color in his own contemplative, psychological prints in 1945. He gave these multiplate intaglios a brooding tone by overprinting them in black or brown. The burin gave intensity to his imagery, as in the dramatic *Pietà* (cat. 67), which he printed from nine plates. Over the decades, Lasansky's color prints became larger, brighter, and more complex, yet they always retained their thoughtful and humanistic attraction.

In 1949, the Walker Art Center in Minneapolis exhibited works from Lasansky's Iowa workshop, including a selection of Lasansky's own prints from the period between 1936 and 1948, as well as works by several of his students: Lee Chesney, John Paul Jones, Ernest Freed, Malcolm Myers, James Steg, Glen Alps, and others destined to be instrumental in American printmaking during the 1950s. The decade was dominated by the academic print workshops that had been established by the students of Peterdi, Lasansky, and others. In intaglio programs, teachers and students concentrated on the working of their plates regardless of whether they planned color or black and white prints. Because color sometimes obscured the distinctive qualities of metalworking, many artists remained wedded to "purist" monochrome printmaking.

Lee Chesney (cat. 64) received recognition as a very young artist; he was represented in the exhibition "A New Direction in Intaglio" in 1949, and his prints were acquired by the Brooklyn Museum the same year. Upon completion of his Master of Fine Arts at the University of Iowa, Chesney first taught at the Iowa workshop and then initiated an undergraduate printmaking program at the University of Illinois. He also organized three national print exhibitions in the 1950s, one of which was circulated by the American Federation of Arts.

The Canadian-born painter and printmaker Wilfred Roloff Beny studied under Lasansky in 1945 and 1946, yet his prints look back to the style of Atelier 17. In 1947, Beny began to combine plates etched with linear, abstract fans and baskets in the manner of Naum Gabo or Harry Bertoia (cat. 54), with nebulas of color printed from lithographic plates.

Malcolm Myers, who left Iowa to teach at the University of Minnesota, created color prints that are unusual in his having worked the color plates in the same manner as the key plate, thereby creating an uncommon harmony. The inking of the key plate often dominated Myers's work, and he kept the relative values of the color areas and key lines quite close. The artist recently commented: "I used a knife instead of an etching needle—I sometimes bit a plate in the acid for several hours—I achieved a nice effect on the *Hundred Guilder Print* [cat. 91] by stepping on a softground area of the plate with my tennis shoe, which worked very well."[14] Although this piece represents the Crucifixion, the artist deemphasized the subject in favor of the landscape background.

The 1950s were an era of economic boom, growth of the mass media, and migration to the suburbs. Science and technology changed life dramatically for the average American; the conveniences of frozen foods and modern appliances and the pleasures of the ubiquitous television set were tempered by knowledge of the devastation made possible by the atomic bomb and of the flight into space by Sputnik. The arts were profoundly transformed by these rapid changes and their attendant moral implications.

In many ways, the 1950s can be seen as a period of proliferation, as printmakers refined the major achievements of the foregoing decade. Prompted by voracious American consumption of the mass media, by the booming economy, and by the scale of New York School painting,

Figure 7
Krishna Reddy (born 1925), *River*, 1960. Etching and aquatint, artist's proof IX/X. Private collection.

printmakers now pushed their art far beyond previous limits of scale and technical complexity. The Brooklyn Museum, a leading supporter of American printmaking through this decade, sponsored an important series of national competitive print exhibition. Una E. Johnson, the influential curator of the museum, described the transitional character of printmaking in this period:

This ferment has brought a veritable clutter of ideas, styles, technical experimentation and the use of newly created materials. . . . Geographical landscapes and sedate portraits have given way to introspective landscapes, psychological portraits and geometric compositions where color alone often creates the desired forms and techniques. . . . Style and content may be achieved through fragmented and disparate objects in unlikely combinations that, in turn, assume a strange life of their own.[15]

Print exhibitions in this era more often included plates and blocks. Critics began to question this new direction and to ask whether "complicated or novel means serve creative ends."[16] Carl Zigrosser wrote:

The public seems to want color; and the resources of all the major techniques, intaglio, relief, lithography, and serigraphy, have been developed to the full for color printing. One sees prints becoming larger and larger in size. They are often enormous, competing in color-weight and impressiveness with paintings. With their exceedingly small editions and great variations of impression, they almost seem to negate the raison d'être of the print as a cheap multi-original. Designed not for the portfolio but for the wall, these abstract color patterns suggest a new decorative convention: they are richly and endlessly pleasing to the eye, but they also appeal to deep subconscious elements, thus being differentiated from the decorative prints of the past.[17]

Just as the 1940s had witnessed an explosion of new images and techniques, the 1950s were a period of market boom, of collaborative printmaking in all media, and of the infusion of a new spirit into lithography in particular.

An Abstract Expressionism rapidly gained ascendancy in American painting, repercussions of the style appeared in printmaking. Jackson Pollock, who also worked at Atelier 17, was less interested in the product than in the process; he carried this attitude over into his action painting of the 1950s. Far more forceful "action" is required to make an intaglio print than to make a painting, but the painterly character of Abstract Expressionism transferred directly to lithography, as in the works of Nathan Oliveira (cat. 87) and George Miyasaki (cat. 90). Influenced by the action painters, printmakers attacked their plates by sanding, scraping, cutting, and grinding them with electric tools. The prints of the 1950s were often tours de force, and their creators were absorbed by every facet in the process of their realization.

The three-dimensional character of intaglio printmaking that had been explored by Hayter's circle was exploited in myriad ways during this period. Peterdi, for example, introduced much larger masses of color into his work of the 1950s than he had previously employed. His extraordinarily rich use of colors and blacks in works like *Glowing Tree* shows a profound understanding of the properties of his materials. Because some artists continued to feel that color sometimes obscured the subtle qualities that metalworking brought forth, vigorous activity in monochrome intaglio printmaking continued despite a proliferation of color work.

Intaglio printmaking flourished in California through the 1950s. Iowa graduate John Paul Jones set up his print shop in Los Angeles, as did Ernest Freed, whose work reflects a

deep interest in combined media. Also active in this area were University of California graduates Leonard Edmondson, who excelled in the complexities of intaglio and mixed-media printing (cat. 77), and Ynez Johnston, whose brilliantly colored prints reveal her exotic fantasy world (cat. 95).

In 1950, Hayter reestablished Atelier 17 in Paris; the New York shop remained in operation until 1955. The desire to print several colors simultaneously continued to haunt studio artists. In the Paris workshop, Krishna Reddy and Kaoko Moti made a startling discovery. They observed that although some inks mixed when layered one upon another, others repelled each other and remained discrete. Mixing occurred when the artists superimposed a thinner ink on a thicker one; but if they reversed the process, the second, thicker ink remained on the surface of, and separate from, the first ink. With this new understanding, Reddy and Moti created a new technique known as color viscosity printing (Fig. 7). Reddy's work fully exploited the tactile qualities of the sculptural plate, and his prints are significant documents in the history of intaglio printmaking. The artists eventually came to the United States, and he now teaches at New York University.

Other printmakers refined the intaglio processes even further. Unquestionably the principal technical contribution of Atelier 17 after 1950, simultaneous color printing quickly spread to other printmaking programs. Having for years mixed printmaking media in order to make color prints, Hayter now found it possible to employ intaglio techniques for the entire process by using viscosity printing. A great catalyst, this master helped many artists surpass the restrictions of engraving and etching. Hayter's great legacy, which he instilled in an entire generation of artists, was his willingness to risk.

In 1952, with the aid of the Rockefeller Foundation, the International Graphic Arts Society was formed for the purpose of educating academic communities about the value of prints as original works of art. Under this program, prints by artists from all over the world were published and widely distributed. Each new IGAS publication was sent to institutions around the United States for exhibition, and gifts were made to public and university museums.

In 1956, largely through the efforts of collector *extraordinaire* Lessing Rosenwald (a founding benefactor of the National Gallery of Art and the donor of an exceptional collection of rare books to the Library of Congress), the Print Council of America was created in order to foster the development of printmaking and encourage scholarship in the field. In 1959, the Print Council sponsored the exhibition "American Prints Today," which was shown throughout the country. Among the artists who exhibited color intaglios therein were Leonard Edmondson, May Janko, Mauricio Lasansky, Malcolm Myers, Barbara Neustadt, Gabor Peterdi, and Michael Ponce de León (cat. 96).

In retrospect, that exhibition has emerged as the definitive survey of American printmaking at the close of an era, for after 1960 the printmaker-technician was overshadowed, in great measure, by the painter-printmaker, and university print shops were augmented by collaborative workshops such as Universal Limited Art Editions (ULAE), Tamarind, and Gemini GEL.

Through programs in the 1950s, the American public became increasingly aware of printmaking as a serious art form, and ever greater numbers of people became interested in prints American and foreign, old and new. Painters' involvement in printmaking extended the arena for color prints, and the Pop and Op artists created an explosive environment for the use of color in the 1960s.

Notes

1. Haverkamp-Begeman 1962, p. 3.

2. Ittmann 1984.

3. Weitenkampf 1970, pp. 89, 103.

4. Seeber 1971, p. 37.

5. Czestochowski 1987, p. 39.

6. Feinblatt/Davis 1980, p. 11.

7. Inman 1963, p. 43.

8. Meyerowitz.

9. Tovell 1980.

10. Watrous 1984, p. 96.

11. Hayter 1949a, p. 158.

12. Becker 1948.

13. Arms 1943, pp. 9–15.

14. Letter to the author from Malcolm Myers, November 1988.

15. Johnson 1968, p. 7.

16. Watrous 1984, p. 192.

17. Zigrosser 1951.

Lithography

During the Etching Revival of the 1880s and 1890s, when many leading artists in the United States turned to the copperplate, few chose to work on stone. "It is a mystery," Frank Weitenkampf wrote in 1903, "that an art so supple in expression, so rich in resources, so absolute in its reproduction of the artist's touch . . . should not have called forth a fuller and readier response to its appeal. . . . With all these advantages, lithography as a painter's art has not made headway here. Why?"[1] Possibly, he suggested, the answer lay in the "commercial use of lithography [which had kept] the glamour of high art [from being associated with a medium] entirely devoted to the spirit of utility."[2]

This legacy lay with particular weight upon color lithography, which in America was so identified with nineteenth-century chromolithography as to be inseparable from it. In 1898, when Joseph and Elizabeth Robins Pennell surveyed the state of the art, they were forced to conclude that "the country was flooded with poor designs, wretchedly carried out. . . . [Lithography] was monopolized by the cigar-box maker, the printer of theatrical posters, or the publisher of chromos and comic prints."[3]

When first used by Godefroy Engelmann in 1847, the term *chromolithographie* described any lithograph printed in colors, whatever its aesthetic character. In America, *chromolithograph* at first had the same meaning.

By the early 1860s, however, it had come to carry a more specific definition: the color-lithographed reproduction of an oil painting or watercolor, or at least the full-color picture of some religious, heroic, or landscape subject. These chromo "paintings" might be glued to a stretched canvas, varnished, embossed with striations to simulate canvas, and framed. Or they might be incorporated into a calendar or some other commercial product. Either way, they were a middle-class medium for disseminating fine-art imagery.[4]

There was little concern as to the origin of an image or the identity of the artist, nor was any great stock placed in originality. What mattered most to the nineteenth-century Americans was the subject matter of a print and the degree of competence and detail with which it was rendered.

It was inevitable, given the vast quantity of chromolithographs, that most were done strictly by formula, and in a manner chosen to satisfy— but not to extend or excite—the taste of the audience for which they were manufactured. By 1890, there were more than seven hundred lithographic printing establishments in the United States, employing some eight thousand people and with a yearly production valued at $20 million in gold—the equivalent of more than $800 million today.[5] Although ardent in his defense of the chromo as "a democratic art," Peter Marzio agrees that by the 1890s, "familiarity [had] bred contempt."[6] The very word *chromo* had become a synonym for the "vulgar,"[7] the "ugly or offensive,"[8] and the prostitution of art.[9]

Given these perceptions, it is hardly remarkable that in the early decades of the twentieth century, American artists actively avoided color lithography. Even in France, where, in contrast to America, the tradition of the painter-printmaker was well established, the makers of color prints were forced to overcome a long-standing identification of their medium with the popular and the commercial. Many artists believed, as did Odilon Redon, that lithography was "cheapened by the addition of color . . . [which destroys] its specific qualities so that it comes to resemble a cheap, colored print."[10]

Ultimately, however, the remarkable "color revolution" of the 1880s and 1890s—the lithographs of Pierre Bonnard, Jules Chéret, Maurice Denis, Henri de Toulouse-Lautrec, Théophile Alexandre Steinlen, Edouard

Vuillard, and others—made it impossible to deny color prints a place in the annual Salon of the Society of French Artists, and in 1899, the statutes of the salon were revised to allow their admission.[11] Ironically, at this moment of triumph, it was already evident that this "phenomenon of immense color lithographic activity was not destined to last beyond the turn of the century."[12] By comparison with lithographs published earlier, many of those included in such late albums as *L'Estampe Moderne* (1897–99) were disappointing, although even here one finds the decorative elegance of Louis John Rhead's brilliantly patterned *Jane* (cat. 5).[13]

In the United States, the influence of the French color revolution was visible only among the poster artists of the 1890s, foremost among them Edward Penfield, who created an outstanding series of monthly posters for *Harper's* magazine (cat. 4). Although lithography gained acceptance as a suitable medium for posters, it was rarely used by other artists in the early 1900s, even for work in black and white. The few who chose to use it were severely handicapped by an absence of supportive printers.

Though simple in principle, lithography is so complex in practice that most artists have found it necessary to work with professional printers. Alois Senefelder, who invented the process, probably in 1798, preferred to call it *chemical printing* because, unlike other print media, it rests upon a chemical, not physical, principle. It is made possible by the fact that grease and water will not mix. When a drawing is made with greasy materials—usually lithographic crayon or a greasy ink called tusche—on a stone or plate, that surface can be chemically treated so that only the image will accept ink. Although the solution used for this purpose is called an etch, it does not bite into the stone, but only chemically separates the image and nonimage areas. After the stone or plate has been etched, a solvent can be used to wash the surface clean, but the greasy areas remain as visible ghosts of the drawing. The image reappears when the surface is inked, with a hand roller. Each stage of the process requires highly critical skills on the part of the printer, who must control the chemistry of the printing element and apply the ink with great care in order to achieve fine and consistent impressions.

To make a color lithograph, the artist must draw a series of stones or plates, one for each color that is to be used; the black materials with which the artist draws are then washed away with solvents and replaced with color inks. Because each color must be printed in perfect registration, color lithography is far more difficult in execution than is work in black and white.

In the United States during the nineteenth century, there were no printers who specialized in work for artists, and, with rare exceptions, commercial printing houses had little interest in such work. It is thus not surprising that among the relatively few American artists who made lithographs during this time, most did so, at least initially, in Europe. James A. McNeill Whistler, arguably the most important American artist-lithographer of the nineteenth century, made his prints in England and France; Joseph Pennell also worked extensively in England; Albert Sterner created his first lithographs in France and Germany. Although Sterner made some prints that employed a tint block,[14] and Whistler made a few in color, including *The Yellow House* (cat. 2),[15] most of their work was in black and white.[16]

Upon his return to the United States, Sterner purchased a press and stones and, lacking alternatives, endeavored to print his own work; twice, in 1911 and again in 1915, he exhibited his lithographs in New York. A key figure in the history of American lithography, it was Sterner who encouraged George Bellows to take up lithography, led the young George C. Miller to become a printer for artists,[17] stimulated (indirectly, through his 1915 exhibition) Bolton Brown to study lithography in London,[18] and in 1917 initiated the

organization of the Painter-Gravers of America.[19]

Bellows's lithographs, most of which were printed by Miller or Brown, have rightly been called "a pivotal achievement in the history of American printmaking."[20] More than any others, his lithographs served to validate the medium in the eyes of critics and the public. Even so, they were in black and white, as were virtually all of the American lithographs printed during the 1920s. During that decade, only Arthur B. Davies seriously explored color lithography, producing a series of multicolor prints in collaboration with Miller.[21] Even for Davies, however, lithography remained secondary to etching and aquatint among the printmaking media (see cat. 13). The many American artists who made lithographs between the end of the World War I in 1918 and the stock market crash of 1929—a list that includes Howard Cook, Stuart Davis, Adolf Dehn, Yasuo Kuniyoshi, Louis Lozowick, Reginald Marsh, Jan Matulka, Charles Sheeler, and Abraham Walkowitz, among others—all chose to work in black and white. Not until the mid-1930s did color lithography emerge as a significant medium of expression.[22]

In 1933, the French-born artist Jean Charlot traveled from New York to Los Angeles where, soon after his arrival, he was introduced to Lynton Kistler, a young lithographic printer whose father, Will A. Kistler, operated a commercial printing plant.[23] A longtime resident of Mexico, Charlot had made lithographs both in Mexico City and New York, where he had worked with Miller, but they were all in black and white.[24]

By conviction a populist, Charlot had as his ambition the creation of an art for the people. Thoroughly conversant with French traditions, he meant in his work "to react against the 'art' lithographs of the Nabis: Bonnard, Vuillard, and Maurice Denis. Granted they are beautiful, [but] they are such obvious works of art."[25] Instead, Charlot conceived of work printed in full, bright, "artistic" colors and in unlimited editions, in order "to give the work as wide a

circulation as possible."[26] In July 1933, soon after his arrival in Los Angeles, Charlot began to work with Lynton Kistler on a stone lithograph, his first in color,[27] and concurrently on the zinc plates for a color lithograph that could be printed on an offset press for the frontispiece of a book by Merle Armitage.[28] These experiences stimulated Charlot to propose the making of a *Picture Book*, a repertory of the motifs derived from his experience in Mexico; this project, printed by Lynton and Will A. Kistler, became a landmark in the history of American color lithography.

In offset lithography, the image on the plate is transferred first to a rubber blanket and thence to paper; the image is thus twice reversed and appears on the paper in the same orientation as it does on the plate. In this respect, it resembles transfer lithography, in which the image is twice reversed when the artist draws on paper (usually a coated transfer paper), then is transferred to the plate, and then to another sheet of paper when printed. Because of this indirectness, transfer lithography was long controversial; indeed, it took a famous trial (Pennell v. Sickert, 1897) to determine that it was legitimate.[29] Because offset lithography is used primarily in photomechanical reproduction, similar questions have been raised about its legitimacy. Characteristically, those who raise such questions fail to understand that in *autographic* offset lithography, no photomechanical processes are used: the artist draws directly on the plates from which the print is made.[30]

Charlot's lithograph *Malinche* (cat. 32), designed for use in a prospectus, and all thirty-two lithographs for his *Picture Book* are completely autographic. They testify both to the artist's technical virtuosity and to the skill and courage of the printers who, without prior experience in autographic offset lithography, undertook so demanding and complex a project.[31]

Following simultaneous completion of *Picture Book* and a series of lithographs on stone, printed by Lynton

Kistler, Charlot returned to New York.[32] The Kistlers, encouraged by their success in the printing of *Picture Book*, undertook work for other artists, notably the young California painter Millard Sheets, who in 1934 drew the plates for *A California Landscape* (cat. 34), which was printed by offset at Will Kistler's printing plant. Within a limited palette, Sheets used simple lithographic means to develop a spirited composition, a vibrant rendition of an idyllic California theme also explored in his watercolors.

Upon his return to New York, Charlot lacked access to a printing plant such as Kistler's. Seeking an alternative way to pursue his work, he took a teaching position at the Florence Cane School, acquired a small Multilith press, and, together with a colleague, the painter Albert Carman, set out to explore its potential. Early in 1935, they were joined by the Mexican artist and printer Emilio Amero, who had come to New York to teach stone lithography at the school.[33] Within months, Charlot, Carman, and Amero were able to overcome the technical problems inherent in an unfamiliar process, and to produce successful editions in color.[34]

Intrigued by his experience with the offset process, Carman abandoned teaching to become a printer.[35] By October 1937, he had printed a sufficient number of offset lithographs to present an initial exhibition by the "Artists Color Proof Associates" at the Charles L. Morgan Galleries on Fifty-seventh Street. At this time, and during the early 1940s, Carmen extended invitations to distinguished artists—among them Howard Cook, Don Freeman, Albert Gallatin, Stefan Hirsch, Louis Lozowick, and George L. K. Morris—to do work with him in color.[36]

Freeman, who by 1937 had made more than one hundred lithographs, most of them printed by George Miller, took particular interest in Carman's offset process, for it suggested to him a means of including original lithographs in *Newsstand*, a personal "magazine" that Freeman published at irregular intervals between 1936 and 1955.[37] With this in mind, Freeman purchased a secondhand Multilith press from the Cane School, and, perhaps as a means of demonstrating its capabilities to the artist, Carman printed *Ladies of the Evening* (cat. 38), a work typically Freemanesque both in the robust good humor of its drawing and in the double entendre of its title.

Of the many ventures initiated during the 1930s for the purpose of publishing prints with popular appeal—"pictures for the masses"—Carman's was alone in its primary emphasis on color.[38] Among the small number of artists of the period whose knowledge of lithographic printing was sufficient to permit work in color were Theodore Roszak, who had taught lithography at the Art Institute of Chicago beginning in 1928,[39] and Emil Ganso, who had studied lithography with Eugene Fitsch at the Art Students League. The contrast between Roszak's striking but little-known lithograph *Staten Island* (cat. 33) and Ganso's more conservative *Still Life with Peaches* (cat. 36) is illuminating. Roszak, though not polished in his technique, produced a "graphic" print that, in the modernist tradition, looks like a print. Ganso, by contrast, apparently strove for the look of a painting, overprinting primary colors in a way that echoes nineteenth-century chromolithography.[40] Despite the limitations of Ganso's work in color (he was an uneven artist), he did much to stimulate the use of color lithography through his exhibitions, which were arranged by Carl Zigrosser at the Weyhe Gallery, and through his friendships with such artists as Konrad Cramer, Albert Heckman, and Yasuo Kuniyoshi, for whom he sometimes printed.

That such projects as Charlot's *Picture Book* and Carman's publishing ventures should have been undertaken in the depth of the Great Depression is in itself remarkable. By the time Franklin D. Roosevelt took office in 1933, many artists were in financial desperation. Their "meager sources of desultory income—dishwashing, house-painting, carpentry, or occasional teaching—were no longer available. Poor as bohemia had been, it had always managed to survive on the left-overs from the affluence of the nineteen-twenties,"[41] but now even that was gone. George Miller's printing business was so reduced that in 1934 he was forced to sell at auction many of the printer's proofs he had acquired over the years.

Within the first year of the Roosevelt administration, a series of programs was begun for the purpose of assisting American artists.[42] It was not, however, until August 1935, when the Federal Art Project (FAP) was created within the Works Progress Administration (WPA), that an active program in printmaking was begun and a workshop established. Audrey McMahon, who was appointed regional director for the New York area, "enlisted the aid of Russell T. Limbach, an artist and printer experienced in all forms of the graphic arts. His job was to plan the shop for maximum working efficiency, to procure the equipment and supplies, and to find skilled printers."[43]

Though the FAP workshop in New York provided facilities for work in all print media, it proved of particular importance to the development of color lithography.[44] Limbach, the workshop's technical adviser, had worked extensively as an artist-lithographer in Cleveland throughout the late 1920s;[45] Gustave von Groschwitz, who served as workshop supervisor from 1935 to 1938, had a particular interest in color lithography, which was stimulated through his association with the painter and printmaker Albert Heckman at Columbia University;[46] and Theodore (Ted) Wahl, who became the workshop's principal printer, had studied lithography with Bolton Brown in Woodstock, New York. Together, they established an environment that made possible the creation of "more fine color lithographs than had ever been made before in the United States."[47]

As early as April 1936, a number of color lithographs were included in exhibitions of the project's work at the Federal Art Gallery on Fifty-seventh Street. Some project artists—Ganso, Limbach, Wahl, Jacob Friedland, and Margaret Lowengrund among them—were themselves able printers; Lowengrund, for example, had studied lithography with Joseph Pennell at the Art Students League and with A. S. Hartrick in London.[48] Her *Interior of a Brickyard* (cat. 37)[49] is typical of the project's work, although more limited in its use of color than most FAP lithographs, a number of which were printed in four and five colors.

Other artists had limited prior experience with the medium; for some, such as Stuart Davis (cat. 88), the prints made at the FAP workshop were their first in color. When the opportunity presented itself, artists who made prints at the FAP collaborated with printers outside the workshop. Some made editions with Carman; others accepted commissions from Associated American Artists (AAA), by far the largest publisher of American prints during the 1930s and 1940s, though seldom of prints in color. An exception is Limbach's *Forest* (cat. 45), a lovely Cézannesque landscape that attests to the artist's solid command of the medium. Like most prints published by AAA, it was printed by George Miller.

After von Groschwitz left the FAP workshop in 1938, it suffered increasing bureaucratic constraints, and by the end of 1940, according to Jacob Kainen, it "began to disintegrate. The war in Europe and Asia, and the obvious determination of the government to discourage artists from continuing on the Project, were reflected in a growing demoralization and loss of focus. No more editions were printed."[50] Even so, Kainen continues:

[The Project's printmaking workshops] were pioneer centers for technical and artistic growth, and the artists who worked there formed a solid base for further development. They popularized lithography, the woodcut, serigraphy, and most of all color printing. When the projects ended they joined the staffs of schools and universities which increasingly added printmaking departments. These artists knew how to set up workshops and they knew all the media. And so, for the first time in the history of American graphic arts, students found a large number of instructors who practiced and welcomed fresh approaches. When Stanley William Hayter came to this country in 1940 to open his experimental graphic arts studio, Atelier 17, he found the artists ready.[51]

The character of American printmaking was profoundly altered by World War II. Even before the Japanese attack on Pearl Harbor, the graphic workshops established by the FAP were closed, and during the war printmakers encountered many problems, not the least of which was interrupted access to papers and other materials formerly imported from France. There were compensations, however, for the émigré artists who came to New York and Los Angeles brought with them the European traditions of the *peintre-graveur*. Hayter's Atelier 17, displaced to New York by the German occupation of Paris, effected a radical transformation of the character of intaglio printmaking in the United States in the 1940s. Simultaneously, the color woodcut was reestablished as an innovative and powerful medium.

By contrast, color lithography remained essentially conservative; the prints made and exhibited during the mid-1940s represented no advance, technically or aesthetically, beyond what had been accomplished in the FAP workshops in the 1930s. Nor did they reflect the radical changes in art that were taking place in New York. The artistic revolution announced by Jackson Pollock in his exhibition at Peggy Guggenheim's Art of This Century Gallery in 1943 found no echo in Benton Spruance's color lithograph *Forward Pass, Football* (cat. 56). Elegant and accomplished though it may be, this lithograph, immaculately printed in Philadelphia by Theodore Cuno in 1944,[52] perfectly represents the stylistic disassociation of American painting from American lithography during the 1940s, a gulf that was not bridged for some years.

In 1947, Gustave von Groschwitz moved to the Cincinnati Art Museum, and in 1948, he organized an exhibition commemorating the 150th anniversary of the invention of lithography. In the process, he became aware of substantially increased activity in color lithography among artists in the United States and Europe. Already committed to the medium as a consequence of his years at the FAP workshop and his subsequent studies,[53] von Groschwitz proposed that the museum "organize a first biennial exhibition of color lithography. It had never been done before."[54]

The first of the five Cincinnati Biennials (the series began in 1950 and continued through 1958)[55] included 235 color lithographs, 103 of these by American artists. The handsome catalogue illustrated six prints in color: two by Fernand Léger and one each by Pablo Picasso, Joan Miró, Emilio Amero, and Rico Lebrun. A similar balance between international and American prints was maintained throughout the series, and in each catalogue only one American print was chosen for illustration: Lebrun's *Villon's Ballad #2 (Man and Armor)*, printed by Lawrence Barrett;[56] Ralston Crawford's *Third Avenue Elevated #2*, printed by Desjobert in Paris (see cat. 71 for Crawford's closely related *Third Avenue Elevated #4*); Alexander Calder's *Composition*: Reginald Neal's *Triptych* (cat. 85), printed by the artist; and Stuart Davis's *Detail Study for Cliché* (cat. 88), printed by Arnold Singer. This selection of illustrations, all abstract or semiabstract, underlines von Groschwitz's evident intention, at a time when lithography was distinctly out of fashion,[57] to create a new perception of the medium.

Taken as a whole, the five Cincinnati Biennials were stylistically mixed; cumulatively, they provided a broad index to American color lithography in the 1950s. A total of 213 American artists were listed in the five catalogues,[58] but of this number only 21 had work in four or more of the exhibitions.[59] The majority of these were artist-teachers of lithography who printed their own work, among them Neal, then at the University of Mississippi;[60] Riva Helfond in Plainfield, New Jersey; Benton Spruance and Jerome Kaplan in Philadelphia;[61] Garo Antreasian in Indianapolis; Emil Weddige in Ann Arbor, Michigan; Eleanor Coen and Max Kahn in Chicago; Mary Spencer Nay in Louisville, Kentucky; and Nathan Oliveira in Oakland, California.

The artists regularly represented in the Cincinnati Biennials made relatively few lithographs in collaboration with professional printers; these included those of Crawford, printed in the Desjobert and Mourlot workshops in Paris; Will Barnet and John von Wicht, printed in Robert Blackburn's workshop in New York; and mine, printed by Lynton Kistler in Los Angeles.

Not coincidentally, the Cincinnati exhibitions reflect the first stirrings of a movement that, after 1960 (and thus beyond the scope of this essay), led to a widely acknowledged renaissance of American color lithography; this came about as a consequence of a series of new workshops established in New York and Los Angeles. Blackburn founded the first of these in 1949 (with financial assistance from Barnet and von Wicht), designing it "not as a printing business, but rather as a counterpart of Hayter's Atelier 17: a place in which artists who sought to make lithographs might gain access to equipment and technical assistance."[62] Barnet's *Spring* (cat. 69), von Wicht's *City* (cat. 75), exhibited in the third Cincinnati Biennial, and Blackburn's striking *Interior* (cat. 93) are three products of that workshop.

Similarly aware of a need for new printing facilities, Margaret Lowengrund established two small workshops in 1952: one in Woodstock, New York, where she was first assisted by Michael Ponce de León (cat. 96) and later by Reginald Neal; and a second in New York City, where John Muench and Arnold Singer printed for a wide range of distinguished artists. It was at the latter that Singer printed Davis's powerful *Detail Study for Cliché*. In 1956, Lowengrund's New York workshop, which had been known as the Contemporaries Graphic Arts Centre, became affiliated with the Pratt Institute and was renamed the Pratt-Contemporaries Graphic Arts Center; following Lowengrund's death in 1957, it was directed by Fritz Eichenberg.[63] A third New York workshop, Tatyana Grosman's Universal Limited Art Editions (ULAE), though of critical importance to the development of American lithography after 1960, did little work in color before that date.[64]

Kistler, who had closed his shop in Los Angeles during the war, resumed printing in 1945 and worked with Charlot, Man Ray,[65] Eugene Berman, George Biddle, and many artists living in southern California, occasionally producing works in color, such as Berman's *Nocturnal Cathedral* (cat. 70). I began my work with Kistler in 1948 and a few months later met June Wayne at his studio. We both continued to work with Kistler into the 1950s; by 1956, however, Kistler, for reasons of health, was forced to stop printing from stone. In 1957, Wayne went to Paris to work with Marcel Durassier, and in April 1958, she wrote to von Groschwitz in Cincinnati: "[I] will rely largely on trips to Europe for my lithography in the future. It seems a long way to go to make a lithograph, but unless someone, somewhere realizes the straits this medium is in, it will have vanished with the present batch of printers."[66]

Wayne and I talked on several occasions in the spring and summer of 1958 about her experience with Durassier and about the sorry state of lithography in the United States.

Subsequently, with encouragement from W. McNeil Lowry, director of the Program in Humanities and the Arts of the Ford Foundation, Wayne wrote a proposal that, upon approval by the foundation, provided funds to establish the Tamarind Lithography Workshop in Los Angeles.[67] Wayne became Tamarind's director, I joined her as associate director, and Garo Antreasian came from Indianapolis to serve as the new workshop's first master printer.

Although Wayne had first intended to bring Durassier from Paris, Antreasian's effectiveness as printer demonstrated that a revival of American lithography could be accomplished without dependence on European sources. Whatever the attrition among professional printers, a substantial reservoir of skills and experience had been developed among American artist-lithographers, with the result that the richest and most complex prints of the 1950s were printed by the artists who conceived them. Among the best of these were Nathan Oliveira's *Man and Drum* (cat. 87), George Miyasaki's *February* (cat. 90), and Antreasian's *View* (cat. 97), lithographs that collectively demonstrate the adaptability of the medium to the demands that were to be made upon it by artists of the 1960s—who, in their work at Tamarind, ULAE, and elsewhere, would make it evident that the French color revolution of the 1890s had found its twentieth-century counterpart in America: "[By 1969, Tamarind] had offered almost 100 artists a unique in-depth experience of working with trained lithographic printers, had invited over 50 additional artists on a shorter visit to Tamarind as guests, had trained 29 curatorial grantees, had conducted extensive research into materials, but, perhaps most important of all, had created a body of competent lithographic printers who, through time, would change the ecology of lithography in the United States."[68]

And so began the experiment that became "the single most important factor in the current vitality of lithography in America."[69]

Notes

1. Weitenkampf 1903, p. 550.

2. Ibid.

3. Pennell/Pennell 1898, p. 246.

4. Marzio 1979, p. 10.

5. This and a portion of the preceding paragraph are taken from Adams 1983, p. 5. The data on nineteenth-century printing establishments are from Marzio 1979, p. 3.

6. Marzio 1979, p. 209.

7. Beraldi 1888, p. 186 note.

8. Wentworth/Flexner 1960.

9. Marzio (1979, p. 210) cites A Supplement to the Oxford English Dictionary (Oxford: Clarendon Press, 1979): "Today in Australia a prostitute is called a chromo."

10. Redon 1922, pp. 119–120.

11. For a discussion of the debate that preceded the admission of color prints to the society's salon in 1899, see Cate/Hitchings 1978, pp. 1–2.

12. Ibid., p. 32.

13. L'Estampe Moderne (1897–99) was unrelated to Loys Delteil's earlier publication of the same name (1895–96). Aimed at a less sophisticated audience, it compromised the reputation of color lithography through its inclusion of collotypes and photo-lithographic reproductions of drawings alongside such original lithographs as Rhead's. See ibid., p. 27.

14. See, for example, Dame am Wasser (1902), a lithograph printed by Klein and Volbert in Munich (illustrated in Adams 1983, p. 18).

15. Allen Staly (1975, pp. 20–22) characterizes Whistler's five color lithographs as "hesitant, thin, and colourless. Personally," he continues, "I think it was a matter of temperament. The process was too involved, too long-winded for his essentially fugitive, mercurial genius." Like Redon, Staly speculates, Whistler may have felt that the addition of color to his lithographs "would merely encumber, and even debase with its additional and complicating dimensions."

16. Despite the prominence of such artists, American lithography received little recognition in major exhibitions. For example, at the Louisiana Purchase Exposition in St. Louis in 1904, "four awards were given to wood engravers compared with seven to etchers (none to lithographers)." Zigrosser 1974, p. 92.

17. Miller (1894–1965) was born into a family of lithographers. He first printed in 1914 for Sterner and in 1916 for Bellows; he opened a lithographic workshop in 1917, the first such enterprise in America that existed for the sole purpose of providing printing services to artists. The firm, now directed by Burr Miller, is still in business in New York. For more about George Miller, see Flint 1976 and Maurice 1976.

18. Brown (1864–1936) was fifty years of age when, in 1915, he began his study of lithography in London. Upon his return to the United States, he was active as an artist; as a printer for George Bellows, John Sloan, Albert Sterner, and other artists; and as author of the most influential book on artists' lithography published in the first half of the twentieth century. For more about Brown, see Adams 1986.

19. For information about the Painter-Gravers of America, see Field 1983, pp. 19–22. Field provides evidence that this organization was founded in 1917, not, as mentioned elsewhere, in 1915.

20. Myers 1988, p. 7.

21. Price 1929 lists only four color lithographs made by Davies between 1920 and 1922. In some cases, Davies would first print an image in black and white, color a few impressions by hand, and several years later decide to print an edition in color.

22. Although the bulk of Miller's work was in black and white, he printed in color more often than is commonly thought. In 1931, Miller proofed a series of multicolor lithographs that Rockwell Kent drew on zinc for the book The Bridge of San Luis Rey; after proofing, the plates were printed on an offset press by Latham Litho & Printing Company (see Jones 1975, nos. 40, 43–47, 49). Miller later collaborated with Kent on several lithographs that employed tint blocks, and also printed color lithographs for Frederico Castellon, Ralston Crawford, Mabel Dwight, William Gropper, Russell Limbach, and Prentiss Taylor. In 1955, Miller acquired an offset press, upon which he printed lithographs for inclusion in books published by Black Sun Press, the Limited Editions Club, and the Heritage Club.

In an interview with this author (May 4, 1979), Burr Miller said that he believed the predominance of black and white lithography in his father's work was caused both by attitude ("[Artists] weren't color oriented, like they are now") and by economics ("[Most] artists had to finance their own printing, and color was expensive, just like it is now. They didn't have the dealers and the publishers backing them up, like they do today. This is one [reason] why there is so much color [now]—we have people who are financing artists' printing today, because color sells").

23. For further information, see Adams 1977a.

24. Charlot worked with Miller from May 1929 through May 1930, producing twenty-five lithographs, all but one on zinc, and all in black and white; he made one additional lithograph with Miller in 1931.

25. Charlot, as quoted in Morse 1976, p. 89.

26. Ibid., p. xiv.

27. Charlot and Kistler encountered technical difficulties in the printing of this lithograph, Woman with Child on Back (Morse 113), and were unable to print a full edition. "I remember the image spread fast on this print, and we only got about thirteen good proofs" (Morse 1976, p. 77).

28. This lithograph, Henrietta Shore (1933; Morse 114), was printed by offset in two colors in an edition of 250, 200 of which were used as the frontispiece of a book about Ms. Shore by Merle Armitage (New York: E. Weyhe, 1933).

29. For an account of the trial from Pennell and Whistler's side, see Pennell/Pennell 1909, 2: pp. 186–192; for Sickert's side, see Brown 1984, pp. 49–71.

30. Burr Miller addresses the issue clearly: "There is, in some circles, a questioning about the use of an offset press to produce originals. Some people use photo offset plates and print them by hand. I, personally, don't believe a plate that is photo-produced is an original. I do believe a hand-drawn plate, printed by offset press, is original." (Miller to Alfred P. Maurice, May 13, 1974; quoted in Maurice 1976, pp. 142–143.)

Louise Sperling and Richard S. Field, in their useful exhibition catalogue (Sperling/Field 1973), mistakenly say that offset lithography has an "inherent photo-mechanical nature" (p. 17); elsewhere they overlook the use of autographic offset lithography in the 1930s, and state that "only during the past few years has it been employed for 'fine' or 'original' prints" (p. 12).

31. For a discussion of the making of Picture Book, see Morse 1976, pp. 80–118.

32. The most ambitious of these lithographs on stone was *Mother with Child in Front* (Morse 230, 66.5 × 44.5 cm.), printed by Kistler in an edition of thirty.

33. Emero had printed for Charlot when the artist was in Mexico City during the summer of 1931.

34. For an account of the problems encountered by Charlot and Carman in use of the Multilith process, see extracts from Charlot's diary quoted in Morse 1976, pp. 142–144, 146–155, 159–161.

35. For information about Albert Carman (1898–1949), see ibid., pp. 142–149, 432–434; Adams 1983, pp. 147–149.

36. Simultaneously, with an eye to the commercial market, Carman chose to produce many meretricious prints that reflected neither the creative potential of color lithography nor the skills of their printer. Perhaps as a consequence, the Artists Color Proof Associates had little success and soon abandoned their association.

37. In addition to offset lithographs by Freeman, issues of *Newsstand* contained lithographs by other artists, photomechanical reproductions, and texts by such authors as e. e. cummings, Carl Sandburg, and William Saroyan. See McCulloch 1988.

38. For a survey of print publishing during the 1920s and 1930s, see Flint 1980.

39. During the summer of 1928, after Roszak graduated from the School of the Art Institute of Chicago with honorable mention in lithography, he worked as an assistant to George Miller. That fall, Roszak returned to the school, where he taught a class in lithography; in the winter of 1929 and 1930, when the school invited Bolton Brown to offer a master class in Chicago, Roszak was among the participants. I am indebted to Janet Flint for information about Roszak's early work in lithography; see also Roszak 1974.

40. Use of chromolike color was encouraged by the judgments of conservative critics. When the American Color Print Society had its first annual exhibition in 1940 (at the Print Club of Philadelphia), Ganso received first prize for his Christmas card landscape *Early Snow*.

41. Ashton 1973, p. 18.

42. For a summary of these programs, see Adams 1983, pp. 121–123. For more detailed information, see O'Connor 1966 and O'Connor 1973.

43. Kainen 1972, pp. 157–158.

44. The FAP workshops have not yet been the subject of research sufficient to permit a full account of their activity. An unpublished manuscript, Northrup 1981, lists a total of 133 color lithographs by 42 artists completed at the New York City workshop between 1935 and 1939. Although it is known that color lithographs were printed in other FAP workshops, their number has not been determined and they have not been catalogued.

45. Limbach's print *Trapeze Girl*, 1935, was the first color lithograph produced by a project artist (for a color illustration, see Adams, 1983, p. 106).

46. Heckman, who had studied lithography at the Leipzig Institute of Graphic Arts, sometimes worked in color; he printed his work on a press in his Woodstock studio.

47. Von Groschwitz 1950.

48. Lowengrund taught lithography at the New School for Social Research in New York, where, in 1938, she offered a "Workshop in Color Lithography," assisted by the printer Irwin Lefcourt.

49. This print was one of three color lithographs included in the exhibition "Prints for the People" at the International Art Gallery, New York, in January 1937. Northrup (1981, no. 79) gives its title as *Interior of a Brick Factory*.

50. Kainen 1972, p. 171.

51. Ibid., p. 175.

52. Little is known about the life of Theodore Cuno, who was active as a printer for artists in Philadelphia during the 1940s and early 1950s. Born in Germany, he was a superior printer of the traditional crayon lithograph.

53. Von Groschwitz completed a master's degree at the Institute of Fine Arts, New York University, in 1947. His thesis topic was nineteenth-century color lithography in Europe.

54. Adams 1977b, p. 86.

55. A summary of the first four Cincinnati Biennials appears in Cincinnati 1958.

56. Unlike Kistler, Miller, and Cuno, Lawrence Barrett (1897–1973) was an artist-printer; he made his own color lithographs and printed in color for a number of other artists, among them Jean Charlot, who, from 1947 to 1949, was director of the Colorado Springs Fine Arts Center, where Barrett served as printer and instructor. For more about Barrett, see Adams 1978, pp. 38–43; Adams 1979, pp. 36–41.

57. In most print exhibitions of the mid-1950s, lithographs were greatly outnumbered by prints in other media.

Lithographs received only 7 percent of the purchase awards given between 1952 and 1956 in the prestigious annual exhibitions at the Brooklyn Museum.

58. Regardless of artists' place of birth, the museum listed them under the United States if they were permanent residents of this country.

59. Only five artists were included in all five exhibitions: Garo Antreasian, Eleanor Coen, Ralston Crawford, Max Kahn, and Benton Spruance.

60. While serving, between 1951 and 1957, as chairman of the Department of Art at the University of Mississippi, Neal produced an influential film, *Color Lithography: An Art Medium*.

61. Earlier, Spruance had collaborated with professional printers, usually with Theodore Cuno, but by the 1950s, he was printing most of his own work.

62. Adams 1983, p. 192. Originally called the Bob Blackburn Workshop, its name was changed first to the Creative Graphics Workshop and later, in 1959, to the Printmaking Workshop.

63. For information about Lowengrund and her workshops, see Adams 1984, pp. 17–23; Adams 1983, pp. 182–189.

64. For more about Grosman, see Tomkins 1976.

65. Man Ray's *Le Roman Noir*, printed by Kistler in 1948, shows an early use of the blended-inking method in an artist's lithograph; for a color illustration, see Adams 1983, p. 186.

66. Letter from Wayne to von Groschwitz, April 2, 1958 (Tamarind Archives, University of New Mexico Library). Wayne's fears were well founded. Over the years, Grant Arnold, Lawrence Barrett, Bolton Brown, Theodore Cuno, Jacob Friedland, Lynton Kistler, Ted Wahl, and many others had either died or retired from the ranks of active printers. Significantly, with the exception of George Miller's son Burr, the departed printers were not replaced.

67. For an account of Wayne's proposal and of the Ford Foundation grant to the Tamarind Lithography Workshop, see Adams 1983, pp. 193–203.

68. Gilmour 1988, pp. 345, 347.

69. Gilmour quotes Barry Walker (1983, p. 14).

Serigraphy

Figure 1
Gilbert R. Tonge (1886–1970), *Covered Wagons*, 1925–35. Serigraph in 105 colors, printed by the Van Ton Company, Los Angeles. Los Angeles County Museum of Art, M.74.147.

Figure 2
Guy Maccoy (1904–81), *Still Life*, 1932. Serigraph. Philadelphia Museum of Art, Thomas Skelton Harrison Fund, 41–53–172.

Of all the techniques used by artists to make prints in color, serigraphy can be characterized as the most distinctively American. Although the invention of the silkscreen-stencil printing method cannot be pinpointed, its refinement as a commercial color process and its early use and development as a medium for artists' prints are known to have taken place in the United States. Silkscreen is a straightforward process, similar to woodblock printmaking in is simplicity and directness. It requires far less training, equipment, and materials than do copperplate printing and lithography. The fact that this full-color process can be learned from books and mastered by practice in isolation has suited the vast geography of this country and the independence of the American character. The events comprising the short history of this technique, with its depression-era struggle for artistic legitimacy and its obstinate associations with commerce, could only have taken place in America.

Stencils were first used for printing multiple impressions in China and Japan, where waterproofed paper templates were cut with such intricacy that they required the support of an open net of horsehair. Simpler stencils, for coloring printed text and images, were used as early as the fifteenth century in Europe, especially in Germany. By the eighteenth century, stenciled decorations were commonly applied to walls and utilitarian objects, as well as to fabric and paper. This process soon spread throughout Europe and the United States. The French term *pochoir* describes the process in which templates of paper or thin sheets of copper are used to stencil an image in watercolor on paper. The use of a sheer, porous fabric as support for thin stencils seems to have developed in the latter half of the nineteenth century. In 1907 in Manchester, England, John Simon was granted a patent for his development of silk mesh as a support for stencils used in the printing of calico.[1]

Richard S. Field's 1972 exhibition at the Philadelphia Museum of Art established the importance of the United States, especially California, in the development of silkscreen printing during the 1910s.[2] This exhibition featured several early commercial screen prints manufactured by the Selectasine and Velvetone companies of San Francisco and the Vitachrome Company of Los Angeles. The Selectasine method, a stencil process utilizing fabric screens to print many colors, was developed by John Pilsworth of San Francisco, who used it for some years before he was awarded a patent in 1918. Designed as signs for shop windows or for advertising displays, placards made by this method were customarily printed in opaque, water-base show card ink. When these companies made pictorial prints for home decoration (Fig. 1), they had more in common with the insipid chromolithographs of the nineteenth century than with contemporary artists' prints: "Stylistically the overwhelming majority of screenprinted works from about 1907 until the late 1930s were conditioned by the flat planes of color laid down by hand-cut and glue-blockout screens (even when painterly effects were sought), and virtually every image was divorced from current international or American regional styles."[3]

Basically, a screen print, or serigraph, is made by pushing ink through a stencil made of fabric mesh that has been stretched taut on a frame. Thick ink is set into one end of the traylike screen, then scraped across and forced through the mesh with a squeegee, or rubber blade. Before 1960, artists prepared their screens in one of two basic ways. In the applied stencil, or film, method, a template is cut from a nonporous material such as paper or lacquer film, then attached to the underside of the screen, thus shielding ink from the paper during printing. In the resist or washout method, the interstices of the fabric weave are stopped up with glue, and the screen itself becomes the stencil. An image is drawn or painted directly on the

surface of the silk with lithographic tusche or crayon, which when dry is resistant to water but soluble in kerosine or turpentine. After the rest of the screen has been blocked out with a squeegeed overlay of glue, the original design is removed from the screen with solvent, leaving a negative stencil.

Generally the inks used were commercial, oil-base "process colors," formulated by several manufacturers to meet the demands of the silk screen method. These inks could be extended, and their opacity and surface sheen controlled, by the addition of a "transparent base" or "medium," a colorless substance with the consistency of petroleum jelly.[4]

Serigraphy has always been a multicolor operation, and printing in colors is made relatively simple with this technique. Because film stencils or glue stop-out can easily be removed from the silk, the same screen can be used to print many colors in succession This method also simplifies registration; the screen is usually hinged onto a tabletop, so that when a sheet of paper is placed in precisely the same position on the table and secured with tape or dimensional tabs, proper registration is assured.

Guy Maccoy was the first to use the commercial silkscreen process as a medium for limited-edition artists' prints (cat. 53). As an art student, he worked in a commercial print shop in Hoboken, New Jersey, in which this method was used to decorate shower curtains.[5] After seeing an exhibition of contemporary French *pochoirs* in 1932, Maccoy tried to achieve similar effects with silkscreens. Using glue to stop out his screens, and thinned oil paint for ink, he printed his first serigraphs, *Still Life* (Fig. 2) and *Woman with Cat*, in editions of about forty impressions. The artist's silkscreen prints of the

Figure 3
Anthony Velonis (born 1911), *Decoration Empire*, 1939. Serigraph. Philadelphia Museum of Art, Harrison Fund, 41–53–266.

following years reveal his constant experiments with procedure and materials. He tried printing with various media in a search for satisfying thickness, opacity, color saturation, and surface texture.

In 1937, Maccoy and his colleague Theodore (Ted) Wahl—a master printer working in the FAP—analyzed commercial silkscreen inks, identifying the ingredients for the purpose of mixing and manipulating their own recipes.[6] Joining in these experiments, Maccoy's old friend and fellow Kansan Bernard Steffen (cat. 61) settled on a variant method utilizing thin, transparent inks that could be printed like washes. An exhibition of Maccoy's prints at the Contemporary Arts Gallery in New York in November 1937 was the first one-man show of serigraphs.[7] After this, the artist traveled around the country, printing and selling new screen prints and presenting lecture demonstrations and art school workshops, which did much to disseminate the process. Settling in Vermont in 1940, Maccoy began a twenty-year career in commercial printing, working chiefly as a color separator. Thus he developed an uncanny ability to plan and organize colors freehand in the preparation of screens for his own prints.[8]

By mid-decade, artists across the country had begun to consider the use of silkscreen in making creative prints. In New York in 1935, Harry Sternberg, who taught printmaking at the Art Students League, experimented with the technique (cat. 35); in St. Paul, Minnesota, the painter Clement Haupers had editions of three silkscreens printed in 1936 by the commercial Bolger Printing Company.[9] Even as these pioneers were experimenting independently with serigraphy, the process was being vigorously developed by the WPA/FAP graphic arts division. In February 1934, a municipal poster workshop was established in New York in conjunction with the Civilian Works Administration, primarily to help promote Mayor Fiorello La Guardia's programs.[10] Although shop

artists at first laboriously painted placards by hand, the introduction of the silkscreen technique quickly magnified their output. This was due largely to the efforts of Anthony Velonis, a young artist familiar with screen printing from commercial employment, who convinced project administrator John Weaver to try the technique. In 1936, this workshop was absorbed by the WPA/FAP, and its services became available to all government agencies needing signs or posters. By the time Bauhaus-trained designer Richard Floethe (cat. 47) became the first FAP project director, the shop was engaged in mass production of screen-printed placards. By June 1938, the division had produced over 370,000 posters.[11]

As Velonis became more skilled, and enthusiastic about silkscreen, he also became convinced of its adaptability to fine printmaking. Hoping to explore this possibility, he determined to introduce the technique to as many artists as possible through the FAP, the only avenue available during the depression. With the support of two of his own prints (cat. 42), Velonis eventually convinced project administrators, and in September 1938, he was reassigned as head of his own pilot silkscreen unit,[12] and given the mandate to introduce the technique to several artists and to produce small editions that would later be evaluated for their artistic and technical merit as fine prints. To find collaborators for this experiment, Velonis approached the Artists Union, which assigned a research committee of six artists—Ruth Chaney, Harry Gottlieb (cat. 48), Louis Lozowick, Eugene Morley (cat. 46), Elizabeth Olds, and Hyman Warsager—each of whom received individual instruction.[13] The simplicity and economy of this full-color process and the range of its expressive capabilities were obvious in the first prints by this disparate group, and the silkscreen unit was duly integrated into the WPA/FAP graphic arts division.

The technology of screen printing grew rapidly as more project artists explored the special characteristics of the process. To coordinate these advances into a comprehensive demonstration, Velonis designed the satirical modernist print *Decoration Empire* in 1939 (Fig. 3), incorporating all of the techniques and printing effects then at his command. He used several methods of screen preparation, including cut lacquer film and tracing paper stencils, and tusche and litho crayon wash-out techniques. He combined screens of very coarse, gauzy fabric with fine, sheer silks, and used both thick and transparent inks, with glossy and matte surfaces, all in this one print. Step-by-step instructions for various procedures were also developed in the FAP workshop, as were tools such as screen frames, squeegee guides, and print drying racks. Velonis assembled this information in his booklet *Technique of the Silk Screen Process*.[14] The mimeographed pamphlet—bound in a color serigraphed cover—was sent out to WPA art centers across the country, where it was made available to the public free of charge. Silkscreen prints were also introduced to the print-buying public through Velonis's illustrated article in the *Magazine of Art*.[15]

In 1940, at the Springfield Museum of Fine Arts, the first museum show devoted entirely to silkscreens was organized by Elizabeth McCausland in conjunction with the Artists Union of Western Massachusetts.[16] This exhibition combined the work of Massachusetts artists such as Philip Hicken, Pauline Stiriss, and Edward Landon (cat. 49) with such leading New York serigraphers as Warsager, Gottlieb, and Olds. Printmaking equipment was shown, and Velonis's pamphlet was featured. Concurrently, at the Weyhe Gallery in New York, another milestone group show included works by eleven area serigraphers. This exhibition was organized by gallery director Carl Zigrosser, who knew all of the artists and had witnessed the development of the technique; in the catalogue of his exhibition, he introduced the term *serigraph*.[17]

Figure 4
Harry Shokler (1896–1978), *Sugaring*, 1949. Serigraph. Worcester Art Museum, Thomas Hovey Gage Fund, 1987.183.

Despite a minor controversy concerning the coinage of this term, it is clear that both Velonis and Zigrosser approved and promoted it in order to distinguish fine arts screen printing from the commercial process, thus establishing some legitimacy for the fledgling medium among connoisseurs, curators, and collectors. The word combines the Greek roots *seri-* (silk) and *-graph* (writing or drawing) by analogy with the term *lithograph* (stone drawing).[18] Shortly after the Springfield Museum show, the new term was introduced to a wider audience by Zigrosser, who had just been appointed curator of prints at the Philadelphia museum of Art, in an article in *Print Quarterly*, which remains the most comprehensive document of the beginnings of serigraphy.[19]

The 1940s were the heyday of color serigraphy. Production skyrocketed as the process spread to schools and art associations throughout the country. In 1942, McGraw-Hill published two handbooks on the technique, one by Jacob Biegeleisen, an instructor at the New York School of Industrial Art, and the other by Harry Sternberg (cat. 35) of the Art Students League. Both widely distributed manuals presented the technique as a self-teachable, straightforward way of making color prints inexpensively and at home.[20] Sternberg's concise book, profusely illustrated with diagrams and photographs, was especially popular.[21]

Its influence is exemplified in the work of Dorr Bothwell, a California painter who used Sternberg's manual to teach herself how to make serigraphs. Quickly mastering the fundamentals, this creative artist soon adapted the technique to her own Surrealist imagery (cat. 63). Similarly, the prints of Thomas Arthur Robertson (cat. 51) reflect the startling sophistication quickly achieved in this medium even in the South, where printmakers worked in relative isolation. This painter translated his modernist watercolors into adept and powerful screen prints and briefly

taught the process to college students. By 1941, many other artists were already working in serigraphy in Richmond, Virginia; Chicago; Iowa City; and Lincoln, Nebraska.[22]

Given its infancy in New York during the depression and its inherent economy and accessibility, serigraphy understandably developed a rather leftist political orientation.[23] This character is reflected in the screen prints of Harry Gottlieb (cat. 48), who, as a chairman of the Artists Union, was one of the first to learn the process in the FAP pilot project. An advocate of art that was accessible and relevant to the broadest range of people, he recognized that serigraphy could exert demystifying and democratizing effects on printmaking. He began his own book on serigraphy, and often gave lecture demonstrations to art students and to the public, in places as remote as Omaha. In August 1940, he presented the process at the New York World's Fair, in association with Elizabeth McCausland's lecture on the social implications of the new medium.

Gottlieb's ethical convictions were also shared by Elizabeth Olds, who had been his close friend since their student days in Minneapolis.[24] They remained close after moving to New York, where Olds studied at the Art Students League with George Luks. In 1937, Gottlieb and Olds traveled together to the coal fields of Pennsylvania to consult with, observe, and depict the organizing miners. Olds concentrated on serigraphy for years, and though her figurative imagery became less insistently political than did her colleagues', she maintained an ingenuous, urban realist style.

Political imagery is also apparent in the prints of Anton Refregier, whose own WPA mural paintings in the San Francisco Post Office—works that depict local labor activism—were the source of many of his provocative serigraphs.[25] A staunch member of the American Communist Party, Hugo Gellert blatantly used printmaking as a propaganda tool. To support the war effort in 1943, he

created the portfolio *Century of the Common Man*, in which the speeches of Vice President Henry Wallace were illustrated with incitive screen prints (cat. 52).

The Social Realist mural painter Ben Shahn began making serigraphs in 1941 and continued for over twenty-five years.[26] His early prints translate all the political bite and social compunction of his paintings and drawings. However, Shahn soon became discouraged by the opacity and saturation of conventional silkscreened color, preferring to print calligraphic outline sketches in black ink, and later hand tint them with watercolor.

The very characteristics that dismayed Shahn made serigraphy ideally suited to the needs of Robert Gwathmey's reductive style and intense palette (cat. 59). The artist used the medium primarily to reproduce and distribute the designs of his paintings in an affordable form. Unceasingly inspired by Southern Black Americans, he represented the daily lives of sharecroppers in a dignified manner that reflected his admiration of this culture born of poverty and racism. Gwathmey was among the artists who came together in New York late in 1939 to establish a cooperative workshop for serigraphy.

The Silk Screen Group, as this coterie of twenty artists was first called, shared shop space by subscription on East Tenth Street.[27] They also shared the finer points of the process, and offered public lectures and printmaking classes. Their inaugural exhibition, the first of many annual shows circulating to libraries and museums, was organized in 1940. By 1944, when the group incorporated as the National Serigraph Society, they had grown to sixty-five members and had moved to larger quarters at 38 West Fifty-seventh Street.[28] There they kept an archive of members' prints and compiled a lending library of slides and

Figure 5
Jackson Pollock (1912–56), *Untitled*,
1951. Serigraph. Private collection.

photographs. From 1946 through 1950, the society published an informative newsletter, the *Serigraph Quarterly*. Ruth Gikow, Leonard Pytlak, Dorie Marder, James Mac-Connell, Mary Van Blarcom, and others exhibited regularly with the National Serigraph Society in the 1940s and 1950s.[29]

Three artists who worked in comparable styles, Sol Wilson, Harry Shoulberg, and Harry Shokler (Fig. 4), are characteristic of the society. The printmakers conceived of serigraphy as a means for mass-producing affordable oil paintings.[30] They prepared their screens in a painterly manner, superimposing numerous layers of color—in both opaque inks and transparent glazes—that gave a thick impasto surface to their prints. Shoulberg usually printed with oil paints and often screened them onto canvas. Perhaps because of the foundation of the group amid depression-era urban realism, or because of its members' determination to remain as accessible as serigraphy itself, the National Serigraph Society encouraged the creation of a great many prints that were more accomplished in their craftsmanship than they were artistically inspired. Accessible and decorative as they were, these prints were often awkwardly drawn and composed.

Especially among these artists, the vigorous development and dissemination of serigraphy in the 1940s descended fairly quickly, during the next decade, into stultifying convention. Although silkscreen had established solid footholds among art teachers and amateur printmakers, most who worked in the medium remained outside the mainstream of American art. A few artists stand out for their creative serigraphs of the 1950s, which in general were more painterly in scale, color, and pictorial means than were the prints that had preceded them. These prints were conceived for the living room wall rather than the library album or solander box.

During this time, Sylvia Wald evolved far beyond her Social Realist background, toward a personal style of nonobjective abstraction. Impatient with the monotonous appearance of conventionally made serigraphs, she started to work with stop-out glue directly on the silk, and to print with great vigor (cat. 82). Later in the decade, in brightly colored serigraphs such as *Devorah's Grave*, Wald used Abstract Expressionist gesture with palpable vitality.

Dean Meeker began teaching at the University of Wisconsin in 1946.[31] Equally accomplished in the intaglio media, he made a considerable contribution as a teacher to American printmaking as it flourished in the university workshops of the Midwest. Technical virtuosity and haunting imagery characterize Meeker's silkscreens of the 1950s, which were inspired by ancient history and mythology. The artist combined screen printing with other media, and his semiabstract prints were often sculptural in conception.

Sister Mary Corita Kent was quite popular in the 1950s for her vivid, elaborately wrought prints of joyful religious subjects.[32] Having entered a convent in 1936, she studied art at the University of Southern California and taught at Immaculate Heart College. Corita based her early prints on Byzantine, early Christian, and medieval art. Her distinctive manner depended on many layers of bright, transparent color, generally produced by the tusche-and-glue method, superimposed to achieve fascinating depth and complexity. Later in her career, under the influence of Pop Art, she experimented with typography and the integration of poetic text in her large screen prints.

Early in the 1950s, the Western Serigraph Institute was founded in Los Angeles by Geno Pettit and Guy Maccoy, who served as its first president. This active group of more than thirty printmakers received wide attention in 1954, when their exhibition "Southern California Serigraphs," organized by the Los Angeles County Museum of Art, was

circulated around the country by the Smithsonian Institution.[33] Member artists Howard Bradford and Dorothy Bowman established national reputations. Their large, semiabstract landscape prints were often similar in technique if not in style. The scraped layers of color in these painterly screen prints approximate the effect of paintings made with a palette knife, a technique popular in the 1950s.[34]

Other artists who made innovative screen prints during this decade include Norio Azuma, Edward Landon, Henry Mark, and Richards Ruben. However, checklists of the National Print Annual exhibitions at the Brooklyn Museum in the 1950s, or of "American Prints Today," an exhibition organized by the Print Council of America in 1959, reveal surprisingly few silkscreens. Serigraphy was used extensively for reproduction in this period, often nearly overshadowing the creative use of the medium. Distinctions between original and reproductive prints were blurred when many artists—such as Charles Sheeler (cat. 84)—created designs specifically for reproduction in silkscreen. Even Jackson Pollock and his brother Sanford MacCoy used photo screens to transform drip paintings into screen prints (Fig. 5).[35]

In New York, several workshops specialized in commercial silkscreen production that was peripherally linked to fine printmaking. In fact, serigraphy had begun its inexorable return to commerce much earlier. In 1939, at the close of his stint in the WPA, Anthony Velonis had joined with four other artists to share print shop facilities.[36] Though at first the Creative Printmakers Group, as they were called, produced editions of their own prints, financial demands soon forced them to print for other artists as well. With contracts from book publishers, galleries, and museum shops, they soon began to make high-quality reproductions.[37] In the following decade, several other workshops sprang up in which the production of original serigraphs was mingled with that of reproductive prints. Among these was Ecran Urban, the screen printing and publishing company of Reva Urban and her husband, painter Albert Urban. At their studio and gallery space on West Tenth Street in New York, reproductions of paintings by modern artists as diverse as Monet, Picasso, and O'Keeffe were screened onto paper and canvas, then sold alongside Albert Urban's excellent original serigraphs (cat. 57).

Esther Gentle, the wife of painter Abraham Rattner, ran a similar business. Her little studio on Grove Street in lower Manhattan also combined workshop space with a sales gallery. She received commissions from book publishers, galleries, and museum shops, and came to specialize in reproductions of watercolors. Her serigraphs after Rattner and other contemporary artists were organized into an exhibition and circulated throughout the country by the American Federation of Arts in 1952 and 1953.[38] A student of Hans Hofmann, the indefatigable Gentle persuaded the master to try his hand at serigraphy at a time when sales of his paintings were slack. Thus they collaborated on an extraordinary print that is part automatist inspiration and part calculated reproduction (cat. 73).

In 1956, Tatyana Grosman also hoped to establish a company for publishing artists' prints. Her first production was a color silkscreen printed by her husband Maurice, which reproduced a drawing by Max Weber (cat. 15).[39] Hoping to illicit more direct involvement from artists, the Grosmans soon turned to lithography and tantalized several painters to become interested by delivering lithography stones to their studios. In this manner, the foundations of the influential workshop Universal Limited Art Editions were established.

At this time, stimulated by their observation of American serigraphs, some European commercial screen printers began to collaborate with artists in making silkscreens.[40] The Stuttgart studio of Luitpold Domberger started producing artists' prints in 1950, and the Wilfredo Arcay workshop in Paris progressed from reproductive prints into editions of silkscreens in about 1954, as did Chris Prater's Kelpra Studio in London in about 1960.[41] Each of these workshops became an important producer of artists' screen prints in the 1960s.

Color silkscreen experienced a stunning revival in the 1960s, when several of the most innovative and influential American artists worked in the medium. Master printers, oriented to efficiency, now concentrated on improved photographic screen preparation as the most responsive, versatile, and precisely controllable process. Although this development is beyond the scope of the present study, it should be observed that the resurrection of screen printing depended on two characteristics inherent in the medium that were suited to the styles of the 1960s. The capability of the technique for producing uniform, opaque passages of saturated color had tremendous appeal for hard edge and color field painters. Along with these brash coloristic capabilities, the ease, economy, and ironically, the commercial character of silkscreen made it the perfect medium for Pop Art.[42]

Notes

1. Biegeleisen/Cohn 1942, p. 10.

2. Field 1972.

3. Ibid.

4. "[Transparent base] is made by combining aluminum stearate with a solution of non-yellowing alkyd or acrylic resin and mineral spirits." Mayer 1969, pp. 401–402; see also pp. 313, 352–354, 358–360.

5. Whitaker 1974, p. 76.

6. Zigrosser 1941b, p. 467.

7. Ibid., p. 442.

8. Whitaker 1974, p. 60.

9. Haupers printed *New Moon*, 52.0 × 37.8 cm. (sheet), *Full Moon*, 51.8 × 37.4 cm. (sheet), and the technically complex *Pine County Barns*, 38.1 × 54.9 cm. (sheet), each printed in editions of fifty on thick poster-card paper. The artist's prints and personal archives are now at the Minnesota Historical Society in Minneapolis. The author is grateful to John Ittmann for bringing these prints to his attention, and to Thomas O'Sullivan for confirming the artist's early interest in serigraphy.

10. DeNoon 1987, pp. 13–17.

11. See Richard Floethe's foreword to Velonis 1938, p. iii.

12. Doris Meltzer, chairperson of the independent lobby Public Use of Arts Committee (1937–38) and an active serigrapher herself, enthusiastically supported Velonis. Two years later, Meltzer served as director of the newly formed National Serigraph Society.

13. Zigrosser 1941b, p. 449; Conkleton/Gilbert 1983, pp. 3–5. Other artists to make screen prints in the FAP graphic arts division were David Burke, Ruth Gikow, Riva Helfond, Florence Kent, Chet LaMore, Joe LeBoit, Nan Lurie, Claire Mahl, Beatrice Mandelman, Leonard Pytlak, Mildred Rackley, and Louis Schanker (cat. 41). Although Russell T. Limbach (cat. 45) and Bernard Schardt were slated to work with Velonis, their serigraphs never materialized.

14. Velonis 1938. This pamphlet discussed the materials for serigraphy and the preparation of screens by the lacquer film (Profilm or Nu-film) technique; a sequel (Velonis 1939) presented such other techniques of screen preparation as tusche and synthetic shellac wash-out, paper stencils, and photo screens.

15. Velonis 1940.

16. Springfield 1940; McCausland 1940. The checklist of the show was bound in a color serigraphed cover by Pauline Stiriss.

17. Weyhe 1940; McCausland 1940.

18. Denoon 1987, p. 78; Tyler 1987, p. 442.

19. Zigrosser 1941b.

20. Biegeleisen/Cohn 1942. Other period publications of this sort include Biegeleisen 1939; Summer/Audrieth 1941; Kosloff 1946; and Shokler 1946.

21. Sternberg 1942; see also Zigrosser 1941b, pp. 461–462. On the artist's opinion of the importance of serigraphy both in education and as the most efficient manner of disseminating information for the war effort, see Sternberg 1943 and Sternberg 1949.

22. Zigrosser 1941b, p. 454.

23. See Francey 1988.

24. See Michigan 1985, pp. 138–139.

25. Ibid., pp. 156–157.

26. Castleman 1988, pp. 124–125.

27. See Zigrosser 1941b, p. 451. The original members of the group were Max Arthur Cohn, Marion Cunningham, Ruth Gikow, Harry Gottlieb (cat. 48), Robert Gwathmey (cat. 59), Mervin Jules, Edward Landon (cat. 49), Guy Maccoy (cat. 53), Doris Meltzer, Reinhold Naegele, Elizabeth Olds, Leonard Pytlak, Harry Shokler, Harry Shoulberg, Bernard Steffen (cat. 61), Harry Sternberg (cat. 35), Mary Van Blarcom, Anthony Velonis (cat. 42), Hyman Warsager, and Sol Wilson.

28. See American Art Annual (1945), p. 169.

29. Williams 1986 provides an extensive census of artists who worked in serigraphy in the 1940s.

30. Shokler 1946, pp. 67, 69.

31. Miami 1964; Haslem 1970; Williams 1987, pp. 28–29.

32. Corita 1984; Galm 1976.

33. Although Feinblatt/Davis 1980 (p. 21) mistakenly places this exhibition in 1953, it was actually on view at the Los Angeles County Museum of Art from January 22 through March 7, 1954.

34. Feinblatt/Davis 1980, pp. 21, 103.

35. O'Connor/Thaw 1978, no. 1094.

36. See DeNoon 1987, pp. 73, 77–78. Joining Velonis were Joseph LeBoit, Eugene Morley (cat. 46), Bernard Schardt, and Hyman Warsager; they began in a rented loft on West Twenty-third Street. LeBoit, Morley, and Schardt dropped out almost immediately, and Velonis and Warsager were joined by Constantine Velonis and Thomas Quinn. By 1941, the burgeoning firm had become known as Creative Printmakers, Inc., and, said Velonis, "we were successful enough that our wives no longer had to support us."

37. For example, reproductions of paintings by Paul Klee for the Nierendorf Gallery (see Nierendorf 1941). In the early 1940s, Bernard Steffen (cat. 61) worked for Creative Printmakers, Inc., in New York, as serigraphy shop supervisor. Also employed by the shop at this time as a paper handler and printer was Jackson Pollock.

38. Rubenstein 1980, p. 96.

39. AFA 1952.

40. Williams 1987, pp. 33–44.

41. Hayward 1970; Tate 1980.

42. See Field 1972. An example of this duality was the portfolio Ten Works by Ten Painters, which was published by the Wadsworth Atheneum in 1964. This varied album of original silkscreens included prints ranging from a photojournalistic quotation by Andy Warhol to a stark color field composition by Ad Reinhardt. The portfolio was produced by Ives/Sillman, a partnership of two artists—Norman Ives and Sewell Sillman—who taught at the Yale University School of Fine Arts. Established in the early 1960s, this firm was among those that exploited silkscreen both for high-quality color reproduction and for artists' prints. Screen printing for Ives/Sillman was done on contract by Scirocco Printers in New Haven. See RISD 1973, no. 25.

Use of the Catalogue

The catalogue has been arranged chronologically. The titles of works given are those assigned by the artists, identifiable by inscription, or by reference to other inscribed impressions or to published descriptions. When this identification has not been possible, the representational prints are given descriptive titles, and abstract images are called *Untitled*. Inscriptions in foreign languages are translated, and those written in foreign scripts are described in transliteration.

A date has been assigned to each undated print, the basis for which can be found in the entry. Edition numbers are recorded whenever possible. Measurements are given in centimeters; height precedes width. Watermarks are described verbally. Whenever possible, reference is made to a catalogue number from a standard definitive exhibition or catalogue raisonné. These sources are described in the entry, and their full references can be found in the bibliography.

Throughout the catalogue, abbreviated bibliographical references are used. Please consult the bibliography for the full corresponding citation of references.

Mary Cassatt

1845–1926

I.

In the Omnibus

1890–91

Drypoint and aquatint on cream laid paper

36.7 × 26.7 cm. (plate)

43.5 × 30.2 cm. (sheet)

Stamped, lower center: artist's monogram (Lugt 604)

In pencil, lower margin: *Edition de 25 épreuves Imprimée par l'artiste et M. Leroy   Mary Cassatt*

Breeskin 145; Matthews/Shapiro 7

Worcester Art Museum, bequest of Mrs. Kingsmill Marrs, 1926.204

The only American to exhibit with the French Impressionists, Mary Stevenson Cassatt was an innovative and imaginative printmaker. A woman of outstanding independence and determination, she always considered herself American even though she lived in France throughout her mature career. Cassatt's indomitable pioneering spirit is apparent in her extraordinary color prints, which brilliantly synthesized the styles and techniques of avant-garde French printmaking with traditional Japanese popular prints.

In the 1880s, Cassatt concentrated her printmaking activities on drypoint, which she seems to have learned from Marcellin Desboutin, who introduced her to Monsieur Leroy, a skilled master printer.

The first documentary evidence of the artist's interest in color prints appeared in her letter to Berthe Morisot in April 1890. Cassatt had gone several times to the impressive exhibition of Japanese prints at the Ecole des Beaux-Arts, and wrote: "You who want to make color prints you couldn't think of anything more beautiful. I dream of it and don't think of anything else but color on copper."[1] In the following months, the artist set to work on a group of large drypoints colored with very fine grained aquatint.[2] For these she drew specifically on the work of Utamaro.[3] The Japanese master's svelte figures and his penchant for mother and child scenes strongly appealed to Cassatt.

Cassatt transformed the aesthetic of *ukiyo-e* to the elegant idiom of fin de siècle Paris. Her organization of a set of prints, related by subject and uniform in format, can be compared with that of Utamaro's series, and the size and shape of her drypoints relate to the standard *oban* format. The Japanese influence also appears in her eloquent draftsmanship and her calculated balances between broad passages of form and color and more detailed decorative patterns. The flat, linear quality of her designs is enhanced by even, shadowless light. Cassatt also derived her palette directly from Japanese prints. However, her pastel tints distinctly resemble those of faded woodcuts that have lost the intensity of their natural pigments by overexposure to daylight.

In this print, she rendered the mother's pale pink dress in a hue identical to that of the Japanese safflower red ink (*beni*) after it had faded; similarly, she admired Japanese purple, a combination of red and dayflower blue (*aigami*) pigments, which aged to the dusty brown of the companion's dress. Cassatt certainly knew how bright pristine impressions of Japanese prints could be, but she preferred these muted, pale colors.

The present composition was forged and refined in preliminary sketches, revealing that the artist had considered including other figures.[4] On the proof of an early state of the print, Cassatt drew in pencil the background landscape, which she later transferred to the plate. Proofs of seven distinct working steps reflect the development of the final version. *In the Omnibus* was printed from three plates. The sheets were pierced in the center at top and bottom by pinholes, which assured precise registration.

Cassatt printed her set of ten color intaglios with the assistance of Leroy on her own press in her family's apartment on the rue Marignan. Leroy exactingly laid the fine aquatint grains, carefully inked each plate in multiple colors *à la poupée*, and printed each in perfect registration. The extent of Leroy's contribution is reflected in the artist's credit to him, which was inscribed in pencil on this example and on every color impression of her prints published in 1891.

Cassatt intended this set of color prints for inclusion in the third exhibition of the Société de Peintres-Graveurs in April 1891. However, when she and Pissarro were barred from this show by the pronouncement that only French-born artists could be included, they arranged to install their prints in adjacent rooms of the Galerie Durand-Ruel. Despite favorable reviews, sales were slow, and the gallery soon began to break up sets in order to sell prints individually.[5]

Notes

1. Matthews 1984, pp. 214–215.

2. Scholars have disagreed about Cassatt's technique for these color prints, but it now seems clear that she combined drypoint with aquatint. The checklist for the exhibition in 1891 at the Galerie Durand-Ruel explicitly describes the prints as such (*pointe sèche et aquatinte*; see Matthews/Shapiro 1989, p. 19, fig. 268). Further, in 1891, in a letter to his son Lucien, Camille Pissarro specifically mentioned Cassatt's use of the aquatint dust box for her prints (see ibid., p. 69).

3. Ives 1974.

4. Fine 1982, pp. 236–242; Matthews/Shapiro 1989, pp. 115–119.

5. The set of Cassatt's color prints in the Worcester Art Museum was one of those sent by the Galerie Durand-Ruel to major galleries in New York as early as May 1891. Mrs. Kingsmill Marrs purchased the set from Keppel and Company in New York. It came to Worcester by bequest after Mrs. Marr's death in 1925. See Riggs 1977.

James McNeill Whistler

1834–1903

2.

The Yellow House, Lannion

1893

Lithograph on cream Japanese
vellum wove paper
24.0 × 16.1 cm. (image)
38.0 × 24.0 cm. (sheet)
In image: butterfly monogram
In pencil, lower margin: butterfly
monogram
Way 101; Levy 196;   state i/iii
Provenance: A.W. Scholle (Lugt
2923a), Emma Regina Martin, C.C.
Cunningham
Private collection

Whistler was first introduced to lithography in about 1855, when he made two prints in Baltimore or Washington.[1] However, it was not until 1878, when the artist's renown as an etcher was well established, that he returned to the stone. He was persuaded to do so by the printer Thomas Way, the only craftsman of the day who produced artist's lithographs in London. At this time, Whistler was occupied with evocative paintings and etchings suffused with atmosphere and light. Way introduced Whistler to the medium of lithotint, a process in which the artist painted on the stone with diluted washes of tusche. This method perfectly provided the soft, misty effects Whistler sought. Way even helped the artist to transport a lithographic stone on a Thames barge to Limehouse, so that he could work directly from nature.[2]

In 1879 and 1887, Whistler collaborated with Way on a group of transfer lithographs.[3] In this technique the artist drew with lithographic crayons on prepared paper; later the printer transferred the image from this paper onto the lithographic stone in a pass through the press; impressions could then be printed in the conventional manner. This technique emancipated the artist from the studio, and eliminated the necessity of transporting cumbersome stones. It was well suited to Whistler's working habits, and he developed a new enthusiasm for lithography. He began to understand the medium as a direct method for producing multiple drawings, preserving the inspiration and immediacy of the original rendering. The artist once wrote in a letter, "Lithography reveals the artist in his true strength as a draughtsman and colourist—for the line comes straight from his pencil."[4]

Whistler began to explore color lithography in 1890, hoping to reproduce the imagery and graphic effects of his pastels. Thomas Way began experimenting with adaptations of the transfer method for color work. However Whistler took his ideas to Paris, where the use of color lithography was far more common, and its technology more so-

phisticated. The artist began to work in the Belfond lithography studio, and he was soon pulling exciting color proofs. Late in 1891, Whistler began to plan a suite of color lithographs to be titled *Songs on Stone*. The set was to be printed at the Belfont studio, and published by William Heinemann in London.

In 1892 Whistler and his wife moved to Paris. There, he continued to make transfer lithographs, which were regularly mailed to London to be proofed by Way, and occasionally to be printed in editions. The subjects of Whistler's Parisian transfer lithographs were widely varied. He depicted scenes of the city, including views in the Louvre galleries and the Luxembourg gardens, and the facades of French shops and houses. These street scenes carried on an interest the artist had developed in a series of etchings of London shop fronts made between 1884 and 1888. Whistler also often represented his wife and her family in pleasant scenes of home, similar in their mood to the color lithographs of Pierre Bonnard and Edouard Vuillard.

In a few of his color lithographs Whistler represented draped female nudes, returning to a theme that had occupied him in the 1860s. At that time, terra-cotta figurines dating from the third century B.C. were unearthed in the vicinity of Tanagra in Greece. They represented elegant dancing women, dressed in sheer, clinging draperies. Whistler was struck not by their classicism, but by their abstract beauty when separated from their cultural context and thus from their meaning. He studied these statuettes closely, and derived a group of figural paintings, pastels, and prints from them. Also in the 1860s, Whistler began to respond to the French enthusiasm for Japanese art, and his female figures were draped in kimonos and carried paper fans. The delicate coloring and selective use of form, as well as the compositional balance of *ukiyo-e* prints were also apparent in Whistler's pastels, and in his color lithographs.

In the summer of 1893 the artist traveled to Brittany. There, he made several drawings for lithographs on transfer paper. Among them were the designs for two color prints, *The*

Red House, made in the Breton village of Paimpol, and *The Yellow House*, drawn in Lannion.

By September 1893 the artist was back in Paris and at work at Belfond's on the two color lithographs of Brittany. The color prints were meant to be included in the Heinemann suite. However, by December 1893 Whistler's relationship with Belfond had ended, and the little mention made of the studio afterward suggests that it closed. The artist was never able to find a printer with whom he could comfortably work on color prints, and later events in his life superseded his interest in *Songs on Stone*, which was never published.

Whistler made seven color lithographs, all taken from transfer drawings. His method of printing each color from a different stone may have begun with the separations of color from a master drawing. The component designs were transferred to as many stones as there were colors, and printed in succession. Registration was achieved by cross marks with pinholes through their centers, visible within the image of the present print. For the production of these experimental works, it seems that Whistler worked in the studio alongside the printer, grinding the colors himself. He avoided the opaque layers and saturated colors of chromolithography, aiming instead for the soft hues of old *ukiyo-e* prints. In their delicacy and their spare economy of line, Whistler's color lithographs were similar to his etched plates.

The rarity of Whistler's color lithographs suggests that only a small number were printed. Indeed, many impressions were unique in their coloration and subtleties of inking. To enhance the deluxe cachet of these prints, Whistler printed them on special papers. Diaphanous sheets made in Asia were used, as well as silky Japanese vellum and leaves of old laid paper removed from books.

Notes

1. Way 1914; Levy 1975.

2. Way 1912, p. 10.

3. Lochnan 1981, pp. 133–137; Smale 1984.

4. Lochnan, 1986, p. 48, note 3.

Maurice Brazil Prendergast

1859–1924

3.

A Mother and Her Two Daughters Beneath an Umbrella

about 1895–97

Monotype on cream Japan paper

14.0 × 8.3 cm. (image)

28.9 × 20.7 cm. (sheet)

In the image, lower right: *MPB*

Collection of Professor and Mrs. Charles H. Sawyer

At the end of the nineteenth century, Maurice Prendergast created a remarkable group of monotypes that brought an unprecedented splash of color to American printmaking. An idyllic world of holidays and haunting romance is represented in these prints, which are sometimes vivid and sometimes pale and delicate in hue. Unexcelled technical mastery and range of expression distinguish Prendergast's monotypes as monuments of the height of American Impressionism in printmaking.

The simplest and most direct of all printmaking techniques, a monotype is basically created from a layer of ink painted on the polished surface of glass or metal and then offset onto a sheet of paper. Though these prints are generally unique, a second, fainter impression can often be pulled from the prepared plate. From the seventeenth to the late nineteenth century, this technique was used only sporadically.[1] However, during the 1870s, the process was employed by a widening circle of artists who created monotypes including Max Weber (cat. 15), Blanche Lazzell (cat. 18), Milton Avery (cat. 83), and Adja Yunkers (cat. 81).

From about 1891 to 1902, Prendergast made as many as two hundred monotypes, nearly a tenth of which were variants of other compositions. He began these prints soon after his arrival in Paris, where he probably learned the technique, for it was a popular practice at the Académie Julian. The artist found inspiration in monotypes by Camille Pissarro, Paul Gauguin, and Edgar Degas. All of Prendergast's monotypes were in color, and he never worked in other print media.

From the beginning these prints were technically accomplished, highly resolved, and distinctly personal in style. Prendergast was drawn to the process as a means for exploring variations on a theme, and for experimenting with effects of tone and color. The artist was undoubtedly intrigued by its peculiar visual qualities, for when the thick, viscous paint is flattened and squeezed deep into the paper, color and line are transformed, and an alluring, luminous quality results. He was also captivated by the unpredictable way in which the paint and paper responded to the action of printing. Prendergast's monotypes always utilized several hues, but one color dominated and unified each composition.

In 1905, the artist briefly described his working procedure in simple terms, in an instructive letter: "Paint on copper in oil, wiping parts to be white. When picture suits you, place on it Japanese paper and either press in a press or rub with a spoon till it pleases you. Sometimes the second or third plate is the best."[2] Prendergast always used oil paint for his monotypes, and printed them on soft, absorptive Japan paper, usually placing the plate on the floor and printing by rubbing with a spoon.

The artist's skill in the subtractive process of the monotype technique is evident in the present print, in areas where strokes of the dry brush and rag used to remove ink are visible, especially in the little girl's white dress. Prendergast also manipulated paint by drawing in the ink film, presumably with the tip of his brush, to outline figures and delineate his monogram. The wide border at the bottom of the print, common to several of his monotypes, often carries a title as well as the artist's signature. Indeed, in the smudged area on the left of this passage, the artist seems to have placed an inscription in the present print, and later, changing his mind, rubbed it away before printing. The placement and size of this border may have ultimately derived from Japanese design and the traditional manner of mounting scroll paintings.

In the present print, an elegant mother and her daughters stroll leisurely away from the viewer across a sun-drenched summer lawn, toward a group chatting in the shade of a large red umbrella.[3] Glaring sunlight is suggested by the richly hued umbrella and dresses, which contrast with the cool, monochromatic figures in the shade. This pleasant vision is typical of Prendergast's monotype oeuvre, which is made up of scenes of elegance, of carefree pastimes, and of charming, romantic locations.

The chronology of Prendergast's monotypes remains uncertain and problematic, for the artist dated just 24 of the 151 prints known today. In subject and style, this print has much in common with a group of monotypes produced between 1895 and 1897. The monotypes in this group represent comparable settings and figures—fashionably dressed women and little girls at leisure on lush green lawns—in similar colors.[4] The subjects often face onto these compositions and away from the viewer. Extensive use of the tip of the brush to outline figures, and other technical traits, are also common to these prints.

Notes

1. MMA/MFA 1980.

2. Rhys/Wick 1960, p. 34.

3. In 1939 this print was given as a Christmas card by Charles and Eugenie Prendergast to Professor and Mrs. Charles H. Sawyer. At that time, Professor Sawyer was director of the Addison Gallery of American Art in Andover, Massachusetts, and had in the previous year organized an important Prendergast exhibition (see Addison 1938).

4. Included in this group are *In the Park* (see Young 1973, p. 140), *Balloons: Park on Sunday* (see Langdale 1979, no. 61), *The Breezy Common* series (see Langdale 1984, nos. 28–30), and others. See also Corcoran 1937; Phillips 1967.

Edward Penfield

1866–1925

4.

HARPER'S NOVEMBER, Young Man in a Hansom Cab

1896

Lithograph on cream wove paper

45.8 × 34.3 cm. (image)

45.8 × 34.1 cm. (sheet)

In the image, upper right: *EDWARD PENFIELD*, and bull's head monogram

Kiehl 186

Worcester Art Museum, Anonymous Fund, 1989.19

In the 1890s, art posters began to change the orientation of American advertising from a narrative to a pictorial mode. Although the public had long responded to brightly colored circus posters and chromolithograph reproductions, the new, fashionable art posters quickly caused excitement and inspired an almost fanatical following. American poster artists introduced avant-garde artistic styles from Europe. They understood the powers of visual imagery to persuade and even educate their audience. With the popularity of art posters in the 1890s, an audience of collectors for color prints in the United States began to be developed.

The American art poster phenomenon grew out of a similar movement in France, which began in the 1860s. In Paris, such artists as Jules Chéret, Eugène Grasset, Theophile-Alexandre Steinlein, and Henri de Toulouse-Lautrec designed posters advertising theatrical entertainments. Hung on street hoardings and kiosks, these powerful images made celebrities of the artists themselves. Decades later, in the United States, art posters came into use primarily as advertising for the publishing industry. In 1890 the Grolier Club in New York mounted the first American exhibition of European art posters. Soon articles in national magazines introduced this art to a wide and receptive American public. Exhibitions of French posters were mounted in East Coast cities and spread progressively across the country. By the middle of the decade, books about poster collecting began to appear, and popular poster shows were seen as far west as Denver.

Edward Penfield was a pivotal figure in the American art poster movement, and he became the arbiter of style in pictorial advertising for two generations. In 1891, he was art editor for *Harper's* magazine in New York, when European posters started to receive wide attention. Penfield briefly visited Paris in 1892, where he directly encountered the influence of the famous French poster artists. He may have helped arrange for the famous Swiss artist

Eugène Grasset to design a placard that advertised the Christmas issue of *Harper's* in 1892.[2] The success of this piece prompted the publisher to print a new poster for every issue of *Harper's*.

When Penfield's first *Harper's* posters appeared in 1893, their radical designs were very European. Most of the compositions represented a sophisticated-looking *Harper's* reader intently absorbed in the magazine; only the name of the month and the magazine's title appeared. This was markedly different from the old-style magazine advertisement, which listed the periodical's contents in detail, sometimes surrounded by decorative marginalia. In the posters that followed, Penfield depicted attractive, stylish members of the upper middle class, shown in casual attitudes that reflected their self-confidence. They often read or carried a copy of *Harper's*, or they were busy in various leisurely activities like riding, boating, or tennis. Penfield's arresting, elegant, often witty images were meant to appeal to a very specific audience, and they subtly flattered the potential *Harper's* reader. These posters seldom related to the features in the magazines they advertised, however their handsome, usually youthful subjects were depicted in simplified seasonal settings or pastimes. For about six years, Penfield created monthly posters for *Harper's*. He also produced magazine covers, illustrations, and calendars.

Young Man in a Hansom Cab is typical of Penfield's distinctive style. Its handsome young traveler is fashionably turned out in a plaid suit, with a homburg, kid gloves, and a cane-handled umbrella. Completely at ease at being driven, he seems intelligent and even pensive. The prominent initials on his suitcases may suggest that he was an acquaintance of the artist.

Bold, legible compositions were the hallmark of Penfield's poster designs. Along with emphasized outlines and flattened forms, they reflected the impact of the English illustrators and poster designers William Nicholson and James Pryde. Over the years, Penfield experimented with his style

and compositional formula. The French artist Theophile-Alexandre Steinlein was also a formative influence. Ultimately Penfield's manner was determined by his purpose. Successful posters were arresting, legible, and memorable enough to be effective advertising.

Penfield was interested in equestrian sports, especially coaching. He studied the history of coach design, and collected historical horse-drawn vehicles. He wrote articles on the subject for *Outing* magazine, and when he died, Penfield was at work on a book about the history of coaches.[3] The artist often represented fancy horses and accurately detailed coaches in his illustrations and poster designs, including *Young Man in a Hansom Cab*.

This poster was printed in four colors, with a commercial lithography process utilizing four zinc plates, a method common in commercial printing by the 1890s. Thin, relatively cheap metal plates could be printed efficiently by mechanized presses, unlike the heavy, unwieldy, and expensive Bavarian limestone of traditional lithography. Penfield and his printers closely simulated the texture of lithographs pulled from stones. To achieve this effect, they used several planographic techniques—including transfer lithography—in combination with plates that were etched, hammered, or cut to print in relief.

The present print was embossed during printing, particularly in the area of the letters, indicating that some relief plates were used. By 1897, Penfield had begun to use the distinctive spatter technique, which approximated the lithographic effect made famous by Toulouse-Lautrec. Poster artist Will Bradley especially admired Penfield's combination of several varied technical effects in his posters and illustrations.[4] Penfield often went to the pressroom himself, to mix and blend the inks for his posters. He stayed there with the pressmen until the machines settled down and the prints were exactly as he wished.

Notes

1. Wong 1974; Kiehl 1987.
2. Kiehl 1987, pp. 11–12.
3. Gibson 1984, p. 13.
4. Bradley 1896.

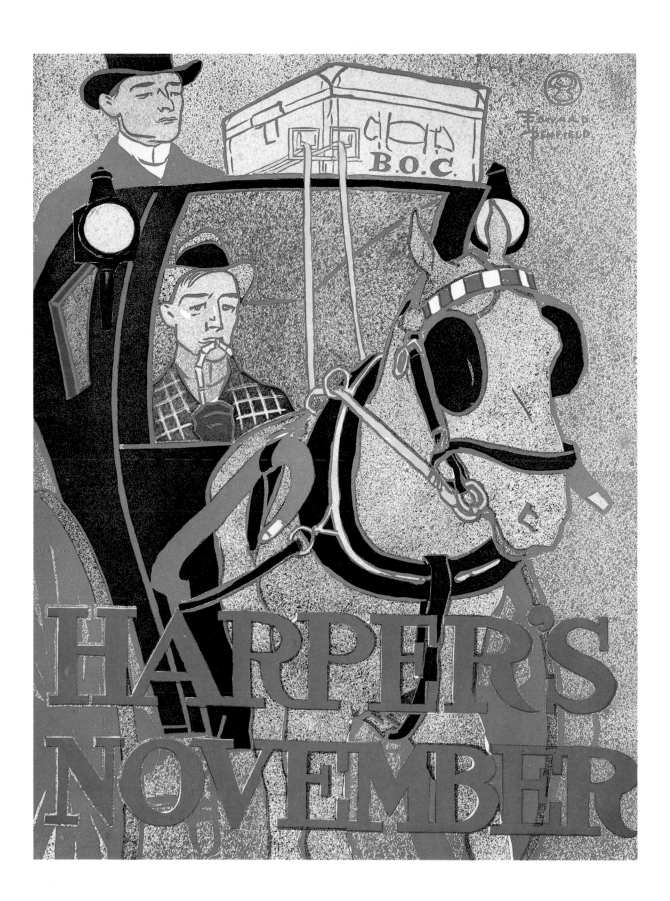

Louis John Rhead

1857–1926

5.

Jane, from L'Estampe Moderne
1898

Lithograph on cream wove paper
40.2 × 31.6 cm. (image)
35.1 × 21.6 cm. (sheet)
In image, lower right: *LOUIS RHEAD*
In margin, lower right: *L'Estampe Moderne*, blind stamp
Worcester Art Museum, bequest of Mrs. Kingsmill Marrs, 1926.404

A prominent figure in the American art poster movement of the 1890s, Louis Rhead was a highly successful commercial designer, and one of the first artists to work in an Art Nouveau style in America. Aside from his famous posters, he also produced designs for decorative arts, calendars, and smaller prints. These graphic works were very popular, and avidly collected in their day.

Jane is a prime example of Rhead's famous idealized women. The striking beauty, splendid costumes, and impassive expressions of these women made them seem unapproachable. They were the descendants of the Gothic virgins of Dante Gabriel Rossetti and the nursery maids of Walter Crane. However, while both of these artists often depicted sympathetic characters, Rhead preferred a cold, haughty elegance. His women were the antithesis of the up-to-date, leisured women of Edward Penfield's (cat. 4) posters and illustrations. It seems that Rhead's subjects were ideals of feminine beauty for Edwardian men, while Penfield sought to represent American women as they wished to see themselves.

Rhead combined the European styles of the English Aesthetic movement and that of the Nabis-influenced poster artist Eugène Grasset, whom he met in Paris. The artist combined bold outlines with strong contrasts of form and color. His distinctive, curving linear rhythms, along with the prominent use of repeated decorative plant motifs, characterize his Art Nouveau style. For example, the screen of lilies in the background of the present print reflects the influence of the Arts and Crafts style of William Morris. The parallel lines behind the flowers, suggesting swirling mists, were ultimately derived from Japanese decorative design. The posture of the figure, facing away from the viewer and twisting around to gaze over her shoulder, also relates to Pre-Raphaelite painting.

An astute businessman, Rhead sustained the demand for his work by wide contacts. Although he lived in New York, his designs were also published concurrently in London and Paris. His work was sold in the Sagot and Arnould galleries in Paris. In 1897, Rhead designed a large lithographic mural panel for the Parisian publisher La Plume. Later, the imperfect impressions of this poster were overprinted with text, and utilized as advertisements for the publisher's magazine *Le Journal de la Beauté*.[1]

The present print was published in the second Parisian serial called *L'Estampe Moderne*, which was issued monthly from May 1897 to April 1899. Each issue contained four prints, usually lithographs, many accompanied by verse or prose. The periodical was moderately priced, and its publishers Charles Masson

and Henri Piazza, intended for the folios to appeal to collectors of posters and popular prints. Rhead published two prints in *L'Estampe Moderne: Jane* was issued in April 1898, following *The Woman of the Pheasants (La femme au paon)* in July 1897.

Jane was created to illustrate a "Scottish ballad," which it accompanied in the folio. This verse specifically mentioned the maid's ruby lips, her long golden tresses, and her piercing blue eyes that "wounded the heart." Rather than dressing her in tartans and lace, Rhead provided Jane with a fanciful Renaissance-style costume. The flat, unmodeled forms of her figure and clothing became decorative patterns. None of the peculiar, interstitial colors were blended or superimposed. However, by repeating many of the outlines of his composition, the artist enlivened this decorative image.

This lithograph was printed from zinc plates on a mechanical press, by professional printers in the Champenois Workshop in Paris. Rhead was intimately aware of the limitations and strengths of this process. Thus he designed his prints so that the slight variations of registration and color during the press run would not ruin prints.

Notes

1. Goddu 1989, p. 75. See also Kiehl 1987, p. 191.

Arthur Wesley Dow

1857–1922

6.

Ipswich Rooftops

about 1904
Woodcut on thin cream Japan paper
12.6 × 5.8 cm. (image)
18.0 × 11.5 cm. (sheet)
In pencil, in image: *Arthur W. Dow*
In black ink, stamped on verso:
ESTATE OF ARTHUR WESLEY DOW
Private collection

The central figure in American color relief printmaking at the turn of the century was Arthur Wesley Dow, an artist who combined the style and technique of traditional Japanese printmaking with concepts derived from the Arts and Crafts movement. His innovative prints, which self-consciously employed craft techniques to create works of fine art, were far-reaching in their influence. The artist was also an important educator, and the effects of his potent aesthetic theories, writings, and teaching methods were felt across the country.

Like many of Dow's color woodcuts, this image includes recognizable buildings that identify its location. The narrow tower of the Ipswich Church and the Gothic spire of the North Church pierce the horizon. The position of these towers suggests that the viewer is looking to the southeast, up the hill and toward the central square of Ipswich. The gleaming, cloudless sky of this image, the billowy shapes of its bushes and trees, and its saturated hues are evocative of a sultry midsummer's day.

This vivid image is exemplary of the artists's personal synthesis of *japonisme* and concepts from the Arts and Crafts movement. It comprises the most basic elements of design, arranged in a manner that uses the alternation of dark and light, or positive and negative. Although some areas of color are edged by other hues, there is no modeling, shading, or detailing of these flat, decorative shapes. The high horizon and empty expanse of foreground draw the viewer into the composition. Its tall, narrow proportions were perhaps suggested by Japanese scroll painting, or by the *ukiyo-e* "pillar print" format.

The bright colors are more decorative than natural, and the artist did not seek to deny the graphic qualities of ink lying on paper. Despite smudges and slight imperfections in registration, Dow signed this print, thus authorizing its legitimacy. This handmade aspect of the woodcut, and Dow's truth to materials of the craft, is a reflection of the influence of the Arts and Crafts movement. Indeed, the artist adamantly undertook every step in the creation of his color woodcuts himself.

Dow used several woodblocks, onto which he expertly spread the watercolor inks with brushes. Placing the thin paper on the inked block, he printed by rubbing the verso by hand. In many ways, inking and printing were for him the most important aspects of the process of creating a color woodcut. Dow called this exercise "painting with woodblocks."[2] It was a creative process, rather than a reproductive one. The artist was enchanted by the quality of color available through this technique, in which he found not only the intensity and subtleties of watercolor, but an added luminosity. In printing itself, and in varying colors from one proof to the next, he was encouraged to concentrate on the colors and their relationships, rather than the subject of the image.

In this process, Dow found a way to produce a given image in several color variations. As his associate Ernest Fenollosa described it: "This method of printing utilizes the lost chances, since the block, once carved, saves the repetition of the drawing, and allows the labor to concentrate on the new color problem."[3] The artist often showed how, by changing colors alone, he could suggest different seasons or times of day. He found that such variation was most effective when the design was simple, and the shapes discrete. In this sense, technique helped determine style. The artist altered his palette drastically when he printed, trying as many as seven or eight color schemes with a single set of blocks.

Dow found that when he changed colors in printing, each new variant defined a new color composition and a different scheme of *notan*, or the arrangement of dark and light masses and hues. Each variant proof begged the artist to try another combination, and by continuing to experiment, he came to understand the effects of colors, alone and in combination.

The artist soon realized that color itself had become the focus of his experiments and, indeed, the very subject of these prints. He observed: "This method of expression would lose all of its charm if obliged to serve the ends of literal representation. Its strength lies in the free interpretations, in playing with colors, so to speak, rather than in a forced realism. It lends itself readily to a suggestive rendering of effects in nature; a twilight, moonlight, sun and shadow, rain, gray days and morning mists, but as easily permits a departure into a purely imaginative treatment as brilliant and unreal as stained glass."[4]

Notes

1. In about 1908, Dow suggested to the governing body of the North Church that they paint the building red. See Moffatt 1977, pp. 115, note 262.

2. Dow 1896, p. 87.

3. Fenollosa 1895.

4. Dow 1896, p. 89.

Arthur W. Dow

Gabrielle De Vaux Clements

1858–1948

7.

Evening Skyline

1907

Etching on cream wove paper

25.0 × 15.9 cm. (plate)

34.4 × 29.3 cm. (sheet)

In plate, lower left:

G. D. Clements 1907

In pencil, lower margin:

Gabrielle D. Clements

Provenance: Stephen Parrish, Maxfield Parrish

Worcester Art Museum, Austin S. Garver Fund, 1988.162

Of the growing number of professional women artists in the latter half of the nineteenth century, Gabrielle De Vaux Clements and her companion Ellen Day Hale gave the most attention to color intaglio prints.

Although Clements painted portraits and figure studies, nearly all of her prints were landscapes, befitting her background in the Etching Revival. These presented her misty, romantic visions of familiar haunts or picturesque views of exotic, faraway places. The artist preferred scenes of civilization to those of nature, and she always implied human activity in her images. Here, the warm glow of the window in the foreground hints of the domestic coziness behind cold, impersonal walls.

This view of the dusk in Baltimore is identifiable by the prominent steeple of the First Presbyterian Church, a landmark that still stands at the corner of Madison Street and Park Avenue.[1] Completed in 1875, the church combined Gothic design with current technology in its soaring spires of stone, built upon a cast-iron framework. Clements created a gloaming atmosphere in order to invest the familiar skyline of Baltimore with all the romance of a medieval French cathedral town.

It has been suggested that Mary Cassatt's color prints (cat. 1) influenced Clements's experiments in color intaglio.[2] Quite probably these two Philadelphians had met in Paris in the 1880s. Cassatt made color prints related to the mural she had painted for the World Columbian Exposition in 1893, and Clements, who painted a mural at the same Chicago fair, likewise derived color aquatints from her church frescoes of the 1920s and 1930s.[3] However, there are more differences than similarities between *Evening Skyline* and Cassatt's color aquatints.

Cassatt employed multiple plates but Clements used just one, which she charged with inks of various colors and overprinted. She printed most of the color using a thin film of ink on the surface of the plate. She inked and printed the entire surface of this plate three times—once each with yellow, blue, and brown—on the same sheet of paper. With each separate inking, she carefully wiped the plate to achieve specific effects of chiaroscuro, tonal modulation, and highlighting. By a purposeful skewing of the registration, the focus of the image was softened, lines were blurred, and an impressionistic effect was achieved. Inevitably, Clements inked and wiped each impression of her color prints somewhat differently.

The artist made *Evening Skyline* quite early in her oeuvre of color prints. During the 1920s, she preferred to apply several colors to the plate at once, *à la poupée*, to be printed in a single pass through the press. Eventually she refined this process even more by using several multicolor inkings and paintings for a single print. Also in the 1920s, in order to capture any accidental felicities, Clements wrote careful accounts of her color intaglio techniques; these are now preserved in the Graphic Arts Division of the National Museum of American Art, Smithsonian Institution.

Notes

1. McCauley 1975, p. 79. I am grateful to Margaret Welch of the Maryland Historical Society for her assistance in identifying this landmark.

2. Peet 1988, p. 22.

3. Matthews/Shapiro 1989, pp. 157–163.

Gabrielle D. Clements

Helen Hyde

1868–1919

8.

A Mexican Coquette

1912

Woodcut on thin cream Japan paper
25.0 × 25.8 cm. (image)
31.4 × 38.4 cm. (sheet)
In the block: *copyright 1912 by Helen Hyde*   HH monogram
In pencil, lower margin: *A Mexican Coquette*
Worcester Art Museum, anonymous gift, 1988.78

A lady of wealth and taste whose willful personality shaped her career as an artist, Helen Hyde was a prolific printmaker and was successful in her own time. She was one of the few American artists who traveled to the East to learn the traditional style and printmaking techniques and to collaborate with native craftsmen.

For the majority of her color woodcuts, Hyde began by preparing a preliminary drawing with brush and ink, from which the key block was carved by Japanese craftsmen. A woodcarver called Matsumoto, and the printer Murata Shojiro, who had worked with Hiroshige III, collaborated with Hyde in the studio upstairs in her Tokyo home. Their names appear on some of her prints, along with the artist's monogram. Later, using watercolor on proof impressions from the key block, Hyde indicated her intentions for the colors of the print. To satisfy her Western, etcher's notion of uniform limited editions, Hyde often supervised the printing of her woodcuts, preventing Murata from creative inking.

For some years, Hyde represented contemporary Japanese subjects in these prints, especially children and their mothers, in a manner that combined a Western illustrative style with compositions adapted from her own collection of traditional *ukiyo-e* prints. However, she soon began depicting the children and adults of other cultures, subjects that were exotic and picturesque to an American. In 1912, after undergoing an operation for cancer in Chicago, Hyde decided to travel to Mexico to escape the severe winter. She was enchanted by this country, despite the raging war of revolution, which severely limited her travels. After her return to Tokyo the artist developed several color woodcuts from drawings she had made in Mexico. Later she wrote a travel article about her experiences in Mexico illustrated with these prints, including *A Mexican Coquette*.[1] In it Hyde wrote: "Romance plays such a part of the life of Mexico. Never in any country have I seen such leisure on the part of a man for the gentle art of wooing. Picturesque they are too, these Mexican lovers, with their tight silver-trimmed trousers, the great rolling hat entrancing with its embroideries of gold and silver. . . . They watch the pretty Señoritas over the garden walls."[2]

The cutting of the woodblocks for *A Mexican Coquette* was remarkably skillful, accurately retaining the character and immediacy of the artist's drawing style. Tonal gradations were achieved both by complicated overlays of color and by the controlled modulation of ink on the printing surfaces. The virtuosity of these techniques is apparent in effects as diverse as those of the purple clouds of bougainvillea hanging on the garden wall, and the pale pastels in the decoration of the coquette's skirt. These subtleties of color depended on absolutely perfect registration.

The ink soaked well into the paper, and visible on the verso of this print are the strokes of the brush that spread and modulated the ink on the block. Scars from the *baren*, or rubbing pad used to print the woodcut, are also apparent. All of these characteristics, and above all the virtuosic cutting and printing, show that the blocks were carved by professional carvers and printed by Japanese printers. Although Hyde experimented with the traditional vertical format, or *oban*, and with narrow pillar print shapes, round images such as this, and elliptical compositions as well, characterize her works as Western designs.

Notes

1. Hyde 1913.

2. Ibid., pp. 32–33. See also Blattner 1911; Emerson 1916.

Edna Boies Hopkins

1872–1937

9.

Fig Leaves

about 1913

Woodcut on cream wove paper

27.9 × 18.6 cm. (image)

37.1 × 26.2 cm. (sheet)

In pencil, lower margin: *Edna Boies Hopkins   10   Fig Leaves*

Private collection

One of a handful of American women of her generation who came under the spell of Japanese prints, Edna Boies Hopkins was so captivated by this art that she traveled to Japan to learn the finer points of the process. Later, in Paris, she developed a very personal style and technique that also incorporated influences from French *japonisme* and from Post-Impressionism. In 1914, she brought this personal stylistic synthesis to Cape Cod, where her teaching provided a foundation for the Provincetown Printers' movement.

Upon her arrival in Paris in 1905, armed with a new expertise in Japanese woodblock printmaking, Hopkins immersed herself in her work. The method she devised combined her experiences in the East with the influences of contemporary French woodcut artists such as Auguste Lepère and Maurice Delcourt, who themselves combined the aesthetics and method of *ukiyo-e* with the current technology of wood engraving. Hopkins chose to focus on floral imagery, traditional to *ukiyo-e* and represented by such artists as Hokusai and Hiroshige.

The elegant composition of *Fig Leaves* has the characteristic flatness, asymmetry, and balance of Japanese design. Hopkins established an elegant tension in the thin, sweeping contour of the web slung from the upper left corner of the image. The gossamer thread seems to suspend the dead fig leaf, balancing it against the weight of the living leaves. The bright yellow abdomen of the spider, which rests near the center of its web, provides the asymmetrical focus of the composition. The creature seems not to have been part of the original conception, for the artist printed its black legs over a complex passage of webbing carved in the blue block. Similarly, the black border line covers tiny inaccuracies of registration. Hopkins always rendered the natural subjects of her prints in soft, pastel hues, contrasting them with a dark or dull-colored, featureless background. Often the modeling of leaves or flowers gives the only sense of naturalistic dimension. Products of long and deliberate processes of refinement, Hopkins's compositions sometimes involved years of sketching and synthesis. The artist was a friend of Claude Monet, and watercolors she made in his famous garden at Giverny provided inspiration for many of her prints.

Although in her earlier floral prints Hopkins used two delicately blended colors for the background, in *Fig Leaves* and other contemporary works, she printed a single color from a block that shows its coarse wood grain. For the mottled texture of the blue ground in this print, she applied a thin film of ink dryly and evenly to the block. She wrote: "Instead of soaking into the paper the color was often caught up, as it were, on the outer fibers only, the very whiteness of those below shining through and diluting it with light."[1]

The cream-colored European wove paper, common among her prints, has a hard surface and is heavily sized.[2] It is interesting that the artist should prefer this unabsorbent paper to Japan paper, or to the readily available French-made, long-fibered *simili* Japan papers. Although the ink sank into the sheet, it did not soak through to the back; nor does the verso show the scars of hand printing. Slight, even embossing is apparent on the recto of the paper surface. These features suggest that at this time Hopkins experimented with printing her woodcuts in a press rather than rubbing them by hand in the Japanese manner. However, she did apply watercolor inks to the block with a brush in the Japanese way, and the soft modulation of colors reflects the subtlety of this inking.

Hopkins's early Parisian prints are also distinguished by a personal, *japoniste* seal of her own design, the image of a pea pod and blossom, which she stamped in red within the image. The absence of the seal, as well as a technical orientation as much to France as to Japan, marks this print as a late product of the artist's first Parisian stay and suggests a date of about 1913.

Notes

1. From notes by the artist, quoted in Ryan 1986, p. 2.

2. Like most of her prints of the period, this sheet has one deckled edge and three askew, suggesting that Hopkins bought large sheets and cut them up for her small prints.

10

George Elbert Burr

1859–1939

10.
Mount Byers, Colorado

about 1915
Etching and aquatint on cream wove paper
17.5 × 25.1 cm. (plate)
26.6 × 35.4 cm. (sheet)
In pencil, lower margin: *George Elbert Burr   Del. et Imp.   No-11*
Watermark: *J. WHATMAN*
Seeber 74
Worcester Art Museum, anonymous gift, 1988.91

In his original technique for printing etchings and aquatints in color, Burr applied his experience as a watercolorist to making color prints of the sort he had seen in France and Germany. There, he had occasionally printed etchings in a single color other than black and soon after his return to the United States, he began experimenting with combinations of color on single plates.[1] In 1904, the artist derived his first successful multicolor intaglio from a watercolor he had painted in Europe, a picturesque view of *Florence from Monte Oliveto* (Seeber 39).

Soon after his move to Denver in 1906, Burr produced *Piñon Trees and Spanish Peaks, Colorado* (Seeber 42). He spent quite a lot of time perfecting his color process even though he made very few prints. By 1908, he had exhibited just five etchings in color. Ultimately the artist printed only about 40 of more than 350 intaglios in color. All of these were made in Denver, though they represented both European and Coloradan subjects. Burr's preoccupation with relationships between color and intaglio techniques and watercolor and etching was underscored by the exhibition of his series *Mountain Moods* in 1916.

No prescriptive academic method for multicolor intaglio existed at that time on either side of the Atlantic; the most prevalent technique was the French manner dominated by aquatint and used by George Senseney.[2] Burr therefore slowly worked out a process that suited him best. A printed description of this technique—prepared by the artist himself "in reply to many inquiries" and probably made for distribution at his exhibitions in Denver before 1910—is preserved at the Denver Public Library. It describes a method for producing monotypes rather than editions of prints from intaglio plates. Burr prepared his plates in the conventional manner, utilizing etching, soft-ground etching, and aquatint, and proofing and often printing impressions in black ink.

For the occasional color proof, he took great care with the processes of inking, wiping, and printing: "I then paint the picture on the copper with ordinary oil colors, removing all color that does not adhere to the granulated surface, and then print on a moistened sheet of Japan paper in an ordinary etching press. By this method each print is a distinct picture, each proof requiring a separate painting on the copper, no two being alike, the pictures varying according to the mood and will of the artist."[3] This involved creative process yielded very few impressions; the artist destroyed each plate after just a few prints, adding cachet and value to those thus produced. Like Davies's color intaglios (cat. 13), Burr's were apparently meant to be precious, deluxe works. The artist's casual printing records make no distinction between color and black ink impressions from each plate, so details of his habits and pleasure in this practice remain unclear, and the exact number of color impressions from any given plate is unknown.

When Burr first arrived in Denver, he settled in Briton Terrace, a picturesque, rather bohemian quarter in the old city. There he became acquainted with Cyrus Boutwell, who with his brother ran a gallery in the neighborhood. Soon Burr's European watercolors were exhibited in the Boutwells' gallery, and his etchings sold well there. Burr and his wife were frequently invited to the Boutwells' mountain lodge in the foothills of the Front Range of the Rockies, west of Denver. In about 1910, the Burrs built their own cabin nearby on land owned by the Pick-Up Club.[4] It was to "Pick-Up Cabin" that they often retreated when summer weather permitted, and in this peaceful, unspoiled wilderness the artist painted watercolors of peaks, forests, and vast skies.

He probably derived this etched view of Mount Byers, a peak in the chain of mountains beyond the Front Range, from a watercolor made at the mountain cabin in the mid-1910s, perhaps one of the documented paintings representing morning or sunrise.[5] Burr transferred the evocative hues and atmosphere of the watercolor to the intaglio plate at his studio in Denver, printing a handful of color etchings.

Notes

1. Seeber 1971, p. 36.

2. Senseney 1910.

3. Seeber 1971, p. 37.

4. Burr's cabin stood above Eldorado Springs, just south of Boulder, about twenty-five miles south of Longs Peak. It was near Tunnel 7 of the Moffat Road branch of the Denver and Rio Grande Western Railroad, which was not finished until after the Burrs left Colorado. See ibid., p. 26.

5. Ibid., p. 170. See also Simmons 1932.

B.J.O. Nordfeldt

1878–1955

11.

Fisherman's Family

1916

Woodcut on cream wove paper
30.5 × 28.1 cm. (image)
35.8 × 33.1 cm. (sheet)
In pencil, lower margin: *Nordfeldt imp the Fisherman's Family no18*
In ink, verso: *BJO Nordfeldt 1916*
Amon Carter Museum, Fort Worth, Texas, 1987.82

Although he considered himself primarily a painter, and his interest in color woodcuts was brief and transitional, B.J.O. Nordfeldt's technical and stylistic contributions to the Provincetown school of color woodcut was pivotal.

Nordfeldt's reputation as a printmaker today is based primarily on his development of the single-block white line woodcut method, of which the present print is a rare example. Although it appears to have been a drastic departure from his *japoniste* prints, the artist's facility and success with this technique grew out of his proficiency with the traditional multiple-block Japanese process. The method was much more appropriate to his spontaneous, Post-Impressionist style of the moment. Frustrated with the involvement and repetition required in cutting and inking a separate block for nearly each color in a print, and with the time-consuming procedure of hydrating, stacking, and interleaving paper, and the care required for proper registration, Nordfeldt developed this process in 1915.[1] It allowed the artist to produce a single impression from start to finish, and to create more readily color variant proofs as Arthur Wesley Dow (cat. 6) had done. Very simply, Nordfeldt could now make either one monotype or a group of them, or produce a uniform edition. His method was parallel to the *à la poupée* manner of printing many colors from an intaglio plate in a single pass through the etching press.

After drawing his composition in outline with pencil on a soft pine woodblock, Nordfeldt cut away these lines with unadorned grooves. These furrows isolated different colors, and made it possible to place several watercolors on the block at once without the wet ink mixing or blurring one another. The paper—usually well moistened first—was tacked to the top edge of the block and folded down on the carved face. In this way, the sheet could be wrapped over the printing surface and removed many times without changing its position on the block itself, and perfect registration was certain. Watercolor was applied to the block with a brush, and the paper was folded down and hand rubbed on the back to print. When the wet paper was forced into the grooves in the block, deep embossed lines were produced that stood out on the surface of the finished print.

By repeating the inking and printing procedure, Nordfeldt layered different colors on his print, in a manner similar to the way that he overlaid oil paints on a canvas. This effect is apparent in the treatment of the shadow of a beard on the fisherman's face, and the blush on the cheeks of his wife and daughter. This process was quite painterly, for the strokes of the inking brush were transferred from the smooth surface of the block to the print, as from a monotype plate. The artist purposely applied his ink dryly to the block, to preserve the physical quality and behavior of the ink for the viewer.

The pencil outline that circumscribes this image is common not only to Nordfeldt's white line prints, but in those of his students like Blanche Lazzell and Ada Gilmore Chaffee (cats. 18, 12) as well. Although the outline's purpose remains uncertain, it would seem to be a fail-safe registration device. The manner in which the artist numbered his prints sequentially but without any indication of complete edition size, was also common to many of his Provincetown colleagues.

The development of the single-block method also depended on the artist's skills as a craftsman interested in wood carving. Like the puppeteer Gustave Baumann (cat. 23), Nordfeldt made wood carvings for other purposes. Throughout his career, he created his own deeply carved, ornamental picture frames, and when he built his own house in Santa Fe, many decorative details of carved wood were incorporated.[2]

Nordfeldt represented anecdotal images of Provincetown life in his white line woodcuts. Work-worn fishermen, playful children, and ladies in brightly patterned summer frocks were depicted before the azure sea, green lawns, and multicolored salt-box cottages. These prints were close to the artist's paintings of the period in style and technique. Large figures were often placed in the immediate foreground, parallel to the picture plane. The figures confronted the viewer with full face or stark profile. Behind them was a large leap of space before the distant background. Thus Nordfeldt's subjects often seem like actors on a stage.[3] It is interesting to recall that Nordfeldt was deeply involved with the Provincetown theater in 1916. Indeed, he was apparently talented enough to seriously contemplate a theatrical career.

These bold and vivid images reflected Nordfeldt's current interest in French modernism. The subdivisions of the composition into simplified, brightly colored forms, and the decorative patterning of many of these surfaces, as seen here in the little girl's dress, identify the style of these woodcuts with Matisse and the Fauves. The painterly layers of color applied to surface of the block relate to the influence of Cézanne.

Perhaps because they were easier to produce, Nordfeldt made his single-block prints larger than his earlier woodcuts, and often square in shape. This format is similar to the black ink prints by artists active in Provincetown like William Zorach and Mildred McMillen. In this sense too, these works became paradigmatic for other Provincetown printmakers, and their white line color woodcuts generally became larger too.

The artist seems to have printed few impressions from his white line blocks. Because he abandoned the technique in 1918, and soon after ceased printmaking altogether, Nordfeldt's own white line color woodcuts are quite rare.

Notes

1. Chaffee 1952.

2. Coke 1972, p. 47.

3. As Coke (1972, p. 46) notes.

Ada Gilmore Chaffee

1893–1955

12.

Provincetown Harbor

1918
Woodcut on thick cream wove paper
25.3 × 34.4 cm. (image)
35.8 × 45.5 cm. (sheet)
In black ink, lower center:
Ada Gilmore
Private collection

One of the original Provincetown printmakers, Ada Gilmore Chaffee made white line woodcuts for about a decade. Her creative prints represent a vision of life in Provincetown, with a peculiar mixture of joyful fellowship, contemplation, and fantasy, that reveals the artist's multifaceted character.

Nearly all of Gilmore's white line prints were made in Provincetown in the late 1910s and early 1920s, and they represent the pleasant storybook life of a little village on the coast of New England. These woodcuts focus on the figure; brightly hued and joyful, many of them represent women in easy camaraderie. Later Gilmore's compositions became more pensive, with muted colors and small figures placed in recognizable local landscapes. Some of these views overlook Provincetown from the hills above the village or from the shore; others represent landmarks such as the town hall, the Pilgrim Monument, or the Octagon House on Commercial Street.

Other woodcuts combine reality with fantasy, giving form to the blithe contentment that Gilmore found in the village. Some represent benign wood nymphs relaxing on hills and in coverts on the outskirts of the enchanted village. *Provincetown Harbor* depicts nereids luxuriating in the sun on the weedy rocks of the shoreline, with the village behind them identifiable by its landmarks. As the local sailors peacefully put in to shore behind them, these mermaids seem to protect them, their ancestors, and their fellows from the perils of the sea. This magical custody is symbolized by the swimming figure on the left. With her hair blowing behind her and her left hand raised to point the way, she is reminiscent of the generations of figureheads that graced the bows of ships that sailed into Provincetown harbor.

Gilmore printed this woodcut on an inexpensive, smooth-surfaced sheet that had been sized like a watercolor paper. Scars from tacks along both the left edge and the bottom of the sheet show that it was fastened to the block twice. The artist may have removed the print from the block to allow it to dry, or to work on its surface during an intermediate stage of printing. Pinholes in each corner and pencil outlines circumscribing the image may have helped her to reposition the sheet precisely.

Broken fibers on the roughened surface of the verso confirm that Gilmore printed this woodcut with vigorous rubbing by hand. Close examination reveals that she used a wide range of pigments, from liquid washes mixed on the block to thick gouches both printed and painted onto the surface of the print. The artist may even have applied the opaque layers of pigment with stencils. She made extensive touch-ups after printing, adding all of the facial details with a brush.

The iridescent glow in many passages resulted from Gilmore's very clear superimposition of color. The white lines often seem to dissolve, perhaps because of the shallowness of the grooves in the block, or because the artist used thin, watery washes. However, she clearly felt that these lines were important to her design, for in some places she used the end of a brush or a stylus to scratch ink off the paper while it was still wet. This effect is apparent in the figure of the swimming mermaid at the left, and Gilmore even scratched additional white lines into this siren's hair after printing. This varied and involved treatment reveals a free, creative attitude to the printmaking process, which resulted in a unique object rather than an edition of multiple prints.

Arthur Bowen Davies

1862–1928

13.
Against Green

1918–24
Soft-ground etching and aquatint on
white wove paper
20.3 × 30.4 cm. (plate)
26.3 × 36.8 cm. (sheet)
In pencil, lower right:
Arthur B. Davies
Price 28 iv/iv?; Czestochowski
58 vi/vi
Private collection

Arthur Bowen Davies, *Without
Pause, Enters, Touches, Passes,* 1928.
Oil on canvas. Worcester Art Museum, 1928.30.

One of the most prominent and influential artists of his day, Arthur Bowen Davies exerted his taste through his own art; through the famous Armory Show, which he helped to organize; and through his thorough counsel of private collectors and patrons. Printmaking was an important phase of the artist's activity, and his style and reputation were spread through the exhibition of his more than two hundred prints. The possibilities of printing in color intrigued Davies, and he marshaled the skills of the most talented printing technicians of the day to create a small but very influential group of color lithographs and intaglios.

From his first experiments with etching, Davies was drawn to the possibilities of color printmaking. He began by occasionally printing on colored papers and adding watercolor washes to his lithographs and etchings. It has been suggested that after critics responded favorably to the results of these watercolored prints, Davies worked with George Miller in about 1920 to add printed color to several of his black and white lithographs.[1] In about 1923, Frank Nankivell began to print all of Davies's intaglios. An accomplished artist in his own right who shared a studio with Walt Kuhn, Nankivell also made original etchings and aquatints in color. It was probably not difficult for him to convince Davies to try printing his earlier plates in color.

Davies's color intaglios reveal extensive involvement of the printer. Nankivell tinted proofs from Davies's plates with watercolor, making suggestions of how the plates might be inked and printed *à la poupée.* A washed impression of the drypoint with aquatint *Iris,* now in the Kresge Art Museum at Michigan State University, was inscribed by Nankivell

with such suggestions for color.[2] The printer submitted tinted proofs for Davies's approval, and occasionally color prints were made on a limited basis. Because the artist wanted to create a cachet for these color prints, he did not print them in full editions as he had the black ink versions from the same plates.

Against Green was probably one of Davies's earliest soft-ground etchings. This technique became his favorite for its combination of immediacy and tonal range. The artist used a soft ground prepared from a mixture of wax and tallow or lard, which he spread evenly onto the plate and then covered with very fine linen. When he drew on this fabric with a pencil, the width and value of his line was modulated by pressure and transferred to the plate. The weave of the linen is still apparent in the print, giving it a stippled quality similar to that of a line made by a roulette. After this initial soft-ground stage, Davies applied aquatint in the conventional manner, often through several states.

Although the sizes of the editions of this print have been recorded, the actual number of impressions has not been determined. In the first state of this print, extant in trial impressions only, Davies had already combined soft-ground etching and aquatint. Such an impression was exhibited at the Anderson Galleries in New York in January 1919. The early black ink impressions in various states were probably printed by Ernest Haskell. There were ultimately six states of the print, of which the color version was the last. Inked *à la poupée,* it was printed in 1924 in an edition of perhaps ten impressions by Frank Nankivell.

Although the figures in *Against Green* are depicted in casual, unposed attitudes, interrelationships of form and space are as important and as balanced as in Davies's more balletic compositions. Until his death, Davies remained intrigued by the use of pose and of relationships between

figures to segment and sculpt space (Fig.). This notion was related to the Cubist use of planes to fragment and model space and to the concept of Futurism in dance, through which the structure of measured time was introduced. Contemporary haircuts also reflect a distillation of the classical and the modern.[3]

Just discernible in the upper-left corner of the present print is a mantelpiece lined with pots or bibelots, showing that the artist originally planned an interior composition. Subsequent changes to the plate obscured these details of setting, fracturing the background with Cubist planes and foliage-like spots of aquatint. Thus, by the third state, Davies had created a smoky, dreamlike space, and the addition of green in the background of the sixth and final state seems to locate the figures in one of his Arcadian gardens.

Between 1923 and 1928, Nankivell printed ten of Davies's aquatints in color. After the artist's death, several of his intaglio plates were reprinted, many of them in color, prior to an exhibition at Kennedy and Company in April 1930. These posthumous impressions bear the printer's signature and the artist's name signed by V[irginia]. M[erriweather]. D[avies].

Notes

1. Czestochowski 1987, p. 39.

2. Despite Nankivell's suggestion, *Iris* (1916; Czestochowski 33) was never printed in color.

3. Berezin 1976. See also Adams 1983, pp. 37–39, 53–54; Phillips 1924.

Margaret Jordan Patterson

1867–1950

14.

Summer Clouds

about 1918

Woodcut on cream laid paper

22.7 × 28.7 cm. (image)

25.4 × 36.8 cm. (sheet)

In pencil, lower margin: *"Summer Clouds" Margaret J. Patterson*

Private collection

Margaret Jordan Patterson, *Poppies and Convolvolus*, about 1925. Woodcut. Private collection.

Patterson seems originally to have conceived of the medium of color woodcut as a means to reproduce her own paintings. Methodical intermediary studies in pencil, pastel, and watercolor were often used to translate her painted compositions into the size and format of the prints. The date of *Summer Clouds* can be determined from the watercolor, dated 1918, from which the print is derived.[1] Though slightly larger than the woodcut, this painting is very similar in coloration. It was created at a time when the artist made most of her landscape sketches on trips to Cape Cod.

The artist achieved remarkable effects of atmosphere and light through the skillful inking and printing of this multiblock woodcut. Lightening the sky slightly at the horizon, she created a subtle atmospheric perspective that emphasizes the sense of spatial depth. On the right shore of the river, the colors are slightly brighter and more intense than on the opposite shore. This makes it seem as if the bright sun, unobscured by clouds, is warming the far shore, again increasing the perception of space. Flat, wispy clouds in a bold diagonal suggest a sense of motion, particularly in juxtaposition with the unmoving, bulbous cumulus clouds.

This impression is notable for its deep and well-preserved embossing. As in all of Patterson's prints, the verso of this sheet is much abraded, showing that the artist printed by rubbing the wetted paper vigorously, and with a great deal of pressure. She applied her watercolor inks to the blocks in delicate, watery washes, except on the horizon in the center of the composition, where a saturated blue line draws the eye of the viewer into the distance. Using white ink against the cream-colored paper, the artist created arresting bright highlights. A more saturated blue was used near the bottom of the block, and a lighter watercolor at the top. The key block was printed last, inked with blue in the manner of color woodcut artists in California such as Frances Gearhart (cat. 16). In other woodcuts, Patterson printed her key blocks in soft blue, lavender, or pale gray. The muted hues softened the contrasting outlines, achieving a more harmonious and unified color scheme.

Similar interests in dimension, luminosity, and sensuous effects of warmth are apparent in Patterson's late floral prints, such as *Poppies and Convolvolus* (sic) (Fig.). In these simple, enchanting still lifes, the artist could disregard her subjects, in order to focus on the relationships of colors and forms and on new technical means to represent them. Vivid colors and silhouetted blooms become almost abstract patterns in contrast to flat backgrounds printed in lavender, deep blue, or black. Patterson still made methodical preparatory watercolor studies in which color and composition were calculated and refined before their transfer to the woodblocks. Although the

artist continued to use the same techniques in the latter part of her career, her compositional aims were slightly different. The subjects were illuminated by bright light falling from one direction. Dark, rich colors contrasted with white printed highlights, giving the viewer not only the perception of space but even a palpable sense of the warmth of the sunlight. For the background of *Poppies and Convolvolus*, Patterson overprinted two shades of bluish lavender and magenta with a saturated black. The sharp contrast of the background emphasized the colors and sense of space in this composition, also isolating the forms of the flowers, and making the image seem quite abstract.

Notes

1. Margaret Jordan Patterson, *River and Clouds*, 1918. Watercolor over charcoal on cream paper, 38.7 × 47.6 cm. (sheet). See Bakker/Coleman 1988, no. 53b.

"Summer Clouds"   Margaret I. Patterson

Max Weber

1891–1961

15.

Seated Woman

1919–20

Woodcut on thin cream Japan paper

10.7 × 4.9 cm. (image)

23.7 × 13.1 cm. (sheet)

In pencil, lower margin: *Max Weber*

Rubenstein 16

Private collection

Working in a personal style forged amid the School of Paris in the first decade of the twentieth century, Max Weber was the first American to demonstrate this modernism in color prints. Unrecognized and meagerly supported for years, this independent artist used humble materials by necessity in his own technique of color relief printmaking.

Weber's personal experiences of the School of Paris, Cubism, Futurism, and African and Oceanic arts are all synthesized in his woodcuts. Like Gauguin and early German Expressionist printmakers, the artist found that the medium itself encouraged simplification of design and that the results were analogous to ethnographic wood carving.

In 1910, Weber found a piece of linoleum in a construction scrap heap near his tenement and used a penknife to cut his first relief print, *Crouching Figure* (Rubenstein 4–5), an isolated experiment.[1] Throughout the decade, the artist continued to work and exhibit regularly, and the influence of Cubism and Futurism are apparent in his work of 1912 to 1916.

Like his single early linocut, Weber's woodcuts began with an experiment. In the winter of 1919, when he had received the gift of some honey in the comb, he became intrigued with its container. This sideless box was made of four thin planks of soft basswood, dovetailed at the corners. The artist freely carved one of the slats with a penknife and applied oil paint to it with his fingers. Placing the inked block beneath a sheet of paper on the floor, he placed a book on top and then stood on it, to offset the ink. His first print, *Head and Shoulders of Figure* (Rubenstein 24), derived its simplified design from Weber's painting *The Egyptian Pot* of 1917. In a flurry of creative activity, he cut and printed twenty-five of these simple woodcuts. The color woodcuts among them were each made from one block in a single printing.

These woodcuts were figurative compositions, which achieved rhythm and balance through the adroit placement of faces, hands and legs in shaped decorative frames. Sensitive, careful inking imparted an added sense of depth to the color impressions. The castellated tops and bottoms in several of these little prints were created by the dovetail cuts in the ends of the side slats of honeycomb boxes that Weber used as blocks. *Seated Woman* is one of this first group of block prints. Its composition, style, and scale derive from Weber's miniature Cubist oils and gouaches of the period between 1917 and 1919.

Weber's woodcuts might be divided into two groups, one that reflects the influence of the style and mood of Gauguin, and another that is much more sophisticated in its Cubist compositions, notions of space, and numbers of colors. The artist had two distinct methods of inking his relief prints, and his approaches to inking and printing paralleled those of Gauguin. Both artists were interested in using the medium to create widely varied versions of the same image, rather than the multiple identical impressions of a regular edition.[2] Both of them also purposely misregistered prints that required more than one imprint from a block.

Notes

1. Originally printed in black ink, this linocut was reprinted in colors in the 1920s, oriented both as a vertical and a horizontal composition depending on the placement of Weber's signature. See Rubenstein 1980, pp. 17–18, 114–115, figs. 2–3.

2. Ibid., p. 13. See also Cahill 1930.

Frances Hammell Gearhart

1869–1958

16.
The Desert Invites

before 1920
Woodcut on cream Japan paper
27.4 × 22.8 cm. (image)
37.0 × 26.6 cm. (sheet)
In pencil, lower margin: *The Desert Invites Frances H. Gearhart*
In dark red ink, stamped on verso: elephant in circle, surrounded by *ALFRED WEINGARTNER*
Worcester Art Museum, anonymous gift, 1988.73

Along with her younger sister May (cat. 22), Frances Gearhart was a pioneer of color printmaking in the West, and her importance to printmaking in California has not yet been fully appreciated. Ubiquitous in print exhibitions on the West Coast beginning in the mid-1910s, she made color woodcuts that a broad audience eagerly purchased. The influence of these prints, in their subjects and compositions, and especially in their palette, was felt across the country by 1925.

Few printmakers have been as eloquent as Frances Gearhart in capturing the majestic spaces and extraordinary atmosphere of the American West. She specialized in landscape prints and was especially fond of dramatic subjects such as the Pacific Coast, Yosemite National Park, the Sonora Desert, and the Rocky Mountains. Composition, technique, and subject all contributed to her mastery of space and atmosphere.

Gearhart often printed her key block in blue rather than black ink, giving her prints a softer and more atmospheric mood. In this print, the artist progressively lightened the tone of the background when wiping the key block, thus enhancing the illusion of distance. The soft tones of her palette accurately depict the bright desert sunlight, muted by haze. In other prints representing mountains or seashore, she adjusted her palette for naturalistic accuracy.

The artist applied the inks to her wooden blocks with a brush in the Japanese manner, often rather dryly, so that the strokes remain quite obvious. This grainy texture is quite appropriate to the subject of *The Desert Invites*. Careful blending of colors on the block reveals the artist's knowledge of Japanese printmaking techniques. Often she blended colors freely on the surface of a single tone block, drawing the composition together with the overprinting of the linear key block. A number of compositional devices mark the influence of Japanese printmaking on her style. Behind the *repoussoir* mounds of earth and heavily fruited prickly pears, a vast leap of space intercedes before the distant mountainside. This central void occurs in many of Gearhart's landscapes, which are generally vertical, with high horizons and elements stacked behind one another. These devices derive ultimately from the prints of Hokusai and Hiroshige— perhaps through Pedro Lemos (cat. 24), Frank Morley Fletcher, or Hiroshi Yoshida—nineteenth-century Japanese master whose vertical landscapes also feature the subtle effects of tonal modulation that Gearhart preferred.

The Desert Invites   Frances H. Gearhart

John Wesley Cotton

1868–1931

17.

Sierra Nevada

1920

Drypoint, soft-ground etching, and aquatint on cream Japanese vellum wove paper

32.4 × 40.2 cm. (plate)

40.8 × 51.8 cm. (sheet)

In pencil, lower margin: *J. Cotton 20*

Worcester Art Museum, Stoddard Charitable Trust Fund, 1987.8

Although John Wesley Cotton was born and died in Canada, he spent many years of his mature activity as a printmaker in California. In the Los Angeles area, in the energized orbit of the California Print Makers Society, he produced all of his color intaglios. Indeed, in some ways, Cotton's prints synthesize the styles and techniques of brothers Benjamin and Howell Brown with those of sisters Frances and May Gearhart (cats. 16, 22), and they must be seen in the context of color intaglio in California in the 1920s.

Cotton's dramatic landscape views of the Southwest combine the imposing imagery of the Browns with the vivid palette of the Gearharts. By comparison with the latter's literal, precise images, the present work seems impressive and its coloration almost arbitrary, although its palette is no more intense. Like George Elbert Burr (cat. 10), Cotton used tone and color to interpret, rather than accurately to capture, the effects of light and atmosphere in a manner bordering on exaggeration.

Photographers who chronicled the majesty of the American West, such as William Henry Jackson and Carleton Watkins, may have been influential to *Sierra Nevada* and other prints of Western subjects by Cotton. The sweeping vista and its distant, monumental peaks contrast with the human scale of *repoussoir* elements such as the rocks and gnarled tree trunks, in a manner parallel to photographers' methods of framing. Cotton imposed organization on the apparent chaos of nature by his use of the tall central tree, which precisely bisects the composition, laterally and in depth, also marking the softening focus from sharp foreground into atmospheric distance. His careful depiction of the effects of light across the landscape enhances the sense of grandeur and scale. Shadows of clouds obscure the lake and forests of the middle ground, while the nearest trees as well as the distant, high snow fields glisten in the sun.

Cotton began this plate, perhaps on site, by sketching with a drypoint needle. Preparation of the soft ground followed in the studio, where the spontaneity of his freely drawn lines, dots, and dashes perpetuated the energy of the drypoint. He also roughly followed the drypoint composition with rather coarse aquatint. The distinctive character of Cotton's technique comes from his bravado inking, wiping, and printing of the plate *à la poupée*; all of the many colors—complex mixtures of plate tone as well as intaglio—were applied to the plate and printed in one pass through the press. The artist laid oil-base inks onto the copperplate in many ways that remain apparent in the print itself. Colored inks were blended directly on the plate using brushes, rags, and sponges to rub and daub ink into the grooves and onto the surface of the copper. Then Cotton delicately manipulated and removed the surface films of ink in order to create tonal modulations, highlights, and even formal effects such as the drifting of snow on the windblown peaks. The strokes of a rag and the artist's fingerprints are further indications of this creative process.

Blanche Lazzell

1878–1956

18.
Tulips

1920–28
Woodcut on white laid paper
30.2 × 29.3 cm. (image)
46.2 × 40.0 cm. (sheet)
In pencil, in image: *Tulips Blanche Lazzell—1928*
In pencil, lower margin: *Tulips cut 1920 Blanche Lazzell 1928*
In pencil, on verso: *Wood Block Print "Tulips" 228/11 Blanche Lazzell Provincetown, Mass. Oct. 10, 1928.*
Private collection

Among the most distinctive works by the printmakers working in Provincetown, Massachusetts, Lazzell's color woodcuts have in recent years become prized by collectors. Their success seems to depend on their directness, and on the joyful vividness of their palette. Amid the often unassuming production of Provincetown artists, Lazzell's 138 color prints stand out for their sophisticated compositions and their virtuosic printing.

Throughout her career, Lazzell felt the compulsion to explore new techniques and fresh visual imagery, an impulse apparent in her passion for education and in her diverse prints. The immediacy and appeal of her prints stem from her resolution of the challenges posed by the method of printing white line woodblocks.

Lazzell planned the compositions of her single-block prints to suit the technique. This process encouraged abstraction in its deletion of details and its reduction of the composition to simple components; it also encouraged a decorative inclination. In this print, gentle arcs, suggested by the stalks of the flowers and the shapes of the petals, partition the entire composition. A deep blue field is broken up by curved, blossom-shaped facets in the spaces around and between the flowers. The artist gave little indication of setting; the central brown passage may represent a vessel, or it may symbolize the fertile soil from which the flowers spring. The image is surrounded by a heavy, dark border line, in the style of the Arts and Crafts movement, which tends to flatten form. The whorls surrounding the brown area are reminiscent of the decoration of Southwestern Indian pottery.

The slightly varied versions of Lazzell's compositions reflect her experimental bent. In 1919, after producing the woodcut *The Red Quill* in the Arts and Crafts style by the customary white line method, the artist cut another block, in which each cell of color was surrounded with a black line. Thus, the second version has a rather flat, decorative character, like stained glass. In 1920 she attempted to replace the white lines with black ones in *Still Life*.

Although Lazzell often worked out her compositions in sketches on quadrille paper, she drew her final design directly on the block. She did her cutting with a straight knife rather than with gouges. The horizontal bands that give this print a corrugated effect resulted from unevenness in the woodblock, a quality probably imposed on the surface of the soft wood, most likely pine, in the milling of the plank. The grooves in the block stand out as bright white lines embossed into the paper.

The artist printed by rubbing the verso of the sheet with a wooden spoon. She preferred French watercolors for printing ink, occasionally adding Chinese white for a more opaque effect.[1] She became masterful at balancing proportions of water and pigment, achieving delicate shifts of color and tone as she brushed ink onto the block. Most of the area of local colors of this woodcut were printed evenly, but the artist modulated others from dusty red to light orange, in transitions as smooth as those made by a Japanese printmaker. Other areas, which are lighter in the middle and darker at their edges, anticipate an effect that Lazzell purposely cultivated in her later prints by thinning ink on the block and lifting it off with a brush or sponge.

The two bronze-colored blooms were shaded in a manner that revealed the brush strokes of the dryly applied watercolor. This modeling enhanced the cupped shapes of the cells, and created a three-dimensional effect that is more striking when viewed from a distance. This is the only passage in *Tulips* that represents effects of light in the modeling of form. The artist gave just the slightest, teasing suggestion of the natural dimension of these objects, preferring a tension between the depth of her shapes and the flat surface of the sheet.

Lazzell often complemented a foundation of primary hues with peculiar interstitial colors. Her early experiences in Paris and her exposure to the paintings of the Fauves may have led her to this preference. The bright, flat, decorative nature of the artist's work certainly has much in common with that of Matisse.

Like many of the Provincetown printmakers, this pragmatic artist kept her woodblocks, so that she could print new impressions later if the demand arose. She printed this impression of *Tulips* eight years after cutting the block. When reprinting from old blocks, Lazzell always carefully inscribed the printing history of the woodcut on the verso of each impression. She taught this procedure to artist Ferol Sibley Warthen, who responsibly followed the ritual of record keeping.

Notes

1. Flint 1983, p. 20. See also Marks 1984.

Tulips   cut 1920   Blanche Lazzell - 1928

Eliza Draper Gardiner

1871–1955

19.

Water Wings

about 1920

Woodcut on cream Japan paper

36.2 × 20.7 cm. (image)

41.4 × 24.5 cm. (sheet)

Falk 45

Worcester Art Museum, anonymous gift, 1988.72

Eliza Draper Gardiner was an artist of national reputation in her day, and her prints were shown throughout the United States and Europe. The artist represented images of childhood, seeking not only to portray typical pastimes, gestures, and attitudes, but to invoke in the viewer memories of the carefree, joyful summers of early youth. A dedicated educator for almost fifty years, Gardiner was cherished by generations of students.

This evocative image exemplifies Gardiner's powers to create ambiance and mood. Like a mirage, a pier disappears into the foggy horizon, and long-rippled reflections in the water suggest the stillness of evening. The artist enhanced this atmosphere with the drab colors of early twilight and the heavy softness of a misty background. With a cartoonist's knack of capturing expression in just a few spare lines, she portrayed relaxation in the face of the little girl, whose mind wanders as she impassively inflates her water wings. The casual posture of her companion and the quiet, lazy sense of their ease and comfort evoke a pleasing, good-humored response in the viewer.

The artist made this print from multiple blocks in a manner very similar to the traditional Japanese method of color printmaking. The surviving blocks are made of cherry, the hardwood favored for *ukiyo-e*. The casual and imprecise character of her outlines suggests that her original drawings were simple and spontaneous. With great economy of form, she achieved an impressive sense of space using very simple tonal modulation.

Gardiner preferred to print on long-fibered mulberry papers. Here, as in most of her woodcuts, there are about eight to ten colors printed from half as many blocks. She applied ink liberally and evenly to the blocks with a brush, and allowed it to soak well into the soft surface of the paper. The background was printed from a single block, with the liquid ink delicately blended upon it. The verso of the print shows no scars from hand printing, proving that the artist used a sensitive touch in rubbing and kept her paper relatively dry during printing. Gardiner hung her prints on a clothesline to dry.[1] This scrupulous adherence to the conventional Japanese printing process supports the notion that she may have learned the technique from Arthur Wesley Dow (cat. 6).

Occasionally Gardiner touched her woodcuts with watercolor ink, pastel, or crayon after printing. Like many of the Provincetown printmakers, she did not limit her editions, but set aside her blocks after printing as many impressions as were immediately needed. Sometimes, in later printings, she used different color combinations. Generally the number of impressions of her prints totaled fewer than fifty; this woodcut was printed in an edition of forty impressions.

Notes

1. She probably did not do this at each stage, as Falk (1987, p. 14) suggests, but only after the final printing. See also Flint 1983, p. 32; Roberts 1920.

Agnes Weinrich

1873–1946

20.

Abstraction

about 1920
Woodcut on cream laid paper
17.9 × 16.7 cm. (image)
33.4 × 24.2 cm. (sheet)
In pencil and traced over with blue ink, lower margin: *Agnes Weinrich*
Worcester Art Museum, anonymous gift, 1988.87

The woodcuts of Agnes Weinrich reflect the advent of modernism in Provincetown, Massachusetts, between 1915 and 1930. An accomplished, indefatigable woman, Weinrich seems to have exerted the force of her convictions not only on her art but on that of others. Scholars are just beginning to appreciate her influential role in the Provincetown Printers' movement.

Weinrich learned the technique of single-block color woodcut, which had been developed by B.J.O. Nordfeldt (cat. 11), from Blanche Lazzell (cat. 18) sometime before 1917. The artist's early prints are similar to those of Nordfeldt in style and technique. Simplified, geometrized figures are represented in scenes of daily life in Provincetown; people stroll in the streets or gather for tea and conversation in cozy sitting rooms. These woodcuts were printed in watercolor ranging from soft pastel washes to dark, saturated hues, which were often dryly applied to the printing surface. Like Nordfeldt, Weinrich layered and mixed colors directly on the woodblock.

A stylistic shift is apparent in such prints as *The Herdsman*, which was exhibited at the Provincetown Art Association in 1920. In this print, which consists of flat shapes strongly isolated by circumscribing white lines, space is confused by the interweaving of forms. Weinrich's imagery had become more decorative and brightly colored, and was fragmented by the rounded fracturing

characteristic of Lazzell. The artist produced an extensive group of still-life woodcuts that relate to other experiments in modernism of the late 1920s. These prints are parallel in style and subject to a few blocks by Karl Knaths, which seem to have been contemporaneous. In the 1920s, Weinrich and her friends in Provincetown struggled to develop their modernist styles in the face of isolation and conservatism. They read Albert Léon Gleizes and Fernand Léger, and the translation of Gino Severini's book *Du Cubisme au Classicisme*.[1]

The backgrounds of Weinrich's landscape prints of about 1920 were subdivided into circumscribed shapes, each asserting its independent planar existence through individual color and modeling. Similarly, in her still-life prints—which generally seem to have succeeded the landscapes—the fruit and flower shapes became progressively simpler and more geometric. The colors were lighter, rendered in thinner, more transparent washes. The artist's tendency to model form with various hues painted onto the block seems to have abated, but she began to add decorative details to her prints, painting them on the block over open passages of color. As with her landscapes, the backgrounds of Weinrich's still lifes gradually became abstract, first by subdivision, and then by the introduction of floating planes. As these flat, geometric forms mingled with flowers and vases, like those in *Abstraction*, elements themselves were simplified and became more Cubist. Finally, all suggestion of representation was removed, and interpenetrating planes floated freely in space.

The pine woodblock for this print survives in a private collection.[2] It is rather simple, and its grooves are shallow and imprecise. The degree of abstraction apparent here is rare in Weinrich's printmaking oeuvre. In style, it is similar to Lazzell's prints of around 1925, but it is simpler, and its execution less exacting. Like her colleague, Weinrich varied some of her forms by adding decorative patterns, here especially in drilling a cluster of holes that read as white spots on the nearest form. Whereas Weinrich made this pattern rather random, enhancing a sense of primitive energy, Lazzell might have placed these spots precisely along a geometric grid.

Notes

1. Kuchta/Seckler 1977, p. 47; see also pp. 31, 45.

2. Thomas 1988, no. 30.

A. Weinrich

John Taylor Arms

1887–1953

21.

Gates of the City

1922

Etching and aquatint on cream laid paper

21.4 × 30.6 cm. (plate)

20.1 × 25.9 cm. (sheet)

In pencil, lower margin: *John Taylor Arms   Gates of the City*

Fletcher 126

Watermark: *F. J. Head & Co.*

Worcester Art Museum, anonymous gift, 1988.89

For three decades, John Taylor Arms maintained a reputation unequaled by that of any other American printmaker. His taste for picturesque architectural views captured the imagination of an audience brought up on the Etching Revival, and his technical virtuosity held the attention of that audience absolutely. The energetic and prolific artist determined, nearly on his own, the taste of a generation of print consumers.[1] Early in his career, Arms was interested in color intaglio, but his experiments ultimately did not satisfy him, and he eventually abandoned the practice of making both color and black ink impressions of the same plates.

Arms worked very slowly and deliberately, never sparing time or compromising quality. His prints always developed from several drawings made on site. To these preparatory sketches, the artist often added details in his studio in Fairfield, Connecticut, occasionally working from photographs. After offsetting his chosen design onto a smoked etching ground, he drew with a needle right onto the ground. The artist preferred to use thin-gauge, common sewing needles set into his own wooden handles.[2]

Arms considered himself a mediocre printer, and on his own he usually pulled only proof impressions of his prints. He engaged professional printers—no fewer than fifteen throughout his career—to help produce the published editions of his work.[3] Frederick Reynolds, the master printer in New York, printed most of Arms's early plates. Later in his career, the artist relied most often on the English printer David Strang.

In the present print, the artist represented the Brooklyn Bridge, one of New York's most recognizable landmarks, as a Gothic drawbridge. Compared with Rudolph Ruzicka's depiction of the bridge juxtaposed with the daily life of the city in *Peck Slip* (cat. 26), Arms's image evokes fantasy and fairy tale.[4]

In *Gates of the City*, a mood of silence and mystery is evoked by softened forms and dulled colors. The atmosphere of dawn is blurred by mist and by vapors spewed from smokestacks and billowing from steam vents into the chill, crisp air. As sunrise breaks through this haze, the tower of the bridge looms in the pale light, its deep recesses and protruding cornices accentuated by long shadows. A vista into depth is framed between the roadbed of the bridge and the shadowed arches. Thus the scale of the tower is emphasized by contrast with the backdrop of distant buildings in lower Manhattan. The size of the tower is also suggested by its geometric dominance over the composition, and the perspectival slant of its side piers. A solitary figure, his head nodding in sleep, affirms the scale of the architecture and the mood of mysterious loneliness.

Like all of Arms's aquatints, this one was made from a single plate, carefully inked in colors by the printer and passed once through the press. Because of this painstaking and laborious process, the editions were relatively small. Nevertheless, the uniformity of color and printing quality within these editions is remarkable. Like most of Arms's color aquatints, this work has a rather narrow palette. Essentially, two colors—tints of tan-yellow and blue—were combined with black ink on the plate. As a complement to the restrained use of color, the inking and wiping of the plate were quite subtle and sensitive. The color and tonal effects enhance and emphasize the evocative mood of the image.

Although the artist was discouraged by the failure of his early color intaglios, he was inspired by eighteenth-century architectural views in color aquatint, and felt that the medium had potential for him. Thus, in his later color prints, he used aquatint for broad passages of soft, subtly modulated tone printed in dull or pale pastel colors, in order to emulate the soft hues of eighteenth-century Japanese woodcuts. These plates were detailed with etching, for this draftsman felt most comfortable with the etching needle and with the linear approach to an image. Even though Arms's aquatints were conceived for color, however, they were also printed in black ink only, as if the effort of producing the plate was not fully justified by a small, precious edition in color.[5] All of Arms's color aquatints were printed by Frederick Reynolds, and after the printer's death in 1929, the artist all but abandoned color intaglio. Of the 446 prints by Arms described by Fletcher, just 47 were printed in color.

Notes

1. In 1936, the magazine *Prints* conducted a wide-ranging survey of the state of American printmaking, and found that only Rockwell Kent had broader national acclaim than Arms had. See Zigrosser 1974, p. 95.

2. Bassham 1975, p. 28.

3. Fletcher 1982, p. 14.

4. Arms's other print representing the bridge, *Cobwebs* (1921; Fletcher 95), is similar to Ruzicka's wood engraving in its depiction of the bridge as one of many structures in a picturesque city. Bassham (1975, p. 21) has suggested that *Cobwebs* conveys the notion of the bridge as the synthesis of Gothic form and modern technology.

5. Fletcher (1982) describes three trial proofs, in etching only, of the first state of *Gates of the City*, four black ink proofs and three color proofs of the second state. The edition included twenty-five impressions in black ink and seventy-five in color. See also Arms 1940; Cary 1931.

John Taylor Arms

May Gearhart

1872–1951

22.
Flower Market, Mexico

about 1923

Soft-ground etching and aquatint on cream Japanese vellum wove paper

13.9 × 15.1 cm. (plate)

20.7 × 21.8 cm. (sheet)

In pencil, lower margin: *Flower Market—Mexico   May Gearhart*

Worcester Art Museum, anonymous gift, 1988.74

May Gearhart specialized in color intaglio prints, working in a personal style notable for its precision, clarity, and vivid palette.

Although her sister Frances and her teacher Benjamin Brown concentrated on landscape, May Gearhart preferred figural compositions, often incorporating romantic or exotic figures. Thus her prints reflect the influence of Helen Hyde (cat. 8) and Bertha Lum, fellow California printmakers. Like Hyde, Gearhart was attracted to the Asian neighborhoods of Los Angeles and San Francisco, which offered vivid glimpses of faraway lands. The artist also traveled regularly to Mexico, and many of her prints represent picturesque views of life south of the border. The bright colors and almost electric intensity of some of Gearhart's prints reflect the quality of the Southwestern light and the bright colors of Mexico, where intense paints and dyes derived from tropical plants were common.

However, Gearhart was also profoundly influenced by the hand-tinted color films of Park French, and their soft, artificial pastel hues are the hallmark of her more luminous prints. The palette in the present print, with its shimmery blue lines, is also similar to that of Frances Gearhart (cat. 16), who preferred to print the key blocks of her multicolor woodcuts in a vivid blue rather than black.

May Gearhart probably learned her color printmaking technique from Brown, who is said to have developed his own process for color intaglio, combining soft-ground

etching, aquatint, and inking *à la poupée*—a process similar to those in use in Paris at the time.[1] *Flower Market* is characteristic of Gearhart's precise, deceptively complex intaglio technique, which incorporated soft-ground etching bitten in stages with very finely grained aquatint. This color print was created from a single plate, bitten in three stages, and very carefully inked and overprinted three times. This long, painstaking method is akin to the personal, essentially monotype process of George Elbert Burr (cat. 10) and other contemporaries of Gearhart. Only a few labored impressions, often unique in their coloration, were printed from many of Gearhart's plates. When she actually produced complete editions, they were fairly small.

Precise registration was achieved by repositioning the plate exactly on the bed of the press using pinholes, which are visible at the top and bottom in the center of the print. In each pass through the press, she printed both intaglio and surface plate tone. Thus, overlapping films of ink and soft, linear imagery printed from vertical wiping scratches created a shimmering, almost iridescent presentation of color. Gearhart added fine aquatint in the last of the three immersions of the plate in the acid. She printed on hard-surfaced paper that would not dry too fast or shrink, in order to make overprinting possible.

Notes

1. Feinblatt/Davis, 1980, p. 10, note 12. "Writing of Brown in 1924, Edna Gearhart defended the artist for combining color with etching, an indication that traditionalists objected to what the then modernists accepted, namely, color as a completion of line and pattern." (Ibid., p. 11).

Flower Market - México   May Gearhart

Gustave Baumann

1881–1971

23.
Cholla and Sahuaro (sic)

1925
Woodcut on oatmeal laid paper
32.5 × 32.9 cm. (image)
43.3 × 36.6 cm. (sheet)
In pencil, upper margin: *Hold for Reprinting*
In pencil, lower margin: *CHOLLA AND SAHUARO 68 III 125 Gustave Baumann*
Watermark: heart and hand
Worcester Art Museum, anonymous gift, 1988.66

Independent, prolific, and influential, Gustave Baumann stands at the center of American color relief printmaking in the first half of the twentieth century, parallel in stature to John Taylor Arms (cat. 21) in intaglio printmaking. However, Baumann's works differ from most American color woodcuts of the period in that they did not evolve from the Japanese tradition of hand-rubbed watercolor prints, but rather from the European tradition of multiple-block, color wood engravings printed on a press.

Cholla and Sahuaro exemplifies Baumann's mature color prints in its size, its vivid palette, and its impressionistic use of color and form to evoke a natural ambiance. Often immediate and sketchy, the artist's graphic style aimed at capturing the essence of a visual experience. However, Baumann tempered his images with an illustrative, decorative sense that is revealed in the systematic patterning of his crosshatching and in the omnipresent dotted border line, which insistently denies the illusion of his compositions.

This striking woodcut was produced in Santa Fe from a gouache sketch made in Florence, Arizona, on March 26, 1925.[1] The dominant bright yellow evokes the warmth of the sun, which is enhanced by the play of shadows on the spiny branches of the cholla and along the sandy ground. This gold is nearly complementary to the deep blue of the sky, and these colors vibrate with a startling intensity peculiar to the dry, thin desert air.

Baumann preferred to work with basswood, which is soft and easy to carve. All of the blocks in a set were made of precisely the same dimensions to achieve correct registration, when printed on Baumann's Reliance Midget letterpress. The artist made his own inks, mixing ground pigments with a varnish base according to a special recipe; this viscous ink remained on the surface of the sized, flaxen paper. Inks were carefully mixed to match the hues of his gouache model, and were applied to the blocks with brayers. Baumann usually printed on fine, German laid papers, often on rag sheets with the Gladbach watermark. Later, distinctive oatmeal laid papers were made to the artist's own specifications in Germany, at a mill destroyed during World War II. These were of linen content, and watermarked with Baumann's hand and heart seal.

This compulsive and methodical craftsman always sought to improve his designs, even during printing; thus he did not always make uniform editions. He occasionally adjusted colors, modified borders, and added or subtracted blocks within an edition.

The note *Hold for Reprinting* in the upper margin of this impression reveals much about Baumann's printing and recording practices. As the artist carved and proofed the blocks of his woodcuts, he often preserved progressive color proofs, along with the gouache model, in files for his own reference. Baumann's editions generally comprised a maximum of 125 impressions, but he never printed an entire edition at once. Like many artists of the period, he pulled prints only as the market demanded, or when he had the time.

In order to control and keep account of his printing, he developed his own system of inscription, in which a Roman numeral indicated a printing campaign within an edition.[2] Thus this impression was produced in the third group of prints made from this set of blocks. Baumann probably retained it for use, perhaps as a color guide, in later reprinting the woodcut.

Notes

1. According to an inscription on the original gouache for Cholla and Sahuaro, which is owned by the Worcester Art Museum, along with six printing blocks and five progressive proofs (accession nos. 1989.164.1–.13).

2. These notations sometimes also include a tiny date after the edition number, indicating the date of the printing. The letters "R. C." before the edition number indicate that the blocks had been substantially recut since their previous printing. Although this record keeping seems careful and systematic, Baumann was often erratic in numbering his prints. See Annex 1981, p. 4. See also Annex 1985; Santa Fe 1972.

CHOLLA AND SAHUARO   48 · III · 125

Gustave Baumann

Pedro Joseph Lemos

1882–1945

24.
Top O' the Hill
about 1925
Linocut on cream Japan paper
22.8 × 30.7 cm. (image)
24.3 × 33.3 cm. (sheet)
In pencil, below image: *Top O' the Hill   Pedro J. Lemos*
Worcester Art Museum, anonymous gift, 1988.80

The leading exponent in California of the Arts and Crafts movement and of Arthur Wesley Dow's (cat. 6) teaching and aesthetic theories, Pedro Lemos also made his own prints. As a printmaker, this versatile artist worked in a variety of media, making etchings, aquatints, and relief prints in color. However, his most influential roles were those of teacher, theorist, author, and arts administrator.

This print exemplifies the subject, style, and technique of most of Lemos's prints in several media, including intaglio, lithography, and relief. The extent of the artist's dependence on the work of Dow is apparent in a few terse imperatives from one of the folios of his instructional series *Applied Art*, words that could describe this very composition: "Sketch landscape in brush and ink. Make every line count. Produce character in each brush stroke. Study Japanese paintings and prints for line rendering."[1]

Lemos's prints also reflect the style and vocabulary of the Arts and Crafts movement. In *Top O' the Hill*, as in many works in this manner, the design of the bold, linear key block is contained by a heavy border line. The synoptic simplicity of design, the use of silhouettes and outlines, and the decorative flourishes are also characteristic of the style.

The artist specialized in depicting the majesty of nature and its constant state of change. In his block prints, wind blows through trees, waves crash against rocky shores, and sunlight flickers through blowing leaves and reflects on water. The landscape of California was the subject of Lemos's prints. Most of his prints represent deserted landscapes; when he did incorporate architecture, figures, or animals, he rendered these elements in a very decorative manner. The artist's first step in the development of a block print was often his own photograph.[2] He would then simplify and transpose these designs on a sketch pad, refining the balance of light and dark according to the principles of *notan*.

A key block printed in black ink dominates the composition of the present print. In isolation it might suggest depth, movement, and effects of light, but in context it also draws the viewer to the inviting, brightly colored distance. However, this linear matrix also tends toward abstraction. Color created the mood, and also added to the abstraction. The unconventional point of view reveals a debt to the Japanese aesthetic.[3] Generally the palette is low in key, and it is punctuated occasionally by bright accents.

Lemos preferred to use linoleum or soft basswood, the simplest and most easily workable materials for making block prints.[4] The design for the key block was drawn with a brush, and the characteristic thickening and thinning of line is apparent. In the area of the tree trunks, for example, this created an effect of luminous, dappled light filtering through high foliage onto roughly textured bark. The artist apparently created this effect by distressing, perhaps with a wire brush, some of the thin, protruding lines in the linoleum block.

The artist usually used oil paint as printing ink. In this print, the image reads almost as clearly from the verso of its very thin, hard-surfaced mulberry paper as it does from the face. Lemos printed many thin layers of ink, often overlapping them to create other colors, and tonal subtlety. A range of hues and tonal effects was achieved by the methodical inking of the blocks. Sometimes the artist used thin washes, which he modulated on the block with a brush as he applied them. Sometimes the inking was dry and the oily ink tacky, leaving a coarse, grainy effect that suggests texture. Peculiarly, the key block of this linocut was printed first, rather than last as is customary. Thus, the overprinted tone blocks softened the linear outlines.

Lemos recommended rubbing the back of the sheet with a pad made from wadded fabric, and from the unscarred appearance of its verso, it would seem that *Top O' the Hill* was printed using this method. The artist also occasionally used a hard rubbing pad. He gave instructions for how to make such a tool—essentially a homemade version of a Japanese *baren*—from corn husks wrapped around a core of cardboard. The stiff, protruding veins of the fibrous husks were much like those of palm or bamboo leaves.[5]

Notes

1. Lemos 1929, pl. 16.

2. Ibid., pl. 13.

3. Lemos 1946.

4. Lemos 1920, pp. 285, 286; Lemos 1931, p. 267.

5. Lemos 1931, p. 267.

Top o' the Hill   Pedro J. Lemos

Tod Lindenmuth

1885–1976

25.

The Harbor at Dawn
about 1925
Linocut on heavy cream Japan paper
24.9 × 19.4 cm. (image)
36.1 × 28.9 cm. (sheet)
In pencil, lower margin: *The Harbor at Dawn   Tod Lindenmuth*
Private collection

A painter and printmaker who concentrated on images of the harbor and seashore, Tod Lindenmuth was the first among the Provincetown Printers to devote himself to linoleum cuts. Lindenmuth conceived of a print as a small painting, an intimate window on another world. He used color and form for all their evocative power, and derived his technical means from Japanese prints. His scenes of harbor life in cool, muted colors seem relatively quiet, naturalistic, and conservative in the context of the often bright, abstract prints of other Provincetown artists.

In this print, the sun rises beyond the Atlantic horizon, silhouetting the fishermen, who load bait into their dory in preparation for the day's work, beneath the flight of scavenging gulls. Soft, chalky colors evoke the effect of blurred boundaries between the watery horizon and the morning mist. The glow of sun on the water is most intense beneath the pilings of the dock, through which peeks a glint of golden light. The hovering birds are echoed by the shapes of reflections in the waves of the foreground. Although this linocut seems simplistic, the artist printed many colors to achieve its soft tonal gradations. Except for the flying gulls, the artist overprinted each form of this composition in a darker tint, isolating a halo of lighter color to soften the outlines.

Lindenmuth printed this linoleum cut from several blocks. The pristine verso of the sheet and the even embossing of the blocks show that he printed the work on a letterpress. The blocks were dryly and evenly inked with a brayer, and the thick, oil-base inks did not soak well into the paper. The influence of other Provincetown printmakers, ultimately Japanese in origin, is apparent in the subtle blending of ink on the block for the background. This passage is darkest at the top of the composition, gradually lightening as it approaches the horizon, which is ever so slightly lighter than the sky above it.

The Harbor at Dawn   Tod Lindenmuth

Rudolph Ruzicka

1883–1978

26.
Peck Slip, New York

about 1919
Wood engraving on cream wove
paper
17.8 × 24.0 cm. (image)
23.4 × 28.2 cm. (sheet)
In pencil, lower margin: *R. Ruzicka
del.sc.imp.   Peck Slip, New York
40/50*
Watermark: *Hon . . . (?) Shokai* (in
Japanese)
Private collection

Rudolph Ruzicka, *Self Portrait*. Wood
engraving. Worcester Art Museum
1986.192.

In a long and rich career as a print-maker, typographer, and book de-signer, Rudolph Ruzicka established himself as an arbiter of style in American graphic design. His large oeuvre of prints was intermingled with his prolific output as a book il-lustrator, and the boundaries be-tween his graphic designs and fine prints are vague. As a printmaker, he made his mark with urban landscapes rendered with great precision in a technique derived from the traditional European methods of chiaroscuro woodcut and from nineteenth-century wood engraving.

Although in his famous keepsakes for the Merrymount Press Ruzicka re-jected human activity in favor of placid, deserted architectural land-scapes, in his own early prints he preferred to represent city scenes teeming with activity. The interac-tions of the inhabitants with their ur-ban environment is a constant theme in these works, and in this regard *Peck Slip* is exemplary. It represents a neighborhood along the East River in New York, where the solid, un-changing monuments of the city are juxtaposed with the myriad activities of daily life. On a dreary winter day, the frigid air causes smoke and steam to billow from chimneys in white clouds. Overcast skies bathe the scene in a gray light, muting colors and blurring the distance. In the misty background, the Brooklyn Bridge looms over Peck Slip, as im-posing and immutable as a mountain.

Bridges held a particular fascination for Ruzicka, and many of his prints represent the spans of New York. His first fine wood engravings rep-resented coal barges loading, off-loading, or navigating the bridges on the East River. The artist made a series of prints representing the pro-gressive construction of the Queens-boro Bridge, then being built near his home on the East Side. The monumental structures offered him an opportunity to experiment with manipulations of scale and peculiar points of view. In many of these prints, the viewer peers up at a bridge from below or overlooks a span from a bird's-eye perspective that Ruzicka could only have imag-ined. In about 1905, the artist sub-mitted a dramatic rendering of the Brooklyn Bridge to the advertising agency of Calkins & Holden. This de-sign eventually became an advertise-ment for the manufacturers of the paint that coated the bridge, and it secured for the artist one of his most important early jobs.

As was his habit, Ruzicka used the rectilinear structure of the buildings to define the space of this composi-tion. He often varied the observed scene, enlarging or tightening com-positional space in order to create the illusion of a broader street or a higher building. He strove to enliven these rigid skeletons by adding mov-ing figures, rendered in a sponta-neous line, in the manner of nineteenth-century wood engravers, whose cuts were facsimiles of brush drawings.

Ruzicka preferred to draw on his blocks with a brush after carefully preparing them for cutting.[1] The material was obtained from a spe-cialist, who supplied boxwood from Turkey. While this exotic variety of wood was available in larger pieces than European boxwood or fruit-wood, it was often knotty, and flaws had to be carefully plugged by the supplier. After sanding the block smooth with progressively finer

abrasives, Ruzicka would coat the face with a mixture of egg white and Chinese white pigment to create a surface as smooth as enamel, on which the artist then drew with black ink and a brush.

Ruzicka's engraved woodblocks are in themselves remarkable feats of craftsmanship. After circumscribing the main lines with a burin and then deepening these grooves with a knife, the artist used an electric routing tool to hollow out deep voids, sometimes to the depth of nearly half a centimeter, between the lines. Fine hatching and details, which were comparatively shallow, were carved with the graver. After printing proofs from the key block and then perfecting these, Ruzicka would transfer his design to the other blocks by offsetting the line block image thickly onto a waxy sheet from which the ink was trans-ferred to blocks in a press. The printing of his multiple-block wood engravings always progressed from light to dark colors, with the key block printed last.

It is likely that Ruzicka's *Self-Portrait* (Fig.) was made at the time of his solo exhibition at the Anderson Gal-leries in New York in 1921.[2] This print shows the artist at work with his burin on a woodblock, which is balanced on the leather pillow of the copperplate engraver; his proofing press is seen in the background.[3]

Notes

1. Lathem 1986, pp. 34–35.

2. Anderson 1921.

3. The engraved woodblock for Ruzicka's *Self Portrait* is in the collection of the Worcester Art Museum (accession no. 1986.193).

William Meyerowitz

1887–1981

27.
Central Park

about 1928
Lift ground, etching, and aquatint,
with touches of graphite, on cream
Japanese vellum paper
25.0 × 20.0 cm. (plate)
29.3 × 23.5 cm. (sheet)
In plate, lower right: *Wm Meyerowitz*
In pencil, lower margin:
Wm Meyerowitz
Private collection

The intaglios of William Meyerowitz perpetuated turn-of-the-century European aesthetics and printmaking techniques well into the 1900s. In style, his early prints combined the picturesque imagery of the Etching Revival with the European modernism of Arthur Bowen Davies (cat. 13), and in technique, they were derived from the color experiments of Charles Mielatz, Gabrielle De Vaux Clements (cat. 7), and Ellen Day Hale.

The artist sketched this view from the eighteenth floor of the Beresford Building on Central Park West at Eighty-first Street.[1] Both Meyerowitz and his wife, artist Theresa Bernstein, favored scenes of city life, especially in the 1920s and 1930s,[2] but these paintings and prints have little in common with the images of Social Realists John Sloan and George Bellows. Meyerowitz preferred to depict the meadows of Central Park before a curtain of vertical buildings, or to represent the skyscrapers of Manhattan as crystalline cubist forms. Although he usually included human figures, they were small and not individualized, thereby fitting comfortably into the context of a harmonious city. In 1945, the artist was commissioned to paint a mural representing vignettes of construction, urban life, and culture for the Office of the Mayor.[3]

Schooled in a tradition of craftsmanship, Meyerowitz undertook every phase of the printmaking process himself, from mixing his own etching grounds, acids, and inks to darkening his grounded plates with soot from a candle flame and printing every proof. The process seems to have been more important than the product for this careful craftsman, for he often pulled just a few proofs. He strove to develop a resolved composition in just one state and hardly ever reworked a plate. The artist's early color etchings were made in multiple printings from the same plate inked with different hues; most of the color was carried in films of ink on the surface of the plate. In later, more sophisticated plates, he printed the color in intaglio rather than in plate tone, and he occasionally utilized multiple plates bitten in several complex stages. Meyerowitz achieved exact registration by making holes at the sides of the plate that fit over pins protruding from the bed of the press. All of these techniques were also utilized by Hale and Clements, who extended French color printmaking practices in their own experiments with intaglio in the 1920s and 1930s.

Meyerowitz created this complex mixed-media intaglio from a single plate bitten in stages, and printed it in at least two passes through the press. For each pass through the press, Meyerowitz applied several colors to the plate *à la poupée*. Most of the color was printed in intaglio, though accents—such as the figures

at the lower right—were occasionally added to the surface of the plate. Intentionally casual inking resulted in lines sometimes printing black, sometimes brown, and often—without inking the intaglio at all—white. The artist wiped his plates carefully, covering his hands with talc to remove ink cleanly. Occasionally he used tools such as a piece of blotter paper rolled into a fine point to remove ink from the plate, thereby creating a highlight.

Notes

1. I am grateful to Theresa Bernstein Meyerowitz, who in a letter of March 20, 1989, kindly identified the location of this view.

2. NYHS 1983.

3. Meyerowitz 1986, p. 49, illus. See also Falk, p. 418; Movalli 1980.

m. Nyeroudf

William Seltzer Rice

1873–1963

28.
White Calla

about 1929
Woodcut on cream Japan paper
22.8 × 19.0 cm. (image)
30.6 × 21.8 cm. (sheet)
In pencil, lower margin: *White
Calla   W. S. Rice*
Worcester Art Museum, anonymous
gift, 1988.83

William Seltzer Rice, *Marsh Moon*,
about 1925. Woodcut. Worcester
Art Museum, 1988.82.

A methodical craftsman who had a long and distinguished career in secondary school education, William Seltzer Rice focused on printmaking as a medium for his private expression. For four decades, he was a leading exponent of the color woodcut in northern California. Rice continually refined his technique, developing the most direct procedures with the intention of teaching them to students. This tendency also affected his style; thus his paintings and prints have a practical purity of design.

By design, most of Rice's color prints are austere, illustrative images.[1] The artist combined one or two tone blocks with a bold, linear key block overprinted in black ink, drawing the composition together and isolating colored cells. Sometimes he exploited the stark outline of the key block for *repoussoir* silhouettes, as in the print *Marsh Moon* (Fig.), a technique that may reflect the influences of Pedro Lemos (cat. 24).[2] Rice always preferred spatial clarity and straightforward relationships between figure and ground.

The artist's books give a very clear picture of his methods. He undertook every step of the printmaking process himself, working woodblocks with German carving tools and methodically inking them with sable brushes. He laid different inks side by side unblended on the block, and printed them as bands of color. In other passages, the brush strokes were preserved, giving a lively, painterly quality to the surface of the prints. Rice preferred to complete each impression before proceeding to the next, rather than printing an entire edition one color at a time. His constant experiments with color resulted in substantial variations among impressions within an edition. These editions seldom exceeded fifteen impressions.

In about 1925, Rice began to experiment with printing color woodcuts from a single block, in a variation of the method of the Provincetown printmakers. The process seems to have occupied him intensely for about five years, although he occasionally returned to the technique throughout his career. He used this method exclusively for floral subjects, making prints that were quite different from his other color woodcuts. Rice isolated flowers and foliage close to the picture plane and before a featureless background, in the manner of Edna Boies Hopkins (cat. 9). Perhaps because these compositions were rather flat and decorative, the artist compensated by printing in inks of varying fluidity in order to expand the tonal range. He carefully built up richly modeled forms by printing many layers of ink, applying both washes and saturated details to the block, and printing by rubbing the back of the sheet. Thus, his white line woodcuts have a tonal range and sculptural subtlety absent from his multiblock prints, and are often unique.

A wide range of inking effects is apparent in *White Calla*. In such areas as the leaves, coarse, dry pigment remained on top of the paper, whereas in passages such as the creamy flowers, thin, liquid ink sank deep into the concavities among the long fibers of the paper. Rice prepared his own pigments, and it seems that he ground the dryly printed colors more coarsely, as evidenced by granular bits of blue apparent in the green ink. The range of absorption, visible on the verso of the sheet, is so varied as to suggest that the artist might have printed on dry paper. The back of the sheet also shows that Rice printed with light, circular strokes of a *baren*, the rubbing pad traditionally used by Japanese printmakers. Areas of misregistration prove that the block was inked and printed several times.

Rice usually printed the background of his single-block prints in colors, and often in blended tones. The delicate modeling of the lily stamens in this print is all the more striking in contrast to the flat, unmodulated background, which contributes to the clean simplicity of the design and to its abstraction.

Notes

1. The artist's talent for succinct, decorative design is apparent in Rice 1946.

2. Printed on cream Japan paper, 22.8 × 26.3 cm. See also Fielding 1986, pp. 769–770; Harlow/Keats 1984, nos. 62–69.

White Calla   W.S. Rice

Cora M. Boone
1865–1953

29.
Morning Glory
1930
Woodcut on cream Japan paper
21.5 × 18.4 cm. (image)
27.1 × 21.0 cm. (sheet)
In pencil, lower margin: *MORNING GLORY   CORA BOONE*
Worcester Art Museum, anonymous gift, 1988.68

Little is known about the northern Californian artist and teacher Cora M. Boone, whose vivid woodcuts of the 1930s and 1940s combined B.J.O. Nordfeldt's (cat. 11) technique for making single-block, white line color woodcuts and the Arts and Crafts style of Pedro Lemos (cat. 24).

The date of this woodcut is inscribed on the pine printing block, which is now in a private collection.[1] Like all white line woodblocks of this sort, the porous wood absorbed the thin watercolors, becoming an art object in itself. Indeed, a diagonal hole in the back of the block indicates that it once hung on a peg on a wall. Four or five sets of holes made by tacks in the top of the block show that very few impressions were made. Like Rice, Boone does not seem to have been concerned with carefully limiting the size of her editions.

Morning Glory was printed on soft Japan paper, perforated along the top where the sheet was tacked to the block. The verso is highly abraded, its long fibers fractured and detached. This reveals the way in which the artist printed: by rubbing the back of the wetted sheet as it lay against the inked block. Boone used saturated, often bright watercolors, occasionally laying two colors next to each other on the printing surface and blending them together with an uncharged brush. By reinking the block and printing the sheet several times, an effect of layering colors was created, modeling form and suggesting depth of color or even dimension. Sometimes the artist layered similar hues, giving certain passages a depth and a glow. In superimposing colors, Boone achieved an iridescent shimmer.

In subject, this woodcut is similar to those of Rice's naturalistic single-block floral prints. However, Boone stylized her flowers, circumscribing their forms with wide, angular outlines, which made the image flatter and more decorative. The artist gave more attention to the decorated vessel holding the bouquet, and she enlivened the featureless background of her print with luminous, opalescent colors. The degree of abstraction in *Morning Glory* approaches that of still-life prints of the 1920s by Agnes Weinrich (cat. 20), an artist whose work Boone probably did not know. However, this relationship may illustrate the manner in which styles and techniques moved across the country over time, from the avant-garde artists in New York City, who introduced modernism to Weinrich in the 1910s, to Boone and others in California in the 1930s.

Notes

1. The woodblock measures 21.5 × 18.4 × 2.1 cm. Sanded smooth on the face, it was roughly cut on the back and edges. See also Fielding 1986, p. 86; Harlow/Keats 1984, nos. 8–9.

MORNING GLORY   CORA BOONE

Cornelis Botke

1887–1954

30.
Eucalypti

about 1930
Linocut on oatmeal laid paper
38.9 × 33.7 cm. (image)
47.8 × 42.4 cm. (sheet)
In pencil, lower margin: *Eucalypti*
Botke Prints   Cornelis Botke
Worcester Art Museum, anonymous
gift, 1988.69

With his masterful, delicate handling of color and light, Botke achieved impressive effects of ambiance and space in his prints. The atmosphere and artificial color of *Eucalypti* mark the print as the creation of an accomplished landscape watercolorist. The artist used no literal colors in this composition, giving the image a pleasing, dreamlike quality. The choice of the tall eucalyptus trees, which flourish in coastal California, exemplifies Botke's preference for local subjects, and suggests that he worked from his own watercolor sketches. The pastel hues and soothing, hazy atmosphere suggest the stylistic influence of the Arts and Crafts movement as well as an association with Pedro Lemos (cat. 24).[1]

Botke created a convincing illusion of space in the curving road, which invites the viewer into the composition, through a misty, light-suffused landscape and toward a shimmering lake. The viewer has the sensation of looking out into hazy morning sunshine from the cool, dewy shade of the tall trees. The overlapping trees, diminishing progressively in scale, measure a recession into depth. The tones gradually become lighter as the view recedes into the distance, and horizontal azure bands confine the top of the composition, drawing the eye to the lighted horizon.

Botke chose arbitrary, rather decorative colors. Lavender, pink, and pale orange hues may reflect the influence of Gustave Baumann's (cat. 23) California woodcuts of the 1920s. Complex overlays of color also evince Botke's experience as a watercolorist. The artist made these soft, light-toned inks more transparent by applying them thinly, superimposing the transparent films to alter the hues and increase their range. For example, he created the brown area at the left edge of the image by laying a deep green over a thin layer of orange. With spots of color rather than solid localized passages, Botke achieved a delicate, impressionistic flickering of color. The artist cut tiny stipples and fine lines in his overprinting blocks in order to allow the colors beneath to peek through the layers.

Botke accurately registered the large linoleum blocks, but their exact placement was not critical. The artist rolled his oil-base ink on the palette for a long time in order to get a very light layer of it on his brayer before applying it to the block. The green of the high, leafy boughs at the left, for example, seems to have been created with a fairly dark, opaque ink, but it was applied so sparingly and dryly that it became transparent and subdued.

Notes

1. One of Botke's paintings was reproduced by Lemos in his instructional folio *Landscape* (Lemos 1929, p. 16).

Augusta Payne Rathbone

1897–

31.

Desolation Valley

about 1930

Etching and aquatint on cream wove paper

32.0 × 24.9 cm. (plate)

50.3 × 40.8 cm. (sheet)

In pencil, lower margin: *artists proof   Augusta Rathbone*

Watermark: *MB* (Arches monogram)

Private collection

Well into the twentieth century, American artists continued to travel to Europe to study art. There, particularly in Paris, they made use of the traditional collaborative relationship between painter and professional printer. Beginning in the 1920s, Augusta Rathbone had her intaglio plates printed by a Parisian shop that normally produced quantities of large, inexpensive, decorative aquatints. Her distinctive prints, which combined quick, expressive, broadly etched lines with brightly colored aquatint passages, were extraordinary among the works of artists both in Paris and in the United States.

Rathbone's first prints, made in Paris in 1927, reproduced drawings and watercolor sketchbooks she had compiled on trips to the Sierra Nevada in California. Her first etching was a smaller, simpler version of the present print: a view of Dick's Peak, a mountain in the Desolation Valley Wilderness, near Lake Tahoe in northern California. One of a series of mountain views, *Desolation Valley* was shown in Paris in 1931 and included in the landmark exhibition "American Color Prints" at the Brooklyn Museum in 1933.[1] Rathbone's early intaglios combined a fashionable, expressive style with the traditional etching and aquatint methods that Gabrielle De Vaux Clements (cat. 7) and George Senseney had learned in Paris. In their combination of quick, spontaneous line and bold patches of local color, these semiabstract compositions were also related to the work of Raoul Dufy.

From the first, Rathbone's plates were printed in color at the atelier of Alfred Porcabeuf, the master printer who had worked with Berthe Morisot. The artist seems to have had a rather formal relationship with her printer. She prepared the plates herself and delivered them to the workshop, but she was not normally present for proofing. A discussion over the proofs concerning colors, paper, and size of edition preceded the final printing. Rathbone determined the number of impressions by virtue of what she could afford (at the rate of about two dollars per sheet in the late 1920s). Thus, her prints were produced in small editions, usually of only about fifteen impressions.

Rathbone confessed that she often had to defer to the taste of the printers, particularly in matters of color, for they were often unwilling to print in the intense, sometimes arbitrary hues that she desired.[2] *Desolation Valley* was one source of disagreement; the artist intended the mountain to be printed in pink, representing the colored granite of Dick's Peak. However, the printer was adamant that it be blue-gray instead. Rathbone's early prints, including the Sierra Nevada series, were executed in muted colors, but her palette became brighter and more saturated in prints made on the Riviera during the late 1930s.

Desolation Valley was printed from a single plate in at least two passes through the press. The rich, burry etched lines show that this artist's proof was one of the first impressions pulled from the plate. Aquatint was layered on the plate in staged biting, and stop-out was not used in the areas of the etched lines; thus, the lines are surrounded by haloes of shading in the finished print. All of the colors were probably applied to the plate at once, with a brush or rag in thin washes, and then printed in the first pass through the press. The black ink intaglio and the shallow aquatint, which gives a gray cast to the image, were printed in a second pass. Registration was achieved using two pinholes through the plate, which were hidden in the etched lines. These are barely visible in the lower center; near the top of the plate in the contour line of the mountain peak; and in the crook just left of the summit.

Notes

1. Brooklyn 1933, no. 232; this was one of six intaglios exhibited by Rathbone.

2. Brokl 1984.

artist's proof   Augusta Rathbone

Jean Charlot

1898–1979

32.

Malinche

1933

Offset lithograph on cream laid paper

15.7 × 20.5 cm. (image)

42.6 × 27.8 cm. (sheet)

In pencil, lower right: *Jean Charlot*

In the stone, lower right: *Jean Charlot*

Watermark: *Utopian* beneath scales in a circle

Morse 116

Private collection

Throughout his career, Jean Charlot was motivated to create quality art that spoke directly to a universal audience. His determination to produce widely accessible original art in full color drew him to the newest lithographic technology and into collaborations with the most talented printers of his day. A learned scholar and persuasive critic, he wrote extensively on art history and aesthetics, and he was also an influential and inspiring teacher.

Charlot's first multicolor offset lithograph was *Malinche*, an experiment in the medium with which the artist would make his great contribution to color printmaking. It was created for the promotional prospectus for *Picture Book*, Charlot's big, inexpensive album of original color prints and a grand attempt to achieve in his own art the popular accessibility of nineteenth-century chromolithographs.[1]

In 1933, Charlot met Lynton Kistler and his father Will A. Kistler, a prominent commercial printer whose shop in Los Angeles contained huge offset presses, and the artist recognized the technology that could help him realize his dream. *Malinche* was a test undertaken to prove that complex offset lithographs in color could be printed from plates drawn by an artist, and to convince Will Kistler of the feasibility of such a project. The work was printed on half a sheet of book paper rather than on artist's paper.[2] The same sheet was printed, opposite the fold on both sides, with text describing the publication and seeking the support of subscribers; an order blank was also attached.[3] Although artist and printers were pleased with the results and most of the run of three thousand prints were mailed out, not a single prepublication order was received for the album.

Printed in an edition of five hundred, *Picture Book* was published by John Becker in New York in April of 1934. Each image was accompanied by a stanza in English written by the artist, and a related descriptive verse in French written by the poet Paul Claudel. Charlot reworked his favorite earlier designs for this compilation, conceiving the album as a survey of his oeuvre "with an emphasis laid upon those Mexican scenes for which he is so justly celebrated."[4]

Charlot's charming figural art represents intimate moments in the simple yet dignified lives of common people. The artist's socialist sympathies, stemming from his Mexican experiences in the 1920s, still echo in these images. However, they also evolved from his observations of contemporary rural life, from folklore, and from Precolumbian terracottas and stone sculpture. A historical figure who gained mythological proportions, Malinche was the native Mayan who served as translator for the Spanish conquerors of Mexico in the sixteenth century, and was said to have been the consort of Hernando Cortes. Reviled as a traitor, Malinche grew in infamy until she became a universal emblem of betrayal and self-destruction in Mexican culture and a common character in folk festivals. The model for this print was a reveler at a Mexican fiesta, a child dressed in festive costume and sporting toy weapons. In her right hand is a rattle, and in her left, a toy sword. Having seen many children dressed as Malinche dancing in a fiesta at the Hacienda de la Llave near Los Angeles, Charlot created a little oil painting that became the model for this print.[5]

Working with this image in mind, the artist made a group of tiny pencil drawings in his sketchbook, which delineated the color separations for this print. His long experiences with mural painting made this approach almost second nature, and this proclivity continually amazed Lynton Kistler. The full-color image was built up in a manner similar to that of fresco painting. First forms were determined, then lines, then details, and in this case, all were drawn together by the final printing of a key plate. Charlot's schematic drawings guided the transfer of his designs to full scale on six zinc plates.[6]

Notes

1. Morse 1976, pp. 88–89.

2. Brown 1930, p. 85, note 1.

3. The complete text of the prospectus is given in Morse 1976, p. 81.

4. Ibid.

5. Ibid., p. 108.

6. These separations were reproduced by Morse (1976, pp. 82–85, color pls. 4–5). A set of four color proofs and the accompanying progressive proofs are in the collection of the Worcester Art Museum (accession nos. 1988.284–.291). See also Adams 1983, pp. 100–103, 147–148.

Jean Charlot

Theodore Roszak

1907–1981

33.
Staten Island
1934
Lithograph on cream wove paper
32.5 × 41.0 cm. (image)
38.5 × 56.2 cm. (sheet)
In pen and black ink, in image, lower
left: *8/20   T. J. Roszak '34*
Watermark: *VAN GELDER ZONEN*
Private collection

Theodore Roszak is best known as a sculptor who produced striking Bauhaus-influenced works in the 1930s and 1940s, and later adopted an Abstract Surrealist style. However, early in his career, the artist studied lithography extensively, and in the late 1920s, he was well on the way to becoming one of this country's few master lithographers. Then the course of Roszak's career was changed by a revelatory trip to Europe, and by his experience of modern art in all its scope of visual richness and intellectual complexity.

In 1931, when he returned to the United States after fifteen months abroad, Roszak settled in Staten Island, New York. There, with the financial support of a Tiffany Foundation grant, he worked for almost two years. In a remarkable outpouring of creativity and energy, the artist gave form to many of the ideas and images conceived in the months of his European sojourn. He experimented with different styles and techniques; he also took up photography and made his first sculptures in clay and plaster, which heralded the direction of his future. Roszak also acquired his own press and produced a handful of remarkable prints, including *Staten Island*. This is an extraordinary work for its time, as very few American artists were then capable of printing their own lithographs, and fewer still were abstractionists.

Roszak depicted his surroundings in Staten Island in several narrative paintings of European modernist style. The present print is adapted from one of these paintings, executed in oil on masonite in 1933.[1] The lithograph was derived from the left half of the painting, and its composition was further simplified. This impression of the print was similar in color to the painting. While Roszak's other paintings of Staten Island included figures, this view was deserted, although city lights and illuminated signs glittered in the distance. The artist removed these lights from the print, deleting even the remote suggestion of active habitation, and further abstracting the image.

Although the painted version of this composition obviously represents a nocturne, the bright colors of the lithograph suggest the sea and sky in glaring daylight. Ripples on the surface of the water—details absent from the painting and some impressions of the print—help the viewer to identify the subject. The navigational landmark of a conical tower is mirrored in the water; and the flag atop a floating buoy hovers on the horizon. In the foreground, an anchored barge or raft is mounted with weather instruments. These devices were meant to detect and record atmospheric changes, yet ironically this image seems quiet and immutable.

While some forms appear flat in this composition, others were made to look three-dimensional with stippled modeling. Roszak used dotted shading and texturing of forms in his paintings and gouaches of this period, in which they often represent flickering city lights. The geometric style of this image signals the artist's developing interest in Constructivism.

This image also reflects Roszak's fascination with measuring instruments, an inclination that anticipated his use of the machine style of the Bauhaus. Measurement was a recurrent theme in Roszak's art of the 1930s. He represented navigational and astronomical tools as allegorical symbols of man's struggle to fix his position in the physical and metaphysical universe.[2] By depicting them prominently in the present print, where landscape was reduced to simple geometry, Roszak implied that there is order to the cosmos, and that man is capable of assessing and understanding his place in that order.

Roszak drew and printed this lithograph himself, from two zinc plates. The primary plate was pierced by holes, two of its corners were rounded, and triangular notches were cut in its sides. This peculiar shape suggests that the lithographic plate might have been a scrap from Roszak's metalworking shop. Smudges of color and fingerprints in the margins of this impression confirm the experimental character of the lithograph, which is printed on a sheet with tattered edges.

The plates were inked to their edges with liquid tusche, applied with a brayer and brush. Some of the white accents were accomplished by the use of resist. Accents were also added to the plate with lithographic crayon. Thick layers of ink show that some passages, particularly the blue, were printed twice. Irregularities in the ink surface suggest that the artist touched up by hand after the first printing, and then ran the sheet through the press once again. Some color accents were later applied through stencils. Finally the artist cropped the lower edge of the image, by painting over it with a brayer charged with black ink.

This highly experimental lithograph is very rare, and seems to exist in just a handful of impressions, despite Roszak's inscription indicating an edition of twenty prints. Each of the known lithographs is uniquely colored. In some impressions, the background was printed in red or pink rather than blue.[3]

Notes

1. Now in a private collection; see Dreishpoon 1989, pp. 42–44.

2. Ibid., pp. 40–41.

3. Examples of the red variant are found at the Amon Carter Museum (accession no. 1989.6), and the British Museum. See also Roszak 1974.

Millard Sheets

1907–1989

34.
A California Landscape

1934
Offset lithograph on cream wove paper
53.6 × 79.0 cm. (image)
64.8 × 100.6 cm. (sheet)
In the stone, lower margin: *PRINTED BY WILL A. KISTLER CO. LOS ANGELES. CONTRIBUTED BY MILLARD SHEETS TO PUBLIC WORKS OF ART PROJECT 14TH REGION*
In the stone, lower right: *M. S.*
In pencil, lower right: *Millard Sheets*
Stamped in black, lower left: *83*
Watermark: *Saxon Japan U.S.A.*
Worcester Art Museum, gift of the Public Works of Art Project, Los Angeles, 1934.52

A leader of a generation of Western artists who depicted California as their native environment, Millard Sheets was remarkably prolific in a wide variety of media throughout a long career. In addition to producing many watercolors and paintings, he was a distinguished teacher and administrator as well as a commercial artist and designer.

In *A California Landscape*, an eerie light and fleeing shadows fall across this view of the California coast, as distant thunderclouds roll in and spew forth showers. This unstable weather excites the horses—Sheet's alter ego and a symbol of freedom—to nervous prancing and pawing. Well acquainted with the anatomy and movement of horses, the artist preferred to treat these figures expressively. The arch of their necks, their rounded, muscular haunches,

and their sweeping tails imply their potential speed and grace. The unspoiled vastness of the land, sea, and sky of Sheets's childhood is represented in this dramatic print. Similar in scale, coloration, and effect to his contemporaneous watercolors, this image evinces the exaltation of youth inspired by nature's majesty.

The influence of Midwestern Regionalism on Sheets's personal style is apparent in the vast perspective of this composition and in the emphatically modeled topography, from towering seaside cliffs to plowed furrows. Also treated as sculptural forms, spare, almost featureless buildings and the abandoned barnyard and buckboard symbolize rather than literally narrate the effect of unrelenting human incursion on the land.

This large and striking print reflects the speedy development of artists' lithographs in Los Angeles after Charlot's introductory offset lithograph (cat. 32), which was made just two years earlier. A constant advocate of this technique was Lynton Kistler, whose father, Will A. Kistler, was proprietor of a flourishing Los Angeles commercial printing plant. There Sheets's fine print was produced in a relatively small edition. Lynton Kistler's working relationship with his contemporary is also apparent in the catalogue of Sheets's solo exhibition in 1935 at the Dalzell Hatfield Gallery, which includes an original offset lithograph, *Kamani Trees.*[1]

A California Landscape was printed in five colors from zinc plates. The artist prepared the plates almost entirely with crayon, although some accents were added with brush and tusche. The use of book paper, the exacting registration of the print, and its mechanical numbering reflect the practices of the Kistler plant, which was oriented to mass production.

As a member of the administrative committee of the WPA in Los Angeles, Sheets designated this lithograph—one of the first products of the project in California—as a donation to schools in the area. Later, other impressions were given to art museums throughout the country, including the Worcester Art Museum.

Notes

1. Hatfield 1935. See also Laguna 1983.

Harry Sternberg

1904–

35.
Riveter
1935
Serigraph on cream laid paper
27.8 × 29.0 cm. (image)
43.3 × 31.4 cm. (sheet)
In pencil, lower margin: *Sternberg*
Watermark: *MANSFIELD VELLUM*
Moore 126
Private collection

A versatile painter and printmaker, Harry Sternberg made his most important contribution to color printmaking as an educator, author, and serigrapher in the 1930s and 1940s. Sternberg's ideas and methods, expressed in his technical manual on the process of serigraphy, had an impact across the country.

This print, one of Sternberg's most dramatic and best-known serigraphs, represents a construction worker building the steel skeleton of a skyscraper in New York. As a student in the 1920s, the artist once worked as field clerk for the Spencer, White, and Prentis Company, construction contractors. His imagination was fired by the workers, who soberly moved the earth and balanced high above the ground on steel beams. The welders and riveters were the elite laborers—brave, agile, and skillful, they were considered superior to the excavators.[1] Sternberg sketched them and remembered them. When his own style took shape in the 1930s, he gravitated to Social Realist images of labor. The artist drew on his personal experiences and visual memories of construction workers to make a group of prints, including this serigraph.

This riveter is a proletarian hero, a virile laborer whose job requires strength, courage, and skill. The stocky, sculpturesque figure is similar in style to those of Hugo Gellert (cat. 52); however, the rivet gun obscures his face, creating an odd tension. This lack of human identification draws the viewer's attention to the activity itself. Like the harvesters in Bernard Steffen's *Haying* (cat. 61), the riveter becomes a symbol of labor, representing the benefits to all society of his toil and skill; conversely, his anonymity also makes him seem a human automaton, like the faceless villains in Sternberg's other prints. Thus this work challenges the viewer to reflect on the exploitation of labor by industrialists for their own gain, in order to raise the disconcertingly large and impenetrable city.

Sometimes called *Steel*, this was Sternberg's first serigraph.[2] Its success depended on its reworking of the earlier intaglio print *Construction* (1932; Moore 89), for the artist admits that his early screen prints included several aesthetically unresolved works as he struggled to learn the new process. Serigraphy entranced Sternberg with its combination of ease and economy and with its relative accessibility. He hoped that this medium might encourage the open production of prints and dispel the convention of small, precious editions.

The artist created this screen print using the tusche and glue method. He printed it in nine colors, and further expanded the palette by overprinting many transparent glazes of ink. Even in his first experiment in the new medium, Sternberg sought its special character. He exploited the textural quality of the silk and was particularly intrigued by the way the tusche could leave brush marks on the screen. This "dry brushing" gave the print a painterly quality.

Sternberg's thoughtful craftsmanship stems from personal discipline and from the influence of his teachers. He has always had heartfelt convictions about the process-oriented art of printmaking, maintaining that the challenge of a difficult technique forces the artist to transcend technical facility: "To conquer the resistance of the materials and to control the technical problems have, I felt, added a special quality to the final results."[3]

Notes

1. Moore 1975, no. 139.

2. Sternberg 1942, pp. 2–5.

3. Letter from the artist to the author, January 9, 1989. See also Landau 1983, pp. 112–113; Zigrosser 1942, pp. 62–69.

Emil Ganso

1895–1941

36.
Still Life with Peaches
1935
Lithograph on cream wove paper
30.8 × 40.2 cm. (image)
38.9 × 47.9 cm. (sheet)
In pencil, beneath image: *Ed.35*
Still Life with Peaches Ganso
Worcester Art Museum, Anonymous
Fund, 1988.164

A versatile printmaker who worked in many graphic media and printed for other artists as well, Emil Ganso was one of the few American artists producing color lithographs in the 1930s.

Ganso's dedicated craftsmanship was most apparent in his printmaking, whether in his own works or in lithographs that he printed for other artists. He mixed his own inks and etching grounds, prepared his own plates and stones, and always pulled entire editions of prints himself.[1] His color lithographs of the 1930s are characteristic of the "Woodstock style," a benign, anecdotal version of Social Realism. Most of these prints are landscapes and still lifes, although the artist occasionally represented his favorite subject, languid, voluptuous nudes. Much more demanding in terms of time and care, these color prints were priced higher than Ganso's black ink lithographs, and the artist hoped to insure their salability by representing more widely appealing and accessible subjects. Several layers of superimposed drawing lent a clarifying effect to these images, giving them a more carefully detailed look than most of his sketchy, draftsmanlike prints of the period.

The high technical quality of *Still Life with Peaches* is proof of Ganso's skill. It was printed in five colors from as many stones by the artist in August of 1935, in Woodstock, New York.[2] Precise registration was achieved by the use of two pins, which pierced the paper through the side margins and fitted into corresponding holes in the stones. All of the images were drawn with crayon directly on the stones. Occasionally the artist added accents in liquid tusche with a brush, which are visible in the blue stone. The somber palette, typical of Ganso's color lithographs, is dominated by yellow and beige with highlights in red and blue. The artist carefully overlapped tints in order to increase the range of colors and tones.

Notes

1. Moser 1980.

2. *Prints* (1936, pp. 43–44) describes an edition of forty for the present lithograph, which contradicts the numbering of this impression.

Margaret Lowengrund

1902–1957

37.

Interior of a Brickyard

1936

Lithograph on cream wove paper

45.5 × 32.2 cm. (image)

38.0 × 28.0 cm. (sheet)

In pencil, lower right: *Lowengrund*

In pencil, lower margin: *Interior of a Brickyard*

Watermark: *NAVARRE*

Worcester Art Museum, anonymous gift, 1988.116

In the review of a historical exhibition of lithographs, Margaret Lowengrund wrote in 1948: "The plea, inspired by this tribute to a great invention, is for more painters to reach out in lithography and more printers to experiment, so that the field in this country is no longer left to the stereotyped printer who refuses to recognize the needs of the artist for free expression."[1] For twenty years, beginning in the mid-1930s, Lowengrund was a diligent champion of lithography. Although she was also an author, critic, teacher, painter, and much more, her most effective and influential activities were as a lithographer and an advocate of printmaking.

In the 1930s, Lowengrund was an enthusiastic member of the Social Realist movement. Her associations with the Art Students League and her membership in the Artists Union and other political organizations brought her into close contact with such activist artists as Harry Sternberg (cat. 35) and Harry Gottlieb (cat. 48). Like them, she worked in a representational, expressive, figural style. At this time, many printmakers with left-wing sympathies concentrated on accessible prints representing heroic American workers

toiling in the cause of personal and national freedom. *Interior of a Brickyard* is the product of this genre; it was included in the union-sponsored exhibition "Prints for the People" in 1937.

The generalized setting and the distortions of background form and space in this print are also characteristic of this style. Sternberg and his colleagues experimented with these devices in order to emphasize, by contrast, the dramatic, naturalistic figure. The muted, earthy palette, so appropriate to this lithograph, was preferred by Lowengrund for most of her color prints. In the coming decades, her paintings and prints remained figurative, and she concentrated on creating anecdotal genre scenes that she may well have observed.

This technically refined lithograph was printed at the FAP workshop in New York. Although Lowengrund was an able lithographer herself, many of the technical characteristics of the present print identify it closely with this workshop and the practices of Russell Limbach (cat. 45), who may have assisted the artist in printing. Lowengrund drew her images with crayon directly onto three lithographic stones. To achieve a richer surface, she varied the quality of her crayon line and hatching, occasionally scraping lines away—as in the sieve held by the figure at the left. In preparing the stone that printed in blue, the artist complemented her crayon drawing with accents in liquid tusche, which she applied with a brush. Nearly perfect registration was achieved by the use of printed cross marks in the top and bottom margins, and perforation of the paper at these points, to fit over pins protruding from the stones.

Notes

1. Lowengrund 1948, p. 19.

Don Freeman
1908–1978

38.
Ladies of the Evening
1937
Offset lithograph on cream wove
paper
23.6 × 16.5 cm. (image)
31.8 × 23.5 cm. (sheet)
In the stone, lower left: *C imp*
In pencil, lower right: *Don Freeman*
McCulloch 117
Worcester Art Museum, anonymous
gift, 1988.114

This color lithograph is unique in Freeman's oeuvre of limited edition prints, although other color offset lithographs did appear in the artist's own magazine of satirical prints, *Newsstand*. Printed from zinc plates on a motorized press, it was created in order to demonstrate the versatility of the printing process of color offset lithography.

The circumstances of the production of this color lithograph were extraordinary. Early in 1937, Freeman decided to acquire a mechanized press, as he wished to produce his own offset lithographs for *Newsstand*. In May of that year, in partnership with Artcraft Litho and Printing Company, the artist purchased a secondhand press from the defunct Florence Cane School of Art. This was probably the Addressograph Multilith 296 machine that Jean Charlot (cat. 32) and Albert Carman had acquired for the school in 1934 and later altered to print handdrawn zinc plates in order to use it for teaching.[1]

It seems that Carman himself printed this five-color offset lithograph demonstrating the use of the modified press and perhaps instructing Freeman in his patented single-plate, multicolor process.[2] Carman's contribution is indicated by the monogram *C imp* in the image at lower left. Inexact registration resulted from the adaptation of the equipment. Carman and Charlot had allowed for this imprecision in the design of their prints, but Freeman was dissatisfied with the effect, and, although a larger edition was planned, he signed only about fifty impressions.

In *Ladies of the Evening*, Freeman closely reproduced his own black ink lithograph, the first print he made for the short-lived New York Public Works of Arts Project in 1934.[3] Another adaptation of this composition was a print representing the charwoman in the aisle of a theater, with her bucket beside her, while her coworkers clean the seats behind her. Published in *Newsstand* in 1937, this early version may have been one of the first produced by Freeman himself on his new press.

This print exemplifies Freeman's ready wit, his love for the theater, and his humanity. He portrayed all of the subjects of his prints sympathetically and always strove to characterize individual personalities, thus revealing himself as a student of John Sloan. His love of verbal and visual puns, also exemplified here, is a common feature in is printmaking oeuvre and distinguished him as an illustrator of children's books.

Notes

1. Morse 1976, pp. 432–434.

2. Such was also the conclusion of Edith McCulloch in a letter dated September 22, 1988.

3. McCulloch 94; see also pp. 119–120, and Freeman 1949.

Grace Martin Taylor

1903–

39.
Old White Art Colony

1937
Woodcut on cream laid paper
30.5 × 35.4 cm. (image)
40.0 × 46.1 cm. (sheet)
In pencil, lower margin: *Old White
Art Colony   1/40   Grace Martin
(Frame* erased)   *1937*
Private collection

Best known as a painter, educator, and administrator, Grace Martin Taylor also made color woodcuts. Her printmaking activities were centered in Provincetown, where along with Angele Myrer and Ferol Sibley Warthen she was one of the second generation of artists to use the single-block white line color woodcut technique for modernist prints.

On the Virginia state line, in the little Appalachian village of White Sulphur Springs, West Virginia, the Old White Art Colony was established in 1933 by artists William C. Grauer and Natalie Enyon Grauer. Privately maintained, this tightly knit creative community was mandated to support and promote contemporary art in the South. The colony's resident membership, limited to one hundred, was divided in half between professional artists and students who worked there year-round. From June to October, exhibitions were changed every two weeks, and additional classes were also conducted later in the summer. Aside from the Grauers, there were two other teachers working at the Old White Art Colony in 1937, when Grace Martin Frame was a student there.

Her style in the present print was similar to those of Ralston Crawford (cat. 71) and especially Niles Spencer. Ultimately derived from Picasso's Analytical Cubism, this manner was suggested by such American Precisionist painters of the preceding generation as Charles Demuth, Patrick Henry Bruce, and Charles Sheeler (cat. 84). Often working in Provincetown between 1924 and 1940, Spencer concentrated on urban architectural landscape paintings comprised of tightly interlocked geometric forms, which were without detail and absent of all traces of human existence. In the 1920s and early 1930s, Spencer gave his canvases active, painterly surfaces, which were moderated in his later style.

Also concentrating on architectural views, Taylor used intuitive perspective to structure her Cubist architectonic forms. She applied paint in a free yet controlled manner, which enhanced the dynamism of her forms and emphasized spatial tensions. Her Cubist distortions were often moderated by sensitively balanced colors. The artist preferred a sharp palette of intense, interstitial hues that are decorative if vaguely naturalistic.

This woodcut was made from a single block in the archetypal manner. The shallow, close grain of the woodblock lacked the parallel ridges or broad whorls of pine, suggesting that the artist may have used an even-grained soft wood like mahogany. Some of Blanche Lazzell's (cat. 18) later prints, made in West Virginia, seem to have been printed from the same material. Taylor's carved lines in the present print randomly vary in their width. Their immediacy and energy suggest that the artist did not painstakingly follow a precise drawing in cutting the block, but carved with some spontaneity. She painted on a stout Western paper, rather than a translucent Japan paper. Scuffing on the verso of the sheet shows that the artist printed with vigorous hand rubbing. Many of the component shapes of this design were printed in two or three thin layers of watercolor wash. This modeling effect, combined with the energized carved line and distorted space, gives this image an alluring vitality.

James Dexter Havens
1900–1960

40.
Wind and Snow
1938
Woodcut on white Japan paper
14.6 × 19.0 cm. (image)
26.1 × 30.2 cm. (sheet)
In the block, lower right: *JH*
monogram
In pencil, lower margin: *19/50-Wind
and Snow-   James D. Havens-Sc.
Imp. 1938–*
Worcester Art Museum, anonymous
gift, 1988.75

James D. Havens, *Wind and Snow*,
about 1938. Graphite and colored
pencils. Worcester Art Museum.
Gift of Bettina Havens Letcher,
1989.129.

The works of Jim Havens are full of
the artist's personal delight at finding
beauty in every cloud and hedgerow.
A solitary, exacting craftsman, he
spared no effort in the production of
his relief prints. They are the works
of one who felt a special compulsion
to celebrate life.

Most of Haven's prints represent still
lifes, landscapes, and scenes from nature that show what a careful and
sensitive observer he was. In these
colorful prints, birds sing as they flit
amid tall grasses, small animals scurry
busily across forest floors, and snows
drifts silently against tree trunks.
The artist strove to depict the dynamic, yet often unseen, processes
of nature: "It's not a picture of a
tree, but of how the tree grows; not
a picture of the sea, but of how a
fluid force meets the ageless edge of
a continent."[1] In *Wind and Snow*, the
artist depicted a neighbor's barn on
an early winter day when squalls
bent the branches of the trees,
bowed and tangled the grasses, and
silently blew the intermittent snow.

In this print, Havens presented the
energy and transience of nature in an
almost palpable manner. Clusters of
farm buildings and the hills themselves seem to huddle against the
wind. The landscape is deserted but
for a single beast, who keeps close
to a barn with its back to the wind.
This mood of desolation evokes a
sense of the silent, inexorable forces
of nature and is reminiscent of the
prints of Regionalist artists such as
Grant Wood, whose barns, rows of
corn, and deserted schoolhouses
suggest rather than depict human
habitation, and the elements of nature enhance feelings of solitude.
The topographical features and the
formal simplicity of the buildings in
Havens's print have almost a sculptural quality. In a small, preparatory

sketch quickly rendered in graphite
and colored pencils, the space was
slightly more compressed than in the
final print (Fig.). However, the colors
in this drawing and the sense of the
movement of the wind were transferred accurately to the woodcut.

The artist became skilled in a variety
of carving techniques. He began cutting linoleum, and in the early 1930s
experimented with carving printing
matrices of Parazin, a similar hard
rubber material. He also made
woodcuts from planks of soft
basswood or acacia. As he became
adept at carving, Havens began to
favor color prints, which he usually
made from three or four separate
blocks. In the mid-1930s, the artist
experimented with leaving one of
the blocks uninked in order to enhance the colors of the print with
surface embossing. He also experimented with printing a solid color on
the verso of such woodcuts as *Night
Watch* of 1937, rendering the Japan
paper opaque and thus strengthening
the colors.

In the late 1930s and early 1940s,
Havens worked briefly in wood engraving, using the copperplate engraver's burin to carve his images in
composite blocks of hard, end-grain
boxwood. His manner in this medium is characterized by parallel
hatching in many directions, and
tonal variation in the frequency and
density of lines. This technique is apparent in the monochrome wood
engraving *Snow Blow*, in which a
broad range of tone delineates the
delicate shadows on wind-sculpted
snowdrifts. In *Wind and Snow*, Havens used similar cutting techniques
in multiple planks of soft wood to
create linear effects that enhance the
design of the images, suggesting the
direction and movement of the wind.
Crisp, v-shaped grooves printed as
negative, or white, lines, overprinting and toning flat areas of color
underneath. The set of three woodblocks for this print, along with two
progressive proofs, are now in the
collection of the Strong Museum in
Rochester, New York.[2]

For the present print, the artist used
just three colors—red, yellow, and
blue—printed from as many blocks.
By isolating and overprinting these,
he skillfully achieved a full range of
hues and subtle tonal effects. Colors
are muted in the dim, diffuse light of
an overcast landscape in early winter.
Havens undertook every step in the
creation of his print. He ground his
own pigments and mixed his own
inks, for he knew that the color letterpress inks—which he often used
for proofing—were fugitive. In the
basement of his house in Fairport,
New York, he printed on his English
letterpress.

It seems that Havens printed open
editions according to need, for he
did not always inscribe his prints as
they were made. This is suggested
by a number of linocuts and woodcuts from the 1930s and 1940s, on
which the artist's signature is followed by the initials A[ssociate]
N[ational] A[cademy], an honor
Havens did not receive until 1951.
Some of his prints, which remained
unsigned at his death, were later inscribed by his wife with the artist's
name and the initials G[ladys]
H[avens], and by his daughter-in-law
A[nne] H[avens].

Notes

1. Croughton 1947.

2. Accession no. 76.1464. The Strong Museum also owns an impression of the print
from the completed edition numbered
14/50 accession no. 74.3504. See Havens
1948; Letcher 1977; Smith 1954; Smith
1960.

19/50 · Wind and Snow.   James D. Havens · Sc Imp 1938 ·

Louis Schanker

1903–1981

41.

Abstraction with Heart

1938

Woodcut on cream Japan paper

23.1 × 30.4 cm. (image)

30.1 × 37.7 cm. (sheet)

In pencil, lower margin: *1/15*

ABSTRACTION WITH HEART

Schanker

Brooklyn 13

Worcester Art Museum, anonymous gift, 1988.85

Louis Schanker stood at the center of the circle of avant-garde woodcut artists in New York in the middle of the twentieth century. Beginning in the mid-1930s, the artist exerted a profound influence on printmaking, through his own technically innovative works and through his activities as a teacher.

This print is exemplary of the mode of European modernism practiced by Schanker in the late 1930s. Earlier in the decade, the artist's imagery was figurative, and he often concentrated on the expression of movement. This print reflects his tendency toward nonrepresentational abstraction, the focus of his prints in the succeeding two decades. In *Abstraction with Heart*, the heavy black lines printed by the key block—lines similar to those circumscribing forms in many of Schanker's earlier prints—were broken up and used to imply spatial ambiguity. Indeed, the theme of this composition, the manipulation of space, was accomplished by effects of overlapping and transparency.

The artist's goals were parallel to those of Blanche Lazzell (cat. 18) and Agnes Weinrich (cat. 20) in their contemporary color woodcuts; however, his means were those of New York painters such as Byron Browne and Arshile Gorky, whose style derived from European modernism. Essentially cubist distortions of space were combined with the bright colors and decorative patterning of the Fauves in Schanker's prints. The hatched lines and checks of Schanker's prints, achieved by a variety of technical means, are reminiscent of Matisse, as are the irregular outlines of form that at times appear scissored. The harmony and joyful mood of this image attest to Schanker's skill as a colorist. The artist used colors to cause forms to seem to advance and recede.

Abstraction with Heart also exemplifies the innovative subtleties of Schanker's technique that impressed Stanley William Hayter (cat. 60).[1] The artist's early woodcuts were printed by hand with small, fabric-covered rubbing pads: his own variation of the Japanese *baren*.[2] During his activity in the FAP workshop, he developed and refined his technique, utilizing several blocks and liberally applying oil-base ink to the blocks. Variations upon this process included printing colors over black ink on undampened paper, in order to achieve new effects of tone and luminosity.

Perhaps the most innovative and effective of Schanker's printing methods was his practice of pressing one layer of ink atop another before the first had the chance to dry. Because he applied his ink thickly to the blocks, some mixing of colors occurred during printing. In the present print, this effect is apparent in passages where red mixed with blue and with yellow. A similar mottled effect resulted from the sticky ink on the block having lifted some of the previously printed color from the paper.

Four blocks were used to print five colors for *Abstraction with Heart*. The oily ink soaked deeply into the paper, and because it was applied so thickly, no wood grain was printed from the surface of the block.[3] Schanker printed by hand rubbing, which is apparent from the verso, where the mottled appearance of ink shows how the sheet was burnished, although on the recto these passages appear flat and saturated.

Schanker's inventive attitude toward technique became a hallmark of his color woodcuts in the 1940s. During this period, he often signed them in the block with an S in a circle, a monogram similar to the Chinese yin-yang symbol. Sometimes Schanker used unconventional tools, such as wire brushes, rasps, and scrapers, to mar the surface of the block. The artist always printed his own blocks and encouraged potentially creative accidents during the process: "The possibility of invention is I believe, one of the most intriguing aspects of woodcut. Traditional tools are no longer sufficient."[4]

Notes

1. Hayter 1962, p. 24.

2. Johnson 1943, p. 4.

3. Aside from the edition of fifteen impressions, there were eight trial proofs. See ibid., no. 7.

4. Lieberman 1955, p. 50. See also AAA 1978 and 1986b; Watrous 1984, pp. 97–98, 178–179.

1/65   ABSTRACTION WITH HEART

Anthony Velonis

1911–

42.

6:30 P.M.

1938

Serigraph on cream China paper

29.3 × 30.9 cm. (image)

21.7 × 28.7 cm. (sheet)

In screen, lower left: *AV* monogram

In pencil, lower margin: *6:30 P.M.*

Anthony Velonis

Worcester Art Museum, anonymous gift, 1988.110

Anthony Velonis was central in the development of serigraphy as a medium for fine art color prints. As director of the FAP silk screen unit, he conducted many experiments that refined the technique, which he taught to numerous artists who came to specialize in it.

In 1934, Velonis was employed by Mayor Fiorello La Guardia's poster project, which was directed by the Civilian Works Administration.[1] Originally the artists of this shop painted posters by hand, one at a time. Despite the speed that resulted from practice, it became clear to them that a more efficient method of production was required. Velonis had learned the silkscreen process while working at Doulberry Brothers, a commercial shop that specialized in wallpapers. He convinced the administrator of the poster project, John Weaver, to try the technique, and soon the shop had markedly increased its production. When this project was reassigned to the FAP in 1936, and Richard Floethe (cat. 47) took over its administration, Velonis found an ally and an advocate.

The young artist's enthusiasm for silkscreen printing grew; he became a proponent of the process as a fine art medium, and hoped to explore its potential within the FAP. In support of his assertion, he made a few of his own prints to show administrators; the first of these was *Auto Motif*, which was soon followed by *6:30 P.M.* Slowly his lobbying had an effect, and in September 1938, FAP executive Audrey McMahon reassigned Velonis for a probationary period as head of his own silkscreen unit in the graphic arts division. His assignment was to introduce the

technique to a handful of artists so that they could each produce an edition of about twenty-five impressions. Velonis went to the Artists Union, which appointed an exploratory committee of six artists, four of whom were already members of the FAP graphic arts division. The first artist to collaborate with Velonis was Louis Lozowick; then followed Harry Gottlieb (cat. 48), Elizabeth Olds, Hyman Warsager, Ruth Chaney, and Eugene Morley (cat. 46).[2] Among the most experimental artists to make serigraphs in the workshop in the late 1930s were Harry Shokler, Leonard Pytlak, and Bernard Steffen (cat. 61).

With the wan palette of this evocative print, Velonis masterfully captured the eerie glow of city lights reflected against an overcast winter sky. Perhaps introduced to these peculiar interstitial hues by Richard Floethe, Velonis was fascinated by them in the late 1930s. These colors appear not only in his own work, but in the prints of several artists who worked with him in the silkscreen unit.

The artist worked the fourteen screens for this print in several different ways, preparing most of them by making stencils of cut gelatin film, a method in which he had become very proficient during his work for the poster project. He meticulously cut the branches of the tree from Profilm in order to show the capabilities of this method.[3] The composition and its illusion of depth

depend on the overlapping of forms and figures, a scheme that echoes the building up of ink layers inherent in the silkscreen process. Generally Velonis laid down background colors first, then superimposed closer tones and forms. He used a fabric of very fine mesh to create even, opaque passages of saturated local color, and printed accents such as the cross-hatched treatment of the bright green sky from a screen prepared with tusche and glue. The dark green and yellow inks appear thicker and pastier than the rest, indicating that the artist used a coarser mesh for these screens.

Velonis's technical vocabulary quickly expanded as he explored the special characteristics of serigraphy in the late 1930s. His experiments coalesced in a single print entitled *Decoration Empire*. Its European modernist design, with motifs derived from "Napoleonic pseudo-classicism," is more satirical than serious. This famous serigraph, never made in a proper edition but printed a few impressions at a time for the purposes of demonstration, combined all of the technical tricks then at the artist's command. Velonis used extremely coarse screens to layer heavy impasto inks over thin, transparent glazes. With thick burlap and organdy screens, he created knobby textures that he juxtaposed against soft gradations printed through sheer silks. In one printing of *Decoration Empire*, he further softened the surfaces by blotting the wet ink with newsprint.

Notes

1. Velonis 1987, pp. 72–79.

2. This is according to Velonis (1987, p. 76). Zigrosser (1941b, p. 459) wrote that Elizabeth Olds was the artist who made the first project print. For Lozowick's print *Roof and Sky*, see Williams 1987, p. 17, fig. 11.

3. Zigrosser (1941b, p. 449) identifies the print incorrectly as *6:30 A.M.* See also O'Connor 1973, p. 294.

6:30 P.M.   Anthony Velonis

Joseph Vogel

1911–

43.

Escape

1938

Serigraph on cream wove paper

25.2 × 32.9 cm. (image)

31.9 × 48.2 cm. (sheet)

In pencil, lower margin: *Escape Joseph Vogel 21* (New York WPA stamp defaced)

Watermark: *NAVARRE*

Private collection

An able painter, printmaker, designer, and filmmaker, Joseph Vogel has also had a varied and distinguished teaching career. His color prints of the late 1930s have their place at the junction of political idealism, a reevaluation of Surrealism, and the technical developments of the FAP.

The most controversial and most widespread artistic movement in the period between the world wars, Surrealism was reevaluated and revived in the late 1930s.[1] This school aimed to broaden the viewer's understanding of reality by examining instinct, dreams, and the subconscious. By merging these realms of experience with those of conscious sense and thought, the Surrealists tried to achieve an absolute or super reality, a more complete experience of life. Shortly before 1940, a reemerging interest in the school was encouraged by the presence in New York of Matta, a Chilean-born painter who promoted his own version of Surrealism.[2] Vogel was drawn to the ideal of an art that could fully reveal the territory of dreams and innermost thoughts, as manifested in the work of Matta as well as that of Fernand Léger, José Clemente Orozco, Alberto Giacometti, and Max Ernst.

Conceived as a reflection of Vogel's wish to be free from the fetters of a constraining relationship, *Escape* is a composition of discord and instability. Throughout this bleak landscape, overlapping forms suggest dimension, but that of an incoherent, confusing, dreamlike space. A green sun, like some nightmarish lunar eclipse, seems to oppress the whole scene. The central monolith is cracked, and the dominant T shape, like a tipped scale, leans precariously, symbolizing imbalance. This dizzying effect is enhanced by the skewed, dark blue rectangle. The figures are dominated by their emotions, the male profile at center haggard and hopeless, the female figure at right attempting to flee. However, the latter seems to be anchored by her right foot, held fast as in a trap; thus her pose becomes one of ranting gesticulation.

This print stands out among the early serigraphs of the FAP for its garish, discordant colors. The hard contours of its forms indicate that, like Velonis's *6:30 P.M.* (cat. 42), it was done primarily with cut Profilm secured to a fine fabric mesh. These sharp edges emphasize the juxtaposition of the bright colors and their message of despair and emotional conflict.

Notes

1. Arnason 1975, pp. 362–375.

2. Frost 1942. See also O'Connor 1972, pp. 117, 166, 174; O'Connor 1973, p. 141.

Hananiah Harari

1912–

44.

Carnival

1939

Serigraph on cream wove paper

17.9 × 24.0 cm. (image)

22.3 × 27.1 cm. (sheet)

In screen, lower left: *Harari*

In pencil, lower margin: *Carnival Harari 39*

Worcester Art Museum, anonymous gift, 1988.105

A painter noted for his fluency in a wide range of styles, Hananiah Harari was, in 1939, among the first artists to make serigraphs in the FAP silkscreen unit. His vivid memories of the period provide a glimpse into the controversy surrounding abstract art in the 1930s and the place of printmaking in this dispute.

A constant dispute raged over the very purpose of art itself, with Social Realists opposing those whose approach was more aesthetic. Many of the former group—including Harry Gottlieb, Harry Sternberg, and Don Freeman (cats. 48, 35, 38)—focused on the traditions and contributions of the Art Students League. Their convictions demanded an art intelligible to the widest possible audience, from the highly sophisticated to the culturally impoverished. Usually working in a realistic manner, they favored themes that commented on social problems.

By contrast, the Abstractionist preferred an aesthetic and psychological visual experience. Stuart Davis, Eugene Morley, Theodore Roszak (cats. 88, 46, 33), and many others were convinced of the abilities inherent in balanced color and form to produce experiences that enhanced life. In his introduction to the catalogue of Harari's exhibition at the Mercury Galleries in New York in 1939, Davis extolled the moral, political, and aesthetic virtues of abstract art.[1]

Like many of his colleagues, Harari was drawn to printmaking in the 1930s by a mixture of practical and ideological concerns. He sought a medium that would allow him to create colorful and alluring original works of art that would be affordable by a broad segment of the public. Many abstract artists hoped in this manner to educate and expand their audience, as well as to generate much-needed income during the depression. Although such prints were made to sell for under ten dollars, a constrained system of distribution found few collectors. Even when hope of selling his prints had faded, Harari remained fascinated by printmaking processes and by the notion of multiple originals.

The first prints Harari made in the FAP silkscreen unit in 1938 were *City Signs* and *Weather Contraptions*, serigraphs derived from contemporaneous paintings and printed in signed and numbered editions. *Carnival*, based on his visits to Coney Island on summer nights, followed in 1939. Gaudy electric lights whirling against the night sky heightened the mystery of this magical place for Harari. In order to create this flashing effect, the artist juxtaposed flat black passages against the keen white of the paper itself, creating a playful, pleasing image. Loopy forms imitate the sinuous track of the roller coaster and the motion of the carousel horses. Flickering parti-colored lights, festive hats, and even the ticket taker's displaced smile are meant to amuse, as are the echoes of the star motif in the Ferris wheel, the spidery hands of the revelers, and the tassel on one figure's hat.

Harari prepared the screens for this print in a straightforward manner, using tusche and glue. His somber colors are unusual for an FAP work made at this time, as is his use of transparent layers of ink rather than flat, opaque passages. The artist pushed inks in thin glazes through the very fine fabric mesh, and overprinted just a few colors in order to achieve different hues, as in the central green forms of the ticket booth.

Notes

1. Reviews for this show can be found in *Art Digest* 1939a, p. 11, and Lowe 1939.

Carnival   Harari 39

Russell T. Limbach

1904–1971

45.
Forest
1939
Lithograph on cream wove paper
40.5 × 30.4 cm. (image)
58.2 × 38.9 cm. (sheet)
In pencil, lower margin: *Forest*
Limbach
Watermark: *RIVES BFK*
Worcester Art Museum, anonymous
gift, 1988.115

As organizer, technical adviser, and a leading printmaker of the FAP workshop, Russell Theodore ("Butch") Limbach introduced color lithography to a number of American artists in the 1930s. His competence as a technician did much to establish the high technical standards early in the history of the graphic arts division of the project, and this goal of excellence was subsequently passed on to generations of students during his teaching career.

Although Limbach has been primarily identified with the fervent political art of New York in the 1930s, a more accurate reflection of his artistic personality can be found in his later nature imagery. Beginning in the late 1930s, he filled many sketchbooks with landscape and nature studies. Unfailingly intrigued by trees, he rendered them in a distinctive personal style, and they became the primary features of most of his later prints. This fascination is most apparent in *American Trees*, a book for young adults, which Limbach wrote and illustrated, and which was published by Random House in 1942. Although the text combines biology and folksy woodcraft, images dominate the book. They range from evocative New England landscapes of changing seasonal foliage to instructive, detailed illustrations of bark, leaves, and seed pods.

Many charcoal studies of trees, from the artist's close observations of nature, are to be found in his archives. The sketches adapted for *American Trees* were refined in the studio into finished charcoal, crayon, or watercolor maquettes that took into account calculations for page design. Many of the illustrations were photomechanically reproduced directly

from these drawings, but Limbach himself made the lithographs for the major color illustrations of the book. Several of these prints were exhibited at the Smithsonian Institution in 1947.

Although it predates the book project by two years, the present lithograph parallels the imagery, style, and even the process of creation of *American Trees*. The original preparatory watercolor for this print is now in the Davison Art Center at Wesleyan University, in Middletown, Connecticut.[1] Rendered in greens, browns, and black, it is slightly smaller, freer, and less detailed than the crayon version of the composition that the artist drew on the lithographic stone. Although the color impressions of this print are titled *Forest*, a black ink impression of the key stone at Wesleyan is titled *Aiken's Woods*, suggesting that the artist made his watercolor in a specific place.

In this print, two great trees stand at the edge of a wood like sentinels. The denuded trunk of the dead tree on the left seems dry, hollow, and spent in the glaring sunlight, in contrast to the curling branches and burly, shaded bark of its flourishing companion. The effects of dappled light, filtering through the lofty foliage and the cool quiet of the shadowy forest beyond, are at once fascinating and forbidding. This five-color lithograph was drawn with fine crayons, occasionally supplemented with brushed-on tusche.[2] Ink was scraped from the stone in many places to approximate the effect of dappled sunlight. A set of fourteen proofs is extant;[3] presumably printed for demonstration, the set comprises an impression in black ink for each of the color separations, and progressive proofs that added each color, beginning with yellow and ending with the key stone, which was printed in gray. Very complicated overlays were exactingly calculated, and the registration perfectly achieved with T marks in the top and bottom margins. The effects of a

variety of lithographic techniques were blended together in order to create an even overall texture that would be unobtrusive to the subject. This virtuosity of draftsmanship and printmaking technique is characteristic of all of Limbach's color lithographs.

In order to demonstrate the capabilities and varied effects of lithography to students, the artist began an extensive series of didactic prints in 1946. The so-called Litho Book consists of nearly one hundred numbered vignettes, each exemplifying a different technical effect of the medium.[4] Other prints in this series graphically reveal how nineteenth-century and contemporary masters of lithography made their prints, contrasting a swatch of characteristic crayon or brush work with a detail copied from a famous lithograph.

Notes

1. Accession no. 1985.1.276, 40.1 × 31.9 cm. (sheet).

2. One impression at the Davison Art Center was inscribed on the verso by the artist with the colors to be used in printing: "sage green, yellow (cold), light brown, blue, gray."

3. Accession nos. 1985.1.277 (1–14), each about 58.0 × 40.0 cm. (sheet).

4. The name "Litho Book" was given to these prints by Jane Bothell, who arranged the archive of Limbach prints at Wesleyan in 1983. Although unaccessioned, this material remains in the collection of the Davison Art Center. Also in this group is a deceptively accurate copy of a lithograph by Toulouse-Lautrec.

Forest   Limbach

Eugene Morley

1909–1953

46.

Execution

1939

Serigraph on cream wove paper

29.4 × 56.2 cm. (image)

39.5 × 41.9 cm. (sheet)

In screen, upper right: *E. Morley*

In screen, upper-right margin: *cut mat to these lines*

In pencil, lower margin: *Execution E. Morley 11 colors*

Watermark: *NAVARRE*

Private collection

After the close of the Federal Arts Project, many artists drifted away from the studio and into more practical careers in commercial art and design, Eugene Morley among them; thus his activity in printmaking was brief. This is unfortunate, for in his six years in the FAP workshops, he created Abstract Surrealist prints that were technically excellent and stylistically progressive. As a workshop technician, Morley assisted in the production of color lithographs under Russell Limbach (cat. 45), and his own color screen prints have long been recognized as outstanding among the first fine art serigraphs.

Before the establishment of the silkscreen unit in the FAP graphic arts division, Morley was one of the committee from the Artists Union initially assigned to learn the process of serigraphy from Anthony Velonis (cat. 42) in 1938. Morley created a pair of screen prints each in a different abstract style, of which *Execution* was the second. He was the only artist in that first group who worked in an abstract or Surrealist manner, and his two prints also stand out for their technical daring. Morley and his prints were favored by Velonis and

Carl Zigrosser,[1] and an impression of this print was included in the ground-breaking show of 1940 at the Springfield Museum of Fine Arts in Massachusetts—the first group exhibition of screen prints.

In his first serigraph, *Harlem Landscape*, Morley used abstraction to reflect on the urban environment and to suggest something of its inhumanity. However, in the more surrealistic *Execution*, the artist aimed inward at a more universal, subconscious vision. An artfully composed abstraction, well balanced in its range of forms, colors, and textures, this print masks a theme of inescapable menace. Morley achieved an intentional ambiguity as to whether the viewer is merely a fascinated witness to the upcoming execution or rather its victim. A rough, immovable window, reminiscent of concrete, frames and confines this brooding image. Beyond a gloomy envelope of interior space the sun shines through prison bars, before which a scaffold is raised above a staircase. The executioner is a brawny, faceless character, his limbs spread in a symbolic manner. Also iconic, his axe has a blunt, blood-red tip matched in hue by the eerie, bifurcated form, perhaps symbolizing a severed head, that hovers over the scaffold.

A pencil inscription states that eleven colors were used, making this one of the most complex prints by the initial FAP group. Morley superimposed three shades of blue in order to create a deep, moody interior. The garish, interstitial accents are similar to the colors in screen prints by Velonis and Joseph Vogel (cat. 43); these drab, sickly hues emphasize the oppressive mood.

The screens for Morley's print were prepared mostly using the tusche and glue process. The technique of texturing frottage with litho crayon was used only for the frame, where grainy black overprinted gray. Some accent colors were printed from screens masked with cut stencil film. An extraordinary scored effect was achieved in the central gray form of the scaffold. Apparently this was first painted onto the screen in tusche, and the striations were then created by lifting the wet ink off the screen, perhaps with the edge of a blotter. Soft, uneven lines were thus left in the tusche, allowing the glue to seep through unevenly into the screen. Oil-base inks were probably supplemented by oil paint to broaden and vary the palette.

Notes

1. Velonis 1987, p. 74; Zigrosser 1941b, p. 460; Zigrosser 1974, p. 94, fig. 640. See also Michigan 1985, pp. 128–129; O'Connor 1972, p. 168; O'Connor 1973, pp. 70, 140.

Execution   E. Morley

Richard Floethe

1901–1988

47.

Polo Still Life

1941

Serigraph on white wove paper

28.3 × 40.2 cm. (image)

32.3 × 48.2 cm. (sheet)

In pencil, lower margin: *39/40*

"Polo Stillife"   Richard Floethe 41

Worcester Art Museum, Helen Sagoff Slosberg Fund, 1988.211

As head of the Federal Arts Project poster division from 1936 to 1939, Richard Floethe exerted subtle, encouraging influences on the development of color serigraphy in the United States. As an administrator, he set a tone of excellence in design and technique, and he inculcated a personal conviction that a graphic design was an artistic creation. His taste steered the output of the project, thus providing an aesthetic foundation that was later perpetuated in the FAP silkscreen unit.

Floethe's work seems sharply divided between the striking, stylized designs of his WPA posters and the prosaic, often saccharine style of his book illustrations. For his deft, elegant poster designs, he favored the typeface *Stencil*, which had been created by Josef Albers at the Bauhaus. Floethe preferred soft, pastel colors and a peculiar interstitial palette, and his flat, decorative, localized areas of color were well suited to serigraphy.

The artist worked in a wide range of graphic media, including woodcut, linocut, and serigraphy. He seems to have begun making serigraphs in 1938, and he continued to produce prints occasionally through the 1940s. Many of the artist's screen prints reflect his interest in horses and equestrian sports. Scenes of fox hunting, the racetrack, driving, and coaching figure among his works, along with several scenes of the polo turf, including *Polo Player* (1938), *Polo Ponies* (1939), and the present print.[1] These suggest that he made prints for his own pleasure rather than merely for profit.

The workmanship of Floethe's serigraphs of the 1940s, including that of the present work, indicates his position at the forefront of screen print technology. The grainy texture, which allows much of the paper to show through, simulates the effect of a crayon on nubbly paper, or the surface of a lithographic stone. The artist achieved this look in the preparation of the screen itself. He used a waxy lithographic crayon to draw directly on the fabric screen, beneath which he had placed a coarse sandpaper, the uneven surface of which was transferred to the silk.

This distilled composition, made of forms stacked up from background to foreground, complements the silkscreen process of overprinting layers of ink. The artist stylized the component shapes by softening their outlines and isolating them with color and modeling. He then accented these generalized forms with details, such as the button atop the polo helmet. Floethe's simplification and balance of form and color force the image to function as an abstraction.

Notes

1. For a partial list of Floethe's serigraphs, see Williams 1986, p. 302. See also De-Noon 1987, pp. 9, 25, 56–57, 73–74, 79, 171; Zigrosser 1941b, p. 447.

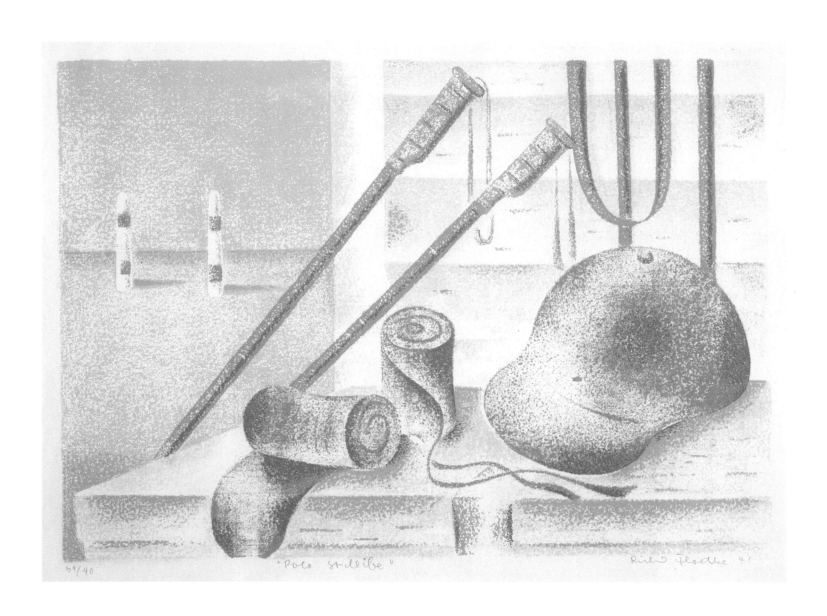

"Polo Stilleben" Richard Floethe 41

Harry Gottlieb

1895–

48.

The Factory

about 1940

Serigraph on cream wove paper

33.0 × 40.7 cm. (image)

41.5 × 53.3 cm. (sheet)

In red crayon, lower right: *Harry Gottlieb*

Worcester Art Museum, anonymous gift, 1988.104

A Social Realist painter and printmaker and a prominent political activist in the 1930s, Harry Gottlieb was among the first to learn the process of serigraphy in the FAP. The medium was particularly suited to the artist's personality and needs, and he continued to make color serigraphs through the mid–1970s. Thus, along with his lifelong friend Elizabeth Olds, Gottlieb was one of a mere handful of serigraphers in the 1930s who maintained their interest and activity in color prints throughout their careers.

From the outset, Gottlieb appreciated the technique of serigraphy for its ease and economy. Inexpensive materials and products offered the exhilarating potential for an easily disseminated, democratic art. Furthermore, the serigraphed image, just like the painted one, could be modified throughout the process, and because the image was not reversed during printing, Gottlieb found it easy to work out his designs in detailed color gouache studies before transferring them to the screen. He could prepare separate studies for single figures and then transfer them to the screen in mid-process. Like Shoulberg, Shokler, and other printmakers in the National Serigraph Society, Gottlieb experimented with simulating the effects of oil painting, perhaps most successfully in his eleven-color print *Winter on the Creek* of 1940. In that serigraph, he combined the painterly effects of tusche applied with a brush, varied transparencies of ink, and several layers of glaze and opaque color.

The present image represents a riverside factory, perhaps a steel mill that the artist saw on his trip to Pennsylvania in 1937, in thunderous production. Although today's viewers may consider an industrial plant ugly, dehumanizing, and environmentally threatening, to Gottlieb and the depression-era Social Realists, a working factory was a thing of potential and awesome beauty.[1] The artist depicted similar industrial Pennsylvanian landscapes in several other prints, including the lithograph *Pittsburgh at Night* (1937) and the serigraph *Steel Town Panorama* (1941).

At night the mill becomes an inferno, eerily illuminated and spouting flames and smoke. The artist tried to suggest the noise, stench, and scale of the place, aspects that rival even the power of nature. Unlike humankind's other technological achievements, this plant has in its productivity an organic, almost biological character, which is suggested by the absence of human figures. To the political Gottlieb, the factory symbolized both the good and the bad aspects of technological and social achievement; it represented productivity, progress, and prosperity for the individual and for society, yet it also stood for the control of these prospects by a chosen few.

Gottlieb thickly layered a variety of effects in this print, creating a complex, sometimes muddy appearance. The artist prepared the screens chiefly with the tusche and glue process, with various texturized overlays. He used stencils for large blocks of color, and superimposed them using screens with bold, spontaneous brush lines in tusche. Gottlieb drew prominent crayon textures against the patterned surface of ross board; these stippled lines create the effect of crosshatching, subtly modeling the forms. The screen that printed the aquamarine passage in the upper center seems to have been offset from the texture of a laid paper.

Notes

1. This perspective is reflected in the artist's statement (Conkelton/Gilbert 1983, p. 22) that the rural landscape of Kingston, New York, was interesting for its coal barges and slaughterhouses. Harry Sternberg (cat. 35) expressed a similar outlook in relation to his lithographs of steel mills; see Moore 1975, nos. 147–149. See also Francey 1988, pp. 38, 39, 73; Williams 1987, pp. 11, 65; Zigrosser 1941b, pp. 455, 460, 462.

Edward Landon

1911–1984

49.
Counterpoint

1942
Serigraph on cream laid paper
31.1 × 32.6 cm. (image)
38.0 × 44.3 cm. (sheet)
In pencil, lower margin:
Counterpoint   Edition 25
E. Landon
Watermark: *Hamilton Andorra*
Private collection

A prodigious serigrapher in the 1940s, Edward Landon made prints that were characterized by high technical quality and stylistic simplicity. Working within the printmaking establishment he sought to raise the standards of the method with the quiet presence of his aesthetically sophisticated and technically uncluttered silkscreens.

Although Landon's early screen prints utilized many colors and overprintings, the artist gradually simplified his technique, restricting his use of the medium to what he thought it did best. Many serigraphers sought technical complexity at the cost of visual clarity and harmony, but Landon came to prefer well-defined, solidly printed areas with minimal texture. By using just a few transparent colors and carefully planning their superimposition, he could achieve sufficient breadth of

color while avoiding the muddiness of surface complexity. "The colors most difficult in painting," he said, "namely green and brown, are exceptionally easy to produce using only primary colors in printing. They have a clarity and depth completely lacking in the pre-mixed opaque greens and browns. Texturing effects should be employed in transparent color printing solely for the purpose of creating additional color."[1] Landon advocated the use of a maximum of three colors, along with black and transparent grays to achieve a range of values.

In *Counterpoint*, these restrictions seem to aim at a simple harmony that is parallel to the balance of forms. White paper offsets the opaque black forms, and against this balance the green and red are almost complementary, thus achieving the opposition implied by the title. With several areas of overprinting, Landon achieved darkened interstitial hues. He prepared the screens for this print with meticulously cut Profilm, which gave sharp edges to the forms. Coarse fabric with a comparatively broad weave lent an open, crosshatched quality to the superimposed, transparent mauve-brown screen.

When Landon returned to New York in 1941, he began a series of stylistic explorations in his prints. The exposure to many styles must have been greatly stimulating to an artist of such catholic tastes. Several of his prints of the 1940s explore the themes of color, music, and dance. Elements both of the abstract surrealism of the School of Paris and of

European modernism appear in many of Landon's serigraphs of this period, and his works of the 1950s show the influences of Scandinavian design and mystical runic calligraphy. The artist's chief models for *Counterpoint* were the works of New York modernists who were associated with the Abstract American Artists group, such painters as Burgoyne Diller and Carl Holty. In this composition, Landon emulated Holty's active, rhythmic curved forms; his limited depth, implied by overlapping forms; and his structural harmony.

Notes

1. Shokler 1946, pp. 66–68, 156. See also Heller 1958, pp. 201, 221, fig. IV–13; Kaye 1977; Williams 1987, p. 67, figs. 22, 28.

Counterpoint   Edition 25   E. Landon

Fletcher Martin

1904–1979

50.

Out at Home

1942

Serigraph on cream wove paper

23.6 × 16.5 cm. (image)

31.8 × 23.5 cm. (sheet)

In screen, lower left: *Fletcher Martin 42*

Worcester Art Museum, anonymous gift, 1988.107

One of the most popular American artists in the 1940s and 1950s, Fletcher Martin was appreciated from the rarefied aesthetic circles of New York to the suburban living rooms of Middle America. Developing from the Social Realism of the 1930s, Martin's paintings transformed the stylized distortions of modernism into an accessible, personal style. Also a teacher, the artist worked as a printmaker in several media. The mature Martin sought to capture the viewer with a spark of energy and to hold the attention through stylistic appeal. Intellectual challenge became less important to his art than the pleasant visual experience.

In the 1940s, Martin began leaning toward pleasing imagery and away from the provocative and morally challenging. He turned from the figural distortions of Social Realism and Regionalism, toward lyrical images and an angular, stocky figure style developed ultimately from his contact with David Alfaro Siqueiros. From the Mexican muralist Martin also learned to represent his own experiences, to strive to capture

that enlivening spark. He tried to recreate his most impressive visual memories and to communicate the energy that made them memorable.

Out at Home is an adaptation of Martin's oil painting of 1940.[1] Similar to the painting in size, the print is slightly more oblong in format, and it differs considerably in composition. In the canvas, the umpire is behind the runner, and the official's arm raised for the "out" call echoes the gesture of the player's arm. The arms of this sliding figure are also in different positions than in the painting, in which Martin broke up the background with the grid of a net backstop. He repeated in the print the dabs of local color that model the figures in the painting.

The artist made this screen print in Kansas City while he was teaching at the Art Institute, and he may well have produced it at this school. Its sporting subject may have been appropriate to the Midwestern art market. The subdued palette and thick application of opaque oil color suggest that Martin may have used an oil-base house paint. The screens were prepared with a straightforward tusche and glue washout process, which the artist varied only by adding a spatter representing the white billows of dust and by modeling the players' uniforms. The opaque, saturated colors and daubed, painterly effect of this print are very similar in quality to Guy Maccoy's serigraph technique (cat. 53).[2]

Out at Home mirrors the artist's manner of developing and repeating patterns over the surface of a painting, an inclination that became dominant in his work of the 1950s. Here, in experimenting with a medium that encouraged such simplification and formulation, Martin chose to render his subject with an almost impressionistic patterning of strokes. This oversize print achieved its success in the vibrancy of its active texture, which resembles brush strokes.

Notes

1. This painting was included in Martin's first solo exhibition in New York at the Midtown Galleries in 1940 (*Art Digest* 1940) and has recently been on the art market (Lublin 1989, pp. 104–105; also Cooke 1977, fig. 40).

2. A graduate of the Kansas City Art Institute, Maccoy made many friends there, including Martin's predecessor Thomas Hart Benton. Maccoy may have visited Kansas City during his travels in 1939 and 1940, and may have taught serigraphy to Martin, or even printed this serigraph for him. See also Ebersole 1954.

Thomas Arthur Robertson

1911–1976

51.
The Orange Point

1941
Serigraph on cream laid paper
26.8 × 18.8 cm. (image)
33.1 × 31.9 cm. (sheet)
In pencil, lower margin: *The Orange Point Ed/54 Tom A. Robertson*
Watermark: *albion laid*
Worcester Art Museum, Anonymous Fund, 1989.8

The dispersion and adaptability of serigraphy are exemplified in the work of Thomas Arthur Robertson, who, working in relative isolation, produced a remarkable group of screen prints in the 1940s. Although this Southern artist was chiefly a painter, his prints resemble his watercolors in style and palette.

Although he seems to have learned the technique of serigraphy in New Orleans, Robertson did not begin to concentrate on his own prints until about 1940, after his return to Little Rock. His first screen print, *Union*, reproduced a painting included in his second solo exhibition at the Delgado Museum. Very quickly, however, the artist's prints became independent works, stylistically related to his small-scale, abstract watercolors. The present work was one of four serigraphs shown in the fifteenth annual membership exhibition of the New Orleans Art League late in 1941.[1] A few months later, the artist presented lecture-demonstrations on silkscreen technique, advocating prints as affordable, original works of art.[2] Robertson may have been drawn to printmaking in search of a broader market for his work, but the fact that many of his prints have only recently come to light, with their editions nearly intact, suggests that sales were disappointing.

The artist employed simple technical means to achieve interesting spatial and coloristic effects in this print, modeling the surface of the yellow field with several colors rather than placing forms before it. The design is primarily linear, however, and the surface contours do not circumscribe forms but instead define ridges, like crests of hills on a topographical chart. The modeling on both sides of these contour lines create spatial ambiguity, the swirling curves reminiscent of markings on a weather map. Robertson looked to Native American art for decorative motifs that bore no recognizable meaning. He derived the arcs, floating circles, serpentine slashes, and meandering lines of his designs of the 1940s from the decoration of pottery made by the ancient Caddoan Indians of southwestern Arkansas.

Despite the apparent simplicity of Robertson's prints, they were very carefully made from high-quality materials. He used bright, opaque colors, and made no attempt to broaden his tonal range by overlapping them. This image was printed in seven colors from as many screens, each prepared by drawing with a litho crayon against a coarse, texturizing surface, perhaps sandpaper. The creamy color of the sheet was part of the design, and the brighter white accents were printed. A grainy void in the center, where the paper peeks through the yellow field, shows that even the screen for this ground was drawn with a crayon.

Notes

1. Robertson's other serigraphs in this exhibition were *Sweet Boy*, *The New Apprentice*, and *Little Willie*.

2. Little Rock 1942.

The Orange Point   Ed / 54   Tom A. Robertson

Hugo Gellert

1892–1985

52.

Modern Science For All

from *Century of the Common Man*,
1943
Serigraph on cream laid paper
38.0 × 33.2 cm. (image)
50.6 × 81.4 cm. (sheet)
Stamped in ink, lower margin:
HUGO/GELLERT
Private collection

Despite his avowed loyalty to the ideals of communism, Hugo Gellert was an American patriot. This became apparent during World War II, when he turned his talents—often used to criticize capitalist society and political convention—to the war effort. Gellert was a prominent member of the Artists for Defense, an organization that in 1942, with the addition of many members of the National Academy of Design, became known as Artists for Victory.[1] For their work in producing war posters, this group was specially commended by Senator Robert Wagner of New York in 1943. In that year, Gellert also produced the portfolio *Century of the Common Man*, an album of nineteen serigraphs that accompanied the text of two speeches by Vice President Henry A. Wallace. This series included images of interracial and interclass harmony, the heroism of American soldiers, anti-Nazi and anti-Axis allegories, and a portrait of President Franklin D. Roosevelt surmounting symbols of the "four freedoms."[2]

Modern Science For All was conceived to complement Wallace's words on the place of science and industry in the twentieth century: "Everywhere the common man must learn to build his own industries with his own hands in practical fashion. . . . Modern science, when devoted wholeheartedly to the general welfare, has in its potentialities of which we do not yet dream."[3] The valiant worker pictured in classical profile is characteristic of Gellert's heroic figure style, a synthesis of widely disparate elements. From the works of American illustrators of the turn of the century, he derived a stocky, handsome figure type, virile men and confident women who were unrealistically attractive. Many artists exploited this classicizing type

between 1910 and 1945, a period during which accessible, uncomplicated, and inspirational art was used to support various political points of view. Elements of the style are apparent in the art of Nazi Germany, Fascist Italy, and Stalinist Russia—and even in the capitalist propaganda of Paul Manship.

Gellert enhanced his figure style with an able facility for design that revealed his knowledge of European poster design and Cubism and Russian Constructivism. From German Expressionist artists, who had themselves reacted to the horror of World War I, Gellert took his unflinching, often violent imagery. Here, his proletarian hero wields the draftsman's pencil and T square rather than the sword and lance. Behind him hangs a blueprint showing his creations, symbols of the products of healthy industry: a child's shoe, a sheaf of wheat, and a light bulb. This characterization depicts the artist as a warrior of industry, a worker-hero.

Gellert was less comfortable with serigraphy than with lithography, a process familiar to him from his work on newspapers and posters. He created three important portfolios of lithographs, *Karl Marx's "Capital" in Lithographs* (1933), *Comrade Gulliver* (1934), and *Aesop Said So* (1936). The use of the litho crayon also dominated the serigraphs of *Century of the Common Man*, for which the artist drew boldly against a rough, texturizing surface, perhaps sandpaper, laid beneath the silkscreen. He used glue to draw the white lines behind the figure on the screen to create the white line drawing of the blueprint. Most of the blocks of local color were set on the screens with cut film. Practical matters partially determined the bright, arbitrary colors and arresting graphic boldness of this print; Gellert used a limited palette throughout the series, perhaps in an effort to contain the cost.

Century of the Common Man was republished by the International Workers Order in a reduced version, a booklet issued as a contribution to the war effort that carried translations of Wallace's text into fifteen languages.

Throughout his career, Gellert's art was met with criticism that often sprang from opposition to his politics.[4] His prints were meant to inflame passions, and whether or not the viewer sympathizes with him, he was certainly an artist convinced of the role of printmaking in social change.

Notes

1. In 1943, Artists for Victory organized the remarkable print exhibition "America and the War." Exploiting the multiple originals of several printmaking media, this show was simultaneously on view at twenty-six museums across the country. See Arms 1943.

2. All of the images from the *Century of the Common Man* are reproduced in Ryan/Kisseloff 1986, pp. 28–32.

3. Excerpt from the quote from Henry Wallace's speech that was printed as a caption to this screen print in the portfolio.

4. See the critical review of Gellert's illustrated edition of Marx's *Das Kapital* (*Prints* 1934), and its comments on the stifling of art by Russian mobocracy. Also see the disagreements in print over the "Call to Action" (Gellert/Clough 1935, p. 15).

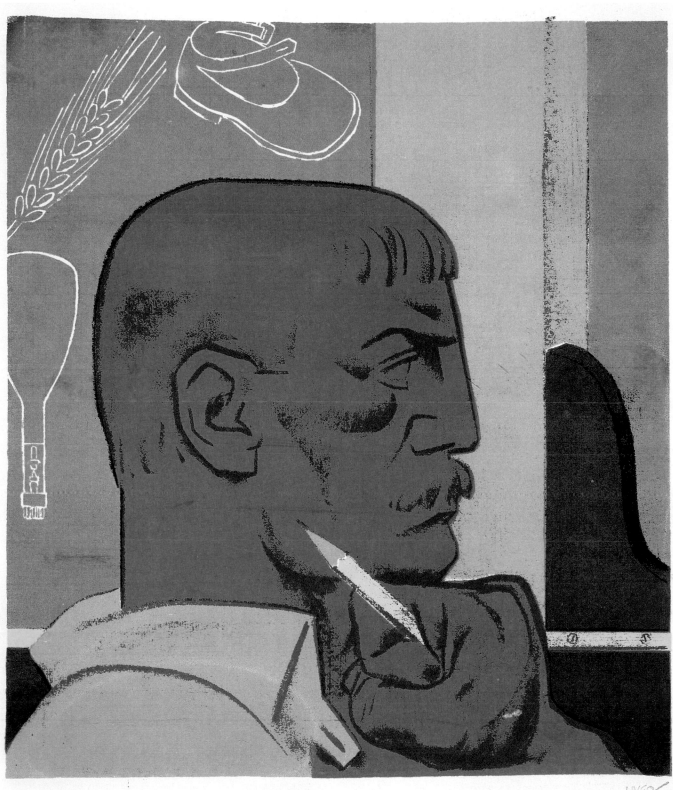

Guy Maccoy

1904–1981

53.

Green Fruit

1943

Serigraph on cream wove paper

27.9 × 35.5 cm. (image)

31.8 × 40.7 cm. (sheet)

In pencil, lower margin: *"GREEN FRUIT" GUY MACCOY 43*

Worcester Art Museum, anonymous gift, 1988.108

Credit for the first use of the commercial process of silkscreen printing as a medium for limited edition artists' prints must be given to the independent and widely admired artist Guy Maccoy. His experiments introduced the most originative American technique for making color prints in the 1930s and 1940s. This development, combined with Maccoy's initiative, determined his direction as an artist.

This print exemplifies Maccoy's technical mastery, his modernist style, and his abilities as a colorist. Like all of his prints, it reveals a debt to Jan Matulka, who exerted the most potent influence on the artist's mature style. Flattened forms and attention to decorative patterns were characteristic of this European modernism,

yet Maccoy always avoided the bright colors of the Fauves in favor of a narrow, muted color scheme. Like Matulka, he was never able to abandon himself to nonobjective abstraction. Rather, he preferred to use still life or landscape as a recognizable point of departure, abstracting his subjects by geometrizing interlocking forms, juxtaposing flat passages against a variety of patterns.

Maccoy's prints exploited the capability of the medium to produce flat, opaque layers of color. Although in the 1930s the artist was drawn to the gouache-like, matte effect of show-card ink, in later prints, such as *Green Fruit*, he used an opaque, shiny oil surface. His painterly manner perhaps related to the work of screen print artists such as Shoulberg and Shokler who looked to serigraphy as a means of producing prints with the look and texture of oil paintings.

Maccoy favored straightforward preparation of the screen with tusche and glue. He seldom resorted to the use of litho crayon or film, and usually achieved the dotted passages in his prints by stippling with the brush. Refinement of this simple method came with a compulsion to use more and more layers of carefully plotted colors.

The artist probably planned the color separations for this print on a stack of transparent celluloid sheets, each painted with a different color.[1] This method allowed for fine adjustments and facilitated the precise

transfer of the design to the screens. Later, after years of working as a color separator in the printing industry, Maccoy developed such an attuned sense of color that he was able to perform separating calculations in his head, a proclivity that astounded other artists.[2] In planning a color scheme, the artist established a basic set of four or five hues, which he then multiplied by lightening them with a medium extender or by tinting them slightly with a small amount of oil paint. Usually the finished print contained ten to fifteen colors, printed from as many screens. Maccoy's abilities as a colorist and his balances of transparency are what distinguish the elegant, personal style of his serigraphs, which he maintained throughout his career.

Notes

1. See Shokler 1946, p. 67.

2. Whitaker 1974, p. 60. See also Williams 1987, pp. 9, 13, 67.

Harry Bertoia

1915–1978

54.
Untitled
about 1943
Monotype on thin white wove paper
21.5 × 29.7 cm. (image)
21.5 × 27.9 cm. (sheet)
Watermark: *FULLERS FALLS*
ONION SKIN   RAG CONTENT
Worcester Art Museum, anonymous
gift, 1988.67

Best known as a designer of furniture and a sculptor, Harry Bertoia was also a creative and prolific printmaker. Preferring the medium of monotype, he made prints continuously throughout his career, always searching for new visual effects from this simple process. The artist made prints for relaxation in his leisure time, and the process itself became his means for developing new design ideas and motifs. The center of Bertoia's creative activity, monotypes were the ultimate source for all his work.

In imagery, style, and technique, this monotype is characteristic of Bertoia's prints of the early 1940s, made soon after his arrival in Los Angeles. Long in the possession of a New York dealer, the present work is one from a series that are similar in style and printed in the same colors on the same paper. It is likely one of many prints sent by the artist to the Nierendorf Gallery in New York in the early 1940s.

Characteristic of these early California prints were floating planes, forms, and lines, that hovered in an expansive, ambiguous void. In his exhibition of monoprints at Cranbrook Academy in Bloomfield Hills, Michigan, in 1943, Bertoia's prints were sandwiched between two sheets of glass in copper frames, meant to be hung in a window so that light could filter through the thin Asian papers on which they were printed.[1] The transmitted light enhanced colors, emphasized the illusion of depth suggested by overlapping forms, and created lighting effects implied in the shading of what seemed to be open space. The result was the sensation that forms and lines seemed to float, like sculpture, in three-dimensional space.

The component forms of the present image seem planar. While the rectilinear forms appear static and fixed, the ovoid shapes seem to move in a silent ballet, intersecting in three dimensions. Linear fancies were a recurrent motive in Bertoia's graphics. There is a fascinating variety to the hovering lines in this image. All of them—lines with knotted ends, the fine, threadlike lines that circumscribe ovoid shapes, hirsute curving ones, and radiating straight lines—were reflected directly in his sculpture. All suggest movement of different quality and speed. They beg for analogy to natural phenomena, such as the feverish activity of microscopic organisms or the slow, rhythmic sway of undersea plants. However, their combination and spatial relationships deny identification. What remains is an abstract, cosmic lyricism.

Ease and immediacy were important to Bertoia in the creation of his monotypes. He called his technique "rapid drawing" and produced many monotypes in quick succession, counting on intuition and momentary inspiration. All of the lines and forms in these monotypes were printed, not applied to the surface of the artwork by hand. The artist used conventional monotype techniques. First he created his image in printer's ink on a smooth plate of glass or hard-surfaced masonite, usually spreading the ink with a brayer. Then a sheet of paper was placed on the plate, and the image was transferred to the sheet by pressure on the verso from a soft roller, or the artist's hands. Although Bertoia preferred hard-surfaced papers, they show no

signs of having been rubbed on the back with a hard implement like a wooden spoon. The ink lays on the surface of Bertoia's prints, indicating that the artist printed on dry paper.

Subtle-toned gradations were achieved with the brayer, which spread a progressively thinning layer of ink across the monotype plate. The hard-edge forms of this print seem to have been produced by rolling the brayer over a masking material, probably a sheet of paper, which protected the plate from ink. The intersecting, central floating forms—shaped like a bifurcated palette, complete with thumb hole—seem to have been rolled onto the plate through two stencils. The brayer's edges, and unevenness caused by its rolling action, are still discernible. Tiny specks of white resulted from grains of sand or other debris, which prevented the flexible rubber surface of the brayer from touching the plate.

All of the lines in this monotype were printed over the forms. The artist routinely executed these by placing his partially printed sheet facedown on an inked plate and drawing lightly on the verso to pick up ink. Bertoia used a variety of tools—including a rounded metal stylus, various balsa-wood sticks, and maybe the edge of a palette knife—to achieve lines of ranging quality.[2] Magnification reveals that these lines either have a grainy appearance determined by the surface texture of the paper, or they are comprised of two fine lines of ink surrounding a furrow, marking the point of pressure of the drawing tool. Because the artist used translucent paper, he could control the placement of his drawn lines from the verso of the sheet. This monotype is printed on a sheet of thin typing paper of weight and translucency similar to those of Japan papers that Bertoia also used. The use of this material underscores Bertoia's orientation to speed, expediency, and volume in his monotypes of this period.

Notes

1. Nelson 1988, p. 24.

2. Ibid., p. 34. See also Nelson 1970.

Werner Drewes

1899–1985

55.
The Jealous Cock

1944
Woodcut and linocut on cream Japan paper
29.0 × 46.0 cm. (image)
34.8 × 61.3 cm. (sheet)
In pencil, below image: *13/xx*
Drewes 44   Werner Drewes "Jealous Cock"
Rose 109
Worcester Art Museum, 1948.26

A prolific printmaker and painter, Werner Drewes brought the influences of the Bauhaus and German Expressionist printmaking directly to the modernists of Manhattan. His artistic versatility complemented a style that was broad yet consistent throughout sixty-five years of printmaking.

Working at Atelier 17 in 1944, Drewes's technical facility with the copperplate developed quickly, and he made his first color intaglio there. At that time Drewes also began to concentrate on color woodcuts, reprinting color variants of several earlier prints, among them *Northern Transitions* (Rose 110), *Curved Shapes* (Rose 112), and the present work. In this early group, the artist used transparent colors. As Drewes progressed, for a time he used many thick, opaque colors for his woodcuts, but in later prints he came back to the simplicity of fewer, more translucent hues. The artist concluded that the latter choice was more effective in this medium and allowed him to be closer to the materials of the process.[1]

Drewes cut the key block for *The Jealous Cock* in 1942, printing about fifteen impressions in black. Some of these are dated 1944, the year when he printed another edition of this work in different color variations, from the key and two additional blocks. Although he projected an edition of twenty impressions, he seems to have printed only about fifteen, several of which were partially hand-colored.

Drewes worked in New York when Louis Schanker, Adja Yunkers, and Seong Moy (cats. 41, 81, 74) were developing a taste and market for color woodcuts. Like these artists, Drewes printed woodcuts by hand, rubbing the back of a wetted sheet directly against the inked block with a wooden tool or, in order to capture the subtleties of the uneven grain, with his fingertips. This effect is apparent in *The Jealous Cock*, especially at the edges of the block.

The artist printed nearly all of his color woodcuts on soft Japan paper. After some experimentation, he came to prefer the unevenness, clarity, and softness of redwood for his blocks. He favored colored oil-base ink, which he occasionally supplemented with oil paint. In the present work, he applied the colors locally onto two blocks with his fingers or a sponge, softening and lightening the ink at the edges of forms. Using the burlap backing of a sheet of linoleum, he printed a layer of thin brown ink over the whole image. The color and texture of this overlaid pattern may remind the viewer of the fenced-in dust of the barnyard.

This image reflects the influence of Kandinsky in its use of radial arcs and hatchings, and in its placement of the abstract figure before a featureless background. The artist played with illusions of dimension and transparency in a web of lines and forms. The diaper pattern of multihued lozenges mimics the rooster's pinfeathers and their iridescent reflections.

The prominent egg seems to be the cause of the cock's jealousy. Green-eyed and gaudy, the rooster apparently sits on the egg as he crows and ruffles his feathers. The egg may even be inside the bird, implying a consuming envy of the hen and her maternal role. Feisty and possessive, the pompous cockerel is the victim of his foolish emotions.

Notes

1. Norelli 1984, p. 31.

13/XX   Drewes - 74 -

Benton Spruance

1904–1967

56.
Forward Pass, Football

1944
Lithograph on laminated white wove
paper
50.8 × 31.8 cm. (image)
59.0 × 39.3 cm. (sheet)
In pencil, lower margin: *Ed 35*
Forward Pass   Spruance '44 PBS
In red ink, lower right: artist's estate
stamp
Fine/Looney 231
Private collection

An eminent painter, teacher, and printmaker, Benton Spruance was one of the most important figures in Philadelphia art circles for nearly forty years. Although he experimented with etchings, woodcuts, and monotypes, his oeuvre of over five hundred lithographs, and his activities as a teacher of the history and techniques of the graphic arts were his great contributions to American printmaking. Late in the 1920s, Spruance was introduced to lithography by the French master printers. Over the next two decade, he produced many editions in collaboration with these craftsmen, and with master lithographer Theodore Cuno in Philadelphia.

During the first decade of his career as a professional artist, Spruance searched for a style and imagery to serve as a personal expression of the American experience. This pursuit was reflected in his social imagery and landscapes, intermingled with depictions of automobiles, airplanes, musical subjects, and especially of football. Spruance loved the game, and prints representing football were the basis of his early reputation.[1] His first football print, *Backfield* (1928; Fine/Looney 4), was made in Paris soon after the artist's initiation in lithography. Between that time and 1940, Spruance made at least twenty-five prints of football subjects. He tried to capture the power, speed, and agility of the players, and to express the excitement of the game in lithographs that were the most vigorous and dynamic of his prints. *Forward Pass* was his last football print, and one of his earliest complex color lithographs.

Spruance treated the theme of football pass receivers leaping over the goal line to grab an airborne ball in his lithograph *Design for America No. 2* (1935; Fine/Looney 118). In this print, the heavyset figures are twisted into a sinuous mass as they jostle one another for the catch. Their limbs radiate in a star-pattern toward the edges of the composition, expressing the burst of energy

of this moment of violent collision. By comparison, the figures in *Forward Pass* seem angular and slightly leaner, and their confrontation less furious. The apparent moderation of activity may result from the segmented cubist background of this image, more complex than that of the earlier print. Spruance used the setting of the shadowed playing field, the gridiron chalk lines, the striped goal posts, and the yard line and goal marker to subdivide the composition. However, by artfully overlapping these elements, the artist achieved a logical organization of this space. Even the five-yard line and goal marker signs were partially covered, to weaken the flattening effect of their typography. Spruance's dedication to the success of this composition prompted him to betray the realism of the image further, for he depicted players in jerseys of three different colors, contradicting the rules of this game that he knew so well.

This lithograph was printed in Philadelphia by Theodore Cuno. An immigrant from Germany, this experienced craftsman worked for the Ketterlinus Lithographic Manufacturing Company in the city, where he had printed for Joseph Pennell.[2] He lived with his married daughter in a row house in northwest Philadelphia, and on his own time, he printed privately for artists in a cramped basement workshop. A solitary character, Cuno seems to have been more comfortable as a contractor than as a collaborator. He preferred to work alone and was secretive about his methods. Nevertheless, Spruance's relationship with the printer was friendly and productive, and they worked together from about 1929 until after 1950.

The technique of *Forward Pass* was characteristic of Cuno's traditional work, for all the stones were prepared with crayon. Passages of tone were laid down by scribbling, not with systematic hatching, and an occasional highlight was created by scraping the ink from the stone. Comparisons of the color proofs for this print reveal that there was no key image; printed alone, none of the stones could represent the complete graphic design.[3] Therefore, precise registration was important to the print's success. Registration was achieved by pins, which pierced the sheet in the top and bottom margins, and fitted into holes in the stones, assuring correct placement of the paper.

Spruance did not inscribe his lithographs as they were printed, but signed them only as they were needed for exhibition or sale. After the artist's death, these prints were marked with the estate stamp in red ink, and signed and titled by the artist's wife W[inifred] G[lover] S[pruance], his son, S[tephen] G[lover] S[pruance], or, as in the present print, his elder son P[eter] B[enton] S[pruance].[4]

As the artist's understanding of the capabilities of lithography developed along with his style, Spruance felt the need for more creative independence in his prints. Building on his long experience, he studied and practiced the lithographic processes in 1950, until he had attained the expertise of a master printer. In 1953, he bought a press in France, which was shipped to Philadelphia and installed at Beaver College. There, until his death in 1967, Spruance printed most of his own lithographs. Working in the school studio, he developed his personal subtractive method for color lithography.[5]

Notes

1. Fine/Looney 1986.

2. Ibid., p. 10; Adams 1983, pp. 115–116.

3. Proofs from each stone for *Forward Pass* and other technical materials are in the Philadelphia Museum of Art.

4. Fine/Looney 1986, pp. 37–38.

5. Ibid., p. 17.

Ed 35   Forward Pass   Spruance '44
                                                                              P 05

Albert Urban

1909–1959

57.
Minnesong

1944
Serigraph on off-white wove paper
19.8 × 28.5 cm. (image)
24.7 × 35.5 cm. (sheet)
In blue ink, lower right: *Albert Urban 44*
Watermark: *Eagle Glendale*
Private Collection

Best known as a painter in the second generation of the New York School, Albert Urban was one of the few artists who used serigraphy for abstract modernist prints in the 1940s and 1950s. Although his screen prints parallel the stylistic development of his paintings, they always seem to have been independent creations. The size, scope, and innovative character of this artist's oeuvre of prints is only now beginning to be understood.

In the mid-1940s, Urban explored musical themes in his paintings and prints. Some of these works sought to relate the character of a specific instrument, and others expressed harmonies, rhythms, and musical dynamics through color, form, and design.[1]

The German title of this theatrical print literally means "love song." It refers to the minnesingers, the German counterparts of French medieval troubadours. These wandering minstrels and lyric poets, who flourished in the twelfth and thirteenth centuries, were the first composers and performers of secular music. Nearly always courtiers of noble birth, they most often wrote songs about courtly love. To modern audiences, the best-known minnesingers have become familiar through the dramas of Wagner. It is this sense of the term that Urban represented in his serigraph, which represents a dramatic scene from a grand opera, perhaps *Tannhäuser*.

Standing before a domed Romanesque building, alongside what is perhaps a bridged canal, the troubadour is dressed in a short tunic, holding his golden lyre. He seems to be engaged in a dramatic confrontation with a white, wraithlike figure before him. Between them there seems to be a funeral pyre, from which a spirit rises amid the flames. The minnesinger's leaning body draws him into the diagonal flames of the undulating fire, linking him to the ascending soul.

Minnesong is technically more complex than most of Urban's serigraphs, which were usually printed in two or three colors. The screens were prepared by the tusche-and-glue wash-out method, and they were printed in layers of oil-base inks that ranged in their thickness, viscosity, and saturation. From the verso of the print, one can see that the first screens to be printed carried linear images, which were hidden by many subsequent layers of ink. This overprinting suggests that the artist continued to develop his design as he worked, in a process similar to painting. The covered layers of ink left an account of the artist's process, and his changing ideas and expectations of this image. At the left edge of the print, where the squeegee ended its trip across the screen, minute bubbles—formed in the vigorous action of printing—burst, leaving miniature craters.

Notes

1. Breuning 1946. See also Reed 1944.

Sue Fuller

1914–

58.
Clown

1945
Aquatint with engraving on cream
laid paper
19.8 × 15.1 cm. (plate)
31.9 × 25.8 cm. (sheet)
In pencil, beneath image: *26/30*
Clown   Sue Fuller '45
Worcester Art Museum, anonymous
gift, 1988.95

Although Sue Fuller made prints for a relatively brief period, she did so in the volatile environment of Atelier 17 in the mid–1940s. The artist flourished in this context of innovation and experimentation, and before her interest shifted to sculpture, she made true technical contributions to intaglio printmaking.

Encouraged by the turbulent, creative atmosphere of Atelier 17 and motivated by her extensive studies of the prints of Mary Cassatt, (cat. 1), Fuller conducted her own printmaking experiments in the 1940s in her favored process, soft-ground etching. In 1945, she combined collage and printmaking, cutting out segments of a lace collar found among her mother's belongings, and pressing them into the soft-ground plate to create the ruffled pinfeathers of *The Hen*.

This inventiveness was also manifested in Fuller's development of "direct blacks aquatint," the widely used method now generally known as sugar lift.[1] Searching for a technique for applying additive rather than subtractive tone to the copperplate, the artist painted an image onto the aquatint-grounded plate with a simple suspension of sugar crystals—Karo syrup. She then covered the entire plate with stop-out varnish; when she immersed the plate in water, the crystalline granules dissolved, dislodging the coat of varnish on top of them. A finely stippled reflection of the brushed lines and forms was thus bitten into the plate. In *Clown*, the artist brushed the zebra-striped figure onto the plate using this method.

In a process similar to that of Stanley William Hayter's *Centauresse* of 1943, Fuller printed *Clown* from two plates. She laid the colors onto an unworked plate through stencils and printed this on the dampened paper; then she overprinted the carefully registered intaglio imagery in black form a separate plate. Although this lengthy process required care and precision, Fuller achieved bright, precise, clearly printed colors, in contrast to the transparent yet often muddy hues of the intaglios Hayter printed in one operation (cat. 60). The clarity of color depended on the use of lithographic or letterpress ink, for intaglio ink was too opaque and gritty, and its colors too unstable. Among the color intaglios made at Atelier 17 in the 1940s, Fuller's prints stand out for their intense, saturated colors.

Notes

1. Hayter 1949a, p. 93.

26/30   Clown   Sue Fuller '45

Robert Gwathmey

1903–1988

59.

Singing and Mending

1946

Serigraph on off-white wove paper

30.7 × 36.3 cm. (image)

38.8 × 47.4 cm. (sheet)

In black ink, lower left: *Gwathmey*

Worcester Art Museum, 1947.3

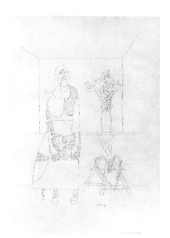

Robert Gwathmey, *Old Woman*, about 1946. Graphite. Worcester Art Museum, gift of Helen Sagoff Slosberg, 1972.1.

In his paintings and prints, Robert Gwathmey consistently maintained a distinctly personal style that grew out of the Social Realism of the 1930s. Although deeply felt social concerns are at the heart of these images, they also function on an aesthetic plane. Bright, flat colors arrest the viewer, and a harmony of two-dimensional forms sustains the pleasant and often provocative experience of Gwathmey's art.

In the mid-1930s, when he was living in Philadelphia, the artist began traveling to the South each summer; there the memories of a lyrical, pleasant childhood were mingled with an adult awareness of the miseries of racism and poverty. Gwathmey felt the presence of black sharecroppers, whose backbreaking, impoverished lives in the tobacco and cotton fields during the depression were as bad as they had been through generations of slavery. Gwathmey was moved by this culture born of adversity, which had been hidden from him in his youth, as well as by racial prejudices different from those he had known up north. His own style was transformed in the discovery of this poignant theme, and refined in the integration of conscience and aesthetic experience. Combining an expressive distortion of the human figure and a focus on the lives of American workers in a particular region, Gwathmey's manner was characteristic of the 1930s, in effect an artistic dialect synthesizing Social Realism and Regionalism. In contrast to these nationalistic movements, however, the means for the artist's personal style derived from Picasso and the Fauves. It was grounded in color and in precise, reductive design.

In many ways, Gwathmey's prints can be seen as the median between his drawings and paintings. First and foremost a draftsman, the artist focused on simplification and reduction, processes that took place on his sketch pad. His paintings were always made in the studio, and invariably based on his drawings. The problems and procedures of drawing, the medium considered by many to be the quintessential artistic experience, were also at the center of his teaching career. Comparing Gwathmey's prints with his drawings, the viewer finds a quality of line similar to that which was often obscured in the upscaled painted versions of these compositions. The spare line of the drawing *Old Woman* (Fig.) has a nervous, jerky quality, indicating that the artist willfully moved his pencil in fits and starts. He reduced the composition to its basic elements in two dimensions, and drew attention to the calligraphic quality of the line itself. This same flat, linear quality is visible in *Singing and Mending* and in Gwathmey's other serigraphs, particularly in the black-key screen of each print.

Gwathmey was also a colorist; his paintings are symphonies of hues carefully selected and placed. His compositional flatness and simplicity were intended, in part, to allow juxtapositions and harmonies of color to occur with as little formal or subjective interference as possible.[1] Serigraphy was the ideal graphic medium for this purpose.

Like all of Gwathmey's silkscreens, this print reproduced a painting. Created in 1945 out of the experiences he had while living and working with the sharecroppers, the canvas is now in the Hirshhorn Museum.[2] Many of the artist's images of this period represent the closeness of the black family and the quiet dignity of their culture. Placed in humble domestic settings suggested by architecture or furniture, seated figures face the viewer directly, functioning as symbols in their frontality. This mood can be found in paintings such as *Family Portrait* (1944), *Lullaby* (1945), and *Woman Shelling Peas* (1945), as well as in *Old Woman* and other drawings. In *Singing and Mending*, the barefoot seamstress represents poverty, the necessity to make do; the song of the blues guitarist symbolizes the wise and handsome culture that grew out of that terrible necessity.

In developing a print from a painting, Gwathmey often simplified the image even more. In this composition, a tall pot was removed from the table, and the background was flattened. Further, although he subdivided his paintings into cells of local color, he usually included some modulation in these areas, and brush strokes are often apparent there. The flat, solid layers of silkscreen ink encouraged the elimination of this modeling in the print. Each of the screens for this serigraph was prepared using the tusche-and-glue method. Gwathmey preferred silk of the finest mesh, because its weave was not apparent on the surface of the print. He occasionally used texturizing methods to prepare his screens, but these are as inconspicuous as the subtle working of paint in his canvases. The artist seems to have achieved the mottling in the floor of this print by offsetting the texture of a coarsely woven fabric onto the screen, perhaps by applying a stop-out of thin glue over the surface of a stretched canvas or a book cover. By contrast, the other local colors are very flat. Gwathmey printed the black contour lines of the composition last, atop the other ink layers, and they retain the character of his distinctive, purposefully drawn line.

Notes

1. McCausland 1946, p. 151; Tully 1985, p. 50.

2. *Singing and Mending*, 1945. Oil on canvas, 76.2 × 92.0 cm. Washington D.C., Hirshhorn Museum and Sculpture Garden, Smithsonian Institution, accession no. 66.2293. See McCausland 1946, p. 146; ACA Gallery 1946, no. 18. See also Landau 1983, pp. 44–45; McGill 1988; Wolf 1946.

Stanley William Hayter

1901–1988

60.
Cinq Personnages

1946
Soft-ground etching and engraving
on cream laid paper
37.9 × 61.6 cm. (plate)
51.5 × 66.8 cm. (sheet)
In pencil, lower margin: *47/50*
SWHayter 46
Worcester Art Museum, 1947.12

Throughout the 1940s, Englishman Stanley William Hayter headed the most innovative workshop for intaglio printmaking in America. The period of his sojourn in New York coincided with his own endeavors in color printmaking, experiments that had deep reverberations for the development of color intaglio in the United States.

In 1940, Hayter made his first color print, *Maternity*—also his first American plate—which combined serigraphy and intaglio. In subsequent experiments, he sought to avoid the registration problems caused by multiple plates or inkings, and these led to new ways of applying several colors to a single plate in order to print them all in one pass through the press. In 1943, Hayter created *Centauresse*, the first print successfully combining intaglio with colored inks printed from the surface of the plate, to which they were applied with stencils.

Cinq Personnages, the artist's first large color intaglio, is considered one of his most important prints. Hayter explained the process of its creation and the development of these techniques in his book, *New Ways of Gravure*.[1] This print was produced between December 1945 and March 1946 at Atelier 17 in New York, with the assistance of Fred Becker, James Goetz, and Karl Schrag. Essentially it combines a complex intaglio image printed in black ink with transparent colors printed from the surface of the plate. The artist carefully chose three colors that would overlap to create five or six hues.

Hayter created *Cinq Personnages* as a requiem for his son David, who had died of tuberculosis at age sixteen. The agonized figure of a dying child reclining at the lower right is related to the broken figure of Christ in Enguerand Quarton's *Pietà* at Avignon, France.[2] Grieving figures surround the youth, whose death is also attended by a little totemic figure—the spirit of a child—in raised relief

near the center of the image. In its emotional response to suffering and death, this work also parallels Hayter's prints of the 1930s depicting the Spanish Civil War.[3]

After originating his figures in paintings and sketches, Hayter combined them in a drawing of the overall composition, which was reversed for transfer to the copperplate. Then he sketched in the outlines of the composition in the plate with a graver and proceeded to fill in details, occasionally printing proofs to check the effect of his progress. Next, the little relief figure was gouged away with a scorper, along with other accents that would be embossed in high relief in the final print. The plate was coated with a soft ground, filling and sealing all the lines made by the burin. The artist impressed a number of textures into the ground using silk, gauze mesh, and crumpled brown paper under the pressure of a roller press, superimposing them in several steps. The plate was then carefully bitten several times in an acid bath, with variations created at each stage by tilting the plate.

Although development of the design was "automatic," the placement and overprinting of colors required careful planning. Hayter applied four different inks to the plate before printing, exploiting the different viscosities of these inks, which prevented them from mixing when they were superimposed. First the artist charged the plate with black etching ink in the conventional intaglio manner and carefully wiped its surface. Then the transparent films of colored inks were superimposed on the plate through silkscreens. The hollows intended for embossing relief accents were then cleaned out and the plate was passed once through a

roller press. The printing was a technical feat in itself, requiring not only precise inking but careful hydration of paper of the proper weight.

All of the experiments and procedures for *Cinq Personnages* took place in Hayter's open workshop with the aid of several of its members, and this exciting event shifted the focus of the studio from black and white engraving and etching to color printmaking.[4] Sue Fuller experimented with syrup in the color sugar-lift process, and Fred Becker devised a method of accurately registering multiple plates. Raoul Ubac and Karl Schrag purposely printed a single plate out of register, charging it with different colored inks to create effects of vibration and depth. Hayter worked with Ruthven Todd and Joan Miró to expand on relief-etching techniques developed by William Blake in the eighteenth century, and Krishna Reddy refined methods of mixing inks for "color viscosity printing."[5] The making of American color prints from intaglio plates had entered an energetic new period.

Many American printmakers, including Gabor Peterdi, Sue Fuller, Fred Becker, Karl Schrag, Mauricio Lasansky, and Garo Antreasian (cats. 79, 58, 62, 80, 67, 97, respectively), were deeply influenced by their experiences at Atelier 17 in New York. They passed on an abstract vocabulary and many new technical procedures to succeeding generations of artists, promulgating Hayter's spirit of experimentation. This is his American legacy.[6]

Notes

1. Hayter 1949a, pp. 155–161.

2. Hacker 1988, p. 84, no. 47.

3. Cohen 1988, p. 29.

4. Moser 1977, p. 36.

5. Ibid., p. 38, notes 36, 37.

6. Moser 1977, pp. 17–19, 43–49. See also Hayter 1962; Moorhead; Reynolds 1967.

47/50   SW Hayter 46

Bernard Steffen

1907–1980

61.

Haying

1946
Serigraph on cream wove paper
25.7 × 20.6 cm. (image)
30.9 × 25.6 cm. (sheet)
In pencil, lower margin: *Haying
Bernard Steffen*
Worcester Art Museum, anonymous
gift, 1988.109

A socially aware artist from the American heartland, Bernard Steffen can be characterized as a Regionalist. In contrast to the fashionable modes of modernism and abstraction, this style advocated a return to the depiction of a familiar reality in a poetic, dignified, and accessible way. In a sense of reactionary attempt to establish an American artistic tradition independent from the traditions of Europe, Regionalism, like its urban counterpart, Social Realism, was grounded in the glorification of the lives of American workers. The everyday existence of prairie farming communities, their history, and their folk traditions were the primary subjects of the Regionalists. Grant Wood, John Steuart Curry, and Thomas Hart Benton, three Midwesterners who worked as muralists and easel painters, spearheaded the movement. They understood the potential of printmaking as an immediate, distributable art form, and each exploited this potential through lithography. Like these masters of the preceding generation, Bernard Steffen depicted images of rural America from his own experience, but unlike them, he began to incorporate elements of modernism into his style, and he preferred the new technique of serigraphy.

Published in Philadelphia as the seventh annual presentation print for the American Color Print Society, this is a reduced version of Steffen's serigraph *Haying Time* of 1941. The original horizontal version of the composition was dominated by a broader wave of grain, which contrasted more subtly with a mottled, azure sky. When the artist altered the format, he removed a trailing

flight of birds, which in *Haying Time* echoed the shape of the wave of grain. It is interesting to see how this cropping transforms the composition. With the image less dramatic and less abstract, the viewer's attention shifts to the workers and their labors. No longer simply elements of design, the people have become the subject of the print.

All of Steffen's prints of the 1930s and 1940s are narrative in content. This fascination with storytelling may have been instilled in him by Thomas Hart Benton. However, though most of Steffen's prints of the period represent rural subjects, they stem from the artist's own experiences rather than from Benton. As a boy, Steffen experienced harvests such as the one in this print on his grandparents' farm in Kansas. His prints often glorify the simplicity and homeliness of the everyday; good-natured and dignified, they are devoid of the satire apparent in Regionalist work by other artists.

Here Steffen depicted a land of plenty, not a depression-ravaged dust bowl. Indeed, belying his activity in the American Artists Congress, he seldom made overtly political or socially critical prints, instead representing workers toiling in harmony with their natural environment. Through works such as this, he and his comrades expressed a hope that all laborers, including artists, would someday be allowed to work in concert with society.

The artist may also have derived from Benton his tendency to distort figures and blend them into a sweeping animation of the natural environment. However, Steffen took this effect even further, twisting and stretching his figures and animals so

that they merged into the expressive rhythm of his overall design. The artist often chose peculiar points of view, or isolated his everyday subjects in ways that removed them from reality and transformed them into abstract forms. His work is always dominated by a stringent compositional foundation, a quality that probably reflects the influence of Stanton Macdonald-Wright (cat. 78). This tendency progressed in Steffen's work until the late 1950s, when he abandoned naturalistic imagery, concentrating instead on swirling, cadenced designs and harmonious balances of color.

A pioneer of serigraphy, Steffen printed his early works in an extraordinary manner. Like a watercolor, this serigraph was printed on thick, stiff paper with a nubbly texture and toothed surface. The transparency of the fourteen colors of ink allows the tone of the paper to show through, giving the effect of watercolor washes.[1] The superimposed layers of color have a saturated look that recreates the intensity of the sun-drenched prairie; the movement and bleached colors of a haymaker's kerchief and overalls contrast slightly with the vast expanses of golden wheat and deep blue sky.

Notes

1. Zigrosser 1941b, p. 465. See also *Art News* 1945; Francey 1988, pp. 64–65; Lowe 1937; Williams 1987, p. 69.

Haying   Bernard Steffen

Fred Becker

1913–

62.

Hooks and Eyes

1947
Soft-ground etching, engraving, and drypoint on thick cream wove paper
7.2 × 6.3 cm. (plate)
13.6 × 11.2 cm. (sheet)
In plate, lower right: artist's monogram
In pencil, lower margin: *Hooks & Eyes   Fred Becker   '47*
Worcester Art Museum, anonymous gift, 1988.90

Prompted by the experiments at Atelier 17, Fred Becker was first drawn to color intaglio in the mid-1940s. He became intrigued by the techniques of the commercial platemakers, who utilized the three primary colors and black ink to achieve a full range of color.

In the summer of 1946, after the artist had concluded his first semester of teaching at the Tyler School, he returned to Atelier 17 in New York. Becker showed his current work to gallery owners, curators, and art directors. Magazine editor Bradley Thompson was receptive to the artist's idea for the preparation of illustrations from original color plates rather than from photographic separations. With slight modifications, one of the artist's images was thus reproduced in the Halloween issue of *Mademoiselle* in 1946. Becker also visited A. Hyatt Mayor, curator of prints and drawings at the Metropolitan Museum of Art. Mayor not only acquired some of Becker's recent prints, he also challenged the artist with a commission to create a four-color miniature intaglio. The curator intended to illustrate the color printmaking process by mounting proofs of the four separations in the corners of a single mat, with the final, full-color print in the center.

To meet Mayor's challenge, Becker created the Surrealist fantasy *Hooks and Eyes*, the theme, imagery, and title of which play wittily on the required scale. Suspended from the edges of the composition, weblike struts grow into miniature nooses in a space complicated by ambiguities of superimposition and transparency. Quivering as on spider's webs, these strange eyelets seem somehow botanical and threatening, like a stand of carnivorous plants. One prominent maw bares menacing fangs. A fan of tensile cords emphasizes the sensitive suspension; this may have been related to the sculptures of Naum Gabo and their reflections in the work of Becker's fellow workshop member Sue Fuller (cat. 58).

In several ways, *Hooks and Eyes* resembles *The Cage*, another color intaglio that Becker created in the summer of 1946. Both prints combine three soft-ground color plates with an engraved key plate printed in black. In preparing the key plate, the artist worked directly on the copper with a burin and a drypoint needle. The plate tone of black ink and the mere pressure of overprinting gave a soft, gray cast to the entire surface of each print. By overlapping the three primary colors, Becker broadened the range of hues to include greens, violets, and oranges.[1] Although for *The Cage* the artist drew the color plates through silk into the ground, he created those for *Hooks and Eyes* by first engraving the composition in a plastic scratchboard and then pressing this image into the soft ground. Thus he reproduced the same basic design on all three plates, and then further modified this in the soft ground or directly in the copper. For both prints, the artist varied each of the three color plates slightly by tilting the image a few degrees in order to achieve a delicate mixture of colors and a subtle effect of vibration.

In his book *New Ways of Gravure*, Stanley William Hayter (cat. 60) described Becker's system of registration.[2] This method used the size and shape of the paper to achieve consistent positioning atop the printing plates. The artist mounted a metal mat to the bed of the press, making an opening into which the plates nested precisely. Three metal tabs, or stops, protruding from the surface of the mat beyond the travel of the printing blankets acted as positioning guides for the paper. With this technique, Becker had to maintain the dampness of the paper throughout the printing process, for if he allowed the drying sheets to shrink, the image would print out of registration. The colors were printed from the surface of the plate with letterpress ink on a type press, and the black was printed in etching ink from the intaglio grooves on a roller press. The artist soon discovered the limitations of this innovative technique, which were caused by the divergent pressures provided by two different presses, and by the aforementioned problems of paper shrinkage. Little prints such as *The Cage* or the present work showed only slight problems, but when Becker later tried the same method on the large *Aerial Jungle* (1948), disparities in pressure became a serious obstacle.

Notes

1. The artist precisely noted the colors of these inks ("Hansa yellow, Talens Rose, Monastral blue, and Intaglio black") on the impressions of these prints, which are mounted together at the Worcester Art Museum (accession nos. 1989.154.1–4).

2. Hayter 1949a, pp. 135–137. See also Johnson 1980, pp. 77–78; Moser 1977, pp. 26, 36, nos. 26, 27; Peterdi 1959a, p. 30.

Hooks &   Fred
Eyes   Becker '47

Dorr Bothwell

1902–

63.

Holiday

1947

Serigraph on off-white wove paper

32.5 × 24.7 cm. (image)

43.3 × 31.7 cm. (sheet)

In screen, upper right: *Bothwell '47*

In pencil, lower margin: *"Holiday"*

D. Bothwell 18/30

Worcester Art Museum, anonymous

gift, 1988.102

Beginning in the 1940s, California painter and teacher Dorr Bothwell created a remarkable group of color serigraphs. These carefully composed and crafted prints depict spare, dreamlike visions. Bothwell's technical mastery of serigraphy was a measure of her own initiative and resourcefulness. Valuing her education profoundly, she perpetuated her knowledge in her art and through her teaching and writings. This intrepid artist also traveled around the world, studying indigenous artistic traditions in order to discover their salient rules of design, which she incorporated and emphasized in her work and teaching.

Bothwell was introduced to serigraphy in 1942 when he friend Marian Osbourne Cunningham returned to California from New York with knowledge of the process; however, it was not until Bothwell obtained Harry Sternberg's (cat. 35) serigraphy manual[1] in that same year that she began her own experiments. Her first print was created in 1943, and during the next year she made three other editions.

Developing her own method amid wartime shortages, Bothwell at first made small prints in editions of few impressions. Paper scarcity led her to use rag book papers with smooth, hot-press finishes and trimmed on all sides; she continued to use such paper until 1948. She came to favor commercial oil-base serigraph inks, but routinely mixed in a small amount of oil paint in order to control color and texture, occasionally using a transparent medium to create thin, extended glazes.[2]

Although Bothwell's prints of the 1940s and 1950s reflect Surrealist influences, the artist synthesized other concepts in these haunting, illusionistic images. She had learned from Rudolph Schaeffer to simplify her designs, disregarding details and secondary features in order to find the simplest recognizable forms. The artist's research into primitive art taught her that this process of refinement can be made more potent by the creation of symbols.

Bothwell's Surrealism is tempered by brightness, humor, and good nature. In *Holiday*, she meant to reveal visual aspects of the interior, psychological world and to express a carefree spirit of celebration. Vivid colors and an open composition express this freedom and happiness. In accordance with the principle of *notan*, Bothwell used the effect of graduated tone, which had been described by Sternberg in his manual, creating ethereal backgrounds of colored mist that dynamized space in the present print and in others.[3] Elongated, triangular human forms were made more palpable by the

simple addition of a web of symbolic crosses representing the spine and rib cage, a suggestion of transparency of the sort that fascinated Bothwell during this period. The artist interwove a linear chassis with overlapping forms of color in this composition, creating shifts between two and three dimensions. In this manner, she tried to integrate figures and ground.

The linear elements of this design were drawn onto the screen with a litho crayon, which was also used to outline forms that were later touched up and strengthened with tusche. The central sculptural form, at once massive and spectrally transparent, was rendered on the screen in the frottage technique, with a litho crayon against a coarse textured material, perhaps sandpaper. Bothwell developed this technique to an extraordinary level in her prints of the late 1940s, offsetting the textures of many materials, including embossed book covers and decorative fabrics such as lace, onto her silkscreens.

Notes

1. Sternberg 1942.

2. Bothwell preferred Naz-Dar 5500 series inks.

3. Sternberg 1942, pp. 58–59.

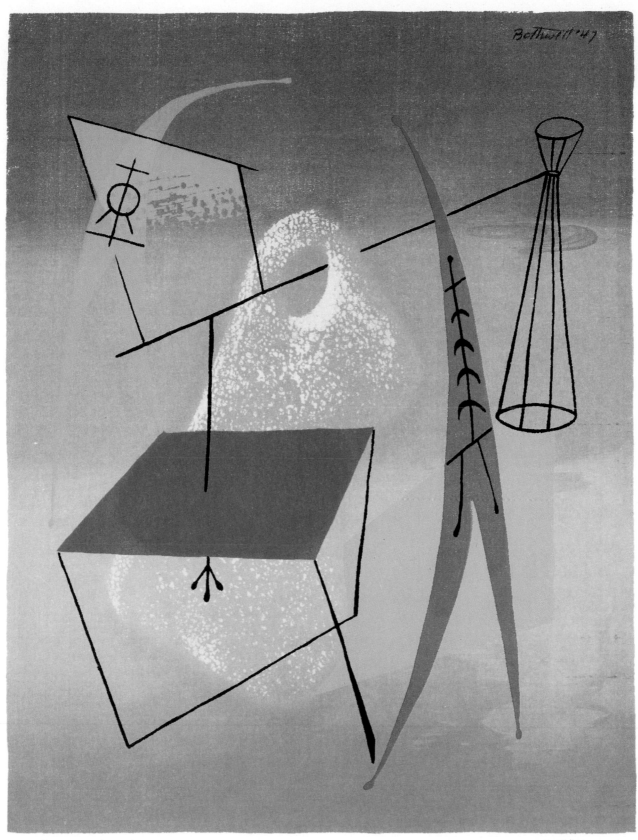

Lee Chesney

1920–

64.

Night Walk

1947

Etching and aquatint with engraving
on cream wove paper
34.9 × 43.1 cm. (plate)
44.2 × 58.6 cm. (sheet)
In pencil, lower margin: *Night
Walk   3/5   Lee Chesney*
Worcester Art Museum, Anonymous
Fund, 1989.16

Executed when Lee Chesney was still a graduate student, *Night Walk* was his first serious attempt at printmaking in color. Although this print does not represent the artist's subsequent achievements in color intaglio, it does reflect the proclivities of a sensitive, creative colorist and an already accomplished technician. The influences of Mauricio Lasansky (cat. 67) and the atmosphere of the University of Iowa workshop are evident in this print. *Night Walk* represents an isolated experiment, for afterward the artist returned to figurative imagery, choosing not to confront pure abstraction again for almost fifteen years. A proper edition of this print was never made, for the artist's curiosity was satisfied by the production of merely five impressions. Like many artists, Chesney has always been impatient with the drudgery of printing, and has preferred to invest himself in more originative pursuits, reflecting the attitude that the printmaking media are but means to creative ends. Unfortunately, therefore, many of his prints exist only in single proofs.

In contrast to most of Chesney's works, which are aesthetic responses to the stimulus of a model, or spring from the creative process itself, *Night Walk* began with an intellectual concept. The artist was fascinated with Einstein's theory of relativity, and challenged himself to express the ideas therein, to create a visit to the realm of stellar physics in visual terms.[1] The result is the haunting image of a cosmic system, constantly vibrating with energy and ever rotating in the black vastness of space.

Ghostly brush strokes suggest veils of particulate matter whirling in celestial clouds, and bundles of stuttering lines impart a sense of motion and pulsating force. In some passages, these strokes were burnished away, and the blurred lines evoke a shimmering aurora. Along with other highlights, deeply etched lines, wiped clean during printing, embossed the paper emphatically. These boldly protruding arcs create a revolving motion and draw the viewer into dark envelopes of space. Powerful burin strokes define a central ladder—a symbolic access into and egress from the vortex of this spacetime continuum. Although some Abstract Surrealist forms and figures appear in this plate, its dominant impression is one of space and energy.[2]

Like Lasansky and most other color intaglio printmakers of the period, Chesney depended on the dominant key plate to transmit meaning and lend coherence to the image. In some characteristics of its style and technique, *Night Walk* is similar to contemporary productions of the Iowa workshop: its palette is dark and somber, and dense veils of black lend mystery to the image. However, unlike Lasansky, Chesney used color to define form and to assert space, denying the dominance of the figure. Color also provided mood and atmosphere, defining geometric forms both transparent and overlapping, creating a palpable spatial tension.

Although Chesney usually began by using a burin, in this print the energized strokes of the graver and the dramatic arc chiseled into the plate with the scorper were "laboriously carved after the etching and aquatint was done as a final dynamic thrust. It was so deep in fact," said the artist, "that the plate almost cracked in two pieces as I printed. . . . Color prints are long in the making, and represent an extended series of experiences rather than a singe experience. A great deal of personal growth occurs during the development of a color print. I approach printmaking as a hunt and seek search for meaning and for appropriate form. The color intaglio, with its multiple plates and consecutive printings only complicates and lengthens the process."[3]

Notes

1. Such problems would not again be addressed by Chesney until 1952 in the print *Engraving*; see Baro 1976, p. 19, illus.

2. The distinctive form at the right—a circle suspended from radiating tensile struts within a crescent—was a haunting motif for Chesney; it reappeared in 1953 in *Specter's Holiday* as the head of a strange Gorkyesque beast. Related to popular tensile sculpture of the day, this notion might have had its ultimate source in Atelier 17, for a similar motif is apparent in Fred Becker's *Hooks and Eyes* (cat. 62).

3. Letter from the artist to the author, December 21, 1988. See also Chesney 1956 and 1959; Print Council 1959, no. 9.

Night Walk   3/5   Lee Chesney

Anne Ryan

1888–1954

65.

Orpheus

1947

Woodcut on thin black wove paper

34.4 × 48.0 cm. (image)

40.7 × 59.0 cm. (sheet)

In white pencil, lower margin: *SIII
Orpheus   Trial I*

Private collection

Anne Ryan is best known for her small mixed-media collages, created in the final six years of her life. However, she was also a painter and printmaker, and her color woodcuts are as technically innovative and eloquent as they are sensitive and individualistic. In these qualities, her prints are characteristic products of the late 1940s in New York, where artists explored European modernism and Abstract Surrealism, and where Abstract Expressionism began. Ryan operated near the center of each of these movements.

Ryan worked in color woodcut between 1945 and 1949. From the beginning of her activity in the medium, she simultaneously created representational pieces and pure abstractions. Ryan looked to the popular, hand-colored "penny prints" of sixteenth- and seventeenth-century Europe, and to the paintings of Georges Rouault, in developing the imagery of her relief prints.[1] In her still-life prints, a subject to which she returned throughout the four years of her interest in woodcut, her models were Cézanne, Matisse, and Picasso. Seemingly late in her activity, Ryan also depicted religious subjects in her color prints.

Her abstract woodcuts display affinities to Stanley William Hayter (cat. 60), Jackson Pollock, Hans Hofmann (cat. 73), and her other friends in the emerging Abstract Expressionist movement. Like Hayter, Ryan preferred to present abstract forms floating freely in the center of her compositions, usually before a mottled ground. This is the case in *Orpheus*, where two yellow forms hover before a moving azure field. However, the abstract forms in this image are unspecific and their relationship too ambiguous to identify them as Orpheus and Eurydice, or to speculate about Ryan's literal representation of the myth. As with her paintings and intaglio prints, many of Ryan's woodcuts have titles that relate to ancient mythology or classical literature.

Ryan preferred the single-block technique, and she never used more than three woodblocks for a single print. She used knives, small chisels, and her intaglio tools to carve freely in the soft blocks of pine and plywood. Inking and printing were active, creative processes for the artist, and each of the woodcuts in her small editions was essentially a monotype. She used Louis Schanker's (cat. 41) technique of printing with oil paints, which she applied freely with her fingers and with small rollers. These were printed in many superimposed layers in a manner similar to that of B.J.O. Nordfelt (cat. 11) and other Provincetown Printers. Ryan printed by rubbing firmly on the verso, usually with the palm of her hand rather than a hard wooden spoon or scraper.

Thick pigments were combined with thin glazes, juxtaposing shiny surfaces with matte passages. Occasionally the artist applied ink so liberally that the surfaces of her prints had vermiculated crusts. Heavy glossy surfaces gave these prints a quality similar to encaustic, a painting technique in which pigments are combined with wax and fixed with heat. After printing, the artist often finished her woodcuts with colored pencils, pastels, and paint. The range of surface quality and texture is similar to the effects Ryan sought in her paintings.

Strong Japan papers, like those used by Schanker and other woodcut artists in New York during this period, were used for Ryan's early woodcuts. When she tried printing on black paper given to her by a photographer friend, she found the final element of her formula. The artist soon preferred this material for

nearly all her color woodcuts. A network of flattened folds, still visible on the verso of *Orpheus*, reveals that the sheet had once been wrapped around a flat package, measuring about 8 × 10 × 1 inches. Clearly a pack of photography paper was once protected from the light by this sheet of black tissue. Similar flattened folds appear in the papers of many of Ryan's prints. The resourceful artist, who never had much money, obtained these used wrappers, much as she would later salvage scraps of fabric to recycle in her collages. She ironed the sheets flat before printing on them. Other woodcut artists such as Adja Yunkers (cat. 81) also printed on black papers, but they did so without Ryan's consistency.

The color of the paper made the lines of Ryan's single-block woodcuts seem drawn, and her colors achieved a saturation and luminosity quite different from those caused by white papers. In Ryan's prints, the black ground read through the thin layers of ink, and an organic mottled texture was effectively achieved. This extraordinary luminosity and the softness and subtlety of hue are what distinguish these woodcuts.

Although Ryan's woodcuts have not been catalogued, she probably produced more than one hundred prints in about four years' work with this medium. These works were the focus of shows at the Kraushaar Galleries in New York in 1957 and 1977.[2] Recently these prints were featured in an exhibition at the Metropolitan Museum of Art in New York.[3]

Notes

1. Johnson 1980, p. 42.

2. Breuning 1957; Brown 1977.

3. Solomon 1989. See also Washburn 1984; Johnson 1956.

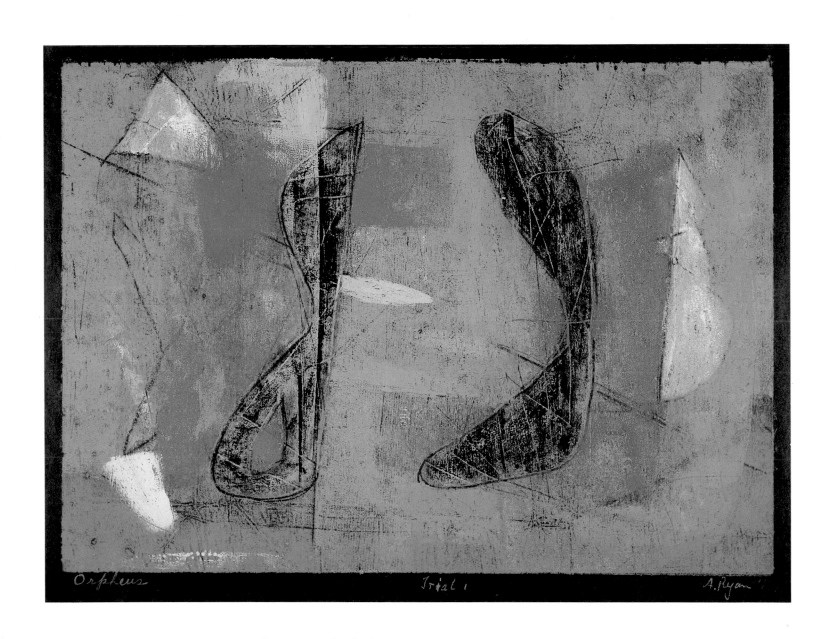

Orpheus   Trial 1   A. Ryan

Boris Margo

1902–

66.
Night and the Atom #2

about 1947

Cellocut on dark cream wove paper

37.6 × 45.3 cm. (image)

44.9 × 58.0 cm. (sheet)

In pencil, lower margin: *Night & the Atom #2   3/15   Cellocut Boris Margo*

Watermark: *HANDMADE SWEDEN*

Worcester Art Museum, anonymous gift, 1988.96

One of the most creative proponents of Surrealism in the United States, Boris Margo was also the inventor of a wholly new graphic medium with which to express his eerie, futuristic visions. In this technique, which he called cellocut, the artist utilized modern, synthetic materials and untried processes, and found a great range of new possibilities.

In the late 1940s, Margo's colorful prints were dominated by spontaneous drawing reminiscent of microscopic biological and atomic forms. Soon these forms were melded with cosmic scientific imagery, as the artist became fascinated by the development of rocketry and by notions of the exploration of space. Margo did not represent specific subjects in his prints, but rather created visual evocations of ideas. In fact the painter, printmaker, and poet Jan Gelb, the artist's wife, created most of the titles for Margo's works out of discussions with him about his conceptual sources.[1]

Night and the Atom #2 was printed from an etched and engraved cellocut plate, which was inked and printed as a relief block rather than as an intaglio. The artist's development of this technique began in 1931. When he found a discarded sheet of celluloid, he wrote to its manufacturer, and received technical descriptions of its properties as well as a bottle of acetone, which dissolved the material.[2]

When Margo dissolved the plastic in acetone to a pourable liquid, he found that he could spread a layer of this varnish on any smooth, flat surface, such as a metal plate or a plank of wood. After the varnish hardened, it could readily be worked with etching or woodcut tools. Acetone squirted from a plastic squeeze bottle could be used to etch the surface in an idiosyncratic liquid line. Thicker celluloid varnish could also be poured or cast on the plate to create designs in high relief. Materials and objects could be embedded in the varnish before it set, creating a collagraph plate. The artist usually printed his cellocuts with oil-base ink, in an etching press. Margo began making color prints with this process in the early 1930s, and over the next thirty years, the majority of his prints were in color.

In *Night and the Atom #2*, a single plate was worked in several ways, inked on the surface with one colorful application, and printed in relief. After creating the cellocut plate on a flat base—probably the patent composition board Prestwood—the artist worked the surface both chemically and mechanically. The main linear matrix was created by dripping liquid acetone directly onto the plate in a spontaneous, automatist manner, and allowing it to chemically etch deep, wide grooves. Tonal etching of the surface of the plate was done with copper chloride in a manner similar to direct-bite etching or aquatint. The artist then worked the plate by hand with engraving and scratching tools, as if he were working a metal plate with a burin and drypoint needle. In some passages, coarse granules were embedded in the celluloid while it was still liquid. In the print, these embossed colored spots are highlighted by halos.

Margo utilized many inking methods for his color cellocuts, including the use of masking stencils, and the application of several colors to a plate *à la poupée*. The inking of the plate for the present print was done in a manner often used in lithography.[3] Several ribbons of color were spread on the ink slab with a palette knife, with spaces reserved between them. When the roller was passed over the slab in parallel strokes, the hues blended in the interval between bands, and the roller was charged with this multicolored layer of ink. The ink was then transferred from the roller to the cellocut plate in one pass, and the cellocut was printed in a single run through an etching press.

Notes

1. Zimiles/Wechsler 1988, pp. 22–23.

2. Schmeckebier/Gelb 1968, pp. 49–51; see also Margo 1947.

3. Antreasian/Adams 1971, pp. 223, 225.

night & the Atom #2   3/15   Cellocut   Boris Margo

Mauricio Lasansky

1914–

67.
Pietà
1948
Etching, soft-ground etching, and aquatint with engraving, drypoint, and roulette on cream wove paper
49.0 × 71.1 cm. (plate)
51.6 × 73.3 cm. (sheet)
In pencil, beneath image: *Pieta 20/35   MLasansky*
Zigrosser 79; Thein 83
Private collection

Lasansky created *Pietà*, one of his most forceful and poignant images, during his period of reflection on the war and the potential of humankind for cruelty. Its brooding subject and dark, obscure forms characterize all his prints of this period. Although a religious interpretation is not explicit in this image, it can be seen as a contemplation of the central tragedy of the Christian mystery, with biblical narrative as the framework for allusions to physical, sacramental, and spiritual aspects of the church.[1]

Inspired by the expressive fifteenth-century *Pietà* at Avignon, France, with its angular anatomy and keenly felt grief, Lasansky created a haunting, dreamlike vision in which sorrow dulled perception, blurring line and obscuring color.[2] The deep hues and compartmentalized composition resemble stained glass, evoking all the trappings and atmosphere of the church. However, the artist did not depict a temple of light and hope but rather a cold and gloomy cathedral, where the shadows of a stony vault, seemingly permeated by stale incense and centuries of desperate prayers, shroud the windows. In the confused and fragmented space of

this composition, flat shapes tug against suggestions of depth from overlapping planes and colors. The artist emphasized this ambiguity by including the transparent ladder, which leans against the base of the cross and is interwoven with the supportive figure of Longinus and the space around it. The wide, staring eyes of Saint John and Mary Magdalene seem to express a kind of disbelieving hysteria. Ingenuous, Picassoesque figures emerge and recede from this ambiguous background.

In the center of the composition, the head of the mourning Virgin seems to dissolve into her circular halo. Her facial features are only vaguely recognizable; her misshapen eyes melt in a watery, downcast gaze. Her triangular form is defined by chevrons that call to mind the embroidered bands on a cope, the outer vestment worn primarily by bishops when celebrating the Mass. Each basal corner of this triangle is marked by hands beneath the body of Christ, although not those of the Virgin. This pyramidal figure and its slightly splayed, pendant feet also bring to mind examples of early Christian art such as the sixteenth-century Italo-Byzantine mosaics at Ravenna, Italy.

Hard-edged and metallic, as if they were cut with a torch from sheets of brass, Christ's head and calves dangle from the central form of his body. The empty gaze of his white, lifeless pupils is accentuated by the halo of red surrounding his head. Lasansky portrayed the horizontal body of Jesus as a weighty, lifeless form, like the stone slab of a church altar. Thus the recumbent figure of Christ and the triangular standing

form of the Virgin behind become a metaphor for a priest standing behind an altar. A point of light blazes in the very center of this print, separating Mary from the figure of Christ. This highlight emphasizes the Virgin's lap, the point of contact between mother and child, and the point of miraculous transsubstantiation during the Mass.

The composition of this remarkable intaglio, which Lasansky printed from nine plates, reflects the process of its creation in its dark, smoky layers and in its emphasis on overlapping planes. Bundles of thin drypoint lines or multiple strokes of the roulette created a soft, blurred effect. The same plates were printed several times, purposely out of registration, to further soften lines and forms.

Notes

1. See Rhoades 1973 on the possible influence of Spanish art and iconography on the printmaker.

2. Ring 1949, pp. 223–224.

Pruppe 20/35   M. [signature]

Minna Citron

1896–

68.

Squid under Pier

1949
Soft-ground etching, etching, and engraving on cream wove paper
37.8 × 45.8 cm. (plate)
49.5 × 56.7 cm. (sheet)
In pencil, lower margin: *etch & engr.   2 color plates   45/50 Hon Mention Boston Printmakers 1st Prize So. of 4 Arts-Palm Beach Squid under Pier   1st Prize Am. Color Print So Dallas Print Annual '53 Minna Citron   '49*
Worcester Art Museum, anonymous gift, 1988.92

In the mid-1940s, when her style was evolving from representation to pure abstraction, Minna Citron joined Atelier 17. In the heady creative atmosphere of this print shop, where artists worked in diverse styles that orbited around Stanley William Hayter's own Abstract Surrealism (cat. 60), the artist felt comfortable enough to explore her own emotions, and experiments with technique helped to inspire and crystallize her ideas of abstraction. Citron was introduced to the processes currently being developed in the workshop, primarily engraving and soft-ground etching with aquatint. Her affiliation with Atelier 17 also roughly coincided with the studio's first experiments with color. *Mime* of 1946, the second print she made there, was her first color intaglio; it is strikingly similar to Sue Fuller's *Clown* (cat. 58) in its subject, imagery, and technique.

As Citron's works became progressively more abstract, she often continued to use recognizable subjects and narrative implied by titles. This was the case with *Squid under Pier*, which combined the artist's lyrical invention with unconscious, automatic aesthetic responses encouraged by Hayter.

In the world just beneath the ocean surface, the sunlight shimmers in blue, green, and gray, filtering through the gently moving water. Peering up from under the brine, we see the shadows of the pier, and beyond the open areas of sea and sky. A squid hovers, motionless but for its slowly writhing tentacles. Predatory and alert even as it floats at rest, its unblinking, piercing eye remains watchful. The squid seems unconcerned by the net that dangles from the pier, twisting in a large helix that echoes the pattern of its knots and cords. However, this is another threat to the viewer, who sees this world through fish's eyes. As the artist once described this image: "It is as though one might escape from those encircling tentacles to a temporary shelter and security under the pier and finally to peace and tranquility in the timeless and limitless space of fair skies and open sea."[1]

The success of this print derives from its imaginative subject, its extraordinary point of view, and its interweaving of narrative and abstraction. Citron carefully balanced form, line, pattern, and color, aiming for dynamic tension and compositional equilibrium. She concentrated on rhythmic sequences of planes and patterns, using transparency to help imply dimension. Her floating, antigravitational world is well represented by ambiguous, interpenetrating shapes, and the drab, restricted palette is characteristic of the artist.

This print utilized many of the techniques developed at Atelier 17. It was printed from one smooth, unetched plate and from one intaglio plate passed twice through the press. The etched plate was prepared in several stages. A lacy, woven net was pressed into the soft ground, precisely transferring its intricate pattern to the plate. The linear structure of the composition was rendered not in discrete lines, but in bundles of etched lines, blurred and variegated with a burnisher and a roulette, so as to seem distorted by the moving water. A scorper was used to carve out deep, emphatic arcs that embossed the paper.

The first pass through the press printed the darker of the two colors, which were applied to the plate through a silkscreen stencil. The second printing was from the intaglio plate, onto which the light blue ink was applied through another silkscreen prepared with washed-out tusche and glue, which masked brush strokes that read as white highlights in the final print. This colored ink was applied only to the surface of the metal and did not penetrate into the intaglio areas. Thus, after printing, the white of the paper showed through, further highlighting the image. The third pass through the press printed the intaglio imagery in black ink. The artist purposely printed the key plate slightly out of register from the color, giving the effect of vibration with the white ghosts of the etched lines in the color plate.

Squid under Pier is the most important print Citron produced at Atelier 17. On this impression, the artist proudly noted a few of the many honors and awards granted to this work.[2]

Notes

1. Kup 1950, p. 6

2. These included an honorable mention from the Boston Printmakers, 1949; first prize from the Society of Four Arts, Palm Beach, 1949; first prize from the American Color Print Society, 1950. This print represented Atelier 17 in an exhibition at Wittenborn and Company, New York, 1949; represented Realités Nouvelles in an exhibition at Wolfe et Cie., Paris, 1949; and was exhibited in the Dallas Print Annual, 1953. See also Landau 1983, pp. 28–29.

Etch & engr. 15/50   Hon Mention   "Squid under Pier"   1st prize Am Color Print S.   Meina ? Eston '49
2 color plates   Boston Printmakers   Dallas Print Annual
                      1st Prize So of Art - Palm Beach   '53

Will Barnet

1911–

69.

Spring

1951

Lithograph on cream wove paper

35.3 × 43.6 cm. (image)

48.0 × 59.7 cm. (sheet)

In pencil, lower right: *Will Barnet*

In pencil, lower left: *Spring*

Watermark: *Rives BFK*

Cole 107

Worcester Art Museum, Anonymous Fund, 1988.168

Will Barnet's status as a master lithographer was solidly established in the late 1930s, when he worked as a printer and then as an instructor of graphic arts at the Art Students League in New York. He introduced many artists to the full range of printmaking techniques. His own prints were distinguished by their technical quality and expressive content. Barnet's early works were sensitive observations of life in the city; Social Realist in style, these prints often had political or moral overtones.[1] Then, late in the 1930s when he became a father, the artist reflected this deeply felt, personal experience in his prints.

During the 1940s, Barnet drifted away from printmaking to concentrate instead on painting, teaching, and his growing family. When he returned to the graphic arts in 1947, his style had become less representational; indeed, he had found his own abstract vocabulary. This development reflected not only the influence of contemporary modernist painting, but also Barnet's experiences with his children and their own art.[2]

Beginning in 1949, Barnet's work was deeply affected by a tumultuous family life, which eventually led to a divorce three years later. The artist found it difficult to paint, and he applied himself again the technical challenges of printmaking.[3] In 1949, Barnet provided financial assistance to his friend Robert Blackburn (cat. 93), who was then able to open his own printmaking studio in New York. This workshop made professional equipment and technical assistance available to artists who wished to make prints. Together, the two artists also carried on their own experiments with color lithography. From 1950 to 1952, they printed seventeen editions of color lithographs by Barnet, *Spring* among them.

Both the subject and style of these color lithographs show how the artist attempted to see the world through the eyes of child. A wide range of emotion was expressed in these prints, from loneliness and melancholy to untroubled confidence. Many of the images were set outdoors, where the figures of children lie in the grass, climb trees, and swing on ropes hanging from their branches. The accessible, evocative mood of these prints was meant to be strengthened by the viewer's nostalgia.

In *Spring*, the artist created a lyrical image of light and atmosphere, as soft as a golden memory. Bright colors seem even to evoke the fresh May air. Although the figures were depicted generally, their relaxed poses and apparent intimacy gave the print a mood of ease and cheerful contentment. Like a child's drawing, this image was freely drawn, and Barnet concentrated on outline rather than three-dimensional form or spatial perspective. In place of modeling and shadow, the artist substituted color.

The products of collaboration between Barnet and Blackburn were always technically elegant. *Spring* was printed in ten colors, and other contemporary lithographs by Barnet used up to fifteen. However, all of these colors were probably printed from fewer stones. John von Wicht (cat. 75), Blackburn, and Barnet experimented with printing several colors from each stone in one pass through the press, in a method similar to the *à la poupée* technique of color intaglio.[4]

The artist prepared all of the stones for *Spring* with crayon, the child's favorite medium. In preparing the stone that printed the brick-red color, Barnet seems to have covered much of the image with crayon, then scraped the ink away from the stone with a comblike tool to crate a crosshatched texture. The paper was registered on the several stones with cross marks in the margins of all four corners of the print, and triangular perforations of the sheet in the upper-left and lower-right corners. The difficulty of printing Barnet's color lithographs is suggested by the small size of the editions, usually from ten to fifteen impressions.

Notes

1. Cole 1972.

2. Doty 1984, pp. 31–49.

3. Ibid., p. 43.

4. Haas 1955. See also Seckler 1952.

Spring   Will Barnet

Eugene Berman

1899–1972

70.
Nocturnal Cathedral

1951
Lithograph on cream wove paper
33.1 × 23.3 cm. (image)
41.9 × 32.0 cm. (sheet)
In pencil, lower margin: *18/100*
Eugene Berman 1951
In image, lower right: printer's
blind stamp
Watermark: *Strathmore Courier*
U.S.A.
Worcester Art Museum, anonymous
gift, 1988.112

Although he was an accomplished painter, Eugene Berman was best known as a designer for the stage. In the course of a theatrical career that spanned almost four decades, he designed stage sets and costumes for such companies as the Ballet Russe de Monte Carlo, the Ballet Theatre of London, La Scala in Milan, and the Metropolitan Opera in New York. Berman's imaginative vision was stimulated by his unswerving love for Italian art, and an insatiable aesthetic curiosity. In the 1920s, he exhibited with a group of young painters who called themselves "Neoromantics," and the fantasy, nostalgia and enchantment of their style never left his art.

Berman worked constantly, filling sketchbooks and producing many ink drawings and watercolors. Late in the 1940s, he began to make prints, perhaps in an attempt to increase his reputation, or to develop his theater-going admirers into a directly supporting audience. Nearly all of Berman's prints were professionally produced lithographs, and among them was one of the most innovative color lithographs of the 1950s, *Nocturnal Cathedral.*

In America, Berman's lithographs were printed in Los Angeles by Lynton R. Kistler, whom Jean Charlot (cat. 32) probably introduced to the painter.[1] Among the first of their collaborations was the suite *Viaggio in Italia*, produced in 1950, prints that were later hand-tinted to simulate watercolor.[2] *Nocturnal Cathedral*, which followed soon after, was their first color print. Afterward Berman and Kistler collaborated on one other color lithograph, *Verona*, which was also published in 1951 in an edition of one hundred impressions. For each of his theatrical projects, Berman created a proliferation of drawings and finished watercolors. In subject and style, the present print is very much like one of these watercolor stage designs.

This evocative image represents the facade of a Baroque cathedral, mysteriously illuminated by the gray light of a full moon. The piazza before the church, which would teem with activity during the day, is now abandoned and melancholy. In the moonlight, the cathedral's many darkened corners and niches seem mysterious and forbidding. There, we imagine, a romantic tryst or a heinous ambush might occur at any moment. Berman set the scene for such events, and provoked the viewer's imagination, but he refrained from storytelling. The architecture is accurate in every detail, from its ornamental pediment to its sculpture-filled niches. This precision was typical of Berman, a perfectionist, who often insisted that even his costumes and stage sets must be historically correct.

The artist placed the viewer across the shadowy courtyard from the facade, which seems to loom above in towering Piranesian scale. The illusionistic space of the image was denied by the overlaid pattern of brickwork, which emphasized the picture plane. Like a gauze scrim in the theater, this transparent curtain increased the mystery of the composition. Scratched in the ink on the prepared stone, this brickwork pattern also distinguished the print technically in its day, as did Berman's multifaceted preparation of the lithography stones. In this sense, the lithograph parallels Berman's drawings, in which diverse media, including crayon, watercolor, gouaches, and colored inks were applied with an array of brushes and pens and often scraped and spattered afterward. Indeed, the artist sometimes splashed, scratched, and distressed even his painted canvases in order to simulate the look of age in the object itself as well as the subject.

Berman painted and drew directly on the four stones for *Nocturnal Cathedral*, which were subsequently printed by Kistler in his workshop in Los Angeles. Mainly he applied liquid tusche, of varied dilutions, to the stones with brushes, afterward detailing the image with crayon and scraping. The artist and printer

proofed this print several times, reducing the strengthening different passages, and adjusting tonal balances. The lithograph was first printed in a black ink edition, then other stones were added. The stones that printed the colors were also prepared with thin washes of liquid tusche, and they printed soft layers of tonal color, like watercolor washes. Berman chose colors and pale tones that are also in his watercolors. This impression is printed on hard-surfaced, laminated book paper, rather than an artist's paper, which may reflect the Kistler family orientation to book printing. Some impressions of the lithograph were printed on blue paper, which enhanced the eerie lighting effects and increased the mystery of the image.

Berman could be a disagreeable character, and a very difficult collaborator. His hubris and surliness are reflected in his correspondence with Rudolf Bing of the Metropolitan Opera, and in his dealings with Lynton Kistler.[3] Berman had long worked in Paris, and had studied under the famous Nabi printmakers Pierre Bonnard and Edouard Vuillard. His initial understanding of lithography was based on his distant memories of the French professional technicians of the beginning of the century. When he began to work with Kistler, Berman's practical knowledge of lithography was slight, but his demands of the medium and of the printer were unremitting. Nevertheless the collaboration was a productive one, and Berman and Kistler undertook several experimental printing projects together. Many of their working proofs, and related technical materials, are now in the National Museum of American Art in Washington, D.C.

Notes

1. Adams 1977b, pp. 105–106.

2. Another suite of hand-colored lithographs by Berman, more closely related to the theater, was *Mozartiana*, published in 1956.

3. Tuggle 1989; Adams 1977b, p. 106, note 18. See also Berman 1971; Levy 1947; Tobin 1984.

Eugene Berman 1951

Ralston Crawford

1906–1978

71.
Third Avenue Elevated #4
1952
Lithograph on white wove paper
43.8 × 25.9 cm. (image)
50.5 × 32.9 cm. (sheet)
In pencil, lower margin: *45/45*
Ralston Crawford   "Third Avenue Elevated #4"
Watermark: *Rives BFK*
Freeman L52.13
Worcester Art Museum, Anonymous Fund, 1986.99

Ralston Crawford, *Third Avenue Elevated*. 1949. Silver gelatin print. Worcester Art Museum, 1987.19.

An innovative modernist painter, Ralston Crawford heroically pursued his personal vision over a long career, often despite critical indifference. He was also a prolific printmaker, who preferred the medium of lithography for its immediacy and it range of visual effects. Although Crawford was fascinated by the peculiar challenges of graphic art, he remained unmoved by the craft of printmaking. In the 1950s, when lithography was not readily available to American artists, he went to Paris to produce most of his prints. Taking advantage of the European tradition, he left the technical intricacies and the tedium of printing to the master printers.

The style of Crawford's lithographs paralleled that of his paintings. Although they seem simplistic, these prints embodied the artist's precisely calculated sense of formal order, and each was the product of a long process of evolution. Crawford's first lithograph was *Overseas Highway* (Freeman L40.1), printed in three colors by George Miller in New York, in 1940. This Precisionist image of the bridge to Key West in Florida was strictly derived from an earlier painting.[1]

The artist's next involved work with lithography came in 1949, when he collaborated again with Miller on two editions (Freeman L49.1 and .2).[2] By this time, Crawford's mature style had developed, and he produced prints with a very different graphic impact. These expressive lithographs represented the artist's visual and emotional memories of the war. Crawford had also become an avid photographer. He always took his camera along in his travels, and he produced thousands of photographs. Beginning in the late 1940s, the compositions of most of Crawford's lithographs, and many of his paintings, were derived from his photographs. Cropped and balanced, reduced and schematized, they were abstracted details of snatches of reality, extrapolated from the artist's experiences. Crawford found in

graphic work—especially the process of lithography—disciplines that improved and purified his painting. He used the medium as a reductive technique for paring away the inessential compositional elements, like a sculptor in the process of carving.

While visiting Cologne in 1951, Crawford was deeply moved when he saw the destruction of the city wrought by three years of Allied bombing during World War II. Proceeding to Paris afterward, he made fourteen lithographs that represented his musings about war and mankind's inclination to violence and destruction. Printed at the studio of Edmond Desjobert, these prints were derived directly from Crawford's photographs taken in Cologne.

This procedure of appropriation and refinement was roughly followed over the years, when Crawford returned periodically to Paris to make prints in the lithographic studios of Desjobert, the Mourlot Brothers, Louis Ravel, and Lucien Detruit. He took the compositions for these prints from his photographs of the ramshackle cemeteries of New Orleans, the freight yards of Minneapolis, the boats and fishing nets on the French seacoast, and demolished buildings in New York City.

Third Avenue Elevated #4 is one from a series of lithographs that Crawford made in 1951 and 1952, at the Desjobert workshop in Paris. The prints of this series were drawn specifically from his photographs of the substructure and tracks of the elevated railroad in New York City, taken in the late 1940s (Fig.).[3] Between the initial photograph and the present lithograph, Crawford created an intermediary version of this composition, *Third Avenue Elevated #3* (Freeman L51.8, .9 and .10), which was printed in black ink and color variants. This version depicted a still-recognizable painted steel pylon.

The technique of this lithograph was suitably elementary. A separate stone was used to print each of the three colors. The opaque lithographic tusche was applied to the stones with a brush. In order to create hard-edged forms, the artist probably painted the tusche onto the stones through masks or stencils. Crawford carefully selected the dull, nearly complementary colors for this print to alternately project and recede, maintaining spatial ambiguity. Registration was achieved by the use of pins projecting from the stones to transfix the paper in the top and bottom margins.

Over the years, Crawford became progressively more comfortable with lithography, his line became more assured, and his drawing on the stone became less inhibited. In his lithographs of 1957, the artist worked in a more spontaneous, painterly style. These lithographs related to the artist's visits to Spain and reflected the influences of Goya and Picasso.

However, even the later prints represented a lean, schematized vision of the world. Like all of Crawford's lithographs, they were images that induce contemplation. Crawford once said of this element of his art: "In a world wracked by unreason, our last hope is to rearrange and bring order to our values, clarity to or lives and logic to our thinking."[4]

Notes

1. In 1940 Crawford also made the first of his two serigraphs, *Grey Street*. With its receding roadway disappearing in the distance, this composition is similar to *Overseas Highway*. The screen print was commissioned and published by the Cincinnati Modern Art Society.

2. Crawford's second and final serigraph, *USS Nevada*, or *Red and Black*, also dates from 1949, and was derived from the artist's observations of the atomic bomb test at Bikini Atoll.

3. Haskell 1985, pp. 110–113.

4. Freeman 1962, p. 8

Worden Day

1916–1986

72.
Arcana

1952

Soft-ground etching with engraving and linoleum block on off-white wove paper

38.5 × 66.8 cm. (plate)

48.5 × 76.7 cm. (sheet)

In pencil, lower margin: *Arcana 2/20 Imp-   Worden/Day/52*

Private collection

An innovator in both imagery and technique, Worden Day constantly allowed her achievements to lead her in new directions in printmaking. Nature and the imagination were her two constant sources of inspiration. Her works ranged from contemplative images of abstract realism, calligraphy, and pictography to observed and imagined landscapes of cosmic or microscopic proportions. Although Day loved to travel, she was drawn to New York and the aesthetic and intellectual camaraderie of her fellow artists.

In the early 1950s, Day maintained a close relationship with Atelier 17. From 1952 through 1954, she traveled several times to Paris to work alongside Stanley William Hayter (cat. 60), and in 1954 the New York shop attempted to expand its activities and membership by having her teach a course in color woodcut. The artist probably created *Arcana* at Atelier 17 in New York.[2]

Day's prints always paralleled her paintings in imagery, pictorial means, and technique. The artist developed her own method of applying paint to canvas, removing it with a scraping tool and blending it with solvents, thereby achieving a soft luminosity of color. She obtained comparable effects in her prints by sensitively inking and wiping her relief blocks and intaglio plates. The linear, pictographic character of Day's early paintings and color woodcuts gave way to more organic, almost microbiological imagery in prints such as *Arcana*. This work is part of a series that included drawings, frottage monotypes, color woodcuts, and intaglio prints ranging in date from the mid-1950s through the 1960s.

The artist conceived many of her works of the 1950s in ongoing suites related to one another in concept and imagery, among them the *Arcana*, *Incunabula*, and *Mandala* series. The well-known *Mandala* group utilized the rugged surfaces of crosscut tree trunks, from which she printed by frottage, supplemented with thin layers of color from other blocks.[3] Her freedom and innovation are also apparent in the remarkable series *Prismatic Presences* of 1957, in which she printed a rugged topographical image using the cracked surface of a plaster wall in her Manhattan studio. Each impression from this series was unique in its use of color and materials.

Arcana seems to evoke a deep, lightless ocean floor, where peculiar fluorescent plants float gently and silently in the mysterious darkness. Even as Day carefully plotted her linear composition, she exploited the random action of the acid in order to create stippling and veils of tone in the plate, which she later supplemented with very fine detail using a burin. By including both positive and negative linear configurations, she created an ambiguous sense of space.

Day apparently printed the color in this impression from an uncut relief block rather than a metal plate. She achieved amorphous veils of color here by freely applying ink in blobs to the block, blending and spreading it afterward with a brayer. The color was printed first, perhaps by rubbing, or under low pressure in a roller press. Then the etched key plate was printed in iridescent black over the thin glazes and washes of color. The unrepeatable character of this method created uniquely colored impressions within the edition.

The Brooklyn Museum has a variant impression of *Arcana* pulled in 1953, for which the colors were printed from another soft-ground plate, which deeply embossed the heavy cream laid paper.[4] Its background colors, dominated by orange and yellow, are quite different from the present impression and were applied to the plate in a more banded, rainbow-roll manner. Scraped out with a scorper and cleaned during the printing of the plate, the white lines of the Brooklyn impression stand out in deep embossing.

Notes

1. Moser 1977, p. 11.

2. Johnson 1959a, no. 33.

3. Johnson 1980, p. 86.

4. Brooklyn Museum, accession no. 65.81.2, the fourth from an edition of seven proofs. Notes at the museum suggest that the edition of 1952 comprised twenty-one, rather than twenty, impressions.

Ariana   4/red imp—Wood cut May 52

Hans Hofmann

1880–1966

73.
Composition in Blue

1952
Serigraph touched with gouache on cream wove paper
43.2 × 35.8 cm. (image)
48.8 × 42.9 cm. (sheet)
In pencil, lower left margin: *74/120*
In brown ink, lower right: *Hans Hofmann*
Worcester Art Museum, Anonymous Fund, 1988.40

Hans Hofmann was the only artist of the New York School to have experienced firsthand the development of modernism in Europe; his career spanned two generations and two artistic worlds. For many years, he was primarily a teacher, and his dissemination of ideas from the artistic revolution that took place in Paris between 1905 and 1915, along with his advocacy of personal style and technical virtuosity, was a formative influence on the American avant-garde in the 1930s and 1940s. Although Hofmann made only one color print, this extraordinary silkscreen represents notions of inspiration and process inherent in Abstract Expressionism.

In the 1940s, many New York artists reevaluated the theories and practices of Surrealism. Though Hofmann could not subscribe to the philosophical foundation of this style, he was intrigued by the process of automatism and the spontaneity of its resultant abstraction. He began to experiment with compositions consisting of linear skeletons of poured and dripped paint, which he created in immediate response to the physical behavior of the paint itself.[1] Gradually the poured web works were replaced by quick, free lines drawn with a crayon or a brush, which were later complemented with painted areas. These drawings still depended on the artist's momentary inspiration: "My work is not accidental and not planned," he said.[2] A series of original, mid-size works on paper followed, which Hofmann called his "free creations."

Hofmann's only screen print is essentially another of these automatist drawings. In its treatment of materials, its size and format, and its imagery and pictorial means, it is similar to his contemporaneous paintings.[3] The artist originated this design on the screen in an immediate burst of creativity, akin to the manner in which Stanley William Hayter (cat. 60) sought form in the engraving process. Hofmann seems to have been fascinated by the behavior of

tusche on the screen, and his varied application of stop-out resulted in a wide range of effects in his impressions of this print. His ink-laden brush quickly created a drawing in which amoebic, or plantlike, forms merge with geometric shapes to suggest depth and model space.

This print was produced by Esther Gentle, the second wife of the painter Abraham Rattner.[4] Gentle was Hofmann's student in the early 1950s, and the proprietor of a small publishing concern that reproduced in screen prints the work of well-known artists. At a time when sales of Hofmann's paintings were slight, Gentle persuaded him to try his hand at printmaking. Working at her studio at 67 Grove Street in New York, the master prepared two screens from which Gentle printed the serigraph.

This print gives the viewer a vicarious sense of the spontaneity of its creation, retained despite the many steps of the printmaking process. Similarly, many separate layers of printed ink mimic the physical effect of gouache and ink washes that were brushed on, had soaked in, and were gradually drying. To achieve the look of such random physical behavior, Hofmann and Gentle used many layers of ink on a hard-surfaced paper. Saturated layers of ink were systematically superimposed over thinner ones. Though the final result appears to consist of just two colors, there were actually seven layers of ink: two of diluted brownish black ink, two of black, and three of different shades of blue. The artist created mottled lines and dappled variations in the background by purposely inking the screens imprecisely, a choice that caused each impression to be in some way unique. This intentionally casual printing is inconspicuous because of the abstract nature of the image.

The first screen—prepared, using the tusche and glue washout method, from Hofmann's unpremeditated drawing on the silk—was printed with a semitransparent, brownish black, oil-base serigraph ink, the tone of which resembled a

watery India ink wash that had soaked into the fibers of an absorbent paper. The silkscreen was then cleaned, and the artist applied the tusche again, this time in the area of the field surrounding his linear brush drawing. The second screen was printed with a diluted greenish blue ink. Succeeding screens alternated black line and form with blue ground, each layer becoming progressively more saturated and opaque. The final, chalky layer of rich blue was not printed with oil-base serigraph ink, but with a water-soluble show card ink taken directly from the jar.

Many impressions of *Composition in Blue* have extensive gouache or ink additions, such as the white area at the middle right of the present impression. Hofmann himself made these touch-ups when he signed the prints. Despite the success of this print, sales were disappointing, and Hofmann never again felt the impulse to try printmaking.

Notes

1. For a discussion of the relationship between Hofmann and Jackson Pollock, see Goodman 1986, pp. 48–52.

2. Kuh 1962, p. 124.

3. See Long 1986, nos. 28–31, for Hofmann's only other prints, three transfer lithographs.

4. Esther Gentle's extraordinary serigraph reproduction of Lyonel Feininger's watercolor *Gothic Spire* is often mistaken for an original. An exhibition of her reproductive prints, "Great Names in Modern Art," was circulated by the American Federation of Arts in 1952 and 1953.

Trimmed away from the bottom margin of the present impression was the following letterpress inscription:
HANS HOFMANN COMPOSITION IN BLUE
Courtesy of 67 Gallery, New York
Publishers Tera-Gentle, New York
A number of impressions of the print also bear a black stamp reading © *Esther Gentle, 1952.* See also Bannard 1976; Greenberg 1961.

74/120   Hans Hofmann

Seong Moy

1921–

74.
Classical Horse and Rider

1952

Woodcut on white wove paper
64.6 × 39.6 cm. (image)
71.4 × 47.8 cm. (sheet)
In pencil, lower margin: *Classical Horse & Rider   II/40–II   S Moy*
Worcester Art Museum, anonymous gift, 1988.81

Though Seong Moy was an accomplished painter and an influential teacher, today his reputation rests chiefly on his distinctive color prints. *Classical Horse and Rider*, which won a purchase award at the Tenth Annual Print National Exhibition at the Brooklyn Museum in 1952,[1] exemplifies Moy's popular and influential woodcuts of the 1950s. These combined vigorous calligraphy with bold, bright colors. Several of his works from this period were inspired by classical themes, as were the prints of Dean Meeker, Anne Ryan (cat. 65), and Adja Yunkers (cat. 81).

Linear drawing in Moy's distinctive style dominates this image, translating plunging figures into sweeping black lines that emulate quick brush strokes. The slashing, exaggerated movement of this drawing has an overrefined, theatrical formality. Figures and background alike are fragmented into distinctive, flamelike lozenges. The figures seem to have been disassembled, mixed with fragments of the background, and twisted in this recombination. The artist used color and effects of overlapping and transparency to give substance to some shapes, and to dissolve adjacent forms into impalpability. The background was laid down first, and the black key block was printed last. Thus, Moy's calligraphy coalesces all elements of the composition into a ceremonial expression of movement.

The artist was innovative in his woodcut technique and was always open to new methods and materials. He experimented with the use of modern wood products, such as plywood, chipboard, and Masonite for his blocks, exploring the qualities of each surface and its response to the knife, seeking new effects.[2] Moy regularly used sheets of cellophane to refine the composition of his prints, and to organize the color separations for his woodblocks. Working from a finished color sketch, the artist would isolate areas of color and trace them onto the thin, transparent material, allotting one color to a sheet. Afterward, by stacking the cellophane sheets, he could visualize the finished print and adjust effects of form and color. Then each of the separate sheets was used to transfer the component designs to the woodblocks.[3] Moy often preferred to use just one or two blocks for his prints, using small brayers to individually ink the cells, which were separated by grooves, with various colored inks and offsetting them onto the paper in only one or two printings. Moy favored peculiar, interstitial colors, and he carefully used extenders to vary the effects of his inks.

Notes

1. Johnson 1956, p. 45. The impression of this print at the Brooklyn Museum (accession no. 53.28) is from an edition of ten; however, the present print comes from a larger edition. The Roman numeral II inscribed on this woodcut also indicates that Moy, like many printmakers of the day, often made more than one edition of his prints, according to the demand of the market.

2. Ibid. 1956, pp. 21–22.

3. Ibid., p. 21. This technique was also used by Guy Maccoy (cat. 53) for his serigraphs.

CLASSICAL Horse + Rider   11/130 · II   Smith

John von Wicht

1888–1970

75.
City

1952
Lithograph on cream wove paper
51.0 × 38.2 cm. (image)
66.2 × 50.9 cm. (sheet)
In pencil, lower margin: *City
1952   v.Wicht*
Watermark: *Basingwerk Parchment*
Worcester Art Museum, anonymous
gift, 1988.118

John von Wicht produced prints sporadically though consistently from the 1930s through the 1960s; these prints always paralleled his paintings in style and technique. The artist combined mastery of technical skill with imagination and intuition and an ever-fresh personal vision. All of his art reflected his enduring fascination with form, pictorial structure, and the representation of space.

Von Wicht learned the technique of lithography as a student in Germany. For many years after his immigration to the United States, the artist worked only occasionally in lithography. Then in 1949, along with Will Barnet, von Wicht helped to provide financial support for the establishment of Robert Blackburn's printmaking studio in New York. Modeled after Atelier 17, this workshop was conceived to make printing equipment and technical advice available to artists, who could have their editions printed by Blackburn and his staff. Classes were offered at the studio, and students often worked side by side with established artists. Von Wicht regularly produced prints at this workshop over a period of more than fifteen years.[1]

In the mid-1950s, the studio established a reputation for its color work, especially in intaglio and lithography. At that time von Wicht, along with Gus Lieber, conducted technical experiments with color lithography. Their work focused on a method for pulling multicolored prints from one stone in a single pass through the press, in a manner akin to the *à la poupée* inking and printing of a color intaglio plate.[2]

Printed with the assistance of Blackburn, *City* was a characteristic production of the Creative Printmaking Workshop in the early 1950s. It was similar in its materials and technique to Barnet's *Spring* (cat. 69) and Blackburn's *Interior* (cat. 93); however, these prints are quite different in style and visual impact. *City* was printed in four colors from four stones. Registration was achieved with Blackburn's distinctive method of triangular perforations of the margins, which fitted over pins protruding from the stones. Von Wicht prepared all of the stones with crayon. He drew with the side of the crayon, with its corners and sharpened point, to create a varied graphic vocabulary and a range of linear and tonal effects. The artist also scraped ink away from the prepared stone, as in the rounded orange triangle in the lower right.

City is one from a series of lithographs by von Wicht representing the city, which were made between 1950 and 1954 and carried similar titles. All of these prints depicted the skyscrapers of Manhattan, and typified the artist's preference for landscape and his practice of developing abstract compositions from his own observation. The present lithograph was the most ethereal of the group, and the most colorful.

In *City*, the streets and buildings were distilled into a Cubist linear gridwork. Equal substance was given to the architectural forms and the voids between them. Von Wicht represented some of the towers as arrows, pointing emphatically into the sky. The delicately drawn lines and soft shading gave the image a foggy obscurity, which evokes the city distorted by atmosphere. This intangibility contributed to an enigmatic and paradoxical sense of transparency and depth.

With selective shading, von Wicht also evoked various effects of light, of beams radiating skyward, and of light reflected off the buildings, highlighting them against the night sky. These effects of reflection and glow are emphasized by the print's soft colors. The luminosity of these hues is also reminiscent of stained glass; they remind us that von Wicht worked as a designer and fabricator of stained glass in the 1920s.

The style and elliptical shape of the composition are reminiscent of the early Cubist experiments of Braque and Picasso. However, its subject, with its energized linear matrix and its shimmering effects of light, are similar to the watercolors and prints of von Wicht's friend Lyonel Feininger.

This lithograph was exhibited in the Third International Biennial Exhibition of Color Lithography at the Cincinnati Art Museum in 1954. Von Wicht's prints were among the largest lithographs produced in the early years at Blackburn's workshop. As time passed, von Wicht felt the need to make bigger prints, analogous in size to his paintings. In the 1960s, he experimented with *pochoirs*, rendered in ink applied with brushes and brayers through stencils of cardboard. These were produced in very small editions and even in unique impressions, which were sometimes touched by hand after printing.

Notes

1. During the 1950s, von Wicht also had lithographs printed at Margaret Lowengrund's (cat. 37) Contemporaries Workshop in New York.

2. Haas 1955.

City 1952   v. Wicht

Reynold Weidenaar

1911–1985

76.
Darkness and Light
1952
Mezzotint on cream laid paper
34.9 × 43.1 cm. (plate)
44.2 × 58.6 cm. (sheet)
In the plate, lower right: *REYNOLD WEIDENAAR*
In pencil, lower margin: *Darkness and Light   Reynold Weidenaar   A.N.A.*
Worcester Art Museum, Anonymous Fund, 1989.5.1

Reynold Weidenaar, *Darkness and Light*, 1952. Mezzotint (proof from red plate). Worcester Art Museum, Anonymous Fund, 1989.5.3.

Choosing to concentrate on the demanding medium of mezzotint, the exceptional craftsman Reynold Weidenaar worked in a personal version of Regionalism. Although his meticulous, sometimes melodramatic manner has not worn well, it was very popular in the 1940s and 1950s, and the artist was highly esteemed in American printmaking circles. Aside from Alessandro Mastro-Valerio, Weidenaar seems to have been the only American artist of his day to focus on mezzotint, a difficult, nearly forgotten printmaking technique. Finding technical manuals to be of little use, he had to develop his own working procedures. He also found it difficult to obtain specialized tools such as mezzotint rockers and scrapers, and eventually had to acquire these—sometimes antique—tools from older artists and craftsmen in England, such as Ernest Stamp.[1] Enthralled by the look of the prints and by the romance of this nearly alchemical process, Weidenaar became almost messianic in his zeal to resurrect it. He published several articles, carefully explaining the process with the aid of his own technical illustrations.

This Piranesian caprice is Weidenaar's largest color mezzotint; one of just a handful of color intaglios, it displays the technical virtuosity that so astounded his fellow printmakers. Unlike the prints of his historical predecessors Christof LeBlon and Abraham Blooteling, who inked a single mezzotint plate *à la poupée* and printed it in one pass through the press, this complex intaglio utilized four plates. Impressions from each of the color plates and

some progressive proofs, now in the collection of the Worcester Art Museum (Fig.), show this print to be a marvel of planning and execution. Each color plate was worked fairly openly with a mezzotint rocker and more extensively with a roulette. However, the key plate was a fully developed mezzotint, also published in an edition of black ink impressions.

Darkness and Light represents the interior of the cathedral in Mexico City, which Weidenaar had seen during his visit in 1944 as a Guggenheim Fellow. The artist continued to depict Mexican subjects until late in his career, mining his old sketchbooks for many years. His most famous color mezzotint, *El Monstro del Parocuti*, depicts the eruption of a Mexican volcano, another scene he had witnessed in his travels.

A smaller version of this subject, *Cathedral Repairs, Mexico City*, was executed in 1949 under commission from the Print Makers Society in California for the annual members' presentation. The artist described the smaller print as "a mezzotint of the interior of the great cathedral of Mexico City, where I took sketches of workmen. They were reinforcing the columns of this massive structure which had been weakened by earthquakes. . . . I think the dusty lighting and the primitive means

to excavate the great pillars of masonry . . . ought to make a good rendering."[2]

Weidenaar's debt to prints of the Old Masters is unmistakable and reflects something of his personality. Fascinated by history and cultural tradition, the artist felt a deep sympathy with the Netherlandish painters and printmakers of the seventeenth century. This sentiment helped form his devotion to craftsmanship, and it was often romanticized in his prints. Another of his favorite subjects was the physical insignificance of man as compared with nature and history. In *Darkness and Light*, this theme is expressed with diminutive figures and dramatic shafts of light, another of Weidenaar's recurrent motifs. Here the light assumes a symbolic role, emphasizing the spiritual life that continues uninterrupted amid the chaos of adversity.

Notes

1. In a letter of 1943, Alessandro Mastro-Valerio asked for Weidenaar's help in obtaining mezzotint rockers. The author is most grateful to Paula Weidenaar Graf, the artist's daughter, for the opportunity to review much of his correspondence.

2. Letter of April 27, 1949, from the artist to Harold Doolittle, president of the Print Makers Society of California. This letter began an extensive correspondence between the two artists, through which Doolittle was encouraged to make mezzotints. Their letters included quite refined technical discussions, references to the trading of tools, and microphotographs of a plate by Blooteling, which fascinated both artists. See also Weidenaar 1948 and 1954; Wolff 1981.

Leonard Edmondson

1916–

77.

Circumstances of Action

1953

Soft-ground etching, etching, and aquatint on cream wove paper

20.2 × 36.7 cm. (plate)

31.3 × 49.8 cm. (sheet)

In pencil, lower margin: *2/50*

Circumstances of Action

EDMONDSON 1953

Worcester Art Museum, anonymous gift, 1988.94

Long a prominent figure in printmaking on the West Coast, Leonard Edmondson has concentrated on color intaglio for forty years. His prolific activity in painting and printmaking has brought him a continual succession of prizes, award purchases, fellowships, residencies, and invitations to exhibit his work. Moreover, this remarkable success is complemented by his distinguished teaching career and his widely read instructional book on intaglio technique. Like his California colleagues Ynez Johnston and Dorr Bothwell (cats. 95, 63), Edmondson based his distinctive style on Abstract Surrealism.

Technical virtuosity and originality are characteristic of Edmondson's etched oeuvre. The artist has acknowledged that landscapes seen from an aerial view were the initial inspiration for his intaglio prints.[1] Onto this topography, however, he superimposed a rich variety of forms and figures, which he perhaps developed from his experience as a calligrapher.

Many of Edmondson's prints of the 1950s represent his own private universe, a realm of what appear to be imaginary microbes teeming in a drop of water. Each print seems to represent a different glass slide, an ecosystem of protoplasmic organisms flourishing among fanciful coral castles. These creatures gradually evolved into larger and more sophisticated animals. The prominent forms of knobbed arms and jawbones in Edmondson's prints of this period are reminiscent of the works of Yves Tanguy and David Smith. In *Circumstances of Action*, these figures may or may not be animate. Together they make up a complex system that resembles a perpetual motion machine. Teetering precariously, the leaning shapes seem poised to tumble and set into motion a clockwork with no obvious purpose.

Edmondson's prints always present rich and fascinating surfaces. Their great variety of textural effects, achieved by soft-ground etching and aquatint, are quite astonishing on close examination. The biting of the plate for *Circumstances of Action* must have been done in numerous stages, followed by reworking with a burnisher and final detailing with an etching needle. The textures are denser in some areas, giving the effect of smoke and haze, and thus implying depth. The artist's use of color is sensitive and restrained, and transparent passages contrast with opaque areas. Not all of his prints are so dark in tone or as restricted in range of colors as is the present intaglio.

By repetition and refinement, Edmondson developed his printing techniques to a virtuosic level. The majority of his color intaglios were made from one plate, with all the colors layered onto the plate and printed in a single operation. It seems incredible that the present image could have been printed in one pass through the press, so integrated are the colors and so precise their registration. The color, usually a mixture of oil-base inks, was rolled through paper stencils onto the plate with small gelatin brayers.[2] Because these films of ink remained very thin, the artist was able to superimpose layers of color. Between about 1955 and 1959, Edmondson experimented with the use of a second soft-ground or aquatint plate, with which he added an overall scrim of tone and pattern to the image.[3]

Notes

1. San Francisco 1967, p. 4.

2. Edmondson 1973, pp. 53–54.

3. San Francisco 1967, p. 4. See also Heller 1958, pp. 116, 120; Print Council 1959, no. 18; Print Council 1962, no. 13.

2/50   Circumstances of Action   EDMONDSON 1953

Stanton Macdonald-Wright

1890–1973

78.

Pomegranate and Persimmons

1953

Woodcut on heavy cream Japan paper

22.4 × 40.0 cm. (image)

40.8 × 50.9 cm. (sheet)

In blue ink, lower margin: *To Lieh (?) – vecchio amico Stanton Kyoto '53*

Private collection

Color was a primary concern in the art of Stanton Macdonald-Wright throughout his eventful career. It was also a main concern of one of the earliest American modernist art movements, Synchromism, which the artist helped to found. His limited color printmaking activity came late in his life, and his woodcuts were personal and eclectic in their style and technique.

Macdonald-Wright's interest in color printmaking probably grew from his exposure to modern Japanese woodcut artists, when he lived in Tokyo in 1952. His earliest prints were made at that time, and *Pomegranate and Persimmons* was among the first of them. Beginning in 1958 and continuing until his death, the artist spent five months of each year at Kenninji, a Zen monastery in the center of Kyoto, Japan. As his knowledge of Asian philosophy continued to deepen, this wisdom and experience was reflected in his art, and he returned to ideas and projects that had occupied him decades earlier. From 1965 to 1967, the artist created *Haiga*, a portfolio of twenty large color woodcuts illustrating classic haiku by Basho, Buson, Issa, Shiki, Chiyoni, and Hokusai. The style of these prints varied from figurative to abstract, and their coloration from lurid to pale pastel. This series was exhibited, along with Macdonald-Wright's watercolors and most of his prints from the 1950s, at the Suzuki Gallery in New York in 1972.[1]

In *Pomegranate and Persimmons*, the artist depicted the brightly colored fruit on a pristine white cloth and bathed in warm, glaring light. The setting was otherwise left to the viewer's imagination. A light gray line used to circumscribe the cloth made it appear white by comparison with its setting, even though subject and ground were with the creamy color of the paper itself. The color of the fruit reflected softly onto the fabric that cradled it, and these warm hues were contrasted with the cool greens and blues that represent shadows. Modeling was done with discrete forms of color, the flatness of which abstracted the image. The elements of this composition—a rhythmic, linear skeleton that structured space, and from which swatches of many different colors radiated in all directions—were the classic elements of Macdonald-Wright's Synchromism.

Macdonald-Wright had returned to this subject—a simple still life of the fruit and a piece of cloth—time and again since the 1910s. This image represents his mature style, in which he strove to unify representation and abstraction and the aesthetics of European and Asian art. Here, the artist combined the analytical structuring of form and space from Cézanne with the simplicity of Chinese Sung Dynasty ink painting. His devotion to Cézanne was lifelong. Shortly after his arrival in Paris in 1907, Macdonald-Wright had purchased four watercolors by the master. Many years later, he stated: "Cézanne began the study of color . . . he was the first man ever in the history of any painting to utilize color as a function."[2] The artist was introduced to Chinese painting in 1912, and though his knowledge of Asian art became wide-ranging, he reserved his highest regard for Sung painting.

The size, palette, and surface effects of this print are analogous to those of Macdonald-Wright's watercolors of the 1950s. This similarity, combined with the stunning virtuosity of the present early woodcut, suggest that it was printed by Japanese craftsmen. The multiple-block woodcut was made on thick, hard-surfaced paper, and was fairly deeply embossed in printing. The remarkably delicate mottling of color on the surface of the print approximates the quality of watercolor painted on paper with a pebbled finish. This effect may have resulted partly from the surface texture of the woodblock. The reticulated effect, along with the delicacy of color, may also have been achieved by the printer's removal of some of the watercolor from the inked blocks with a textured blotter paper.

The prints of Macdonald-Wright's *Haiga* series were generally bolder in design and color than this early woodcut. However, they were made in exactly the same manner, with similar materials, and were signed in the same way, with blue ballpoint pen. Many of them derived from full-scale oil sketches made between 1965 and 1967. Though these prints are technically competent and effective, many seem to lack the consummate precision and control of the present woodcut.

Notes

1. Crimp 1972, p. 72.

2. Walker 1974, p. 64.

To hich rechio amdo -
Stanton Kyoto '53.

Gabor Peterdi

1915–

79.
The Vision of Fear

1953

Etching and engraving on cream wove paper

58.7 × 90.2 cm. (plate)

75.0 × 103.3 cm. (sheet)

In pencil, beneath image: *16/20*

The Vision of Fear   Peterdi 53 Imp

Watermark: *Arches*

Johnson 92

Lent by the artist

Upon becoming an American citizen in 1944, Gabor Peterdi was drafted into the army. Assigned to the anti-tank infantry, he witnessed the destruction of war firsthand. Soon, however, he was transferred to an intelligence unit in the Seventh Army, working first as a cartographer. Then, attached to the Office of Strategic Services, he was involved in the capture and repatriation of Hungarian war criminals who were to stand trial.

One of Peterdi's most technically innovative prints, this powerful vision grew out of a wartime experience. The artist's infantry unit was strafed by German fighter planes in 1945, and the visual impression of this terrifying moment stayed with him, eventually to be combined with and intensified by his reactions to the use of the atomic bomb.[1] Peterdi conceived of a cosmic landscape dominated by the destructive potential of humankind—eerily beautiful but polluted by the threatening presence of the bombers hovering in the glowing sky. "When you are a soldier," he wrote, "nature is hostile."[2]

The artist expressed the implications of this theme through an ambiguous space that merged points of view. He integrated a view from below, looking up at the annihilators, with one from above, hovering over a decimated, infernal landscape. The horizon is low and the perspective broad-ranging. From below, the viewer sees the cross-shaped symbols of the bombers as circling raptors, watchful and deadly. Like tracer bullets, dotted streaks of light surround the planes, piercing the night sky. From above, the viewer witnesses explosions in midair and on the ground. Smoke and debris from surface explosions rise into the air like whitecaps on a windy day, each indicating the impact of a bomb and the indiscriminate destruction of life, nature, and the works of man. As colorful and spectacular as fireworks, aerial explosions energize the sky. Trailing rockets and flashing bombs describe whirling arabesques and crosses, symbols of the airplanes that have delivered them and, inescapably, of the sacrifice of Christ. Thus Peterdi created a mystical vision of human annihilation and final judgment.

The artist's vision of this image was well formed before he began this print, but the means of expression emerged through the creative process.[3] Peterdi worked the large zinc plate deeply and with vigor, using the staccato stippling of the electric drill to simulate the trailing explosions of fireworks. In order to represent these aerial explosions, the artist had originally intended to use stenciled passages of color, but these created an unsatisfying flat, muddy effect.

After much trial and error, Peterdi realized that intaglio color would be most effective, and so he developed a way for small thin copperplates, inked separately and superimposed upon the main plate, to be printed in a single operation. He cut four little plates from twenty-gauge copper

sheets and etched and engraved them with cruciform explosions in precise relationships to the large plate. The white halos surrounding these color passages highlight the shape and height of the small plates from which they were printed. The artist integrated these areas more fully into the composition by applying black lines to two plates by offset, and he achieved a unifying effect by applying color to the surface of the large plate with a rubber mold cast from yet another, specially prepared intaglio plate. Fiery orange ink was rolled onto the rubber mold and then offset onto the inked intaglio plate behind one of the superimposed crosses.

Notes

1. Yale 1964, p. 17.

2. Peterdi 1963, p. 40.

3. Peterdi (1959a, p. 212) described in some detail the process of creating this print. See also Peterdi 1959b; Prasse/ Richards 1962.

6:20   The Vision of Four   Robert B Cops

Karl Schrag

1912–

80.

Evening Radiance

1953

Etching and aquatint with engraving
and drypoint on cream wove paper
48.2 × 67.8 cm. (plate)
55.4 × 75.4 cm. (sheet)
In pencil, lower margin: *Evening
Radiance   No 11 Ed. 30   Karl
Schrag   1953*
Watermark: *Arches*
Freundlich 81
Worcester Art Museum, anonymous
gift, 1988.99

The landscape prints of Karl Schrag represent the seamless union of inspiration and technical virtuosity. Years of drawing, painting, and printmaking preceded the effortless elegance of these evocative prints.

In *Evening Radiance*, the autumn sun sets over the northern woods, its rays represented in a calligraphic, linear manner, as are the branches of the bare trees, the forest underbrush, the eddies of wind through the crisp air, and the waves rippling on the surface of the distant lake. The light falling on every element of this vibrant landscape integrates them and draws them together. They all function as one harmonious system, droning in unison like a musical composition.

In his more than forty summers on the coast of Maine, Schrag has tirelessly sketched and painted the landscape, and his immersion there in the beauty of nature contributed to the evolution of his personal style. This development began in the mid-1940s, when the artist made careful studies in which he sought linear means to express the fluid movement of water. These exercises were concurrent with his experiments in etching and engraving at Atelier 17, and with the inevitable inspiration of Stanley William Hayter's presence (cat. 60).[1] From the idea of rhythms in water, Schrag began to find rhythms in clouds and land formations, in rain, wind, and the very ether.

The artist was strongly influenced by Asian calligraphy, and its basis in spontaneous inspiration combined with long, diligent practice. Practice (a physical search) and introspection (an emotional search) brought him some insight into what is essential in a landscape. Schrag learned to sum up his visual experience; thus his landscapes and seascapes often do not represent specific places or moments, but rather are vehicles for the expression of his thoughts, moods, and emotions. *Evening Radiance* is an example, the lyrical evocation of the sensual, and emotional experience of a dusky twilight.

Despite its seeming simplicity, *Evening Radiance* is technically quite complex. It was printed in three colors from three intaglio plates, each of which was prepared with mixed techniques, on the big press at Atelier 17. The artist's son Peter took time off from school at the Friends Seminary to assist in the two days of printing.[2]

The intaglio plate, inked with yellow, was printed first. The subtle texture of this plate was achieved overall by shallow-bitten soft-ground etching. In some places, such as the area of the sun, the plate was not treated, and was wiped during printing so that the film of ink was very thin, allowing highlights of the white paper to show through it. Other areas, etched with crosshatching, created deep yellow highlights. The second pass through the press printed the orange passages. On this plate, finely grained lift-ground aquatint was often accented by bundles of etched lines, imparting a sense of density and vibration to each of the energized orange brush strokes. The black key plate was printed last and was prepared chiefly with lift-ground aquatint, a technique that allowed the artist to apply his vibrant, calligraphic lines directly to the plate using a brush. Afterward, this plate was enhanced and detailed with a burin and a drypoint needle. So complex was the printing procedure for this intaglio that the wiping and printing of the plates made a great deal of difference to the final effect. Thus, some variation in effect occurred among prints in this edition.

Notes

1. Burrey 1956, p. 39.

2. Letter from the artist to the author, December 6, 1988. See also Schrag 1966 and 1977.

Evening Radiance   Nº 11 Ed. 30   Karl Schrag, 1953

Adja Yunkers

1900–1983

81.
Nocturne

1953
Woodcut on cream Japan paper
53.0 × 38.0 cm. (image)
59.9 × 43.7 cm. (sheet)
In pencil, lower margin:
"Nocturne"   AP   Yunkers – 53
Johnson/Miller 72
Worcester Art Museum, anonymous
gift, 1988.88

Adja Yunkers began making color woodcuts in Europe, under the influence of the German Expressionist printmakers and Edvard Munch. After his arrival in New York in 1947, he continued to develop woodcut as a creative medium, producing ever larger prints with up to twenty colors. Nocturne was created at the technical apogee of the artist's activity in this medium. A few impressions printed from the same blocks in deep green and brown are entitled Catching Grunions and Grunion Fishing.[1] This suggests that he was inspired by the spectacle of the late-night gathering of fish on the shores of southern California.

The woodcut depicts several figures gathering fish on the beach. The sky above is punctuated by diagonal slashes of purple, suggesting clouds that range into the distance above the beach, as well as the constant cadence of waves lapping on the shore. Darkness obscures the figures, entangling them and their movements, distorting line and muting color, and giving the whole scene a ghostly or dreamlike quality. Distant figures at the right, their position marked by the diminished triangle of the beam from their flashlight, give a sense of depth to the composition. The female figure standing at center holds up another flashlight, casting a triangle of illumination over her companion, who bends forward to gather the wriggling fish.

This figure recurs in several of Yunkers's woodcuts of the 1950s, including Miss EverReady and Succubae. Her companion wears a striped shirt, which calls up associations with the French Riviera and Picasso's Night Fishing at Antibes, a painting that was on view at the Museum of Modern Art in New York in the mid-1940s. So similar is Yunkers's print to this work that the painting seems likely to have been an inspiration for him.[2] The cubist fragmenting of the background and the palette of the earlier version of this print, Grunion Fishing, are both analogous to Picasso's painting.

In one impression of Grunion Fishing, most of the tone blocks are complete, and additional drawing in charcoal and pastel mark where the artist intended the key block to be cut for Nocturne, the final edition. This shows the way in which Yunkers built up his woodcut compositions, layering tones and colors, and allowing these forms to suggest the ultimate composition. The artist deeply scored the tone blocks that printed the background, perhaps

with a wire brush; these grooves allowed fine shafts of the white to show through, creating texture on the surface. Yunkers printed his woodcuts in many layers, with saturated and opaque inks superimposed upon thin, translucent colors. The surfaces of these prints always have a fascinating variety, for the artist contrasted glossy and soft, matte inks.

Each of the blocks carried two or more colors, and the artist generally applied ink to their surfaces with brayers. To Yunkers, inking was itself a creative act, often inspired though unmethodical. In this period, each impression may have been uniquely colored, and occasionally the blocks were even altered between printings. Quite casual about the control of his editions, Yunkers often made impressions that, although seemingly from the same edition, were inscribed as artist's proofs and assigned alternate titles. This confusion may have arisen when prints were not signed until several years after their production.

Notes

1. The year 1948, inscribed on one impression, is probably incorrect.

2. See Barr 1946, p. 223. See also Robinson 1983.

"Nocturne" Nb.

Sylvia Wald

1915–

82.
Dark Wings

1953–54
Serigraph on cream wove paper
46.5 × 60.5 cm. (image)
50.9 × 66.5 cm. (sheet)
In pencil, lower margin: "*Dark Wings*" *Artist's Proof* *Sylvia Wald*
Private collection

The originative, abstract prints of Sylvia Wald gave a new direction to serigraphy in the early 1950s. With a distinctive painter's approach to silkscreen and its materials, the artist made free, creative use of the process in a way that suggested the breadth of possibilities available to it.

Around 1950, Wald was deeply absorbed in the technique of serigraphy. In isolated, inventive experiments, she explored untried methods and visual effects. The artist moved to a studio in the woods where she could be close to nature,

and all of her prints from the period reflect this direct inspiration. More than the rugged, formal beauty of the natural world, Wald stove to capture its animating, energetic spark in her abstractions. Derived from landscapes, some of these essentially Abstract Expressionist compositions depict microscopic subjects, and others broad vistas, as suggested by their titles. The best known of these are *Tundra, Sun Caught in a Rock*, and the present serigraph. These remarkable prints were first exhibited at the Serigraph Gallery in Manhattan in February 1951.[1]

In *Dark Wings*, the many superimposed layers create vacillating effects of opacity and transparency. Through screens of fine mesh fabric, Wald laid a foundation of very thin ink, over which she layered progressively thicker pigments. Various techniques and materials were used for masking the screen, such as stencil film, which created the hard-edged forms in the lower left. The viscous top layer of ink, with its raised veins, achieves a peculiar organic freedom and delicacy. The artist created the arborescent impasto pattern by printing with thick, sticky ink, and by lifting the screen from the surface of the sheet with a sudden movement, pulling up ridges and peaks of ink that resemble the veins of leaves or insects' wings. This painterly method created great variations among prints within an edition, each impression being essentially unique.

In contrast to Wald's earlier representational prints, her abstract serigraphs of the 1950s were restricted, muted, and earthy in their palette, evoking the hues of the woods in autumn and spring. Like rocks or leafless trees, black forms and lines give a foundation to this composition, which is occasionally accented by a bright note of color, reminiscent of a spring flower emerging from the fertile forest floor.

Notes

1. Haas 1951; Cole 1951. See also Heller 1958, pp. 222, 225; Landau 1983, p. 120; Williams 1987, pp. 17, 69, and pl. 10

"Dark Wings"   Artist's Proof   Sylvia Wald

Milton Avery

1885–1965

83.
Dancer

1954
Woodcut on cream Japan paper
31.1 × 24.9 cm. (image)
42.4 × 31.9 cm. (sheet)
In pencil, lower margin: *Trial Proof Milton Avery 1954*
Johnson/Miller 89; Lunn 56
Private collection

Long before his critical recognition, Milton Avery had won the respect and adulation of his fellow artists. His figural style was intuitive and poetic, qualities also present in his charming, optimistic prints. His mode of printmaking was personal, minimal, and eloquent, and so was his use of color.

Although Avery's print oeuvre is small, it includes intaglios, lithographs, and relief prints. The artist's fascination with the boundaries between drawing and printmaking gave his prints their fresh, exploratory quality. The printmaking techniques that he preferred were the simplest: drypoint, with its spare, keen scratching of a needle in metal; lithography, with its direct, spontaneous drawing with crayon or brush; and woodcut, with its free seemingly random drawing in soft pine with knives and gouges. His uncomplicated, direct approach to each of these processes paralleled his instinctive, childlike drawing style.

Avery was more interested in the creative act of preparing a plate or stone and finding out whether it could print a satisfactory image than he was in the laborious, mechanical craft of printing. Thus his drypoints and lithographs were usually printed by others working from an authorized proof. By contrast, he found the processes of both cutting and printing woodcuts engaging. He was fascinated by the qualities and range of effects available from the subtle variations of the many stages of the process. Like Max Weber (cat. 15),

Avery seems to have found in woodcut the equivalent of a new drawing medium and an intuitive link to the pure inspiration of primitive art. He was absorbed by the decorative qualities that the materials imparted to the prints. In cutting the block, the artist often stressed—or even mimicked with his parallel strokes of the knife—the grain of the wood.[1] Occasionally, he also texturized the block with tools that left decorative patterns such as round pits, squiggles, and crescent shapes. Sometimes the back of the key block was used to print the color; it was oven carved with a shallow pattern or texture but not with a supplementary image.

Avery began making woodcuts in 1952 when Emily Francis asked him to try the process, in commissioning an edition for the Collectors of American Art, the organization she headed. Artist Steve Pace instructed Avery and printed two different versions of the woodcut *Dawn*, one of them utilizing a tone block printed in solid yellow.[2] The print, depicting a bird rising among the stars, was quite successful, and the artist would maintain its technical formula through all of his woodcuts.

These woodcuts were all printed by hand with the back of a tablespoon, sometimes with the aid of Avery's wife and daughter. The artist enjoyed printing because of the range of graphic effects available to him in the variation of the inking, the modulation of the printing pressure by rubbing, and the alteration of the register. Each impression was perceived as a unique opportunity; no two impressions were exactly alike. Many of the blocks were inked with a brush in a manner akin to the practice of the Provincetown Printers. Sometimes his woodcuts were methodically printed, properly signed, and numbered in editions, but often proofs were pulled only as needed.

The joyful and exuberant *Dancer* embodies a sense of balance and quiet control in the midst of almost frenetic movement. The dancer's body molds the space through which it moves, before a background of two large red forms, which insistently impart depth to the composition. He seems to have been captured in the midst of a pirouette, for his twisting feet, placed close together, do not seem steady enough to support his undulating body. The edge of the composition, beyond which the dancer's arm disappears, also suggests motion, as does the contrast of the solid human form with the nervous patterning of the background, the double outline of the figure, and the checkered pattern of his costume. Nevertheless, all the vibrating energy seems under control, judging by the graceful pose of the confident dancer's exaggerated arms.

Notes

1. Lunn 40. Printed in editions of fifteen impressions in black and one hundred impressions in yellow and black, *Dawn* is a variant of the lithograph *Soaring Bird* (1952; Lunn 35).

2. Lunn 1973, p. 14. See also Greenberg 1957; Kramer 1962.

Milton Avery '54

Charles Sheeler

1883–1965

84.
Architectural Cadences
1954
Serigraph on cream wove paper
15.8 × 22.2 cm. (image)
21.7 × 26.6 cm. (sheet)
In pencil, lower margin: *100/78*
Charles Sheeler 1954
Gordon 6
Private collection

Charles Sheeler is best known as a painter and photographer who worked in a range of styles, from avant-garde modernism to precise naturalism. His printmaking activity was slight but noteworthy. Over the period of a decade beginning in 1918, Sheeler made five lithographs in collaboration with master printer George Miller in New York.[1] These images, meticulously rendered on stone with crayon, were very much like the artist's exacting drawings in pencil and Conté crayon. In their choice of subject, composition, and tonality, they are also similar to his photographs. Among them were a stark still life, a semiabstract motion study of sailboats, and three architectural landscapes. Some of these prints were specifically derived from paintings, or their preparatory studies.[2]

Architectural Cadences was the artist's only serigraph, his only color print, and his final experiment with printmaking. In 1954 Frederick S. Wight organized a retrospective exhibition of Sheeler's work for the Art Gallery at the University of California, Los Angeles, where he was director.[3] The artist's dealer in New York, Edith Halpert, suggested that in conjunction with this project, Sheeler produce a print. *Architectural Cadences* was tipped in to a special edition of the exhibition catalogue, which was distributed to special contributors and supporters of the UCLA Art Gallery, particularly those who had helped to provide for the color reproductions in Wight's catalogue.[4]

The screen print reproduced an oil painting on canvas of the same title, now in the Whitney Museum of American Art in New York.[5] This painting was said to have been inspired by an industrial plant in Wisconsin.[6] The serigraph simplified the design of the painting slightly, expanding the composition on the left side and changing its coloration. Sheeler gave a little study, closer to the print than to the Whitney painting, to Wight; it is still owned by his widow. There were at least three other studies for the print. Two sketches in tempera on artist's board and one in tempera on glass were comparable in size to the serigraph itself; their whereabouts are unknown.

Although Sheeler may have initially developed this image from observation, his simplified shapes and schematized space shifted the subject of the image to a geometric dance of color and form. The range of colors in the print was more restricted than in his painting, and the image became all the more abstract and remote from naturalism.

During the 1950s, several workshops in New York specialized in commercial silkscreen work and were linked to the art world. However, it is uncertain just where this print was

made. The silkscreens for *Architectural Cadences* were prepared by the cut-film stencil technique. Eleven colors were printed from as many screens, achieving a subtle balance. Many of the lighter hues were transparent and transmitted the rich tone of the paper. The darker colors were more saturated, and also superimposed earlier layers of ink.

It is unclear whether Sheeler thought of this serigraph as a reproduction or as a work of art. It subtly adapted and interpreted the design of the painting rather than attempting to reproduce it exactly. He created the simplified scale design for the reproductive print. The soft palette and the careful adjustment of colors to create spatial effects suggest that the artist himself had the opportunity to proof the print. Although the degree of his association with the production of the screen print is unknown, Sheeler was certainly involved to some extent; and the artist's signature gave the serigraph the legitimacy of an original print, a distinction that it has retained.

Notes

1. Adams 1983, pp. 82–84. There is no discursive catalogue of Sheeler's prints; for an illustrated checklist, see Gordon 1976.

2. See Troyen/Hirschler 1987, pp. 68–69, for background on Sheeler's print *Barn Abstraction* (1918; Gordon 1), and ibid., pp. 90–93, for the lithograph *Yachts* (1924; Gordon 3).

3. Wight 1954.

4. Sims 1980, p. 29, note 25.

5. Whitney Museum Purchase, accession no. 54.35; reproduced in Sims 1980, p. 29.

6. I am thankful to Carol Troyen of the Museum of Fine Arts in Boston, for information regarding the preparation and production of this print.

 Charles Sheeler 1954

Reginald Neal

1909–

85.

Triptych

1955

Lithograph on cream wove paper

50.6 × 38.0 cm. (image)

59.7 × 45.5 cm. (sheet)

In pencil, lower margin: *"Triptych"*

8/10   Reginald H. Neal '55

Lent by the artist

One of the most able artist-lithographers working at mid-century, Reginald Neal was very influential in the promotion of color lithography in the United States. Having taught himself the technique early in the 1930s, and having refined his skills as a printer over years of study and practice, Neal printed his own lithographs for almost thirty years. His most influential contributions to the promotion of lithography, and to the use of color, came in the mid–1950s, when he was one of the few artists working in this country capable of printing his own lithographs. At this time, he taught printmaking at the University of Mississippi in Oxford, and his summers were spent working as a printer or teaching the process in various summer school programs. In 1954, Neal was director and principal lithographic printer at Margaret Lowengrund's (cat. 37) printmaking workshop in Woodstock, New York. There he printed editions for several artists, some of which utilized two colors.

In 1955 Neal produced the film "Color Lithography: An Artist's Medium" at the University of Mississippi. Widely praised as clear, concise, and instructive, this award-winning film featured a technical demonstration of the creation of Neal's lithograph *Reflections*. The movie was presented in New York in 1956, at the opening celebrations for Lowengrund's printmaking workshop at the Contemporaries Gallery.

In the early 1950s, the artist turned away from Regionalist landscapes printed in black ink, and first made abstract color lithographs. His evocative, nonrepresentational prints of this period derived from observed nature. Although some were semi-abstract, lyrical images and others were essentially calligraphic, Neal never pursued gestural abstraction.

Triptych is perhaps the best known of Neal's abstract prints.[1] Its linear abstraction may have been suggested to the artist by the prints of David Smith, which Neal printed in Woodstock in 1954. Smith's prints represented bands of energized linear calligraphy, each character of which can be read as the notation of a sculptural form.

Neal achieved a similar illusion of three-dimensional space in his columns of hovering shapes in *Triptych*. The careful placement of the sketchy forms over pale green vertical bands, as well as the intervals between these registers, implied a sense of depth and movement. Tattered edges preserved the brush-stroke quality of these forms; the artist removed some of the ink from the interior of these calligraphic shapes to emphasize this character. By using two colors, and occasionally superimposing them, Neal also enhanced the illusion of depth. The three vertical panels of Neal's composition also evoke Japanese calligraphy scrolls, the tall, narrow paintings that were sometimes mounted side by side on folding screens.

Neal worked directly on the three stones for this print. The narrow vertical blocks of the background were rendered on the stone with crayon. Afterward, these passages were textured by the removal of the waxy ink with an abrasive, perhaps sandpaper, which left a network of tiny scratches. This texture softened the color, and seemed to push forward the shapes superimposed on them. The calligraphic forms were applied to their stones with brushes, and also modulated by scraping. Perforations in the upper and lower margins of the present print show that Neal used pins, which pierced the paper and fitted into holes in the stones, to achieve proper registration. The artist printed *Triptych* himself, in the graphics studio at the University of Mississippi at Oxford.

Interrelationships of form and color became primary subjects of Neal's abstract prints. The present lithograph exemplifies the nature of his experiments with the interrelationships of imagery and technique.[2] After he had finished the edition of ten impressions of *Triptych*, he experimented with printing color variations from the same stones. A second edition of ten impressions was printed, entitled *Calligraphy* (Boyer/Capasso 20). In this set, the background bands were eliminated, and the calligraphic shapes, printed from two stones in black and dark gray, stood out boldly against the white of the paper. In a third variant edition, Neal reintroduced the light green field, but printed the calligraphic forms in deep green and pink. This lithograph (Boyer/Capasso 21) was also printed in an edition of ten impressions.

Notes

1. The print is reproduced in color in von Groschwitz 1956, cat. 390.

2. Boyer/Capasso 1986, p. 11.

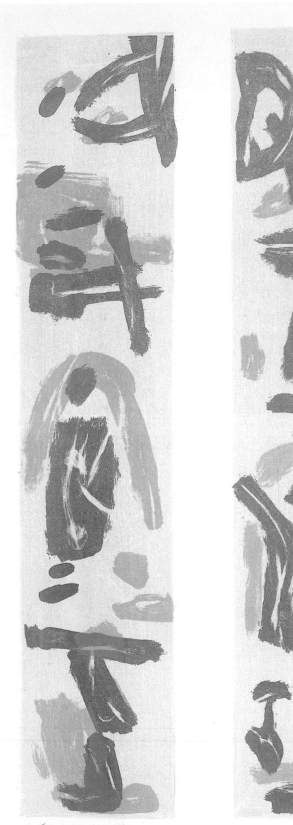

"Triptych" 8/10   Reginald H. Neal '55

Clinton Hill

1922–

86.
Title Page, or **First Page**
1956
Woodcut on blue-gray Japan paper
88.1 × 29.8 cm. (image)
93.9 × 31.9 cm. (sheet)
In pencil, lower margin: *Title Page Proof 1956   C Hill*
Worcester Art Museum, anonymous gift, 1988.77

The first in a series of color woodcuts, this print brought Hill early recognition as a printmaker when it was awarded the purchase award in the Tenth Print National at the Brooklyn Museum in 1956.[1] The calligraphy of this image has much in common with the style of contemporaneous woodcuts of Vincent Longo and Arthur Deshaies. All three artists were drawn to such imagery for its gestural abstraction. Hill wrote: "Though the images are invented I probably have to give credit to the calligraphy of Persia and the many languages of India. . . . I was attracted to oriental calligraphy I think not only for the speed, poise and elegance of line, but for the accumulation of marks on the page."[2] Full of indecipherable symbolic implications, the image conjured up many literary and loric associations.

The artist found a provocative paradox in the contrast between the spontaneous quality of calligraphic line from a brush loaded with paint, and the slow, mechanical, subtractive process of carving a woodcut. The halo of yellow surrounding each character creates an illusion of dimension and a sense that it was carved in relief. The artist also utilized the rough, knotted surface and open grain of the wood to enhance this effect. Thus it seems almost as if he carved the characters on a wooden plaque or stela. The narrow vertical format of the print invokes the shape of a scroll, an association supported by the material, a richly colored *washi* paper. Set apart and dignified in its frame, the print seems like a *sutra*, or the revered ceremonial writings of some sage mystic.

Hill carried on this theme in a handful of woodcuts with related imagery and similar technique. In the 1960s, when he lived in the Southwest, his color woodcuts on Asian papers reflected associations with the geology of that region. To this day, the artist finds occasional delight in relief printmaking, the most direct and intimate of the graphic processes.

Notes

1. Johnson 1980, pp. 116, 118, 162.

2. Letter from the artist to the author, April 14, 1989. See also Flint 1977, p. 10; Pearl 1984 and 1988.

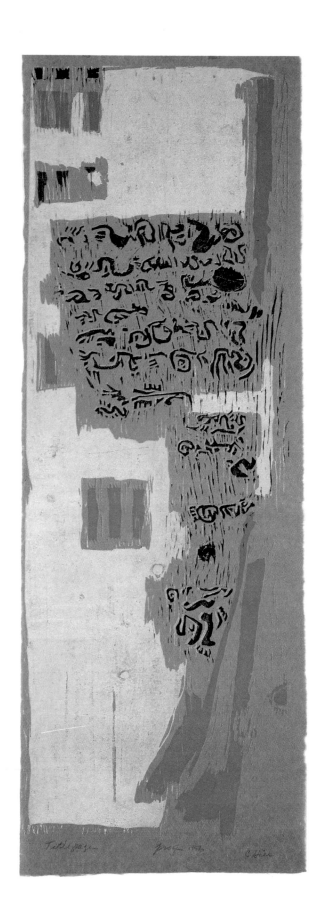

Nathan Oliveira

1928–

87.

Man and Drum

1956

Lithograph on cream wove paper

82.2 × 61.5 cm. (image)

92.7 × 66.2 cm. (sheet)

In pencil, lower margin: *Man and Drum   N. Oliveira 56*

Watermark: *Basingwerk Parchment*

Ball 20

Lent by the artist

Nathan Oliveira, an eminent painter and an influential teacher, produced a fascinating oeuvre of prints over a period of thirty years.[1] All of his work in etching, monotype, and lithography issued from his activity as a painter. During the 1950s, Oliveira began printing his own lithographs, many in color, using a relatively uncomplicated method that closely paralleled his manner of painting.

After his first experiments with lithography, Oliveira quickly rejected the crayon, preferring the painterly freedom of the brush and tusche. His first color lithograph was made in 1951. The style of his prints reflected the influence of the Bay Area Figurative School of painting, which sought the spark of inspiration in an unpremeditated, spontaneous manner of working. Retaining legible representations of landscape or figure, these painters focused on the activity of painting and on the physical nature of the paint itself. For them, the work of art recorded the process by which it was made, and symbolized its creator's unconscious mind. Oliveira's personal style used this gestural, intuitive manner of working to represent the unseen dimensions of the human psyche, the spiritual, the romantic, and the spectral.

In 1956 Oliveira bought an old lithographic press, stones, and materials from a defunct art school and began to make his own prints. In lithography, he found another painting medium, with its own distinctive physical and visual qualities and the provocative ability to replicate itself in multiple originals. Like many painters, the artist was frustrated by the task of printing and the tedium of organizing editions of identical impressions. For some time he sought

to resolve this dilemma by collaborating with various master printers. However, it remained difficult for Oliveira to relinquish any decisions that might have effected the final prints.

Working with master printer Irwin Hollander at Tamarind Lithography Workshop in Los Angeles, Oliveira produced eight editions. Among them was the famous *Homage to Carrière* (Ball 68), a tribute to the French nineteenth-century printmaker, whose influence on Oliveira was notable. Eugène Carrière was well known for his romantic lithographic portraits in which highlighted faces emerged from mysterious gloom. He often used a subtractive *manière noire* technique, in which the drawing was rubbed or scraped from a solid black image in gradations toward white. Successive printings were essential for extending tone, further enriching the black background and thus heightening and defining the figure. Carrière's images fascinated Oliveira, not only for their mystical appearance, but also because they disclosed their own evolution to the viewer.

This quality of disclosure is apparent in *Man and Drum*, a nine-color lithograph printed by Oliveira himself. Even in his early prints, the artist used the evolutionary system of color lithography.[2] It was appropriate for Oliveira, who worked alone with a massive, unwieldy lithographic stone. He painted on the printing surface with liquid tusche and asphaltum, pouring, dripping, and brushing these solutions with vigor and immediacy. Several layers of different-colored inks were superimposed, printed from a single counter-etched stone. Oliveira reworked the stone after printing each color. He deleted inked passages with an abrasive block of pressed pumice—called a scotch hone or snakeslip—and added new details by selectively counteretching and resensitizing the surface in order to introduce new painted passages. To draw details in the area of the figure's eye and on his shoulder, the artist scraped and pulled wet tusche across the stone, probably with the end of a brush.

In this direct process, each layer of imagery and each successive color evolved from the one before it. Oliveira made decisions concerning his changing design spontaneously as he worked on the stone. This process was analogous to his method in painting, in which he sought inspiration by visually, aesthetically, and physically reacting to an existing image of his own creation. Through this process of sequential development, the artist reached for a certain ineffable presence and vitality.[3] Unlike painting, printmaking allowed the artist to document the progressive transformation of an image in working proofs and changing states.

The somber, sometimes discordant palette of *Man with Drum* and the figure's haunting visage created a serious mood rather than a celebratory one. With this shaman, the artist enticed the viewer enticed viewer with unsettling fascination. Spontaneous brush strokes emphasized the swirling motion of the drummer's arm, suggesting the intensity of his playing. The profile head was a recurrent theme in Oliveira's lithographs. It often depicted a mask, prompting associations with ritual and the theater. Here, the elongation of the head was also reminiscent of an African ceremonial mask. The piercing eye flashing from the drummer's skull-like face also evoked the mystery of death. Costumed and entranced for a mystical, ancient ritual, the drummer seems to have been transported to an altered and impenetrable state of consciousness. Part of the power of this image lies in our uncertainty whether this trance is one of enlightenment or of possession.

Notes

1. Antreasian/Adams 1971, p. 35.

2. Ibid., p. 191; Eichenberg 1976, pp. 395, 397.

3. Ball 1980, p. 11.

Stuart Davis

1892–1964

88.
Detail Study for Cliché
1957
Lithograph on cream wove paper
32.0 × 37.9 cm. (image)
35.8 × 41.9 cm. (sheet)
Stamped in blue ink, lower right:
Stuart Davis
In pencil, lower right: (*E. D.*)
Myers/Cole 24
Private collection

One of the leading modernist painters of the twentieth century, Stuart Davis was passionately devoted to abstraction, and to the ideal that an image had its own independent reality. During an era when abstraction was thought to be foreign, this artist boldly strove to reconcile the modernist aesthetic with American culture. He was an important printmaker who concentrated primarily on lithographs. Davis was a superlative colorist, and he sensitively applied his intuitive command of the balance and interrelationships of color to his color prints. Four of Davis's twenty-five prints were made in color, and two other serigraph reproductions were made after his small paintings.[1] The artist's first color print was *Shapes of Landscape Space* (Myers/Cole 22), made in the New York City FAP graphic arts division in 1939. Of all of his color work, *Detail Study for Cliché* was perhaps the print on which he expended the most effort and exerted the most control.

In the mid-1950s, when Margaret Lowengrund (cat. 37) of the Pratt-Contemporaries Graphic Arts Center in New York organized her Master Print Series, Davis was invited to participate at the suggestion of the center's master printer Arnold Singer. In developing his design for the print, Davis adapted a composition he had used in 1955 for the lower halves of two paintings: *Cliché*, now in the Solomon R. Guggenheim Museum in New York, and *Ready to*

Wear, now in the Art Institute of Chicago. The artist utilized this method of appropriation and meticulous revision to develop the compositions of many of his prints. A preparatory drawing for this print as well as a gouache study are extant in private collections.[2]

Simple shapes of flat color were placed together, and seem as if they were a collage of cut paper. The final image has a careful, controlled balance of form and color that is decorative and harmonious. The collage quality of this lithograph, and other color prints by Davis, is reminiscent of the rightly hued *Jazz* series of *pochoir* prints by Matisse. Among the component forms is a curling red shape resembling a pair of fishhooks, one of the characters in Davis's own imaginary alphabet. Some of the shapes seem to overlap, and others appear transparent, causing the entire image to vacillate between flatness and illusory depth. The delicate balance of color and form achieves a satisfying cohesion.

Detail Study for Cliché was printed from three zinc plates. Working in his studio, Davis cut stencils from one sheet of material, probably heavy paper, and used them to mask the plates, which were then prepared with liquid tusche applied with a brush. When the three plates were overprinted, the composite image was reassembled. The jigsaw quality of this image, and the inaccurate matching of the edges of many of the forms, resulted from this process. An intentional imprecision gave the image a subtle tension and energy. After the plates were completed, they were taken to the Pratt-Contemporaries workshop,

where they were printed by Arnold-Singer. Davis was present for the proofing; he insisted on mixing the colors himself, and many trial proofs were required before the artist was satisfied.

Detail Study for Cliché was printed in an edition of forty, with two signed artist's proofs. This uncataloged proof apart from the edition was left unsigned at Davis's death. Thus the estate stamp, representing a facsimile of the artist's signature, was affixed later, and then endorsed with the initials of his son E[arl] D[avis].

The lithograph was exhibited in the fifth International Biennial of Color Lithography at the Cincinnati Art Museum 1958. The clarity and graphic impact of *Detail Study for Cliché* made the print an ideal design for a commemorative U. S. postage stamp. Davis approved the final design for the stamp shortly before his death, and it was issued in December 1964.

Notes

1. Myers/Cole 1986, p. 73.

2. Ibid., pp. 76–77. See also Kelder 1980.

Antonio Frasconi
1919–

89.
14th Street Meat Market, N.Y., #1
1957
Woodcut on cream Japan paper
87.2 × 58.7 cm. (image)
91.6 × 61.0 cm. (sheet)
In pencil, lower margin: 7/10
"14th Street Meat Market, N.Y. #1"
Frasconi 57
Baltimore 381
Worcester Art Museum, anonymous
gift, 1988.71

There are two sides to Antonio Frasconi's artistic personality. His passionate, poetic reaction to the beauty of life has always flourished alongside constant concerns about oppression, social injustice, and his personal commitment to human dignity. The vehicle for these messages has been a direct, heartfelt style, expressed through mastery of the medium of woodcut, in prints, portfolios, and illustrated books.

Throughout his career, the artist has worked in an expressive semi-abstract style, derived from German Expressionist printmaking and journalistic social criticism. When he worked in Uruguay as a political cartoonist, Frasconi's style developed out of the tradition of social commentary formed from the left-wing Mexican muralist revival of the previous generation. After his arrival in the United States in 1945, the artist was encouraged by vestiges of American Social Realism.

The present print is one from a series of six large-scale color woodcuts, representing Frasconi's observations of the meat market in New York City. Executed in 1957, these woodcuts straddled the boundary between still life and abstraction. In this nocturne, the hanging sides of beef and the undulating forms of the hardware suspending them were rendered in the artist's distinctive, confident drawing. Many of the component forms of this image were outlined and isolated by the color of the background. Pushed toward the picture plane, these shapes created a strong surface pattern.

The poetic side of Frasconi's personality is apparent in this Carracci-esque still life, where he discovered beauty in everyday life. His humanist side is present here too, for literally and figuratively the cuts of meat in the *14th Street Meat Market* series represent the butchers and meat vendors. This is quite apparent in the present print, where white-smocked butchers stands in the shadow of the

hanging carcasses. However, in other prints in the series, the repeated meat hooks and inspection tags and stamps affixed to the meat also symbolize the workers and the repetitive routines of their jobs.

Perhaps through his background as a journalist and his literary bent, Frasconi recognized that one of the extraordinary capabilities of the graphic arts was to express the passage of time.[1] The reproductive process of printmaking encouraged him to reuse and vary his images, replicating and altering his printing blocks to create different states and renditions of a given composition. This quality of variation better reflected Frasconi's own experiences as an observer, and as a craftsman engaged in a time-consuming process. A group of prints, mounted as a series or bound in a folio to be perused slowly, provided an experience fundamentally different from the immediate reading of a painting.

To further explore this notion, the artist adapted some of the visual techniques of the cinematographer. For example, in his woodcut series *Lettuce Workers* (1953; Baltimore 305–309), Frasconi first represented the farm laborers from a distance, scattered among endless rows of plants in vast fields, often bending to pick the lettuce. In subsequent prints, the artist zoomed in on the workers like a cameraman, so that details of their stooped figures comprised entire compositions. This device not only emphasized the experience of the laborers, but also symbolized the seeming endlessness of their task. For exhibition, Frasconi printed several blocks from this series on large canvases, to be viewed at once. Later the suite was printed on separate sheets of paper and compiled in the folio *Lettuce Country* (1954; Baltimore 337).

Frasconi often used this and similar effects of variation and repetition to express the passage of time, or the complexity and multiple viewpoints on a given subject. The *14th Street Meat Market* series provided a similar, multifaceted experience. Thus, unfortunately, when removed from its context in the suite, the present print loses one aspect of its impact.

The artist always favored bright, primary colors. These were often emphasized by the use of an even, overall composition in balanced, relatively dull tones, which the bright hues accented by juxtaposition. To achieve a satisfying intensity in his prints, the artist preferred oil colors for their versatility and their range of opacity and translucency.

Frasconi carved his woodcuts from planks of pine.[2] He began the process by drawing directly on the plank with charcoal, or ink applied with a pen or brush. The artist usually worked from preparatory sketches, and blocked in gray and black areas with hatching. The blocks were cut with a variety of carving tools, for each knife and gouge produced a different texture. Frasconi was extraordinarily sensitive to the wood itself; he often found in its grain the suggestion of a composition.

The blocks were charged with oil-base printer's ink with a brayer. They were then fitted into a jig or registration frame to insure correct placement of the sheets on the multiple blocks. Placing the sheet face down on the inked block, Frasconi printed by rubbing the back of the paper with a wooden dowel.

To some extent, he also tried to allow the medium to form his imagery. Thus, his prints were often abstracted by the idiosyncrasies of a woodblock, by the character of the form and texture caused by the carving knife, and by the distinctive appearance of ink on the surface of the paper. Because he cut, inked, and printed all of his own work, imbuing each impression with the sensitivity of his touch, Frasconi's editions are small, usually limited to twenty impressions or fewer.

Notes

1. Tonelli 1987, p. 22.

2. Hentoff/Parkhurst 1974, pp. 148–155.

George Miyasaki

1935–

90.

February

1958

Lithograph on cream wove paper

63.5 × 48.4 cm. (image)

66.3 × 52.0 cm. (sheet)

In pencil, lower margin: *8/10*

February   Miyasaki '58

Watermark: *Basingwerk Parchment*

Worcester Art Museum, Helen

Sagoff Slosberg Fund, 1988.210

During the 1950s, George Miyasaki was one of the few Abstract Expressionist painters who succeeded in transferring the full impact of his painterly style and method to his prints. Soon after his introduction to lithography in 1956, this young artist began to create eloquent color prints, which gained a wide reputation for him as a printmaker.

Abstract Expressionism was the style developed in the mid-1940s by artists of the New York School, including Franz Kline, Jackson Pollock and Willem de Kooning. Adopting some tenets of Surrealism, these painters believed that by working in an unpremeditated, automatist manner, they could tap into the universal creativity of the unconscious mind. The evolution of their style toward complete abstraction coincided with their growing fascination with the sensuous qualities of the paint itself, and with the techniques of its manipulation. They began to think of a work of art as a record of the process by which it was made and a symbol of the inner mental states of the artist.

The first generation of Abstract Expressionists concluded that printmaking was incompatible with their intellectual and aesthetic ideals.[1] The democratizing aspects of printmaking were contrary to their highly personal aims. Further, it was believed that the involved techniques required to make prints suppressed the intuitive spontaneity of creation central to action painting. However, this New York School prejudice did not accompany the dissemination of the style. In 1948, a group of artists in San Francisco, including Richard Diebenkorn and Frank Lobdell, created the suite *Drawings*, a series of original offset lithographs that proved how the medium could reproduce spontaneously created images while preserving all of the power and energy of automatism.[2]

In the 1950s, Diebenkorn and Nathan Oliveira (cat. 87) pointed the way to Miyasaki's use of lithography in an Abstract Expressionist mode. Like those of his teachers, Miyasaki's prints grew directly out of his painting. Unlike relief or intaglio techniques, lithography retained every gesture and nuance of the artist's drawing. It was also significant that Miyasaki himself undertook every step of the process, preparing and printing from the stones.

In his early prints, Miyasaki was inspired by the beauties and forces of nature, which he sought to represent in a symbolic manner. By their titles, many of the prints of this period allude to landscapes, seasons, or times of the day. However, seldom did their compositions, forms, or colors have any direct relationship to these ostensible subjects. The energy, subtlety, and complexity of his work functioned allegorically. The process of the print's creation, the qualities of the materials, and their handling were the primary subjects of such lithographs as *February*.

This print was produced from a single stone by the evolutionary system of color lithography, also used by Garo Antreasian (cat. 97).[3] This method was well suited to an artist who worked alone, printing large lithographs from stone. The composite image was made up of many layers of superimposed printing in different-colored inks. After printing each color, the stone was chemically defaced and its ability to print negated, although the image remained legible. The surface of the stone was then resensitized, and the next color image was applied. Working from

the shadows on the stone and from proofs, the artist could introduce new imagery, strengthen early elements of the design, or cover and obscure old passages. Thus, each layer of imagery evolved from the one before it. In this direct process, all the decisions about design and color were made actively and immediately by the artist during the preparation of the stone.

In *February*, what appears to be opaque blocks of color are revealed, on close inspection, to be richly layered passages of transparent tones. Despite its abstraction, this image achieves the illusions of depth and space. Miyasaki's color prints are most intriguing because they combine, paradoxically, the immediate and spontaneous in an overlayered complexity.

The artist prepared his stones with both crayon and liquid tusche, which was dripped, poured, painted, and scumbled onto the stones with brushes. Tusches were applied in varied dilutions, but most were fairly transparent, veil-like washes. Miyasaki often drew freely on the stone with crayons. Sometimes he also scratched and scraped tusche from the stone, in a sort of negative drawing. With adroit judgement, the artist instinctively adjusted the superimposition of imagery and the balance of colors.

Miyasaki inked the entire stone, and the distinctive chipped edges became the borderline of the lithograph. Ink built up at the edges of the stone, producing staggered lines when the sheet was printed slightly off register. Several lines reveal how many times the stone was printed. The complexity of this process was also reflected in the small size of Miyasaki's editions, which seldom included as many as twenty impressions.

Notes

1. Graham 1987, pp. 10–11.

2. Ibid., pp. 11, 38; Adams 1983, pp. 161–163.

3. Antreasian/Adams 1971, pp. 192–193.

Malcolm Myers

1917–

91.
Hundred Guilder Print

1957

Soft-ground etching, open bite, etching, aquatint, and engraving with gold leaf on cream wove paper

60.7 × 65.7 cm. (plate)

65.9 × 73.6 cm. (sheet)

In pencil, lower margin: *"Hundred Guilder Print" 10/30 1957 Malcolm H. Myers*

Watermark: *J. WHATMAN*

Helsell 29

Worcester Art Museum, Anonymous Fund, 1989.6

One of the most outstanding teachers of intaglio printmaking in America, Malcolm Myers helped perpetuate the influence of Atelier 17 by initiating the graphic arts workshop and study program at the University of Minnesota. Infatuated by the addition of printed color to his own intaglios, the artist consistently produced captivating color prints from the late 1940s through the 1980s.

As early as 1946, Myers expressed his thorough knowledge of printmaking history in prints such as *Saint Anthony* (Helsell 10), which was inspired by Martin Schongauer's famous engraving, and later in *Knight, Death and the Devil* (1956 and 1961; Helsell 36) after Albrecht Dürer.[1] The work of Rembrandt served as both the source of inspiration and the subject of lighthearted parody in *Improvisation on the Night Watch* (1961) and in the present plate. Extended study of art history in an academic environment may have perpetuated this leitmotif in Myers's prints up through the 1960s.

This print takes its name from Rembrandt's famous etching *Christ Calling the Children to Him*, a work so prized that during the artist's lifetime one hundred guilders was paid for an impression.[2] Unlike that of Rembrandt's, the ostensible theme of Myers's print is the Crucifixion. Its mood and treatment of the subject also parallel *A Procession to Calvary*, a panel painting of 1564 by Pieter Bruegel the Elder, which is now in Vienna.[3] Like Bruegel, Myers obscured his subject in a vast and teeming summer landscape, making it seem as if the primary theme of the image were the season itself. The printmaker also adopted Bruegel's anonymous crowds, which lead the viewer from the foreground to the base of the cross. Myers represented the period of eclipse, the sixth to the ninth hour of the Crucifixion, when "the sun's light failed" (Luke 23:44–45). Rembrandt, in his large etching *The Three Crosses*, depicted this interval with tenebrous, dramatic light, and Myers attempted in his print to create a similar effect in colors.

A solar disc in gold leaf surmounts the figure of Christ, and a black sun is reflected in the central lake before Golgotha. The eclipse casts a pallid green light and eerie shadows over the forests, lakes, and meadows. Reflecting the universality of this event, the birds and beasts all pause in alarm and nervous wonderment. Despite the animals' awareness, the crowds of people seem ironically oblivious to this terrible miracle. A strangely glowing light hides the crosses of the two thieves, but the fruit-laden trees flanking the Crucifixion stand out as symbols of the fallen man now redeemed.

As always, Myers approached the creation of this print without any preconceptions, preparatory drawings, or even a compositional scheme. He allowed the image to evolve organically through many revisions, with an openness to inspiration and change that can also be seen in Rembrandt's printmaking process. Myers worked the soft ground of the key plate using a wide variety of techniques and tools. Patterned objects that happened to be lying about the studio were pressed into the soft ground. The artist preferred to use a penknife to draw in the ground and to engrave the plate at a later stage. A buff color was stenciled onto the aquatint tone plate; he inked and wiped the plate as spontaneously as he had worked it.

This print was included in *American Prints Today*, the influential exhibition organized by the Print Council of America in 1959.[4] As well, it won the purchase prize at the Brookhaven Museum Print National exhibit of 1960.

Notes

1. Johnson 1980, p. 203.

2. With characteristic irony, Myers first offered the print for sale at a price of one hundred dollars.

3. Friedländer 1976, pp. 25–26, pls. 32, 33.

4. Print Council 1959, no. 41. See also MIA 1958; Swanson 1962.

"Hundred Guilder Print"　　　　　10/30　　　　　1957　　　Malcolm H. Myers

Carol Summers

1925–

92.
Dark Vision of Xerxes
1958

Woodcut on cream Japan paper
94.8 × 63.7 cm. (image and sheet)
In pencil, lower margin: *Proof   Dark Vision of Xerxes   Carol Summers*
Summers 30
Private collection

Immediately arresting and emotionally accessible for their bold, flowing designs and vivid colors, Carol Summers's prints hold the viewer's attention with their tonal and textural subtleties. The artist's technical innovations depended on the nature of his medium. His prints reveal a sensitivity to wood, the subtleties of its grain, its various absorptive qualities, and the ways in which it responds to sculpting tools.

The king of Persia in the fifth century B.C., Xerxes was immortalized by Herodotus and Aeschylus, and his military exploits became part of Hellenic folklore. Determined to conquer the Greek Empire, Xerxes amassed the biggest fighting force of ancient times. Crossing the Hellespont on a bridge of boats, the Persians marched all the way to Athens, forcing the Greeks back to their last line of defense, the Isthmus of Corinth. However, in a dream, the king foresaw the destruction of his great fleet and army by cataclysmic storms and tidal waves. Indeed, the Persian navy, crippled by devastating storms, was defeated by the Greeks at the battle of Salamis. Xerxes witnessed this rout from a lofty vantage on Mount Aegaleos, and when his vision became reality, he was forced to retreat.

In one sense, the artist conceived of Xerxes's lust to conquer the world as his "dark vision."[1] He represented this story as a lyrical vision of deluge. With overwhelming force, an impenetrable blue wall closes the top of the composition and descends ragingly upon the viewer. A sliver of space at the left enhances this precipitous sensation of movement. Undulating bands of yellow and pink beneath represent the bobbing bridge of boats, but the swirling blue billows are ambiguous. They may represent roiling clouds surging with

frightening speed over the sea and land, or a cataclysmic tidal wave whipped up by an ocean storm. Unlike the golden bands beneath, the softened edges of these azure forms enhance their duality.[2]

Summers produces his woodcuts by hand, usually from a single block of quarter-inch pine plywood, using oilbase printing inks and Japanese papers. The artist makes his block slightly larger than the paper, and before printing, he centers the dry sheet on the cut block and secures it with clips. Summers refers to his own printing technique as "rubbing." The ink is applied directly to the front of the sheet with small, thinly charged brayers. Pressure against the protruding relief areas deposits ink on the paper, which also bends into the concavities of the block to escape the ink. Essentially this process is more like painting than printmaking, for the artist applies color to the paper itself. Thus, he can see the pigment and can directly control it. Summers then atomizes mineral spirits onto the sheet, and the ink becomes dye. The absorptive fibers of the paper draw the thinned ink away from the surface, diffusing and muting colors.[3] By varying the volume of the solvent spray, the artist can control the dissolution of the ink and its bleeding into the paper. This process always produces unique impressions, and the artist accepts the inevitable variations.

When Summers made his first conventionally printed woodcut in 1950, he was strongly attracted by the materials, but uncomfortable with the

reversal of the process. Irregularities of the wood grain and surface enthralled him, and the soft, curving lines they suggested were more alluring than the straight ones traditionally imposed on the material. A master carpenter and cabinetmaker, Summers depended on carpentry for his livelihood in the years before he was able to support himself through printmaking.[4]

For several years, the artist sought his own formal vocabulary in concert with the nature of the wood itself. He cut with dull carving tools and filed with rasps to soften the edges of forms. His woodcut *Rainbow* (1957; Summers 29) was the first in which he rolled several colors onto the surface of a sheet set atop a woodblock. For *Dark Vision of Xerxes*, his next print, Summers wanted to soften the edges of form even more, so that they might suggest pounding waves and billowing clouds. He pushed his technique one step further, dissolving the wet ink with mineral spirits to blur these forms. This additional step made this print the first to integrate all the elements of Summer's innovative color woodcut technique.[5]

Notes

1. Letter from the artist to the author, May 11, 1989.

2. In a letter of December 12, 1988, to the author, the artist divulged that when the print was complete, he recognized overtones of germination that may relate to the birth of his son shortly thereafter.

3. This is a common variation of color in Summers's prints, here apparent in the iridescent, dark blue area at the upper right, which seems to glow with a pink cast, the result of a chemical reaction between the ink and the mineral spirits. The diluent broke down the ink into its component pigments, causing the pink hues to leach out and rise to the surface.

4. ADI Gallery 1977, p. 8.

5. Summers's bleeding effects have technical affinities with the prints of Kosaka Gajin (1877–1953), the Japanese master whose water-base inks were absorbed in the paper in similar manner, achieving ghostly, feathered edges. See Jenkins 1983, pp. 70–71.

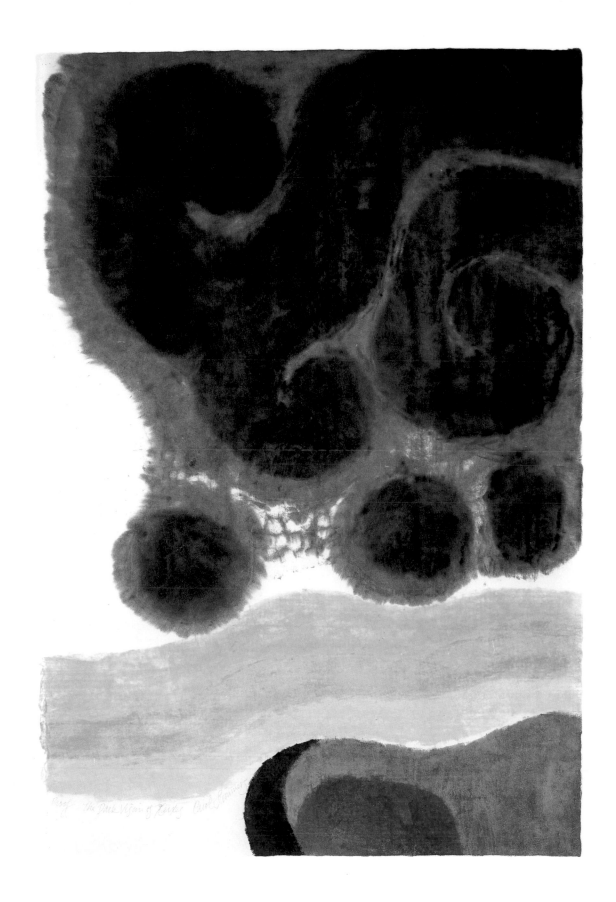

Robert Blackburn

1920–

93.

Interior

1958
Lithograph on cream wove paper
30.3 × 22.5 cm. (image)
45.2 × 31.7 cm. (sheet)
In pencil, lower margin: *"Interior"*
Bob Blackburn
Watermark: *Rives BFK*
Private collection

Robert Blackburn is the proprietor of the oldest collaborative lithography workshop in continuous operation in the United States. The longevity of this studio, and its considerable influence on American printmaking, has depended on his personal commitment to sharing the joys of printmaking and to the creation of an expressive, distributable, accessible art. The Printmaking Workshop opened in New York in 1949, with the financial assistance of Will Barnet (cat. 69) and John von Wicht (cat. 75). It was conceived on the model of Atelier 17 (see cat. 60), and organized as an open, cooperative workshop where artists could find professional equipment and technical assistance. Private donations and the subscription fees paid by a group of artists and students for the use of the shop have always been its main sources of support.

However, during the 1950s, it was a difficult task to keep the studio open, and only Blackburn's personal industry and economy met the challenge. The artist earned supplementary income by printing at the New School for Social Research, the National Academy, and Cooper Union. In 1953 and 1954, he was in Paris, working at the Desjobert lithography studio, sharpening his technical skills and observing the collaborative practice of the famous master printers. However, when he returned to New York in 1955, Blackburn found little demand for his expertise. Still, he persisted, and somehow the workshop slowly continued to grow. Soon there were five presses, with facilities for intaglio and relief printing as well as lithography. The studio developed a reputation for color printmaking,

based on Blackburn's achievements and the experiments of John von Wicht, Gus Lieber, and Harold Paris.[1] The master lithographer Arnold Singer (see cats. 37, 88) printed at the studio at this time. Among the many other artists who worked there in the 1950s were Will Barnet, Bernard Childs, Minna Citron, and Boris Margo (cats. 69, 94, 68, 66). Under the influence of the School of Paris, Blackburn's own prints of this period became more organic in their imagery, more abstract and brightly hued.

In 1957, Blackburn became the first master printer for Tatyana Grosman's new Universal Limited Art Editions (ULAE).[2] He commuted from Manhattan to West Islip, Long Island, to work with a secondhand press in a succession of makeshift studios in Grosman's house. There, he printed editions—many of them in color—for Sam Francis, Fritz Glarner, Grace Hartigan, and Larry Rivers, and later for Helen Frankenthaler, Jasper Johns, and Robert Rauschenberg. Blackburn helped these painters, most of whom had never made prints before, with patient encouragement. Although he may have been at odds with them stylistically, the craftsman's respect for creative freedom and his high standards for technical quality were apparent in many early masterpieces published by ULAE. When Blackburn decided to return to his own studio full-time in 1962, he was succeeded at ULAE by his assistant Zigmund Priede.

Despite his collaborations with these New York School painters, *Interior* reflects the European modernist style that Blackburn developed during his studies at the Art Students League during the 1940s. Its Analytical Cubism characterized many of the artist's prints of the 1950s, most of which were still lifes or figurative compositions. In the succeeding years, Blackburn progressed away from this style, along with the School of Paris, toward a more organic abstraction that was always lyrical and colorful.

Interior was printed in four colors from four stones. The sheet was pierced by pins in the top and bottom margins, to affect the placement of the paper on the stone and assure proper registration. The artist prepared the stones with crayon only. Using the point and edge of the crayon to achieve varied qualities of line and modeled form, Blackburn created a remarkable range of linear and tonal effects. The artist used crosshatching extensively, and deepened the shading and colors with overprinted layers of hatching. Some stones were printed very slightly off register on this impression. This imprecision adds a slight sense of tension to the image, and an added sense of depth. However, the precision of the drawn line and the accuracy of the printing tighten and contain this quiet, restful image.

This lithograph is one from an edition of ten. Blackburn's prints were usually printed in small editions, often in just a handful of impressions. Blackburn sometimes neglected to inscribe edition numbers on his prints.

As his career has progressed, the artist has been gradually swept up by the administrative duties of the workshop and drawn away from his own artwork. "But running the place," he once said, "teaching and interacting with other artists is a rewarding experience that sometimes supplants my own creative urge. It gives me something back."[3]

Notes

1. Haas 1955, p. 15.

2. Tomkins 1976.

3. Glueck 1988, p. 15. See also Johnson 1980, p. 167; Adams 1983, pp. 191–193.

"Interior"   Bob Blackburn

Bernard Childs

1910–1985

94.
Persephone

1958

Drypoint on cream wove paper
22.6 × 29.8 cm. (plate)
49.3 × 69.4 cm. (sheet)
In pencil, lower margin: *Childs '58*
épreuve d'artiste "Persephone" 3/10
Watermark: *Rives BFK*
Private collection

Bernard Child's approach to printmaking, like all of his artistic activities, was characterized by the integration of traditional working methods with the newest technology, by the transformation of a mechanical process into a personal mode of expression.[1] The artist experimented with mixing materials in order to give texture to painted surfaces, and in sculpture, he combined Plexiglas with transmitted and projected light. In intaglio printmaking, Childs used up-to-date metalworking tools and techniques, and lavished his attention on inking and printing. This innovative, typically American attitude contrasted glaringly with the European context the artist chose for himself in the 1950s, when his creative experiments in printmaking began.

The titles of Child's prints reflect his inexhaustible fascination with universal and cosmological themes. The spontaneous, intuitive quality of these works, especially his early drypoints, seems to reveal the artist reaching within to a deep reservoir of creativity.

In ancient Greek mythology, the beautiful Persephone was queen of the underworld, having been abducted by Pluto and forced into this regal role. When her mother, Demeter, goddess of agriculture and the harvest, mourned the loss of her daughter, her fertility ceased, and a period of barrenness fell on the earth. Yet Persephone was allowed to visit her mother each spring, for one-third of the year, and Demeter's jubilation caused the earth to grow and flourish again. Thus, ancient Greek cosmology explained the passage of the seasons.

Childs's lyrical image therefore represents a personification of joy, an explanation of the return of life in the spring. The musical, dancelike quality of the image implies some sense of the limitation of this pleasure, for summer passes as inevitably as the dance is measured by its musical score.

The soft, pastel hues of *Persephone* are gay and heartening; it is an energized, kinetic image. The artist's dotted, calligraphic lines are botanical in their graceful, arching curves. By careful inking and wiping of the plate, Childs defined a fairylike pink form. The cloud of blue plate tone surrounding this form has a windy, watery feeling. The emerging shape marks *Persephone* as a transitional print, between works made in Childs's gestural style and those in his later style, which was dominated by form and dimension.

The plate for *Persephone* was chiefly prepared with an electric drill in the artist's Paris studio. Childs insistently described this process as "power drypoint," acknowledging the use of the drill and distinguishing the quality of line and stipple from that of plates made by hand with a needle or roulette. He felt that conventional drypoint lines were feeble. In making such plates, the artist worked on zinc, brass, or copper, without preliminary drawings or designs or preconceived notions of composition. He used a broad variety of tools with his drill, including straight bits and rotary burrs made of steel, carborundum, and wire, and he supplemented these with burin work.

Despite their freshness and immediacy, Child's intaglios resulted from long processes of refinement. The artist would work and rework a plate, striving for an elegant poise between spontaneity and compositional balance. The layers of strokes and gestures were often made over months, and in one instance the artist spent four years on one plate. Childs also conducted careful and methodical experiments with wiping and printing in colors. A great many variant impressions were pulled before he settled on the manner of inking and printing for an edition. He customarily applied all of the colors to the plate at once, and printed it in one pass through the press. The artist modulated tone and blended colors directly on the plate, sometimes creating new lines and forms in the course of wiping away the evenly applied film of ink. He once wrote that it took him about five years to perfect his skill in inking, wiping, and printing a plate.[2]

Childs found that it was nearly impossible for another printer to duplicate in quantity his original intention and effects, so he preferred to pull each print himself. In fact, he used the term "artist's proof" or *épreuve d'artiste* to indicate an impression printed by the artist himself. This process demanded enormous concentration of labor, time, and spirit, and determined that the size of the edition would be small, fifteen or fewer impressions. Yet only very slight variations exist among impressions within Childs's editions. It is the passion apparent in his prints that makes his intaglios so extraordinary.

Notes

1. I am indebted to Judith Childs for her assistance in the preparation of this essay.

2. Letter from the artist to Joan Hansrath, November 17, 1965, now in the Archives of American Art.

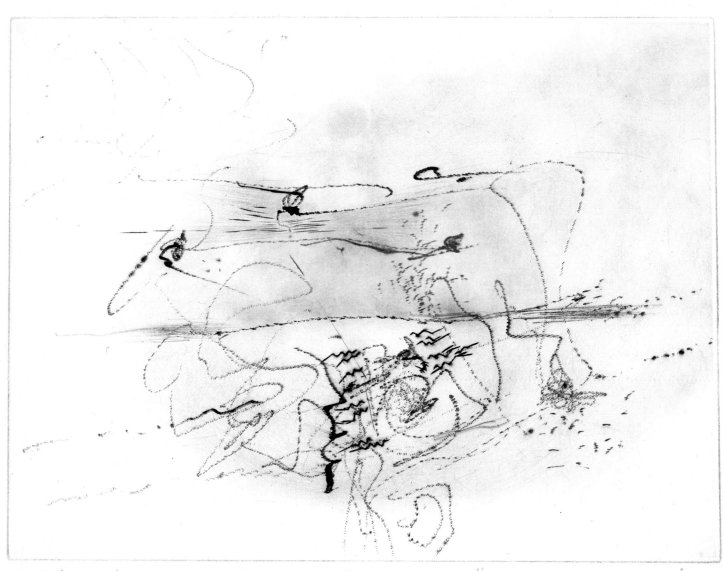

Childs — '58   Épreuve d'artiste   " Persephone "   3/10

Ynez Johnston

1920–

95.
Dynastic Scene

1958

Soft-ground etching, etching, and aquatint on cream wove paper
29.9 × 22.6 cm. (plate)
43.7 × 32.4 cm. (sheet)
In pencil, lower margin: *26/35
Dynastic Scene   Ynez Johnston*
Private collection

A perennial fantasist, Ynez Johnston produced a wonderful group of color intaglios in the 1950s and 1960s. These prints, always parallel to her paintings, evoke her own imaginary world. Deceivingly unimposing, they are actually masterful technical achievements; their range of texture and subtlety of color help create a provocative effect.

Johnston's very personal images sprang both from her dreams and from her imagination: "My involvement of form may be compared to the idea of doodling, in which shapes and symbols appear in unpremeditated fashion as continuously self-propagating forms."[1] The linear aspect of etching encouraged her flat, calligraphic orientation. She named her works so as to conjure up associations in the viewer; often title preceded image, contributing to its inspiration.[2] Sophisticated implications—sociological, anthropological, and even spiritual—seem to emerge from these visions. However, although this well-read and widely traveled artist drew on a vast body of knowledge and experience in forging her prints, they came fundamentally from her own universe. Thus they invite viewers to explore and to fantasize, to concoct their own explanations, indulge in games of association, and narrate their own

stories as part of the visual experience.[3] The use of color, though not essential to these images, is sensitive and rich, with the opulence of a tapestry.

The title of the present work suggests the cumulative achievements of an honored family, or perhaps the civilization and culture ruled by such a dynasty. A calligraphic inscription at the top of the plate evokes a Mogul miniature, yet this legend also seems weathered and deeply etched, like some stone inscription or pictograph, a commemorative legend carved by a mysterious antediluvian or Incan civilization. A city emerges from a mountain, chiseled and terraced into the rock through generations, with castellated palaces separated by streams and precipitous pathways. The elegant structures and exotic written language seems to reflect a culture of wisdom and ritual formed around the legends of an ancient dynasty. Mysteries lurk in this paradise, a forbidding and yet strangely alluring place.

The technique of *Dynastic Scene* is as provocative as its imagery. Deceptively simple, this intaglio exemplifies the elegant integration of stylistic and technical aspects in Ynez Johnston's mature prints. Her experiments with this medium often focused on achieving in her prints effects and impact similar to those of her mesmerizing canvases. The artist constantly played the capabilities and limitations of the media against one another. She worked intensely with color intaglio from about 1957 to 1965, combining aquatint, sugar lift, and soft-ground and standard etching with inventive inking and printing techniques. Johnston produced each of her color prints from one plate in a single pass through the press.

Here, a heavily printed, deeply etched matrix provides the framework for delicate drawing and for textures from lightly bitten etching and aquatint. The heavy black embossed lines and forms of Johnston prints were achieved by deeply etching the plates in a variant of the lift-ground process parallel to the dimensional impasto of her casein paintings. She charged the single plate with black ink, wiped it clean, then applied oil colors onto it through paper stencils with her fingers or with little gelatin brayers. The shiny quality of the dense black lines and passages, printed from the deeply etched areas of the plate, was a result of the quality of the French ink.

Notes

1. Loran 1950.

2. Ibid.

3. Wolff 1978. See also Ikeda 1977; Langsner 1951; Berry 1975; Pousette-Dart 1956.

26/35   Dynastic Scene   Ynez Johnston

Michael Ponce de León

1922–

96.
Wounded Mountain

1958
Collagraph on cream handmade paper
60.9 × 42.1 cm. (plate)
64.8 × 50.4 cm. (sheet)
In pencil, lower margin: *9/10 Wounded Mountain   Ponce de León*
Worcester Art Museum, anonymous gift, 1988.98

Late in the 1950s, Michael Ponce de León made innovative prints that challenged the conventional limitations of intaglio, blurring the boundaries among sculpture, painting, and printmaking. These works also heralded experiments with paper pulp as a medium.

In his first series of collagraphs, Ponce de León represented monoliths, especially mountains, which he remembered from his travels in the American West, Mexico, and Norway. Prints such as *Mountain Woman*, *Once Upon a Mountain*, and *Enchanted Mountain* reflect his movement toward abstraction and more conceptual interpretations.[1] The artist endowed some of these mountains with human characteristics; they became personalities shaped by the geological processes that made them, with events evident on their weathered surfaces like experiences on the face of an old man.

Wounded Mountain grew directly out of personal experience. While Ponce de León was living in Norway, a close friend was killed in a mountain accident, and the event inspired the creation of this collagraph.[2] The gaping wound in the mountain suggests an opening into the volcanic innards of the earth, yet the blood-red color also reinforces a human identity for this subject. The artist wrote of this print: "I have tried to evoke in this tragic proud shape a poetic metaphor of the human drama with all the directness and simplicity of a spear thrown by a savage."[3]

When creating his collagraphic plates, the artist was more interested in sculptural and formal problems than in graphic concerns. He created a relief sculpture for its own sake, and only later was it transformed into a printing matrix. Similarly, color came under consideration only when the artist began to ink the plate and then only as "dictated by the disposition and relationship of the shapes."[4]

The plate for *Wounded Mountain* comprises three main components welded together. The dividing white lines of the print reflect the seams between these elements, crevices whose depth was beyond the reach of the malleable, wetted paper. Striations in the blue field were printed by shallowly etched grooves that held a thicker film of ink than did the surface of the zinc plate. This background, like a raging rainstorm falling from darkened skies, lends a sense of majestic scale to the image. Discernible among the objects that make up the mountain's surface are tangled bits of wire, swatches from various wire screens, a zipper, and a fragmented ball chain.

Ponce de León himself made the viscous, slow-drying, oil-base inks for his collagraphs. These were methodically applied to the printing matrix with little gelatin rollers, rags, and brushes, a painstaking inking process that sometimes took up to four hours. The artist printed his plates in one pass through a modified etching press fitted with sensitive springs, allowing a broad variation in the height of the sculpted plates while maintaining constant and consistent pressure. It was also necessary to pad the press with thick blankets in order to absorb this variation.

Through the years, Ponce de León continued to modify and develop the technology of the press, eventually devising a hydraulic machine that could apply ten thousand pounds of vertical pressure. This process required very special paper, a sensitive, heavy sheet as much as a quarter-inch in thickness, that would conform to the deep crevices of these relief plates and could withstand great pressure without tearing. After some difficulty, the artist found a source for such paper from Douglass Howell, who made the required material from long-fibered linters in his paper mill on Long Island. Like his teacher, Rolf Nesch, Ponce de León printed his uniquely colored collagraphs in small editions, usually of ten impressions or fewer.

Ponce de León has often referred to the "magic" of printmaking, the bewildering technical complexity that makes it possible to create powerful, reproducible works of art. A comfortable familiarity with technique, along with the open-mindedness required to develop individual solutions to technical problems, is what the artist continues to instill in his students at the Atelier Ponce de León in New York.[5]

Notes

1. Cochrane 1974, p. 40.

2. Letter from the artist to the author, June 22, 1989.

3. Print Council 1959, no. 47.

4. Ponce de León 1959.

5. Cochrane 1975, p. 54. See also Gray 1969; Ponce de León 1967.

Wounded Mountain   Ponce de León

Garo Z. Antreasian

1922–

97.
View

1959
Lithograph on cream wove paper
66.2 × 86.5 cm. (image)
79.9 × 90.0 cm. (sheet)
In pencil, lower margin: *8/15*
View   G. Antreasian 59
Worcester Art Museum, Anonymous
Fund, 1988.209

Like many of Antreasian's prints of the late 1950s, *View* resulted from his efforts to transfer the impact and appearance of his paintings to lithography. His prints of this period became progressively larger, more colorful, and more abstract, and he sought painterly effects in the special capabilities and characteristics of lithography. The artist also preferred printmaking techniques that were analogous to the process of painting as a creative experience.

View was given a purchase award in the Twelfth National Print Exhibition at the Brooklyn Museum.[1] This print presents a very romantic, wholly imaginary vision. Like Antreasian's other prints of this time, such as *Limes, Leaves, and Flowers*, *View* was composed of basic forms in lyrical colors, with a focus on the painterly surface quality. Despite the abstracted two-dimensionality of this print, an illusion of depth is strongly exerted by the central road leading to the high horizon, and by the contrasting linear details and jewellike colors of the distant city.

To achieve the freedom of painting, Antreasian approached the creation of this print with no preconceived design, just as he would have confronted an unmarked canvas. Rather than beginning with a finished color model, which would have been separated into individual component colors and then precisely reproduced, the artist allowed the design and colors of the print to develop during the process of creation itself. The image emerged progressively from both additions and deletions, each suggested by the preceding phase. In this manner, Antreasian also permitted the physical properties and behavior of the materials to determine the image.[2]

View was made from just one large, repeatedly counteretched stone, which the artist reworked for each overlaid color. Made directly on the stone with tusche, asphaltum, and touches of crayon, each image was then adjusted with scraping, sandpapering, and scratching of details that were afterward mostly obscured by superimposed layers of ink. After printing, the image was chemically defaced from the stone, which was then resensitized for the next color. Thus the work emerged from a minimum of resurfacings of the stone.

A combination of overprinted, impasto-like inks contribute to this print's painterly effect. A rich and dense body of resonant color was built up from many layers in contrast with the thinness often associated with color lithography. Though some of the layers were laid on the stone with opaque tusche, others were applied in thin washes. These veils of ink allow for shimmery effects of transparency as imagery from lower layers shows through. The last three or four layers were printed in transparent white ink, with modifications to the image in between printings, to achieve a scrim of milky washes that heightens the mystery of the setting.

Antreasian also tried to find a sharper, etching-like linear structure that would overcome the characteristic soft, insubstantial tonalities of lithography at that time. To achieve such a bold, crisp delineation, he printed the linear key drawing twice. Numerous transparent veils of color followed, and then the linear key, somewhat modified, was superimposed once again, further strengthening and amalgamating the overall structure. In *Rock Cliff* (1958), Antreasian used the same combination of layered, painterly washes along with an overprinted key image in brown and black with dramatic effectiveness.

Like many of Antreasian's early techniques, the evolutionary method developed largely out of technical limitations. Before 1961, the artist worked in a tiny studio at the Herron School of Art, in which efficiency of setup and operation were paramount. Working alone in this cramped space, without benefit of dollies or hydraulic lifts, Antreasian had to improvise in order to produce from stone a multicolor lithograph of this size. To avoid moving the ungainly stone repeatedly from press to graining sink, he decided to print from just one surface and to minimally adjust his imagery between printings by chemical means rather than the standard mechanical method of regrinding and re-etching for each color.

Notes

1. Baro 1976, no. 10.

2. Antreasian/Adams 1971, pp. 192–193.

Edmond Casarella

1920–

98.

Triggered

1959

Paper relief print on cream Japan paper

68.8 × 52.4 cm. (image)

86.8 × 61.2 cm. (sheet)

In pencil, lower margin: *15/20 "Triggered" E. Casarella '59*

Worcester Art Museum, anonymous gift, 1988.70

In the 1950s, Edmond Casarella used an interesting variation of relief printmaking to make large, powerful, vividly colored prints. A talented sculptor, he independently developed an additive method for producing relief-printing blocks from cardboard in a manner that was essentially the opposite of the customary procedure of carving a relief block and analogous to modeling in sculpture. In this sense, Casarella's printing matrices parallel Michael Ponce de León's (cat. 96) contemporary metal collagraph plates and their relationship to conventional intaglio.

The style of Casarella's prints reflects the development of imagery in his paintings. In the early 1950s, in prints such as *Civitavecchio* and *A Moment of Panic*, he stacked rectilinear and angular forms in rickety constructions that seem to tremble with tension. Later in the decade, in large-scale color prints such as *Blue Vein* (1957), *Departure* (1958), and *Signal* (1959), the artist represented more organic, rounded forms and painterly, sweeping arcs. *Triggered*, one of his most gestural prints, also belongs to this group from the late 1950s, which are similar to Will Barnet's contemporary woodcuts (cat. 69).[1] The floating forms multiplied progressively in Casarella's prints, eventually subsuming the entire composition. Through their titles, many of Casarella's works of the period represent themes of change, sometimes violent, or of geological transformation. A taut balance permeates these big evocative images. The sweeping gesture of *Triggered* is tense, like a wound-up spring or a cocked trap.

Casarella's method for making his paper relief prints began with a full-scale color sketch, usually in gouache.[2] Designs would be continually adjusted and refined throughout the process of building the printing blocks. The artist made several tracings from the primary model, representing the number of blocks used to delineate the color separations. Often inessential shapes and details were eliminated from the design in the preparation of these tracings. At this stage, the artist also decided on the number of colors to be printed from each block, as well as on the placement of those colors and the transparent and opaque areas. Casarella's most complex prints utilized eight blocks, with a total of up to sixty different colors.

The construction of the printing blocks began when Casarella transferred his composition from the traced drawings onto a double-weight, laminated illustration board. Working from the reverse of the translucent tracing paper, he thus arranged for the reversal of the printmaking process, so that his prints would be oriented as his original gouache was. The components of the design were cut out of the illustration board in sizes slightly larger than the traced shapes and glued with rubber cement onto supports of chipboard.

The composite blocks thus assembled, Casarella proceeded to precisely cut them, usually on a slight bevel away from the compositional forms. The excess cardboard was carefully peeled away in layers. By varying the depth of the cut and the amount of paper removed, the artist created interesting effects. By removing only one or two layers, he formed areas that were only slightly recessed and printed as faint, secondary shapes or shadows. Sometimes he also gave texture to the printing surface by distressing the cardboard with the point of a nail or with an awl.

The sequence of printing proceeded from the blocks bearing the largest shapes, usually printed in opaque inks, to those with smaller forms printed in translucent inks. Because of the absorptive nature of cardboard, water-base inks could not be used with these paper blocks. Instead, Casarella used oil-based industrial printing inks. These pigments were applied directly to the uncoated or unsealed paper blocks, which were cleaned with turpentine between printings. However, these oily inks, applied in many layers, often did not fully dry, and the surfaces of Casarella's prints remained tacky for many years. The artist favored the use of a transparent medium to reduce his colors and extend them into glazes. By cutting the inks with this medium, he could control the shiny or matte surface of the printed color.

Ink was applied liberally, for it soaked well into the undampened paper. Small gelatin rollers, some specially made by the artist, were used to apply the ink to the blocks. Printing was done by rubbing the back of the sheet by hand, with a wooden spoon, or by a roller. Brayer marks on the verso of *Triggered* show that it was printed under the pressure of a hand-held roller. Vestiges of ink on the verso, which can be read through the sheet in the area of the artist's signature, also signal this manner of printing. Twenty-four hours of drying time was allotted between the printing of each color.

Casarella used strong, long-fibered mulberry papers. He exploited the absorptive quality of this material and the adjustable transparency of the ink to create tonal shifts and effects of depth. His blocks were quite durable and were able to withstand the printing of fairly large editions. Customarily the artist produced editions of about fifty impressions.

Notes

1. This is especially true of such prints by Barnet as *Wine, Women and Song* (1958; Cole 115) and *Province by the Sea* (1959; Cole 120).

2. Chaet 1958. See also Johnson 1956, pp. 17–19; Johnson 1980, pp. 134–137, fig. 6; Peterdi 1959a, pp. 261–262.

15/20   "Triggered"   E. Casarella '59

Ansei Uchima

1921–

99.
Nostalgia in Black
1960
Woodcut on cream handmade wove paper
39.4 × 32.9 cm. (image)
44.9 × 58.0 cm. (sheet)
In pencil, lower margin: *Nostalgia in Black* (in Japanese: Kuroi no natutarajia) 20/50   A. Uchima, 1960
Watermark: *UCHIMA*
Worcester Art Museum, anonymous gift, 1988.86

Ansei Uchima's point of view, as expressed in his art, is a synthesis of Eastern and Western cultural idioms and ways of seeing, and it represents a fascinating instance of the direct intercourse between Japanese and American printmaking in the twentieth century.

Americans living in postwar Japan were intrigued to discover a flourishing tradition of modernist printmaking there. Concerts and art exhibitions were organized for occupation forces; these included shows of prints by Onchi Koshiro and other artists of the "creative print" or *sosaku-hanga* movement. These prints appealed to the Americans, and the exhibitions were well received. Many of the prints were even offered for sale in the military base post exchanges, and soon Americans were collecting them more avidly than the Japanese. During a period of economic crisis in Japan, this new source of interest made it possible for printmakers to support themselves by their artwork.[1]

The *sosaku-hanga* movement had been growing in Japan since its foundation in 1918. Artists of this school attempted to synthesize Western modernist aesthetics with those of traditional Japan. They broke decisively from the past in that they did their own carving and printing; they often leaned toward spontaneous methods of carving and used the full range of inking techniques. One of the American servicemen to discover this art was Oliver Statler, who built up an enviable collection of prints and published several critical essays about them. In about 1954, he began to interview the printmakers in order to gather information for a book about *sosaku-hanga*.[2] Statler engaged the services of Uchima to serve as translator in his meetings with the artists. In this way, Uchima was introduced to printmaking, and it was through the extraor-

dinary opportunity to watch artists at work and to intimately discuss their prints with them that he became enchanted with printmaking and with the possibility of designing, cutting, and printing his own woodcuts.

Many of Uchima's prints of the 1950s, executed in Japan, were open and airy compositions, in which brush strokes and abstract shapes seemed to float in space, frozen in moments of delicate balance and dancelike grace. Often these were poetic landscapes, as balanced and simple as Zen gardens. To a Japanese viewer, these prints suggested the open space of America,[3] yet to Western eyes, they represented the sensitive Japanese celebration of nature. These woodcuts may have reflected the artist's longing for emancipation from his cramped existence amid the concrete walls and streets of Tokyo.[4] They had clear relationships to *sumi* painting and to the balance of calligraphy on a field of white paper.

By comparison, *Nostalgia in Black*, produced soon after Uchima's return to the United States in 1959, is a closed and confined composition that expresses tension and excitement. An illusion of space is achieved with overlapping forms and transparent textures. Its central wreath, bracketed by heavy angular bars, gives the composition a sense of confinement, and the angled placement of the rectilinear shapes suggests an almost jerky vibration.

Though they could still be characterized as poetic responses to the natural world and their palette was still restrained, many of the woodcuts of this period were less open and vaporous. During the 1960s, the artist was influenced by Abstract Expressionism, and his works explored spatial and formal relationships emerging from the gestural movements of the activity of painting. The stylistic means of the present print are also linked to *sosaku-hanga*. The fretted texture and brush-stroke-like lines and forms are reminiscent of the prints of Rikio Takahashi.

Uchima was in the habit of recording his thoughts and visual ideas in tiny watercolor sketches in pocket notebooks.[5] These miniature compositional and color studies were later transformed into large oil paintings or finished maquettes for his prints. The small size and seeming spontaneity of these little studies belie the care and time the artist gave them. He would spend hours calculating his compositions and delicately placing layers of color in thin washes. In conception and process, these studies parallel the woodcut technique of overprinting many layers of transparent watercolors.

Uchima's techniques, based closely on the traditional methods of *ukiyo*-e, are explained in a chapter written by the artist for a recent book on printmaking history and techniques.[6] After 1955, many of his woodcuts were printed on paper made specially for him in the village of Imadate-cho by the late Ichibei Iwano, a craftsman who had been named a Living National Treasure of Japan. The lower right corner of the present sheet was cut square so that it could be fitted perfectly into the *kento*, or triangular notch cut into the blocks in order to assure proper registration. The verso of this print shows that the ink soaked well into the paper. Its surface was roughed where the artist printed by rubbing, and it shows the circular scars of the *baren*, or printing pad. *Nostalgia in Black* is titled in pencil in Japanese, indicating that it was intended for distribution in Japan as well as in the United States.

Notes

1. Jenkins 1983, pp. 21–22.

2. Statler 1956.

3. Kawakita 1967, p. 186.

4. Oliver Statler, "Ansei Uchima: A Friendship," in Philipps/Ryan 1985.

5. Philip Gould, "The Sketchbooks of Ansei Uchima," in Philipps/Ryan 1985.

6. Uchima 1976, pp. 144–153; Saff/Sacilotto 1978, pp. 53–68.

Nostalgia in Black (黒のノスタルジー) 20/50   A. UeNo, 1960

Clinton Adams
1918–

100.
Window Series III
1960

Lithograph on cream wove paper
36.9 × 28.0 cm. (image)
46.2 × 38.3 cm. (sheet)
In pencil, lower margin: *Artist's Proof   Window Series III   Clinton Adams '60*
In image, lower left: printer's blind stamp
In margin, lower left: Tamarind blind stamp
Watermark: *Rives BFK*
Tamarind 124A
Worcester Art Museum, Anonymous Fund, 1988.149.3

Few people have been so influential in the field of lithography in this country as Clinton Adams. He has been actively making lithographs since 1948. As a teacher and administrator, his contributions were fundamental to the successful foundation of the Tamarind Lithography Workshop and its first decade of operation. Adams's comprehensive studies of the history of American lithography greatly broadened our understanding of a long-neglected subject. However, first and last, Clinton Adams is a painter. Despite all his other commitments, he has always found time to heed his compulsion to paint.

In 1960, along with June Wayne and Garo Antreasian (cat. 97), Adams helped to establish the Tamarind Lithography Workshop in Los Angeles, an organization that fundamentally changed the course of lithography in this country.[1] Lithography, a complex process, requires great expertise, and equipment and materials that are prohibitively expensive, so it was often difficult for American artists to find the necessary resources to make lithographs. Consequently there was little market for the prints, and the handful of master printers who labored in relative isolation across the country were often ignored. Like the professional lithography studios in Europe, Tamarind made quality printing facilities and expertise available to many artists. However, more important was Tamarind's printer-training program, which eventually produced a distinguished lineage of American master printers. This achievement provided the foundation for the American print boom of the 1960s.

Color prints were made at Tamarind almost from its inception. In 1959, workshop founder and director Wayne had experimented only with chiaroscuro lithographs. However, both associate director Adams and technical director Antreasian had previously created color lithographs. Their first collaboration was Adams's *Window Series*, which were among the first color prints made at Tamarind, the present print among them.

Though this series represented a beginning for Tamarind, the sophisticated *Window Series* was a stylistic culmination for Adams. Following World War II, he painted in a geometric abstract style, under the influence of Stuart Davis (cat. 88). Adams's brightly colored cityscapes were punctuated by details from billboards and building facades. Beginning in 1949, he concentrated on empty interiors and still lifes, eventually focusing on the objects. His early experiences with lithography had repercussions in his paintings. In a series of finely finished works in egg tempera, he adopted a precise manner of crosshatching, similar to his intricate crayon drawings on stone.

In the late 1950s, geological imagery began to appear in Adams's paintings and prints. Driving through northern New Mexico and Arizona, he was impressed by the broken land of ancient lava flows and by the towering walls of multicolored sandstone, laid down by the waters of long-vanished oceans, all illuminated by the ever-changing light of vast open skies. These mountains first inspired the monumentality and dimension that Adams sought to achieve in his still-life elements. Adams began to paint the schematized forms of rectilinear peaks, mesas, and canyons, and varied them with shadows and reflected light.

In an attempt to visually and intellectually reconcile the impact of these vast geological landscapes with the geometry and intimacy of his still lifes, Adams began the *Window Series* of paintings and prints in 1958. He combined still-life objects in an interior, placed before a window, allowing a framed view of the landscape beyond. This formula encompassed several of the perennial concerns of the artist, including the still life, the landscape, and the dilemma of framing in a single composition. In the *Window Series*, Adams explored relationships of form and space, of literal representation and abstraction.

In 1959 Adams explored the window theme in a series of intaglio prints, his first work in that medium. The Tamarind suite of lithographs, including the present print, was produced in Los Angeles between July 12 and December 1, 1959, and printed by Antreasian, and Joe Funk produced the present impression. It is one of thirty-four prints that make up the edition and proofs. Throughout the suite of lithographs, the compositional formula was maintained. However, still-life objects and landscape elements became almost interchangeable, differentiated only by their positions.

This lithograph was a technical tour de force. Adams worked the stones in many different ways to achieve a wide range of textures. He drew with crayon and occasionally altered his drawing by scraping; he brushed on liquid tusche, sometimes with additives to break down and separate the ink, creating random organic patterns; he used spatter techniques, in combination with objects that masked the stones from the sprayed-on ink. The artist achieved a great variety of delicate effects, but he employed them all with a care and precision meant to leave little trace of his execution. He aimed to focus the viewer on formal and spatial relationships.

Adams delighted the eye with myriad textures and color patterns. All these textures seem organic in their random modulations, similar to the varied surfaces of rock. But the stark geometry of their arrangement in the composition calls up the all-pervading order of the universe. This print was meant to reveal its internal logic and compositional cohesion, to express the order in nature beneath apparent chaos.

Notes

1. Adams 1983, pp. 196–203.

Artists' Biographies

■

Clinton Adams

Clinton Adams was born on December 11, 1918, in Glendale, California.[1] He studied at the University of California in Los Angeles with George J. Cox, Helen Chandler, and Anita Delano. He earned a bachelor's degree in education in 1940, and a master's degree in 1942. In that year he had his first exhibition at the American Contemporary Gallery in Los Angeles, and joined the arts faculty at UCLA. His teaching career was soon interrupted by military service, and he served as the sergeant-major of an engineer camouflage battalion in the Army Air Force.

In 1946 Adams returned to UCLA and taught courses in design, technique, and art history. At the suggestion of his colleague Stanton Macdonald-Wright (cat. 78), Adams began to make lithographs in the shop of Lynton R. Kistler in 1948. In 1950 the artist's first solo exhibition was mounted at the UCLA Art Gallery, and his work was featured in the First International Biennial of Color Lithography at the Cincinnati Museum of Art. At this time, Adams participated extensively in group exhibitions around the country. He also taught at the Otis Art Institute in Los Angeles in 1953 and 1954. In that year, Adams became chairman of the art department at the University of Kentucky in Lexington. In 1957 he became head of the department of art at the University of Florida in Gainesville.

In the summer of 1959 Adams began discussions with June Wayne about her plans to establish a lithography workshop and printer training program under the sponsorship of the Ford Foundation. In 1960 Adams returned to Los Angeles to become associate director of the Tamarind Lithography Workshop, working closely with the Director June Wayne and Technical Director Garo Antreasian (cat. 97). In 1961, Adams took the position of dean of the College of Fine Arts at the University of New Mexico in Albuquerque. With foundation support for Tamarind soon to expire, plans were for-

mulated to move the shop to Albuquerque, where its programs could continue under the auspices of the University of New Mexico in 1962. Thus, the Tamarind Institute reopened with Adams as director.

During the 1970s, Adams was drawn away from his own art and concentrated on administration, teaching, research, and writing. He worked with Antreasian on *The Tamarind Book of Lithography: Art & Techniques*, a technical manual based on the experiences and innovations at the workshop.[2] A monograph on the prints of Fritz Scholder followed in 1973. In the following year, Adams founded the scholarly journal *The Tamarind Technical Papers*.

Adams became interim associate provost and dean of faculties at the University of New Mexico during 1976–77, and afterward returned to teaching. His third book, *American Lithographers, 1900–1960: The Artists and Their Printers*, was published in 1983.[3] A retrospective exhibition of his paintings was organized by the University of New Mexico Art Museum in 1987.

Since his retirement from teaching and administration in 1985, Adams returned to his own artwork and today continues to paint, make prints, and exhibit regularly, as well as maintaining his scholarly activities.

Notes
1. Walch 1987, pp. 10–26.
2. Antreasian/Adams 1971.
3. Adams 1983.

■

Garo Z. Antreasian

Garo Zaren Antreasian was born on February 16, 1922, in Indianapolis, Indiana,[1] where he was introduced to the graphic arts at Arsenal Technical High School. In 1941 he entered the John Herron School of Art. There, in a class taught by Maxil Ballinger, Antreasian made his first color lithograph,[2] which was shown in the First National Exhibition of Prints at the Library of Congress in 1943. In that year, Antreasian joined the United States Coast Guard, in which he served as a combat artist in the Pacific Theater, recording the invasions of Iwo Jima and Okinawa and the occupation of Japan.

He returned to Indianapolis and the John Herron School in 1946, where he graduated and began teaching in 1948. In New York in the summer of 1949, he studied printmaking at the Art Students League with Will Barnet (cat. 69) and worked with Stanley William Hayter (cat. 60) at Atelier 17.

Antreasian's first solo exhibition of prints was in 1952 at the Esther Gentle Gallery in New York. Since that time, he has had over 70 one-man exhibitions and has participated in more than 130 group shows. In the 1950s and 1960s, he executed several mural commissions in Indiana. By the late 1950s, he had developed remarkable technical sophistication in his use of lithography, and strove to achieve the creative immediacy, scale, and coloristic range of painting in his prints.[3] In 1959 June Wayne invited Antreasian to become the first technical director of the Tamarind Lithography Workshop in Los Angeles.[4] He printed many of the first color lithographs to be produced at Tamarind. Antreasian's own color print *The Land and The Sea*, printed at the workshop in 1960, was outstanding for this period for its size and complexity.

In 1961, continuing as technical advisor to the Board of Directors of Tamarind, Antreasian returned to his teaching position at the John Herron School of Art, and soon began offering introductory training programs for Tamarind Printer Fellows. In 1964 he became an associate professor at the University of New Mexico in Albuquerque, later attaining the rank of full professor.

In 1970 Antreasian became technical director of the reorganized Tamarind Institute in Albuquerque. The landmark *Tamarind Book of Lithography: Art & Techniques*, written by Antreasian with Clinton Adams, was published in 1971.[5] In the 1970s, he held numerous residencies and presented many exhibitions, workshops, lectures, and critiques. From 1981 through 1984, he was chairman of the art department at the University of New Mexico. His NEA grant sponsored visits to Izmir and Istanbul were influential on many of his later paintings and prints. In 1987, Antreasian retired from the University of New Mexico.

In 1988 a comprehensive retrospective exhibition of his work was presented by the Albuquerque Museum and the University of New Mexico Art Museum.[6] Still living in Albuquerque, Antreasian continues to paint, make prints, and exhibit extensively, and he often presents lectures and workshops.

Notes

1. Lewis 1973; Moore 1988; *Who's Who* 1986, p. 25.
2. Adams 1983, pp. 166–167.
3. Print Council 1959, no. 3.
4. Adams 1983, pp. 200–203.
5. Antreasian/Adams 1971.
6. Moore 1988.

■

John Taylor Arms

Born in Washington, D.C. on April 19, 1987, John Taylor Arms attended the Lawrenceville School and began the study of law at Princeton University.[1] However, in 1907, he transferred to Massachusetts Institute of Technology and took up the study of architecture. Arms developed his unique drafting style, with its precise detail and carefully observed effects of light, from his experience and practice as an architectural student. He graduated in 1911, and completed a master's degree the following year. He then worked as a draftsman with the well-known Carrère and Hastings Company in New York.

In 1913 Arms was given a hobbyist's etching set, and he began to dabble with copperplate and acid. In 1915, after copying a handful of prints by Jongkind and other Etching Revivalists, Arms created his first original etching. His early experiments were picturesque views of European villages, reflecting the influence of Whistler (cat. 2). He inked and printed several of these plates in color in the manner of Charles Mielatz. Arms formed a short-lived partnership with Cameron Clark, specializing in domestic architecture. In 1916 he joined the United States Navy; seeing Europe fueled his fascination with French architectural printmakers, and after the war he devoted himself wholly to printmaking.

Arms was directly influenced by many artists: from Eugene Higgins he learned the fine points of intaglio technique, the eloquence of detail, and the allure of the miniature print;[2] from Bolton Brown, he learned the technique of lithography.

Inspired to capture the romantic ambience of Gothic architecture, Arms developed a plan to represent in etching all the major Gothic cathedrals of Europe. His thorough knowledge, his remarkably precise draftsmanship, and his growing command of the medium made his prints fascinating and broadly appealing.

In the 1920s, his most productive period, Arms traveled throughout Europe, and produced almost half of his nearly 450 prints. Two travel books written by his wife were illustrated with heliographic reproductions of his intaglios.[3]

In the 1930s Arms became a highly visible champion of printmaking. He was the author of *The Handbook of Print Making and Print Makers*, and as editor of *Prints* magazine he produced many articles of opinion and criticism and reviews of books and exhibitions.[4] He was a prominent member and officer of many print organizations. In 1938 and 1939, Arms was a visiting lecturer at Wesleyan University,[5] and spoke widely on printmaking history for many years. He died on October 13, 1953, in New York.

Notes

1. A detailed biography of the artist is provided in Bassham 1975, pp. 1–34.
2. Fletcher 1982.
3. Arms 1932 and 1937.
4. Arms 1934.
5. Outstanding holdings of Arms's prints, given in bequest by the artist, can be found at Wesleyan University.

■

Milton Avery

Milton Clark Avery was born on March 7, 1885, in Sand Bank, New York, where his father worked as a tanner.[1] His family moved to Wilson Station, Connecticut, where he began working in a factory at the age of sixteen. While working in a succession of mechanical jobs in industry, Avery studied at the Connecticut League of Art Students in Hartford until 1918. His work was first exhibited in 1915 at the Wadsworth Athenaeum Annual Exhibition.

In 1918 he transferred to the School of the Art Society of Hartford, and worked in the evenings so that he could paint during the day. Avery became a member of the Connecticut Academy of Fine Arts in 1924. That summer in Gloucester, Massachusetts, he met the artist Sally Michael, who became his wife in 1926. They moved to New York, and Avery began attending evening drawing classes at the Art Students League several times a week, while his wife worked as an artist for *Progressive Grocer* magazine to enable him to paint full-time.

In 1928 Avery showed two paintings in a group exhibition at the Opportunity Gallery. He made his first print in 1932—a drypoint scratched into a copperplate that had been discarded by the printer of the *Progressive Grocer*.[2] Between 1933 and 1950 Avery intermittently made drypoints, however editions of most of these prints were not pulled until the early 1960s. In 1935 the artist had his first solo exhibition at the Valentine Gallery in New York.

The Philips Memorial Gallery in Washington, D.C., mounted Avery's first one-man museum exhibition in 1944. In 1948, a portfolio of five of his drypoints was published by the Laurel Gallery.[3] After a major heart attack in 1949, the artist created just one more drypoint. However, during his recuperation he began experimenting with monotypes. Over the next two years the artist produced over two hundred of these unique prints.

In 1950 Avery donated his work on a lithograph advertisement for the souvenir catalogue of the fundraising ball sponsored by the Artists Equity Association. He continued to create such prints until 1953, and they accounted for six of his eight

lithographs.[4] The artist began making woodcuts in 1952, and continued on an experimental basis for three years, completing twenty-one prints.

A major retrospective of Avery's paintings opened at the Baltimore Museum of Art in December of 1952.[5] Through the decade, the artist continued to work diligently despite poor health. A retrospective exhibition, organized by the American Federation of Arts, was presented by the Whitney Museum of American Art in New York in 1960.[6] Late in that year, the artist suffered his second heart attack. Avery died in New York on January 3, 1965; he was buried in the Artists Cemetery in Woodstock, New York.

Notes

1. For the most complete biography of the artist see Haskell 1982, pp. 185–192.
2. Johnson/Miller 1966, p. 11.
3. Ibid., no. 72.
4. Lunn 1973, nos. 31–38.
5. Wight 1952.
6. Breeskin 1960.

■

Will Barnet

Will Barnet was born on May 25, 1911, in the industrial coast town of Beverly, Massachusetts, where his father was a master mechanic.[1] The boy inherited a ready dexterity, and his poetic curiosity and imagination drew him to the study of art. At sixteen Barnet began his formal studies at the School of the Boston Museum of Fine Arts, where he was the pupil of painter Philip Hale. His success in Boston won him a three-year, out-of-town scholarship in 1930 to study at the Art Students League in New York, where he learned the process of lithography from Charles Locke. His first prints represent Social Realist subjects then current at the League, carefully observed vignettes of city life and the interactions of people, rendered with increasing command of the crayon on the stone.

His capability as a technician won Barnet an appointment as printer at the Art Students League in 1934, and he began to exhibit his prints in New York group exhibitions. The budding professional married in 1935 and began a family. In the following year, he joined the faculty of the League, becoming its youngest instructor of graphic arts. His first one-man show was at the Hudson Walker Gallery in New York in 1938, the year that he began teaching at the New School for Social Research. A revealing duality began to emerge in Barnet's prints of the late 1930s: an increasing contrast between his figural scenes of intimate everyday moments and the stark, ravaged industrial landscapes of Social Realism. Resigned self-possession in Barnet's figures began to give way to a more positive mood of quiet, personal dignity. This was certainly due to the artist's constant observation, for he was able to represent the bleakness of his surroundings alongside the private, quiet joys of his young family. As the decade progressed, this sympathy turned to open affection, as Barnet's wife and infant children became his primary models. The artist also expanded his technical scope in this period, creating alongside his masterful lithographs several etchings, aquatints, and woodcuts, some of them in color.[2]

A distinguished career as a teacher always coincided with Barnet's painting, printmaking, and active exhibition schedule. In the 1940s he also shifted his primary attention from printmaking to painting, from more technical media to one that allowed more creative immediacy. He relinquished his teaching position in the graphic arts in 1946, to become an instructor of painting at the Art Students League. Barnet's growing circle of artist friends, and colleagues from his various teaching appointments, exposed him to many new ideas and painting styles, and he was drawn among the abstractionists late in the 1940s. When a five-year hiatus in his own printmaking activity was broken in 1947, the influence of his abstract painting experiments was striking.

This shift was moderated in a group of prints from 1947 to 1951 that sought to synthesize the tenets of

abstraction with the figural style that Barnet had always found most comfortable. While pure abstraction dominates his prints of the 1950s, this and a simplified representational style are concurrent in Barnet's paintings and prints of the 1960s. In large color lithographs, intaglios, and woodcuts, flat, elementary forms are carefully balanced in shape, color, and texture. The representational compositions of the period similarly reduce and simplify the draped human figure and elements of setting into flat, formal compositions. The subjects of these prints, the artist's family and close friends, are still captured in silent moments of introspection of reverie. Safe and confident, they are also somehow strangely guarded. It is this imagery that would come to dominate Barnet's art in the 1970s and 1980s, an appealing and accessible style in which the artist created many large color lithographs and screen prints that are moody and evocative.

Notes
1. Doty 1984.
2. Cole 1972.

■

Gustave Baumann

Born on June 27, 1881, in Magdeburg, Germany, Gustave Baumann was the son of a craftsman.[1] His family immigrated to the United States when he was ten and settled in Chicago. From 1897 to 1904 he studied in the evenings at the Art Institute of Chicago, working during the day in a commercial printmaking shop. In 1905 he returned to Germany to attend the Kunstgewerbe Schule in Munich, and decided on a career in printmaking. Returning to Chicago in 1906, he worked for a few years as a designer of labels.

Baumann made his first limited edition prints in 1909, and exhibited at the Art Institute of Chicago the following year.[2] In 1910 he moved to the artists' colony of Nashville, Indiana. There, he explored the creative

Gustave Baumann, *Packard Twin Six*, 1917. Woodcut. Worcester Art Museum, 1987.157.

and commercial possibilities of a career as a printmaker. Baumann's experiments may have been encouraged by Louis O. Griffith, leader of the Brown County Art Gallery Association, a group of printmakers who worked chiefly in color intaglio. Baumann exhibited color prints at the Panama-Pacific International Exposition in San Francisco in 1915 and won the gold medal.

Among Baumann's ongoing commercial activities was his work for the Packard Motor Car Company from 1914 to 1920.[3] He produced designs, illustrations, and color woodcuts such as *Packard Twin Six* (Fig.), one image from a calendar to be distributed to dealers in 1917. The artist continued to produce such commercial woodcuts at least until 1923.

In 1919 Baumann's work dominated the important exhibition of American color woodcuts at the Detroit Institute of Arts,[4] which included twenty-six of his prints, far more than those of any other artist. He also loaned a set of blocks to the exhibition, along with a preparatory drawing and seven progressive proofs. In that year Baumann worked in New York and, over the summer, in Provincetown, Massachusetts. His airy images of Cape Cod employ soft, pastel colors and occasionally show the influence of the white line technique.

Strongly attracted by the magnificent landscape, climate, and supportive community, Baumann moved to Santa Fe, New Mexico, in 1918. Later in the decade, after traveling to the West Coast, he made prints of California landscapes.

In the 1930s Baumann became interested in puppet theater. He designed and carved his own marionettes, and established a little traveling company.[5] From 1943 to 1945, the artist carved an altarpiece for the Episcopal Church of the Holy Faith in Santa Fe. In 1952, a retrospective exhibition of his prints was mounted at the New Mexico Museum of Fine Arts. In the course of his career, Baumann executed nearly four hundred color woodcuts.[6] He died in Santa Fe on October 8, 1971.

Notes
1. *Who's Who* 1947; Flint 1983, p. 27. The artist wrote an autobiography which was never published; see Baumann/Griffiths 1983.
2. Baumann also began to illustrate books at this time. For a list of his book illustration projects, see Annex 1981, p. 2.
3. Baumann/Griffiths 1983, pp. 22–28.
4. DIA 1919.
5. Flint 1983, p. 27.
6. A catalogue raisonné of Baumann's woodcuts is currently being compiled by the Annex Galleries in Santa Rosa, California.

■

Fred Becker

Born in Oakland, California, on August 5, 1913, Fred Becker was raised in Hollywood. His father was an actor and director in silent films. The young artist began his studies at the Otis Art Institute in Los Angeles in 1931; there he was introduced to printmaking in about 1933.[1] In 1934, at the Beaux-Arts Institute of Design in New York, he studied with Eugene Steinhof. Becker received his first recognition as a printmaker for wood engravings and linocuts he made in the FAP graphic arts division, which he joined the following year. These relief prints represent jazz musicians, reflecting the artist's experiences moonlighting as a caricaturist in New York nightclubs. The satirical depictions elongate and distort figures to emphasize their creative abandon, but the knowing smirks of these worldly wise musicians imply that they are in on Becker's joke.[2] Several of these prints are straightforward depictions printed in both white line and black line, but others are more complex, decorative compositions.

Becker first exhibited his work at the Willard Gallery in New York in 1938. In 1941, soon after his establishment at the New School for Social Research, the artist became a member of Atelier 17. The profound influence of Stanley William Hayter appears in a group of Abstract Surrealist intaglios that show Becker's quickly developing technical virtuosity. In some of these prints, he carried on his interest in jazz themes in an appropriately improvisational, automatist mode. By middle of the decade Becker had become one of the most versatile technicians of the workshop, and he was among the artists who assisted Hayter with the printing of *Cinq Personnages* (cat. 60).

Becker began teaching at the Tyler School of Art at Temple University in Philadelphia in 1946. He received a Tiffany Fellowship in 1948, and took a teaching position at Washington University in St. Louis. With the support of a Guggenheim Fellowship, the artist traveled to Paris in 1957 to work at the original Atelier 17; he returned to the United States in 1958 to teach a session at Yale-Norfolk summer school. A visiting lecturer and instructor at Brandeis University and the Portland School of Art in Maine, the artist also received a fellowship from the National Endowment for the Arts in 1975. From 1968 until his retirement in 1986, Becker taught at the University of Massachusetts in Amherst.

Still very active as a painter and printmaker, he continues to live and work in Amherst. In collaboration with Robert Blackburn (cat. 93), Becker has recently completed a group of prints at the Printmaking Workshop in New York.

Notes

1. *Who's Who* 1962, p. 42. The author is grateful to Fred Becker for providing information that contributed much to this entry, and to several others in this catalogue.
2. See, for example, *At the Jazz-Band Ball*, reproduced in Zigrosser 1941a.

Eugene Berman

Eugene Berman was born on November 4, 1899, in St. Petersburg, Russia.[1] There, he studied art between 1915 and 1918 with several academic masters. In 1919, after the Russian Revolution, he moved with his family to Paris and enrolled at the Académie Ranson, where he was a pupil of Pierre Bonnard, Félix Vallaton, and Edouard Vuillard; he also studied privately with the architect Emilio Terry. In 1922 the young artist made his first visit to Italy. He was enchanted, and returned there nearly every year until 1938. Italian art of the Renaissance and Baroque periods provided the foundation for his developing style.

In the 1920s Christian Berard became one of his closest friends, and along with Pavel Tchelitchew, Berman's brother Leonide, and others, these artists shared ideas and called themselves Neoromanticists. Inspired by Giorgio de Chirico, Salvador Dali, and the early work of Picasso, these painters represented narrative subjects in surrealistic and fantastic styles. They exhibited together at the Galerie Druet in Paris, in 1924. Berman's first solo exhibition was mounted at the Galerie Granoff in 1927. Two years later he drew the illustrations for Gertrude Stein's book of poems *Ten Portraits*.[2]

Berman's work was first shown in the United States in 1930 at the Julien Levy Gallery in New York. Briefly visiting this country in 1935, the artist met A. Everett Austin of the Wadsworth Atheneum, who arranged for his first theatrical commission, to design scenery for the Second Hartford Music Festival in 1936.[3] Other offers for theatrical projects came to the artist after his return to Europe. In 1937 he de-

signed sets for the Théâtre de l'Etoile in Paris, and in 1938 and 1939 he worked for the Ballet Russe de Monte Carlo.

The artist left Paris in 1939 and immigrated to the United States in the following year, to remain for the duration of the war. Before 1950 his frequent theatrical commissions were chiefly for the ballet. Notable among his projects were the Ballet Theatre production of *Romeo and Juliet* in 1943 in Renaissance style, and his designs for *Giselle* in 1946 in Gothic Revival style.

A selection of the many sketches and finely finished watercolors produced for Berman's theatrical commissions made up an exhibition at the Institute of Modern Art in Boston in 1941.[4] After World War II, the artist was attracted to California and the prospect of theater and set design work in Hollywood. He became an American citizen in 1944, and six years later, he married actress Ona Munson in the living room of the Beverly Hills home of his friend Igor Stravinsky. In 1945 and 1947 the artist won two Guggenheim Fellowships, which enabled him to travel to Mexico in order to study colonial architecture. In 1947 a retrospective exhibition of his paintings and theatrical designs was organized by the Museum of Modern Art in New York.[5]

The later phase of Berman's career in theatrical design concentrated on opera. His first major project, for the Metropolitan Opera in New York, was the design for Rudolf Bing's production of Verdi's *Rigoletto*, which Berman set in late-Renaissance Italy. The artist also worked extensively for La Scala in Milan. Berman's designs for the Metropolitan Opera production of Mozart's *Don Giovanni* in 1957 were considered the height of his theatrical career.

After 1958 Berman lived in Rome, surrounded by his vast collections of paintings, sculpture, and decorative arts from all historical periods and

cultures, which provided material for his own artwork. Berman focused on painting late in his career, rejecting most theatrical projects. In his last work for the stage, the Metropolitan Opera production of *Pulcinella* in 1972, he was reunited with his friends George Balanchine and Igor Stravinsky. Berman died in Rome on December 14, 1972.

Notes

1. Cummings 1971, pp. 66–67.
2. Stein 1930.
3. Tuggle 1989.
4. Soby 1941.
5. MoMA 1947.

Harry Bertoia

Arieto Bertoia was born on March 10, 1915, in San Lorenzo, Italy.[1] He came to the United States in 1930, to join his brother in Detroit. Soon he was enrolled in a special program for outstanding students in the arts at Cass Technical High School. In 1936 he attended the School of the Detroit Society of Arts and Crafts.

In 1937 Bertoia began teaching metalworking at the Cranbrook Academy in Bloomfield Hills, Michigan, while studying painting on a scholarship. He began to explore printmaking, working evenings in the graphic studio. Beginning with conventional carved woodcuts, he taught himself the full range of printmaking techniques. Soon he was making multicolor monotypes stamped by hand with small blocks of inked wood. In 1943 Bertoia's monotypes were exhibited at Cranbrook, at the Guggenheim Museum and the Nierendorf Gallery in New York.[2]

Late in 1943 the artist moved to Los Angeles, where he made major contributions to the design and fabrication of the steel support systems for Charles Eames's furniture. He continued to produce monoprints, which became his formative activity of creation. Between 1945 and 1947 Bertoia was provided with a monthly stipend from the Nierendorf Gallery in exchange for a steady flow of his work. An exhibition of his monotypes was mounted at the

San Francisco Museum of Art in 1945. The "Eames chair" began production at this time, and was exhibited at the Museum of Modern Art in New York in 1946.[3]

In 1947 Bertoia began making his own welded sculptures. Their designs grew out of his monotype experiments, and many utilized the metal rods he had used in furniture fabrication. In 1950 the artist was invited by Hans and Florence Knoll to create his own line of furniture and help to engineer its production. Bertoia moved to a farm near Barto, Pennsylvania, and for two years dedicated himself to this project. The pivotal chair design was based on a cupped latticework of welded steel rods suspended on thin legs of similar wire, a functional version of Bertoia's sculpture.[4]

His first important sculpture commission, completed in 1953, was for a decorative wall screen in the General Motors Center in Warren, Michigan. During the 1950s Bertoia created more graphic works than in any other period of his career. His sculptures and prints were exhibited at the Museum of Modern Art and Massachusetts Institute of Technology. In 1957 the Smithsonian Institution Traveling Exhibition Service circulated a solo exhibition of Bertoia's sculptures, monotypes, and furniture to ten American museums.

During the 1960s he concentrated on sculpture. He became fascinated by the ability of his metal sculpture to produce musical sound, and made various chiming, clanking, and resonating pieces which were assembled in sound environments and recorded.[5]

Bertoia executed fewer commissions but compiled more exhibitions in the 1970s. He died of bronchial cancer in Barto, Pennsylvania, on November 6, 1978. In 1988 a major circulation exhibition of Bertoia's monotypes was organized by the Detroit Institute of Arts.

Notes
1. Nelson 1988.
2. Riley 1943.
3. Kane 1976, pp. 282–284.
4. Ibid., pp. 286–289.
5. Eger 1971.

■

Robert Blackburn

Born in Summit, New Jersey, on December 10, 1920, Robert Blackburn grew up in Harlem.[1] He was profoundly influenced by his English teacher at P.S. 139, poet Countee Cullen, who instilled in him a determination to become an artist. In high school Blackburn worked on a literary magazine and attended classes at the WPA-operated Harlem Community Art Center, where, in 1938, he was introduced to the process of lithography by the painter and printmaker Riva Helfond.[2]

In 1941 Blackburn won a scholarship to the Art Students League, where he studied painting with Vaclav Vytlacil. Gradually he developed a European modernist style of the sort taught by Vytlacil and Jan Matulka. Blackburn also studied printmaking with Will Barnet (cat. 69), who introduced him to the intaglio processes, and a range of other printmaking techniques. These two artists became close friends, and Blackburn worked as Barnet's assistant as a lithographic printer. Although fine art lithography was still rare in the 1940s, the artist recognized the vast creative potential of the medium.

When Blackburn concluded his studies, teaching positions for black artists were nonexistent. He took odd jobs in commercial lithography shops, and his technical knowledge progressively increased. In 1949, with the financial assistance of Barnet and John von Wicht (cat. 75), he established his own self-supporting cooperative printmaking workshop in lower Manhattan, specializing in lithography. The Bob Blackburn Workshop, as it was originally called, was organized on the model of Stanley William Hayter's Atelier 17 (cat. 60). Later the studio's name was

changed to the Creative Graphics Workshop, and in 1959 it became the Printmaking Workshop.

In the early years Blackburn struggled to keep the studio in operation, succeeding only through painstaking economy and heroic diligence. His own color lithographs won purchase prizes at the Brooklyn Museum Annual National Print Exhibitions in 1950 and 1951. In 1953 and 1954 the artist was in Paris, working at the famous lithography studio of Edmond and Jacques Desjobert, sharpening his technical skills and observing the collaborative practice of the master printers.

From 1957 to 1962 Blackburn served as the first master printer for Tatyana Grosman's Universal Limited Art Editions (ULAE).[3] When many more artists were drawn to printmaking in the 1960s, and a new audience of collectors sprang up, lucrative opportunities arose for Blackburn. However, the artist avoided changing his ideals and the objectives of his workshop, preferring to focus on providing opportunities in printmaking for young, local, and disadvantaged artists.

In 1987 the Printmaking Workshop moved into expanded quarters on West 17th Street in New York. In the following year, a retrospective exhibition of the artist's prints was mounted by the Alternative Museum in New York. At that time, Blackburn and the Printmaking Workshop were awarded the Governor's Art Award by the New York State Council on the Arts.

Robert Blackburn still runs the nonprofit Printmaking Workshop, which gains momentum each year. Today his warmth and encouragement continue to inspire yet another generation of young artists.

Notes
1. Jones 1982–83, pp. 10–14.
2. Glueck 1988.
3. Tomkins 1976.

■

Cora M. Boone

Little is known about the northern Californian artist and teacher Cora M. Boone, whose vivid woodcuts of the 1930s and 1940s combined B.J.O. Nordfeldt's (cat. 11) technique for making single-block, white line color woodcuts and the Arts and Crafts style of Pedro Lemos (cat. 24). Boone was born in St. Louis on November 18, 1871, and at the age of five, she moved with her family to California.[1] In the 1890s she attended the Mark Hopkins Institute in San Francisco, and afterward traveled to Paris to continue her studies. In 1912 she was a student at the Central Arts and Crafts School in London.

Returning to California in the following year, Boone took up the position of art supervisor in the Oakland public schools; she would retain this post until 1935. Boone also taught art in the schools of Danville and Benicia, California. At the Panama-Pacific International Exposition in San Francisco in 1915, her decorative bronze work and copper enamels were exhibited. One of Boone's watercolors was shown at the Pennsylvania Academy of Fine Arts in 1922, and her work was regularly included in local exhibitions, including those at the Oakland Art Gallery and the Golden Gate International Exposition, in 1928 and 1939, respectively.

Although the artist's most widely exhibited works were watercolors of naturalistic still lifes and California landscapes, she also made handicrafts. Late in the 1920s Boone learned techniques of relief printmaking from William S. Rice (cat. 28), and she became proficient in making single-block and multiblock color woodcuts. Her early prints were representational and rather decorative, in the style of the Arts and Crafts movement. The influences of modernism are apparent in her later paintings and prints, which were slightly more abstract. The artist died in Oakland, California, on December 7, 1953.

Notes
1. Hughes, p. 52; *American Art Annual* 1919, p. 314; *American Art Annual* 1923, p. 447.

Dorr Bothwell

Born in San Francisco on May 3, 1902, Dorr Bothwell began her studies in 1921 at the California School of Fine Arts, where she was the student of Rudolph Schaeffer.[1] After a year at the University of Oregon in Eugene, she returned to the School of Fine Arts, and in 1924, she enrolled at Rudolph Schaeffer's own School of Design. His methods were derived in part from the work of Ernest Fenollosa and Arthur Wesley Dow (cat. 6), and also focused on the rudiments of Japanese design, especially the concept of *notan*.[2]

In 1927 Bothwell's paintings were first exhibited at the Modern Gallery in San Francisco. In 1928 she journeyed to American Samoa, where for two years she painted and studied native arts. Intrigued by the primitive artist's impulse to achieve carefully balanced decorative, symbolic shapes, she recognized therein the principle of *notan*. Her works from Samoa were exhibited in San Diego and in San Francisco upon her return. She traveled and studied in Europe in 1930 and 1931.

In the 1940s Bothwell explored the artistic traditions of the Native American tribes of the northwest coastal regions. She began making her own serigraphs in 1943. The following year, she joined the faculty of the California School of Fine Arts, where she continued to present Schaeffer's teachings. Later in the decade Bothwell exhibited regularly with the National Serigraph Society, and in 1948 she had the first of many exhibitions at the Serigraph Gallery in New York. Among numerous awards for her prints was a purchase prize in the Second National Print Exhibition at the Brooklyn Museum in 1948. After a yearlong teaching appointment at the Parsons School of Design in New York, Bothwell returned to teach at the California School of Fine Arts until 1961. Throughout her career the artist presented many symposia on painting, design, and color.[3]

From 1949 to 1951 Bothwell painted and studied in Paris, and continued working with serigraphy. Concerned about wasting the leftovers of unobtainable silkscreen inks, she began spreading them on glass, printing monotypes by hand.[4]

In 1958 a solo exhibition of Bothwell's paintings was mounted at the De Young Museum in San Francisco.[5] The artist studied the traditional crafts of decorative weaving and dyeing, pottery, and gravestone carving in Nigeria and Tunisia in 1966–67. In 1974 she went to Bali, Java, and Sumatra in order to study folk design and observe the manufacture of batik and wood carving. A retrospective of her screen prints was mounted in Mendocino, California, in 1985.

The artist distilled many of her observations of traditional arts from all over the world both in her teaching programs and in the book *Notan, the Dark-Light Principle of Design*, which was coauthored by Marlys Frey.[6] Still active as a painter and printmaker, Bothwell now divides her time between studios in Mendocino and Joshua Tree, California.

Notes
1. Falk, p. 68; *Who's Who* 1947, p. 69.
2. On Rudolph Schaeffer see *Who's Who* 1947, p. 407.
3. Bothwell's article "So You Love Color!" (Bothwell 1940) presents many of the concepts she taught in her well-known workshops on color.
4. Johnson 1956, p. 35.
5. Chipp 1958.
6. Bothwell/Frey 1968.

Cornelis Botke

The son of a horticulturist, Cornelis J. Botke was born in Leewarden, in the Dutch province of Friesland, on July 6, 1887.[1] He began his studies of art as a teenager at the School of Applied Design in Haarlem, where he was the pupil of Chris Le Beau. He had just begun a career in commercial design when his family emigrated from Holland to the United States, settling in Chicago in 1906. Botke was able to find enough work as a graphic and decorative arts designer to establish a modest studio while continuing his studies at the Art Institute of Chicago. At this time, several of the artist's decorative landscape paintings were acquired by public institutions, including the Oak Park High School in Illinois and the public library in Ponca City, Oklahoma.

In Chicago, Botke met fellow art student Jessie Arms, and they were married in about 1916. Jessie Arms Botke established a successful career of her own, producing intaglio prints and specializing in vivid, decorative watercolors and color relief prints of birds.[2] During this time Cornelis Botke made landscape intaglios in the academic style of the Etching Revival, and he exhibited these with the Chicago Society of Etchers.

In 1919 the artist accepted a teaching position at the Carmel Club of Arts and Crafts, and he and his wife moved to California.[3] His watercolors and picturesque etchings of this period reveal his delight in the landscape of California. After an extended trip to Europe in 1927, the Botkes bought a working ranch near Santa Paula in southern California and settled there. They both continued to produce oil paintings, watercolors, etchings, and color relief prints, which were exhibited mostly on a local basis.

One of Botke's prints took first prize at the Sacramento State Fair in 1929; his work also won an award from the California Society of Etchers in 1934, and the Shope Prize from the Society of American Etchers in 1935. The artist exhibited with the California Art Club, the California Society of Etchers, the California Watercolor Society, the Society of Graphic Arts, and the California Print Makers. He died at his ranch in Santa Paula on September 16, 1954.

Notes
1. Falk, p. 68; Hughes, p. 56; *Who's Who* 1936, p. 54.
2. On Jessie Arms Botke (1883–1971), see Falk, p. 68; Hughes, p. 56.
3. *American Art Annual* 1920, p. 111.

George Elbert Burr

George Burr was born on April 14, 1859, in Munroe Falls, Ohio, a suburb of Cleveland.[1] When he was ten, his family migrated westward to Cameron, Missouri. His father opened a hardware store, which quickly became a success. In the tin shop of this store, at the age of fifteen, Burr made his first etchings. In 1876 he left home to attend business college in Iowa, and then to study at the Chicago Academy of Design, returning three years later to help manage the family business.

It looked as if Burr would become a local businessman like his father, but by 1885, he was actively teaching drawing classes and had sent some of his sketches to publishers and art galleries. In 1888 he won commissions from both *Harper's* and *Scribner's* magazines, and he published his first book illustrations. By the end of that year Burr was living in New York, and he was an established magazine illustrator, working steadily for *Cosmopolitan* and *Frank Leslie's Illustrated Newspaper*. He preferred to work in pen and ink or wash, but he also managed to maintain his etching activity. His interest in photography also grew during these years, and he used his own photographs to develop illustrations.

In 1896 Burr sailed to Europe, where he stayed for four and a half years, traveling widely. The artist sketched and painted constantly, occasionally dispatching illustrations to American magazines. Returning to America in 1901, he established a new career as a watercolorist and printmaker in Toms River, New Jersey. The wide distribution of his prints and paintings on paper brought him success quite rapidly.

In 1906 Burr moved to Denver. He exhibited twenty-two etchings, several of them printed in color, at the Panama-Pacific International Exposition in San Francisco in 1915. The following year his *Estes Park*, or *Mountain Moods*, series was shown; this group comprised sixteen watercolors complemented by renderings of the same landscapes in etching.

Late in the 1910s the artist began to travel to the deserts of Arizona, New Mexico, and California, and documented these travels in *The Desert Set*, a series of thirty-five dramatic etchings published in 1921. This set is remarkable in Burr's oeuvre in that the unusually large editions were carefully numbered.[2] This much-publicized series established and spread Burr's reputation, and he became further identified with the Southwest and desert imagery.

In about 1920 the artist's health declined appreciably; he suffered from a chronic respiratory ailment and a disabled arm. These complaints prompted him to move to Phoenix in 1924. Burr never again attempted a large series of prints or any other project of similar scope, but he remained remarkably active through the final days of his life. In 1928 and 1929 his etchings were exhibited in Paris, Washington, D.C., and London.

In 1930, in a letter to Bertha Jacques of the Brooklyn Society of Etchers, Burr related that during his career he had printed and mounted more than seven hundred etchings.[3] He died in Phoenix on November 17, 1939.

Notes
1. Seeber 1971.
2. Ibid., p. 44.
3. Ibid., p. 30.

Edmond Casarella

Born in Newark, New Jersey, on September 3, 1920, Edmond Casarella studied art at Cooper Union in New York from 1938 to 1942.[1] In the early 1940s he was enrolled in the National Youth Administration, and was employed by Anthony Velonis (cat. 42) at Creative Printmakers as a silkscreen printer. After serving in the Army from 1944 to 1946, Casarella settled in Brooklyn. He continued his studies on the GI Bill at the School of the Brooklyn

Museum from 1949 to 1951, where he studied printmaking with Gabor Peterdi (cat. 79), Louis Schanker (cat. 41), and Vincent Longo.[2] Drawn to the technique by a desire to produce large-scale prints in color independently and economically, Casarella made his first paper relief print as early as 1949. Over the next ten years, he gradually developed a range of his own techniques for paper relief cut printmaking, constantly refining his method.

With the support of a Fulbright Fellowship in 1951 and 1952, Casarella traveled in Italy and Greece. Among the works resulting from this trip was *Civitavecchio*, a paper relief print made in 1952, which was awarded a purchase prize at the Print National Exhibition at the Brooklyn Museum the following year. The artist's paintings were featured along with those of Longo in a two-man exhibition at this museum in 1952.[3] and the following year in a solo exhibition at the Zabriskie Gallery.

Casarella taught in the Brooklyn Museum graphic workshop from 1956 to 1960 and concentrated on his own paper relief cut technique. In 1959 he won a Guggenheim Fellowship grant and traveled in France. From 1969 through 1974 the artist taught at Finch College in New York City. In 1963 he began teaching at Cooper Union, the Art Students League, and Hunter College in New York. Over the years Casarella also held a number of temporary teaching positions, including appointments at New York University, Columbia University, Yale University, Rutgers University, Queens College, the Pratt Institute, and Manhattanville College of the Sacred Heart.

Among several retrospective exhibitions of Casarella's work were those organized by the Naroden Muzej in Skopje, Yugoslavia, in 1967, and at Edward Williams College in Hackensack, New Jersey, in 1979. His paintings, prints, and sculptures have also been featured in more than twenty-five solo exhibitions and in many group shows in the United States and abroad, especially in Eastern Europe.

Since the mid-1960s Casarella has given his attention almost exclusively to sculpture. In the 1960s he occasionally made intaglio prints related to his metal Constructivist relief sculptures. The artist has also made lithographs, monotypes, and etchings. Now living in Englewood, New Jersey, he concentrates chiefly on sculpture in steel and bronze.

Notes
1. *Who's Who* 1986, p. 160; Cummings 1988, pp. 171–172.
2. Some stylistic cross–influences between Longo and Casarella in the 1950s are apparent. Although Longo produced an outstanding group of woodcuts during this period, only a few were in color. See Corcoran 1970.
3. Holliday 1953.

■

Mary Cassatt

The daughter of a prosperous businessman, Mary Stevenson Cassatt was born on May 22, 1845, in Allegheny City, Pennsylvania, just outside Pittsburgh.[1] Her family lived in Europe through much of her childhood, and she learned to speak both French and German. Between 1860 and 1862, when they lived in Philadelphia, Cassatt attended classes at the Pennsylvania Academy of Fine Arts. Late in 1865 she returned to France, studying with Jean Léon Gérome and Charles Chaplin in Paris, and with Paul Soyer and Thomas Couture in art colonies north of the city. In 1858 Cassatt's painting *The Mandolin Player* was accepted for exhibition at the Paris Salon.

In 1870 Cassatt returned to Philadelphia where she became a close friend of Emily Sartain, a painter and engraver who exposed her to current fashions in American printmaking. At the end of 1871 the two young women traveled to Italy together, where they worked with Carlo Raimondi, a reproductive engraver and teacher, from whom Cassatt may have learned printmaking techniques. In 1874, after travels in Italy, Spain, and the Netherlands, she settled permanently in Paris.

There she met Edgar Degas, who welcomed her into his coterie of independent artists; she first exhibited with the Impressionists in 1879. Close relationships of style and technique show that several of these artists collaborated in experiments with intaglio printmaking. They even tried printing their plates in color, and Cassatt learned a creative and unrestrained attitude to printmaking. In 1879 and 1880, under Degas's influence, she created several experimental intaglios in soft-ground etching and coarse aquatint.[2]

In about 1885, after a respite from printmaking, Cassatt began to experiment with drypoint. Her prints were exhibited in the landmark exhibition Women Etchers of America, mounted in Boston in 1887, and in 1889 at the Galerie Durand-Ruel in Paris, in the first exhibition of the Société de Peintres-Graveurs Français, a fulcrum for the Parisian print revival. Organized by Félix Bracquemond and Henri Guérard, this group was dedicated to creative, original printmaking, as opposed to conventional, stilted reproductive intaglio work. In 1890 Cassatt began to add color aquatint to her drypoint plates. A few years later she was commissioned to paint *Modern Woman*, a mural for the Woman's Building at the World Columbian Exposition in Chicago. Cassatt's large solo exhibition in Paris in 1893 featured thirteen color prints, and her show at the Durand-Ruel Gallery in New York in 1895 included eighteen.

In 1898 the artist traveled to the United States for the first time in over twenty years. By the time of her last visit to America in 1908, she was already experiencing the eyestrain that would soon force her to abandon printmaking. Shortly thereafter, she had to stop painting, and cataract operations were performed on both her eyes. In 1914 Cassatt was awarded the Gold Medal of Honor by the Pennsylvania Academy of Fine Arts. She died at the Château de Beaufresne, her country home at Mesnil-Théribus, on June 14, 1926.

Notes

1. Matthews 1987. The standard study of Cassatt's prints, Breeskin 1970, has been superseded in its treatment of the color prints by the research of Matthews/Shapiro 1989. The author is grateful to Barbara Shapiro for guidance in the preparation of this entry.
2. Matthews/Shapiro 1989, pp. 57–59.

■

Ada Gilmore Chaffee

Born Ada Gilmore in Kalamazoo, Michigan, on June 17, 1883, she was one of four children of a prominent local merchant.[1] When Ada was just eight years old, her mother died, and four years later her father died. She and her siblings were taken to live with an aunt near Belfast, Ireland. Gilmore attended the Belfast School of Design, where she studied drawing and watercolor.

Returning to Kalamazoo in 1900, she taught a few private pupils and in 1903 continued her studies at the School of the Art Institute of Chicago. She found lodgings in the home of a fellow student, Mildred "Dolly" McMillen, and the two women became friends. In 1910 Robert Henri organized an exhibition of the Independent Artists, in which Gilmore's works were included.[2] Living on Long Island in 1912, the artist studied with Henri, and the following year she went to Paris. There, after seeing an exhibition of color woodcuts by Ethel Mars, Gilmore became her student.[3]

When World War I began, Gilmore and many of her friends returned to the United States, and settled in Provincetown, Massachusetts. She was one of the first to wholeheartedly embrace B.J.O. Nordfeldt's method of printing color woodcuts from a single block (cat. 11). In 1915 Gilmore's prints were exhibited at the Panama-Pacific International Exposition in San Francisco and at the inaugural exhibition of the Provincetown Art Association. She sent work to the annual exhibition of the New York Watercolor Club in December 1915, and showed color prints at the Berlin Photographic Company in New York the following

spring.[4] Indeed, the artist contributed to all the early exhibitions of the Provincetown group,[5] including a show at Ambrose Webster's oceanside studio that excited much local interest, and gallery exhibitions in New York and Boston from 1918 through 1922.

In 1923, while visiting Mars at Vence in southern France, Gilmore renewed her acquaintance with Oliver Newberry Chaffee, Jr. They were married that same year in Vence, where they lived and worked together. Gilmore became artistically oriented to the work of her husband and of his French and American colleagues, modernists such as Albert Gleizes, Chaim Soutine, Jules Pascin, and Marsden Hartley. She then turned to watercolor, concentrating on still lifes and floral subjects. Although she occasionally printed from old blocks in later years, she had essentially stopped making color woodcuts by 1923.

Gilmore and Chaffee returned to Provincetown in 1928. There, following the rift in the Provincetown Art Association, they were drawn to the modernists with whom they exhibited in the 1930s. They wintered at a cottage in Ormond Beach, Florida, spending their summers on Cape Cod, and Gilmore continued to produce watercolors. After her husband died in April 1944, Gilmore spent most of her time in Provincetown. She continued to paint watercolors and was a visible member of local art circles until her death in 1955.

Notes

1. Falk, pp. 107, 233; Fielding 1986, p. 327.
2. Parker 1988, p. 6.
3. Flint 1983, pp. 12–13, 28, 39.
4. Chaffee 1952; see also Flint 1983, p. 14.
5. *New York Times* 1916.

■

Jean Charlot

Jean Charlot was born in Paris on February 7, 1898. As a teenager, he purchased a group of *Images d'Epinal* at a flea market and began a lifelong fascination with these inexpensive,

popular, hand-colored French woodcuts.[1] He began his studies at the Ecole des Beaux-Arts in Paris, and made his first prints in 1915 when he carved several woodcuts representing religious subjects.

Charlot moved to Mexico in 1921. At the Academy of San Carlos in Coyoacán, he experimented with drypoint and simple lithographs and produced several woodcuts. He joined in the populist artistic movement of postrevolutionary Mexico and became a colleague of Diego Rivera, David Alfaro Siqueiros, and José Orozco.[2] Like these artists, Charlot represented genre or pre-Hispanic subjects in large-scale frescoes.

In 1926 Charlot won the position of archaeological draftsman for excavations of the twelfth-century Mayan temple at Chichén Itzá in the Yucatán.[3] The experience of the dig and of ancient Mayan art and culture profoundly influenced his style. Charlot went to New York in 1928 to correct proofs for the archaeological report. In 1929 he began working with George Miller on lithographs of Mayan and Mexican subjects. Several prints representing the ancient Mayans building their sacred pyramids, reflected the artist's preoccupation with the almost mystical process of unearthing an ancient civilization.[4] Charlot and Miller collaborated until 1931, producing twenty-seven prints. The artist alternated between living in Mexico and New York, where he taught at the Art Students League and lectured at Columbia University. In 1933 Charlot met Lynton R. Kistler in Los Angeles. They made many color prints together, including the landmark *Picture Book*, of offset lithographs, published in 1933.

The artist returned to New York in 1934 to take a teaching position at the Florence Cane School, where he initiated a printmaking program with fellow teacher Albert Carman. A Multilith Offset lithograph press was purchased for the school and was modified, for instructional purposes, to print from hand-drawn plates.[5] Charlot and Carman were cosigners of a patent for using the offset

lithographic process to make hand-drawn—as opposed to a photomechanically transferred—full-color lithographs.[6]

A decade of productive painting, printmaking, and teaching followed for Charlot at several colleges and universities throughout the country. For the academic year 1945 to 1946, he won a Guggenheim Fellowship to work in Mexico, where he produced *Mexihkanantli (Mexican Mother;* Morse 487–502), a portfolio of sixteen color lithographs. In 1947 the artist was appointed head of the Colorado Springs Fine Arts Center.

In 1949 Charlot moved to Hawaii. In 1961 he produced illustrations of Thorton Wilder's *The Bridge of San Luis Rey;* these fifteen color offset lithographs were printed by George Miller in New York (Morse 596–610).[7]

The thirty-two color offset lithographs of *Picture Book II* were drawn by Charlot in Hawaii and printed by Kistler in Los Angeles in 1972 and 1973 (Morse 659–694). Charlot's printmaking activity lasted into his final days; his last major project was another portfolio depicting Hawaiian culture, *Kei Viti* of 1978, completed just months before the artist's death in Honolulu in March 1979.

Notes

1. Morse 1976 (pp. vii–viii); Morse catalogued 714 prints by Charlot, including woodcuts, etchings, drypoints, lithographs, and serigraphs.
2. Charlot 1963.
3. Morris/Charlot 1931.
4. Morse 74–75 (1927); Morse 83 (1929); and Morse 93 (1929).
5. This was probably the very press, an Addressograph Multilith 296, that Don Freeman (cat. 38) purchased in 1937 to produce his magazine *Newsstand*. Three of Charlot's own major projects were completed using this technique: an edition of Hillaire Belloc's *Characters of the Reformation* illustrated with twenty-three original color lithographs (Belloc 1936; Morse 279–318); *A Catalogue of Prints*, representing Charlot's oeuvre to date (1936–37; Morse 321–362); and *Carmen* (1939–40; Morse 407–441).
6. Morse 1976, pp. 432–434.
7. Wilder 1962.

■

Lee Chesney

The son of a civil servant, Lee Chesney was born on June 1, 1920, in Washington, D.C.[1] His college education was interrupted by the war; working in the Medical Administration Corps from 1942 through 1945, he achieved the rank of captain. After his discharge, Chesney attended the University of Colorado, receiving a bachelor's degree in 1946. He then pursued graduate studies in printmaking with Mauricio Lasansky (cat. 67) at the University of Iowa, where he was awarded his Master of Fine Arts in 1948. Chesney worked as an assistant and instructor in a print shop while completing his degree, and he continued to teach in Iowa City until 1950. He then took a position at the University of Illinois, where he outfitted and organized a printmaking workshop and initiated teaching programs. The artist continued to hone his own technical skills in postgraduate studies at the Mill Race Studio in San Antonio, Texas, and at the Universidad de Michoacán in Morelia, Mexico.

Chesney's first solo exhibition was held early in 1954 at the Newman Brown Gallery in Chicago. During the 1950s he helped organize three national exhibitions of contemporary prints, two of which were later circulated by the American Federation of Arts.

A Fulbright Research Award made possible the artist's visit to Japan in 1956 in order to study traditional and contemporary Japanese printmaking. However, calligraphy and *sumi* painting were what most captivated and influenced the artist during his stay there. He also acquired a new sensitivity to nature and a desire to adapt responsively to his environment and circumstances. As a member of the Japan Print Association (*Nihon Sosaku Hanga Kyokai*), he has since exhibited regularly in the East.[2] After serving as visiting professor at the Otis Art Institute in Los Angeles in 1966, the artist was lured by the University of Southern California to accept the position of associate dean of fine arts there in 1967.

In 1972 Chesney began a decade of teaching at the University of Hawaii. A major retrospective exhibition of his prints opened at the Florida Technological University in Orlando in November 1977, and afterward circulated throughout the country.[3] A Ford Foundation Grant in 1978 took the artist to Paris, and with the support of Gardilanne Foundation-Moffat Studio Awards, he has returned there frequently to work and exhibit. Chesney's prints have been shown in more than 140 national and international group exhibitions, and he has had more than 30 solo exhibitions. Currently living in Los Angeles, the artist continues to teach, paint, and produce intaglio prints with unabated vigor.

Notes
1. *Who's Who* 1986, p. 174.
2. Chesney's second one-man show was at the Yoseido Gallery in Tokyo in May 1957.
3. Miyamoto 1978.

■

Bernard Childs

Born in Brooklyn, New York, on September 1, 1910 to Russian immigrant parents, Bernard Childs moved with his family to Harrisburg, Pennsylvania, in 1921.[1] After studying for two years at the University of Pennsylvania, he pursued his artistic career in New York. Studying by night at the Art Students League with Kimon Nicolaides, Childs met the Danish silversmith Per Smed, who instilled in him a love of metals and a respect for traditional art and craftsmanship.

In 1941 Childs learned about industrial tools and the metalworking processes while working as a machinist in a factory. In 1943 he joined the navy, and he suffered injuries during the war that required a long convalescence. In 1947 he began studies in New York with Amédée Ozenfant. Childs moved to Europe in 1951; living in Italy, he had his first solo exhibition at the Galleria dell'Obelisco in Rome in 1952. In the following year he moved to Paris.

Late in 1954 Childs first combined his interest in metalworking with his painting experience, in original intaglio prints. He worked at Atelier 17 while studying printmaking history on his own. At first drawn to the direct techniques of engraving and drypoint, he later sought a freer process with which he could prepare his plates in a manner parallel to the calligraphic style of his current paintings. Before long, Childs began experiments with electric tools,[2] and set up an old printing press in his studio. Although most of his prints were produced in the 1960s and 1970s, the artist created about twenty purely experimental plates and twenty-seven published prints before 1960, most of them in color.

Child's first solo museum exhibition was mounted at the Stedelijk Museum in Amsterdam in 1959.[3] During the 1960s he created about seventy-four editions. Childs made progressively denser and more textural prints, incorporating very deeply cut engraving, aquatint, and collagraph. He also began to shape his plates, piercing them with holes and sawn slots. Late in 1968 the artist began making his sculpture *Images in Light*, thick sheets of polymer acrylic engraved with electric tools, through which colored light was transmitted. He developed a different sort of printing matrix for use with a mechanized letterpress, as exemplified by *Magic Over the Mountain*, an intaglio produced for the catalogue of his exhibition at the Storm King Art Center in 1969.[4]

Most of Child's prints of the 1970s incorporated collagraph. In 1978 he suffered a stroke; however, he returned to painting until his death in New York on March 27, 1985.

Notes
1. Johnson 1969b.
2. This search and evolution are recounted in a letter written by the artist on November 17, 1965, to Joan Hansrath, preserved in the Archives of American Art. See also Graham 1987, pp. 20, 27.
3. Stedelijk 1959.
4. Johnson 1969a.

■

Minna Citron

Born on October 15, 1896 in Newark, New Jersey, Minna Wright began her art studies at the Brooklyn Manual Training High School and continued them at the Brooklyn Institute of Arts and Sciences, the College of the City of New York, and the New York School of Applied Design for Women.[1] After her marriage to Henry Citron in 1916, she attended the Art Students League, where she was the pupil of John Sloan, Kenneth Hayes Miller, Reginald Marsh, and Kimon Nicolaides.

In the mode of the Fourteenth Street School, Citron's paintings and prints of the 1930s and 1940s were observations of human character, ranging from scathing satire to the optimism of the New Deal. Her early etchings were Social Realist images of life in the city, in the manner of Sloan and Miller. In the 1930s she won federal painting commissions and executed murals in the post offices of Newport and Manchester, Tennessee, depicting the activities of the Tennessee Valley Authority. Her first solo exhibition, at the Midtown Galleries in New York in 1935, was followed by one-person shows there every other year until 1943. During this time Citron was a staff lecturer at the Art Students League, and from 1942 to 1946, she taught life drawing at the School of the Brooklyn Museum.

By 1945 Citron had begun to work in a more abstract style, though her paintings and prints were still imbued with fantasy and humor. Linear elements, often expressive and calligraphic, dominated her work. Her fascination with peculiar points of view is apparent in several paintings from aerial or submarine perspectives.

In 1946 Citron served as the Paris correspondent for the art magazine *Iconograph*. In 1947 she exhibited with the 14 Painter-Printmakers group, of which she was a founding member.[2] In the 1950s the artist's style was progressively simplified, as linear elements were replaced by form and color. Citron steadily produced color intaglios through the decade.

Early in the 1960s she experimented with collage paintings that utilized such materials as tar paper, which she tore, crumpled, and overpainted with bright, gestural splashes of pigment. She also added sand and other materials to her paint in order to give a range of texture to her canvases. In 1962 these paintings were exhibited at the Ruth White Gallery in New York, and in 1963 a retrospective exhibition of Citron's work was organized by Howard University in Washington, D.C.[3] Later in the decade, she began to work with metal foil, embossing and distressing the material from the back, creating shallow reliefs in a clean, simple, Constructivist style.

Citron's prints of the 1970s reflect a continuing impulse to explore new techniques and styles. This lifetime of youthful curiosity and creativity was celebrated in 1986 when Rutgers organized an exhibition of her work to mark her ninetieth birthday, and she served for a year as artist in residence at the Mason Gross School of the Arts.[4] The artist continues to live and work in New York.

Notes

1. Falk, p. 115; Who's Who 1947, p. 103.
2. Gordon/Johnson 1955, nos. 7–12.
3. Howard 1963.
4. Rutgers 1986.

■

Gabrielle De Vaux Clements

Born in Philadelphia on September 11, 1858, Gabrielle De Vaux Clements was the daughter of a physician and a Southern lady of means.[1] She was introduced to printmaking in 1875 by Charles Page at the Philadelphia School of Design for Women, and she continued her artistic studies at Cornell University, creating scientific illustrations in preparation for her Bachelor of Science degree, which she was awarded in 1880. From 1880 to 1883 she studied with Thomas Eakins at the Pennsylvania Academy of Fine Arts, where she won the Toppan Prize for the best student painting.

In 1883 Stephen Parrish invited five of Eakins's female students, Clements among them, to learn etching at a weekly class in his studio.[2] At this time, Clements developed a close friendship with painter Ellen Day Hale, who had her own portrait studio in Boston. When Clements and her parents left for Europe in 1884, Hale accompanied them. In Paris the two women studied together at the Académie Julian under Tony Robert-Fleury and William Bouguereau.

In the late 1880s Clements and Hale collaborated on two miniature etching portfolios for Louis Prang & Company, representing scenes of the Massachusetts shore and of Newport, Rhode Island. Twenty-one of Clements's prints were included in the landmark exhibition Women Etchers of America at the Museum of Fine Arts, Boston in 1887. In the 1890s she began to execute commissions for the prominent New York publisher Christian Klackner and the Bendann Galleries.[3] By 1895 the artist was in Baltimore, beginning a long teaching career at the Bryn Mawr School for Girls.

During World War I, Clements and Hale began spending their winters in Charleston, South Carolina, and their summers in Rockport, Massachusetts. Soon they became enthusiastic about printing in color. They used as their point of departure René Ligeron's treatise Original Engravings in Colours, which was published in Paris in 1924, and which Hale translated.[4] Both made many experimental color plates, reworking images from sketchbooks of South Carolina and travels in Europe, the Middle East, and North Africa. Technical experiments were shared with an array of younger Cape Ann artists—Margaret Yeaton Hoyt, Lesley Jackson, William Meyerowitz (cat. 27), and Theresa Bernstein—all of whom also had the use of their etching studio. Similarly, Clements and Hale trained printmaking students in Charleston, including Elizabeth O'Neil Verner and Alice Ravenel Huger Smith.

Clements tried to exhibit her prints as widely as possible, entering them in many shows in the vicinity of her homes on Cape Ann, in Charleston, and in the Baltimore area. The artist died in Rockport on March 23, 1948.

Notes

1. Falk, p. 118; Bernstein 1976, p. 5. Peet 1988, pp. 15–18, 29–30, 53, provides further references.
2. Peet 1988, p. 15.
3. The Maryland Historical Society possesses nine prints by Clements representing scenes of Baltimore, along with nine etched plates and annotated proofs. Most of these were commissioned by David Bendann between 1924 and 1931.
4. Speed 1935.

■

John Wesley Cotton

Born on October 29, 1868, in Simcoe County, Ontario, John Wesley Cotton began his schooling in Toronto at the Art Students League in 1886.[1] He went on to study at the Art Institute of Chicago, exhibiting his prints there with the Chicago Society of Etchers. In 1911 and 1912 Cotton studied with E. Marsden Wilson in London. This training in the tradition of the Royal Society of Painter-Etchers is evident in Cotton's prints in the still-fashionable Barbizon-influenced style of the Etching Revival. The artist traveled in Britain and on the Continent, producing etched views of picturesque architecture in London and Bruges and of landscape vistas in Cornwall.[2] Returning to Toronto, he had his first solo exhibition at the Métropole Galleries in 1912.[3] Cotton was awarded a medal for etchings exhibited at the Panama-Pacific International Exposition in 1915. He may have visited that fair in San Francisco, and would have been exposed not only to the dramatic natural beauty of the American West and its hospitable climate, but also to the prints of George Elbert Burr (cat. 10), Pedro Lemos (cat. 24), and Benjamin Brown, among others. In about 1918 Cotton left Toronto for southern California.[4]

The artist quickly developed a reputation and a following of collectors in the West for his broadly etched views of the picturesque pueblos and old Spanish churches of New Mexico and his lyrical vistas of the Western coastline, sierras, and deserts. He settled in Glendale, California, which was close to Pasadena, the home of the Browns and the Gearharts (cats. 16, 22), artists who were at the center of the California Print Makers in the 1920s. The subjects of Cotton's prints show that he traveled throughout the Southwest, but he always maintained his home and studio in Glendale, printing on a press that had once belonged to Auguste Lepere. Unlike many of his colleagues, Cotton did not distribute his prints much beyond California. He exhibited with the California Art Club and the California Watercolor Club; one of his prints was awarded the gold medal at the Southwest Exposition in Long Beach in 1928. The artist may have been in failing health when, in 1930, he returned to Toronto. He died there on November 24, 1931.

Notes

1. Falk, p. 132; Hughes, p. 102; Samuels 1976, p. 109.
2. Ontario 1970, pp. 83–84.
3. Métropole 1912.
4. This is suggested by Cotton's resignation from the Ontario Society of Artists in 1918. He was reelected to the society when he returned to Toronto in 1930, shortly before his death. See Miller 1931; Skelinghaus 1924.

■

Ralston Crawford

Ralston Crawford was born on September 5, 1906, in St. Catherines, Ontario, Canada.[1] He grew up in Buffalo, New York, and as a child he explored the Great Lakes with his father, a ship captain. In 1926 Crawford went to sea on a tramp steamer, and sailed in the Caribbean and the Pacific. Settling briefly in Los Angeles, he found work at the Walt Disney Studios while studying at the Otis Art Institute.

From 1927 to 1930 scholarships enabled Crawford to study at the Pennsylvania Academy of Fine Arts in Philadelphia, where he was the pupil of Hugh Henry Breckenridge, and at the Barnes Foundation in Merion, Pennsylvania. He first became interested in modernism at this time. After painting in New York briefly, Crawford won a Tiffany Foundation Grant and traveled to Europe in 1932. In Paris he attended the Académie Colorossi and the Académie Scandinave.

Crawford worked in a representational style when he returned to New York in 1933. His first one-man show was held at the Maryland Institute of Art in Baltimore in 1934. He attended the first American Artists Congress in New York in 1936, and for some time he was allied with the active left-wing artists of New York City.[2] Until 1939 he painted at Chadds Ford and Exton, Pennsylvania. The artist taught briefly at the Art Academy of Cincinnati and at the Albright School in Buffalo. After 1940, between his wide and frequent travels, New York City remained Crawford's base. There, in 1942, he began to experiment with Synthetic Cubism in his paintings.

During World War II, Crawford worked in the Weather Division of the Army Air Force in Washington, D.C. His experiences in charting weather movements changed his concepts of graphic form and expression. He was then posted to the China-Burma-India theater of war; as an artist-correspondent for *Fortune* magazine, he witnessed the test explosion of an atomic bomb at Bikini Atoll in the Marshall Islands in 1946.

After his discharge, Crawford served as director of the Honolulu School of Art in 1947. At this time his paintings depicted ships and industrial landscapes in a Cubist-Precisionist manner. His style evolved progressively toward flatter colors and bolder outlines. Sales of his artwork were seldom enough to support Crawford, so he held many temporary teaching jobs and residencies at colleges and universities throughout the country. Between 1948 and 1950 he taught at the Brooklyn Museum School, the Art Academy of Cincinnati, and the University of Minnesota. When he was at Louisiana State University in Baton Rouge in

1949 and 1950, Crawford first encountered Dixieland jazz. Afterward, he remained fascinated by this music and its culture, and returned frequently to New Orleans to extensively photograph the musicians.

In 1951 Crawford returned to France. He found Paris particularly conducive to his work, and he went there to paint and to collaborate with the French master lithographers in 1954–55, 1957, and 1959. The artist taught at the New School for Social Research in New York from 1952 to 1957. Although he worked incessantly, sales of Crawford's paintings were slight during the 1950s; however, demand for his prints was consistent, and he was encouraged to continue making lithographs. His first solo exhibition, which included many prints, was held at the University of Alabama in 1953, and marked the publication of Richard B. Freeman's monograph on Crawford.[3]

In 1958 an important retrospective of Crawford's paintings, lithographs, photographs, and drawings was mounted at the Milwaukee Art Center.[4] After a residency at the University of Colorado, he joined the faculty of Hofstra College in 1960. He later taught briefly at the University of Kentucky and the University of Southern California. Sixty-five of Crawford's lithographs were featured in a traveling show organized by the University of Kentucky at Lexington in 1961.[5] In that year another retrospective of paintings and lithographs was held at the Tweed Gallery of the University of Minnesota in Duluth, where Crawford taught during the summer.

During the last years of his life, Crawford spent more time traveling than teaching; he journeyed in North Africa, the South Pacific, and the Far East. In 1971 the artist learned that he had cancer; however neither his travels nor his work abated. Crawford died in Houston, Texas, on April 27, 1978, where he had gone to arrange for an exhibition. In accordance with his wishes, he was buried

in St. Louis Cemetery in New Orleans, and a full brass band played at his funeral.

Notes

1. Haskell 1985, with extensive bibliography.
2. Ibid., pp. 35–36.
3. Freeman 1953.
4. Dwight 1958.
5. Freeman 1961 and 1962.

Arthur Bowen Davies

The son of British immigrants, Arthur Bowen Davies was born in Utica, New York, on September 26, 1862.[1] As a child, his parents provided him with private drawing lessons. When his family moved to Chicago, he continued his studies at the Chicago Academy of Design. In 1882 Davies began studies at the School of the Art Institute of Chicago with Charles Corwin.

In 1886 he moved to New York, where he took classes at the Gotham Art Students School and the Art Students League. He supported his studies through a brief career in magazine illustration and began to exhibit his paintings in 1888.[2] In 1892 Davies married a physician, Virginia Merriweather, and they moved to upstate New York. A year later, he set up a studio in the city and visited his wife on weekends.

Davies's first prints, created in 1884, were etchings after his own earlier drawings. A few experiments with woodcut related to his designs for magazine illustrations.[3] In the mid-1890s he was also an avid amateur photographer, and he made his initial experiments with lithography.

After a trip to Europe in 1895, Davies exhibited a group of small paintings in his first one-man show, at the Macbeth Gallery in New York. Visiting Europe again the following year, he was influenced by Pierre Puvis de Chavannes. He also responded deeply to the frescoes of Pompeii, and he began to distill from them a classicizing style based on the idealized nude depicted in an idyllic garden. This personal version of European Symbolism became popular

almost immediately, and the artist maintained its essential formula throughout his career.[4]

In 1900 Davies and his wife separated, and two years later he met dancer Edna Potter. By 1905 they were living together in New York City under assumed names, and later they had a child together. Davies never divorced his wife and for the rest of his life he supported two families. Through Potter he became interested in the work of Isadora Duncan and was one of several artists to represent her style and choreography. In 1908 Davies was included in the landmark exhibition of "The Eight," which he helped to organize at the Macbeth Gallery.

In 1912 Davies became president of the Association of American Painters and Sculptors. He spearheaded the idea of expanding the show of this association into an international exhibition of modern art—the famous Armory Show of 1913 in New York.[5] In 1916 Davies created a group of Cubist-influenced drypoints with aquatint. The artist returned to lithography in 1919, collaborating first with Bolton Brown. Later, working with George Miller, he produced more than fifty prints, including several color lithographs, between 1919 and 1921. The first comprehensive exhibition of Davies's prints was mounted at the Weyhe Gallery in New York in 1921.

Beginning in 1923 the artist divided each year between New York and Europe. In 1928, during his annual stay in Florence, Davies died of a heart attack on October 28, with Edna Potter and their daughter at his side.

Notes

1. A complete biography is given in Czestochowski 1987, pp. 11–48. This catalogue supersedes that of Price 1929.
2. Czestochowski 1987, pp. 12, 80–85.
3. Ibid., p. 19.
4. Wattenmaker 1975, pp. 194, 195.
5. Brown 1963, p. 40.

Stuart Davis

Stuart Davis was born in Philadelphia, on December 7, 1892.[1] His father was art director of the Philadelphia Press, and his mother was a sculptor. When he was seven years old, his family moved to East Orange, New Jersey. From 1909 to 1913 Davis studied with Robert Henri in New York. He then began working as an illustrator for *Harper's Weekly*, and the left-wing magazine *The Masses*, for which he worked until 1916.[2] Afterward, Davis continued to make a living as a free-lance illustrator for several other periodicals.

Five of Davis's Social Realist watercolors were included in the Armory Show in New York in 1913. This exhibition introduced the artist to modernism, challenging all of his aesthetic values and assumptions, and profoundly affecting him. His work soon reflected the influence of such Post-Impressionist painters as Gauguin and van Gogh, and of the Fauvism of Matisse. Davis conducted his own thoughtful experiments with abstraction. Exploring Cubism, he made painted imitations of collages, representing such elements as package labels and billboard fragments. During World War I, Davis served as a cartographer in the Army Intelligence Corps. His first solo exhibition was held at the Sheridan Gallery in New York in 1917.

Around 1927 the artist began his famous series of analytical paintings, compositions derived from still-life images of a percolator and an eggbeater. He progressively simplified the representation of these objects until they became lean, geometric forms, delicately balanced in their shape, hue, and relation to one another.

In 1928 and 1929 Davis was in Paris. There he painted rather picturesque urban views in which form and space were schematized. In Paris he also made his first lithographs, probably at the studio of Edmond Desjobert.[3] Upon his return to New York, the artist entered a new phase; his paintings were now oriented to Synthetic rather than Analytical Cubism. The artist's powerful abstractions were distilled from observed reality, often from landscapes that were particularly American in their character. Flat, vividly colored, and precisely outlined shapes were arranged in Matisse-like decorative patterns. The artist continued to produce modernist lithographs after his return to New York, in 1930 and 1931. More abstract than his Parisian prints, these prints were straightforward in their technique. They were probably printed by George Miller.[4]

Davis taught at the Art Students League in New York in 1931 and 1932. He worked as a muralist, executing abstract wall paintings in the men's lounge at Radio City Music Hall and other commissions. In 1933 Davis was one of the first artists to join the WPA/FAP, for which he worked as an instructor in New York. He also worked in the mural painting division and in the graphic arts division.

During the 1930s Davis was a prominent figure among the politically active artists of New York City. He was a leader of the emerging United American Artists union, and editor of its *Art Front* magazine in 1934. Beginning in 1936 Davis also became active in the Artists Congress.[5] He began teaching at the New School for Social Research in 1940. At this time his palette became brighter, and he represented themes based on jazz, which he considered to be the truest and most American mode of expression. The artist's first important retrospective exhibition was organized in 1945 by the Museum of Modern Art in New York.[6]

In the 1950s Davis's paintings expanded in scale, their component forms became relatively larger, and the compositions became more stable. In 1957 retrospective exhibitions of Davis's paintings were held at the Walker Art Center in Minneapolis and at the Whitney Museum of American Art in New York. The artist was awarded Guggenheim International Awards in 1958 and in 1960.

Davis died on June 24, 1964 in New York. In the following year, a large memorial exhibition was organized by the National Collection of Fine Arts, Smithsonian Institution, in Washington, D.C.[7]

Notes

1. Kelder 1971.
2. Zurier 1985, p. 164, passim.
3. Myers/Cole 1986, pp. 24–26.
4. Adams 1983, p. 76.
5. Davis 1973, pp. 249–250.
6. Sweeney 1945.
7. Arnason 1965.

Worden Day

The daughter of a traveling Methodist minister, Worden Day was born on June 11, 1916 in Columbus, Ohio.[1] When her family moved to a rural community near Alexandria, Virginia, she found a whole new world in the museums of Washington, D.C. After graduating from Randolph-Macon College in Richmond, Virginia, in 1934, Day went to New York. There she studied drawing with Maurice Sterne and George Grosz, and then attended the Florence Crane School, where she learned mural painting and lithography from Jean Charlot (cat. 32) and Emilio Amero.

In 1936 Day supervised a newly organized color offset-lithography shop for the WPA. From 1937 to 1940 she studied at the Art Students League, learning printmaking from Will Barnet and Harry Sternberg (cats. 69, 35) and painting from Vaclav Vytlacil; she also studied with Hans Hofmann (cat. 73) at his school.

In 1940 Day won a fellowship from the Virginia Museum of Fine Arts in Richmond, where she had her first solo exhibition. A one-person show at the Perls Gallery in New York followed shortly. When the war began, she taught at the Richmond Professional Institute of William and Mary College in Virginia. There she began her first experiments with sculpture. She won a fellowship from the Julius Rosenwald Foundation of Chicago in 1941, and traveled around the South before returning to New York in 1943.

"The excitement here," Day later wrote, "was between the whole international atmosphere of . . . the Hofmann Studio, Atelier 17, and the Art of This Century Gallery established by Peggy Guggenheim."[2] In 1943, working at Atelier 17, she met Sue Fuller and Anne Ryan as well as Stanley William Hayter (cats. 58, 65, 60). After several short teaching appointments, Day took a position at the University of Wyoming at Laramie in 1949.

Returning to New York after three years, the artist quickly rejoined the art scene, which revolved around the Artists Club, Atelier 17, and the Cedar Tree Bar on East Eighth Street. Along with Minna Citron (cat. 68), Day started the 14 Painter-Printmakers group.[3] With the support of two Guggenheim Fellowships in 1952 and 1953, she was able to concentrate on painting and printmaking in a stimulating creative environment that included the most influential printmakers of the day.

When Day turned to sculpture in the 1950s, she learned casting techniques from Fred Farr and welding from Abraham Lassaw. From 1961 to 1966 she taught classes in woodcut and watercolor at the New School for Social Research. She received her long-awaited master's degree from New York University in 1966, and began teaching at the Art Students League, where she was an instructor until 1970.

After 1968 Day no longer produced editions of prints, but confined herself to sculpture and occasional monotypes.[4] A solo exhibition of her sculpture was mounted at the Sculpture Center in New York in 1972. She contributed to the organization and to the accompanying catalogue of a retrospective of her work held at the New Jersey State Museum in Trenton, but died of cancer on January 27, 1986, shortly before its opening.

Notes

1. The most complete biography of the artist can be found in Johnson/Day 1986.
2. Ibid., p. 13.
3. Johnson 1956, nos. 13–18.
4. Day 1963.

Arthur Wesley Dow

The son of a merchant and seasonal farm laborer, Arthur Wesley Dow was born in the little coastal town of Ipswich, Massachusetts, on April 6, 1857.[1] When he was in his twenties, he began to make drawings of the houses and historical landmarks of Ipswich. After private studies in Boston, Dow departed for France in 1884. In Paris he studied at the Académie Julian, and he painted at Pont Aven on the coast of Brittany. In 1889 he returned to Boston, where he set himself up as a painter, designer, and private teacher.

Dow was drawn to the Museum of Fine Arts and to its curator of Oriental art, Ernest F. Fenollosa, who provided the artist with a thorough understanding of Japanese art. Together they conceived the idea of combining the purest and most inspired elements of Eastern and Western traditions, in a new style they called "Synthesism." Dow began to practice *sumi* painting and to study Japanese principles of design, which he applied to his own work. The artist sought to reduce and simplify the elements of design, codifying their structure and the process of their combination. He abandoned Western, linear systems of modeling in favor of flat, decorative compositions derived from *ukiyo-e* prints. The idea was that the basic elements of design were line, color, and *notan*, the Japanese term for the arrangement of dark and light.

The artist was also acquainted with S. R. Koehler, curator of graphic arts at The Boston Museum and an expert on the technique of *ukiyo-e*.[2] Using the traditional methods of Japanese printmaking to implement his Synthesist style, Dow began to make color woodcuts in 1891.[3] Approaching the printmaking process as an expressive tool, the artist called his prints "color themes." In 1895 nearly two hundred of them were exhibited at the Museum of Fine Arts in Boston.[4]

As his theories became more resolved, Dow's commitment to teaching increased. In 1895 he became an instructor at the Pratt Institute in Brooklyn. In 1897 the artist taught at the Art Students League in New York, and served as curator of Oriental art at the Museum of Fine Arts in Boston. His instructional book *Composition*, published in 1899, became immensely popular and influential.[5] The following year, Dow founded the Ipswich Summer School of Art. The artist produced the first of his *Ipswich Prints* folios in 1902. These small, unbound albums of prints were intended to be used as exercise and study guides in public school art programs.

In 1903 Dow sailed to Tokyo, where he met Helen Hyde (cat. 8), who arranged lessons for him from her painting master Kano Tomonobu, and for a demonstration by her printer Murato Shojiro. At that time, Dow was appointed director of the department of fine arts of the Teachers College at Columbia University. He established a program that used his book *Composition* as the basic text. Thus Dow's own ideas and methods were passed on to a legion of art teachers who fanned out across the country to disseminate his teachings.

Dow insistently reserved time to devote to his own art. In 1908 a one-man exhibition of his oil paintings, prints, and photographs, as well as his book *By Salt Marshes*, was presented by the Montross Gallery in New York. Dow's health progressively deteriorated during the late 1910s. He died suddenly in New York on December 13, 1922.

Notes
1. Moffatt 1977.
2. In 1889 the government of Japan presented the American National Museum of the Smithsonian Institution, at which Koehler was curator of graphic arts, with the gift of a collection of woodcutting and printing equipment. These technical materials were accompanied by a written explanation of their use, edited and published by the curator. See Tokuno 1893.
3. Dow 1896, p. 87.
4. Fenollosa 1895.
5. Dow 1899.

Werner Drewes

Werner Drewes was born on July 27, 1899, in Canig, Niederlausitz, in eastern Germany.[1] He had his first art instruction in 1907 at the Saldria Gymnasium in Brandenburg-Havel. Soon after graduation, he joined the German Army.

In 1919 Drewes studied architecture and design at the Technische Hochschule in Charlottenburg and made his first experimental linocuts, woodcuts, and etchings on his own soon after he arrived. In 1920 he took classes at the Stuttgart School of Architecture, and in the following year he enrolled at the Stuttgart School of Arts and Crafts. In 1921 and 1922 he studied at the Bauhaus at Weimar, where he was a pupil of Johannes Itten, Paul Klee, and Oskar Schlemmer.[2]

Earning his way by selling etchings and portrait paintings, Drewes traveled widely from 1924 to 1927, visiting the United States. He stayed for a year in St. Louis, where he published his intaglio series *Latin America* (Rose 51–77) and *Saint Louis Cathedral* (Rose 81–87). He traveled around the country, and then visited Asia before returning to Berlin.

Drewes reenrolled at the Bauhaus, now at Dessau, to attend Hinnerk Scheper's mural tutorials and Wassily Kandinsky's weekly painting classes. For about two years after leaving the Bauhaus, he lived in Frankfurt am Main, teaching and exhibiting widely.

In 1930 he moved to New York. Continuing his active career as a printmaker, Drewes made woodcuts and studied lithography with Eugene Fitsch at the Art Students League. The Société Anonyme provided the artist with his first exhibition of paintings in 1931. In 1934 he published *It Can't Happen Here* (Rose 87–96), a series of ten block prints commenting on the rise in Nazism in Germany.

From 1934 to 1936 Drewes taught drawing and printmaking, first at the Brooklyn Museum School, then under the administration of the FAP. In 1937 he became an American citizen, and began to teach painting at Columbia University. He was director of the graphic arts division of the New York City FAP in 1940 and 1941. Joining Atelier 17 in 1944, he experimented with engraving and soft-ground etching.[3] Also in 1944 the artist taught design and printmaking at Brooklyn College, and design at the Institute of Design in Chicago, the "New Bauhaus."

From 1946 to 1965 Drewes taught at the School of Fine Arts of Washington University in St. Louis. The artist maintained an energetic schedule of printmaking, painting, and exhibitions throughout the 1950s and 1960s. In 1969 the National Collection of Fine Arts of the Smithsonian Institution organized a retrospective exhibition of Drewes's prints,[4] which was circulated internationally by the federal government in 1974 and 1975. The artist moved to Reston, Virginia, near Washington, D.C., in 1972. In 1984 a major retrospective of his prints was mounted at the National Museum of American Art in honor of his eighty-fifth birthday. Drewes died on June 21 of the following year.

Notes
1. A comprehensive chronology of Drewes's career can be found in Rose 1984, pp. 27–36.
2. Norelli 1984, pp. 11–13. I am grateful to Martina Norelli for her assistance in the preparation of this entry.
3. Ibid., pp. 25–26.
4. Dreyfuss 1969.

Leonard Edmondson

Leonard Edmondson was born in Sacramento, California, on June 21, 1916.[1] He attended Los Angeles City College in 1934, and went on to study art at the University of California at Berkeley in 1937, where he received a bachelor's degree in 1940 and his master's in 1942. He served in Army Intelligence for four years and traveled in Europe, where he encountered the works of Old Masters and of Paul Klee. When, in 1947, the artist began teaching at Pasadena

City College, he studied Klee's *Pedagogical Sketchbook* and Kandinsky's theoretical writings in order to formulate his own teaching methods.[2]

Edmondson had his first solo exhibition at the Felix Landau Gallery in Los Angeles in 1950. The following year, he learned how to etch in a course taught by Ernest Freed at the University of Southern California. In 1952 the artist won his first print award at the annual exhibition of the Brooklyn Museum, for his color intaglio *Heralds of Inquiry*.[3] Edmondson's first one-man museum exhibition was mounted at the De Young Museum in San Francisco in 1952.[4] This was followed by solo shows at the Pasadena Art Museum and the Santa Barbara Museum in 1953, the year he won his first Tiffany Fellowship. In 1954 the artist was hired by Millard Sheets (cat. 34) to teach design at the Otis Art Institute in Los Angeles, where for two years he taught alongside Freed. Edmondson won a second Tiffany Fellowship in 1955. In the mid-1950s Ynez Johnston (cat. 95) worked in the artist's studio, learning a variety of intaglio techniques.[5] Edmondson returned to his teaching position at Pasadena City College in 1956, remaining there until 1964; he served on the Board of Directors of the Pasadena Art Museum from 1957 to 1963.

In the late 1950s Edmondson's style gradually changed, his imagery became flatter, more calligraphic, and purged of minute detail. With the support of a Guggenheim Fellowship in 1960, the artist was able to concentrate on printmaking, and among the several editions he produced in that year was one executed for the International Graphic Arts Society. Edmondson taught at the University of California at Berkeley during the summers of 1960 and 1964, and at the Pratt Institute in New York in 1961. In 1964 the artist was appointed chairman of the printmaking department at California State University in Los Angeles, and he remained there until his retirement in 1986.

A major retrospective exhibition of Edmondson's prints was organized by the San Francisco Museum of Art in 1967.[6] In 1973 his book *Etching*, a compilation of his technical knowledge and teaching experiences, was published.[7] Edmondson still lives in southern California, where he continues to work and exhibit.

Notes

1. Cummings 1988, pp. 231 232; *Who's Who* 1986, p. 280.
2. San Francisco 1967, p. 10.
3. Johnson 1956, pp. 44–46. Edmondson's color intaglio *Flying Machine* won another purchase award at the Brooklyn Museum in 1956.
4. Loran 1952.
5. Wight 1953; Wooster 1978.
6. San Francisco 1967.
7. Edmondson 1973.

■

Richard Floethe

Born on September 2, 1901, in Essen, Germany, Richard Floethe began his studies at the Dortmund Art School.[1] He traveled from one art academy to another, seeking outstanding instructors. At the Munich State School of Art, he learned graphic techniques from Willie Geiger and Edward Ege, and at the Bauhaus in Weimar, he studied design with Paul Klee and color theory with Wassily Kandinsky, both of whom exerted a permanent influence on his work.

Floethe struggled to find employment as a commercial artist in Germany, painting a large mural for the International Exposition at Cologne in 1928. Later that year, the artist was granted a visa to immigrate to the United States, where he eventually became a naturalized citizen. Settling in New York, Floethe had greater success in finding commercial work; supporting himself by doing free-lance graphic design and book illustration.

In 1936 the artist accepted the offer of the directorship of the fledgling FAP poster division.[2] By this time, the shop was engaged in large-scale production of silkscreens, and

Floethe's primary duties were production management and the selection of designs. By all accounts an effective and affable director, he sought to provide an environment in which artists would be encouraged to experiment creatively. He mounted a persistent but ultimately frustrated campaign to allow the artists to sign their posters.

Influences of the Bauhaus style are apparent in Floethe's own work of the 1930s, including his poster designs. In 1937 he had a one-man show at Pynson Printers in New York that included both his continuing private work and his WPA posters. The artist married and acquired a small, dilapidated farm in Orange County, New York, to which he moved in 1939 when he decided to retire from the poster division. He then returned to commercial graphic design, especially book illustration.

Floethe's work as a printmaker flourished throughout his activity in America. He made woodcuts as well as limited edition serigraphs that grew out of his production of WPA posters. Straddling the boundaries between a poster and a fine print, Floethe's serigraph *The Liberator* was an outstanding contribution to the widely seen exhibition America and the War, of 1943.[3] The artist designed and illustrated over fifty books, among them *Tyl Ulenspiegl* (1935), *Pinocchio* (1938), and *Robinson Crusoe* (1945). In the 1950s he also illustrated several books written by his wife Louise Floethe.

The artist taught design at Cooper Union School of Art in 1941 and 1942. In 1955 he moved to Florida, where he taught illustration and painting at the Ringling School of Art in Sarasota until his retirement in 1967. He died in Middletown, Connecticut, in 1988.

Notes

1. Falk, p. 206; Floethe 1987.
2. Floethe 1973 and 1987.
3. This exhibition of prints, sponsored by the Artists for Victory, took advantage of the ability of printmaking to produce multiple originals, allowing the show to open simultaneously at twenty-six museums throughout the country. Floethe's *The*

Liberator was reproduced on the cover of *Art News* when this exhibition was reviewed. See Arms 1943; Landau 1983, pp. 38–39.

■

Antonio Frasconi

Antonio Frasconi was born into an Italian family in Montevideo, Uruguay, on April 28, 1919.[1] After several years of working for a printer, he enrolled at the Architecture Academy in Montevideo in 1936. The modernist, expressive art led by the socialist–inspired Mexican muralist revival sparked his imagination.[2] In 1938 Frasconi went to work as a draftsman of graphs in a government office, while on his own he was also a free-lance political cartoonist.[3] His first prints were made in 1944, inspired by the woodcuts of Paul Gauguin and Uruguayan artist Carlos Gonzalez. Frasconi began to make single-sheet linocuts representing images of biting social commentary. He was also encouraged by German Expressionist prints by Erich Heckel and George Grosz.

In 1945 Frasconi came to the United States to study with Grosz at the Art Students League in New York; however he studied instead with Yasuo Kuniyoshi. In 1946 he traveled to California, where he made his first rural landscape prints and began experiments with color woodcuts. His first solo exhibition in the United States was mounted at the Santa Barbara Museum of Art in 1946.[4]

Frasconi's prints became larger and more complex, inspired by the flourishing activity in color woodcut in New York. An intermittent series of prints representing Don Quixote embodied the artist's response to Spanish culture and history. In 1948 he attended the New School for Social Research and studied mural painting with Camilo Egas. In Vermont the following summer, he produced several prints reflecting his fascination with farmers. These were his first prints to represent a general theme upon which he produced many variations: the American worker.

Frasconi began teaching at the New School in 1951. With the support of a Guggenheim Fellowship, he illustrated the poetry of Walt Whitman and Frederico Garcia Lorca.[5] In 1952 an important retrospective exhibition of Frasconi's works, including paintings, drawings, monotypes, and technical materials, was organized by the Cleveland Museum of Art.[6] A series of woodcuts representing autumn bird migrations visible from his Connecticut studio, was begun in 1959, and included several color woodcuts.

In 1961 the artist mounted a retrospective exhibition of his work from 1943 to 1951 in Montevideo. In 1962 he worked at the Tamarind Lithography Workshop in Los Angeles, producing a suite of lithographs dedicated to the poet Lorca. An exhibition of Frasconi's prints and books produced from 1953 to 1963 was mounted at the Baltimore Museum of Art.[7]

In the later 1960s Frasconi's prints represented his reactions to the Vietnam War and to the political unrest of the day. In the 1970s, Frasconi experimented with the medium of color Xerox. His most recent prints, *Los Desaperecidos*, depict the missing persons in Latin America and were the focus of a powerful recent solo exhibition.

Notes

1. *Who's Who* 1984, p. 304; see also Tonelli 1987.
2. Charlot 1963.
3. Tonelli 1987, pp. 17–18.
4. Ibid., p. 20, note 25.
5. Frasconi, 1953.
6. Cleveland 1952.
7. Baltimore 1963.

■

Don Freeman

Don Freeman was born on August 11, 1908, in San Diego.[1] While taking his first art classes at the San Diego Art Institute, he saved the money to move east. In 1928 he arrived in New York, began studies at the Art Students League, and managed to publish his first design on the theater page of the *New York Herald Tribune*. Over the next ten years, the artist continued his studies at the League with John Sloan and Harry Wickey, and he published his drawings of city life and theatrical subjects in many periodicals. A vivacious character, a natural performer, and an observant draftsman, Freeman also created an oeuvre of lithographs illustrating urban life. He habitually carried sketchbooks in travels throughout the city to record his observations. Freeman's love of the theater, his sympathy with his subjects, and his humor and knack for visual storytelling made his illustrations ideal for books and magazines.

Freeman's activities as a printmaker began under the aegis of John Sloan, and a handful of etchings produced from 1930 to 1933 emulated the master's subjects, style, and technique.[2] However, the artist soon gravitated to lithography, a process he learned from Charles Locke. Freeman's first prints were clearly experimental. As he became comfortable and proficient with the technique, he came to appreciate the spontaneity and freedom it allowed him, and to exploit the range of tonal qualities available. In September of 1932 he began making prints at George Miller's lithography workshop. These were refined versions of his sketchbook observations, or of his most successful newspaper illustrations.

In 1934 Freeman worked briefly in the New York City FAP graphic arts division, creating eleven lithographs. After a disagreement with the administration of the workshop, he resigned from the graphic arts division, and took a position as an artist in the Federal Theater Project.

In the late 1930s and early 1940s Freeman's career as an illustrator flourished; this was also his most productive period as a printmaker. During the war, the artist made paintings and drawings of naval aviation subjects, commissioned by the Abbott Foundation and the *New York Times*, and in 1943 and 1944 he served in the United States Army. In 1951 he and his wife collaborated on the first of more than twenty-five children's books.[3] Freeman also illustrated about thirty-five books by other authors.

During the next thirty years, the artist's lively personality and his talents as a performer and ready draughtsman were combined in his well-known "chalk talks," story telling sessions for children. Freeman was active working and traveling, until his death on February 1, 1978, in New York.

Notes

1. McCulloch 1988, pp. 128–131, provides a comprehensive chronology of the artist as well as a list of his exhibitions, publications, and bibliography.
2. McCulloch 1988 describes 14 etchings in Freeman's oeuvre of 146 editioned prints.
3. Freeman 1951.

■

Sue Fuller

Sue Fuller was born in Pittsburgh on August 11, 1914. She studied at the Carnegie Institute of Technology, where she received a bachelor's degree in 1936.[1] Early in her undergraduate career, she spent a formative summer studying with Hans Hofmann (cat. 73) in Gloucester, Massachusetts. Continuing her studies at the Columbia University Teachers College in 1939, she worked with Arthur Young, from whom she learned the history and processes of printmaking.

In 1943 Fuller joined Atelier 17, which was then under the administration of the New School for Social Research in New York. After just one semester she became an assistant to Stanley William Hayter (cat. 60), working in exchange for tuition. She mixed acids, managed shop supplies, and instructed beginners. This experience coincided with the arrival of Josef Albers in New York, and Fuller became a member of a privately arranged Bauhaus class. Working within the framework of Albers's well-known teaching program, she made folded-paper collages and experimented with color and the processes of perception.

The artist's exposure to Albers encouraged her personal impulse to explore sculptural concepts in printmaking. Her prints began to incorporate the tensile line of her contemporary sculpture.

In the mid-1940s Fuller independently developed an interest in the prints of Mary Cassat (cat. 1). In attempting to understand how these prints were made, she was drawn to curator Adelyn Breeskin, whose study of Cassatt's prints was published in 1948.[2] The two became lifelong friends, and Breeksin encouraged Fuller's research and her original theory that Cassatt's color prints were soft-ground etchings.[3]

By the time she won Tiffany and Guggenheim Fellowships in 1948 and 1949, Fuller had already moved away from printmaking. Inspired by the work of Naum Gabo and Antoine Pevsner, the artist experimented with string constructions stretched on pegged frames, which became progressively more dimensional. In her early string reliefs she struggled with problems of fading dyes and rickety stretchers and so conceived of enclosing her pieces in transparent capsules. To this end, Fuller studied glassblowing in Italy and England in 1950, calligraphy in Japan in 1953, and lace making in 1960. Experiments with glass and Lucite led the artist to embed her smallest pieces in plastic in 1960, and her sculpture finally became fully three-dimensional.[4]

Following her first solo exhibition at the Bertha Schaefer Gallery in New York in 1949, Fuller continued to exhibit continuously for the next thirty years. She taught at the University of Minnesota, the University of Georgia, Columbia University Teachers College, the Pratt Institute, and the Museum of Modern Art, New York. She has also been honored by the Women's Caucus for Art and the National Sculpture Conference.

Notes

1. *Who's Who* 1986, p. 343.
2. Breeskin 1948.
3. Fuller 1950.
4. Browne 1972.

Emil Ganso

Emil Ganso was born on April 14, 1895, in Halberstadt, in the Harz Mountains of Germany.[1] There, at the age of fourteen, he was apprenticed to a baker. In 1912 he came to the United States with his family, settling in New York. He found night work in a bakery and concentrated on his art in the daytime. He studied briefly at the National Academy of Design, but was mostly self-taught.

In 1924 Ganso showed a large group of his drawings to Carl Zigrosser at the Weyhe Gallery, who organized the artist's first solo exhibition. Soon afterward, Ganso enrolled in Eugene Fitsch's printmaking class at the Art Students League.[2]

Although he considered himself primarily a painter, Ganso made prints in all media, including relief and stencil prints, lithographs, and complex intaglios. His approach to printmaking was consistently that of a painter, not a draftsman, but as time progressed his prints became technically more sophisticated.[3] In the 1920s Ganso's aquatints were influenced by those of Arthur B. Davies (cat. 13) in subject, style, and technique. The artist began his experiments in color lithography late in the 1920s. In about 1926 he met an engineer with whom he worked on the design and fabrication of a new etching press.[4]

Also in 1926 Ganso attended the summer session of the Art Students League in Woodstock, New York. There he met Jules Pascin, and the two artists began a close and influential friendship; they briefly shared a studio, and Ganso followed Pascin to Europe in 1928.

In 1929 Ganso returned to New York, and his work appeared regularly in group exhibitions. In the summer months he also continued to work in Woodstock, where he often printed lithographs for other artists. The Cleveland Print Club commissioned him to produce an edition of wood engravings for their members' presentation print in 1932. In the following year Ganso won a Guggenheim Fellowship and traveled to Europe. After his return, he worked in the FAP, and in 1936 he was one of the artists to contribute to the first flourish of color lithography in the New York City FAP workshop.

A print by Ganso was awarded the Pennell Memorial Medal from the Pennsylvania Academy of Fine Arts in 1938. He was appointed artist in residence at Lawrence College in Appleton, Wisconsin, in 1939, and presented a one-man exhibition at Lawrence and at the Milwaukee Art Institute.

Although Ganso had abandoned graphic arts in order to concentrate on painting, his talents as a printmaker helped him win a teaching position at the University of Iowa in 1939. In 1940 Ganso published a brief article in *Parnassus* reflecting on problems in teaching printmaking.[5] Lester Longman, chairman of the art department at Iowa, wanted him to develop a teaching lithographic shop, but these plans were left unfulfilled when Ganso died suddenly of a heart attack in Iowa City on April 18, 1941.

Notes
1. Moser 1980.
2. Adams 1983, p. 68.
3. Moser 1980, p. 8.
4. Ibid., p. 5.
5. Ganso/Janson 1940.

Eliza Draper Gardiner

Born on October 29, 1871, in Cranston, Rhode Island,[1] Eliza Draper Gardiner studied art with Sophia L. Pittman at the Friends School in Providence. She continued at the Rhode Island School of Design, where she earned her degree in 1897. In accordance with the arts curricula of the day, Gardiner's education was broad and crafts-related. Her first exhibited work of art, included in the inaugural exhibition of the Boston Society of Arts and Crafts in 1897, was a piece of decorative ironwork. After brief studies in Europe, the artist studied in Boston with Charles H. Woodbury, who probably introduced her to etching.

Gardiner's early prints reflect the influence of Arthur Wesley Dow (cat. 6) and his notions of design and coloration.[2] Although there is no evidence of direct contact between the two, Dow's prestige and Gardiner's proximity to him would have made a meeting likely. Seven of her woodcuts were included in an exhibition at the Berlin Photographic Company in New York in 1916, in which she was first associated with the Provincetown Printers.[3] Four of her prints were also shown in the first exhibition of the Provincetown Art Association in 1919. In that year, twelve other woodcuts by Gardiner were included in the landmark exhibition of American color woodcuts at the Detroit Institute of Arts, and her first solo exhibition was mounted at Goodspeed's in Boston.

Gardiner's teaching career began in Providence at her old secondary school. In 1908 she took an appointment at the Rhode Island School of Design, teaching drawing, watercolor, and relief printmaking; she remained there until 1939. As a printmaker, the artist was most active in the late 1910s and 1920s and was encouraged by the enthusiasm and popularity of the Provincetown printmakers. She settled on a technical process derived from traditional Japanese methods, and seems never to have experimented with the white line technique. Gardiner found her favorite imagery at the beach, on the shores of duck ponds in parks, in flowery meadows, and especially in the lighthearted activities of childhood. At Pawtucket Cove, near Edgewater, Rhode Island, she converted a large barn into a studio. Her home became a gathering place for generations of students.[4]

Gardiner endeavored to exhibit her prints widely, sending woodcuts to exhibitions of the Providence Art Club, the Providence Print Club, the Rhode Island Art Teachers Association, the Philadelphia Print Club, the Philadelphia Woodcut Society, the American Color Print Society, and the California Print Makers.

In 1932 she produced a number of lithographs, which were printed in New York by George Miller.[5] She created at least ten prints, delicately drawn on the stone with a fine crayon. The following year, her work was featured in the pivotal color print exhibition at the Brooklyn Museum. The artist died at her home in Edgewater on January 14, 1955.

Notes
1. Falk, p. 223; *Who's Who* 1947, p. 184.
2. Falk (1987, p. 9) also suggests the influence of the English illustrator Sir William Nicholson.
3. *New York Times* 1916; Flint 1983, p. 16.
4. Lawrence 1975.
5. Falk 1987, pp. 24, 25, note 6.

Frances Hammell Gearhart

The eldest daughter of a merchant, Frances Hammell Gearhart was born in Sagetown (later Gladstone), Illinois, on January 4, 1869.[1] Although her family moved to southern California before 1890, she studied with Charles H. Woodbury and Henry R. Poore, two painters from the East Coast who were educated in Paris in the 1890s, although exactly when she did so is unclear.[2]

For many years Gearhart taught English history in the Los Angeles public schools, but when her artistic activities became more lucrative, she retired and devoted herself wholly to printmaking. In 1911 Frances and her sister May mounted an independent exhibition of watercolors at the Walker Theatre Building in downtown Los Angeles. In 1914, along with Benjamin and Howell Brown, Frances helped organize the Print Makers of Los Angeles, a steadily growing club that was later renamed the California Print Makers. Gearhart was first listed as secretary of the organization in 1921, and she held this post through 1928.[3] For several years she lived with May (cat. 22) on West California Street in Pasadena, and their studio served as the headquarters and meeting place for this club. In 1932 this organization's annual competitive exhibition, which circulated throughout the country, was confined to prints in color.

Gearhart may have taught herself to make woodcuts around 1919 or 1920. Stylistic and technical affinities suggest, however, that she may have been introduced to the process by Pedro Lemos (cat. 24). She may also have been influenced by Frank Morley Fletcher, the English artist who made color woodcuts in the Japanese manner and who founded the Santa Barbara School of Arts in 1923.[4] In addition, there are noticeable relationships between Gearhart's woodcuts and the prints of Hiroshi Yoshida, a Japanese painter and printmaker in the occidental style who visited the American West and made popular prints depicting its dramatic landscapes.[5]

Gearhart also exhibited with the Prairie Printmakers, and at the Brooklyn Museum and the American Institute of Graphic Arts. In 1923 the artist showed twenty-seven of her color block prints in an exhibition shared with her sister at the Los Angeles County Museum of History, Science, and Art.[6] In 1930 her color prints of California subjects were organized into a circulating exhibition by the American Federation of Arts.[7] Gearhart showed her work in New York at the Grand Central Galleries, where a solo exhibition opened in February 1933, the year in which she won a purchase prize in the annual exhibition of the California Print Makers at the Los Angeles museum.[8] She died in Pasadena on April 6, 1958.

Notes

1. Falk, p. 227; *Who's Who* 1938, p. 200. Concerning the birthplace of the Gearhart sisters, see biography of May Gearhart, note 1.
2. Hughes, p. 173.
3. See biography of May Gearhart, note 4.
4. LeJeune 1970; Knowles 1970.
5. Yoshida (1876–1950) had already had a successful career as a painter when he began making woodcuts in 1920. His reputation was considerable in this country, and his prints were avidly collected by Americans. These woodcuts, many of which were derived from travels in the American and Canadian West, were prominent in two *Shin Hanga* or "New Print" move-

ment exhibitions in 1930 and 1936 at the Toledo Museum of Art. See Jenkins 1983, pp. 48–50; Smith 1983, p. 102.
6. Los Angeles 1923.
7. *Prints* 1931, p. 16.
8. *Prints* 1933, p. 13. See also Harlow/Keats 1984, nos. 27–31.

May Gearhart

The second daughter of a merchant, May Gearhart was born in Sagetown (later Gladstone), Illinois, in 1872.[1] She moved with her family to southern California before 1890. One of three sisters, May had the most extensive art education. She attended the Los Angeles State Normal School, the School of the Art Institute of Chicago, and the California School of Fine Arts in San Francisco, where she was the pupil of Rudolph Schaeffer. In 1911 the Gearhart sisters exhibited their watercolors together at the Walker Theatre Building in downtown Los Angeles.[2] May went to New York one summer late in the 1910s to study at Columbia University Teachers College with Arthur Wesley Dow (cat. 6). She probably also studied with Walter Shirlaw during this visit. May served as a delegate to the International Art Congress at London in 1908, at Dresden in 1912, at Prague in 1928, and at Paris in 1937.

In 1900 Gearhart began teaching art in the Berkeley Public Schools, and in 1903, she became supervisor of art programs for the Los Angeles City Schools, a position she held until 1939. She taught children the basic rudiments of design and color, and then encouraged unbounded creative freedom. This outlook was considered rather advanced in Gearhart's time.[3] In the summer of 1930 she studied with Hans Hofmann (cat. 73) at the University of California at Berkeley.

Gearhart learned to etch from Benjamin Chambers Brown, a Pasadena neighbor who was cofounder of the Print Makers of Los Angeles (later the California Print Makers Society) in 1914. By 1919 she was living with her sister in Pasadena, and the studio of this house served as the meeting place and headquarters for the

group.[4] Soon printmaking had become Gearhart's primary artistic activity and she exhibited her prints widely. She showed her color etchings regularly with the California Print Makers at the Los Angeles County Museum of Art, and in 1923 exhibited ten color prints in an exhibition at that museum.[5] Gearhart was also a member of the Pacific Artists Association, the Chicago Society of Etchers, and the Society of American Etchers. She died in retirement on April 14, 1951, in Altadena, California.

Notes

1. The likely birthplace of the Gearhart sisters can be deduced from the Register of Births for Oquawka, Illinois, in which the birth of the youngest, Edna Gearhart, was recorded as having occurred in Sagetown on August 12, 1879. Their father was the merchant S. M. Gearhart, born in Iowa in 1843, and their mother was Emma Darch Gearhart, born in the same year during the passage of her immigrant parents from England. On May Gearhart, see Falk, p. 227; Hughes, p. 173; Dawdy 1974, p. 93.
2. See Feinblatt/Davis 1980, p. 11.
3. Ibid.
4. *American Art Annual* 1919, p. 378. By 1923 May and Frances both lived in the same house on California Street (ibid., 20: 529), but they also shared a studio at 611 South Fair Oaks in Pasadena. By 1925 they were living together down the street from the studio, at 595 South Fair Oaks (ibid., 22: 501).
5. Los Angeles 1923.

Hugo Gellert

The son of a tailor, Hugo Gellert was born on March 3, 1892, in Budapest, Hungary. He came to the United States with his family in 1907, and was soon at work in New York, first in a machine shop, then in a lithography shop printing movie posters.[1] Gellert enrolled at the National Academy of Design in 1909, and he also took classes at Cooper Union. As a student, he designed theater posters and stained-glass windows, the latter for Tiffany Studios. In 1914 he studied at the Académie Julian in Paris.

After his return to the United States in 1915, Gellert rooted his personal and professional life in his leftist political convictions. He created antiwar cartoons and lithographed posters, and contributed to the Hungarian workers' paper, *Elöre*. Magazine illustration soon became Gellert's primary activity. In 1916 his work began to appear in *The Masses*, and in 1918 he joined the editorial board of *The Liberator*. Through membership in the American Communist party, the artist became a friend of activist leaders John Reed, Louise Bryant, and Michael Gold. After traveling to Mexico in 1919, Gellert moved to the commune of the Modern School in Stelton, New Jersey, where he taught art to children.

Beginning in the late 1920s Gellert became more politically active. In 1928 he cofounded the Anti-Horthy League, the first American antifascist group. In 1936 the artist led the famous protest against the destruction of Diego Rivera's mural at Rockefeller Center. Gellert was also chairman of the Artists Committee of Action, and a founding member of the American Artists Congress.[2]

From 1920 to 1923 Gellert was on the staff of *Pearson's Magazine* and contributed to a score of other periodicals. He had his first one-man exhibition at the Kevorkian Gallery in New York in 1923. In 1926 Gellert became a contributing editor to *The New Masses*. Late in the decade, he gravitated toward mural painting, creating murals for the Workers' Cafeteria at Union Square in 1928 and a fresco in the Center Theater at Rockefeller Center in 1932. His murals created a controversy when they were exhibited at the Museum of Modern Art in 1931 and 1932.[3] Gellert joined the National Society of Mural Painters, and in 1934 he helped form the Mural Artists Guild of the United Scenic Painters of the AFL-CIO in order to insure that wall paintings for the World's Fair would be contracted through the union. Working in the FAP mural division in 1938, the artist painted a fresco in the Communications Building of the World's Fair.[4]

In 1950 Gellert traveled throughout Australia, the Middle East, and Southeast Asia. During the next two decades, he continued to use his art for political means, designing many posters, banners, and murals in protest of racism and militarism. Until the end of his life Gellert remained active in labor and political organizations and in the Hungarian community. Retrospective exhibitions of his work were held at the Marx-Lenin Institute in Moscow in 1967 and at the National Gallery in Budapest in 1968. The artist painted his last mural at Hillcrest High School in Jamaica, New York. He died on December 6, 1985, in Freehold, New Jersey.

Notes

1. Falk, p. 228; Zurier 1985, p. 165; Ryan/Kisseloff 1986.
2. Gellert 1973, pp. 251, 255–257, 277, 298.
3. Ryan/Kisseloff 1986, p. 2.
4. Gutthcim 1937.

■

Harry Gottlieb

Born in Bucharest, Romania, on January 23, 1895, Harry Gottlieb moved with his family to Minneapolis in 1907.[1] He grew up in severe poverty, and he had to shine shoes and sell newspapers throughout his school years. In 1915, after his high school graduation, he attended the School of the Minneapolis Institute of Arts, where he was introduced to lithography. Gottlieb joined the Navy in 1917 and worked as a draftsman, producing technical diagrams.

After his discharge, Gottlieb went to New York, working first as a wallpaper designer, then as a costume and set designer for Eugene O'Neill's Provincetown Theatre group. In 1923 he moved to the artist's colony at Woodstock, New York, where he had his first one-man exhibition in 1929. With the support of a Guggenheim Fellowship, the artist was able to travel and study in Europe in 1931. At the Atelier Desjobert in Paris, he made several lithographs that represented landscapes and people at leisure.

Gottlieb returned to Woodstock in the middle of the depression, but in 1935 moved to New York, where he worked in the FAP and soon became a political activist. Involved with the formation of the Artists Union, he served as its president in 1936.[2] Gottlieb was a speaker at the first meeting of the Artists Congress in 1936, and he worked to establish Artists Equity. Appointed to the FAP graphic arts division in 1936, he worked with lithography, participating in the color prints project spearheaded by Russell Limbach (cat. 45).[3]

Gottlieb's prints now depicted images of industry and of people at work coping with the depression. Following Harry Sternberg (cat. 35), Gottlieb journeyed to the coal fields of Pennsylvania in 1937 to meet workers and make sketches of them. Some of these were made into color lithographs after his return to New York.[4]

In 1938 Gottlieb joined Anthony Velonis (cat. 42) to make prints for the pilot project of the FAP silkscreen unit.[5] His first print was the nine-color serigraph *On the Beach*. He immediately took to the process of serigraphy, recognizing that the easy and inexpensive technique could exert a remarkable, democratizing effect on printmaking. Gottlieb's one-man exhibition of screen prints at the ACA Galleries in New York hung simultaneously with ground-breaking group shows at the Weyhe Gallery and Springfield Museum of Fine Arts in 1940.[6] Gottlieb began to write his own technical manual on the silk-screen process, but never finished. In 1940 he was among a group of printmakers in New York who came together to establish the Silk Screen Group, later the National Serigraph Society.

Despite the decline of FAP programs, Gottlieb continued his work in serigraphy. Beginning in the 1940s he occasionally presented lecture-demonstrations of the process at art schools around the country for the Association of American Colleges. The artist worked in serigraphy until the mid-1970s.

Notes

1. Falk, p. 240; *Who's Who* 1947, p. 196; Conkelton/Gilbert 1983, p. 20 and passim.
2. On the violent artists' demonstrations of December 1, 1936, and the roles of Gottlieb and the union in these events, see Conkelton/Gilbert 1983, p. 13.
3. Kainen 1972, p. 167; Adams 1983, pp. 124–125.
4. For the artist's anecdotal memories of this trip, see Conkelton/Gilbert 1983, p. 3, fig. 1, and pp. 24–25.
5. Ibid., pp. 3–5.
6. McCausland 1940, pp. 34–36.

■

Robert Gwathmey

Robert Gwathmey was born in Richmond, on January 24, 1903, into an eighth-generation Virginian family.[1] His father was killed at work on the railroad before he was born, and so Robert often had to work as a child, while his mother taught school. Still, a strong extended family provided the boy with a secure childhood, and his artistic interests became apparent very early. He attended North Carolina State College for one year, and then went to the Maryland Institute in Baltimore, where he began his studies of art in 1925. That summer, working on an Atlantic freighter, Gwathmey first visited Europe. A four-year course followed at the Pennsylvania Academy of Fine Arts, where he was influenced by Franklin Watkins. In 1930 the artist began teaching at Beaver College in Jenkintown, Pennsylvania, where Benton Spruance (cat. 56) was among his colleagues. Gwathmey joined the Artists Union and became more active politically, and his mature style gradually emerged. His figures began to acquire their attenuation, and his palette its famous intensity. In the mid-1930s the artist began traveling to the South each summer, and was inspired by the black American culture there.

From 1938 to 1942 Gwathmey taught drawing and painting at the Carnegie Institute of Technology in Pittsburgh. In 1939 he won the annual exhibition competition at the American Contemporary Arts Gallery, and had his first one-man exhibition there in 1941. Soon after, he began teaching drawing at Cooper

Union, a job he held until his retirement in 1968. In 1944 and 1945, with the support of a Rosenwald Fellowship, the artist lived on a Southern tobacco farm and worked alongside the sharecroppers, deepening his experience of the life and culture that he felt compelled to represent. Among the protesters of the sale of WPA paintings as surplus property by the federal government in 1946, he also picketed with the Artist Union against sweatshop conditions in New York in 1949.

Gwathmey was a visiting professor at Boston University in 1968 and 1969 and at Syracuse University in 1972. He was elected to the American Academy and Institute of Arts and Letters, and in 1976, he became an associate of the National Academy of Design. That year a major retrospective of his work was organized at Saint Mary's College in Maryland.[2] Gwathmey's retirement was spent mostly in his studio in Amagansett, Long Island. His enduring concentration on bright, modernist pictures of Southern blacks continued through the civil rights movement of the 1960s and beyond. As Paul Robeson wrote in the introduction to an early exhibition of the artist's paintings: "In the coming years, when as we all hope, true equality and the brotherhood of man will be a reality, Gwathmey's paintings will have earned him the right to feel that he has shared in the shaping of a better world."[3] The artist died on Long Island, on September 21, 1988.

Notes

1. McCausland 1946, p. 149; *Who's Who* 1986, p. 406.
2. Saint Mary's 1976.
3. ACA Gallery 1946, p. iii.

■

Hananiah Harari

Born on August 29, 1912, in Rochester, New York, Hananiah Harari studied at the College of Fine Arts of the University of Syracuse.[1] After graduation, he traveled to France to study at the Ecole de Fresque at Fontainebleau and with Fernand Léger, André Lhote, and Marcel Gromaire in Paris. Returning to New York, he made a tenuous living in the FAP projects but drew strength from the community of artists in Greenwich Village who met and socialized in Washington Square and at the headquarters of the Artists Union on Sixth Avenue.

Although Harari was a capable Realist, his knowledge of the work of the School of Paris made him a fervent supporter of abstraction. In his early shows the artist emerged as a facile modernist in the European manner as well as an able colorist. A member of the Artists League of America, Harari was also among the founders of the American Abstract Artists group. In the 1930s this group met monthly, usually in Albert Swinden's loft on East Seventeenth Street, where they discussed aesthetic ideology, exhibition prospects, and their relationships with the artistic establishment.[2]

Harari was inspired by European modernism; he characterized his style as "transfigurative," choosing not to abstract his subjects beyond recognition. He described this viewpoint in 1937 in a letter advocating abstract art and artists. This declaration, undersigned by six other American Abstract Artists, was printed in the 1937 issue of *Art Front*, the publication of the Artists Union, and was submitted to the *New York Times* in 1939.[3]

Harari was employed by the FAP mural and the graphic arts divisions, where, in 1938, he was one of the first artists to whom Anthony Velonis (cat. 42) introduced serigraphy. This exhilarating experience prompted a desire to explore other graphic media, and he studied etching with Ernest Roth. Despite their vastly different aesthetic orientations, Harari learned much from this disciplined craftsman.[4]

From 1938 to 1940 Harari taught painting at the American Artists School. By this time he had begun to paint *trompe l'oeil* still lifes in the manner of the late nineteenth-century Realist William M. Harnett. Six of these illusionistic paintings were included in the exhibition American Realists and Magic Realists in 1941, and another won the Hallgarten Prize at the National Academy in 1943. Harari's work was also included in group exhibitions at the Whitney Museum of American Art in 1942 and 1944 and at the Museum of Modern Art in 1943.

Drafted in 1943, Harari served two and a half years in the army; when he returned to New York, he found a very different artistic climate from the one he had left. His successful exhibition at the Laurel Gallery in 1948 showed him to have settled on abstraction. In many of his paintings, the artist aimed at evoking physical sensations by using images representing the themes of balance, weightlessness, and flight.[5] From 1950 to 1952, Harari was an instructor of illustration at the Workshop School of Art in New York. In the 1950s he created several paintings for the Coca-Cola Company that were widely reproduced.[6] The artist taught painting and drawing at both the New School for Social Research and the School of Visual Arts in 1974, and at the Art Students League in 1984. Now living in Croton-on-Hudson, New York, Harari continues to paint and to teach at the School of Visual Arts and the Art Students League.

Notes

1. Falk, p. 261; *Who's Who* 1947, p. 210.
2. Harari 1987, p. 3.
3. Rosalind Bengelsdorf, Byron Browne, Hartzel Emanuel, Leo Lances, Jan Matulka, and George McNeil cosigned this letter.
4. Harari 1987, p. 2.
5. Breuning 1948.
6. Sharp 1950.

James Dexter Havens

Born in Rochester, New York, on January 13, 1900, James Dexter Havens was the son of a prominent attorney.[1] As a teenager, confined to his bed by diabetes, he passed the hours by drawing. With difficulty, he attended the University of Rochester for three years. Illness increasingly limited Haven's life, but in May of 1922, he became the first American to receive experimental insulin therapy, and the disease was soon brought under control.[2] Through the cooperation of a Pullman porter in Toronto and Great Lakes rum runners, the drug was imported from Canada until it was fully developed, tested, legalized, and made available in this country.

With his returning health, Havens resumed his studies at the Mechanics Institute (now Rochester Institute of Technology), where he was enrolled from 1922 to 1925. He later studied privately with Thomas Fogarty, Troy Kinney, John E. Costigan, and Grant Reynard. In eight successive summers, Havens traveled to Ogunquit, Maine, to continue his studies with Charles H. Woodbury.

Shortly before 1930 Havens was drawn to printmaking. His first prints were bookplates, illustrative vignettes, and greeting cards. Soon the artist progressed to making portraits of his family and to landscape and nature subjects in multicolor linocuts and woodcuts. Havens was essentially self-trained as a printmaker, and his technique was the result of independent dedication. Nevertheless, his work had much in common with a group of contemporary American relief printmakers who represented images of the countryside with a virtuosity of technique approaching that of the nineteenth-century masters of the medium.

Before 1933 Havens's family moved to Fairport, New York. The rustic surroundings became the source for most of his paintings and prints. Later in the decade, the artist and John Menihan founded the Print Club of Rochester. Havens exhibited with the club annually, and his prints won the Ewald Eiserhardt Memorial Award in 1936 and 1939. During the war, Havens worked as an inspector in the parachute manufacturing business owned by the Menihan family.

Havens contributed a chapter about linoleum block printmaking to *The Relief Print*, an instructional book published in 1945.[3] He also taught occasionally, in the Fairport Public Schools, at Nazareth College, and at the Rochester Institute of Technology. His color woodcut *Rabbit Fence* of 1946 won a purchase award at the first National Print Annual Exhibition at the Brooklyn Museum in 1947.[4] In 1948 the artist executed a color woodcut for the membership of the Prairie Printmakers. The following year he produced editions for the Woodcut Society and the Print Club of Rochester, and in 1950 he was commissioned to produce a color woodcut for the American Color Print Society. In 1951 Havens was elected Associate of the National Academy of Design. The artist continued to produce multiple-block woodcuts into the final months of his life. He died of cancer on November 30, 1960, in Fairport.

Notes

1. Falk, pp. 269–270; *Who's Who* 1959, p. 244.
2. Woodbury 1962.
3. Watson/Kent 1945.
4. Baro 1976, p. 54.

Stanley William Hayter

Born in a suburb of London on December 27, 1901, Stanley William Hayter studied chemistry and geology at King's College.[1] After working as a chemist, he went to Paris in 1926, where he studied briefly at the Académie Julian. Soon he began to concentrate on engraving, and in 1927 his first one-man show was mounted at the Galerie Sacre du Printemps in Paris.

Hayter realized that the extensive demands of printmaking in equipment, labor, and materials could be eased by the collaborative atmosphere of a workshop, so he established his own teaching shop in 1927. When, in 1933, the studio moved to 17, rue Champagne-Première, near Montparnasse, a new name was taken from its address. Thus Atelier 17 became the name of Hayter's workshop through the next fifty years and various changes of location.

Though his association with the Surrealists was temporary, their ideas about the subconscious led to his own notions of automatism, and became central to his aesthetic theory. Hayter sought to understand and exploit the resources of the unconscious mind and the automatic processes that underlie reasoning and activity. He wrote about this phenomenon and its significance for printmaking in "The Interdependence of Idea and Technique in Gravure."[2]

In 1940 Hayter moved to New York.[3] There he set up a studio and offered a printmaking course at the New School for Social Research. This workshop retained the open practices of the Paris operation—as well as its French name—bringing together carefully selected students and mature visiting artists in order to produce collaborative editions. The workshop benefited from its proximity to other artist-printmakers teaching at the New School, including Stuart Davis, Will Barnet, and Louis Schanker (cats. 88, 69, 41). Hayter continued his own experiments, developing new technical variations on ever larger plates. By 1944 enough innovative prints had been produced at the workshop to warrant an important exhibition at the Museum of Modern Art.[4]

By 1946 Atelier 17 was operating independently in larger and more versatile facilities. Engagements and temporary appointments kept Hayter traveling all over the country. In 1949 the artist published *New Ways of Gravure*, a book that included a short history of intaglio techniques as well as a description of the experiments and achievements of Atelier 17.[5] In 1950 Hayter returned to Europe, and Atelier 17 was reestablished in Paris. Without him the New York shop began a steady decline until its closing in 1955. In Paris, however, the studio flourished.

Throughout the 1980s Hayter continued to work with his customary drive and openness, consistently responding to currents of style and technique, eventually gravitating back to painting. In 1987, with the

purchase of four hundred prints ranging in date from 1926 through 1960, the British Museum became the most important repository of Hayter's work. When the artist died in London, on May 4, 1988, work was well under way on a major retrospective of his prints at the Ashmolean Museum at Oxford.[6]

Notes
1. A complete chronology of Hayter's life can be found in Hacker 1988, pp. 105–112. See also Moser 1977.
2. Hayter 1949b.
3. Ibid., pp. 17–19, 45–47; Cohen 1988, pp. 18–33.
4. MoMA 1944.
5. Hayter 1949a.
6. The catalogue of this exhibition is included in Hacker 1988, pp. 73–101.

■

Clinton Hill

Clinton Hill was born on a cattle ranch in Payette, Idaho, on March 8, 1922.[1] He served as the captain of a minesweeper during World War II.[1] After the war Hill pursued his education on the GI Bill at the University of Oregon, where, although he was an art major, he was awarded a Bachelor of Science degree in 1947. He moved to New York in 1949, and attended the School of the Brooklyn Museum. There, in about 1950, along with Edmond Casarella (cat. 98), the artist was introduced to the technique of color woodcut by his contemporary Vincent Longo.

In 1951 Hill went to Europe, where he studied at the Académie de la Grande Chaumière in Paris, and in 1952 at the Istituto d'Arte Statale in Florence. In 1954 the artist had his first one-man show of paintings at the Korman Gallery in New York; more than thirty-five solo exhibitions followed. During this period he combined a great variety of papers with his oil paintings on canvas, to create mysterious abstract collages.[2]

In the 1960s Hill lived in Phoenix, Arizona, where he continued to paint and make prints, exhibiting regularly in New York and throughout

the country. The artist experimented with intaglio printmaking at this time. While making large paintings on panels of fiberglass, he decided to experiment with that material as a printmaking surface. Hill stretched the fiberglass mesh over plates of metal or cardboard, stretching and twisting the gridded matrix and then securing the desired patterns with resin.[3] He applied thinned inks to these collagraph-like plates and printed them as intaglios.[4] In 1968 the artist began teaching at Queens College of the City University of New York.

In the early 1970s, while continuing his experiments with collages of torn and cut paper, Hill conceived of the similar manipulation of wet paper pulp during the formation of a sheet. He contacted John and Kathryn Koller, students of Lawrence Barker at the Cranbrook Academy, who had set up their own experimental papermaking workshop in Woodstock, Connecticut. Visiting their paper mill, the artist found that it mattered little if his ideas differed from the realities of papermaking, for he had discovered a new and comfortable medium.[5] Hill has continued to work with handmade paper pulp ever since; his works evolved from drawings in the mold that produced watermarks to multisheet constructions of colored pulp. All along he has maintained interests in painting, sculpture, and woodcut, and has pursued a vigorous schedule of shows.

A solo exhibition of Hill's paintings and works in handmade paper was mounted at the Montclair Art Museum in New Jersey in 1981.[6] The artist still lives in New York, and is very active as a painter, sculptor, papermaker, and printmaker. A retrospective of his woodcuts was recently exhibited in New York.[7]

Notes
1. *Who's Who* 1986, p. 452.
2. Longo 1956.
3. Gilbert-Rolfe 1973.
4. Johnson 1980, p. 62.
5. Farmer 1978, p. 39; Long 1979, p. 105.
6. Montclair 1981.
7. Pearl 1989.

■

Hans Hofmann

The son of a government official, Hans Hofmann was born on March 21, 1880, in a small town in Bavaria, Germany.[1] He excelled in his studies of science in Munich. From 1896 to 1898 he served as assistant to the Bavarian state director of public works; he also invented several mechanical instruments. However, when in 1898, his father sent him money to continue his scientific experiments, he enrolled instead in Mortiz Heymann's art school.

Hofmann went to Paris in 1903, where he attended evening drawing classes at the Académie Colarossi and the Académie de la Grande Chaumiere. His friends Sonia and Robert Delaunay influenced Hofmann's understanding and use of color. Although the artist's first paintings were conventional and naturalistic, he gradually succumbed to the spatial concepts of Paul Cézanne and incorporated the bright palette of the Fauves. His first one-man exhibition was held at the Paul Cassirer Gallery in Berlin in 1910. Hofmann established his own School for Modern Art in Munich in 1915. There he strove to introduce to his students the elements of Parisian modernism that he had learned and practiced.

Hofmann first came to the United States in 1930 to teach at the University of California at Berkeley. He immigrated permanently to America in 1932, and began teaching at the Art Students League in New York. The artist opened his own school in New York in the fall of 1933, and in 1935 he offered the first of his summer courses in Provincetown, Massachusetts. Hofmann's school struggled financially, until an influx of GI Bill students brought new strength in the 1940s.

As a teacher Hofmann advocated introspection and technical prowess. At the center of his curriculum was an understanding of the visual dynamics of movement, the development of composition from planar components, and the manipulation of positive and negative space with color and form. He set forth his theories in his book *The Search for the Real and Other Essays*.[2]

In Hofmann's painting of the late 1930s, recognizable subjects progressively dissolved into abstract experiments in formal and spatial distortion, usually in vivid, Fauvist colors. In 1941 the artist became an American citizen, and his first solo exhibition in New York was held in 1944 at Peggy Guggenheim's Art of This Century Gallery.[3] This show revealed that he was working at the forefront of the progressive movement in New York. The term *Abstract Expressionism* was first used to describe a solo exhibition of Hofmann's paintings at Mortimer Brandt Gallery in 1946.[4]

A major retrospective of Hofmann's work was mounted at the Whitney Museum of American Art in 1957.[5] Soon after, the artist retired from teaching in order to devote himself full-time to his own painting. The Museum of Modern Art held a retrospective of his work in 1963, and organized a circulating exhibition of paintings by the artist and his students.[6] Hofmann remained active until his death in New York City on February 17, 1966.

Notes
1. An excellent chronology of Hofmann's career and account of his achievements is provided by Goodman 1986, pp. 117–122 and passim.
2. Hofmann 1948.
3. *Art News* 1944; Goodman 1986, pp. 8–9.
4. Coates 1946.
5. Wight 1957.
6. Seitz 1963.

■

Edna Boies Hopkins

Born Edna Bel Beachboard in Hudson, Michigan, in 1872,[1] her father, David Jackson Beachboard, was a merchant and banker whose success

afforded his daughter broad opportunities.[2] When she was twenty, she moved to Chicago, having married John Henry Boies, who died just two years later of tuberculosis.[3]

From 1895 through 1898, the artist studied at the Art Academy of Cincinnati, where she began enduring friendships with several artists, including Ethel Mars, Maud Squire, and James R. Hopkins. The following year, as a student of Arthur Wesley Dow (cat. 6) at the Pratt Institute in New York, she was first exposed to the tradition of Japanese printmaking. In 1900 she taught at the Veltin School for Girls in New York.

After marrying James Hopkins in 1904, she traveled widely. In Japan she undertook a methodical study of traditional woodcut techniques. Settling afterward in Paris, Hopkins devoted herself to mastering Japanese technique. Soon she was showing and selling her floral prints with some success. The artist's prints became popular in Paris, and although she worked slowly, she produced many editions.

At the outbreak of World War I, the Hopkinses returned to Cincinnati, where James took a teaching job at the Art Academy. However, the cosmopolitan Edna was uncomfortable with the life of a staid midwestern academic matron. In the summer of 1914 she was in Provincetown, Massachusetts.[4] There she taught printmaking to several artists, and in the fall she rented an apartment in Manhattan and began to exhibit actively. In 1915 her work was included in the Provincetown Printers' exhibition at the Berlin Photographic Company in New York, and the following year her first solo exhibition was mounted there.

Although Hopkins regularly visited her husband in Ohio, she seldom lingered. Still, their relationship remained strong, and James helped arrange a solo exhibition of her

woodcuts at the Cincinnati Art Museum in 1917. That year they traveled together in the Cumberland Gap in Kentucky, and Edna made white line color woodcuts representing lives of the mountain people, a marked diversion from her floral imagery.

In 1919 the artist's prints were featured in the landmark exhibition at the Detroit Institute of Arts, and she first exhibited with the Provincetown Art Association in 1920. In that year, the Hopkinses returned to Paris together. Reverting to floral imagery, Edna printed with a single block in the white line method. The contours of her forms became harder, her palette brighter, and the overall impact of her designs more decorative, perhaps under the influence of Art Nouveau. Hopkins's printmaking activities seem to have ceased by the time she returned to the United States in 1923.[5] It seems that her career was cut short by disability. Hopkins died in New York in 1937.

Notes
1. Falk, p. 291.
2. Bonner 1909, pp. 35–36.
3. Ryan 1986. Adrian 1894 relates how Boies's body was brought home to Adrian, Michigan, from Chicago.
4. Flint 1983, pp. 13–14, 32–33.
5. Although the artist is thought to have remained in Ohio after 1923, her father's obituary notice in 1926 notes that she was still a resident of France (see Adrian 1926).

■

Helen Hyde

Helen Hyde was born in Lima, New York, on April 6, 1868.[1] Her artistic talents were recognized early, and at the age of twelve, she began studies with Joachim Ferdinand Richardt.[2] After the death of her father in 1882, Hyde moved to San Francisco to live with her paternal grandparents, and there entered the orbit of her Aunt Gussie, a good-natured pioneer dowager who loved art. Augusta Hyde had married attorney David Bixler in Nevada, who later amassed a sizable fortune from the silver mines of the Comstock lode and moved afterward to California.

Thus, substantial family resources were available for Helen's education and artistic endeavors. She studied at the San Francisco School of Design with Emil Carlsen.

In 1888 she went to New York to study at the Art Students League with Kenyon Cox. The following year she was in Berlin, where she studied for two years with Franz Skarbina; then she went to Paris, where for three years she worked with Raphael Collin and Albert Sterner. In Paris Hyde was acquainted with Félix Regamey, a painter, illustrator, and etcher who had been to Japan. He introduced her to *ukiyo-e* prints and passed on his infectious enthusiasm for all things Japanese. After ten years of study, Hyde returned to San Francisco, where she continued to paint and began to exhibit her work.

Helen Hyde learned to etch from her friend Josephine Hyde in about 1885.[3] Her first plates, which she etched herself but had professionally printed, represented children. On sketching expeditions, she sought out quaint subjects for her etchings and watercolors.[4] In 1897 Hyde made her first color etchings—inked *à la poupée* and printed from one place—which became the basis for her early reputation. At this time, she began a career illustrating childrens' books, and her images sometimes represented the children of Chinatown.[5]

After the death of her mother in 1899, Hyde sailed to Japan, accompanied by her friend Josephine. Today, she established herself in luxury. In the Akasaka district of the city, she built a house, and each summer until 1914 she retired to Nikko. She adopted a monogram crest, and had it dyed on her servants' robes and emblazoned in gold on her rickshaw.

For over three years, the artist studied ink painting with the ninth and last master of the great Kano school of painters, Kano Tomonobu. Hyde learned to handle the brush with ease and grace, and her forceful calligraphic line contributed much to the success of her woodcuts. These collaborative prints were produced in the traditional *ukiyo-e* manner, for Japanese craftsmen cut the multiple woodblocks and printed the editions, under Hyde's supervision.

In these days of steamship travel, she occasionally returned to America for extended visits. Back in Tokyo in 1903 Hyde played hostess to Arthur Wesley Dow (cat. 6), whose prints she admired. In 1912 she returned to the United States to undergo cancer surgery; she spent the spring in Chicago and the winter in Mexico.

In October 1914 Hyde moved permanently to Chicago. She abandoned the medium of woodcut, and returned to color intaglio printmaking. One of her prints was awarded a medal at the Panama–Pacific International Exposition in San Francisco in 1915. In 1916 Hyde was in delicate health; to escape the winter, she traveled to the Carolinas. Her drawings and watercolors of Southern subjects were later translated into color intaglios and transfer lithographs. During World War I, the artist designed posters for the Red Cross, and made color prints that extolled the virtues of home-front diligence.

In ill health, Hyde traveled to be near her sister in Pasadena a few weeks before her death on May 13, 1919. She was buried in the family plot near Oakland, California.

Notes

1. Dinwiddie 1906; Wright 1930. I am grateful to Tim Mason who contributed information for this biography.
2. van der Veer 1905.
3. Jacques 1922, p. 10.
4. Ibid.
5. Clark 1900.

■

Ynez Johnston

Ynez Johnston was born on May 12, 1920, in Berkeley, California.[1] In 1943, shortly after graduating from the University of California, she had her first solo exhibition at the San

Francisco Museum of Art. She continued her studies at Berkeley, working with Margaret Peterson and receiving her master's degree in 1946. Having learned the fundamentals of etching in college, Johnston experimented on her own in 1948 and found a great affinity for this versatile medium. Later, working in the studio of her friend Leonard Edmondson (cat. 77) in Los Angeles, she quickly evolved her individual printmaking manner.

All of Johnston's compositions depict a magical world: a private realm of labyrinthine medieval cities, turreted castles, and fantastically rigged sailing ships. Constructions with their walls removed reveal the secret activities within. These essentially flat line drawings combine the free naïveté of a child's hand with the spontaneous inspiration of Oriental calligraphy. Influenced by Klee, Klimt, Picasso, and Braque, Johnston also studied Byzantine icon painting.

The artist often compressed or contorted space in her prints, so that the scale of her figures and constructions seemed arbitrary and bewildering. In the 1950s she concentrated on a pictographic language, and her compositions opened up, becoming less congested by detail. As this runic calligraphy began to dominate Johnston's images, they took on the beguiling character of petroglyphs.

Both in paintings and in prints, she accompanied this scriptural orientation with experiments in visual and physical surface textures. She preferred to paint with casein, which allowed a wide variety of surface effects. She also experimented with oil painting in the early 1950s, employing sun-thickened linseed oil to achieve a heavy, impasto surface. Johnston combined soft-ground etching with finely grained aquatint, long-etched plates, and refined inking procedures in order to produce fascinatingly textural intaglios.

Johnston lectured at the University of California at Berkeley in 1949 and 1950. As a Guggenheim Fellow in 1952, she worked in Italy. She taught printmaking at the Colorado Springs Fine Arts Center in the summers of

1954 through 1956, and in 1956 at the Chouinard Art Institute in Los Angeles. In 1959 Johnston was named Woman of the Year in Art by the *Los Angeles Times*. Between 1966 and 1973 she taught painting and printmaking at California State College, and in 1967 she taught at the University of Judaism in Los Angeles. In 1966 Johnston made her first lithographs at Tamarind Lithography Workshop; later Lynton Kistler printed her lithographs. In 1967 a major retrospective exhibition was mounted at the San Francisco Museum of Art.

In the early 1970s sawn and carved wood reliefs became the supports for Johnston's abstract paintings.[2] The calligraphy of her etchings became more representational, forming amorous, intertwined figures, engaged in the often humorous contortions of some imaginary Tantric cult.[3] She taught at the Otis Art Institute in Los Angeles from 1978 through 1980, and she was artist in residence at Fullerton College in 1982 and at the Laguna Beach School of Art in 1984. Still productive, inventive, and fanciful, Johnston now lives and works in Los Angeles.

Notes

1. *Who's Who* 1986, p. 213.
2. Leopold 1973.
3. Hotaling 1970; Young 1970.

■

Edward Landon

Edward August Landon was born on March 13, 1911, in Hartford Connecticut.[1] His father, who was a foreman in a drop forge, died when Edward was fifteen years old. Anxious to pursue the career of an artist, he dropped out of high school and took a job to pay his tuition at the Hartford Art School. In 1930 and 1931 he was the student of Jean Charlot (cat. 32) at the Art Students League in New York. Afterward, he traveled to Mexico to study privately for a year with Carlos Merida.

In 1933 Landon settled near Springfield, Massachusetts, painted murals in the local trade school, and exhibited with the Springfield Art League.

His painting *Memorial Day* won first prize at the fifteenth annual exhibition of the League at the Springfield Museum of Fine Arts.[2] Landon became one of the most visible and active members of the Artists Union of Western Massachusetts, serving as president from 1934 to 1938.

Landon acquired Anthony Velonis's (cat. 42) instructional pamphlet on the technique of serigraphy in the late 1930s. With such colleagues as Philip Hicken, Donald Reichert, and Pauline Stiriss, he began to experiment with technique and had soon amassed a body of work. These prints formed the nucleus of the landmark group exhibition of serigraphs at the Springfield Museum of Fine Arts in 1940.[3]

Landon had his first one-man show at the Museum of Fine Arts, Boston, in 1934.[4] At this time he ran the Little Gallery in Springfield, where he made picture frames and sold his prints. His next solo exhibition was mounted at Smith College in Northampton, Massachusetts, in 1941. He moved to New York later that year.[5] There he worked in the easel and mural painting divisions of the FAP, and later supported himself as an industrial designer.

A founding member of the National Serigraph Society, Landon served as editor of its publication, *Serigraph Quarterly*, in the late 1940s, and as president in 1952 and 1953. A one-man show of his prints hung at the Norlyst Gallery in Manhattan in 1945. Landon also published his first book, a manual on picture framing, that year.[6]

In 1950, with the support of a Fulbright grant, Landon traveled to Norway, where he researched the history of local artistic traditions, resulting in the book *Scandinavian Design: Picture and Rune Stones, 1000 B.C. to 1100 A.D.*[7] In Norway, Landon also taught serigraphy and organized print exhibitions, including a show of his own work at the Unge Kunstneres Samfund in Oslo. In

Stockholm, Sweden, he lectured on serigraphy under the auspices of the United States Information Agency.

The artist exhibited with the National Serigraph Society (1940–60), the American Color Print Society (1945–65), the Boston Printmakers (1955–70), and the Northwest Printmakers (1950–60). The Philadelphia Print Club sponsored a solo show of his work in 1953.

In 1958 Landon's legs were paralyzed when surgeons encountered complications during an operation to correct a back ailment. Nevertheless, he continued to produce paintings, sculpture, and a steady output of color serigraphs. In 1965 the artist moved to Weston, Vermont, into a house designed to accommodate working in a wheelchair. Landon died on October 18, 1984.

Notes

1. Falk, p. 356; *Who's Who* 1983, p. 531; Cummings 1988, p. 388. The author is indebted to Rachel Landon, the artist's widow, who provided many biographical details.
2. *Art Digest* 1934.
3. McCausland 1940.
4. *Parnassus* 1938.
5. Zigrosser 1941b, p. 451.
6. Landon 1945.
7. Landon 1951.

■

Mauricio Lasansky

Born on October 12, 1914, in Buenos Aires, Argentina, to an Eastern European immigrant who worked as an engraver of bank notes, Mauricio Lasansky began attending the Superior School of Fine Arts in 1933.[1] Drawn to printmaking by his background and inclination, Lasansky first concentrated on woodcuts. Later, he began to use drypoint in an unusual way, building up fully modeled, volumetric forms in large, romantic, Italianate prints. His first solo exhibition was presented at Fort General Roca, Argentina, in 1935.

At the age of twenty-two, Lasansky became director of the Free Fine Arts School at Córdoba. He married and began a family, and in 1939, he

became director of the Manual Training School in Córdoba. In 1940 Francis Henry Taylor, director of the Metropolitan Museum of Art in New York, met Lasansky and sponsored his Guggenheim Fellowship application, enabling him to come to the United States.

In 1943 Lasansky arrived in New York to study the vast print collection at the Metropolitan while maintaining his printmaking activity with Stanley William Hayter (cat. 60) at Atelier 17. His prints soon reflected the current style and techniques of the workshop: expressive, Surrealist abstractions rendered in bold softground etching, with extensive burin work.

The artist explored new methods of deeply sculpting his plates and texturizing their surfaces, along with *retroussage* and other printing procedures that produced rich, dark images. In 1944 he began to experiment with color, preferring multiple-plate techniques. These prints merged the childlike, Cubist figures of Picasso with the distinctive geometry of Atelier 17.

In 1945 Lasansky was a visiting lecturer at the University of Iowa and began to establish a graphic arts department there. That year his first solo exhibition in the United States was mounted at the Whyte Gallery in Washington, D.C. In 1946 he became an assistant professor of art at Iowa, and by 1948 he was a full professor. An extensive exhibition mounted in 1949 at the Walker Art Center in Minneapolis included a selection of his prints along with works by sixty-five of his students, including Lee Chesney and Malcolm Myers (cats. 64, 91).[2] In 1957 an important retrospective exhibition of the artist's prints were mounted at the University of Iowa.[3]

In the 1950s Lasansky's intaglios remained dark, passionately wrought images expressing his feelings about the spiritual and psychological effects of war. His *Nazi Drawings* was a

powerful, often horrific series executed between 1961 and 1966.[4] Soon thereafter, the artist moved toward a wider and more vivid range of hues, and he established an entirely new graphic vocabulary. His prints were larger, representing the human figure in unflinching, full-face poses or in strict profile. These enormous, parti-colored prints were created with several shaped plates, individually inked and secured on the bed of the press.

In 1960 the Ford Foundation sponsored a retrospective exhibition of Lasansky's work, documented by a monograph.[5] The artist retired from teaching in 1985, but maintains close ties to the university as a professor emeritus. Still living in Iowa City, as prolific as ever, Lasansky is currently engaged in a series of large intaglio portraits representing *The Great Thinkers*.

Notes

1. Thien/Lasansky 1975. I am grateful to the artist and to his son, Phillip Lasansky, for their help with this entry.
2. Longman/Friedman 1949; see also Friedman 1959.
3. Longman 1957.
4. Honig 1966. A sense of personal resolution can perhaps be seen in Lasansky's intaglio series *Kaddish*, completed in 1978. See Barragan 1978.
5. Zigrosser 1960.

■

Blanche Lazzell

Nettie Blanche Lazzell was born on October 19, 1878, near the village of Maidsville, West Virginia. She studied at West Virginia Conference Seminary, where she was awarded a liberal arts degree in 1898.[1] She continued her education at the South Carolina Co-educational Institute and at West Virginia University, where she studied art history, drawing, and painting with Eva E. Hubbard and William J. Leonard. By the time Lazzell decided on a career as an artist, at the age of twenty-seven, she had earned degrees in literature, liberal arts, and fine arts. In 1908 she attended William Merritt Chase's classes at the Art Students League in New York. She then journeyed to

Paris, where from 1912 to 1914 she studied with Charles Guérin and David Rosen at the Académie Moderne.

Lazzell was one of the many American artists who, at the outbreak of World War I, returned from the Continent and gathered in Provincetown, Massachusetts.[2] She learned the white line color woodcut technique from Oliver Newberry Chaffee in 1916. Lazzell also took classes from Charles W. Hawthorne, and exhibited her prints at the Provincetown Art Association.

During the winters of 1916 and 1917 the artist studied in New York with Homer Boss, and in the summer of 1917 she was the student of William E. Shumacher in Woodstock, New York. In Provincetown the following summer, Lazzell began to teach the woodcut technique in her little wharf studio. She was a member of the Société Anonyme, the international organization that promoted abstract art.

In 1923 she returned to Paris, where she studied with Fernand Léger, Albert Gleizes, and André Lhote, and her style became more abstract. Léger wrote an essay especially for Lazzell formalizing his teachings, explaining how to organize and develop an abstract composition.[3] She followed these instructions closely in her paintings, simplifying everyday objects into geometric shapes and stacking these planar forms atop a fulcrum at the center.[4] These were shown at the Salon d'Automne in Paris in 1923. She continued to submit works to this annual exhibition through the mid-1930s.

In the winter of 1933 Lazzell moved to Morgantown, West Virginia, to work for the Public Works of Art Project and the WPA, for which she made prints and painted murals. In 1935 Lazzell used the technique of white line woodcut for nonobjective abstractions. Although she gradually returned to more conventional landscapes and still lifes, the influence of modernist planar abstraction remained with her. The artist continued to offer classes in block printmaking, painting, and composition. For more than forty years she returned to Provincetown in the summertime, continuing to produce color woodcuts and focusing on still lifes and local imagery. She never lost her youthful curiosity; at the age of fifty she took Hans Hofmann's (cat. 73) painting course in Provincetown. Lazzell died in Morgantown on June 1, 1956.

Notes
1. Clarkson 1979; Flint 1983, pp. 34–35.
2. Flint 1983, p. 14.
3. Campbell 1986.
4. Fort 1982.

■
Pedro J. Lemos

Pedro Joseph Lemos was born in Austin, Nevada, on May 25, 1882.[1] He grew up in Oakland, California, and attended the public schools there. Lemos began his studies of art in San Francisco with Mary P. S. Benton and Harry Stuart Fonda. In 1900 he was the pupil of Arthur Matthews at the Mark Hopkins Institute. In about 1903 he went to New York and studied with George Bridgman at the Art Students League, and Arthur Wesley Dow (cat. 6) at Columbia University Teachers College. Dow's influence on Lemos was profound, and it would remain obvious in every phase of the artist's activity throughout his career.

Returning to Oakland, Lemos began a career as a painter, illustrator, and designer. He contributed illustrations to a variety of publications, particularly children's books.[2] In 1911 he began conducting classes in etching and decorative design at the San Francisco Institute of Art, where he continued to teach until 1917. He helped found the California Society of Etchers in 1913, and in 1914 he became director of the San Francisco Institute of Art. For the Panama-Pacific International Exposition of 1915, the artist was chief organizer of the California print exhibition. One of Lemos's own prints won an honorable mention at this exhibition.

Late in the decade Lemos founded the Rionido Summer School of Art, where he practiced many of Dow's teaching methods.[3] In 1919 he was appointed director of the Leland Stanford Junior Museum (now the Stanford Museum of Art). There, his career as a theorist and educator flourished. His reputation and influence became widespread through a series of textbooks written primarily for teachers of art in grammar and secondary schools,[4] often illustrated with his own artwork and line drawings.

As editor of *School Arts Magazine*, Lemos published many articles about teaching art. In 1901 he produced a series of folios entitled *Applied Art*, based on Dow's books *Composition* and *Ipswich Prints*.[5] Each of Lemos's albums, organized by subject, included about twenty illustrative plates, unbound so they could be mounted on schoolroom walls. The majority of the illustrations reproduced projects successfully completed by Lemos and his students.

Lemos was the first president of the Carmel Art Association. He exhibited his paintings and prints with the Bohemian Club, the California Society of Etchers, the Chicago Society of Etchers, the Palo Alto Art Association, and the California Print Makers. A solo exhibition of his work was mounted at Stanford University in 1928.

By 1943 Lemos was a fellow of the Royal Society of Art in London. The artist died in Palo Alto on December 5, 1945.

Notes
1. Hughes, p. 274; Falk, p. 367; *American Art Annual* 1923, p. 592; Fielding 1986, p. 533. The artist occasionally signed his name as Pedro de Lemos.
2. Miller 1904; Bralliar 1908.
3. There were notable similarities between this curriculum and that of Dow's Ipswich Summer School. See Moffatt 1977, pp. 92–103.
4. Among the most important of these were Lemos 1920 and 1931.
5. There were at least fourteen *Applied Art* folios. They were published between 1920 and 1930 by *School Arts Magazine* and Davis Press in Worcester, Massachusetts.

■
Russell T. Limbach

Russell Theodore ("Butch") Limbach was born in Massillon, Ohio, on November 9, 1904. He made his first lithographs when he was a teenager, even before his enrollment at the Cleveland School of Art in 1922.[1] Beginning in 1926 Limbach worked for a few years in professional workshops, gaining experience in the full range of printmaking media. His own prints were widely exhibited and won awards from the California Print Makers, the Cleveland Museum of Art, and the Art Institute of Chicago.

In 1929 the artist studied in Vienna and in Paris, where, in 1930 he probably made his first color lithograph. By 1933 Limbach had returned to New York, where he contributed a lithograph to the second portfolio published by the Contemporary Print Group.[2] He now supported himself primarily as an illustrator, and his political cartoons, fillers, and illustrations appeared regularly in *The Masses* from 1934 to 1936.

In 1934 Limbach was commissioned to organize the first centralized FAP print shop in New York. He designed and outfitted the workshop and sought out artists to work there.[3] The shop opened on February 6, 1936, with Gustave von Groschwitz as supervisor and Limbach as technical advisor.

Color lithography was introduced into the workshop because of Limbach's inclination and expertise. Late in 1936 he began a series of satirical prints representing the circus. One print from this series, *Trapeze Girl*, was the first color lithograph ever made in the FAP workshop.[4] With the realization of this expanded capability, FAP artists were invited early in 1937 to make color lithographs from stones under Limbach's technical direction and assistance. The immediate and eager response generated was reflected in the exhibition Printmaking, a New Tradition held in 1938 at the Federal Art Gallery on Fifty-seventh Street and which included twenty-three color lithographs by sixteen project artists.[5]

Soon the artist's own work shifted decisively from figural, often political imagery to landscape and nature subjects. In 1939 he began teaching at Walt Whitman High School in New York City. He remained in this position after his release from the WPA in March of 1940. Limbach became artist in residence at Wesleyan University at Middletown, Connecticut, in 1941; two years later he joined the faculty.[6]

Limbach was elected an Associate of the National Academy of Design in 1952. He actively taught at Wesleyan and produced artwork until his death in Sherman, Connecticut, on January 10, 1971.

Notes
1. Falk, p. 372; *Who's Who* 1962, p. 378; *Who's Who* 1970, p. 260; Michigan 1985, pp. 104–105. I am grateful to Ellen D'Oench and Elisabeth A. Swaim for making materials available from Limbach's archives at Wesleyan University.
2. Adams 1983, p. 136.
3. Kainen 1972, pp. 157–158.
4. Ibid., p. 167. A set of progressive color proofs of this lithograph can be found at the Davison Art Center, Wesleyan University; see Adams 1983, p. 106.
5. Kainen 1972, p. 167.
6. For an account of the Art Laboratory program, which Limbach headed from 1943 to 1966, see Wesleyan 1971.

■
Tod Lindenmuth

Born on May 4, 1885, in Allentown, Pennsylvania, Tod Lindenmuth was the son of a painter-photographer, who taught him the techniques of photography.[1] He studied at the Chase School of Art in New York with William H. W. Bicknell, George Elmer Browne, Robert Henri, and E. Ambrose Webster, artists who had close connections with Provincetown. Lindenmuth first exhibited there in 1915, and the following year his block prints were featured at the Berlin Photographic Company in New York, in what was essentially the first exhibition of the Provincetown Printers group. The artist produced the covers for the annual catalogue of the Provincetown Art Association in 1916 and 1917. His prints were featured in the landmark exhibition of color woodcuts at the Detroit Institute of Arts in 1919.

Although Lindenmuth's work seems conservative, he was an outspoken advocate of modernism in Provincetown, and in 1926 he was one of the authors of a petition, undersigned by thirty local artists, advocating that four painters of modernist style and sympathy be added to the jury of the Provincetown Art Association.[2] In the following month a fragile resolution of this controversy came with the decision that separate exhibitions would be mounted for conventional and modernist artists. Lindenmuth's work was included in the First Modernistic Exhibition the following summer, alongside pieces by Blanche Lazzell (cat. 18), Agnes Weinrich (cat. 20), and other Provincetown printmakers.[3]

In the mid-1920s Lindenmuth married Elizabeth Warren, a painter and printmaker who had studied with Bicknell in Providence. He was employed by the Public Works Administration and the WPA in the 1930s. Six of his prints were included in an important exhibition of American color prints at the Brooklyn Museum in 1933. In 1940 Lindenmuth stopped making prints and moved to Rockport, Massachusetts, where he concentrated on painting.

Lindenmuth exhibited with the St. Augustine Art Club in Florida and with the Rockport Artists Association, and one of his prints exhibited at the Pennsylvania Academy of Fine Arts won a prize. From the late 1940s until 1971 the artist spent his winters in St. Augustine and his summers in Rockport. He died in St. Augustine on November 6, 1976.

Notes
1. *Who's Who* 1962, p. 378; Flint 1983, pp. 36–37.
2. Kuchta/Seckler 1977, pp. 19–30.
3. Ibid., p. 47. See also Falk, p. 371; Johnson 1980, pp. 15, 17.

■
Margaret Lowengrund

Margaret Lowengrund, born in Atlantic City on August 24, 1902, grew up in Philadelphia.[1] She studied at the Pennsylvania Academy of Fine Arts, and wrote and illustrated a column called "Sketches about Town" for the *Philadelphia Ledger*. In 1923 she moved to New York to study at the Art Students League, where she learned the technique of lithography from Joseph Pennell.[2] She then supported herself by writing a newspaper column for the *New York Post*.

Lowengrund traveled to England in 1925, enrolled at the London County Council School of Arts and Crafts, and studied lithography with A. S. Hartrick. She published her drawings piecemeal in several London newspapers. In 1926 she proceeded to Paris and studied painting under André Lhote and Leopold Gottlieb.

In 1927 Lowengrund's first solo exhibition was mounted at the Kleeman-Thorson Galleries soon after her return to New York. In the 1930s Lowengrund was active as a painter, illustrator, critic, author, and radio interviewer. Though she continued her interest in printmaking, more attention was given to painting, and she executed several murals. Lowengrund had solo exhibitions at the Philadelphia Print Club and at the Baltimore Museum. She worked in the New York City FAP graphic arts workshop, where she was one of the first artists to make color lithographs. Her color prints were included in the exhibition Printmaking, a New Tradition at the Federal Art Gallery in 1938.[3] At this time Lowengrund taught a workshop in color lithography at the New School for Social Research. She also taught at the American Artists School.

The artist undertook many commercial projects.[4] She worked as a courtroom artist for Paramount News, and as a book illustrator. From 1948 to 1950 she was an associate editor of *Art Digest*, writing reviews of exhibitions and a column about the graphic arts. Lowengrund

was also registrar and assistant director of the National Academy of Design School of Fine Arts for the 1950–51 academic year.

In the 1950s Lowengrund was a zealous advocate of printmaking. She envisioned a lithography workshop which, functioning together with a sales gallery, could provide facilities for artists to economically produce creative prints in color. In 1952 she opened a small gallery called The Contemporaries, where she represented American graphic artists. The gallery had a little print shop in the back room, where ancient, rickety equipment was used to produce lithographs and intaglio prints. The artist John Muench, who worked as associate director of the gallery, printed the lithographs and taught this process, while Michael Ponce de León (cat. 96) taught classes in intaglio printmaking.

In the summer of 1952, Lowengrund also reopened a lithography workshop in the basement of the Woodstock Artists Association, a program that continued over the next three summers.[5] A solo exhibition of Lowengrund's paintings and prints was organized by the Smithsonian Institution in 1954. In 1955 she moved her gallery to a larger, more accessible space. The workshop now became a prominent school, and several of New York's finest printmakers worked there as instructors. Some of the most accomplished and beautiful prints of the day were produced at this workshop, including works by Stuart Davis (cat. 88) and Milton Avery (cat. 83). However, facing financial difficulties, Lowengrund enlisted the support of the Rockefeller Foundation, and the studio merged with the Pratt Institute in 1956. The artist died from cancer in New York on November 20, 1957.

Notes
1. Adams 1984.
2. Lowengrund 1951, p. 151.
3. Adams 1983, p. 125.
4. Landau 1983, pp. 65–66.
5. See Adams 1983, p. 185.

■
Guy Maccoy

Guy Maccoy was born in Valley Falls, Kansas, on October 7, 1904. When he was twelve, a private tutor provided his first lessons in drawing and painting.[1] He undertook a four-year BFA degree course at the Kansas City Art Institute, followed by two years of study with Ernest Lawson at the Broadmoor Art Academy in Colorado.[2] In New York, he studied at Columbia University, and at the Art Students League with Jan Matulka and Vaclav Vytlacil.

The artist was first exposed to the silkscreen process in 1932, when he worked for a printer in Hoboken, New Jersey.[3] Seeing an exhibition of contemporary French *pochoir* prints at the Weyhe Gallery in New York, Maccoy wondered whether he could achieve the same effects with silkscreens. He produced two prints in 1932, using glue as the stop-out and thinned oil paint as ink.[4] Maccoy continued to play with the process, producing several editions independently of Anthony Velonis (cat. 42) and the development of serigraphy in the FAP graphic arts workshop.

Maccoy was dissatisfied with commercial inks, and experimented to achieve the combination of soft surface and saturated hues of the watercolor *pochoirs*. In 1937 he analyzed commercial water-base silkscreen inks, chemical dryers and extenders, and developed recipes for mixing and manipulating similar preparations.[5]

Maccoy was employed by the FAP mural division in New York from about 1934 to 1939, and he painted a large fresco in the entranceway of the Brooklyn Museum.[6] His first one-man exhibition of easel paintings was mounted at the ACA Gallery in New York in 1936.[7] The following November this gallery exhibited sixteen prints by Maccoy, the first one-man show to be devoted solely to serigraphs.[8] Dismissed by the WPA in 1939, Maccoy and his wife, artist Geno Pettit, traveled around the country by trailer, making prints that they sold at lecture demonstrations, and teaching serigraphy to eager amateurs.

Maccoy graduated from Columbia University with a teaching certificate in 1940. Working as a color separator at the Poligraphic Lithograph Company, a commercial firm in Bennington, Vermont, he developed a remarkable analytical sensibility for the makeup of colors. His own prints from this period were landscapes that incorporated stylistic elements derived from Chinese painting. In 1941 the Maccoys' paintings and prints dominated the annual exhibition of the Cleveland Museum of Art.[9]

In 1947 the artist moved to California and worked at the Bolter Lithograph Company in Los Angeles. At that time Maccoy and Pettit helped form the Western Serigraph Society. In 1951 the artist began teaching at the Jepson Art Institute. He taught at the Otis Art Institute in Los Angeles from 1958 until his retirement in 1969. He also conducted serigraphy classes at the Los Angeles County Art Institute.

In 1970 Maccoy's home and studio in Chatsworth, California, were destroyed by fire, and the body of his work was lost. He then resumed teaching private students and printed reproductive serigraphs after the works of other artists. The technical standard of these reproductions—often utilizing more than forty colors—was remarkable.[10] Maccoy died in 1981 in Canoga Park, California.

Notes
1. The best account of Maccoy's career is given in Whitaker 1974.
2. Falk, p. 386.
3. Whitaker 1974, p. 76.
4. Zigrosser 1941b, pp. 465–466. Both of Maccoy's first two prints are reproduced in Williams 1987, p. 6.
5. Zigrosser 1941b, p. 465.
6. Maccoy also executed two large map frescoes at the Brooklyn Industrial High School for Girls. See Watson 1935; *Art Digest* 1939b.
7. In 1936 Maccoy also worked briefly in Colorado Springs. See Adams 1983, p. 112.
8. Zigrosser 1941b, p. 442.
9. Maccoy's landscape painting *White Horses* won first prize. Milliken 1946, pp. 57, 59, 63, 65, 70, 72.
10. Whitaker 1974, p. 76.

Stanton Macdonald-Wright

Stanton Macdonald-Wright was born in Charlottesville, Virginia, on July 8, 1890.[1] He took his first art classes at the age of five. He moved with his family to Santa Monica, California in 1900. Four years later, he ran away from home and signed on as cabin boy on a schooner bound for Japan, eventually landing in Maui.

Returning to Los Angeles in 1904, Macdonald-Wright enrolled at the Art Students League and studied with Warren Hedges. In France in 1907 he studied at the Sorbonne, and briefly at the Académie Colarossi, the Académie Julian, and the Ecole des Beaux–Arts. He also frequented museums and carefully studied the work of Seurat and Cézanne. One of his paintings was exhibited at the Salon d'Automne in 1910, and another at the Salon des Indépendants two years later.

Macdonald-Wright's fascination with color began late in 1910, when he met the American painter Morgan Russell. Together they studied color theory with Percyval Tudor-Hart, and learned the color systems of several other theorists. They developed a painting style in which form was generated by color, not based on observed nature. They called this manner syn-chromy (meaning "with color"), by analogy with the musical sym-phony ("with sound").[2] In 1913 the first Synchromist group exhibition was mounted at the Neue Kunst Salon in Munich, and another followed at the Galerie Bernheim-Jeune in Paris.

Later that year he returned to New York, and the following March, his Synchromist canvases were shown in a solo exhibition at the Carroll Galleries. In 1914, in London, he collaborated with his brother Willard Huntington Wright on books concerning aesthetics and art theory.[3]

In 1916 Macdonald-Wright settled in Manhattan, exhibiting at Stieglitz's 291 Gallery, the Montross Gallery, and the Daniels Gallery. In 1919 he moved to Hollywood, where he experimented with color film, and produced the first full-length, stop-motion color movie, which required thousands of hand-drawn images. The artist also helped develop an additive cinematic color process and planned a kinetic color projection machine.

From 1922 to 1930 Macdonald-Wright was director of the Art Students League in Los Angeles. He compiled his ideas and experiences on color theory in *A Treatise on Color*, published privately for students in 1924.[4]

The artist executed a mural in the Santa Monica Library in 1935, and his drawings of this period reveal a broad, eclectic range of styles. He also became director of the southern California FAP in 1935.

Macdonald-Wright joined the faculty at the University of California at Los Angeles in 1942, where he taught art history, Oriental aesthetics, and iconography. A solo exhibition was organized by the Honolulu Academy of Art in 1949. In 1952, as a Fulbright exchange professor, Macdonald-Wright lectured at the Tokyo University of Education (Kyoiku Daigaku). There his interest in color woodcut was aroused, and his fascination with Buddhist art deepened. The artist resigned his appointment at UCLA in 1954, and dedicated himself to painting. A major solo exhibition was organized by the Los Angeles County Museum in 1956.

Beginning in 1958 and continuing until his death, the artist spent five months of each year at a Zen monastery in the center of Kyoto, Japan. In 1962 a heart attack forced him to work on smaller paintings and watercolors. He established a home in Florence, and for the remainder of his life Macdonald-Wright divided most of his time between Italy and Japan. Important retrospective exhibitions of his work were shown by the Smithsonian Institution in 1967 and at UCLA in 1970.[5] Macdonald-Wright died of a heart attack in Los Angeles on August 22, 1973.

Notes
1. A biographical chronology, written by the artist, is found in Scott 1967, pp. 21–24.
2. Agee 1965; Levin 1978.
3. Wright/Macdonald-Wright 1916 and 1923.
4. Macdonald-Wright 1924.
5. Scott 1967; UCLA 1970.

Boris Margo

Boris Margo was born in Wolotschisk, in the Russian Ukraine, on November 7, 1902.[1] He began his studies in Odessa at the Polytechnik School of Art in 1919. In 1924, in Moscow, he studied briefly in the avant-garde group Futemas and there he came under the spell of the sixteenth-century artists of fantasy Hieronymus Bosch and Pieter Bruegel.

From 1927 to 1929 while in Leningrad, he studied at the Hermitage. There he became associated with the Analytical School of Art operated by Pavel Nikolaevich Filinov, who advocated a Protosurrealist style that combined intellectual and intuitive reactions to human experience, and an innovative, experimental approach to materials and techniques.

With a student visa, Margo came to New York in 1930, and began studies at the Roerich Museum. Two years later he was teaching there. At this time Margo worked in a naturalistic Surrealist style, often with found or recycled materials. In 1931 the artist began experiments that led to his development of the cellocut.[2] Soon printmaking became the center of his technical experiments and prolific output.

In 1940 Margo first went to Provincetown, Massachusetts, with Jan Gelb, whom he married the following year. He would return to Cape Cod in the summers over the next thirty years. He gathered driftwood and assembled it into sculptures, and drawings of these were later transformed into new paintings and prints. In 1942 the Metropolitan Museum of Art purchased his canvas *Floating Objects Illumined*, from the Artists for Victory exhibition. He became an American citizen in 1943.

Margo's work was included in the exhibition Abstract and Surrealist American Art at Peggy Guggenheim's Art of This Century Gallery in 1947. He also won the first of several purchase awards in the Brooklyn Museum's Print National exhibition of 1947, and a solo exhibition of his prints was organized by this museum.[3] Margo was the chief organizer of the Graphic Circle, a group of printmakers who gathered to share ideas about new materials and techniques, and exhibited their work together at the Jacques Seligmann Galleries; he was also an active member of the 14 Painter–Printmakers Group.[4] In 1948 a solo exhibition of Margo's graphic work was organized by the Smithsonian Institution. The following year he began teaching in the dunes near Provincetown, and a popular school developed which was continued over many successive summers.

In the 1950s Margo's style evolved toward a quieter, monochromatic, more sculptural imagery. Deep reliefs embossed in thick papers were usually printed in one pale hue, or were completely without color. He also created free standing sculptures covered with calligraphy, made of canvas stretched over wooden armatures, and covered with fiberglass and cellocut plates. Margo undertook several temporary teaching appointments and residences in the 1950s and 1960s. In 1966, when he was a visiting professor at Syracuse University, a documentary film about his life was produced, and a retrospective exhibition of his graphics was mounted, accompanied by a catalogue raisonné of his prints.[5]

In his paintings and prints of the 1970s Margo's distinctive calligraphy was organized in columns and bands, seemingly adrift in water or ether. After he suffered a stroke in the decade, his artistic activity ceased. In 1988 a retrospective exhibition of his work was mounted at the Provincetown Art Association, which later traveled to the Museum of Fine Arts in St. Petersburg, Florida.[6] Margo currently lives in Venice, Florida.

Notes
1. *Who's Who* 1982, p. 623.
2. Parsons 1955.
3. Brooklyn 1947.
4. Kup 1947; Gordon/Johnson 1955, nos. 37–42.
5. Schmeckebier/Gelb 1968.
6. Zimiles/Wechsler 1988.

■

Fletcher Martin

Born on April 29, 1904, in Palisade, Colorado, Fletcher Martin grew up in a succession of rugged frontier villages, where his father struggled with a string of small-town newspapers.[1] At these presses, Martin first became acquainted with printing processes. When he was thirteen, he worked with the Western Show Print Company in Seattle, a firm that printed big, colorful outdoor posters from large basswood blocks. Drifting around the Northwest, Martin often amused himself by sketching. He joined the navy in 1922.

Having married in 1925, Martin settled in Los Angeles. He worked as a printer, producing all sorts of props for the movie industry. Martin began to study art, to paint, and to make prints in his spare time. Attracted by David Alfaros Siqueiros's murals, fiery personality and philosophical approach to art and life, Martin spent many evenings with him and was briefly his assistant.

In 1933 Martin visited New York, and he had his first solo exhibition of woodcuts in Los Angeles. His first one-man show of paintings, at the San Diego Fine Arts Gallery in 1935, was followed almost immediately by a solo exhibition at the Los Angeles County Museum. The FAP provided Martin with his first full-time job as an artist. In 1936 he painted a large fresco cycle in the auditorium of North Hollywood High School,[2] which attracted government-sponsored commissions for five major frescoes between 1937 and 1940.

In 1938 Martin took his first teaching position, a two-year appointment at the Art Center School in Los Angeles, and during the next four decades he taught at the Kansas City Art Institute, the Albany Institute of History and Art, the Los Angeles

County Institute, and the University of Bridgeport. In 1939, his painting *Trouble in Frisco* was purchased by the Museum of Modern Art.[3] His first one-man show in Manhattan hung at the Midtown Galleries, from which the gouache *Juliet* was purchased by the Metropolitan Museum of Art, in 1940. That year Martin became artist in residence at the University of Iowa.

In 1943 he traveled to North Africa as a war artist-correspondent for *Life* magazine. Many more magazine assignments followed. In 1945 Martin moved to New York and began to work for *Sports Illustrated*.[4] At this time he also took on his first projects in book illustration.

In 1946 Martin moved to Woodstock, New York, where he built a house and studio. Soon he joined the teaching staff of the Art Students League in Woodstock. He was very active through the 1950s, dividing his time among many teaching positions, working residencies, diverse commercial commissions, and his own painting. This period witnessed a new lyricism in Martin's work. A spiky modernism came to dominate his representational style, along with ever-increasing tendencies to flatten form and to divide compositions into repeated decorative patterns. During the next three decades Martin remained in demand as an instructor and an artist in residence. He died on May 30, in Guanajuato, Mexico, in 1979.

Notes
1. For the most complete chronology of Martin's life see Cooke 1977, pp. 223–225.
2. Ibid., figs. 18–25.
3. *Art Digest* 1940. An adaptation of the painting *Trouble in Frisco* (Cooke 1977, fig. 27) became Martin's best-known lithograph.
4. Taylor 1956.

William Meyerowitz

William Meyerowitz was born on July 15, 1898, in the Ukrainian village of Ekaterinslav. He emigrated with family in 1908, and settled on the Lower West Side of Manhattan.[1] He was a cantor in the synagogue, and

during his student years he also supported himself by singing in the chorus of the Metropolitan Opera. Relationships between music and the visual arts always fascinated the artist, and he conceived many of his paintings and prints in musical terms.

From 1912 to 1916 Meyerowitz studied at the National Academy of Design, and his academic painting *Drama as a Teacher* won an honorable mention in the Prix de Rome competition of 1916. He first encountered color intaglio in the work of Charles Mielatz at the National Academy of Design. The budding artist became serious about printmaking when he was given an old printing press that had already seen long service at the U.S. Mint.

His early prints—landscapes and character studies reflecting the influences of Whistler and Hassam—were first exhibited in 1918 with the Brooklyn Society of Etchers. The following year the artist's first one-man show was mounted at the Milch Gallery, and he continued to exhibit almost annually for the next sixty-five years.

In 1919 Meyerowitz married artist Theresa Bernstein; they went to Gloucester, Massachusetts, and became close to artists Ellen Day Hale and Gabrielle De Vaux Clements (cat. 7) who owned a printing press. There Meyerowitz experimented with color etching that summer. He moved his own press to Gloucester in 1921 and began his most productive period of printmaking.

Meyerowitz was also an accomplished portraitist. Following his first important commission, from Oliver Wendell Holmes, the artist went on to portray the other justices of the Supreme Court, as well as scientist Albert Einstein, on both canvas and copperplate. In 1925 Meyerowitz's printmaking was the subject of an early educational film produced by the Fox Film Company, *The Magic Needle*.

Late in the decade, the artist began to experiment with Analytical Cubism, subdividing his compositions into sharp, polygonal facets, as shown in several paintings and in a remarkable aquatint of 1929 representing the Rockport quarry, which he printed in several color variations. In the 1930s Meyerowitz spent several summers in Ridgefield, New Jersey, where he produced a series of bucolic aquatints, landscapes permeated with the glow of sunshine, which often dissolved into Cubist fragments.

As artist for the WPA Meyerowitz produced mural paintings, including a fresco in the post office in Clinton, Connecticut, in 1933. That same year a group of his intaglios were featured in the pivotal exhibition of color prints at the Brooklyn Museum.[2] Along with Robert Henri and George Bellows, Meyerowitz helped to found the People's Art Guild, an association dedicated to making art more accessible. From 1940 to 1945 he taught painting and etching at the Modern School of Self-Expression in the Bronx. In 1943 the artist was elected to the National Academy of Design.

His etched oeuvre has been said to number more than one thousand plates, many of which were printed in only a few impressions.[3] Meyerowitz died in New York on May 28, 1981.

Notes
1. Meyerowitz 1986.
2. Brooklyn 1933; Bernstein 1933.
3. Meyerowitz.

■

George Miyasaki

George Joji Miyasaki was born on March 24, 1935, in Kalopa, Hawaii.[1] He enrolled at the California College of Arts and Crafts in Oakland in 1953, to study commercial art. His friends Billy Al Bengston and Manuel Neri soon convinced him to change his major to fine arts. He studied under Richard Diebenkorn and Nathan Oliveira (cat. 87), and set up a studio to paint seriously in 1955.

Oliveira introduced Miyasaki to lithography in 1956, and he began to make color prints almost immediately. His early work was shown in the Fourth International Biennial of Contemporary Color Lithography at the Cincinnati Art Museum in 1956. Miyasaki's first solo exhibition was presented at Gump's Gallery in San Francisco in 1957. In the following year he won a purchase prize at the Eleventh Print National Exhibition at the Brooklyn Museum for his lithograph *Autumn*. After completing his master's degree in 1958, Miyasaki joined the faculty of the California School of Arts and Crafts, and began to teach printmaking, painting, and drawing.

In 1959, when his work was featured in the traveling exhibition American Prints Today, Miyasaki quickly gained national recognition.[2] A Ford Foundation grant enabled the artist to work at the Tamarind Lithography Workshop in 1961. A major solo exhibition of his paintings was mounted at the Paul Kantor Gallery in Los Angeles the same year.

The artist received a Guggenheim Fellowship in 1962, and won a Ford Foundation purchase prize at the San Francisco Museum of Art's Eighty-second Annual Exhibition. In 1963 solo exhibitions of Miyasaki's paintings and prints were mounted at the University of California and at the Achenbach Foundation for Graphic Arts in San Francisco.[3] At this time he also taught briefly at Stanford University.

Miyasaki traveled in Europe in 1964. Influences of the geometric imagery of ancient Etruscan frescoes and Greek vase painting appeared in the prints he created at the Clot lithography studio in Paris. On his return, Miyasaki began to teach printmaking at the University of California, Berkeley. Figures appeared in his work; soon he began to use images appropriated by transfer methods in his paintings and prints, and he also experimented with stencils and spray effects.

Around 1965 Miyasaki and Harold Paris worked together to produce several editions of large lithographs printed from zinc plates. Miyasaki exhibited widely in the late 1960s, and among his many awards was the purchase prize at the Sixteenth Print National Exhibition at the Brooklyn Museum in 1968.

A period of introspection for the artist followed in the early 1970s, resulting in a softer, more stable imagery. He studied color theory, and developed an analytical approach to color. After a visit to Japan in 1978, he began to experiment with handmade paper. In 1980 and 1985 the artist received grants from the National Endowment of the Arts to support his painting projects.

Miyasaki currently lives in Berkeley, where he continues to paint actively and teach at the University of California.

Notes
1. *Who's Who* 1986, p. 706; Wirtz 1981, pp. 8–9.
2. Print Council 1959, no. 38; see also Print Council 1962, nos. 32–33.
3. Troche/Beall 1963.

■

Eugene Morley

Born in Scranton, Pennsylvania, on November 10, 1909, Eugene Morley honed his printmaking and design skills in studies at the Art Students League in New York.[1] In his first lithographs, he represented the hardships of life in the city, the countryside, and the coal mines of Pennsylvania in a personal version of Social Realism that already tended to the dismal and macabre.[2] Conscientious and politically active, like many of his colleagues in the FAP, Morley was a member of the American Artists Congress and the New York Artists Union. Born of personal experience, his convictions held him to the imagery of social commentary in his prints even as he was drawn more and more toward abstraction.[3]

Morley joined the FAP workshops in 1935. Working in the mural division, he executed wall paintings for the Williamsburg Housing Project in Brooklyn, New York.[4] In 1936 the

artist also began to work in the graphic arts division, where his skills as a master lithographer were apparent not only in his own prints, but in his technical assistance to many other project artists. The record of Morley's production of prints in the workshop lists just four lithographs and two serigraphs. In September 1940 he became a project supervisor in the FAP, and he was dismissed from the project the following year.

Morley was associated with the stage designer Norman Bel Geddes, and he taught drawing and lithography at the American Artists School, which he helped organize. In the late 1940s he became art director at Covington Fabrics in New York. He continued to paint in a nonobjective, abstract style. After the war, however, he did not exhibit his work or have a dealer. He died in New York City in 1953.

Notes
1. *Who's Who* 1940, p. 456; Falk, p. 431; O'Connor 1973, pp. 286–287.
2. *Prints* 1936.
3. Ward 1939.
4. Diller 1973.

■

Seong Moy

Seong Moy was born in Canton, China, on April 12, 1921.[1] When he was ten, he came to the United States to join other members of his family who had settled in St. Paul, Minnesota. He studied under Ben Swanson at the WPA/FAP school in St. Paul in 1935, and under Cameron Booth at the St. Paul School of Art from 1936 to 1940. Moy worked in the FAP print shop in Minneapolis from 1939 to 1941.

With a scholarship Moy went to New York to study at the Art Students League, under Vaclav Vytlacil in 1941. He was also a pupil of Hans Hofmann (cat. 73). His first solo exhibition was at the Carmel Art Association in California in 1943. That year the artist joined the armed forces, serving in the 14th Air Force—the "Flying Tigers"—in the China-Burma-India Theater.

A one-man show of Moy's paintings and prints was exhibited at the Ashby Gallery in New York in 1947. In the late 1940s the artist often represented characters or moments from Chinese theater, in an abstract figurative style related to Arshile Gorky and Joan Miró. In 1948 Moy joined Atelier 17.[2] In 1950 he won an Opportunity Fellowship from the John Hay Whitney Foundation. The same year he executed commissioned editions for the International Graphic Art Society, Associated American Artists, the Pratt Graphic Center, and SAGA.

Moy taught painting at the University of Minnesota in 1951. Although Chinese themes continued to inspire his works, their style became oriented to the New York School. In 1952 he executed five multicolor woodcuts conceived for a popular market, which were published as one of the Rio Grande Graphics portfolios.[3]

He exhibited with the 14 Painter-Printmakers group.[4] In the 1950s and 1960s Moy taught part time at Indiana University, Smith College, Vassar College, Cooper Union, Columbia University, the Pratt Graphic Center, and the Art Students League. In 1954 he established his summer art school in Provincetown, Massachusetts. There, for more than twenty years, he offered instruction in painting and drawing, and also specialized in teaching printmaking.[5] The artist won a Guggenheim Fellowship in 1955, the year he executed a mural painting at the Architectural League of New York.

In 1958 Moy took up book illustration, sometimes representing Chinese subjects.[6] However, his paintings and prints generally progressed toward poetic interpretations of nature, and he began to incorporate collage into his paintings. The characteristic carved lines in his woodcut blocks now approximated broad, gestural swaths of color, the strokes of brush or palette knife on canvas.

In 1970 Moy became professor of art at the City College of New York. His work concentrated on contemplative abstractions in muted hues, executed in acrylic with collage on canvas. Many of his late color prints were made from cardboard reliefs, with painterly surfaces built up in modeling paste or acrylic medium and collage.[7] Moy is presently recovering from a stroke suffered in 1987.

Notes
1. *Who's Who* 1986, p. 722; Cummings 1988, p. 460. I am grateful to Jackie Moy, the artist's daughter, for her assistance and information.
2. Reed 1950.
3. Fitzsimmons 1952a.
4. Gordon/Johnson 1955, no. 53 and pp. 49–54.
5. Kuchta/Seckler 1977, p. 93.
6. Among the books that the artist illustrated were Moy 1958; Bro 1965; Dolch 1964.
7. Saff/Sacilotto 1978, pp. 77–78, 85–86.

■

Malcolm Myers

Malcolm Hayne Myers was born in Chillicothe, Missouri, on June 19, 1917.[1] His youthful drawings and watercolors reflected many of the subjects and moods that would engage him as a mature artist.[2] He began his studies of art at Wichita State University. Although this school offered no printmaking courses, Myers engaged Bill Dickerson, a local artist, to teach him the processes of relief printmaking and lithography. After receiving a Bachelor of Fine Arts in 1939, he attended the University of Iowa, where he studied with Emil Ganso (cat. 36). Concentrating on watercolor, Myers received a Master of Fine Arts in 1941. He assisted in the workshop and served as instructor while completing his degree.

After serving in the armed forces during World War II, Myers returned to Iowa City, where he met Mauricio Lasansky (cat. 67), who introduced him to the mysteries of intaglio, which have fascinated him ever since. The stylistic and technical influence of Lasansky is apparent in Myer's prints of the late 1940s, such as *Perlandra* (1947; Helsell 11), a dark, deeply etched color intaglio, the imagery and Abstract Surrealism of which also parallel Lee Chesney's

Night Walk (cat. 64). However, the artist's own eccentricity and humor soon asserted themselves in bright, blithe images and technical improvisation.

In 1948 Myers developed a graphic arts program at the University of Minnesota in Minneapolis.[3] A third-generation descendant of Atelier 17, this renowned workshop introduced graphic arts to the upper Midwest. Two solo exhibitions in 1949, at the College of Saint Catherine in St. Paul and the Walker Art Center in Minneapolis, marked his arrival in Minnesota. In 1950 Myers created a series of prints based on the Black American folk ballad "John Henry," combining elaborate intaglio plates with silkscreened color (Helsell 16–20). He also began adding gold leaf to his prints, impressing the delicate foil into the sheet during the printing process.

In 1950 a Guggenheim Fellowship enabled Myers to go to Paris. He made his first color lithograph, *Gold Horns* (1951; Helsell 23) at the Atelier Desjobert, and he worked extensively at Atelier 17. A passionate devotion to jazz had already disposed him toward notions of the intuitive process in creation, and both technical and stylistic improvisation became progressively more manifest in his art. With a second Guggenheim Fellowship, he lived in Mexico City in 1954 and 1955.

In 1960 Myers became a tenured professor at the University of Minnesota, and he served as chairman of the art department from 1965 to 1970. His prints of the 1960s, included an extended series of satirical color intaglios representing anthropomorphized forest creatures, which characterized his mischievous humor. These large, facetious images have an intuitive, childlike quality that conceals their technical intricacy. For many years, Myers also found inspiration in the mythology of the American West.

A retrospective of Myers's prints was mounted at the University of Minnesota in 1982.[4] The artist still occasionally produces intaglios, but focuses chiefly on painting.

Notes
1. *Who's Who* 1986, p. 726.
2. Helsell 1982, p. 7.
3. Myers 1962.
4. Helsell 1982.

Reginald Neal

Reginald H. Neal was born in Leicester, England, on May 20, 1909. He immigrated to the United States with his family when he was about three years old, and settled in the Midwest. In 1929 he enrolled in the School of Fine Arts at Yale University; however it was Bradley University in Peoria, Illinois, that awarded him his bachelor's degree in 1932. After graduation, Neal taught art at Moline High School in Illinois. In 1934 the artist purchased an old lithography press and set out to learn the complex process himself. His earliest prints were landscape and genre scenes in the Regionalist style. These were among the first of his works to be widely exhibited, and in the course of his career the artist has participated in over fifty group exhibitions.

In 1936 Neal studied with Grant Wood at the State University of Iowa at Ames. Afterward, while working toward his master's degree at the University of Chicago, he pursued further research on lithography. His thesis on "The Technique of Lithography for Artists," completed in 1939, was accompanied by a portfolio of forty original prints. Neal became professor of art at Millikin University at Decatur, Illinois, in 1940. In the summer of 1941 he worked with Lawrence Barrett at the Colorado Springs Fine Arts Institute; he assisted the master printer in the production of editions for artists and students who were being introduced to lithography in a course taught by Adolf Dehn.[1] In 1946 and 1947 two of Neal's lithographs were included in the "five-dollar print series" published by Associated American Artists in New York, a noted vehicle for Regionalist printmaking.

From 1943 to 1948 Neal also served as director of the Decatur Art Center, where he had a one-man show in 1945, the first of over twenty solo exhibitions. In that year his prints were included in the widely circulated Artists for Victory exhibitions. In 1948 and 1949 he served as chairman of the Department of Fine Arts at the Memphis Academy of Arts in Tennessee. Neal's last Regionalist-style works were created at this time. These were chiefly landscapes representing the bucolic countryside, small towns, and changeable weather of the Midwest. He also often depicted grand Revivalist architecture, which he found on the campuses of heartland colleges. In 1951 the artist joined the faculty at the University of Mississippi in Oxford, where his arrival was celebrated by a solo exhibition of his paintings and prints.

Early in the 1950s Neal began to make abstract color lithographs. Beginning in 1954, these were regularly featured in the biennial exhibitions of contemporary color lithography at the Cincinnati Art Museum, organized by Gustave von Groschwitz. During his summer breaks, Neal taught lithography at the Escuela des Bellas Artes in San Miguel de Allende, Mexico, at Margaret Lowengrund's (cat. 37) graphic workshop at the Woodstock Art Association, and later at her Contemporaries Graphic Center in New York City.[2] Neal's first solo exhibition in New York was presented at the Salpeter Gallery in 1953.

After brief teaching appointments at the State University of New York in New Paltz, and at Southern Illinois University in Carbondale, Neal became chairman of the art department of Douglass College at Rutgers University, in New Brunswick, New Jersey, in 1955. There he founded a graduate program in fine arts. In the 1960s the artist worked in a coloristic Op Art style in his paintings and prints. In 1962 Neal worked at the Tamarind Lithography Workshop in Los Angeles, where for the first time he experienced the luxury of collaborating with another master printer.

In 1977 Neal retired from active teaching at Rutgers, and was named professor emeritus. A retrospective exhibition of his prints was organized by the university's Jane Voorhees Zimmerli Art Museum in 1986.[3] Another retrospective comprising paintings and prints created from 1958 to 1989, was organized by the New Jersey State Museum in Trenton.[4] Still quite active as a painter and printmaker, Neal currently lives in Lebanon, New Jersey.

Notes
1. Adams 1983, pp. 112–113.
2. Adams 1984, p. 21, note 18.
3. Boyer/Capasso 1986.
4. Naar 1989.

B.J.O. Nordfeldt

Bror Julius Olsson was born in Tullstrop, Skåne, Sweden on April 13, 1878.[1] In 1891 his family came to the United States and settled in Chicago. Olsson worked as a compositor and printer's devil for the Swedish-language newspaper *Hemlandet*, and enrolled at the Art Institute of Chicago in 1899. In 1900 he was in Paris, where he briefly attended the Académie Julian, and then painted on his own. He traveled to England to study the technique of color woodcut from Frank Morley Fletcher at the Oxford Extension College in Reading.[2] Olsson's prints of this period were closely based on *ukiyo-e* and *shin hanga* models, in their composition and palette, as well as their technique.

The artist returned to Chicago in 1903, where he produced color woodcuts, etchings, and occasionally painted portraits. At this time he began to use his mother's maiden name, Nordfeldt, to distinguish himself from another artist named Julius Olsson. Soon his career became centered on his activity as an etcher.[3] Nordfeldt worked as a journeyman etcher for *Harper's*, where he produced illustrations in the style of the Etching Revival, and he was sent to Europe in 1908 to illustrate travel articles.

After his return to Chicago in 1911, Nordfeldt's paintings became brighter and more painterly, reflecting the influences of Matisse. Solo exhibitions of his paintings and prints were presented at the Thurber Gallery, the Albert Roullier Gallery in Chicago, and the Milwaukee Art Society. Beginning in 1914 the artist went during the summer to Provincetown, Massachusetts. He helped found the Provincetown Players, and afterward to establish the Provincetown Theatre in New York City. In 1915 Nordfeldt originated the technical innovation that soon became the hallmark of printmaking in Provincetown: the single-block, white line color woodcut process.[4]

Nordfeldt's prints were prominent in the group exhibitions organized by artists who worked in Provincetown. One of his color woodcuts won a silver medal at the Panama-Pacific International Exposition in San Francisco in 1915. During World War I the artist became assistant district camofleur for the U.S. Shipping Board in San Francisco. While traveling through New Mexico, he decided to stay. His first paintings there represented Indian dances. His last series of etchings, made in the 1920s, represented New Mexico subjects. A solo exhibition of Nordfeldt's etchings and woodcuts was presented by the Smithsonian Institution in 1926.

In 1920 Nordfeldt had a one-man show at the Chicago Arts Club. In 1926 he won the bronze medal at the sesquicentennial exposition in Philadelphia, and the Logan Medal at the Art Institute of Chicago. In 1927 he won the first annual prize from the Brooklyn Society of Etchers, and the following year he won first prize from the Chicago Society of Etchers. In 1929 Nordfeldt had a one-man show at the Denver Art Museum.

After this time, the artist devoted himself to painting, in an Expressionist style. In the early 1930s Nordfeldt taught briefly at the University of Utah, the Minneapolis Institute of Art, and the Wichita Art Association. During this period, he also executed some lithographs for the PWAP. From 1941 to 1943 he taught briefly at the Minneapolis School of Art. Nordfeldt died of a heart attack on April 21, 1955, in Henderson, Texas.

Notes
1. Coke 1972.
2. On Fletcher, see Knowles 1970; LeJeune 1970.
3. Bruère 1915.
4. Flint 1983, pp. 15, 42–43.

Nathan Oliveira

Nathan Oliveira was born in Oakland, California, on December 9, 1928.[1] In 1947 he enrolled at the California College of Arts and Crafts, where he studied lithography under Raymond Bertram and Leon Goldin. Oliveira's style grew out of the Bay Area Figurative School of painting, and was especially influenced by David Park. In 1950 he studied with Max Beckmann at Mills College. Two years later Oliveira made his first etching, and he has returned to this technique periodically throughout his career.

After receiving his master's degree in 1952, Oliveira joined the faculty of the California College of Arts and Crafts. After military service he taught at the California School of Fine Arts in San Francisco, where he became head of the graphic arts department in 1956. That year he began to make prints on his own lithographic press. Oliveira's first solo exhibition was a show of lithographs, held at the Eric Locke Gallery in San Francisco in 1957, the year in which he won the Tiffany Foundation Grant for lithography.

With support from a Guggenheim Fellowship in 1958, Oliveira traveled to Europe, hoping to learn the techniques of the French master printers. However, he returned to San Francisco in 1959 without making a single lithograph. Soon he captured the Norman Wait Harris Bronze Medal for painting at the Chicago Art Institute. He continued to make his own prints until 1963, when he won an artist-fellowship at the Tamarind

Lithography Workshop in Los Angeles. In the following twelve years, Oliveira produced many editions in collaboration with master printers, including Irwin Hollander, Serge Lozingot, Ernest de Soto, Bohuslav Horak, Joseph Zirker, Kenjilo Nanao, and William Laws. In 1963 Oliveira began teaching at Stanford University. A retrospective exhibition of his works on paper was organized by the San Francisco Museum of Art in 1969.[2]

Around 1970, Oliveira's interest in his early lithographic techniques was rekindled. This, combined with a love for the works of Poe, and of Odilon Redon who made prints inspired by the author, impelled him to embark on the suite *To Edgar Allan Poe*. Although he was assisted in printing, Oliveira himself organized and published the series of forty prints, the apogee of his career as a lithographer.

Turning to the technique of monotype, Oliveira's first exhibition of these prints was held at the Smith-Anderson Gallery in 1971.[3] Two years later a retrospective exhibition of his paintings was mounted at the Oakland Museum.[4] In 1974 he won a grant from the National Endowment for the Arts for paintings and monotypes. The following year he worked at the Tamarind Institute in Albuquerque, producing five editions, his last lithographs. One of the etchings from Oliveira's series executed in 1979 at 3EP, Ltd., in Palo Alto, was adopted as the commemorative print for the inauguration of the Archives of American Art at the Smithsonian Institution.

In 1984 a major retrospective exhibition of Oliveira's work was held at the San Francisco Museum of Modern Art.[5] He continues to paint, produce monotypes, and teach at Stanford University, where he is head of the graphic arts department.

Notes
1. Ball 1980, pp. 24–25.
2. Humphrey 1969.
3. Baxter 1979.
4. Jones 1973.
5. Garver/Neubert 1984.

■

Margaret Jordan Patterson

Margaret Jordon Patterson was born in November, 1867 on a ship near the port of Surabaja, Java. As a child, she sailed around the world with her father and grandfather, who were both sea captains, yet she spent mostly her youth in Maine and Boston.[1] She taught art in the public schools of Portsmouth, New Hampshire, and Southbridge, Massachusetts. In 1895 Patterson attended the Pratt Institute, where she came under the influence of Arthur Wesley Dow (cat. 6).[2]

In 1899 Patterson made her first trip to Europe, and Continental subjects became predominant in her paintings. Over the next decade, she traveled abroad nearly every summer from Boston, where she taught in the public schools. She studied in Italy with Claudio Castellucho and in Paris with Ermenagildo Anglada-Camarasa. In about 1910 Patterson met Ethel Mars in Paris, and learned the color woodcut process from her.[3]

Patterson's first prints, created in 1911, translated her paintings of picturesque European views. Mars helped arrange Patterson's first solo exhibition of prints, at the Galerie Levesque in Paris in 1913; this was soon followed by a show at the Galerie Barbazanges. In 1914 another group of prints was shown in Boston at Herman Dudley Murphy's studio gallery, and soon after Patterson's first American solo exhibition of color woodcuts opened at the Louis Katz Gallery in New York.

At the beginning of World War I, the artist became director of the art department at the Dana Hall School for Girls in Wellesley, Massachusetts. She now found her subjects on outings in the New England countryside, especially on Cape Cod. She won an honorable mention for a color print at the Panama-Pacific International Exposition in San Francisco in 1915.

From 1922 to 1929 Patterson made annual trips to Italy, seeking out picturesque landscapes for her paintings and prints. In their bright, impressionistic palette, her plein-air color studies of this period reveal the influence of the French painter Albert Bésnard.[4] Gradually floral still-life prints began to supplant her landscape woodcuts. In the 1920s and 1930s, Patterson exhibited her work widely. Her color woodcuts received acclaim in the Second International Exhibition of Lithographs and Woodcuts in Chicago,[5] and in 1939 at the annual exhibition of the Philadelphia Watercolor Club, her entry was awarded a medal.

Patterson retired from teaching in 1940, but painting and printmaking continued to occupy her until the end of her life. The artist died in Boston on February 17, 1950.

Notes
1. The most comprehensive published biography of the artist is in Bakker/Coleman 1988, pp. 6–22. I am grateful to James Bakker for assistance with this biography.
2. Coleman observes (ibid., p. 7) that Patterson always identified Dow as her teacher, even though she was never enrolled in any of his classes at Pratt. Her extant student works are clearly related to the sort of compositional exercises that Dow set his students.
3. Bakker/Coleman 1988, p. 10, note 8.
4. Ibid., p. 21, note 14.
5. *Prints* 1931, p. 43.

■

Edward Penfield

Edward Penfield was born in Brooklyn, New York, on June 2, 1866.[1] When he was a child, his delicate health limited his public school attendance, and its seems that he spent much time drawing and reading alone.[2] Between 1889 and 1895 he studied intermittently at the Art Students League in New York. There, he was a pupil of George de-Forest Brush, who probably introduced the youth to French art and graphic design.

In 1891 Penfield became art editor at Harper and Brothers Publications in New York, which produced *Harper's* magazine and several other literary journals catering to a growing middle-class American market. The artist created his own illustrations, designed magazine layout, supervised other illustrators and graphic artists, and sometimes even monitored the printing of the magazine. Penfield briefly visited Paris in 1892, where he directly encountered the work of the French poster artists and printmakers. Their influence was apparent in Penfield's posters advertising *Harper's* magazine, which first appeared in 1893, beginning a long series that became the basis for his growing popular reputation. Soon he instituted monthly posters to advertise other Harper's magazines. In the ensuing art poster rage, Penfield was a celebrity. He wrote the introduction for *Posters in Miniature*, a collectors' anthology of recent designs represented in tiny reproductions.[3]

In April of 1897 the artist married Jennie Judd Walker, the daughter of a prominent Civil War veteran and railroad executive, Major Charles A. Walker. The authoritative character of his father-in-law became an important factor in Penfield's life. Major Walker accompanied the newlyweds on their honeymoon to Europe.[4] Later the artist and his family often lived in Walker's grand house in Pelham Manor, New York, where Penfield maintained a large upstairs studio.

Penfield's last poster for *Harper's* was issued in 1899, although he remained art director for the publisher until 1901. His popular reputation assured his success as a free-lance artist after leaving Harper's. The artist eventually set up a successful commercial studio on West 23rd Street in New York. His illustrations and designs regularly appeared in an array of magazines, including *Scribner's* and *Harper's*. Penfield also continued his output of posters and produced a series of calendars, published by R. H. Russell.

While at Harper's, Penfield had begun to produce book illustrations for the work of several authors, including John Kendrick Bangs.[5] Now he illustrated several of his own children's books. In contrast to his advertising imagery, Penfield's book illustrations depicted a greater range of emotion and character. The artist chronicled his travels in Europe in drawings and prose, which were later transformed into the book *Holland Sketches*, published in 1907. Many of the illustrations depicted the Dutch in their native costumes, posed in picturesque settings. In a sequel, *Spanish Sketches*, which followed in 1911, Penfield combined a livelier narrative with more varied and colorful illustrations.[6]

Beginning in 1908 and for over a decade to follow, the Beck Engraving Company of New York and the Franklin Printing Company of Philadelphia were Penfield's most important clients, for whom he designed promotional posters, calendars, and typography. Until about 1915 the artist frequently executed magazine covers, especially for *Collier's*, *Saturday Evening Post*, *Life*, and *Ladies' Home Journal*. No longer straightforward color lithographs, these illustrations were now photomechanically reproduced from Penfield's watercolors, utilizing the halftone process.

In 1915 the artist began teaching courses in commercial draftsmanship, poster design, and lettering at the Art Students League in New York. He continued to offer these classes intermittently until 1921, when he collaborated on a class on lettering with the famous typographer and type designer Frederic W. Goudy. During World War I, Penfield designed posters encouraging enlistment and home-front vigilance for the federal Division of Pictorial Publicity. From 1921 to 1923 the artist served as president of the Society of Illustrators in New York. Penfield died in Beacon, New York, on February 8, 1925.

Notes

1. Gibson 1984; Kiehl 1987, pp. 138–162, 190.
2. Rowland 1958.
3. Pollard 1896.
4. Gibson 1984, p. 14. The *Harper's* poster for July 1897 depicts Mrs. Penfield and her father aboard ship.
5. Bangs 1899a and b.
6. Penfield 1907 and 1911.

■

Gabor Peterdi

Born in Budapest on September 17, 1915, Gabor Peterdi began his studies at the Hungarian Academy. His first solo exhibition was mounted at the Ernst Museum when he was just fifteen years old.[1] In 1930 Peterdi won the Prix de Rome for painting and continued his studies at the Academia delle Belle Arti. The following year he went to Paris to attend the Académie Julian and the Académie Scandinavien. There, the young artist met Szenes and Maria Helena Vieira da Silva, and was thrust into the avant-garde.

Peterdi joined Atelier 17 in Paris in 1933, and through Stanley William Hayter (cat. 60) he became enchanted with the burin and the plate. Gradually developing an intimacy with engraving, he explored every phase of the technique. Notable among Peterdi's early engravings is the series *Black Bull*, published in 1939 (Johnson 15), expressive, semi-abstract caprices drawn from nature and from the artist's experience.

In 1939 Peterdi emigrated to the United States. Later that year, his first American one-man exhibition of paintings opened at the Julien Levy Gallery in New York. Seven years later, having served in the army, Peterdi resumed his printmaking career at Atelier 17 in New York. He found working with the copperplate cathartic after his military experiences. His first prints reflected the horrors and destruction of war, but he soon began representing natural awakenings and biblical beginnings in such works as *Adam and Eve* (Johnson 35). At this time, the artist created his first color intaglio, *Sign of the Lobster* (Johnson 29), which incorporated eight stenciled colors and an etched and engraved key plate. Here Surrealism resurfaced in a distinctive, personal response to Hayter and Miró.

Maintaining his activity at Atelier 17, Peterdi began teaching at the Brooklyn Museum in 1948, organizing the graphic arts workshop there. His paintings and prints of this period were dominated by his own gestural imagery, the result of exposure to Abstract Expressionism. Peterdi's creative approach to intaglio continued to expand as he invented new techniques and printed from ever-larger plates. In 1952 he became an associate professor of art at Hunter College, where he taught until 1959. In 1953 he also began teaching at the Yale-Norfolk summer school, and he joined the art faculty of Yale University as a visiting professor, gaining a full-time appointment in 1960. Today Peterdi sustains a close association with Yale through his position as professor emeritus.

In 1959 Peterdi's book *Printmaking Methods Old and New* was published. It remains a standard technical reference for both printmaking students and professionals.[2] Peterdi has also exerted his influence on American printmaking in well over a hundred solo exhibitions. Currently living in Rowayton, Connecticut, the artist continues to work and exhibit widely.

Notes

1. The most complete biography of the artist is provided by Johnson 1970. For the artist's personal reminiscences, see Peterdi 1963.
2. Peterdi 1959a.

■

Michael Ponce de León

Born in Miami, Florida, on July 4, 1922, Michael Ponce de León is a direct descendant of the Spanish explorer who discovered Florida in the sixteenth century.[1] He grew up in Mexico and first studied art at the University of Mexico. In New York in the late 1940s, he studied at the National Academy of Design, and the Art Students League with Harry Sternberg and Will Barnet (cats. 35, 69). After World War II, Ponce de León worked as a syndicated cartoonist, producing a widely published series called *Imp-ulses*. In 1951 he resumed his concentrated study of printmaking under Gabor Peterdi (cat. 79) at the School of the Brooklyn Museum, and two years later he worked with Margaret Lowengrund (cat. 37) at the Contemporaries Workshop, which evolved into the Pratt Graphics Center.

Working at Pratt in the 1950s as a master printer, Ponce de León collaborated with many artists to produce editions of both lithographs and intaglio prints. Tiffany Fellowships in 1953 and 1955 enabled the artist to travel widely and experiment with style and technique. He concentrated on lithography, combining collage with planographic printing techniques. From experiments with transferring the textures of found objects onto lithographic plates, Ponce de León was drawn to photoengraving. He combined printed typography and photographic reproductions in visually complex montage prints with many levels of meaning. He also became intrigued with molded, three-dimensional prints suggested by the experimental embossings made from metal and plaster at Atelier 17.[2]

With the support of Fulbright Fellowships in 1956 and 1957, Ponce de León visited Rolf Nesch in Norway. This artist made metal collagraph printing plates. Cutting and shaping wires and metal fragments, Nesch soldered them to the surface of his plates, engraving, punching, or distressing the uneven surfaces, and then printing from the resultant bas-relief sculpture. Ponce de León made this technique his own by incorporating discarded metal objects. When he became enthralled by an object that was neither metal nor printable, he made a metal casting and welded this onto his collagraphic plate.

Ponce de León taught in New York at Hunter College and the Pratt Graphics Center from 1959 to 1966. In 1977 he taught at Columbia University and in the following year at the Art Students League. In the 1960s he traveled to Europe and Asia in cultural exchanges sponsored by the Smithsonian Institution and the U.S. Department of State, lecturing and leading innovative printmaking workshops.

In the mid-1960s Ponce de León began to experiment with cast paper pulp, using very different means to achieve goals similar to those he had in making his collagraphs. These deeply embossed, vividly colored editions are exemplified by the extraordinary *Succubus* of 1967.[3] The artist lives in New York City, and continues to teach, work, and exhibit.

Notes

1. Cochrane 1974 and 1975; *Who's Who* 1986, p. 806.
2. Hayter 1949a, pp. 146–154.
3. Johnson 1980, p. 106.

Maurice Brazil Prendergast

Maurice Brazil Prendergast was born on October 10, 1859, in St. John's, Newfoundland, Canada, where his Irish-born father was the proprietor of a trading post.[1] When the business failed in 1860, the family moved to Boston, Mrs. Prendergast's hometown.

After completing the eighth grade Maurice began working. Soon he was an apprentice in a commercial art firm, where he painted show cards and learned the fundamentals of illustration and graphic design. In Paris in 1891, he studied at the Academie Colarossi under Gustave Courtois, and at the Académie Julian with Jean Paul Laurens, Joseph-Paul Blanc, and Benjamin Constant. Prendergast became friends with the Canadian painter James Wilson Morrice, who introduced him to the city, his favorite artists, and his own manner of working. In the cafés of Montparnasse, they gathered with an international circle of artist friends. At this time Prendergast created his first monotypes.

Several formative influences are apparent in Prendergast's art in the early 1890s. The stylish elegance of Whistler (cat. 2) was combined with the decorative poise of Japanese prints.[2] However, most prominent was the influence of the Nabis, especially the painter-printmakers Pierre Bonnard and Edouard Vuillard.[3]

Prendergast returned to Boston in 1894 and was able to support himself by his art. He illustrated several books for the publisher Joseph Knight. At this time he began his well-known *Boston Sketchbooks* of watercolors.[4] Prendergast returned to Europe six more times over the next fifteen years. In the summer of 1898, he worked mostly in Venice, making lyrical watercolors and prints, which contributed to the artist's burgeoning reputation. Soon after the turn of the century, Prendergast abandoned the medium of monotype and turned to oil painting.

In 1914 Prendergast moved to New York. The manner of oil painting that occupied his final decade is often called his "tapestry style." The artist now freely applied paint to the canvas in heavy layers of impasto. Colors were vivid and opaque, the brush strokes terse and rhythmic. Prendergast's late style also affected his watercolors which became broader and more loosely painted.

Although deteriorating health curtailed Prendergast's artistic activities, his reputation continued to grow in the 1910s. His last solo exhibition was mounted in 1922, and his work was honored at the Corcoran Gallery in Washington, D.C., in 1923. The artist died in New York on February 4, 1924.

Notes

1. Some discrepancies among biographical details are found in monographic studies of Prendergast. Although Green (1976) gives more details, Langdale (1984) reflects most accurately the current scholarship and chronology of the artist.
2. Whistler, in turn, unwittingly admired Prendergast's work. See Langdale 1984, p. 12.
3. Ibid., pp. 28–30.
4. MFA 1960; Szabo 1987.

Augusta Payne Rathbone

Augusta Payne Rathbone was born on December 30, 1987, in Berkeley, California, where she was raised by

"traveling aunts and a feminist-inclined father."[1] She enrolled at the University of California at Berkeley, intending to major in French, but because she was already fluent in the language she had to select another field and serendipitously chose art. After her graduation in 1920, she went to Paris to live with relatives and attended the Académie de la Grande Chaumière, where she studied with Claudio Castellucho and Lucien Simon. Rathbone set up a painting studio in Reid Hall, the center for expatriot Americans in Paris. In 1927 she learned etching and aquatint from Norah Hamilton, an artist from Chicago who also had a studio there. However, for many years her intaglios were printed by professional craftsmen in Paris.

Rathbone first exhibited her paintings and prints at the Paris Salon in 1930. Though her work was shown regularly at the Galerie Jean Charpentier and the Galerie Ecalle in Paris, her first solo exhibition was at the Elder Gallery in San Francisco in 1930.

Late in the 1930s Rathbone was in the south of France, painting and etching views of the Côte d'Azur. She collaborated on the travel book *French Riviera Villages*, which was illustrated with reproductions of her color intaglios.[2] In San Francisco during the war, she continued to paint and learned intaglio printing techniques. Returning to France fortified with a solid knowledge and experience of technique, she could not find a collaborator in Paris, so she set up her own press on the Riviera.[3]

A solo exhibition of Rathbone's work was mounted at the San Francisco Museum of Art in 1940. About that time, she made etched fashion portraits under commission from City of Paris, a department store in San Francisco. In 1944 and 1945 she was the head of Tyler House, a dormitory at Smith College in Northampton, Massachusetts, and the following year she supervised at Morrow House. She made a few color aquatints representing buildings at the college. Although Rathbone returned often to San

Francisco to care for her convalescent father, she traveled frequently to New York and Paris in continued pursuit of her artistic career.

The artist was very active in the 1950s. She exhibited at the National Arts Club in New York, the Oakland Museum, the De Young Museum, and the California State Library in San Francisco. As financial success eluded Rathbone, her exhibition activities waned. In the 1970s and 1980s, however, her prints enjoyed a revival, with exhibitions in California and Maryland, and she was involved in collaborative printmaking projects well into her eighties.[4] Although she has ceased to work, Rathbone still lives in northern California.

Notes

1. Hughes, pp. 378–379; *Who's Who* 1962, p. 498; Brokl 1984, pp. 6–7.
2. Rathbone/Thompson 1938; see also *New York Times* 1938.
3. On her return, Rathbone found that the shop of her printer M. Porcabeuf had been sold to M. Leblanc—seemingly Charles Leblanc, proprietor of Leblanc et Trautmann, at 26, rue des Fossés-Saint-Jacques—who could not satisfy the artist.
4. Rathbone had successful exhibition at Gallery 261 in Palo Alto, California; the Bethesda Gallery in Maryland; and the Annex Galleries in Santa Rosa, California. See Shaw-Eagle 1984.

Louis John Rhead

Louis John Rhead was born on November 6, 1857, in Etruria, Staffordshire, the English village in which the famous pottery factory founded by Josiah Wedgwood had been in operation for a century.[1] He studied in London with Edward J. Poynter and Alphonse Legros at the National Art Training School in South Kensington. There he was instructed in the style of the English Arts and Crafts movement, and learned its philosophical foundations. In 1883 Rhead came to the United States to become an illustrator and then art director for the publisher D. Appleton and Company in New York. In this position, he created illustrations and organized the layout of *Appleton's* magazine. He was also active as a free-lance designer, creating designs for a range of applied arts, from patterns for needlework and ceramic decoration published in women's magazines to decorative book bindings. At this time, Rhead's style derived from such Aesthetic Movement artists as Walter Crane and William Morris.

From 1891 to 1894 Rhead lived in England and in France. He studied French posters closely, and fell deeply under the influence of the Swiss-born poster artist Eugène Grasset. He also encountered *japonisme*, which he gradually and selectively incorporated into his own style.

Upon his return to New York in 1894, the artist found many commissions for posters from the magazines *St. Nicholas*, *Century*, *Harper's*, the *New York Sun*, and *Scribner's*, and for the Boston publishers Louis Prang & Company. Rhead's experience and reputation in England also placed him in demand as a designer for advertising, which was unusual at this time for an independent artist in the United States. He designed advertisements and posters for Lundborg Perfumes, Pearline Washing Powder, Packer's Soap, and other products.

In 1895 a solo exhibition of Rhead's posters was held at the Wunderlich Gallery in New York.[2] Soon afterward, his work won a gold medal at the International Exhibition of Posters in Boston. Thus the artist's reputation grew quickly, and along with Edward Penfield (cat. 4), he became a prominent figure in the American art poster rage. Rhead's tall reputation and accompanying command of expensive fees may be reflected in the fact that the artist's work appeared primarily in the most lavish holiday editions of magazines. A solo exhibition of Rhead's posters was mounted in London in 1896, and his triumph was a one-man show at the Salon des Cent in Paris in 1897. Prolific and ambitious, Rhead pushed

the limits of his art, designing a poster the size of a billboard for *Cassel's* magazine, and producing a *Poster Calendar* for 1897, published by Prang in Boston.

Like John Ruskin and William Morris, Rhead believed that all art—particularly widely distributed and visible applied and commercial art—exerted profound moral influences upon its viewers. He lectured on the moral functions of all aspects of design. His writings also included criticisms of the styles of other poster artists; he condemned Jules Chéret for gratuitous sensuality, and Will Bradley for decorative superficiality.[3] Rhead's certainty about the importance of his art was reflected in his declaration that the poster was the harbinger of a new artistic Renaissance.[4]

After 1900 the artist concentrated more upon book illustration. He illustrated Harper's juvenile classics, editions of *Robin Hood*, *Grimm's Fairy Tales*, and several books on angling.[5] Rhead died in Amityville, New York, on July 29, 1926.

Notes
1. Falk, p. 514; White 1896.
2. Wunderlich 1895.
3. Rhead 1895.
4. Wong 1974, p. 12.
5. Scholz 1985.

■

William Seltzer Rice

William Seltzer Rice was born on June 23, 1873, in Manheim, Pennsylvania, where his father where his father worked as a painter and decorator of carriages.[1] His artistic inclinations were recognized at an early age, and he took lessons from itinerant artists. In 1893 he received a scholarship to the Pennsylvania School of Industrial Art in Philadelphia. Afterward, he was the student of Howard Pyle at the Drexel Institute. Rice worked as an artist on the staff of the *Philadelphia Times* until 1901, when he moved to California to become supervisor of art

for the Stockton Public Schools. In 1910 he became head of the art department at Alameda High School.

Rice had experimented with relief printmaking, and he became captivated by the technique after his introduction to traditional Japanese prints at the Panama-Pacific International Exposition in San Francisco in 1915. The influence of *ukiyo-e* prints is strong in his early work, but the aesthetic of the Arts and Crafts movement gradually came to dominate as his technique became simpler and more direct. The designs for the artist's block prints came from his own watercolors or pastel drawings, which were always done on site: "He perched on the rocks above the ocean with a black umbrella overhead or sat astride a small campstool which he had toted up a mountain trail."[2] The first solo exhibition of his prints was mounted at the California Palace of Fine Arts, in San Francisco in 1917.

In 1919 Rice began teaching at Fremont High School in Oakland, and twelve of his prints were featured in the important exhibition of color woodcuts at the Detroit Institute of Arts. He taught a simplified version of his block-printing process to his students, and this technique, as well as the projects that he developed, became the basis for his book *Block Printing in Schools*.[3] In the 1920s Rice frequently taught summer sessions at the California College of Arts and Crafts. He conducted printmaking classes for half the day and then took classes himself in the afternoon. This study led to a Bachelor of Fine Arts degree, granted to Rice in 1929. In 1930 he was art instructor at the Castlemont High School in Oakland. Two years later he began a decade of teaching in the extension programs at the University of California.

In 1933 six of Rice's woodcuts were featured in the important exhibition of color prints at the Brooklyn Museum, and in 1939 his prints were seen at the Golden Gate International Exposition and the New York World's Fair. His influential instructional manual *Block Prints—How to Make Them* was published in 1941 and became quite popular in the next decade.[4] In 1945 the Smithsonian Institution presented a one-man show of his woodcuts.

In the course of his career, Rice produced more than three hundred color woodcuts and linocuts. He died in Oakland, California, on August 27, 1963.

Notes
1. *Who's Who* 1962, p. 509; Hughes, p. 385; Falk, p. 514. I am grateful to Roberta Rice Treseder, the artist's daughter, who contributed much information to this study.
2. Annex 1984, p. 3.
3. Rice 1929.
4. Rice 1941.

■

Thomas Arthur Robertson

Born in Little Rock, Arkansas, on July 19, 1911, Thomas Arthur Robertson was the son of an attorney.[1] Although his father, the co-owner of the Arkansas Law School, insisted that his son study there, after graduating Robertson enrolled at the Adrian Brewer School of Art in Little Rock, where his studies were supported by scholarships. He probably first learned about printmaking from the illustrator and woodcut artist Howard Simon.

In 1933, along with painter Howard Bragg and author Arthur Halliburton, Robertson helped found the Little Rock Art League and served as its first president. Modeled after the Art Students League in New York, this nonprofit organization offered art instruction and mounted annual exhibitions. Robertson won first prize in the spring exhibition of the Fine Arts Club of Arkansas in 1935, and his award-winning painting *Summer Interlude* hung in the annual exhibition of the Pennsylvania Academy of Fine Arts.

Robertson moved to New Orleans in 1935 to study with Paul Ninas. There he established himself as a portraitist, and became an active member of the New Orleans Art League.[2] Robertson's first one-man show was held at the Delgado Museum in 1937, an event sponsored by the Art Association of New Orleans.

In 1937 Robertson married and returned to Little Rock, but he long maintained his connections with New Orleans. In 1940 the artist became an instructor of art at Little Rock Junior College. His second solo exhibition at the Delgado Museum that year, sponsored by the New Orleans Art League, consisted solely of abstract paintings. In 1942 Robertson began working as a civil service draftsman in the office of the Army Corps of Engineers in Little Rock. For a time, he sustained his artistic activity by concentrating on smaller and less demanding watercolor and tempera paintings on paper. In 1945 an exhibition of twenty of his nonobjective watercolors was mounted at the Addison Gallery in Andover, Massachusetts.[3] Along with his serigraphs, these comprised a one-man exhibition at the Little Rock Public Library later that year.[4]

In about 1946 Robertson was transferred to the Corps of Graves Registration Command in Paris. It seems that he should have flourished there, but mysteriously he ceased painting and turned away from art at this time. Robertson returned to the United States in 1957, and eventually settled in California. There he seems to have continued working for the Corps of Engineers, until his retirement shortly after 1960. He lived the remainder of his life in the small town of Albion in northern California, where he died on May 25, 1976.

Notes
1. *Who's Who* 1940, p. 542; Falk, p. 23.
2. Cooper 1935; Hutson 1937. See also the file at the Historic New Orleans Collection
3. One of these watercolors, *Composition No. 32*, was acquired at this time by the Addison Gallery (accession no. 1945.11).
4. *Arkansas Gazette* 1945; Fletcher 1945.

Theodore Roszak

Theodore Roszak was born on May 1, 1907, in Poznán, Poland.[1] When he was two years old, Roszak's family immigrated to the United States and settled in Chicago. There, he grew up in a home full of music and art. In 1919 Roszak became a U.S. citizen.

In 1923 Roszak began taking evening classes at the School of the Art Institute of Chicago. After his high school graduation in 1925 he became a favored full-time student at the Art Institute, where he was the pupil of John W. Norton and Boris Anisfeldt. In 1925–26 he studied at the Art Students League in New York with Charles Hawthorne, and had private lessons from George Luks.[2] The youth also attended philosophy lectures at Columbia University.

Returning to the Art Institute school in 1927, Roszak also became a part-time instructor of drawing and lithography. His first exhibition was a show of lithographs at the Allerton House Gallery in Chicago in 1928. At this time he worked in a personal, Symbolist-influenced, figurative style, enlivened by an expressive Eastern European flavor. After graduation in 1928, an American Traveling Fellowship enabled Roszak to go to New York City, where he worked as an assistant to the master lithographer George Miller, and to Woodstock, New York, where he studied lithography with Bolton Brown. Returning to Chicago in the fall of 1929, Roszak began to teach full-time. A few months later, Bolton Brown visited the Art Institute school to offer a master class in lithography.

In 1929 Roszak won the Anna Louise Raymond Fellowship from the Art Institute, allowing him to spend fifteen months abroad. Only in Europe did the artist become aware of modernism. After several weeks of travel, he lived and worked in Prague for nine months and in Paris for six months more. At this time the influence of Synthetic Cubism became apparent in his work.

Roszak married soon after his return to New York in 1931. A Tiffany Fellowship enabled him to work in relative financial freedom. In 1932 Roszak's work was included in the first Biennial of the Whitney Museum of American Art; his entry in the second Whitney Biennial was purchased for the museum's permanent collection. Working in Staten Island, New York, the artist tried out new materials, processes, and styles. He also began to work in sculpture, and by 1934, Roszak had outfitted his own workshop and was at work on metal constructions. In his early sculpture, the artist combined geometric forms with abstract mechanistic details, reflecting his growing interest in Constructivism and in the machine aesthetic of the Bauhaus. In 1935 the Roerich Museum in New York organized Roszak's first retrospective exhibition.[3]

After 1937 the artist moved gradually away from narrative painting and focused more on sculpture. In 1938 Roszak met László Moholy-Nagy and became an instructor in composition and design at the Design Laboratory in New York, Moholy-Nagy's school conceived to the perpetuate Bauhaus design and teaching principles. Roszak also collaborated with Norman Bel Geddes on the Futurama diorama at the General Motors pavilion for the New York World's Fair in 1939.

During World War II, Roszak taught aircraft mechanics and built airplanes at the Brewster Aircraft Corporation in New York. He taught at Sarah Lawrence College from 1941 until 1956. After 1945 his style progressed away from Constructivism and returned to the symbolic content and organic imagery of his earlier work. He rendered expressive, biomorphic forms in welded steel, brazed alloys, and cast bronze.

In 1953 Roszak was commissioned to design the bell tower for Eero Saarinen's chapel at Massachusetts Institute of Technology. In 1956 he won a gold medal for sculpture at the Pennsylvania Academy of Fine Arts. In that year, a circulating retrospective exhibition of Roszak's work was organized by the Whitney Museum of American Art.[4] Another circulating show was organized by the Boston Institute of Contemporary Art in 1959, and in 1960 Roszak had a solo exhibition at the Venice Biennale. The artist taught at Columbia University from 1970 to 1972. Late in his life, he returned to lithography, producing large, dramatic prints related to his biomorphic sculptures. Theodore Roszak died in New York on September 3, 1981.

Notes
1. Cummings 1971, p. 280.
2. Dreishpoon 1989, p. 70, note 5.
3. Roerich 1935.
4. Arnason 1956.

Rudolph Ruzicka

The son of a tailor, Rudolph Ruzicka was born on June 27, 1883, in the village of Kourim, in central Bohemia.[1] His family came to Chicago in 1894. In only three years of public school he reached the seventh grade-level, while also attending Saturday drawing classes at Hull House. At the age of fourteen he left school and worked at the Franklin Engraving Company, and other commercial printing shops and design studios.

In 1903 Ruzicka moved to New York and took a job at the American Banknote Company. Afterward, he worked as a free-lance commercial artist. Ruzicka began to make reproductive prints in the manner of the nineteenth-century "new school" of American wood engravers. He experimented with style and technique, cutting in planks of wood and rubber and making monochromatic and multicolor prints.

In about 1905 Ruzicka began working at the advertising agency of Calkins & Holden, where he was first exposed to typography. Under the spell of Auguste Lepére, Ruzicka then began making wood engravings. In 1908 he went to London where he met Walter Sickert and Lucien Pissarro; at the British Museum he studied the history of color in prints. He also traveled in Europe. Back in New York in 1910 he received his first major commission for four illustrations from the business magazine *System*.

Ruzicka was hired by Daniel Berkely Updike, the typographer, printer, and historian, to create wood-engraved views of Boston landmarks as "keepsakes" for Updike's Merrymount

Press.[2] Ruzicka sent six prints to the Société de la Gravure Bois Originale for their first exhibition in Paris in 1912. The prestigious Grolier Club of bibliophiles commissioned him to represent New York City in a series of wood engravings to be compiled in an elegant book.[3]

In 1916 the artist moved to Dobbs Ferry, New York, where he eventually set up a workshop in his home. He produced a series of wood engravings representing landmarks of Newark, New Jersey, and the first solo exhibition of Ruzicka's prints was mounted in 1917 at the Newark Public Library.[4]

Ruzicka's many projects of the 1930s included a series of prints of the United States Military Academy and drawings of the gardens at Dumbarton Oaks. The American Institute of Graphic Arts awarded its gold medal to Ruzicka in 1935, and a print retrospective was mounted at the Architectural League in New York.[5] Late in the decade he was engaged by the Mergenthaler Linotype Company to create the *Fairfield* typeface, the first of his three type designs.[6]

The artist concentrated on book and commercial projects during the 1940s, undertaking major commissions for the *Encyclopaedia Britannica* and *Reader's Digest*. Late in the decade he moved to the Boston area.

In the 1950s Ruzicka was retained by Charles Scribner and Company. He worked increasingly for libraries, colleges, and universities during this period, designing diplomas and commemorative medals. In 1962 he moved from Boston to Hanover, New Hampshire.

The final exhibition of Ruzicka's work during his lifetime was held at the Century Association in New York in 1977. He died quietly in Hanover on July 10, 1978.

Notes
1. Lathem 1986.
2. Updike 1917 and 1922.
3. Ruzicka 1915. Many of his subsequent book illustration projects are listed in Bolton 1938; see also Lathem 1986, index.
4. Ruzicka 1917.
5. Kent 1935; Hofer 1935.
6. Lathem 1986, pp. 110, 114–115.

■
Anne Ryan

Anne Ryan was born into a prosperous Irish Catholic family in Hoboken, New Jersey, on July 28, 1888.[1] In 1909 she studied literature at St. Elizabeth's College, but left school in her junior year to get married. Though she assumed the role of wife and mother, her writing aspirations never waned. After her turbulent marriage ended, Ryan returned to writing, and her book of poetry, *Lost Hills*, was published in 1925.[2]

In 1931 Ryan moved to Majorca; there she worked on a novel, supporting herself with essays and articles for American magazines. Traveling to Spain and Paris she was first exposed to European modernism and the spectrum of contemporary art. Back in New York in 1933 she began to explore the plastic arts. In 1938, under encouragement from her neighbors Hans Hoffman (cat. 73) and Tony Smith, she began to paint.

Ryan joined Atelier 17 in 1941 and began to make prints. Stanley William Hayter's (cat. 60) devotion to Abstract Surrealism and his technical skills were revelatory to her. Her work at Atelier 17 was typical for the workshop at this time— automatist abstractions, imbued with Hayter's stylistic influence, rendered in soft-ground etching and aquatint, with deeply cut burin lines. Notable among her intaglios are two series of small round prints representing ancient mythological figures transformed into constellations.

The artist's first solo exhibition, mounted at the Marquis Gallery in New York in 1943, included paintings and intaglio prints.[3] The canvases were primarily still lifes, and critics commented on the surfaces of these works, which she varied by mixing cement and sand with her oil paint.

Ryan learned the techniques of color woodcut from Louis Schanker (cat. 41) in 1945. While her first woodcuts resembled his work in style and technique, she quickly gravitated to the same effects of texture and color of her paintings. Her color woodcuts quickly eclipsed her intaglio prints.

The artist exhibited with VANGUARD, a group of experimental printmakers that included Schanker and Werner Drewes (cat. 55).[4] Her solo exhibition at the Marquis Gallery in 1946 comprised twenty-two color woodcuts, including modernist still lifes, figurative pieces and abstractions.[5] In 1948 Ryan's color woodcut *In A Room* won a purchase award at the Second Annual Print National Exhibition at the Brooklyn Museum.

That same year Ryan became enthralled by Kurt Schwitters's collages. She began experimenting with her own collages made of found papers, at first preferring wrinkled wrappers and newspapers printed with interesting or foreign type, and then gravitating to unmarked papers, which she chose for the colors and varied textures.[6]

In her last six years, Ryan may have produced over four hundred miniature collages. The last exhibition during her lifetime, comprised of paintings and small collages, was mounted at the Betty Parsons Gallery in New York.[7] Ryan died on April 18, 1954, in Morristown, New Jersey.

Notes
1. *Who's Who* 1953, p. 365.
2. Ryan 1925.
3. Roswell 1943.
4. Brooklyn 1946.
5. Lansford 1946.
6. A major exhibition of Ryan's collages was held at the Brooklyn Museum in 1974; see Faunce 1974.
7. Guest 1954.

■
Louis Schanker

Born in New York on July 20, 1903, Louis Schanker left school as a teenager to join the circus.[1] Two years later, he labored on farms, on the Erie Railroad, on a steamship, and crisscrossed the country on the railroad as a hobo. Back in New York by 1920, Shanker began four years of part-time studies at Cooper Union and the Education Alliance. In 1925 he also took classes at the Art Students League.[2]

Schanker's first prints were Social Realist–style etchings, made when he was a student. A handful of experimental lithographs, printed in 1928, reflect the artist's inclinations to modernism and the work of the School of Paris. He painted and traveled in Europe in 1931.

His first solo exhibition was mounted at the Contemporary Art Gallery in New York in 1933.[3] Another one-man show, at the New School for Social Research in 1934, chiefly included paintings made in Spain.

Schanker became a member of the WPA mural division, and in 1934 began a series of wall panels for Neponsit Bay Hospital on Long Island.[4] Other important projects were to follow, including murals for the lobby of radio station WNYC and at the New York World's Fair in 1939. In 1935 Schanker was one of the "Ten Whitney Dissenters;"[5] He was also a founding member of the American Abstract Artists group.

In 1935 the artist made his first woodcut, *Trio* (Brooklyn 7), to which he added seven colors printed from as many blocks. In developing his own style and technique in this unfamiliar medium, he studied German Expressionist and traditional Japanese woodblock prints.

By mid-1938 Schanker was employed by the New York City WPA/FAP graphic arts division. When the workshop moved, he took over as supervisor of color block printing, and he remained in the division until 1941.[6] In 1943 a solo exhibition of the artist's color woodcuts was mounted at the Brooklyn Museum.[7] He began teaching printmaking courses at the New School for Social Research. His *Abstract Landscape, No. 1* (Brooklyn 92) was awarded a purchase prize at the Brooklyn Museum's first Print National Exhibition in 1947. The artist organized Studio 74 at the New School, his own experimental workshop, modeled after Atelier 17.

Schanker taught briefly at the School of the Brooklyn Museum in the late 1940s, and beginning in 1949 at Bard College. As a teacher, he attracted many outstanding students, including Anne Ryan (cat. 65) and Carol Summers (cat. 92). Schanker was an active member of the Graphic Circle, and the 14 Painter-Printmakers group.[8] Many of his prints of the 1950s focused on abstract circular forms and the expression of the sense of revolution. In mid-decade, Schanker developed his own variation of the plaster relief print technique.[9]

In the 1960s and 1970s Schanker expanded his activities as a sculptor, and experimented with relief prints from plastic plates. A major retrospective exhibition of his prints was organized by the Brooklyn Museum in 1974.[10]

The last solo exhibition during the artist's lifetime featured paintings from the 1930s and 1940s.[11] Schanker died in New York on May 7, 1981.

Notes

1. See Schanker/Nathan 1938.
2. *Who's Who* 1980, p. 658; Cummings 1971, p. 286.
3. *Art Digest* 1933.
4. Schanker/Nathan 1938, p. 16.
5. Larsen 1983, pp. 20–21.
6. Kainen 1972, p. 160.
7. Johnson 1943.
8. *Art News* 1947; Gordon/Johnson 1955, nos. 61–66.
9. Johnson 1956, pp. 37–38; Johnson 1980, p. 153, 155.
10. Johnson/Miller 1974.
11. Yeh 1981.

■

Karl Schrag

Karl Schrag was born in Karlsruhe, Germany, on December 12, 1912.[1] Upon graduation from the Humanistisches Gymnasium in 1930, he attended art school in Geneva. Later in Paris, he studied at the Ecole Nationale Supérieure des Beaux–Arts with Lucien Simon, the Académie Ranson, and the Académie de la Grande Chaumière with Roger Bissière. Schrag's first solo exhibition was held at the Galerie Arenberg in Brussels in 1938.

At the Art Students League in New York in 1938, he learned etching from Harry Sternberg (cat. 35). The following year, Schrag's work was included in the annual exhibition of the Society of American Etchers, and in 1942 he showed a print in the annual exhibition at the Whitney Museum. His intaglios of this period represent dramatic, often tragic images in a poignant Social Realist style.

After having met Stanley William Hayter (cat. 60) in 1944, Schrag joined Atelier 17 in 1945, and this had a profound influence on his art. The discipline of constant work on intaglio plates drew Schrag toward abstraction, and helped develop and refine his faculty for making decisions about design. His first one-man show in the United States was presented in 1945 at the Smithsonian Institution.[2]

Schrag began to settle on landscape as the means for his distinctive personal expression; however, portraits of himself, his family, and friends were also a recurring subject. His first solo exhibition of painting was presented at Kraushaar Galleries in New York in 1947. In 1950, Schrag succeeded Hayter as director of Atelier 17 in New York, though his own work and teaching commitments drew him away after one term.[3] In 1953 he taught graphic arts at Brooklyn College.

Schrag was an active member of the 14 Painter-Printmakers group.[4] In 1954 he joined the faculty of Cooper Union, where he continued to teach until 1968. In 1960, the American Federation of Arts sponsored a retrospective exhibition of Schrag's work, documented by a monograph.

He worked at the Tamarind Lithography Workshop in Los Angeles in 1962, producing eleven lithographs, some of which were in color.[5] In 1966 he published *By the Sea*, a portfolio of eighteen intaglios accompanied by his own poetry.

A comprehensive retrospective of Schrag's prints was organized by Syracuse University in 1971.[6] In 1981, he was elected to the National Academy of Design. In 1986 a retrospective selection of his prints was presented by the Associated American Artists gallery. At this time his work was also in exhibitions at the Metropolitan Museum of Art, the Museum of Modern Art, the Brooklyn Museum, the National Portrait Gallery, and the British Museum.[7] Today Schrag remains active as a painter and printmaker, dividing his time between New York and Maine.

Notes

1. Gordon 1960; *Who's Who* 1986, p. 904; Cummings 1988, pp. 575–576.
2. See Mellow 1945.
3. Moser 1977, p. 10.
4. Gordon/Johnson 1955, nos. 67–72.
5. Bloch 1971, p. 75; Lieberman 1969, pp. 31, 63.
6. Freundlich 1970 and 1980.
7. AAA 1986a.

■

Charles Sheeler

Charles Rettew Sheeler, Jr., was born in Philadelphia on July 16, 1883.[1] At age seventeen he enrolled in the School of Industrial Art. Three years later he began studies at the Pennsylvania Academy of Fine Arts with William Merritt Chase. Although his early works were academic in style, from several trips to Europe between 1904 and 1909 he gradually developed a more modernist outlook. Sheeler graduated from the Pennsylvania Academy in 1906. His first solo exhibition was held at McClees Gallery in Philadelphia in 1908; concurrently, five of his paintings were shown at the Macbeth Gallery in New York. Sheeler's six paintings featured in the famous Armory Show in New York in 1913, revealed the influence of Cézanne. In that year he became an assistant in Marius de Zayas's Modern Gallery.

Sheeler began to work as a professional photographer around 1910, specializing in architectural work. His photographs were first shown in

1917 at the Modern Gallery. In 1918 Sheeler moved to New York, and soon he began work with Paul Strand on the film of *Manhatta*, one of the first cinematic portraits of New York as an architectural environment. Sheeler remained active as a painter, and organized annual solo exhibitions.

He found inspiration for his paintings of this period in the lean elegance and American spirit of Shaker crafts and design. Through the 1920s the artist occasionally experimented with lithography.[2] In 1926 he began working as a photographer for Condé Nast Publications. Among his important photographic projects of this period were essays on the Ford Motor Company River Rouge Plant (1927), and on Chartres Cathedral (1929), selections from which were featured in the Film und Foto exhibition in Stuttgart. In 1931 the artist had his first exhibition at the Downtown Gallery in New York, which began a long association with dealer Edith Halpert.

Gradually Sheeler's interest shifted away from historical Americana to contemporary industrial and architectural landscapes. In 1939 his first important retrospective was organized by the Museum of Modern Art in New York.[3] In 1942 he began to work at the Metropolitan Museum of Art as a senior research fellow in photography.

Color became more important in Sheeler's painting during the 1940s. His palette became brighter and his style became much more abstract, representing architecture fragmented in interpenetrating planes, from which rays projected. The artist held residencies at the Phillips Academy in Andover, Massachusetts (1946), and the Currier Gallery of Art in Manchester, New Hampshire (1948). In 1948 Eastman Kodak commissioned him to create color photographic series depicting Shaker architecture, and the U.N. Building in New York. Important retrospective exhibitions of Sheeler's work were held at the University of California at Los Angeles in 1954,[4] and at the University of Iowa in 1963.[5] The artist died in Dobbs Ferry, New

York, on May 8, 1965. His paintings and photographs were gathered for a definitive retrospective at the Museum of Fine Arts in Boston in 1987.[6]

Notes
1. Troyen/Hirschler 1987, pp. 2–49.
2. Adams 1983, pp. 83–84.
3. MoMA 1939.
4. Wight 1954.
5. Dochterman 1963.
6. Troyen/Hirschler 1987; Stebbins 1987. See also Sims 1980; Friedman 1968.

■

Millard Sheets

Millard Sheets was born on June 24, 1907, in Pomona, California, and was raised by his grandparents.[1] After taking private lessons, from Theodore B. Moda and Clarence Hinkle, Sheets attended the Chouinard School of Art in Los Angeles, where he learned the practice of mural painting. He made extra money by working part-time as an architect's draftsman, and joined an independent etching class. For three years at Chouinard, he taught watercolor classes.

In 1929 Sheets's first solo exhibition was mounted at Dalzell Hatfield's Newhouse Galleries in Los Angeles, and he won a cash prize in the annual Davis Competition at the Witte Museum in San Antonio. He sailed to Central and South American and Caribbean ports, and traveled widely in Europe, sketching and visiting museums. Sheets's painting *Women of Champerico* was exhibited in Paris at the Salon d'Automne in 1929. He sought out the print shop of Gaston Dorfinant, and there he learned the technique of lithography.[2] Sheets returned to New York, where architect Cass Gilbert helped to place his drawings in professional magazines.[3]

In 1930 Sheets returned to Los Angeles, where he had a solo exhibition at the Los Angeles County Museum of Art. He executed several commissions for large public murals. In 1932 he began teaching at Scripps College in Claremont, California, and from 1936 to 1955 was the director of the art department there. He first exhibited in New York in 1934 at the

Whitney Museum, and in a one-man show at the Milch Gallery. Such Social Realist painters as Eugene Speicher and Leon Kroll influenced Sheets's art in this period.

When WPA/FAP programs were instituted in California in 1934, Sheets helped organize the program and select artists to participate. He also continued his steady production of watercolors, which dominated his exhibition at Hatfield's Gallery in 1935.[4] The artist took on his first design project for the air force in 1939, and managed the design of seventeen flying schools over the next decade.

In 1943 under the sponsorship of *Life* magazine, Sheets was sent to the China-Burma-India Theater, where he made drawings representing the secondary effects of the devastation—famine and disease.[5] Late in 1945 Sheets returned to California, where he resumed his position as art director of the Los Angeles County Fair, a job he had begun in 1940.

During his tenure as director of the Los Angeles County Art Institute in the mid-1950s, the school was reorganized as the Otis Art Institute. Sheets's architectural design firm, a business specializing in mural, mosaic, stained glass, and sculptural decoration of architecture, opened in 1953. In 1960 and 1961 the artist lectured and taught in Turkey and the Soviet Union. From 1964 to 1973 he was director of design for the Interpace Corporation.

Sheets's position at the center of the California art world for over forty years was documented when his reminiscences were recorded by the oral history program at the University of California at Los Angeles.[6] The artist continued to paint large, vivid watercolors into his final months. He died in Gualala, California, on March 31, 1989.

Notes
1. Lovoos/Penney 1984.
2. Adams 1983, p. 103.
3. *Pencil Points*.
4. Hatfield 1935.
5. These drawings and sketches were published in *Life* on November 22, 1943. See also Lovoos/Penney 1984, pp. 35–43.
6. Goodwin 1977.

■

Benton Spruance

Benton Murdoch Spruance was born in Philadelphia on June 25, 1904.[1] He studied architecture at the University of Pennsylvania School of Fine Arts, earning his tuition as an architectural draftsman. From 1925 to 1929 he attended the Pennsylvania Academy of Fine Arts, and took classes at the Graphic Sketch Club.

In 1926 Spruance began teaching part-time at Beaver College in Glenside, Pennsylvania. Two years later he won a William Emlen Cresson Scholarship, and traveled to Paris, where he made his first lithographs at the Desjobert workshop. These lithographs represented landscapes and city and genre scenes in a figurative style that reflected the influence of George Bellows.

Working at a furniture and interior design firm in Philadelphia, Spruance was determined to continue making prints and sought out Theodore Cuno, the only master lithographer in the city who worked with artists. Among his earliest prints were portraits and other figurative compositions, several representing football.

Spruance's first solo exhibition was presented at the Edward Side Gallery in Philadelphia in 1930. He received his second Cresson Scholarship and returned to Paris along with Robert Gwathmey (cat. 59), where he made prints at the Atelier Desjobert and studied painting with André Lhote. Spruance had a solo exhibition at the Philadelphia Print Club in 1932. The following year his work was featured in the first Biennial exhibition at the Whitney Museum of American Art, and his first one-man show in New York was mounted at the Weyhe Gallery. In 1933 Spruance became chairman of the department of fine

arts at Beaver College and also began teaching at the Philadelphia Museum School of Industrial Art.

In the 1930s and early 1940s Spruance's style was influenced by Synthetic Cubism and by the work of such Precisionist printmakers as Louis Lozowick and Charles Sheeler (cat. 84). Alongside his naturalistic images, Spruance consistently produced images in which stretched and elongated forms expressed movement or energy. He was a founding member of Artists Equity in Philadelphia, and from about 1935 to 1940 his political activism was reflected in his prints. In 1939 he executed a major public mural in the Philadelphia Municipal Court Building, and produced his first book illustrations.

In the mid-1940s Spruance's awareness of modernism and abstraction became more apparent in his art, and he also began to represent religious themes in his prints. In 1947 he had a solo exhibition in Washington, D.C., at the division of graphic arts of the United States National Museum. The following year he was elected an associate of the National Academy of Design.

In 1950, with the support of a Guggenheim Fellowship, Spruance took time to study and practice his printing skills, and he began to print his own lithographs. Soon he was producing color prints from a single stone, by his own special subtractive process. In 1953 Spruance returned to Paris where he made lithographs at the Atelier Desjobert, and intaglios with printer Roger Lacourière. He purchased a lithographic press in France, which was brought back to the United States and installed at Beaver College. From this time forward, he did his own printing on this press.

Spruance was a close friend and colleague to such renowned connoisseurs as Carl Zigrosser and Lessing J. Rosenwald. His prominence in print circles was reflected in his position as an adviser later in his career; from

1955 until 1962 he served on the Pennell Fund Purchase Committee at the Library of Congress, and he was one of the original members of the Board of Directors of the Tamarind Lithography Workshop. The artist's crowing achievement as a printmaker was his series of twenty-seven lithographs, *Moby Dick: The Passion of Ahab*, completed shortly before his death in Philadelphia, on December 6, 1967.

Notes
1. Fine/Looney 1986.

■

Bernard Steffen

Bernard Joseph Steffen was born on November 24, 1907, in Neodesha, Kansas, where his father was a teacher and superintendent of schools.[1] In 1929 and 1930 he was the pupil of Thomas Hart Benton at the Kansas City Art Institute. A scholarship took him to New York to study at the Art Students League with Ernest Lawson and Boardman Robinson,[2] and he also studied with Stanton Macdonald-Wright (cat. 78). Steffen was a founding member of the American Artists Congress, an association established in 1935 to encourage government support for artists' unions and to promote the style of Social Realism in American painting.

A skilled painter who worked comfortably in watercolor, tempera, oils, and fresco, Steffen was awarded the silver medal at the Midwestern Exhibition at the Kansas City Art Institute in 1929. His prints also took second prize at the Philadelphia Art Alliance and first prize in the Printmaking Competition at the Museum of Modern Art, New York, in 1940. His first one-man exhibition of paintings in New York was presented at the Contemporary Arts Gallery in October 1937. In 1936 and 1937 Steffen served as instructor and staff artist in painting and the graphic arts with the Federal Resettlement Administration and traveled all around the country. Between 1935 and 1941 he worked with the FAP as a muralist. In 1938 he worked in Colorado

Springs, where he contributed a print to a portfolio of lithographs printed by Lawrence Barrett. Steffen later painted a fresco in the post office in Neodesha, where his father was then postmaster. This work represented the Native Americans and European settlers of southwestern Kansas.

In 1945, while living in New York, the artist exhibited his serigraphs and watercolors along with those of his longtime friend Guy Maccoy (cat. 53) at the Weyhe Gallery. At this point Steffen was an active member of the Color Print Society and the National Serigraph Society, which he served as treasurer and trustee. Beginning in the 1950s he lived in Woodstock, New York, continuing to exhibit his Regionalist screen prints widely. In 1963 his technical manual *Silk Screen* was published.[3]

By this time the artist had turned to abstraction, and had gravitated away from printmaking to oil painting.[4] The rhythm and pattern of his compositions, and color balances themselves, became the subjects of his later work. In 1977 his studio was destroyed by fire, and thousands of paintings and prints were lost. However, the artist continued to work steadily until his death on July 10, 1980, just two days before the opening of his last exhibition in New York. He was buried in the Artists Cemetery in Woodstock.[5]

Notes
1. According to sheet 4A of the federal census of Neodesha City, Kansas, April 20, 1910. I am grateful to Donna J. Bressie, Dr. Lawrence Steffen, and Mrs. Eleanor Steffen for providing much biographical information.
2. Falk, p. 593.
3. Steffen 1963.
4. Mellow 1959.
5. Neodesha 1980.

■

Harry Sternberg

Born in New York on July 9, 1904, Harry Sternberg began his studies of art in grade school, attending the

free life-drawing classes at the Brooklyn Museum. At the Art Students League, he studied with George Bridgman and Harry Wickey, who introduced Sternberg to printmaking in 1927 and remained his private tutor for two years.[1] His first one-man exhibition was at the Weyhe Gallery in New York in 1932, and was followed by a long procession of solo shows at the ACA Gallery in New York.

In the late 1920s Sternberg became an adherent of Social Realism. The artist's earliest prints represent the urban neighborhood of his youth. Somber moods of resignation are also visible in his many intaglios, which he explored the expressive possibilities of the human form. At this time, Sternberg was also influenced by the political leanings of the Art Students League and the artists' community of Greenwich Village. His lithograph *Industrial Landscape* of 1934 (Moore 114) represents the bewildering, tragic relationships between the individual and society and its politics.

In 1933 Sternberg replaced Wickey as instructor of graphic arts at the Art Students League. Following his mentor's example, he strove to instill a dedication to creativity, technical mastery, and a thoughtful approach to printmaking.[2] With the support of a Guggenheim Fellowship in 1936, Sternberg lived among the coal and steel workers of Pennsylvania, and made paintings, drawings, and prints that were often sinister and powerful.[3]

Sternberg was one of the first artists to experiment with offset lithography processes.[4] In 1936 he won the WPA competition for the mural commission in the offices of the federal Treasury Department in Sellersville, Pennsylvania. He also created murals for post offices in Chester, Pennsylvania, and Chicago in 1938. An advisor to the FAP graphic arts division in New York, he experimented there with monotypes.[5]

In 1942 Sternberg began teaching at the New School for Social Research and he published his first book, *Silk Screen Color Printing*, the first techni-

cal handbook to be widely distributed to artists, teachers, and students.[6] Sternberg's own work became more vital and resolved during the 1940s, and he promoted serigraphy as an economical means to produce posters for the war effort.[7]

In the 1950s Sternberg continued to teach and exhibit paintings and prints. In 1953 the ACA Gallery held a retrospective exhibition of Sternberg's graphics. In the summer of 1958, when he taught at Brigham Young University in Utah, the colors and luminosity of the Southwest began to appear in his work. In 1959 the artist moved to California to head the art department at the Idyllwild School of Music and Art of the University of California.

Major retrospective exhibitions of Sternberg's graphics have been held at the Walker Art Center in Minneapolis and at the Edwin A. Ulrich Museum of Art at Wichita State University. From 1980 to 1983 Sternberg taught courses at the Palm Springs Desert Museum. The artist currently lives in Escondido, California, where he actively continues to paint and make prints.[8]

Notes
1. Cummings 1988, p. 614; *Who's Who* 1986, p. 981; Moore 1975. I am grateful to Harry Sternberg for much information on his life and work.
2. Sternberg 1949.
3. *Art Digest* 1937b.
4. Moore 1975, no. 139.
5. Floethe 1987, p. 76.
6. Sternberg 1942; for a review of this book, see Hoeckner 1943, pp. 61–62.
7. Sternberg 1943.
8. See Freudenheim 1989, a review of Sternberg's retrospective exhibition at the Night Gallery in San Diego.

■

Carol Summers

The son of two artists living in Woodstock, New York, Carol Summers was born on December 26, 1925.[1] His father, a painter and medical illustrator, introduced him to printmaking in the late 1930s. The youth learned about etching when his father taught copperplate printmaking at the Arizona State Teachers College at Flagstaff.[2] During World War II Summers served in the marines; in 1944, he was a navigator-bombardier stationed in the South Pacific. In 1948 he attended Bard College, where he studied painting with Stefan Hirsch and printmaking with Louis Schanker (cat. 41). Summers studied at the Art Students League in Woodstock with Arnold Blanch in 1949, and in 1952 with Daniel Rhodes at the College of Ceramic Design at Alfred University.

In 1954, the artist taught at the Haystack Mountain School of Crafts in Maine, and in the fall at the Brooklyn Museum school. His first solo exhibitions were mounted in 1954 at the Art Society of Albany, New York, and the Contemporaries Gallery in New York. In this period the artist experimented with adding collage to his woodcuts. In *Still Life* (1953; Summers 10), he combined simple forms with a Picassoesque contact paper printed with wood grain.

Summers went to Italy in 1955 where he was profoundly impressed by the quiet, dignified beauty of Siena, and the local paintings of the early Renaissance. Tiffany Fellowships in 1955 and 1960 and a Guggenheim Fellowship in 1959 also helped support the artist's travels and printmaking. By this time his formal vocabulary and technical means had coalesced.

In 1962 Summers taught part-time at the Pratt Graphics Center, and the following year he was an instructor at Hunter College in New York. An exhibition of his prints was circulated by the Museum of Modern Art between 1964 and 1966. He produced a series of nine widely varied prints (Summers 71–78) for publication by Associated American Artists in 1967. The same year, a retrospective exhibition of the artist's prints was organized by the San Francisco Museum of Art, and he also worked and taught in Paris, and began to experiment with serigraphy.[3] The following year he taught at Pennsylvania State University.

In 1974 and 1979, under the sponsorship of the United States Information Agency, Summers traveled to India to teach and demonstrate his printmaking method. In 1980 he published the portfolio *Inside the Palace, A Bow to India* (Summers 163–168). These six colorful woodcuts reflect the influence of Indian miniature painting—particularly the vivid, expressive miniatures of the Malwa School—in their palette and composition. Indian imagery recurred in Summers's prints of the 1980s, and the artist often depicted landscapes. A catalogue raisonné of Summers's more than two hundred editions was published in 1988.[4]

Notes

1. *Who's Who* 1986, p. 997; Cummings 1988, pp. 618–619.
2. Summers 1988, p. 7.
3. San Francisco 1968.
4. Summers 1988.

■

Grace Martin Taylor

Grace Martin Taylor was born in Morgantown, West Virginia, on February 11, 1903.[1] She studied at West Virginia University, where she received both bachelor's and master's degrees. After working briefly on the editorial staff of *Dominion News* in Morgantown, she decided to pursue a career in art. In 1922 Martin enrolled at the Pennsylvania Academy of Fine Arts in Philadelphia, where over the next two years she studied with Hugh Henry Breckenridge, Arthur B. Carles, and Henry McCarter. She first went to Provincetown, Massachusetts, in 1925 to visit artist Blanche Lazzell (cat. 18), a distant relative, who taught her the single-block white line printmaking method.[2] Martin returned regularly to Cape Cod in the summer throughout her life, and she was an active member of the Provincetown Art Association. There, she studied painting with Fritz Pfeiffer in 1930. One of her prints was placed among the Fifty Color Prints of the Year by the California Print Makers in 1933.

In the 1930s and 1940s Martin was married to Wilbur Frame and lived in Charleston, West Virginia. In 1934 she began teaching painting and drawing at Mason College of Music and Fine Arts in Charleston, and later she became the head of the department. A member of the Allied Artists of Charleston, she served this local artists' association as president in 1935 and 1936. Her first solo exhibition was mounted at the College of William and Mary in 1938. The following year the artist was one of the founders of the American Color Print Society in Philadelphia.

Martin studied with Hans Hofmann (cat. 73) at his summer school in Provincetown during the 1940s. She also journeyed to Taos, New Mexico, to attend the Emil Bistram School of Art. The artist strove to exhibit her work widely, showing with the American Color Print Society, the California Print Makers, the Southern Printmakers, and the New England Printmakers Association. Her work was shown at the Metropolitan Museum of Art in 1943, and at the National Academy of Design in New York in 1944 and 1948. A solo exhibition of her paintings and prints was organized by Ohio University in 1945.

Sometime around 1950 major changes took place in the artist's personal life, and she now signed her work Grace Martin Taylor. In 1950 she became dean at Mason College, a position she maintained for five years. For the 1955–56 academic year she served as president. In 1956 after retiring from Mason College, Taylor became associate professor of art at Morris Harvey College (later the University of Charleston), a position she held until 1958. In that year Taylor's work was featured in a one-person exhibition organized by West Virginia University in Morgantown, in celebration of her being honored as Artist of the Year in that state. From 1967 to 1971 Taylor lectured in the West Virginia University Extension Program.

The artist was named Distinguished West Virginian of the Year in 1982. Her work was shown at the

Smithsonian Institution in Washington, D.C., in 1985. She is still living and working in Charleston.

Notes

1. *Who's Who* 1986, p. 1010.
2. Flint 1983, pp. 20, 49.

■

Ansei Uchima

The son of Japanese immigrants, Ansei Uchima was born in Stockton, California, on May 1, 1921.[1] He grew up in Los Angeles, where he attended public schools. In 1940, in accordance with his father's wishes, he went to Tokyo, to study architecture at Waseda University. When war broke out two years later, Uchima was cut off from home. He soon gravitated from the study of architecture to an interest in painting, which he pursued under the tutelage of Japanese masters and later on his own. His paintings won awards at the Jiyu Bijitsu Art Association annual exhibitions in 1953 and 1954.

Uchima began to experiment with printmaking in Japan in 1957, and his work was immediately successful with collectors there and abroad. The same year he shared an exhibition at the Yoseido Gallery in Tokyo with the sculptor Masayuki Nagare, and showed his woodcuts in the Tokyo International Print Triennials in 1957 and 1960.

In 1959 he returned to the United States with his family and settled in New York. The following year the Art Institute of Chicago organized the exhibition Japan's Modern Prints—Sosaku Hanga, a project with which Uchima's friend Oliver Statler was involved as an adviser and a lender.[2] Nine of Uchima's prints were included in this landmark exhibition, which introduced these works to a progressively widening American audience. In 1962 the artist won a Guggenheim Fellowship, which helped him to complete his first American portfolio of prints, *Evening Calm*. In that year he began teaching at Sarah Lawrence College in Bronxville, New York, where he would continue to teach actively for twenty years. In 1967 he became an adjunct professor of printmaking at Columbia University. In 1970 Uchima won another Guggenheim award, which allowed him to travel and teach in Europe.

In 1977 Uchima began a series of twenty-five large prints entitled *Forest Byobu*, or *Forest Screen*. Compared to most of his earlier prints, these woodcuts were more vividly colored, and their compositions denser. The artist arranged fragments of delicately graduated color in vertical and horizontal courses, resembling geological strata or the layers of rain forest overgrowth. Thus, the viewer was simultaneously presented with a panorama of nature from several perspectives. Saturated bands of color were graded into soft, washlike passages, giving these prints an expansive sense of space.

Uchima has had more than forty solo exhibitions in the United States and Japan, including a circulating show of his prints, which traveled to ten museums and galleries in Japan in 1982 and 1983. The artist suffered a debilitating stroke in 1982, from which he is currently recovering. A retrospective of his printmaking career was mounted at Sarah Lawrence College in 1985, and he was named professor emeritus in 1988.

Notes

1. *Who's Who* 1986, p. 1042; Uchima 1982; Philipps/Ryan 1985.
2. AIC 1960.

■

Albert Urban

Born in Frankfurt-am-Main, Germany, on July 22, 1909, Albert Urban began his studies of art at the Frankfurt Kunstschule, where he was the pupil of Max Beckmann and Willi Baumeister.[1] His first solo exhibition was mounted at the Schneider Galleries in Frankfurt when he was just nineteen. After graduation, he became an assistant instructor at the

academy. Urban was one of many modern artists condemned by the Nazis, and his work was confiscated and included in the Degenerate Art exhibition that opened in Munich in July 1937. With Hitler in power, the artist was forbidden to paint, and eventually exiled from Germany. After almost a year in London, he came to the United States in 1940.

Urban's expressive paintings of the early 1940s reflected influences not only of Beckmann and the Expressionists, but of Rouault and Braque as well. They were generally figural compositions, with heavy, abstracted forms placed before diaphanous scrims of muted colors. From 1941 to 1948 the artist had five solo exhibitions in New York and Philadelphia. He was recognized as a virtuosic technician: "a painter's painter, whose brilliant color, vibrant forms, swiftly spontaneous design, and general technical inventiveness must win the respect of all informed scholars of painting."[2] In 1942 he was already at work on a series of four- and five-color serigraphs. These were small prints, conceived to be affordable.[3] The artist's interest and facility in serigraphy were complemented by those of his wife Reva, who used the process to reproduce the paintings of modern artists ranging from Claude Monet to Georgia O'Keeffe. In Greenwich Village, the couple ran a gallery where these reproductive prints were sold alongside Albert Urban's original serigraphs.[4]

Urban's silkscreens of the 1950s developed from figural compositions of theatrical subjects into larger, flatter abstractions in which spare, delicate calligraphic lines floated before fields of color. Between 1948 and 1958, although he continued to produce color prints, the artist secreted himself in his studio, refusing to share his paintings with anyone but his closest friends. A one-man exhibition at the Zabriskie Gallery in 1958 revealed Urban's large, abstract paintings with elementary, centrifugal compositions of a single hue.[5]

After his untimely death in New York on April 4, 1959, Urban's work was reevaluated and deemed significant. His paintings were featured in the major exhibitions Sixteen Americans at the Museum of Modern Art and American Abstract Expressionists and Imagists at the Guggenheim Museum.[6]

Notes

1. Vollmer 1961, 6:457.
2. *Art News* 1946.
3. *The First Portfolio of Ten Color Prints*, 1942, serigraphs on cream wove paper, 20.6 × 26.9 cm. (sheet), can be found at the Brooklyn Museum (accession nos. 44.12–1).
4. The screen printing and publishing company was called *Ecran Urban*, and it incorporated an exhibition space, Gallery Urban, located at 16 West Tenth Street in New York. In 1955, it was renamed the Ganymede Gallery.
5. Porter 1958; Ventura 1958.
6. Miller 1960, pp. 80–84, 96; Arnason 1961, pp. 79, 95, 130.

■

Anthony Velonis

Anthony Velonis was born on October 20, 1920, in New York.[1] He studied in the College of Fine Arts at New York University. In 1934 he began working for the Civilian Work Administration as a poster artist, where Velonis spearheaded the use of silkscreen to print posters. In 1936 this program was reassigned to the FAP.

The stimulating environment of the FAP brought new incentive to Velonis. He conducted experiments that completed the transformation of silkscreen printing from a commercial process to a fine art medium. In his own work of the period, Velonis experimented with combinations of screen printing and *pochoir*.[2]

The artist authored a pamphlet, *Technical Problems of the Artist: Technique of the Silkscreen Process*, which described the method, and answered many questions repeatedly encountered in its introduction.[3] Distributed to WPA art centers across the country, this booklet contributed greatly to the spread and popularity of the medium in the 1940s. Velonis also introduced silkscreen to the art-consuming public in an article in the *Magazine of Art*.[4]

In the spring of 1939 Velonis was among the artists who received pink slips from the WPA. He and four colleagues who were released from the graphic arts division established the Creative Printmakers Group, which shared a screen-printing studio and commissions.[5] They began by producing their own prints, but it soon became clear that they needed more commercial work to pay the rent. Soon, they printed several editions for other artists, such as Adolf Dehn and Federico Castellano, and they undertook commissions from the Nierendorf Gallery and from Hyperion Press to print high-quality color reproductions. They carried out other illustrative projects for Saks Fifth Avenue, Tiffany & Company, and the Metropolitan Museum of Art.

Velonis's works were included in the two landmark exhibitions of serigraphs in 1940, held at the Weyhe Gallery in New York and at the Springfield Museum of Fine Arts in Massachusetts. By this time, however, commercial work had begun to monopolize his time and energy. In the 1940s he was a member of the National Serigraph Society, but his artistic activity had begun to wane.

In 1942 Velonis and his business partner Hyman Warsager were drafted into the Air Force. Working first at Lowry Field, the artist designed training aids and recruiting posters; later, at Wright Field, he rendered graphs and statistical charts.

After his discharge, Velonis returned to Creative Printmakers, which had flourished and grown, by that time engaging about a hundred employees. This business demanded so much of him that he found very little time to devote to his own artwork. Nevertheless, his technical innovations continued during his commercial career, as documented in 1959 by an article in the professional journal *Print*, which reviewed the latest developments in screen printing.[6] Retired from a successful business career, Velonis now divides his time between Glen Rock, New Jersey, and St. Croix in the Virgin Islands.

Notes
1. Falk, p. 646; *Who's Who* 1940, p. 661.
2. Shokler 1946, p. 69.
3. Velonis 1938.
4. Velonis 1940; see also Velonis 1973.
5. The five original members of the Creative Printmakers Group, Joseph LeBoit, Eugene Morley, Bernard Schardt, Hyman Warsager, and Velonis, set up shop on West Twenty-third Street. Soon the first three artists dropped out, and Thomas Quinn and Constantine Velonis, Anthony's brother, joined them. By 1942, their primarily commercial business a success, they became Creative Printmakers, Inc.; greatly expanded, the workshops occupied three lofts on Seventeenth Street.
6. Velonis 1959. Today the company is in operation as Ceragraphic, Inc. Although Velonis sold his interest in the business some years ago, he is still occasionally called in as a consultant.

Joseph Vogel

Born in Austria on April 22, 1911, Joseph Vogel moved with his family to Poland as a young boy.[1] The family immigrated to the United States in 1927, settling in New York. Vogel studied at the National Academy of Design from 1929 through 1932. Passionate and idealistic, he was active in the politics of art and was a founding member of the American Artists Union in 1931. In 1933 he studied at the Art Students League, and he worked with Ben Shahn and Lou Block on a mural painting at Riker's Island under the Temporary Emergency Relief Administration in 1934 and 1935.[2] In 1935 Vogel became a member of the FAP graphic arts division, remaining there until 1938.

The artist produced his entire oeuvre of about twenty prints, including the well-known *Solicitations*, during the late 1930s in New York.[3] Vogel contributed to the color lithography project led by Gustave von Groschwitz and Russell Limbach (cat. 45) in 1935 and 1936. As an Artists Union activist, Vogel went to Spain in 1937 to join the Abraham Lincoln Brigade and fight against the Fascists.

He returned to New York and to his artistic career in 1938; his first one-man show was at the New School

for Social Research soon after his arrival. He became a member of both the National Society of Mural Painters and the Mural Artists Guild in that year. In 1939 he exhibited prints at the New York World's Fair and in the Whitney Museum Invitational Exhibition, to which he contributed for several years. In that year Vogel went to Mexico, to experience firsthand the charged, creative environment of the populist mural painters Diego Rivera and José Orozco.

When the United States entered the war, Vogel went home, finding work in southern California in the film industry. In 1942 he enlisted in the armed forces and served in the European and Pacific Theaters, first in the Signal Corps, then as a cameraman and a combat artist. After his discharge in 1946 he returned to Los Angeles, and resumed his career as a painter and teacher. He taught documentary filmmaking at the University of Southern California from 1946 to 1948. He returned to Europe, where he came to know André Lhote and Fernand Léger in Paris. After traveling through France and visiting England and Italy, the artist returned once again to California in 1954 to resume painting and teaching. He offered private classes at his studio and was an instructor of painting at the Chouinard Art Institute between 1961 and 1963.

Vogel taught drawing and painting at Beverly Hills High School from 1963 to 1965 and at Culver City High School from 1963 to 1966. He lived in France and Italy from 1972 through 1976, and since 1981 has lived in Roswell, New Mexico, where he continues to paint and exhibit actively. A retrospective exhibition of his paintings and drawings was recently mounted at the Roswell Museum and Art Center.

Notes
1. *Who's Who* 1940; Falk, p. 648; O'Connor 1973, p. 295.
2. Adams 1983, pp. 124–125.
3. *Prints* 1937, p. 222; Adams 1983, p. 127, fig. 77.

Sylvia Wald

Sylvia Wald was born on October 30, 1914, in Philadelphia.[1] She studied at the Moore Institute of Art, Science, and Industry from 1931 to 1935, and then taught for the FAP in Philadelphia. The artist moved to New York in 1937, where she continued teaching in the FAP. Her works of this period fit comfortably into the dramatic genre of American Scene painting, yet they were more humorous or optimistic in mood than most contemporary works of Social Realism. Wald's first solo exhibition, at the ACA Gallery in New York in 1939, included both painting and sculpture.

The artist had no background in printmaking when, in about 1939, she was drawn to the new method of silkscreen, which made it possible for artists to make prints independently in their studios. Although Wald's introduction to the medium was conventional, she advanced very soon to a high level of technical sophistication, utilizing as many as twenty-five colors in her prints.

At first her serigraphs were essentially reproductions of her own paintings. For example, in the bright and joyful serigraph *Tag, You're It!* of 1941 (Fig.), a peculiar point of view and distortions of the urban setting parallel the expressive poses and the proportions of the figures. The screens for this print combined the tusche and glue washout method and texturizing effects achieved with the litho crayon. The palette is broad and high in key. Like many of Wald's serigraphs of the 1940s, the print stands out for its energy and spirit, and its evocative light and atmosphere. Two prints of this period were included in the pivotal exhibition at the Springfield Museum of Fine Arts in 1940.[2] A recognized member of the National Serigraph Society by 1941, the artist continued to exhibit with this group for over fifteen years.[3]

Sylvia Wald, *Tag, You're It!*, 1941. Serigraph. Worcester Art Museum, 1947.2.

By the end of the decade, Wald's work had begun to progress away from an emphasis on the figure and toward an organic, nonobjective abstraction. At the same time the artist was becoming impatient with the conventional techniques of color serigraphy and their predictable results. She took a more direct approach to screen preparation, and began to work with glue directly on the silk, using brushes, squeegees, and even her fingers to manipulate stop-out on the screen in a manner that retained a focus on form.

In the 1950s and 1960s Wald employed similar experimental means to explore natural themes in her large, intensely colored canvases. Sometimes she incorporated elements of collage and built up a wide range of textures on the surface of the canvas. The artist occasionally represented these subjects and effects simultaneously in serigraphs and woodcuts.

Wald has had over fifteen solo exhibitions in the United States and Germany; her work has been featured in group shows and is represented in museum collections throughout the world. She is a seasoned traveler, and her journeys have taken her through Europe, Central and South America, and Asia. Still very active, she lives in New York, where she now concentrates on painting and sculpture.

Notes
1. Cummings 1988, p. 649; *Who's Who* 1986, p. 1063.
2. These were *Fuel* (thirteen colors) and *Gardening* (sixteen colors). See McCausland 1940.
3. Zigrosser 1941b, p. 451.

Max Weber

Max Weber was born in Bialystok, in western Russia, on April 18, 1881.[1] When he was ten, his family came to America, settling in Brooklyn. Studying at the nearby Pratt Institute from 1898 to 1900, he was a student of Arthur Wesley Dow (cat. 6). He became an art teacher, first in the public schools in Lynchburg, Virginia, and beginning in 1903, at the Minnesota Normal School in Duluth. The artist dreamed of continuing his studies in Europe, and after years of prudent saving, he sailed for Paris in 1905.

In Europe, Weber fell under the influence of Gauguin, Cézanne, Picasso, and Rousseau. He was a pupil in a painting class taught by Matisse in 1908, and his style was influenced by his teacher's expressive freedom and boldness of color. In 1907 one of Weber's paintings was accepted for exhibition at the Salon d'Automne.

Weber returned to New York and had his first one-man show at the Haas Gallery in April of 1909, which revealed him as one of the first American artists working in a modernist style. Though hostilely criticized, this show introduced the artist to Arthur B. Davies (cat. 13), who bought two paintings and became a friend and supporter. Weber maintained that Davies taught him to make lithographs in 1916, which were perhaps the earliest American modernist lithographs.

In 1919 Weber produced his first group of woodcuts, many of them in color, which were exhibited in 1920 at the Montross Gallery in New York. Davies purchased woodcuts, and Carl Zigrosser took other prints to sell at the Weyhe Gallery. That spring, ten of Weber's poems were published along with ten woodcuts—including *Seated Woman* (cat. 15)—in the Yiddish literary serial journal *Schriften*.

Executed soon afterward, Weber's next group of relief prints represented Jewish themes, reflecting his heritage and spiritual convictions. These prints, closely related to his contemporaneous paintings, often depicted several figures in more complex compositions. The artist frequently published his prints in small literary magazines. Weber's book *Primitives*, published in 1926, integrated his poetry and woodcuts.[2]

In 1925 the artist taught at the Art Students League. From 1928 to 1933 he produced thirty-four black ink lithographs, printed from zinc plates.

In 1930 Weber finally began to enjoy some long-awaited recognition. That year, the Museum of Modern Art mounted a retrospective exhibition of his work,[3] and four years later the Metropolitan Museum of Art in New York purchased a painting. This interest was sustained through several important exhibitions in the 1940s and 1950s. Weber died on October, 4, 1961.

Notes

1. Rubenstein 1980, with further bibliography.
2. Weber 1926.
3. Barr 1930. *Seated Woman* appeared on the cover of this exhibition catalogue.

Reynold Weidenaar

Born in Grand Rapids, Michigan, on November 17, 1915, Reynold Henry Weidenaar was the son of a minister.[1] He studied at the Kendall School of Design in Grand Rapids. From 1938 to 1940, he attended the Kansas City Art Institute, where he was introduced to printmaking. In 1940, Weidenaar learned important lessons in intaglio technique and practice from James Swann, and decided on printmaking as a career.

Bertha Jacques, doyenne of the Chicago Society of Etchers, helped Weidenaar acquire an etching press; later she showed his work to Ruel Pardee Tolman, curator of prints at the National Collection of Fine Arts in Washington. A solo exhibition of Weidenaar's prints at the Smithsonian Institution followed in 1941. Another staunch supporter, John Taylor Arms (cat. 21), corresponded regularly with the artist and traded prints with him beginning in 1942, when Weidenaar won the Kate A. Arms Prize from the Society of American Etchers. In 1944 a Guggenheim Fellowship took him to Mexico, where the traditional peasant way of life, basically unchanged over the past two centuries, gave him the thrilling sensation of being transported back in time.

Weidenaar won the Noyes Prize in 1945 for his print *El Monstro del Parocuti*. He also won a Tiffany Foundation scholarship in 1948. In 1950, he was elected an associate of the National Academy of Design after winning the Arms Prize. His large mezzotint self-portrait, executed to fulfill the requirement of the academy, won wide acclaim. In 1956 the artist joined the faculty of the Kendall School of Design, where he continued to teach life drawing and painting courses until 1974. However, this was a frustrating period for Weidenaar, who, disillusioned by trends in the art world, waged a spiteful, unsuccessful campaign against Abstract Expressionism. A consummate craftsman who had dedicated himself to the most challenging technique among the laborious graphic arts, Weidenaar could not understand the aesthetics of modernism. This struggle became a crisis in 1957, when his work was denied entry in an exhibition of abstract art at Western Michigan University. He spoke out indignantly, and in the ensuing turmoil, he resigned as president of the Friends of American Art.

Weidenaar created a series of mezzotints representing scenes of Michigan, including *Bridgebuilders, Mackinac Straits*, which won an award from the Society of American Etchers in 1958.[2] In 1959 the artist traveled in Europe, studying the history and technique of fresco painting. He executed four murals, depicting church history in the La Grave Avenue Christian Reformed Church in Grand Rapids. In the late 1950s he became more occupied with watercolors, chiefly landscapes painted outdoors. He was elected to the American Watercolor Society in 1965. In the mid-1960s Weidenaar traveled around the country alone, completely immersed in his cathartic, personal art. His fascination with the American landscape was reflected in two books, *Our Changing Landscape* and *A Sketchbook of Michigan*.[3] The artist died suddenly of a heart attack in Grand Rapids on April 23, 1985.

Notes

1. *Who's Who* 1984, p. 984.
2. An account of the making of this print is given in Weidenaar 1956.
3. Weidenaar 1971; Zeller/Weidenaar 1980.

Agnes Weinrich

Agnes Weinrich was born on a prosperous farm near Burlington, Iowa, on July 16, 1873.[1] Her parents were immigrants from Prussia. After graduating from Burlington Institute College, Weinrich continued her studies at Iowa Wesleyan College. After the death of their father in 1899, Weinrich and her sister Helen went to Berlin to study art and piano respectively. Afterward they traveled through Europe.

In 1905 Weinrich was back in Chicago, where she studied until 1908 at the School of the Art Institute under Ralph Clarkson, Frederick W. Freer, and John H. Vanderpoel. The artist was profoundly influenced by the Armory Show in New York in 1913, and fell under the influence of Cézanne and the Cubists. She was also attracted to the abstractions of the artists in the circle of Alfred Stieglitz, including Max Weber (cat. 15).

The Weinrich sisters moved to Provincetown in 1914. On Cape Cod, the artist studied with Charles W. Hawthorne and became a close friend of Blanche Lazzell (cat. 18), who taught her how to make woodcuts.[2] In 1914 she enrolled at the Art Students League in New York, where she studied with George Bridgman and William De Leftwich Dodge. In 1917 she exhibited two color woodcuts in the annual exhibition of the Provincetown Art Association. These picturesque vignettes of life in the New England village were similar to the three color prints she exhibited at the Detroit Institute of Arts two years later.[3] It is likely that Weinrich's enthusiasm for modernism and her knowledge of New York art circles induced Max Weber to exhibit his work with the Provincetown Printers.[4]

At this time, Weinrich was artistic mentor of Karl Knaths, who married her sister Helen in 1924. The three of them lived together in a house he built in west Provincetown. Both artists had studios in the house, and worked there for the rest of their lives. In about 1925 Weinrich spearheaded the modernist movement within the Provincetown Art Association. In 1927, under growing pressure from its membership, the conservative organization finally relented and sponsored an independent exhibition of modernist art. Weinrich and Knaths were both members of the jury for this exhibition. Of the four color woodcuts by Weinrich exhibited in the landmark print show at the Brooklyn Museum in 1933, three were modernist still lifes.[5]

Weinrich had solo exhibitions of her paintings and prints in Boston, Chicago, and Washington, D.C. Thirty color woodcuts by the artist have been described, and the titles of perhaps ten other prints can be found in the records of various exhibitions. It is likely that Weinrich continued to make woodcuts into the 1940s. She also printed color monotypes and etchings, but these prints are very rare. Weinrich died in Provincetown on April 17, 1946. She was buried near Yarmouth, Iowa.

Notes

1. Weinrich's birth date is given in an obituary in the Burlington, Iowa, *Hawkeye* 1946. Falk, p. 667; Ness/Orwig 1939, p. 217; Who's Who 1938, p. 554; Flint 1983, pp. 50–51.
2. Flint 1983, p. 16; Thomas 1988.
3. DIA 1919, nos. 166–168.
4. Flint 1983, p. 23, note 15; Rubenstein 1980, pp. 37–38.
5. Brooklyn 1933, nos. 292–295.

■

James McNeill Whistler

Born on July 11, 1834, in Lowell, Massachusetts, James Whistler was the son of a prosperous civil engineer and artist.[1] From 1843 to 1849 when his father worked as a construction supervisor on the railroad from Moscow to St. Petersburg, Whistler lived in Russia. His father's death left the family in financial difficulties, and they returned to America. The youth attended School at Christ Church Hall in Pomfret, Connecticut and the United States Military Academy at West Point. When he failed chemistry there in 1854, he was dismissed.

Whistler worked briefly in Washington, D.C., for the U.S. Coast and Geodetic Survey, where he was trained as a draftsman and cartographer. He was also introduced to etching, used in the reproduction of maps. This experience helped to confirm his aspirations of becoming an artist, and he went to France in 1855.

In Paris, he was briefly the pupil of Charles Gabriel Gleyre, however, he soon set out to study and work on his own. Whistler became friends with young French artists Henri Fantin-Latour and Alphonse Legros, who introduced him to many leading artists, including Gustave Courbet. From Courbet's Realism and the influences of Velasquez and other Old Masters, Whistler formed his own style. The artist was introduced to etching by his brother-in-law Francis Seymour Haden. In 1858, Whistler published his *French Set* of etchings. He executed his *Thames Set* of etchings between 1859 and 1861.

Whistler settled permanently in London in 1859, although he traveled frequently to the Continent and remained a part of Parisian art circles. He made friends with Dante Gabriel Rossetti, and was influenced by the Pre-Raphaelite painters and their notions of "art for art's sake." In the 1860s the artist studied with the classicizing painter Albert Moore. At this time he was also affected by the influence of *japonisme*.

In 1874 Whistler's first solo exhibition, comprising a series of landscapes called *Nocturnes*, *Arrangements*, and *Symphonies*, shocked the English public and critics. In 1877, when the leading critic of the day, John Ruskin, condemned his painting as a hoax, Whistler lost commissions. In one of the period's most celebrated court cases, the artist sued Ruskin for libel. Whistler won a moral victory and damages of just one farthing, but he was bankrupted by legal costs. Fortunately he was commissioned by the Fine Art Society to go to Venice in September 1879 and create a series of twelve etchings; the *First Venice Set* was published in 1880.

In 1888 Whistler married Beatrice Philip Godwin. He published a book of his writings, *The Gentle Art of Making Enemies*, in 1890. In 1892 Whistler moved to Paris. A retrospective exhibition in that year helped to develop his recognition and patronage in Europe and the United States. When his wife died in 1896, the artist was devastated. He traveled widely in Europe and northern Africa. In 1898 Whistler founded a school in Paris. In its three years of operation, it was only marginally successful.

In the course of his career Whistler produced over 400 etchings and about 178 lithographs, and his influence as a printmaker was universal. Whistler died in London on July 17, 1903.

Notes

1. Pennell/Pennell 1909; Lochnan 1984.

■

John von Wicht

John von Wicht was born on February 3, 1888, in Malente, in the province of Holstein in northern Germany.[1] His father was a minister, who moved his family of eight children to nearby Oldenburg when John was two years old. Without instruction the boy became an outstanding draftsman, and in 1905 one

of his meticulous drawings was purchased by the Bremen Kunsthalle. His obvious talent made it possible for von Wicht to attend the private art school sponsored by Ernst Ludwig Hohe, grand duke of Hesse, in Darmstadt. There, before 1911 he was introduced to the technique of lithography. In 1912 von Wicht continued his studies at the State Schools of Fine and Applied Arts in Berlin. In the summer, the artist often traveled to the Orkney Islands of Scotland, where he painted in quiet and isolation. He had his first one-man show in Scotland, and it was followed by solo exhibitions in Berlin and Stockholm.

While serving in the German army during World War I, von Wicht was severely wounded, and he spent several years in therapy to overcome paralysis.[2] In 1923 he immigrated to the United States, and settled in Brooklyn Heights, New York. He found work as a mosaicist and designer of mosaics and stained glass for architectural decoration, and gained experience that helped him to develop a new understanding of color. Occasionally he was able to make lithographs, which were sold at the Weyhe Gallery in New York. Von Wicht became a U.S. citizen in 1936.

The artist was a member of Burgoyne Diller's FAP mural painting division. Along with Stuart Davis, Louis Schanker (cats. 88, 41), and Byron Browne, he executed one of the abstract murals at radio station WNYC in New York; the geometric design of von Wicht's mural, which decorated the broadcasting booth, featured concentric circles that implied the forms of record discs.[3] Among his other mural projects were paintings in the Pan Am terminal in Miami, Florida; at the Pennsylvania Railroad Station in Trenton, New Jersey; and at the New York World's Fair in 1939. The artist was an early member of the Abstract American Artists group.

Von Wicht's first solo exhibition in the United States was held at the Theodore A. Kohn Company in New York in 1939. During World War II, he worked for the army as the captain of a supply barge in the vicinity of New York. Through the early 1940s von Wicht exhibited widely with the Abstract American Artists and the Society of Mural Painters. In 1942 he was invited to exhibit his paintings in the Whitney Museum of American Art Biennial exhibition; he won first prize in the Brooklyn Museum watercolor exhibition of 1945.

During the 1950s von Wicht experimented with paintings in oil and wax on paper and canvas. Perhaps under the influence of Abstract Expressionism, his style became more organic, and gestural forms replaced carefully measured Cubist shapes. He continued to represent landscapes, and formal balance remained fundamental to his art. Von Wicht's prints became larger, and he experimented with stencil techniques. These striking works won awards from the Society of Graphic Artists (1953), the Print Club of Philadelphia (1957), and the Brooklyn Museum (1951, 1956, 1958).[4]

The artist taught painting at the Art Students League in New York in 1951 and 1952. The following year, when he offered a course on color lithography at the John Herron Institute of Art in Indianapolis, a solo exhibition of his prints was mounted there. He contributed to several notable group shows by New York painter-printmakers, including Color Prints by Ten Well-Known Painters at the Contemporaries Gallery in 1950. Von Wicht was also an active member of the 14 Painter-Printmakers group.[5] In 1959 his work was shown in California in solo exhibitions at the Esther Robles Gallery in Los Angeles and the Pasadena Museum of Art, and in a retrospective at the Santa Barbara Museum.

John von Wicht died in Brooklyn on January 22, 1970. At the time of his death, he was busy on a series of large screen prints, which advanced notions of scale, form, and space begun in his earlier lithographs and stencil prints.

Notes

1. Cummings 1971, p. 323; Who's Who 1970, pp. 445–446.
2. Seckler 1957.
3. Lane/Larson 1983, p. 23.
4. Johnson 1956, pp. 44, 47; Baro 1976, p. 121.
5. Gordon/Johnson 1955, nos. 79–84.

Adja Yunkers

Adja Yunkers was born on July 15, 1900, in Riga, Latvia.[1] At the age of fourteen, he began his studies of art at the Petrograd Art Academy in Russia. After fighting in the revolution of 1917, he fled to Berlin and then to Hamburg. There he became the protégé of Emil Nolde, who helped arrange his first solo exhibition, at the Maria Kunde Gallery in Hamburg in 1921.

In the 1920s Yunkers traveled widely, eventually settling in Paris, where he stayed from 1928 to 1938. There he won an important commission to paint murals in the city hall at Ivry. In Sweden in 1939, he made his first color woodcuts, which reflected the influence of Munch and the artists of Die Brücke in their moody, expressive imagery. In Stockholm, Yunkers produced a number of artists' magazines with original prints.

In 1947 he arrived in New York, and produced six editions of woodcuts and many monotypes in his first year there. He began teaching at the New School for Social Research and exhibiting with dealer Henry Kleeman. Through his colleague Louis Schanker (cat. 41), Yunkers quickly became acquainted with the most creative group of woodcut artists in the city.

While artist in residence at the University of New Mexico in 1948, he became enchanted with the Southwest. Native American and desert imagery appeared in his prints, and his palette became muted, occasionally accented by the magenta or yellow of a desert sunset. After returning to New York in the fall, he came back to Albuquerque in 1949 with a Guggenheim Fellowship, and helped organize a private art school. Prints in the Desert, a magazine compiled by Yunkers and his students, documented the activities of this short-lived school. In 1952, the year in which Yunkers became an American citizen, he produced his Rio Grande Portfolio.[2]

Back in New York Yunkers began a single work that comprised five large woodcuts, each handprinted in more than twenty colors,[3] However, when his studio ceiling collapsed, most of the edition of Polyptych was destroyed, and just three complete sets are known. In 1954 Yunkers traveled to Rome on another Guggenheim Fellowship, and created the series of monotypes and woodcuts entitled Ostia Antica.

In 1956 the artist began teaching at Cooper Union, in New York. Large, gestural pastels, created by mixing dry pigments with liquid media directly on the canvas, now occupied him. The Abstract Expressionist imagery of these chalk paintings is reflected in his first lithographs, the

Skies of Venice series, made at Tamarind in 1960.[4] A major retrospective of Yunkers's prints was mounted at the Brooklyn Museum in 1969.[5]

In the 1970s the artist made brightly painted canvases that included elements of torn-paper collage. In big, vivid serigraphs, he transferred these effects to prints. The artist illuminated the writings of the Mexican poet Octavio Paz in the mixed media prints and unique paintings of his portfolio Blanco of 1974. Two years later Yunkers began a series of deeply—etched intaglios that again translated his contemporary collage paintings into prints.

After 1980 Yunkers's compositions became sparse, centralized, and iconic as a result of failing eyesight. The artist died in New York in 1983.

Notes

1. Who's Who 1980, p. 822; AAA 1989.
2. Fitzsimmons 1952b.
3. Breeskin 1953.
4. Lieberman 1969, nos. 166–167.
5. Johnson/Miller 1969.

Bibliography

AAA 1978
Associated American Artists. *Louis Schanker*. New York: Exhibition cat., 1978.

AAA 1986a
Associated American Artists. *Karl Schrag, A Retrospective Exhibition of Prints with Monotypes and Related Drawings 1939–1986*. New York: Exhibition cat., 1986.

AAA 1986b
Associated American Artists. *Louis Schanker, Prints and Drawings*. New York: Exhibition cat., 1986.

AAA 1989
Associated American Artists. *Adja Yunkers, Woodcuts 1927–1966*. New York: Exhibition cat., 1989.

ACA Gallery 1946
ACA Gallery. *Gwathmey* (introduction by Paul Robeson). New York: Exhibition cat., 1946.

Adams 1977a
Adams, Clinton. "Color Lithography in the 1950s. The Cincinnati Biennials: A Conversation with Gustave von Groschwitz." *Tamarind Papers* 1 (Summer 1977): 86.

Adams 1977b
Adams, Clinton. "Lynton R. Kistler and the Development of Lithography in Los Angeles." *Tamarind Papers* 1 (Winter 1977–78): 100–109.

Adams 1978
Adams, Clinton. "Lawrence Barrett: Colorado's Prophet of Stone." *Artspace* (Fall 1978): 38–43.

Adams 1979
Adams, Clinton. "Rubbed Stones, Middle Tones, and Hot Etches: Lawrence Barrett of Colorado." *Tamarind Papers* 2 (1979): 36–41.

Adams 1983
Adams, Clinton. *American Lithographers: The Artist and Their Printers, 1900–1960*. Albuquerque: University of New Mexico Press, 1983.

Adams 1984
Adams, Clinton. "Margaret Lowengrund and The Contemporaries." *Tamarind Papers* 7 (Spring 1984): 17–23.

Adams 1986
Adams, Clinton. "Bolton Brown: Artist-Lithographer." In David Tatham (ed.), *Prints and Printmakers of New York State, 1825–1940*. Syracuse, N.Y.: Syracuse University Press, 1986.

Addison 1938
Addison Gallery of American Art. *Retrospective Exhibition of the Work of Maurice and Charles Prendergast* (with essay by Van Wyck Brooks). Andover, Mass.: Exhibition cat., Phillips Academy, 1938.

ADI Gallery 1977
ADI Gallery. *Carol Summers: Woodcuts* (introduction by Gene Baro). San Francisco: Exhibition cat., 1977.

Adrian 1894
"Sad Home Coming." *Adrian Daily Times and Expositor* (December 14, 1894), n.p.

Adrian 1926
"David Beachbord of Hudson is Dead." *Adrian Daily Telegram* (January 26, 1926), p. 1.

AFA 1952
American Federation of Arts. *Great Names in Modern Art*. New York: Exhibition cat., 1952.

Agee 1965
Agee, William C. *Synchromism and Color Principles in American Painting, 1910–1930*. New York: Exhibition cat., M. Knoedler, 1965.

AIC 1960
Art Institute of Chicago. *Japan's Modern Prints—Sosaku Hanga*. Chicago: Exhibition cat., 1960.

American Art Annual
American Art Annual. 1–9 (1898–1912). New York: American Art Annual. 10–37 (1913–48). New York: American Federation of Arts.

Anderson 1921
Anderson Galleries. *Catalogue of an Exhibition of Wood Engravings, Etchings, and Drawings by Rudolph Ruzicka* (organized by Walter Monroe Grant and Mollie Higgins Smith). New York: Exhibition cat., 1921.

Annex 1981
Annex Galleries. *Gustave Baumann, A Catalogue of 60 Color Woodcuts*. Santa Rosa, Calif.: Exhibition cat., 1981.

Annex 1984
Annex Galleries. *William S. Rice, An Exhibition of Color Woodcuts from 1910 to 1940*. Santa Rosa, Calif.: Exhibition cat., 1984–85.

Annex 1985
Annex Galleries. *Gustave Baumann: An American Master Printmaker*. Santa Rosa, Calif.: Exhibition cat., 1985.

Antreasian/Adams 1971
Antreasian, Garo Z. and Clinton Adams. *The Tamarind Book of Lithography: Art and Technique*. Los Angeles: Tamarind Lithography Workshop, 1971.

Arkansas Gazette 1945
"Modern Art Means What It Means." *Arkansas Gazette* (1945), n.p.

Arms 1932
Arms, John Taylor. *Hill Towns and Cities of Northern Italy*. New York: Macmillan, 1932.

Arms 1934
Arms, John Taylor. *The Handbook of Print Making and Print Makers*. New York: Macmillan, 1934.

Arms/Arms 1937
Arms, John and Dorothy Noyes Arms. *Design in Flower Arranging*. New York: Macmillan, 1937.

Arms 1940
Arms, John Taylor. "John Taylor Arms Tells How He Makes an Etching, Part 1." *American Artist* 4 (December 1940): 16.
"Part 2." 5 (January 1941): 10.

Arms 1943
Arms, John Taylor. "Printmakers' Processes and a Militant Show." *Art News* 42 (October 1, 1943): 9–15.

Arnason 1956
Arnason, H. H. *Theodore Roszak*. Minneapolis: Exhibition cat., Walker Art Center, 1956.

Arnason 1961
Arnason, H. H. *American Abstract Expressionists and Imagists*. New York: Exhibition cat., Guggenheim Museum, 1961.

Arnason 1965
Arnason, H. H. *Stuart Davis Memorial Exhibition*. Washington, D.C.: Exhibition cat., National Collection of Fine Arts, Smithsonian Institution, 1965.

Arnason 1975
Arnason, H. H. *History of Modern Art*. Englewood Cliffs, N.J.: Prentice-Hall, 1975.

Art Digest 1933
"Schanker Shows his Abstractions." *Art Digest* 7 (April 1, 1933): 17.

Art Digest 1934
"Sur-realist Wins Springfield Prize." *Art Digest* 8 (March 1, 1934): 17.

Art Digest 1939a
"Abstract Democracy." *Art Digest* 13 (March 1, 1939): 11.

Art Digest 1939b
"White Slips for Pink." *Art Digest* 13 (August 1, 1939): 12.

Art Digest 1940
"New York Introduced to Fletcher Martin." *Art Digest* 15 (November 15, 1940): 6.

Art Digest 1949
"Studio 74." *Art Digest* 1923 (January 15, 1949): 26.

Art News 1944
"Hans Hofmann." *Art News* 43 (March 25, 1944): 20.

Art News 1945
"The Passing Shows: Guy Maccoy and Bernard Steffen." *Art News* 44 (May 15–31, 1945): 27.

Art News 1946
"The Passing Shows: Minna Citron; Harry Shokler; Albert Urban." *Art News* 44 (January 15–31, 1946): 24.

Art News 1947
"The Graphic Circle." *Art News* 45 (February 1947): 44.

Ashton 1973
Ashton, Dore. *The New York School: A Cultural Reckoning*. New York: Viking, 1973.

Bakker/Coleman 1988
Bakker, James R. *Margaret J. Patterson, 1867–1950, Retrospective Exhibition* (essay by Feay Shellman Coleman). Cambridge, Mass.: Exhibition cat., 1988.

Ball 1980
Ball, Maudette W. *Nathan Oliveira, Print Retrospective: 1949–1980*. Long Beach: Exhibition cat., Art Museum and Galleries, and Center for Southern California Studies in the Visual Arts, California State University, 1980.

Baltimore 1963
Baltimore Museum of Art. *The Works of Antonio Frasconi, 1953–1963*. Baltimore: Exhibition cat., 1963.

Bangs 1899a
Bangs, John Kendrick. *The Dreamers*. New York and London: Harper, 1899.

Bangs 1899b
Bangs, John Kendrick. *Peeps at People*. New York and London: Harper, 1899.

Bannard 1976
Bannard, Walter Darby. *Hans Hofmann*. Houston: Exhibition cat., Museum of Fine Arts, 1976.

Barbin 1976
Barbin, Madeleine. "Des Américaines à Paris." *Nouvelles de l'estampe* 28 (July–August 1976): 16–19.

Baro 1970
Baro, Gene. *Vincent Longo Print Retrospective*. Washington, D.C.: Exhibition cat., Corcoran Gallery of Art, 1970.

Baro 1976
Baro, Gene. *30 Years of American Printmaking*. Brooklyn: Exhibition cat., Brooklyn Museum, 1976.

Barr 1930
Barr, Alfred H., Jr. *Max Weber: Retrospective Exhibition, 1907–1930*. New York: Exhibition cat., Museum of Modern Art, 1930.

Barr 1946
Barr, Alfred H., Jr. *Picasso, Fifty Years of His Art*. New York: Exhibition cat., Museum of Modern Art, 1946.

Barragan 1978
Barragan, Nina (Rocia Lasansky Weinstein). *Mauricio Lasansky's Kaddish Prints*. Iowa City: Exhibition cat., University of Iowa Museum of Art, 1978.

Bassham 1975
Bassham, Ben L. (ed.). *John Taylor Arms, American Etcher*. Madison, Wis.: Exhibition cat., Elvehjem Art Center, 1975.

Baumann/Griffiths 1983
Baumann, Ann and Gwilym G. Griffiths. "Packard's Artists: Gustave Baumann, Master of the Colored Woodcut." *The Packard Cormorant* 30 (Autumn 1983): 25.

Baur 1961
Baur, John I. H. *Bernard Reder*. New York: Exhibition cat., Whitney Museum of American Art, 1961.

Baxter 1979
Baxter Art Gallery. *Nathan Oliveira, A Survey of Monotypes 1973–1978*. Pasadena: Exhibition cat., California Institute of Technology, 1979.

Becker 1948
Becker, Fred. The artist's introductory notes to 1948 exhibition in vertical files. Washington, D.C.: National Museum of American Art, Smithsonian Institution, 1948.

Beraldi 1888
Beraldi, Henri. *Les Graveurs du XIXe Siècle*. Paris: Librairie L. Conquet, 1888.

Berezin 1976
Berezin, Ellen. "Arthur B. Davies, Artist and Connoisseur." *Worcester Art Museum Bulletin* 6 (November 1976): 8–9, 14–15.

Berman 1971
Berman, Eugene (introduction by Russell Lynes). *The Graphic Work of Eugene Berman*. New York: Clarkson N. Potter, 1971.

Bernstein 1976
Bernstein, Judy et al. *19th Century American Women Artists*. New York: Exhibition cat., Whitney Museum of American Art, 1976.

Bernstein 1933
Bernstein, Theresa F. "American Color Print Exhibition." *The Brooklyn Museum Quarterly* 20 (April 1933): 24–29.

Berry 1975
Berry, John. "View from the Wind Palace." *Mankind Magazine* (March 1975): n.p.

Biegeleisen/Cohn 1942
Biegeleisen, Jacob Israel and Max Arthur Cohn. *Silk Screen Stenciling as a Fine Art*. New York: McGraw-Hill, 1942.

Blattner 1911
Blattner E. J. "Helen Hyde, An American Artist in Japan." *International Studio* 45 (October 1911): 51–57.

Bloch 1971
Bloch, E. Maurice. *Tamarind: A Renaissance in Lithography*. Baltimore: Exhibition cat., International Exhibition Foundation, Garamond/Pridemark Press, 1971.

Bolton 1938
Bolton, Theodore. *American Book Illustrators*. New York: R. R. Bowker, 1938.

Bonner 1909
Bonner, Richard Illenden. *Memoirs of Lenawee County, Michigan*. Madison, Wis.: Western Historical Society, 1909.

Boston Sunday Herald 1886
"Art of the Dead Wall." *Boston Sunday Herald* (November 21, 1886), p. 5.

Bothwell 1940
Bothwell, Dorr. "So You Love Color!" *California Arts and Architecture* 57 (March 1940): 10–13.

Bothwell/Frey 1968
Bothwell, Dorr and Marlys Frey. *Notan, The Dark-Light Principle of Design*. New York: Van Nostrand Reinhold, 1968.

Bowles 1927
Bowles, J. M. "The Art of Allen Lewis." *The Print Connoisseur* 7 (April 1927): 62–78.

Boyer/Capasso 1986
Boyer, Patricia Eckert and Nicholas J. Capasso. *Reginald Neal, A Retrospective of his Prints*. New Brunswick, N.J.: Exhibition cat., Jane Voorhees Zimmerli Art Museum, Rutgers University, 1986.

Bradley 1896
Bradley, Will H. "Edward Penfield: Artist." *Bradley: His Book* 1 (May 1896): n.p.

Breeskin 1948
Breeskin, Adelyn Dohme. *The Graphic Work of Mary Cassatt, A Catalogue Raisonné*. New York: H. Bittner, 1948.

Breeskin 1953
Breeskin, Adelyn Dohme. "Adja Yunkers, Pioneer of the Contemporary Color Woodcut." *Baltimore Museum of Art News* 16 (June 1953): 4–7.

Breeskin 1960
Breeskin, Adelyn Dohme. *Milton Avery*. New York: American Federation of Arts, 1960.

Breuning 1946
Breuning, Margaret. "In Musical Terms." *Art Digest* 20 (January 1, 1946): 7.

Breuning 1948
Breuning, Margaret. "Harari Turns Abstract." *Art Digest* 22 (March 1, 1948): 23.

Breuning 1957
Breuning, Margaret. "Margaret Breuning Writes." *Arts* 32 (December 1957): 51.

Bro 1965
Bro, Margueritte. *The Animal Friends of Peng-U*. Garden City, N.Y.: Doubleday, 1965.

Brokl 1984
Brokl, Robert. "Augusta Rathbone: Rediscovered Printmaker." *California Printmaker* (October 1984): 6–7.

Brooklyn 1933
Brooklyn Museum. *American Color Prints*. Brooklyn: Exhibition cat., 1933.

Brooklyn 1946
"VANGUARD." *The Brooklyn Museum Bulletin* 8 (November 1946): n.p.

Brooklyn 1947
Brooklyn Museum. *Boris Margo, Graphic Work 1934–1947*. Brooklyn: Exhibition cat., 1947.

Brown 1930
Brown, Bolton. *Lithography for Artists*. Chicago: University of Chicago Press, 1930.

Brown 1984
Brown, Bolton. "Pennellism and the Pennells." *Tamarind Papers* 7 (Fall 1984): 49–71.

Brown 1977
Brown, Gordon. "Anne Ryan." *Arts* 52 (March 1977): 35.

Brown 1963
Brown, Milton Wolf. *The Story of the Armory Show*. New York: Joseph H. Hirshhorn Foundation, 1963.

Browne 1972
Browne, Rosalind. "Sue Fuller." *Art International* 16 (1972): 37–40.

Bruère 1915
Bruère, Robert W. *The Etchings of B.J.O. Nordfeldt*. New York: Exhibition cat., Arthur Hahlo, 1915.

Bruhn 1983
Bruhn, Thomas P. *The Art of Al Frueh*. Storrs, Conn.: The William Benton Museum of Art, The University of Connecticut, 1983.

Bryan 1957
Bryan, Kirke. *The First American Color Printer*. Norristown, Pa.: Kirke Bryan, 1957.

Burrey 1956
Burrey, Suzanne. "Karl Schrag, Movement Above and Below." *Arts* 30 (June 1956): 38.

Cahill 1930
Cahill, Holger. *Max Weber*. New York: Exhibition cat., Downtown Gallery, 1930.

Campbell 1986
Campbell, Lawrence. "Blanche Lazzell at Martin Diamond Fine Arts." *Art in America* 74 (July 1986): 122–123.

Capasso 1988
Capasso, Nicholas J. *Relief Printing in the 1980s*. New Brunswick, N.J.: Exhibition cat., Jane Voorhees Zimerli: Art Museum, Rutgers University, 1988.

Cary 1931
Cary, Elizabeth Luther. "The Work of John Taylor Arms." *Prints* 1 (September 1931): 1–13.

Castleman 1988
Castleman, Riva. *Prints of the Twentieth Century*. Rev. ed. London and New York: Thames & Hudson, 1988.

Cate/Hitchings, 1978
Cate, Phillip Dennis and Sinclair Hamilton Hitchings. *The Color Revolution: Color Lithography in France, 1890–1900*. Santa Barbara and Salt Lake City: Exhibition cat., Peregrine Smith, 1978.

Chaet 1958
Chaet, Bernard. "Interview with Edmond Casarella: Paper Relief Cuts in the Renaissance of Printmaking." *Arts* 33 (November 1958): 66–67.

Chaffee 1952
Chaffee, Ada Gilmore. "Cape End Early Cradled Gifted Groups of Print Makers Who Added to Art." *The Advocate* [Provincetown, Mass.] (October 30, 1952): 5.

Chapman 1857
Chapman, John Gadsby. *The American Drawing Book: A Manual for the Amateur, and Basis of Study for the Professional Artist: Especially Adapted to the Use of Public and Private Schools, as well as Home Instruction*. New York: J. S. Redfield, 1857.

Charlot 1963
Charlot, Jean. *The Mexican mural renaissance, 1920–1925*. New Haven: Yale University Press, 1963.

Chesney 1956
Chesney, Lee. "Lee Chesney" (artist's statement). *Art in America* 44 (February 1956): 52.

Chesney 1959
Chesney, Lee. "Printmaking Today." *College Art Journal* 19 (1959–1960): 158–165.

Chipp 1958
Chipp, Herschel B. "San Francisco: One Man Shows." *Art News* 57 (April 1958): 48.

Cincinnati 1958
The Cincinnati Art Museum. *Fifth International Biennial of Contemporary Color Lithography*. Cincinnati: Exhibition cat., 1958.

Clark 1900
Clark, G. Orr. *The Moon Babies*. New York: H. Russell, 1900.

Clarkson 1979
Clarkson, John. *Blanche Lazzell*. Morgantown: Exhibition cat., West Virginia University, Creative Arts Center Galleries, 1979.

Cleveland 1952
Cleveland Museum of Art. *The Work of Antonio Frasconi* (introduction by Leona E. Prasse). Cleveland: Exhibition cat., 1952.

Coates 1946
Coates, Robert. "The Art Galleries: Abroad and at Home." *The New Yorker* 22 (March 30, 1946): 83.

Cochrane 1974
Cochrane, Diane. "Michael Ponce de León: Metal Intaglio Collage." *American Artist* 38 (October 1974): 38–43, 77–83.

Cochrane 1975
Cochrane, Diane. *Michael Ponce de León at the Pioneer-Moss Gallery*. New York: Exhibition cat., Irwin Rothman and Stanley Tankel, 1975.

Cohen 1988
Cohen, David. "S. W. Hayter and Atelier 17 in America." In Hacker 1988.

Coke 1972
Coke, Van Deren. *Nordfeldt the Painter*. Albuquerque: University of New Mexico Press, 1972.

Cole 1951
Cole, Mary. "Henry Mark, Sylvia Wald." *Art Digest* 25 (February 15, 1951): 25.

Cole 1972
Cole, Sylvan, Jr. *Will Barnet, etchings, lithographs, woodcuts, serigraphs, 1932–1972, catalogue raisonné*. New York: Associated American Artists, 1972.

Conkelton/Gilbert 1983
Conkelton, Sheryl and Gregory Gilbert. *Harry Gottlieb, The Silkscreen and Social Concern in the WPA Era*. New Brunswick, N.J.: Exhibition cat., Rutgers University, Jane Voorhees Zimerli Art Museum, 1983.

Cooke 1977
Cooke, Hereward Lester, Jr. *Fletcher Martin*. New York: Abrams, 1977.

Cooper 1935
Cooper, Irene. "Arkansas Artist Archives Desire for Studio Here." *New Orleans Times-Picayune* (December 29, 1935), n.p.

Corcoran 1937
Corcoran Gallery of Art. *Special Exhibition of Monotypes by Maurice Brazil Prendergast*. Washington D.C.: Exhibition cat., 1937.

Corcoran 1970
Corcoran Gallery of Art. *Vincent Longo: Print Retrospective, 1954–1970* (introduction by Gene Baro). Washington D.C.: Exhibition cat., 1970.

Corita 1984
Corita Prints 1951–1984. North Hollywood, Calif.: 1984.

Crimp 1972
Crimp, Douglas. "News and Reviews." *Art News* 71 (December 1972): 72.

Croughton 1947
Croughton, Amy H. "Beauty Everywhere; Says James Havens." [Rochester] *Times-Union* (July 25, 1947), p. 7.

Cummings 1971
Cummings, Paul. *Dictionary of Contemporary American Artists*. 2nd ed. New York: St. Martin's Press, 1971.

Cummings 1988
Cummings, Paul. *Dictionary of Contemporary American Artists*. 5th ed. New York: St. Martin's Press, 1988.

Czestochowski 1987
Czestochowski, Joseph S. *Arthur B. Davies, A Catalogue Raisonné of the Prints*. Newark: University of Delaware Press, 1987.

Dailey 1989
Dailey, Victoria. "Early California Color Prints." *Antiques & Fine Art* 7 (February 1989): 87–95.

Davis 1973
Davis, Stuart. "American Artists' Congress." In O'Connor 1973, pp. 249–250.

Dawdy 1974
Dawdy, Doris Ostrander. *Artists of the American West: A Biographical Dictionary*. Chicago: Swallow Press, 1974.

Day 1963
Day, Worden. "Why Painters Turn Sculptors." *Art Voices* (1963): 7.

DeNoon 1987
DeNoon, Christopher. *Posters of the WPA*. Los Angeles: Wheatley Press, 1987.

DIA 1919
Detroit Institute of Arts. *Wood Block Prints in Color by American Artists* (with introduction by Claude Burroughs). Detroit: Exhibition cat., 1919.

Diller 1973
Diller, Burgoyne. "Abstract Murals." In O'Connor 1973, pp. 69–71.

Dinwiddie 1906
Dinwiddie, William. "Miss Helen Hyde of Japan." *Harper's Bazzar* 40 (January 1906): 12–18.

Dochterman 1963
Dochterman, Lillian. *The Quest of Charles Sheeler; 83 Works Honoring his 80th Year*. Iowa City: Exhibition cat., University of Iowa, 1963.

Dolch 1964
Dolch, Edward W. *Stories from Old China*. Champaign, Ill.: Garrard, 1964.

Doty 1984
Doty, Robert. *Will Barnet*. New York: Abrams, 1984.

Dow 1896
Dow, Arthur Wesley. "Painting with Wooden Blocks." *Modern Art* 4 (Summer 1896): 85–90.

Dow 1899
Dow, Arthur Wesley. *Composition: A Series of Exercises Selected from a New System of Art Education*. Boston: J. M. Bowles, 1899.

Dreishpoon 1989
Dreishpoon, Douglas. *Theodore Roszak, Paintings and Drawings from the Thirties*. New York: Exhibition cat., Hirschl & Adler Galleries, 1989.

Dreyfuss 1969
Dreyfuss, Caril. *Werner Drewes Woodcuts*. Washington, D.C.: Exhibition cat., National Collection of Fine Arts, Smithsonian Institution, 1969.

Dwight 1958
Dwight, Edward H. *Ralston Crawford (paintings, prints, drawings)*. Milwaukee: Exhibition cat., Milwaukee Art Center, 1958.

Ebersole 1954
Ebersole, Barbara. *Fletcher Martin* (foreword by William Saroyan). Gainesville: University of Florida Press, 1954.

Edmondson 1973
Edmondson, Leonard. *Etching*. New York: Van Nostrand Reinhold, 1973.

Eger 1971
Eger, Jeffery. *Sonambients: The Sound Sculpture of Harry Bertoia* (film). Kenesaw Films, 1971.

Eichenberg 1976
Eichenberg, Fritz. *The Art of the Print*. New York: Abrams, 1976.

Emerson 1916
Emerson, Gertrude. "Helen Hyde and her Japanese Children." *The American Magazine of Art* 7 (September 1916): 429–435.

Falk
Falk, Peter Hastings. *Who Was Who in American Art*. Madison, Conn.: Sound View Press, 1985.

Falk 1987
Falk, Peter Hastings. *Eliza Draper Gardiner, Master of the Color Woodcut*. Madison, Conn.: Sound View Press, 1987.

Farmer, 1978
Farmer, Jane M. *Paper, Art as Medium*. Washington D.C.: Exhibition cat., National Museum of American Art, Smithsonian Institution, 1978.

Faunce 1974
Faunce, Sarah. *Anne Ryan Collages*. Brooklyn: Exhibition cat., Brooklyn Museum, 1974.

Feinblatt/Davis 1980
Feinblatt, Ebria and Bruce Davis. *Los Angeles Prints, 1883–1980*. Los Angeles: Exhibition cat., Los Angeles County Museum of Art, 1980.

Fenollossa 1895
Fenollossa, Ernest F. *Special Exhibition of Prints, Designed, Engraved, and Printed by Arthur Wesley Dow*. Boston: Exhibition cat., Museum of Fine Arts, 1895.

Field 1972
Field, Richard S. *Silkscreen: History of a Medium*. Philadelphia: Exhibition cat., Philadelphia Museum of Art, 1972.

Field 1983
Field, Richard S. et al. *American Prints 1900–1950*. New Haven: Exhibition cat., Yale University Art Gallery, 1983.

Fielding 1986
Fielding, Mantle. *Mantle Fielding's Dictionary of American Painters, Sculptors, and Engravers* (ed. Glenn B. Opitz). 2nd rev. ed. Poughkeepsie, N.Y.: Apollo, 1986.

Fine 1982
Fine, Ruth E. *Lessing J. Rosenwald, Tribute to a Collector.* Washington, D.C.: Exhibition cat., National Gallery of Art, 1982.

Fine/Looney 1986
Fine, Ruth E. and Robert F. Looney. *The Prints of Benton Spruance, A Catalogue Raisonné.* Philadelphia: University of Philadelphia Press, 1986.

Fitzsimmons 1952a
Fitzsimmons, James. "Seong Moy/New Gallery." *Art Digest* 26 (May 1, 1952): 26.

Fitzsimmons 1952b
Fitzsimmons, James. "Print Project Launched." *Art Digest* 27 (October 1, 1952): 10.

Fletcher 1945
Fletcher, John Gould. "Robertson Paintings at Library." *Arkansas Gazette* (June 3, 1945), n.p.

Fletcher 1982
Fletcher, William Dolan. *John Taylor Arms, A Man For All Time, The Artist and His Work.* New Haven: Eastern Press, 1982.

Flint 1976
Flint, Janet Altic. *George Miller and American Lithography.* Washington, D.C.: Exhibition cat., National Collection of Fine Arts, Smithsonian Institution, 1976.

Flint 1977
Flint, Janet Altic. *New Ways with Paper.* Washington, D.C.: Exhibition cat., National Collection of Fine Arts, Smithsonian Institution, 1977.

Flint 1980
Flint, Janet Altic. *Art for All: American Print Publishing between the Wars.* Washington, D.C.: Exhibition cat., National Museum of American Art, Smithsonian Institution, 1980.

Flint 1983
Flint, Janet Altic. *Provincetown Printers: A Woodcut Tradition.* Washington, D.C.: Exhibition cat., National Museum of American Art, Smithsonian Institution, 1983.

Floethe 1973
Floethe, Richard. "Posters." In O'Connor 1973, pp. 177–178.

Floethe 1987
Floethe, Richard. "A Remembrance of the Federal Art Project." In DeNoon 1987, pp. 128–131.

Floud 1955
Floud, Peter, C.B.E. "International Colour Woodcuts." *Studio* 149 (1955): 10–17.

Fort 1982
Fort, Susan Ilene. "Blanche Lazzell." *Arts* 57 (October 1982): 20–21.

Francey 1988
Francey, Mary. *Depression Printmakers as Workers, Re-defining Traditional Interpretations.* Salt Lake City: Exhibition cat., Utah Museum of Fine Arts, University of Utah, 1988.

Frasconi 1953
Frasconi, Antonio. *2 Poems de Garcia Lorca.* A limited edition portfolio with 17 woodcuts printed from the original blocks by the artist, text printed by John Muench at The Contemporaries. New York: 1953.

Freeman 1949
Freeman, Don. *Come One, Come All!* New York: Rinehart, 1949.

Freeman 1951
Freeman, Don and Lydia. *Chuggy and the Blue Caboose.* New York: Viking Press, 1951.

Freeman 1953
Freeman, Richard B. *Ralston Crawford.* Tuscaloosa: University of Alabama Press, 1953.

Freeman 1961
Freeman, Richard B. *The Lithographs of Ralston Crawford.* Lexington: Exhibition cat., University of Kentucky Art Gallery, 1961.

Freeman 1962
Freeman, Richard B. *The Lithographs of Ralston Crawford.* Lexington: University of Kentucky Press, 1962.

Freudenheim 1989
Freudenheim, Susan. "Still Painting after all these years." *San Diego Tribune* (January 25, 1989), pp. D1–2.

Freundlich 1970
Freundlich, August L. *Karl Schrag, A Catalogue Raisonné of the Graphic Works, 1939–1970* (with commentary by Una E. Johnson). Syracuse, N.Y.: Syracuse University, 1970.

Freundlich 1980
Freundlich, August L. *Karl Schrag, A Catalogue Raisonné of the Graphic Works, Part II, 1971–1980.* Syracuse, N.Y.: Syracuse University, 1980.

Friedländer 1976
Friedländer, Max J. *Pieter Brueghel (Early Netherlandish Painting,* vol. 14) (trans. Heinz Norden). 2nd ed. New York: Praeger, 1976.

Friedman 1978
Friedman, Joan M. *Color Printing in England, 1486–1870.* New Haven: Exhibition cat., Yale Center for British Art, 1978.

Friedman 1968
Friedman, Martin et al. *Charles Sheeler.* Washington D.C.: Exhibition cat., National Collection of Fine Arts, Smithsonian Institution, 1968.

Friedman 1959
Friedman, William. *Intaglios—The Work of Mauricio Lasansky and Other Printmakers Who Studied with Him at The State University of Iowa.* Buffalo, N.Y.: Exhibition cat., Albright-Knox Art Gallery, 1959.

Frost 1942
Frost, Rosamund. "Matta, Furious Scientist." *Art News* 41 (April 15, 1942): 26–27.

Frueh 1917
Frueh, Alfred Joseph. *Portraits in Caricature of Stage Celebrities.* New York: Frueh, 1917.

Frueh 1922
Frueh, Alfred Joseph. *Stage Folk.* New York: Lieber & Lewis, 1922.

Fuller 1950
Fuller, Sue. "Mary Cassatt's Use of Soft-Ground Etching." *The Magazine of Art* 43 (February 1950): 54–57.

Galm 1976
Galm, Bernard. *Corita Kent.* Los Angeles: University of California, Los Angeles Oral History Program, 1976

Ganso/Janson 1940
Ganso, Emil and H. W. Janson. "The Technique of Lithographic Printing." *Parnassus* 12 (November 1940): 67.

Garver/Neubert 1984
Garver, Thomas H. and George W. Neubert. *Nathan Oliveira: A Survey Exhibition, 1957–1984.* San Francisco: Exhibition cat., San Francisco Museum of Modern Art, 1984.

Gellert 1973
Gellert, Hugo. "Artists' Coordination Committee." In O'Connor 1973, pp. 255–257.

Gellert/Clough 1935
Gellert, Hugo and F. Gardner Clough. "Another Dispute." *Art Digest* 10 (November 15, 1935): 15, 19.

Gibson 1984
Gibson, David. *Designed to Persuade, The Graphic Art of Edward Penfield.* Yonkers, N.Y.: Exhibition cat., Hudson River Museum, 1984.

Gilbert-Rolfe 1973
Gilbert-Rolfe, Jeremy. "Clinton Hill, Zabriskie Gallery." *Artforum* 12 (December 1973): 86–87.

Gilmour 1988
Gilmour, Pat. "Lithographic Collaboration: The Hand, The Head, The Heart." In *Lasting Impressions: Lithography as Art.* Canberra: Exhibition cat., National Gallery of Australia, 1988.

Glueck 1988
Glueck, Grace. "Printmaking for the Love of It." *New York Times* (July 12, 1988), p. C15.

Goddu 1989
Goddu, Joseph. *American Art Posters of the 1890s.* New York: Exhibition cat., Hirschl & Adler Galleries, 1989.

Goodman 1986
Goodman, Cynthia. *Hans Hofmann.* New York: Abbeville Press, 1986.

Goodwin 1977
Goodwin, George M. *Millard Sheets.* Los Angeles: University of California, Los Angeles Oral History Program, 1977.

Gordon 1960
Gordon, John. *Karl Schrag.* New York: Whitney Museum of American Art, American Federation of Arts, 1960.

Gordon 1976
Gordon, Martin. "A Catalog of the Prints of Charles Sheeler." *Photo/Print Bulletin* 1 (Fall–Winter 1976): 4.

Gordon/Johnson 1955
Gordon, John and Una E. Johnson. 14 *Painter–Printmakers.* Brooklyn: Exhibition cat., Brooklyn Museum, 1955.

Graham 1987
Graham, Lanier. *The Spontaneous Gesture: Prints and Books of the Abstract Expressionist Era.* Canberra: Exhibition cat., Australian National Gallery, 1987.

Gravalos
Gravalos, Mary E. O. *Bertha Lum: Smithsonian Institution Press Series of American Printmaking.* Forthcoming.

Gray 1969
Gray, Cleve. "Experiments in Three Dimensions—Michael Ponce de León." *Art in America* 57 (May 1969): 72–73.

Green 1976
Green, Eleanor, Ellen Glavin, S.N.D., and Jeffrey R. Hayes. *Maurice Prendergast: Art of Impulse and Color.* New York: Exhibition cat., Davis & Long, 1976.

Greenberg 1957
Greenberg, Clement. "Milton Avery." *Arts* 32 (December 1957): 40–45.

Greenberg 1961
Greenberg, Clement. *Hofmann.* Paris: Editions Georges Fall, 1961.

Groce/Wallace 1957
Groce, George C. and David H. Wallace. *Dictionary of Artists in America, 1564–1860.* New Haven: Yale University Press, 1957.

von Groschwitz 1950
von Groschwitz, Gustave. *First International Biennial of Contemporary Color Lithography.* Cincinnati: Exhibition cat., Cincinnati Art Museum, 1950.

von Groschwitz 1956
von Groschwitz, Gustave. *Fourth International Biennial of Color Lithography*. Cincinnati: Exhibition cat., Cincinnati Art Museum, 1956.

Guest 1954
Guest, Barbara. "Anne Ryan." *Art News* 52 (January 1954): 69.

Guttheim 1937
Guttheim, F. A. "Architecture, Art, Life." *Magazine of Art* 30 (May 1937): 308.

Haas 1951
Haas, Irvin. "Henry Mark & Sylvia Wald." *Art News* 49 (February 1951): 47.

Haas 1955
Haas, Irwin. "The Print Collector." *Art News* 54 (May 1955): 15.

Hacker 1988
Hacker, Peter M. S. (ed.). *The Renaissance of Gravure, The Art of S. W. Hayter*. Oxford: Clarendon Press, 1988.

Hamilton 1958
Hamilton, Sinclair. *Early American Book Illustrators and Wood Engravers, 1670–1870*. Princeton: Princeton University Library, 1958.

Harari 1987
Harari, Hananiah. "WPA-AAA." Unpublished essay. 1987.

Harlow/Keats 1984
Harlow, Ann and Terry Keats. *The Color Woodcut in America 1895–1945*. Moraga, Calif.: Exhibition cat., Hearst Art Gallery, Saint Mary's College, 1984.

Haskell 1982
Haskell, Barbara. *Milton Avery*. New York: Exhibition cat., Whitney Museum of American Art, 1982.

Haskell 1985
Haskell, Barbara. *Ralston Crawford*. New York: Exhibition cat., Whitney Museum of American Art, 1985.

Haslem 1970
Jane Haslem Gallery. *Dean Meeker, Sculpture*. Washington, D.C.: Exhibition cat., 1970.

van Hasselt 1965
van Hasselt, Carlos. *Clairs-Obscurs, Gravures sur bois imprimées en couleurs de 1500 à 1800*. Paris: Exhibition cat., Institut Neerlandais, 1965.

Hatfield 1935
Dalzell Hatfield Gallery. *Millard Sheets* (articles by Arthur Millier, Dr. Hartley Burr Alexander, and Merle Armitage, portrait photograph by Edward Weston). Los Angeles: Exhibition cat., 1935.

Havens 1948
Havens, James D. "Reject Insincere Art, Keep Vigor." [Rochester] *Times-Union* (January 30, 1948), p. 18.

Haverkamp-Begeman 1962
Haverkamp-Begeman, Egbert et al. *Color in Prints*. New Haven: Exhibition cat., Yale University Art Gallery, 1962.

Hawkeye 1946
"Agnes Weinrich Dies in the East." [Burlington, Iowa] *Hawkeye* (April 18, 1946), n.p.

Hayter 1949a
Hayter, Stanley William. *New Ways of Gravure* (preface by Herbert Read). New York: Pantheon, 1949.

Hayter 1949b
Hayter, Stanley William. "The Interdependence of Idea and Technique." *Tiger's Eye* 1 (1949): n.p.

Hayter 1962
Hayter, Stanley William. *About Prints*. London and New York: Oxford University Press, 1962.

Hayward 1970
Hayward Gallery. *Kelpra Prints*. London: Exhibition cat., 1970.

Heller 1958
Heller, Jules. *Printmaking Today*. New York: Holt, Rinehart & Winston, 1958.

Helsell 1982
Helsell, Charles Paul. *Mr. Possum and Friends: Prints by Malcolm Myers*. Minneapolis: Exhibition cat., University Gallery, University of Minnesota, 1982.

Hentoff/Parkhurst 1974
Hentoff, Nat and Charles Parkhurst. *Frasconi, Against the Grain*. New York: Collier, 1974.

Hills 1983
Hills, Patricia. *Social Concernn and Urban R/*ealism, American Painting of the 1930s*. Boston: Exhibitionn cat., Boston University Art Gallery, 1983.

Hoeckner 1943
Hoecckner, Carl. "Book Review." *College Art Journal* 2 (January 1943): 61–62.

Hofer 1935
Hofer, Philip. "On Rudolph Ruzicka." *American Society of Graphic Arts Newsletter* 37 (1935): 8–9.

Hofmann 1948
Hofmann, Hans (eds. Bartlett H. Hayes, Jr., and Sara T. Weeks). *The Search for the Real and Other Essays*. Andover, Mass.: Addison Gallery of American Art, 1948. Reprint Cambridge, Mass.: MIT Press, 1968.

Holliday 1953
Holliday, Betty. "Casarella and Longo." *Art News* 52 (June 1953): 61–62.

Honig 1966
Honig, Edwin. *Mauricio Lasansky—The Nazi Drawings*. Iowa City: Exhibition cat., Lasansky Foundation, 1966.

Hotaling 1970
Hotaling, Ed. "Los Angeles." *Art News* 69 (May 1970): 168.

Howard 1963
Howard University, Gallery of Art. *16 Years After . . . Minna Citron*. Washington D.C.: Exhibition cat., 1963.

Hughes
Hughes, Edan Milton. *Artists in California, 1786–1940*. San Francisco: Hughes, 1986.

Hughes 1978
Hughes, Sukey. *Washi, the World of Japanese Paper*. Tokyo: Kodansha International, 1978.

Humphrey 1969
Humphrey, John. *Nathan Oliveira: Works on Paper 1960–1969*. San Francisco: Exhibition cat., San Francisco Museum of Art, 1969.

Hunter 1943
Hunter, Dard. *Papermaking, The History and Technique of an Ancient Craft*. New York: Knopf, 1943.

Hutson 1937
Hutson, Ethel. "Current Exhibitions of the Art Association of New Orleans." *The Warrington* [Louisiana] *Messenger* (February 1937), pp. 6, 13.

Hyde 1913
Hyde, Helen. "The Colour Lure of Mexico." *International Studio* 51 (November 1913): 26–35.

Ikeda 1977
Ikeda, Masuo. *Ynez Johnston*. Tokyo: Exhibition cat., Mitsukoshi Gallery, 1977.

Inman 1963
Inman, Pauline Winchester. "A History of the Society of American Graphic Artists." *Artist's Proof* 6 (Fall-Winter 1963–64): 43.

Ittmann 1984
Ittmann, John W. "The Triumph of Color: Technical Innovations in Printmaking." In *Regency to Empire, French Printmaking 1715–1814*. Minneapolis: Exhibition cat., Minneapolis Institute of Arts, 1984, pp. 22–24.

Ives 1974
Ives, Colta Feller. *The Great Wave: The Influence of Japanese Woodcuts on French Prints*. New York: Exhibition cat., Metropolitan Museum of Art, 1974.

Jacques 1922
Jacques, Bertha E. *Helen Hyde and Her Work, An Appreciation*. Chicago: Libby, 1922.

Jenkins 1983
Jenkins, Donald. *Images of a Changing World, Japanese Prints of the Twentieth Century*. Portland, Ore.: Exhibition cat., Portland Art Museum, 1983.

Johnson 1943
Johnson, Una E. *Abstraction, The Woodblock Color Prints of Louis Schanker*. Brooklyn: Exhibition cat., Brooklyn Museum, 1943.

Johnson 1956
Johnson, Una E. *Ten Years of American Prints, 1947–1956*. Brooklyn: Exhibition cat., Brooklyn Museum, 1956.

Johnson 1959a
Johnson, Una E. *Worden Day, Paintings, Collages, Drawings, Prints*, Montclair, N.J.: Exhibition cat., Montclair Art Museum, 1959.

Johnson 1959b
Johnson, Una E. *Gabor Peterdi, Twenty-five Years of his Prints, 1934–1959*. Brooklyn: Exhibition cat., Brooklyn Museum, 1959.

Johnson 1968
Johnson, Una E. *Sixteenth National Print Exhibition*. Brooklyn: Exhibition cat., Brooklyn Museum, 1968.

Johnson 1969a
Johnson, Una E. *Bernard Childs, Paintings/Prints/Images in Light*. Mountainville, N.Y.: Exhibition cat., Storm King Art Center, 1969.

Johnson 1969b
Johnson, Una E. "The Intaglio Prints of Bernard Childs." *Art in America* 57 (November–December 1969): 118–121.

Johnson 1970
Johnson, Una E. *Gabor Peterdi, Graphics, 1934–1969*. New York: Touchstone, 1970.

Johnson 1980
Johnson, Una E. *American Prints and Printmakers*. Garden City, N.Y.: Doubleday, 1980.

Johnson/Day 1986
Johnson, Una E. and Worden Day. *Worden Day, 40-Year Retrospective: 1946–1986. Drawings, Paintings, Prints, and Sculpture*. Trenton: Exhibition cat., New Jersey State Museum, 1986.

Johnson/Miller 1966
Johnson, Una E. and Jo Miller. *Milton Avery, Prints and Drawings, 1930–1964*. Brooklyn: Exhibition cat., Brooklyn Museum, 1966.

Johnson/Miller 1969
Johnson, Una E. and Jo Miller. *Adja Yunkers, Prints 1927–1967*. Brooklyn: Exhibition cat., Brooklyn Museum, 1969.

Johnson/Miller 1974
Johnson, Una E. and Jo Miller (research by Tom Jagger). *Louis Schanker, Prints, 1924–1971*. Brooklyn: Exhibition cat., Brooklyn Museum, 1974.

Jones 1975
Jones, Dan Burne. *The Prints of Rockwell Kent: A Catalogue Raisonné*. Chicago: University of Chicago Press, 1975.

Jones 1982
Jones, Elizabeth. "Robert Blackburn: An Investment in an Idea." *Tamarind Technical Papers* 6 (Winter 1982–83): 10–14.

Jones 1973
Jones, Harvey. *Nathan Oliveira, Paintings 1959–1973.* Oakland, Calif.: Exhibition cat., Oakland Museum of Art, 1973.

Kainen 1972
Kainen, Jacob. "The Graphic Arts Division of the WPA Federal Arts Project." In O'Connor 1972.

Kane 1976
Kane, Patricia E. *300 Years of American Seating Furniture.* Boston: New York Graphic Society, 1976.

Kawakita 1967
Kawakita, Michiaki. *Contemporary Japanese Prints.* Tokyo: Kodansha International, 1967.

Kaye 1977
Kaye, Evelyn. "Master of the Silk Screen." *Boston Sunday Globe* (September 11, 1977); pp. 42, 44.

Kelder 1980
Kelder, Diane. *Stuart Davis: Prints and Related Works.* Staten Island, N.Y.: Exhibition cat., Staten Island Museum, 1980.

Kelder 1971
Kelder, Diane (ed.). *Stuart Davis: A Documentary Monograph.* New York, Washington D.C., and London: 1971.

Kent 1935
Kent, Henry Watson. *An Exhibition of the Work of Rudolph Ruzicka.* New York: Exhibition cat., American Society of the Graphic Arts, 1935.

Kiehl 1987
Kiehl, David. *American Art Posters of the 1890s.* New York: Exhibition cat., Metropolitan Museum of Art, 1987.

Knowles 1970
Knowles, Joseph. "Santa Barbara's Historic Link to Color Wood Block Printing." *Noticias, Quarterly Bulletin of the Santa Barbara Historical Society* 16 (Winter 1970): 10–20.

Kosloff 1946
Kosloff, Albert. *Silk Screen Printing with Mimeograph Type Stencils.* Chicago: Industrial Arts Laboratory, Waller High School, 1946.

Kramer 1962
Kramer, Hilton. *Milton Avery: Paintings, 1930–1960.* New York: Thomas Yoseloff, 1962.

Kuchta/Seckler 1977
Kuchta, Ronald A. and Dorothy Gees Seckler. *Provincetown Painters, 1890s–1970s.* Syracuse, N.Y.: Exhibition cat., Everson Museum of Art, 1977.

Kuh 1962
Kuh, Katherine. *The Artist's Voice: Talks with Seventeen Artists.* New York: Harper & Row, 1962.

Kup 1947
Kup, Karl. "New York Commentary." *Print* 5 (1947): 71.

Kup 1950
Kup, Karl. *The Graphic work of Minna Citron, 1945–1950.* New York: Exhibition cat., New School for Social Research, 1950.

Laguna 1983
Laguna Museum of Art. *Millard Sheets, Six Decades of Painting.* Laguna Beach, Calif.: Exhibition cat., 1983.

Landau 1983
Landau, Ellen G. *Artists for Victory.* Washington, D.C.: Exhibition cat., Library of Congress, 1983.

Landon 1945
Landon, Edward. *Picture Framing.* New York: American Artists Group, 1945.

Landon 1951
Landon, Edward. *Scandinavian Design: Picture and Rune Stones, 1000 B.C. to 1100 A.D.* New York: American-Scandinavian Foundation, 1951.

Lane/Larson 1983
Lane, John R. and Susan C. Larson. *Abstract Painting and Sculpture in America, 1927–1944.* Pittsburgh: Exhibition cat., Museum of Art, Carnegie Institute, 1983.

Langdale 1979
Langdale, Cecily. *The Monotypes of Maurice Prendergast.* New York: Exhibition cat., David & Long, 1979.

Langdale 1984
Langdale, Cecily. *Monotypes by Maurice Prendergast in the Terra Museum of American Art.* Chicago: Terra Museum of American Art, 1984.

Langsner 1951
Langsner, Jules. "Ynez Johnston." *Arts and Architecture* 68 (June 1951): 30–31.

Lansford 1946
Lansford, Alonzo. "Printed Paintings." *Art Digest* 21 (December 1, 1946): 29.

Lathem 1986
Lathem, Edward Connery. *Rudolph Ruzicka: Speaking Reminiscently.* New York: Grolier Club, 1986.

Lawrence 1975
Lawrence, Edna W. *Bulletin of the Rhode Island School of Design* 62 (December 1975): 28.

LeJeune 1970
LeJeune, Arnold and Gladys. "Woodblock Printing in Santa Barbara." *Noticias, Quarterly Bulletin of the Santa Barbara Historical Society* 16 (Winter 1970): 4–9.

Lemos 1920
Lemos, Pedro Joseph. *Applied Art: Drawing, Painting, Design and Handicraft Arranged for Self Instruction of Teachers, Parents, and Students.* Mountain View, Calif.: Pacific Press, 1920.

Lemos 1929
Lemos, Pedro Joseph. *Landscape in Decoration.* Worcester, Mass.: Davis Press, 1929.

Lemos 1931
Lemos, Pedro Joseph. *The Art Teacher, A Book for Children and Teachers.* Worcester, Mass.: Davis Press, 1931.

Lemos 1946
Lemos, Pedro Joseph. "Oriental Art and the American Art Teacher." *School Arts Magazine* 47 (September 1946): 30.

Leopold 1973
Leopold, Michael. "Los Angeles Letter." *Art International* 17 (Summer 1973): 86.

Letcher 1977
Letcher, Bettina Havens. "James D. Havens, Woodcut Artist." *Yearbook of the American Society of Bookplate Collectors and Designers* (1977): 45–50.

Levin 1978
Levin, Gail. *Synchromism and American Color Abstraction, 1910–1925.* New York: Exhibition cat., Braziller/Whitney Museum of American Art, 1978.

Lewis 1973
Lewis, Louise M. *Garo Z. Antreasian: A Retrospective Exhibition of Lithographs.* Albuquerque: Exhibition cat., University of New Mexico Press, 1973.

Levy 1947
Levy, Julien. *Eugene Berman.* New York: Julien Levy Gallery, 1947.

Levy 1975
Levy, Mervyn. *Whistler Lithographs, An Illustrated Catalogue Raisonné.* London: Jupiter Books, 1975.

Lieberman 1955
Lieberman, William S. "Printmaking and the American Woodcut Today." *Perspective U.S.A.* 12 (Summer 1955): 50.

Lieberman 1969
Lieberman, William S. *Tamarind: Homage to Lithography.* New York: Exhibition cat., Museum of Modern Art, 1969.

Linton 1882
Linton, William James. *History of Wood Engraving in America.* Boston: Estes & Lauriat, 1882.

Lippencott 1941
Lippencott, Margaret E. "Dearborn's Musical Scheme." *New York Historical Society Quarterly Bulletin* 25 (1941): 134–142.

Little Rock 1942
"Robertson Lands Prints for Student Collection." *College Chatter* [Little Rock, Ark., Junior College] (February 17, 1942), p. 2.

Lochnan 1981
Lochnan, Katherine A. "Whistler & the Transfer Lithograph: A Lithograph with a Verdict." *The Print Collector's Newsletter* 12 (November-December 1981): 133–137.

Lochnan 1984
Lochnan, Katherine A. *The Etchings of James McNeill Whistler.* Toronto: Exhibition cat., Art Gallery of Ontario, 1984.

Lochnan 1986
Lochnan, Katherine A. *Whistler and his Circle.* Toronto: Exhibition cat., Art Gallery of Ontario, 1986.

Long, 1979
Long, Paulette. *Paper—Art & Technology.* San Francisco: Exhibition cat., World Print Council, 1979.

Long 1986
Long, Stephen. *Abstract Expressionist Prints.* New York: Exhibition cat., Associated American Artists, 1986.

Longman 1957
Longman, Lester. *Lasansky: Twenty-four Years of Printmaking.* Iowa City: Exhibition cat., University of Iowa, 1957.

Longman/Friedman 1949
Longman, Lester and William Friedman. *A New Direction in Intaglio: The Work of Mauricio Lasansky and His Students.* Minneapolis: Exhibition cat., Walker Art Center, 1949.

Longo 1956
Longo, Vincent. "Collage Combined with Painting: Interview with Clinton Hill." *Arts* 30 (September 1956): 64–65.

Loran 1950
Loran, Erle. "Art News from San Francisco." *Art News* 49 (October 1950): 52, 58.

Loran 1952
Loran, Erle. "Art News from San Francisco." *Art News* 51 (September 1952): 39.

Los Angeles 1920
Los Angeles Museum of History, Science and Art, Department of Fine and Applied Art. *Exhibition of Woodblock Prints by Bertha Lum.* Los Angeles: Exhibition cat., 1920.

Los Angeles 1921
"Bertha Lum." *Bulletin of the [Los Angeles] Museum of History, Science and Art, Department of Fine and Applied Art* 2 (January 1921): 45.

Los Angeles 1923
Los Angeles Museum of History, Science and Art. *Colored Etchings by May Gearhart, Block Prints by Frances H. Gearhart.* Los Angeles: Exhibition cat., 1923.

Lovoos/Penney 1984
Lovoos, Janice and Edmund F. Penney. *Millard Sheets, One Man Renaissance.* Flagstaff, Ariz.: Northland Press, 1984.

Lowe 1937
Lowe, Jeanette. "Rhythmic Play of Line and Color in Paintings by Bernard Steffen." *Art News* 36 (October 16, 1937): 15–16.

Lowe 1939
Lowe, Jeanette. "Hananiah Harari." *Art News* 37 (March 4, 1939): 14.

Lowengrund 1948
Lowengrund, Margaret. "Metropolitan Surveys the Art of Lithography." *Art Digest* 23 (December 15, 1948): 19.

Lowengrund 1951
Lowengrund, Margaret. "Fine Art and Commercial Art." In Arthur Zaidenburg (ed.), *The Art of the Artist*. New York: Crown, 1951.

Lublin 1989
Lublin, Mary. *19th and 20th Century Paintings*. New York: Exhibition cat., Jordan-Volpe Gallery, 1989.

Lum 1922
Lum, Bertha. *Gods, Goblins and Ghosts, The Weird Legends of the Far East*. Philadelphia and London: Lippincott, 1922.

Lum 1981
Lum, Peter. *My Own Pair of Wings*. San Francisco: Chinese Materials Center, 1981.

Lunn 1973
Lunn, Harry H., Jr. *Milton Avery, Prints 1933–1955* (introduction by Frank Getlein and essay by Alan Fern). Washington, D.C.: Exhibition cat., Graphics International, 1973.

Lynn 1980
Lynn, Catherine. *Wallpaper in America, from the Seventeenth Century to World War I*. New York: Norton, 1980.

Macdonald-Wright 1924
Macdonald-Wright, Stanton. *A Treatise on Color*. Los Angeles: Stanton Macdonald-Wright, 1924 (reprinted in Scott 1967).

Margo 1947
Margo, Boris. "My Theories and Techniques." *The Magazine of Art* 40 (November 1947): 272–273.

Marks 1984
Marks, Matthew. "Provincetown Prints." *Print Collectors' Newsletter* 15 (September-October 1984): 132–133.

Marzio 1979
Marzio, Peter. *The Democratic Art: Pictures for a 19th-Century America*. Boston: David R. Godine, 1979.

Matthews 1987
Matthews, Nancy Mowll. *Mary Cassatt*. New York: Abrams, 1987.

Matthews 1984
Matthews, Nancy Mowll (ed.). *Cassatt and Her Circle: Selected Letters*. New York: Abbeville Press, 1984.

Matthews/Shapiro 1989
Matthews, Nancy Mowll and Barbara Stern Shapiro. *Mary Cassatt: The Color Prints*. New York: Exhibition cat., Abrams, in association with Williams College Museum of Art, 1989.

Maurice 1976
Maurice, Alfred P. "George C. Miller and Son, Lithographic Printers to Artists since 1917." *American Art Review* 3 (March-April 1976): 133–144.

Mayer 1969
Mayer, Ralph. *A Dictionary of Art Terms & Techniques*. New York: Crowell, 1969.

McCauley 1975
McCauley, Lois B. *Maryland Historical Prints 1752–1889*. Baltimore: Maryland Historical Society, 1975.

McCausland 1940
McCausland, Elizabeth. "Silk Screen Color Prints." *Parnassus* 12 (March 1940): 34–36.

McCausland 1946
McCausland, Elizabeth. "Robert Gwathmey." *Magazine of Art* 39 (April 1946): 149.

McClelland 1924
McClelland, Nancy. *Historic Wall-Papers from Their Inception to the Introduction of Machinery*. Philadelphia: Lippincott, 1924.

McCulloch 1988
McCulloch, Edith. *The Prints of Don Freeman: A Catalogue Raisonné*. Charlottesville: University Press of Virginia, 1988.

McGill 1988
McGill, Douglas C. "Robert Gwathmey, 85, an Artist of Social Passions and Style, Dies." *New York Times* (September 22, 1988), p. B11.

Mellow 1945
Mellow, James R. "Schrag Exhibition at Smithsonian." *Art News* 44 (November 1945): 20.

Mellow 1959
Mellow, James R. "Schrag Exhibition at Smithsonian." *Arts* 33 (September 1959): 64.

Métropole 1912
Métropole Gallery. *Exhibition of Original Etchings by John W. Cotton*. Toronto: Exhibition cat., 1912.

Meyerowitz 1986
Meyerowitz, Theresa Bernstein. *William Meyerowitz, The Artist Speaks*. Philadelphia: Art Alliance Press, 1986.

Meyerowitz
Meyerowitz, Theresa Bernstein. *William Meyerowitz, Etchings in Color*. Unpublished manuscript in vertical files. Washington, D.C.: National Museum of American Art, Smithsonian Institute, n.d.

MFA 1960
Museum of Fine Arts. *Maurice Prendergast Water-Color Sketchbook 1899* (with essay by Peter A. Wick). Boston and Cambridge: Harvard University Press, 1960.

MIA 1958
Minneapolis Institute of Arts. *Exhibition of Painting and Prints by Malcolm H. Myers* (preface by Harold Joachim). Minneapolis: Exhibition cat., 1958.

Miami 1964
Dean Meeker. Miami: Exhibition cat., Washington Federal Bank, 1964.

Michigan 1985
Ruby, Christine Nelson, Arnold Lauren, and Victoria Weston Julius. *The Federal Art Project: American Prints from the 1930s*. Ann Arbor: Exhibition cat., University of Michigan Museum of Art, 1985.

Miller 1931
Miller, Arthur. "Far-Western Print Makers." *Prints* 1 (January 1931): 20.

Miller 1960
Miller, Dorothy C. (ed.). *Sixteen Americans*. New York: Exhibition cat., Museum of Modern Art, 1960.

Miller 1904
Miller, H. B. *Uncle Ben's Cobblestones: Familiar Talks About Unfamiliar Things*. Mountain View, Calif.: Pacific Press, 1904.

Milliken 1946
Milliken, William M. "Review of the [Annual] Exhibition." *Bulletin of the Cleveland Museum of Art* 33 (May 1946): 57–72.

Miyamoto 1978
Miyamoto, Wayne A. *Lee Chesney–25 Years of Printmaking* (introduction by Kenneth A. Kerslake). Orlando: Exhibition cat., Florida Technological University, University Presses of Florida, 1978.

MMA/MFA 1980
Metropolitan Museum of Art and Museum of Fine Arts. *The Painterly Print: Monotypes from the Seventeenth to the Twentieth Century*. New York and Boston: Exhibition cat., 1980.

Moffatt 1977
Moffatt, Frederick C. *Arthur Wesley Dow (1857–1922)*. Washington, D.C.: Smithsonian Institution Press, 1977.

MoMA 1939
Museum of Modern Art. *Charles Sheeler; Paintings, Drawings, Photographs*, statements by Charles Sheeler and William Carlos Williams, New York: Exhibition cat., 1939.

MoMA 1944
"Hayter and Studio 17." *Museum of Modern Art Bulletin* 12 (August 1944): 3–15.

MoMA 1947
Museum of Modern Art. *The Theatre of Eugene Berman*. New York: Exhibition cat., 1947.

Montclair 1981
Montclair Art Museum. *Clinton Hill, Paintings and Paperworks*. Montclair, N.J.: Exhibition cat., 1981.

Moore 1975
Moore, James C. *Harry Sternberg: A Catalogue Raisonné of His Graphic Work*. Wichita, Kans.: Exhibition cat., Edwin A. Ulrich Museum of Art, Wichita State University, 1975.

Moore 1988
Moore, James. *Garo Z. Antreasian, A Retrospective, 1942–1987*. Albuquerque: Exhibition cat., Albuquerque Museum, 1988.

Moorhead
Moorhead, Désirée. *The Prints of S. W. Hayter, A Catalogue Raisonné*. Forthcoming.

Moran 1973
Moran, James. *Printing Presses, History and Development from the 15th Century to Modern Times*. Berkeley and Los Angeles: University of California Press, 1973.

Morris/Charlot 1931
Morris, Earl Halstead, Jean Charlot, and Ann Axtell Morris. *The Temple of the Warriors . . .* Washington, D.C.: Carnegie Foundation, 1931.

Morse 1976
Morse, Peter. *Jean Charlot's Prints: A Catalogue Raisonné*. Honolulu: University Press of Hawaii, 1976.

Moser 1977
Moser, Joanne. *Atelier 17, A 50th Anniversary Retrospective Exhibition*. Madison, Wis.: Exhibition cat., Elvehjem Art Center, 1977.

Moser 1980
Moser, Joanne. *The Graphic Art of Emil Ganso*. Iowa City: Exhibition cat., University of Iowa Museum of Art, 1980.

Movalli 1980
Movalli, Charles. "A Conversation with William Meyerowitz and Theresa Bernstein." *American Artist* 44 (January 1980): 62–67, 90–92.

Moy 1958
Moy, Seong. *Uncle Remus*. New York: Limited Edition Club, 1958.

Myers 1988
Myers, Jane. "Lithographs of 1916–1918." In Jane Myers and Linda Ayres, *George Bellows: The Artist and His Lithographs, 1916–1924*. Fort Worth: Exhibition cat., Amon Carter Museum, 1988.

Myers 1962
Myers, Malcolm H. "Graphic Workshops: The University of Minnesota." *Artist's Proof* 1 (1962): 37–38.

Myers/Cole 1986
Myers, Jane (ed.) and Sylvan Cole. *Stuart Davis, Graphic Work and Related Paintings with a Catalogue Raisonné of the Prints.* Fort Worth, Tex.: Amon Carter Museum, 1986.

Naar 1989
Naar, Harry I. *Reginald Neal, Works from 1958 to the Present.* Trenton: Exhibition cat., New Jersey State Museum, 1989.

Nelson 1970
Nelson, June Kompass. *Harry Bertoia, Sculptor.* Detroit: Wayne State University Press, 1970.

Nelson 1988
Nelson, June Kompass. *Harry Bertoia, Printmaker, Monotypes, and Other Monographics.* Detroit: Wayne State University Press, 1988.

Neodesha 1980
"Famous Local Artist Dies in New York." *The Neodesha [Kansas] Sun-Register* (July 29, 1980), p. 1.

Ness/Orwig 1939
Ness, Zenobia B. and Louise Orwig. *Iowa Artists of the First Hundred Years.* Des Moines: Wallace-Homestead, 1939.

New York Times 1916
"Art at Home and Abroad." *New York Times* (May 14, 1916), section 5, p. 18.

New York Times 1938
"The Villages of the French Riviera." *New York Times Book Review* (April 17, 1938), p. 8.

Nierendorf 1941
Nierendorf, Karl (ed.) *Paul Klee: Paintings, Watercolors, 1913 to 1939.* New York: Exhibition cat., Nierendorf Gallery, Oxford University Press, 1941.

Norelli 1984
Norelli, Martina Roudabush. *Werner Drewes, Sixty-Five Years of Printmaking.* Washington, D.C.: Exhibition cat., National Museum of American Art, Smithsonian Institution, 1984.

Northrup 1981
Northrup, C. Van. *Colour Lithographs of the Works Progress Administration Federal Art Project: New York City, 1935–1942.* (Unpublished manuscript). San Diego: San Diego State University, 1981.

NYHS 1983
New York Historical Society. *New York Themes: Paintings and Prints by William Meyerowitz and Theresa Bernstein.* New York: Exhibition cat., 1983.

O'Connor 1966
O'Connor, Francis V. (ed.). *Federal Art Patronage, 1933–1943.* College Park: Exhibition cat., J. Millard Tawes Fine Arts Center, University of Maryland, 1966.

O'Connor 1972
O'Connor, Francis V. (ed.). *The New Deal Art Projects.* Washington, D.C.: Smithsonian Institution, 1972.

O'Connor 1973
O'Connor, Francis V. (ed.). *Art for the Millions: Essays from the 1930s by Artists and Administrators of the WPA Federal Art Project.* New York: New York Graphic Society, 1973.

O'Connor/Thaw 1978
O'Connor, Francis V. and Eugene Thaw. *Jackson Pollock, A Catalogue Raisonné of Paintings, Drawings and Other Works.* New Haven: Yale University Press, 1978.

Ontario 1970
The Art Gallery of Ontario, the Canadian Collection. Toronto and New York: McGraw-Hill Book Company of Canada, 1970.

Parker 1988
Parker, Barbara. *Ada Gilmore, Woodcuts and Watercolors.* New York: Exhibition cat., Mary Ryan Gallery, and Provincetown, Mass.: Art Association and Museum, 1988.

Parnassus 1938
Parnassus 10 (October 1938): 34.

Parsons 1955
Betty Parsons Gallery. *Boris Margo.* New York: Exhibition cat., 1955.

Pasko 1894
Pasko, Wesley Washington (ed.). *American Dictionary of Printing and Bookmaking.* New York: Howard Lockwood, 1894.

Pearl 1984
Marilyn Pearl Gallery. *Clinton Hill, Paintings, Paperworks, Constructions.* New York: Exhibition cat., 1984.

Pearl 1988
Marilyn Pearl Gallery. *Clinton Hill, Recent Work.* New York: Exhibition cat., 1988.

Pearl 1989
Marilyn Pearl Gallery. *Clinton Hill: Woodcuts 1958–1988.* New York: Exhibition cat., 1989.

Peet 1988
Peet, Phyllis. *American Women of the Etching Revival.* Atlanta: Exhibition cat., High Museum of Art, 1988.

Pencil Points
Pencil Points 10 (March 1930): 155–160.

Penfield 1907
Penfield, Edward, *Holland Sketches.* New York: Scribner's, 1907.

Penfield 1911
Penfield, Edward. *Spanish Sketches.* New York: Scribner's, 1911.

Pennell/Pennell 1898
Pennell, Joseph and Elizabeth Robins Pennell. *Lithography and Lithographers.* London: T. Fisher Unwin, 1898.

Pennell/Pennell 1909
Pennell, Joseph and Elizabeth Robins Pennell. *The Life of James McNeill Whistler.* 3rd ed. 2 vols. London: William Heinemann, 1909.

Pepper 1905
Pepper, Charles Hovey. *Japanese Prints.* Boston: Walter Kimball, 1905.

Peterdi 1959a
Peterdi, Gabor. *Printmaking, Methods Old and New.* New York: Macmillan, 1959.

Peterdi 1959b
Peterdi, Gabor. *Great Prints of the World.* New York: Macmillan, 1959.

Peterdi 1963
Peterdi, Gabor. "A Biography of My Landscape." *Art in America* 51 (June 1963): 38–43.

Philipps/Ryan 1985
Philipps, Kris and Gillian Ryan et al. *Ansei Uchima: A Retrospective.* Bronxville, N.Y.: Exhibition cat., Sarah Lawrence College Gallery, 1985.

Phillips 1924
Phillips, Duncan et al. *Arthur B. Davies: Essays on the Man and His Art.* Cambridge, Mass.: Riverside Press, 1924.

Phillips 1967
Phillips, Matthew. *Maurice Prendergast: The Monotypes.* Annandale-on-Hudson, N.Y.: Exhibition cat., William Cooper Proctor Art Center, Bard College, 1967.

Pollard 1896
Pollard, Percival (introduction by Edward Penfield). *Posters in Miniature.* London: John Lane, 1896.

Ponce de León 1959
Ponce de León, Michael. "An Artist-Teacher Explains . . ." *Print* 13 (January 1959): 30–31.

Ponce de León 1967
Ponce de León, Michael. "The Metal Collage Intaglio Print." *Artist's Proof* 7 (1967): 52–54.

Porter 1958
Porter, Fairfield. "Albert Urban." *Art News* 57 (October 1958): 46.

Pousette-Dart 1956
Pousette-Dart, Nathaniel (ed.) *American Painting Today.* New York: Hastings House, 1956.

Prasse/Richards 1962
Prasse, Leona E. and Louise S. Richards. *Prints and Drawings by Gabor Peterdi.* Cleveland: Exhibition cat., Cleveland Museum of Art, 1962.

Price 1929
Price, Frederic Newlin. *The Etchings and Lithographs of Arthur B. Davies.* New York: Mitchell Kennerly, 1929.

Print Council 1959
Print Council of America. *American Prints Today/1959* (introduction by Lessing J. Rosenwald). New York: Exhibition cat., 1959.

Print Council 1962
Print Council of America. *American Prints Today* (introduction by Lessing J. Rosenwald and catalogue by Grace M. Mayer). New York: Exhibition cat., 1962.

Prints 1931
Prints 1 (January 1931): 16, 43.

Prints 1933
Prints 3 (March 1933): 13.

Prints 1934
Prints 4 (March 1934): 41–42.

Prints 1936
Prints 6 (February 1936): 43–44, 131.

Prints 1937
Prints 7 (April 1937): 222.

Rathbone/Thompson 1938
Rathbone, Augusta, Virginia Thompson, and Juliet Thompson. *French Riviera Villages* (illustrated by reproductions of aquatints by Augusta Rathbone and photographs by Juliet Thompson). New York: Mitchell Kennerley, 1938.

Redon 1922
Redon, Odilon. *A Soi-même.* Paris: H. Floury, 1922.

Reed 1944
Reed, Judith Kaye. "Urban Impresses." *Art Digest* 19 (December 1, 1944): 30.

Reed 1950
Reed, Judith Kaye. "Sound Abstractions by Seong Moy." *Art Digest* 24 (June 1, 1950): 17–18.

Reed/Wallace 1989
Reed, Sue Welsh and Richard Wallace. *Italian Etchers of the Renaissance and Baroque.* Boston: Exhibition cat., Museum of Fine Arts, 1989.

Rewald 1953
Rewald, John. *Bernard Reder, Woodcuts.* New York: Exhibition cat., Grace Borgenicht Gallery, 1953.

Reynolds 1967
Reynolds, Graham. *The Engravings of S. W. Hayter.* London: Exhibition cat., Victoria and Albert Museum, 1967.

Rhead 1985
Rhead, Louis John. "The Moral Aspect of the Artistic Poster." *The Bookman* 1 (June 1895): 312–314.

Rhoades 1973
Rhoades, Stephen L. *Mauricio Lasansky, 43 Prints, 1937–1972.* Fort Dodge, Iowa: Exhibition cat., Blanden Art Gallery, 1973.

Rhys/Wick 1960
Rhys, Hedley Howell and Peter A. Wick. *Maurice Prendergast, 1859–1924.* Boston: Exhibition cat., Museum of Fine Arts, 1960.

Rice 1929
Rice, William Seltzer. *Block Printing in the School*. Milwaukee, Wis.: Bruce, 1929.

Rice 1941
Rice, William Seltzer. *Block Prints—How to Make Them*. Milwaukee, Wis.: Bruce, 1941.

Rice 1946
Rice, William Seltzer. *Block Printing Designs for Use on Textiles*. Milwaukee, Wis.: Bruce, 1946.

Riggs 1977
Riggs, Timothy A. "Mr. Koehler and Mrs. Marrs: The Formation of the Mrs. Kingsmill Marrs Collection." *Worcester Art Museum Journal* 1 (1977–78): 3–13.

Riley 1943
Riley, Maude. "Non-Objective Museum Holds Loan Show." *Art Digest* 18 (November 1, 1943): 12.

Ring 1949
Ring, Grete. *A Century of French Painting 1400–1500*. New York: Oxford University Press, 1949.

RISD 1973
Museum of Art, Rhode Island School of Design. *Selection III: Contemporary Graphics from the Museum's Collection*. Providence: Exhibition cat., 1973.

Roberts 1920
Roberts, Mary Fanton. "Studies of Childhood in Block Prints: The Work of Eliza Gardiner." *Touchstone* 8 (December 1920): 210–214.

Robinson 1983
Robinson, William. *A Cloud in Pants, Adja Yunkers and Abstract Expressionism*. Ph.D. diss., Case Western Reserve University. Ann Arbor, Mich.: UMI Press, 1983.

Roerich 1935
Roerich Museum. *Theodore J. Roszak: Exhibition of Paintings, Drawings, Lithographs, and Studies in Color*. New York: Exhibition cat., Polish Institute of Arts and Letters and International Center of the Roerich Museum, 1935.

Rose 1984
Rose, Ingrid. *Werner Drewes, A Catalogue Raisonné of his Prints*. New York and Munich: Verlag Kunstgalerie Esslingen, 1984.

Roswell 1943
Roswell, Helen. "Still Lifes by Anne Ryan." *Art Design* 17 (April 15, 1943): 21.

Roszak 1974
Roszak, Theodore. *Lithographs and Drawings, 1971–1974*. New York: Pierre Matisse Gallery, 1974.

Rowland 1958
Rowland, Earl. "Edward Penfield, An American Master Illustrator." *American Artist* 22 (April 1958): 46–51, 60–64.

Rubenstein 1980
Rubenstein, Daryl P. *Max Weber, A Catalogue Raisonné of his Graphic Work*. Chicago and London: University of Chicago Press, 1980.

Rutgers 1986
Rutgers, State University of New Jersey. *Minna Citron at 90*. New Brunswick: Exhibition cat., Mabel Smith Douglass Library, 1986.

Ruzicka 1915
Ruzicka, Rudolph. *New York, A Series of Wood Engravings in Color*. New York: Grolier Club, 1915.

Ruzicka 1917
Ruzicka, Rudolph. *Newark, A Series of Engravings on Wood* (with an essay by Walter Prichard Eaton). Newark, N.J.: Cartaret Book Club, 1917.

Ryan 1925
Ryan, Anne. *Lost Hills*. New York: The New Door, 1925.

Ryan 1986
Mary Ryan Gallery. *Edna Boies Hopkins: Color Woodcuts, 1900–1923*. New York: Exhibition cat., 1986.

Ryan/Kisseloff 1986
Ryan, Mary and Jeff Kisseloff. *Hugo Gellert*. New York: Exhibition cat., Mary Ryan Gallery, 1986.

Saff/Sacilotto 1978
Saff, Donald and Deli Sacilotto. *Printmaking, History and Process*. New York: Holt, Rinehart and Winston, 1978.

Saint Mary's 1976
Saint Mary's College of Maryland. *Robert Gwathmey*. Mary's City: Exhibition cat., 1976.

de Salle 1929
de Salle, Albert. "Paul Honoré, Muralist and Xylographer." *The Print Connoisseur* 9 (January 1929): 51–83.

Samuels 1976
Samuels, Peggy and Harold. *The Illustrated Biographical Encyclopedia of Artists of the American West*. Garden City, N.Y.: Doubleday, 1976.

San Francisco 1967
San Francisco Museum of Art. *Leonard Edmondson, Color Etchings 1951–1967*. San Francisco: Exhibition cat., 1967.

San Francisco 1968
San Francisco Museum of Art. *Carol Summers, Woodcuts 1950–1967*. San Francisco: Exhibition cat., 1968.

Santa Fe 1972
Santa Fe, Museum of New Mexico. *Gustave Baumann* (reprinted from *El Palacio* 78, includes "Concerning a Small Untroubled World" by Gustave Baumann, and "Gustave Baumann" by Calla Hay). 1972.

Savage 1818
Savage, William. *Practical Hints on Decorative Printing*. London: Longman, Hurst, Rees, Orme, and Brown, 1818–23.

Schanker/Nathan 1938
Schanker, Louis and Walter L. Nathan. "Controversy Concerning a Coincidence." *Art News* 37 (October 29, 1938): 16.

Schmeckebier/Gelb 1968
Schmeckebier, Laurence, Jan Gelb, and Alexandra Schmeckebier. *Boris Margo: Graphic Work/1932–1968*. Syracuse, N.Y.: Exhibition cat., School of Art, Syracuse University, 1968.

Scholz 1985
Scholz, Lynn. "Louis Rhead's First Career." *The American Fly Fisher* 12 (Winter 1985): 18–25.

Schrag 1966
Schrag, Karl. "Happiness and Torment of Printmaking." *Artist's Proof* 6 (1966): 12–13.

Schrag 1977
Schrag, Karl. "Light and Darkness in Contemporary Printmaking." *Print Review* 7 (1977): 44–48.

Scott 1967
Scott, David W. *The Art of Stanton Macdonald-Wright*. Washington, D.C.: Exhibition cat., National Collection of Fine Arts, Smithsonian Institution, 1967.

Seeber 1971
Seeber, Louise Combes. *George Elbert Burr, 1859–1939: A Catalogue Raisonné and Guide to the Etched Work*. Flagstaff, Ariz.: Northland Press, 1971.

Seckler 1952
Seckler, Dorothy Gees. "Will Barnet makes a lithograph." *Art News* 51 (April 1952): 38–41, 62–64.

Seckler 1957
Seckler, Dorothy Gees. "John von Wicht." *Arts* 32 (November 1957): 32–37.

Seitz 1963
Seitz, William. *Hans Hofmann*. New York: Exhibition cat., Museum of Modern Art, 1963.

Senseney 1910
Senseney, George E. "Etching in Color." *Palette & Bench* 2 (May 1910): 192–194.

Sessler 1988
Sessler, Alfred. *The Prints of Alfred Sessler, from 1935 to 1963*. Madison: Exhibition cat., Wisconsin Academy of Sciences, Arts, Letters, 1988.

Sharp 1950
Sharp, Maynell. "Harnessed Harari." *Art Digest* 24 (May 1, 1950): 16.

Shaw-Eagle 1984
Shaw-Eagle, Joanna. "Bethesda Gallery rediscovers two artists." *The Montgomery Journal* (February 17, 1984), p. B6.

Shokler 1946
Shokler, Harry. *Artist's Manual for Silk Screen Printing*. New York: American Artists Group, 1946.

Silverman 1972
Silverman, Maxwell. *Frueh on the Theater* (introduction by Brendan Gill). New York: New York Public Library, 1972.

Simmons 1932
Simmons, Will. "The Etchings of George Elbert Burr." *Prints* 3 (November 1932): 1–9.

Sims 1980
Sims, Patterson. *Charles Sheeler, A Concentration of Works from the Permanent Collection of the Whitney Museum of American Art*. New York: Exhibition cat., Whitney Museum of American Art, 1980.

Skelinghaus 1924
Skelinghaus, Jessie A. "Etchers of California." *International Studio* 78 (February 1924): 384–387.

Smale 1984
Smale, Nicholas. "Whistler and the Transfer Lithograph." *The Tamarind Papers* 7 (Fall 1984): 72–83.

Smith 1945
Smith, Joseph Coburn. *Charles Hovey Pepper*. Portland, Maine: Southworth-Anthonensen Press, 1945.

Smith 1983
Smith, Lawrence. *The Japanese Print Since 1900, Old Dreams and New Visions*. New York: Harper & Row, 1983.

Smith 1954
Smith, Virginia Jeffrey. "Fairport's Jim Havens, A Much-Honored Artist." [Rochester] *Times-Union* (October 21, 1954), p. 41.

Smith 1960
Smith, Virginia Jeffrey. "James D. Havens Dies; Prominent Graphic Artist." [Rochester] *Times-Union* (December 1, 1960), p. 36.

Soby 1941
Soby, James Thrall. *Eugene Berman, Catalogue of the Retrospective Exhibition*. Boston: Exhibition cat., Institute of Modern Art, 1941.

Solomon 1989
Solomon, Deborah. "The Hidden Legacy of Anne Ryan." *The New Criterion* (January 19, 1989), pp. 53–58.

Speed 1935
J. B. Speed Memorial Museum. *Exhibition of Etching in Color by Ellen Day Hale, Gabrielle DeVaux Clements, Lesley Jackson, Margaret Yeaton Hoyt, Theresa F. Bernstein, and William Meyerowitz*. Louisville, Ky.: Exhibition cat., 1935.

Sperling/Field 1973
Sperling, Louise and Richard S. Field. *Offset Lithography*. Middletown, Conn.: Exhibition cat., Davison Art Center, Wesleyan University, 1973.

Springfield 1940
Springfield Museum of Fine Arts. *Exhibition of Silk Screen Prints* (foreword by Elizabeth McCausland). Springfield, Mass.: Exhibition cat., 1940.

Staly 1975
Staly, Allen. "Whistler as Printmaker." In Mervyn Levy (ed.), *Whistler Lithographs: An Illustrated Catalogue Raisonné*. London: Jupiter Books, 1975.

Stapleton 1906
Stapleton, Ammon. "Gustav Sigismund Peters, Pioneer Stereotyper and Color-Printer." *Pennsylvania-German* 7 (1906): 177–178.

Statler 1956
Statler, Oliver. *Modern Japanese Prints: An Art Reborn*. Rutland, Vt.: Charles E. Tuttle, 1956.

Stebbins 1987
Stebbins, Theodore E. *Charles Sheeler, the Photographs*. Boston: Exhibition cat., Museum of Fine Arts, 1987.

Stedelijk 1959
Stedelijk Museum. *Childs*. Amsterdam: Exhibition cat., 1959.

Steffen 1963
Steffen, Bernard. *Silk Screen*. New York: Grosset & Dunlap, 1963.

Stein 1930
Stein, Gertrude. *Ten Portraits*. Paris: Editions de la Montaigne, 1930.

Sternberg 1942
Sternberg, Harry. *Silk Screen Color Printing*. New York: McGraw-Hill, 1942.

Sternberg 1943
Sternberg, Harry. "War from the Bottom Up . . ." *Magazine of Art* 36 (January 1943): 3–5.

Sternberg 1949
Sternberg, Harry. "Craftsmanship, Printmaking, and Contemporary Education." *College Art Journal* 9 (1949): 204–205.

Summer/Audrieth 1941
Summer, Harry and Ralph M. Audrieth. *Handbook of Silk Screen Printing Process*. New York: A. Brown, 1941.

Summers 1988
Summers, Carol. *Catalogue Raisoné [sic], Woodcuts 1950–1988*. Milwaukee, Boston, and New York: Exhibition cat., David Barnett Gallery, 1988.

Swanson 1962
Swanson, Dean. *Recent Prints and Drawings by Malcolm Myers*. Minneapolis: Exhibition cat., Walker Art Gallery, 1962.

Sweeney 1945
Sweeney, James Johnson. *Stuart Davis*. New York: Exhibition cat., Museum of Modern Art, 1945.

Szabo 1987
Szabo, George. *Prendergast: The Large Boston Public Garden Sketchbook*. New York: Braziller, 1987.

Tamarind
Tamarind Archives. Albuquerque: University of New Mexico Library.

Tate 1980
Tate Gallery. *Kelpra Studio: An Exhibition to commemorate the Rose and Chris Prater Gift*. London: Exhibition cat., 1980.

Taylor 1956
Taylor, Rex. "Fletcher Martin: Sports King of the Art World." *Famous Artists Magazine* 5 (Autumn 1956): 13–15.

Thieme/Becker
Thieme, Ulrich and Felix Becker et al. *Allgemeines Lexikon der bildenden Künstler von der Antike bis zur Gegenwart*. 37 vols. Leipzig: Wilhelm Engelmann, (after vol. 4, E. A. Seemann), 1907–50.

Thien/Lasansky 1975
Thien, John and Phillip Lasansky. *Lasansky: Printmaker*. Iowa City: University of Iowa Press, 1975.

Thomas 1988
Thomas, Steven. *Provincetown Printing Blocks*. Woodstock, Vt.: Exhibition cat., 1988.

Tobin 1984
Tobin, Robert L. B. *Eugene Berman and the Theatre of Meloncholia*. San Antonio, Tex.: Exhibition cat., Marion Koogler McNay Art Museum, 1984.

Todd 1948
Todd, Ruthven. "The Techniques of William Blake's Illuminated Painting." *Print Collector's Quarterly* 29 (November 1948): 25–37.

Tokuno 1893
Tokuno, T. (ed. S. R. Koehler). "Japanese wood-cutting and wood-cut printing." *Report of the United States National Museum of 1892*. Washington D.C.: Smithsonian Institution, 1893, pp. 221–244.

Toledo 1930
Toledo Museum of Art. *Modern Japanese Prints*. Toledo, Ohio: Exhibition cat., 1930.

Tomkins 1976
Tomkins, Calvin. "Profiles [Tatyana Grossman]: The Moods of a Stone." *The New Yorker* 7 (June 1976): 62–76.

Tonelli 1987
Tonelli, Edith A. (ed.). *IN VOL VE MENT, The Graphic Art of Antonio Frasconi*. Los Angeles: Exhibition cat., Wight Art Gallery, University of California, 1987.

Tovell 1980
Tovell, Rosemarie L. *Reflections of a Quiet Pool, The Prints of David Milne*. Ottawa: National Gallery of Canada, 1980.

Troche/Beall 1963
Troche, E. Gunter and Dennis Beall. *Prints by George Miyasaki*. San Francisco: Exhibition cat., Achenbach Foundation for the Graphic Arts, 1963.

Troyen/Hirshler 1987
Troyen, Carol and Erica E. Hirshler. *Charles Sheeler: Paintings and Drawings*. Boston: Exhibition cat., Museum of Fine Arts, 1987.

Tuggle 1989
Tuggle, Robert. *Eugene Berman, Drawings for the Stage*. New York: Exhibition cat., Wheelock Whitney, 1989.

Tully 1985
Tully, Judd. "Robert Gwathmey." *American Artist* 19 (June 1985): 47–50, 88–92.

Tyler 1987
Armstrong, Elizabeth, Pat Gilmour, and Kenneth E. Tyler. *Tyler Graphics: Catalogue Raisonné, 1974–1985*. New York and Minneapolis: Abbeville Press, 1987.

Uchima 1976
Uchima, Ansei. "My Use of Japanese Techniques." In Eichenberg 1976.

Uchima 1982
Uchima, Ansei. "Thirty Years: My Journey with Woodblocks" (trans. William Masuda). *Hana Geitjutsu* (Summer 1982), pp. 224–225.

UCLA 1970
The UCLA Galleries. *Stanton Macdonald-Wright, A Retrospective Exhibition, 1911–1970*. Los Angeles: Exhibition cat., Grunwald Graphic Arts Foundation, 1970.

Updike 1917
Updike, Daniel Berkeley. "Rudolph Ruzicka—An Appreciation." *Printing Art* 30 (1917): 17–24.

Updike 1922
Updike, Daniel Berkeley. *Printing Types, Their History, Forms and Use, A Study in Survivals*. Cambridge: Harvard University Press, 1922.

V & A 1956
Victoria and Albert Museum. *International Colour Woodcuts*. London: Exhibition cat., Her Majesty's Stationers Office, 1956.

Velonis 1938
Velonis, Anthony. *Technical Problems of the Artist: Technique of the Silk Screen Process*. New York: Federal Art Project, 1938.

Velonis 1940
Velonis, Anthony. "Silk Screen Process Prints." *The Magazine of Art* 33 (July 1940): 408–411.

Velonis 1959
Velonis, Anthony. "A Screen Process Printer Explains . . ." *Print* 13 (January 1959): 32–33.

Velonis 1973
Velonis, Anthony. "A Graphic Medium Grows Up." In O'Connor 1973, pp. 154–156.

Velonis 1987
Velonis, Anthony. "A Remembrance of the WPA." In DeNoon 1987, pp. 72–79.

Ventura 1958
Ventura, Anita. "Albert Urban." *Arts* 33 (October 1958): 56–57.

van der Veer 1905
van der Veer, L. "Miss Helen Hyde's Chromoxylographs in the Japanese Manner." *International Studio* 24 (January 1905): 240.

Vollmer
Vollmer, Hans A. *Allgemeines Lexikon der bildenden Künstler des XX. Jahrhunderts*. Leipzig: A. Seeman, 1953–62 (various eds.).

Waite 1951
Waite, Emma Forbes. "Benjamin Dearborn: Teacher, Inventor, Philanthropist." *Old-Time New England* 42 (1951–52): 44–47.

Walch 1987
Walch, Peter (introduction by Van Deren Coke). *Clinton Adams: Paintings and Watercolors 1945–1987*. Albuquerque: Exhibition cat., University of New Mexico Art Museum, 1987.

Walker 1974
Walker, John. "Interview: Stanton Macdonald-Wright." *American Art Review* (January–February 1974), p. 64.

Ward 1939
Ward, Lynd. "Printmakers of Tomorrow." *Parnassus* 11 (March 1939): 8–12.

Washburn 1984
Washburn Gallery. *Anne Ryan & Circle* (with an essay by Elizabeth McFadden). New York: Exhibition cat., 1984.

Watrous 1984
Watrous, James. *American Printmaking: A Century of American Printmaking 1880–1980*. Madison: University of Wisconsin Press, 1984.

Watrous
Watrous, James. "The Woodcuts of Alfred Sessler in the Elvehjem Collection." *Elvehjem Museum of Art, University of Wisconsin-Madison Bulletin/Annual Report, 1987–88*. Forthcoming.

Watson 1935
Watson, Forbes. "Art and the Government in 1934." *Parnassus* 6 (January 1935): 12–16.

Watson/Kent 1945
Watson, Ernest W. and Norman Kent (eds.). *The Relief Print*. New York: Watson-Guptill, 1945.

Wattenmaker 1975
Wattenmaker, Richard J. *Puvis de Chavannes and the Modern Tradition.* Toronto: Exhibition cat., Art Gallery of Ontario, 1975.

Way 1912
Way, T. R. *Memories of James McNeill Whistler.* London: John Lane, 1912.

Way 1914
Way, T. R. *The Lithographs by Whistler.* New York: Kennedy, 1914.

Weber 1926
Weber, Max. *Primitives.* New York: Spiral Press, 1926.

Weidenaar 1948
Weidenaar, Reynold H. "The Forgotten Art of Mezzotint Engraving." *American Artist* 12 (September 1948): 52–55, 70–71.

Weidenaar 1954
Weidenaar, Reynold H. "Scraping a Mezzotint." *Today's Art* 2 (February 1954): 8–10.

Weidenaar 1956
Weidenaar, Reynold H. "The Art of Mezzotint." *American Artist* 20 (December 1956): 24–31, 70–73.

Weidenaar 1971
Weidenaar, Reynold H. *Our Changing Landscape.* Cape Cod, Mass.: Wakebrook House, 1971.

Weitenkampf 1903
Weitenkampf, Frank. "Painter-lithography in the United States." *Scribner's Magazine* 33 (May 1903): 550.

Weitenkampf 1970
Weitenkampf, Frank. *American Graphic Art.* New York and London: Johnson Reprint, 1970.

Wentworth/Flexner 1960
Wentworth, Harold and Stuart Flexner (eds.). *The Dictionary of American Slang.* New York: Crowell, 1960.

Wesleyan 1971
"Private Press Books at Wesleyan: The Art Laboratory." *Wesleyan Library Notes* 7 (Autumn 1971): 11–20.

Weyhe 1940
Weyhe Gallery. *First Exhibition of Silk Screen Stencil Prints* (introduction by Lynd Ward). New York: Exhibition cat., 1940.

Whitaker 1974
Whitaker, Frederic. "Guy Maccoy: Printing with a Screen." *American Artist* 38 (October 1974): 60–65, 76–77.

White 1986
White, Gleeson. "The Posters of Louis Rhead." *The Studio* 8 (August 1986): 156–161.

Who's Who
Who's Who in Art. London: Art Trade Press, 1927–72 (various eds.). *Who's Who in American Art.* Washington, D.C.: American Federation of Arts, 1936–89 (various eds.) (after 1947, New York: R. R. Bowker).

Wight 1952
Wight, Frederick S. *Milton Avery.* Baltimore: Exhibition cat., Baltimore Museum of Art, 1952.

Wight 1953
Wight, Frederick S. "Los Angeles." *Art Digest* 28 (December 1, 1953): 34.

Wight 1954
Wight, Frederick S. *Charles Sheeler: A Retrospective Exhibition.* Los Angeles: Exhibition cat., Art Galleries, University of California at Los Angeles, 1954.

Wight 1957
Wight, Frederick S. *Hans Hofmann.* New York: Exhibition cat., Whitney Museum of American Art, 1957.

Wilder 1962
Wilder, Thornton. *The Bridge of San Luis Rey.* New York: Limited Editions, 1962.

Williams 1986
Williams, Reba and Dave. "The Early History of the Screenprint." *Print Quarterly* 3 (December 1986): 287–321.

Williams 1987
Williams, Reba and Dave. *American Screenprints.* New York: National Academy of Design, 1987.

Wirtz 1981
Stephen Wirtz Gallery (with introduction by Rudy H. Turk). *George Miyasaki.* San Francisco: Exhibition cat., 1981.

Wolf 1946
Wolf, Ben. "Gwathmey Employs Heart and Head." *Art Digest* 20 (February 1, 1946): 16.

Wolff 1978
Wolff, Theodore F. "Engendering Life in Strange Places." *Christian Science Monitor* (November 24, 1978), p. 24.

Wolff 1981
Wolff, Theodore F. "Art that is small, intimate and black and white." *Christian Science Monitor* (February 5, 1981), p. 18.

Wong 1974
Wong, Roberta Waddell. *American Posters of the Nineties.* New York and Boston: Exhibition cat., Boston Public Library, 1974.

Woodbury 1962
Woodbury, David O. "Please Save My Son!" *Liberty* (June 1962), pp. 157–162.

Wooster 1978
Wooster, Ann Sargent. "Henry Guerriero, Ynez Johnston, Leonard Edmondson, Walter Askin." *Artnews* 77 (May 1978): 188.

Wright 1916
Wright, Helen. "Bertha Lum's Woodblock Prints." *American Magazine of Art* 8 (1916–17): 408–411.

Wright 1930
Wright, Helen. "Helen Hyde." *Dictionary of American Biography* 5 (1930): 449–450.

Wright/Macdonald-Wright 1916
Wright, Willard Huntington and Stanton Macdonald-Wright. *The Creative Will: Studies in the Philosophy and Syntax of Aesthetics.* New York: John Lane, 1916.

Wunderlich 1895
Wunderlich Gallery. *Catalogue of an Exhibition of Original Designs from Posters by Louis J. Rhead . . .* New York: Exhibition cat., 1895.

Yale 1964
Yale University Art Gallery. *Gabor Peterdi: Paintings, Drawings and Prints.* New Haven: Exhibition cat., 1964.

Yeh 1981
Yeh, Susan Fillin. *Louis Schanker.* New York: Exhibition cat., Martin Diamond Fine Arts, 1981.

Yoshida 1939
Yoshida, Hiroshi. *Japanese Woodblock Printing.* Tokyo: Sanseido, 1939.

Young 1970
Young, Joseph E. "Los Angeles." *Art International* 14 (Summer 1970): 111–115.

Young 1973
Young, Mahonri Sharp. *The Realist Revolution in American Painting, The Eight.* New York: Watson-Guptill, 1973.

Zeller/Weidenaar 1980
Zeller, Anne and Reynold H. Weidenaar. *A Sketchbook of Michigan.* Grand Rapids, Mich.: Baker, 1980.

Zigrosser 1941a
Zigrosser, Carl. "Renaissance of the Wood-Engraving in the United States." *The Studio* 121 (June 1941): 181.

Zigrosser 1941b
Zigrosser, Carl. "Serigraph—A New Medium." *Print Collector's Quarterly* 28 (December 1941): 422–477.

Zigrosser 1942
Zigrosser, Carl. *The Artist in America: Twenty-four Close-Ups of Contemporary Printmakers.* New York: Knopf, 1942.

Zigrosser 1951
Zigrosser, Carl. "American Prints Since 1926." *Art Digest* 26 (November 1, 1951): 71.

Zigrosser 1960
Zigrosser, Carl. *Mauricio Lasansky.* New York: Exhibition cat., American Federation of Arts, 1960.

Zigrosser 1974
Zigrosser, Carl. *Prints and Their Creators: A World History.* 2nd rev. ed. New York: Crown, 1974.

Zimiles/Wechsler 1988
Zimiles, Murray and Jeffery Wechsler. *Boris Margo, A Retrospective.* Provincetown, Mass.: Exhibition cat., Provincetown Art Association and St. Petersburg, Florida, Museum of Fine Arts, 1988.

Zurier 1985
Zurier, Rebecca. *Art for the Masses (1911–1917): A Radical Magazine and its Graphics.* New Haven: Exhibition cat., Yale University Art Gallery, 1985.

Artists